Methods in Behavioural Research

SECOND CANADIAN EDITION

PAUL C. COZBY, Ph.D.

California State University, Fullerton

CATHERINE D. RAWN, Ph.D.

University of British Columbia

Mc
Graw
Hill
Education

ISBN-13: 978-1-25-9088469
ISBN-10: 1-25-908846-4

1 2 3 4 5 6 QVS 20 19 18 17 16
Printed and Bound in the United States of America.

Director of Product Management: *Rhondda McNabb*
Product Manager: *Jason Chih/Scott Hardie*
Senior Marketing Manager: *Margaret Greenfield*
Senior Product Developer: *Jennifer Cressman/Brianna McIlwain*
Senior Product Team Associate: *Marina Seguin*
Supervising Editor: *Stephanie Gay*
Copy Editor: *Mike Kelly*
Plant Production Coordinator: *Tammy Mavroudi/Scott Morrison*
Cover Design: *Dianne Reynolds*
Cover Image: *Dwight Nadig/Getty Images*
Page Layout: *Aptara*
Printer: *Quad/Graphics*

Dedication

To Kathleen D. Vohs,
For your mentorship and encouragement.
–C.D.R.

For Ingrid and Pierre.
–P.C.C.

About the Authors

Paul C. Cozby is emeritus professor of psychology at California State University, Fullerton. Dr. Cozby was an undergraduate at the University of California, Riverside, and received his Ph.D. in psychology from the University of Minnesota. He is a fellow of the American Psychological Association and a member of the Association for Psychological Science; he has served as officer of the Society for Computers in Psychology. He is executive officer of the Western Psychological Association. He is the author of *Using Computers in the Behavioral Sciences* and co-editor with Daniel Perlman of *Social Psychology*.

Catherine D. Rawn is senior instructor of psychology at the University of British Columbia, Vancouver. Dr. Rawn was an undergraduate psychology major at the University of Waterloo, and received her master of arts in social/personality psychology at the University of British Columbia. She continued at UBC and received her Ph.D. in social/personality psychology with a minor in quantitative methods. Her publications appear in journals such as *Teaching of Psychology* and *Personality and Social Psychology Review*. She regularly teaches undergraduates research methods, introductory statistics, and introductory psychology. She also facilitates professional development in teaching for graduate students and faculty.

Brief Contents

Contents

4   Research Design Fundamentals   68

5   Measurement Concepts   95

6 Observational Methods   113

7 Asking People about Themselves: Survey Research   131

11   Research Designs for Special Circumstances   220

12   Understanding Research Results: Describing Variables and Relationships among Them   246

Preface

Learning about and teaching research methods can be greatly challenging and incredibly rewarding. As a young learner, with each step I took toward participating in the research process, I realized I was learning an incredibly useful way to think about the world. The cover image of this second Canadian edition of *Methods in Behavioural Research* offers a metaphor for what this text aims to do: Illuminate core concepts and current issues to help readers navigate the path toward using research methods effectively. This path also can be viewed as depicting the process of research itself: Sometimes research investigations are clear and straightforward, but more often the path toward understanding an aspect of behaviour is winding and uncertain.

WHY A CANADIAN EDITION?

The second Canadian edition of *Methods in Behavioural Research* offers a Canadian perspective on conducting research in psychology. Three benefits emerge from a Canadian edition. First, by incorporating Canadian examples, researchers, and cultural references, this text will more effectively reach our students and instructors in Canada. I grew up reading texts brimming with American references. I can still recall the first time I realized–with great excitement–that I personally knew a researcher cited in my Canadian text. By highlighting the Canadian context of research, we can avoid subtle yet unnecessary barriers to the enlightening world of research methods. Second, a Canadian research methods text offers the chance to illuminate the rich Canadian research landscape while preparing readers to engage in it. Researchers across our country are conducting rigorous, interesting, impactful work; plenty of high-quality examples are available to incorporate. Third, a Canadian research methods text gives a voice to Canadian reviewers. I am thankful for the three rounds of peer reviews the Canadian editions have received so far. By incorporating most of their ideas and feedback each time, this text is becoming stronger. You are shaping the very text our students use.

Notably, I have maintained the features of previous American editions that have been appreciated by instructors and students, including clarity, brevity, and repetition of key ideas (e.g., operationalization, validity). Below is a summary of the text's features and major changes for the second Canadian edition.

ORGANIZATION

The organization generally follows the sequence of planning and conducting a research investigation. Chapter 1 gives an overview of the scientific approach to knowledge and distinguishes between basic and applied research. Chapter 2 discusses sources of ideas for research including reading the literature. Ethical issues are covered in depth in Chapter 3 and emphasized throughout the book. Chapter 4 highlights the fundamental features of experimental and non-experimental approaches to studying relationships among variables. Chapter 5 focuses on measurement issues, including reliability and validity. Observational research approaches, including systematic observation and content analysis, are described in Chapter 6. Chapter 7 explores sampling as well as the design of questionnaires and interviews. Chapter 8 adds depth to experimental design, and Chapter 9 helps readers prepare studies for data collection. Factorial designs are explored in Chapter 10. Chapter 11 features designs for special circumstances where random assignment is impossible (e.g., quasi-experimental designs). Chapters 12 and 13 introduce the use of statistics, including effect size and confidence intervals, to help students understand research results. Finally, Chapter 14 discusses generalization issues, meta-analyses, and the importance of replications. Appendices on writing research reports, conducting statistical analyses, and using *PsycINFO* to search for journal articles are included for reference.

FLEXIBILITY

Chapters are relatively independent to provide instructors maximum flexibility in assigning the order of chapters. For example, chapters on observational and survey research methods are presented in the middle of the book, but instructors who wish to present this material earlier or later in a course can easily do so. It is also relatively easy to eliminate sections of material within most chapters. This book is particularly useful for courses in which students conduct their own research projects. Chapters 4 and 9 highlight key concepts for conducting experimental and non-experimental research; I assign these early in my course to help students kick off their projects. More nuanced details (e.g., Chapter 10, factorial designs) are then saved until later in the course.

FEATURES

- *Clarity.* The second Canadian edition retains the strength of direct, clear writing. Concepts are described in different contexts to enhance understanding. Some chapters have been reorganized to enhance overall clarity and reduce redundancy.
- *Decision-making emphasis.* Distinguishing among a variety of research designs helps students understand when to use one type of design over another.
- *Strong pedagogy. Learning Objectives* are highlighted throughout each chapter and mirrored in end-of-chapter self-test *Review Questions.* End-of-chapter *Deepen Your Understanding* questions prompt students to apply material from the chapter, and also can be used as in-class activities. All boldface key terms are listed at the end of each chapter, with prompts that encourage students to test their knowledge. Each key term is defined in the Glossary at the end of the book.

NEW TO THE SECOND CANADIAN EDITION

- *Features current controversies.* The last three years have been pivotal for research methods. Major cases of fraud, controversial publications, and failures to replicate some high-profile studies have triggered an explosion of interest in improving our own and other sciences. I see no need to shield students from these controversies and "in-progress" improvements; consequently, I have featured them throughout this edition. Many new references are included to help instructors and students alike learn more about these hot ongoing debates.
- *Current, Canadian context.* Updated research examples have been carefully selected to help students interpret challenging concepts and complex research designs. Remaining outdated or difficult examples have been replaced by new research conducted in Canada and occasionally by Canadians working abroad. Thirty percent of research featured throughout this edition is Canadian, representing 37 universities plus partnering institutions from all provinces. Note that not every Canadian reference is indicated as such. Sometimes institutions are mentioned, but highlighting every reference would create a sense of artificiality that could distract from the main purpose of teaching research methods.
- *Improved flow within chapters.* The sequencing and hierarchy of headings within each chapter has been carefully reconsidered for logical flow. Adjustments were made in many chapters to enhance flow by ensuring concepts build on each other in a stepwise manner.

Some changes to specific chapters are outlined below.

- *Chapter 1.* A new figure offers an overview of the scientific process that is revisited in Chapters 9 and 14. Clarified and better organized discussion of the ideal process of science. Shifted focus of basic versus applied research to emphasize continuum. Changed examples to highlight these different approaches to the same topic.
- *Chapter 2.* Reorganized structure to improve flow. Moved *PsycINFO* search steps to Appendix D. Highlighted importance of references and in-text citations for situating new work in the context of existing research. A new table compares the usefulness of different search engines (e.g., GoogleScholar vs. *PsycINFO*).

- *Chapter 3.* Refocused section on scientific misconduct to include publication ethics. Updated major cases. New feature on disciplinary reform initiatives. Brief treatment of big data controversy.

- *Chapter 4.* Changed title to better reflect chapter's purpose. Improved flow to emphasize key role of operational definitions. Added more examples of confounds and third-variable problem. Updated examples.

- *Chapter 5.* Updated some brief examples, including replacing a fictional example.

- *Chapter 6.* Updated to feature technology-driven innovations in observation and archival methods.

- *Chapter 7.* Updated examples to feature recent controversies. New figure to clarify cluster sampling technique. Changes to headings improve organization.

- *Chapter 8.* Updated all major examples to feature recent research. Re-emphasized confounds with a controversial example. New figures illustrate contrast effects and Solomon four-group design.

- *Chapter 9.* Reframed chapter to facilitate the decision-making process when finalizing a design for data collection. Two new checklists help readers organize tasks and make final decisions.

- *Chapter 10.* Minor changes to enhance organization and clarity.

- *Chapter 11.* Changed title to better reflect content. Improved example and graphs of single case designs. New tables organize and compare all special-case designs as well as threats to internal validity. Elaborated on ways threats to internal validity can affect interpretation of experimental designs too.

- *Chapter 12.* Replaced all fictional data with real data to illustrate concepts throughout the chapter. Some reorganization to enhance flow.

- *Chapter 13.* New emphasis on problems caused by seeking statistical significance, including publication bias and file drawer problem. Explicitly addressed the appropriate interpretation of a p value. Reinforced disciplinary reform initiatives.

- *Chapter 14.* Thorough revision highlights current controversies and disciplinary reform regarding replication and generalizing beyond convenience samples. Expanded final section encourages readers to "generalize" knowledge beyond course, including revisiting what they have learned about the whole process of research.

- *Appendices.* Updated Appendix A to emphasize the importance of audience and the broader purposes of APA style conventions; replaced sample paper. Clarified and updated Appendix B, particularly regarding effect sizes. Moved Latin square construction online to make room for new Appendix D that offers tips on conducting a *PsycINFO* search.

MARKET-LEADING TECHNOLOGY

◼ connect®

Learn without Limits

McGraw-Hill Connect® is an award-winning digital teaching and learning platform that gives students the means to better connect with their coursework, with their instructors, and with the important concepts that they will need to know for success now and in the future. With Connect, instructors can take advantage of McGraw-Hill Education's trusted content to seamlessly deliver assignments, quizzes, and tests online. McGraw-Hill Connect is a learning platform that continually adapts to each student, delivering precisely what they need, when they need it, so class time is more engaging and effective. Connect makes teaching and learning personal, easy, and proven.

Connect Key Features

SmartBook®

As the first and only adaptive reading experience, SmartBook is changing the way students read and learn. SmartBook creates a personalized reading experience by highlighting the most important concepts a student needs to learn at that moment in time. As a student engages with SmartBook, the reading experience continuously adapts by highlighting content based on what each student knows and doesn't know. This ensures that he or she is focused on the content needed to close specific knowledge gaps, while it simultaneously promotes long-term learning.

Connect Insight®

Connect Insight is Connect's new one-of-a-kind visual analytics dashboard–now available for instructors–that provides at-a-glance information regarding student performance, which is immediately actionable. By presenting assignment, assessment, and topical performance results together with a time metric that is easily visible for aggregate or individual results, Connect Insight gives instructors the ability to take a just-in-time approach to teaching and learning, which was never before available. Connect Insight presents data that helps instructors improve class performance in a way that is efficient and effective.

Simple Assignment Management

With Connect, creating assignments is easier than ever, so instructors can spend more time teaching and less time managing.

- Assign SmartBook learning modules.
- Instructors can edit existing questions and create their own questions.
- Draw from a variety of text specific questions, resources, and test bank material to assign online.
- Streamline lesson planning, student progress reporting, and assignment grading to make classroom management more efficient than ever.

Smart Grading

When it comes to studying, time is precious. Connect helps students learn more efficiently by providing feedback and practice material when they need it, where they need it.

- Automatically score assignments, giving students immediate feedback on their work and comparisons with correct answers.
- Access and review each response; manually change grades or leave comments for students to review.
- Track individual student performance–by question, by assignment, or in relation to the class overall–with detailed grade reports.
- Reinforce classroom concepts with practice tests and instant quizzes.
- Integrate grade reports easily with Learning Management Systems including Blackboard, D2L, and Moodle.

Instructor Library

The Connect Instructor Library is a repository for additional resources to improve student engagement in and out of the class. It provides all the critical resources instructors need to build their course.

- Access instructor resources.
- View assignments and resources created for past sections.
- Post your own resources for students to use.

INSTRUCTOR RESOURCES

- **Instructors Manual.** Written by this text's author, this in-depth Instructors Manual offers numerous student activities and assignment suggestions as well as demonstrations, discussions topics, reference articles, and sample answers for questions in the text.

- *Computerized Test Bank.* Prepared by Chantal Merner of University of Windsor, the Test Bank contains over 700 multiple choice questions, each categorized according to Bloom's Taxonomy. The Test Bank is available within Connect and through EZ Test Online–a flexible and easy-to-use electronic testing system–that allows instructors to create tests from book-specific items. Test items are also available in Word (rich text format).
- *Microsoft® PowerPoint® Lecture Slides.* Prepared by Craig Blatz of Grant MacEwan University, these customizable PowerPoint presentations represent the key concepts in each chapter.

SUPERIOR LEARNING SOLUTIONS AND SUPPORT

The McGraw-Hill Education team is ready to help instructors assess and integrate any of our products, technology, and services into your course for optimal teaching and learning performance. Whether it's helping your students improve their grades, or putting your entire course online, the McGraw-Hill Education team is here to help you do it. Contact your Learning Solutions Consultant today to learn how to maximize all of McGraw-Hill Education's resources.

For more information, please visit us online: http://www.mheducation.ca/he/solutions.

ACKNOWLEDGMENTS

Many people helped to produce this second Canadian edition. First, I am indebted to the author of previous American editions, Paul C. Cozby, and to all who contributed to them. At McGraw-Hill Ryerson, product manager Jason Chih and senior product developer Jennifer Cressman provided invaluable support. I particularly thank the following people who provided detailed reviews for the second Canadian edition:

Craig Blatz
Grant MacEwan University

Connie Boudens
University of Toronto, Scarborough

Patrick Brown
University of Western Ontario

Keith Busby
University of Ottawa

Laura Dane
Douglas College

Lucie Kocum
Saint Mary's University

Guy Lacroix
Carleton University

Chris Montoya
Thompson Rivers University

Margarete Wolfram
York University

I would like to thank my family, friends, students, and colleagues, who have helped me in various ways to produce the second Canadian edition. My colleagues, especially Jaclyn Rea, Eric Eich, and Victoria Savalei, deepened my understanding of disciplinarity and issues in the discipline, both of which influenced this book. My students, including Preet Pandher, Robin Richardson, and Andre Beukers, help motivate my drive to engage undergraduates in disciplinary controversies and inspire me to produce the best work I can. I thank my husband Russell Ball for ongoing encouragement and patience throughout this process. To Donna Bilton, for helping me put all these hours of work into perspective. More broadly, many people have played important roles in my life, helping prepare me to be able to create a work like this. I especially thank Dr. Kathleen Vohs, to whom I dedicate this edition. Your years of mentorship have made me a better scientist, writer, and academic. I am forever grateful.

–Catherine D. Rawn

1

Scientific Understanding of Behaviour

LEARNING OBJECTIVES

Keep these learning objectives in mind as you read to help you identify the most critical information in this chapter.

By the end of this chapter, you should be able to:

1	Explain reasons for understanding research methods.
2	Describe the scientific approach to learning about behaviour and contrast it with pseudoscience.
3	Define and give examples of the four goals of scientific research in psychology.
4	Compare and contrast basic and applied research.

What makes people happy? How do we remember things, what causes us to forget, and how can memory be improved? What are the effects of stressful environments on physical health and relationships? How do early childhood experiences affect later development? What are the best ways to treat depression? How can we reduce prejudice and war? Curiosity about questions like these is probably the most important reason many students decide to take courses in the behavioural sciences. Scientific research provides us with a way to address such questions and find answers. Throughout this book, we will examine methods of scientific research in the behavioural sciences. In this introductory chapter, we will focus on the ways in which knowledge of research methods can be useful for understanding the world around us. Further, we will review the characteristics of a scientific approach to the study of behaviour and the general types of research questions that concern behavioural scientists.

LOI

WHY STUDY RESEARCH METHODS?

Understanding research methods can help you become an informed consumer of products, services, health care, and news. Research is continually reported by news organizations, popular magazines, bloggers, and advertisers. Headlines claim "Study finds that lonely women use Facebook all the time," assert "When drugs and therapy don't cure depression, running will," and question "Do cellphones cause brain cancer?". Articles, television commercials, books, and websites make claims about the beneficial or harmful effects of particular diets or vitamins on one's personality, health, or sex life. Survey results are frequently reported that draw conclusions about our beliefs and attitudes. How do you evaluate such reports? Do you simply accept the findings because they seem scientific? Can you detect pseudoscientific claims (as we will explore later in this chapter)? A background in research methods will help you to read these reports critically, evaluate the methods, and decide whether the conclusions and headlines are appropriate.

Understanding research methods can give you a competitive edge in various career paths. Many occupations require the ability to interpret, appropriately use, and create sound research. For example, mental health professionals must make decisions about treatment methods, medications, and testing procedures—all of which require the ability to read relevant research literature and apply it effectively. Similarly, people who work in business frequently rely on research to make decisions about marketing strategies, ways of improving employee productivity or morale, and methods of selecting and training new employees. Educators must keep up with research on topics such as the effectiveness of different teaching strategies or programs to deal with special challenges that some students are facing. *Program evaluation* (discussed further later in this chapter) is a career that is centred on conducting research to evaluate the efficacy of government and other programs to ensure that funding is well-spent. Knowledge of research methods and the ability to evaluate research reports are useful in these and other careers.

Understanding research methods can help you be an informed citizen and participate in public policy debates. Legislators and political leaders at all levels of government often take political positions and propose legislation based on research findings. Research can also influence legal practices and decisions. For example, numerous wrongful convictions triggered the use of psychological research to inform police investigation and courtroom procedures (Public Prosecution Service of Canada [PPSC], 2011; U.S. Department of Justice, 1999;

Wells, 2001; Yarmey, 2003). In one case, Thomas Sophonow was wrongfully convicted of murder by a Manitoba jury in 1983. After serving four years of his life sentence, his conviction was overturned. In the inquiry to follow (Cory, 2001), a retired Supreme Court of Canada justice used psychological science as the basis of numerous recommendations to prevent the kind of wrongful conviction that Sophonow endured. One of the studies that influenced these recommendations was conducted at Queen's University and showed that people make fewer false identifications of suspects when they are presented with a set of photographs one at a time rather than simultaneously (Lindsay & Wells, 1985; see also Steblay, Dysart, Fulero, & Lindsay, 2001). Since the inquiry was published, police have been required to present photographs sequentially when asking eyewitnesses to identify a suspect (PPSC, 2011). Another way that psychologists influence judicial decisions is by providing expert testimony and consultation on a variety of issues, including domestic violence (e.g., *R. v. Lavallee*, 1990), risk for violence (e.g., *R. v. Berikoff*, 2000), and evaluation of hypnotically recovered memory evidence (e.g., *R. v. Trochym*, 2007).

Understanding research methods can help you evaluate the efficacy of programs in which you may choose to participate or that you may implement in your community. For example, there are programs to enhance parenting skills for parents of youth engaged in aggressive and antisocial behaviour (Moretti & Obsuth, 2009), to influence people to engage in behaviours that reduce their risk of contracting HIV, and to enable employees in a company to learn how to reduce the effects of stress. We need to be able to determine whether these programs are successfully meeting their goals, and the application of research methods helps us do just that.

METHODS OF ACQUIRING KNOWLEDGE

We opened this chapter with several questions about human behaviour and suggested that scientific research is a valuable means of answering them. How does the scientific approach differ from other ways of learning about behaviour? People have always observed the world around them and sought explanations for what they see and experience. In this quest, relying on intuition and authority can be helpful sometimes, yet can lead to biased conclusions. Science offers a way to avoid some of these biases while systematically seeking high-quality evidence.

Intuition

Many of us have heard about someone who, after years of actively pursuing a long-term partner, stops looking for love. Then within a very short period of time, this person happens to find the love of his or her life. This observation contributes to a common belief that love arrives just when one is not looking for it.

Such a conclusion seems intuitively reasonable, and people can easily create an explanation for this event (see Gilovich, 1991). Perhaps stopping the hunt reduces a major source of stress, then the stress reduction increases confidence in social interactions, making people more desirable to potential partners.

This example illustrates the use of **intuition** based on anecdotal evidence to draw general conclusions. When you rely on intuition, you accept unquestioningly what your personal judgment or a single story about one person's experience tells you about the world. The intuitive approach takes many forms. Often, it involves finding an explanation for our own or others' behaviours. For example, you might develop an explanation for why you keep having conflicts with a co-worker, such as "that other person wants my job" or "having to share an office puts us in a conflict situation." Other times, intuition is used to explain intriguing events that you observe, as in the case of concluding that no longer looking for long-term love increases the chances of finding it.

A problem with intuition is that many cognitive and motivational biases affect our perceptions, and so we are likely to draw erroneous conclusions about cause and effect (cf., Gilovich, 1991; Nisbett & Ross, 1980; Nisbett & Wilson, 1977). So why do we believe that no longer looking for love leads to finding love? Most likely it is because of a cognitive bias called *illusory correlation* that occurs when we focus on two events that stand out and occur together. When a decision to stop looking is followed closely by finding a long-term mate, our attention is drawn to the situation, but when a decision to stop looking is *not* closely followed by finding a long-term mate, we don't notice this non-event. Therefore, we are biased to conclude that there must be a causal connection when in fact no such relationship exists. Such illusory correlations are also likely to occur when we are highly motivated to believe in the supposed causal relationship. Although this way of thinking comes naturally, it is not scientific and can lead us to make inaccurate assumptions. A scientific approach requires much more rigorous evidence before drawing conclusions.

Authority

When we make a decision based on **authority,** we place our trust in someone else who we think knows more than we do. For example, people tend to trust a physician's recommendations, particularly when they view that physician as being a specialist in that area (Barnoy, Ofra, & Bar-Tal, 2012). Such blind trust in medical authority is problematic. Ample research has shown that many health care workers (and patients alike) are prone to drawing incorrect conclusions from health-relevant statistics (e.g., when assessing survival rates versus length of life after cancer diagnoses; Gigerenzer, Gaissmaier, Kurz-Milcke, Schwartz, & Woloshin, 2007). Similarly, many people readily accept anything they encounter from the news media, books, government officials, or religious figures. They believe that the statements of such authorities must be true. Advertisers know this and therefore use endorsements by authorities to sell products. The problem, of course, is that the statements by the authority may not be true. The scientific approach rejects the notion that one can accept on faith the statements of any authority; again, more evidence is needed before we can draw scientific conclusions.

The Scientific Method: Be Skeptical, Seek Empirical Data

LO2

The scientific method of acquiring knowledge includes both intuition and authority as sources of ideas about behaviour. However, taking a scientific approach means avoiding the unquestioned acceptance of anyone's intuitions—including one's own. Ideas must be evaluated on the basis of careful logic and results from structured investigations. Throughout this book, we invite you to try out a mindset of **scientific skepticism** (if you haven't already!). Recognize that our own ideas are just as likely to be as wrong as anyone else's, and question other people's pronouncements of truth, regardless of their prestige or authority.

If scientific skepticism involves rejecting intuition and the blind acceptance of authority as ways of knowing about the world, how does knowledge develop? The fundamental characteristic of the scientific method is **empiricism:** knowledge is based on structured, systematic observations. The process of conducting research is complex and involves many steps. In its basic form, a scientist develops a *hypothesis* (an idea that might be true; see Chapter 2), then carefully collects data to evaluate whether that hypothesis accurately reflects the nature of the world. See Figure 1.1 for an overview of the many steps involved in conducting research. Although these steps may seem daunting, the scientific method includes a number of useful rules for developing theories and hypotheses, designing studies, collecting and evaluating data, and writing up results for publication. We will explore many of these rules together throughout this book.

Thousands of individual scientists worldwide—in disciplines as varied as psychology and physics—use the scientific method to understand the world. Regardless of the topic being studied and the specific procedures used, there are some broad characteristics that guide the ideal process of scientific inquiry (Goodstein, 2011; Merton, 1973). It is important to note at the outset that scientists are human and science is an imperfect enterprise. These ideals are not meant to be a fully exhaustive list. Moreover, they are not always perfectly reflected in reality, and they are often met with counterpressures, such as the pressure to publish many studies to build a career as a scientist. Yet the majority of scientists across various disciplines agree that the following four norms (Merton, 1973) should characterize scientific inquiry at its best (Anderson, Ronning, DeVries, & Martinson, 2010).

1. *Universalism:* Scientific observations are systematically structured and evaluated objectively using accepted methods of the discipline. By relying on empiricism in this way, we expect that scientists can conduct research to test any idea, other scientists can disagree, and the research reported from both sides can be objectively evaluated by others to find truth.

FIGURE I.I
Overview of
the process of
conducting
research,
scientist's
perspective
*Ask your
instructor to
identify which
step in this pro-
cess is most or
least fun for him
or her. Which
do you think
will be most fun
for you?*

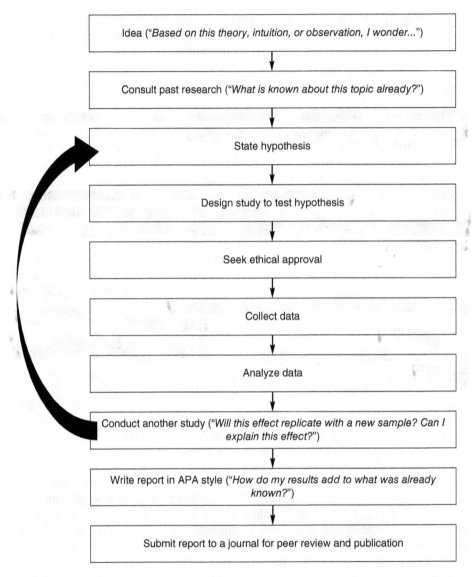

Idea (*"Based on this theory, intuition, or observation, I wonder..."*)

Consult past research (*"What is known about this topic already?"*)

State hypothesis

Design study to test hypothesis

Seek ethical approval

Collect data

Analyze data

Conduct another study (*"Will this effect replicate with a new sample? Can I explain this effect?"*)

Write report in APA style (*"How do my results add to what was already known?"*)

Submit report to a journal for peer review and publication

2. *Communality:* Methods and results are to be shared openly. One major benefit to open reporting is that others can **replicate** the methods used to check whether they obtain the same results (see Chapter 14 and Collaboration, 2013). Replications help to ensure that effects are not just false positives or random flukes (see Chapter 13). Another major benefit to open reporting is that the results of many studies can be combined

in *meta-analyses,* which are studies that combine results from many studies of the same phenomenon to examine the overall effect (see Chapter 14). No single study provides a perfectly accurate answer to a complex question; a meta-analysis is an important tool in the search for knowledge that relies crucially on communality (see Braver, Thoemmes, & Rosenthal, 2014; Cumming, 2014). Some researchers have begun posting data sets and full study procedures online after a study is published for others to use.

3. *Disinterestedness:* Scientists are expected to search for observations that will help them make accurate discoveries about the world. They develop theories, argue that existing data support their theories, conduct research to evaluate propositions of their theories, and revise their theories as needed to more accurately account for new data. Scientists should be rewarded for their honest and careful quest for truth, and ideally are not motivated primarily for personal gain.

4. *Organized skepticism:* All new evidence and theories should be evaluated based on scientific merit, even those that challenge one's own work or prior beliefs. Science exists in a free market of ideas in which the best ideas are supported by research, and scientists can build upon the research of others to make further advances. Of all the ideals, organized skepticism is the one that most directly underlies the practice of **peer review.** Before a study is published in a scientific journal, it must be reviewed by other scientists who have the expertise to carefully evaluate the research and recommend whether the research should be published. This review process, although imperfect, helps to ensure that research with major flaws in theory, methodology, analyses, or conclusions will not become part of the scientific literature.

Science as a Way to Ask and Answer Questions

The main advantage of the scientific approach over other ways of knowing about the world is that it provides an objective set of rules for gathering, evaluating, and reporting evidence. In its ideal form, science is an open system that allows ideas to be refuted or supported on the basis of available evidence. Researchers are only interested in **falsifiable** ideas. If an idea is falsifiable, then it can be either supported or refuted using empirical data (Popper, 1968). Sometimes, scientific evidence is not obtainable, as, for example, when religions ask us to accept certain beliefs on faith. It is possible to design a study to test whether belief in god(s) increases peoples' willingness to help others; however, it is not possible to design a study to test whether such a god (or gods) exists. The former idea is falsifiable; the latter is not. Many of Freud's ideas were unfalsifiable, and therefore fell out of favour as psychology distinguished itself as a science. For example, the idea of repression is unfalsifiable: How can we ever prove or disprove that someone has buried a memory deep in the unconscious mind where it can never be accessed? Only ideas that are falsifiable—where data can reveal whether they are truth or fiction—can be tackled by science. Some ideas, even some very good ideas, may prove to be false if empirical research continually fails to provide support for them. If an idea is falsified when it is tested, science is also advanced because this result will spur the development of new and better ideas.

Our emphasis on science is not meant to imply that intuition and authority are unimportant; indeed, scientists often rely on them for research ideas. There is nothing wrong with accepting the assertions of authority as long as we do not accept them uncritically as scientific evidence. Likewise, there is nothing wrong with having opinions or beliefs as long as they are presented simply as opinions or beliefs. When we take on the scientific mindset, we should always ask whether the assertion or opinion can be tested scientifically, or whether scientific evidence exists that relates to the opinion. For example, opinions on whether exposure to video game violence increases aggression are only opinions until scientific evidence on the issue is gathered—and indeed such research has demonstrated this causal link (Anderson et al., 2010).

Truly embracing scientific skepticism will mean questioning the claims of scientists themselves. Scientists can become *authorities* when they express their ideas. Because someone claims to be a scientist, should we be more willing to accept what he or she has to say? Consider the person's credentials. Does he or she have an established reputation in the field? A position at a reputable institution? Who funds the person's research? You might be somewhat skeptical when research funded by a drug company supports the effectiveness of a drug manufactured by that company. Similarly, when an organization with a particular socio-political agenda funds the research that supports that agenda, you may be skeptical of the findings and closely examine the methods of the study.

As you practise scientific skepticism and learn more about scientific methods, you may increasingly question claims reported in the media. The reputable website www.snopes.com can be helpful for evaluating urban legends and scams often circulated online (e.g., that you can earn cash by buying a $2 kit from Google and posting links online). Be vigilant for **pseudoscience,** which uses scientific terms to make claims look compelling, but without using scientific data. Ranging from astrologers to some marketers, pseudoscientists ask you to purchase products and experiences to improve your life without appropriate evidence to back up their claims. Detecting pseudoscience can be challenging. Figure 1.2 lists some of the many warning signs suggesting that a claim is pseudoscientific. For example, consider the claim that people can learn complicated material (e.g., a second language) while sleeping. Before reading further, try visiting the

* Claims are not falsifiable.
* If tests are reported, methodology is not scientific and accuracy of data is questionable.
* Supportive evidence is anecdotal or relies heavily on authorities who are "so-called" experts in the area of interest. Genuine, peer-reviewed scientific references are not cited.
* Claims ignore conflicting evidence.
* Claims are stated in scientific-sounding terminology and ideas.
* Claims tend to be vague, rationalize strongly held beliefs, and appeal to preconceived ideas.
* Claims are never revised to account for new data.

FIGURE 1.2
Checklist for detecting some warning signs of pseudoscience

website www.sleeplearning.com with a *scientifically skeptical* mindset, and using Figure 1.2 to detect evidence of pseudoscience.

The authors of the website imply their claim is based on science: "Latest research proves there is a link between sleep and learning." Such a vague and non-directional claim is actually consistent with copious evidence that sleep helps consolidate waking memories (Rasch & Born, 2013). To their credit, this website paraphrases and quotes from some of these studies, but a major problem remains: Missing is evidence that listening to recordings (like their product) during sleep can produce complex, long-term learning. Without any supporting evidence, this website claims that you can "master another language, cram up on any subject," and more while sleeping. Research that is somewhat relevant (along with other non-scientific features such as testimonials) is used deceptively to increase the website's credibility while it leaps to a pseudoscientific claim. Other websites will offer more subtle examples of pseudoscience. A general rule is to be highly skeptical when scientific assertions are made that are supported by only vague or improbable evidence.

GOALS OF SCIENTIFIC RESEARCH IN PSYCHOLOGY

LO3

Four general **goals of scientific research** guide much of psychology and the behavioural sciences: (1) to describe behaviour, (2) to predict behaviour, (3) to determine the causes of behaviour, and (4) to understand or explain behaviour.

Describing Behaviour

The first goal of scientific research in psychology is to describe events, which involves careful observation and measurement. For example, University of Alberta researcher Connie Varnhagen and her colleagues explored new language use in instant messaging among teenagers (Varnhagen et al., 2010). Teens saved their instant messages for one week, and researchers analyzed the types of unconventional words used. Reflecting an emphasis on efficiency of communication, shortcuts represented the most frequent new language category, including abbreviations (e.g., *prolly*) and acronyms (e.g., *bf, ttys*). Adding emotion to bland text was also a frequent occurrence through the use of uppercase letters, emotion punctuation such as :) and emotion acronyms (e.g., *lol*). Using new language in this way was related to poor spelling among boys but not among girls.

Descriptive research like this study can provide a foundation for future work. Consider how results may inform research into these questions: Does learning new language for brief communications interfere with people's formal writing skills? Do people use new language only with others they think are "in-group" members? Do people like other people who use new language more often than those who use only formal language? Does the use of new language mean that people's spelling ability will suffer? How is interpersonal conflict affected by low levels of nonverbal communication in instant messaging situations?

Predicting Behaviour

Another goal of scientific research in psychology is to predict future behaviour. Once it has been observed with some regularity that two events are systematically related to one another (e.g., a more credible speaker is associated with greater attitude change among listeners), it becomes possible to make predictions and, therefore, to anticipate events. If we know a woman's symptoms of depression and post-traumatic stress disorder when she leaves an abusive partner, we can predict how likely she is to return to an abusive relationship within a year (Alhalal, Ford-Gilboe, Kerr, & Davies, 2012). If we know how long children can resist the temptation of eating a marshmallow, we can predict their academic success in adolescence (Shoda, Mischel, & Peake, 1990). However, we must be careful not to assume that such predictive relationships imply causation. We will explore appropriate conclusions from these *correlational* research designs in more detail in Chapter 4.

Determining the Causes of Behaviour

A third goal of scientific research in psychology is to determine the causes of behaviour. Although we might accurately predict the occurrence of a behaviour, we might not have correctly identified its cause. For example, high school grades do not cause university grades, although they are related. There are likely various causes of grades achieved at both education levels (e.g., motivation, study skills); research may be undertaken to study these factors. Similarly, research shows that a child's aggressive behaviour may be predicted by knowing how much violence the child views on television. Unless we know that exposure to television violence is a *cause* of behaviour, we cannot assert that aggressive behaviour can be reduced by limiting scenes of violence on television. Thus, to know how to *change* behaviour, we need to know the *causes* of behaviour. Experiments help us to identify cause-and-effect relationships (see Chapter 4).

Criteria for Causal Claims   To make a causal claim, it is not enough to know that two events occur together. Cook and Campbell (1979) describe three criteria (drawn from the work of philosopher John Stuart Mill) that must be satisfied to identify a cause. For example, consider research showing that multitasking on a laptop during a lesson predicts worse test scores than strictly taking notes on a laptop during a lesson (Sana, Weston, & Cepeda, 2013). These researchers made a claim that multitasking *causes* worse test scores by meeting the three criteria:

1. When the cause (i.e., multitasking) is present, the effect (i.e., low test score) occurs; when the cause is not present, the effect does not occur. This is called **covariation of cause and effect.** Sana and colleagues showed that people who were multitasking on their laptop scored, on average, 55 percent correct on the lesson comprehension test, and people who were not multitasking scored higher (an average of 66 percent correct).

2. There is a temporal order of events in which the cause precedes the effect. This is called **temporal precedence.** In Sana and colleagues' study, listening to the lesson while multitasking (or not) occurred before the comprehension test. Test scores could not have reached back in time and affected learning during multitasking.

3. Nothing other than a causal variable could be responsible for the observed effect. This is called *elimination of alternative explanations.* There should be no other plausible **alternative explanation** for the relationship. Consider this hypothetical alternative explanation in Sana and colleagues' study: Suppose that the people who multitasked were all people who had no prior knowledge of the topic, whereas the people who did not multitask had all taken a course in the topic before. In this case, difference in test scores could have an alternative explanation: amount of prior knowledge. To avoid this and many other alternative explanations, Sana and colleagues randomly assigned research participants to either multitask or not during the experiment, thereby creating equivalent groups. Causation, including methods like *random assignment* used to achieve it, will be discussed again in later chapters.

Explaining Behaviour

A final goal of scientific research in psychology is to explain *why* the events and behaviours occur. Consider the relationship between television violence and aggression; even if we know that television violence is a cause of aggression, we need to explain this relationship. Why does it occur? Is it due to imitation of the violence seen on television? Does viewing television violence desensitize people to violence, which then leads to more aggressive behaviour when given the chance to aggress? Or does watching television violence lead to a belief that aggression is a normal response to frustration and conflict, and that belief is what ultimately triggers aggressive acts? Do all three of these possibilities (modelling, desensitization, and believing aggression is normal) combine to jointly explain why aggression increases after viewing television violence? Additional research is often needed to explore possible explanations of the causal relationship. Such research often involves testing theories that are developed to explain particular relationships. Experiments and mediation analyses can help us explain behaviour (see Chapter 4).

Description, prediction, determination of cause, and explanation are all closely connected. Determining cause and explaining behaviour are particularly closely related because it is difficult to ever know the true cause or all the causes of any behaviour. An explanation that appears satisfactory may turn out to be inadequate when other causes are identified in subsequent research. For example, when early research showed that speaker credibility is related to attitude change, researchers explained the finding by stating that people are more willing to believe what is said by a person with high credibility than by a person with low credibility. This explanation was inadequate, but it formed the basis of a more complex theory of attitude change that includes many other factors related to persuasion (Petty & Cacioppo, 1986). There is a certain amount of ambiguity in scientific inquiry. New research findings almost always invite new questions to be addressed by further research; explanations of behaviour often must be discarded or revised as new evidence is gathered. Such ambiguity is part of the excitement and fun of science.

LO4

BASIC AND APPLIED RESEARCH

There are differences in the extent to which research is readily applicable to everyday contexts. The terms *basic* and *applied* research are often used to denote the ends of this continuum. To illustrate the distinctions between these approaches, we will consider different examples drawn from research using virtual reality.

Basic Research

The four goals of scientific research in psychology capture much of the focus of **basic research,** which attempts to answer fundamental questions about the nature of behaviour. Studies are often designed to develop and test aspects of *theories* (see Chapter 2) about phenomena such as cognition, emotion, motivation, learning, psychobiology, personality development, and social behaviour. In the following example of basic research, notice that the purpose is theory testing rather than a specific application. Results might be used to inform research on a variety of different phenomena (e.g., gaming, GPS navigation tools, post-brain injury rehabilitation), but these applications are not its primary purpose.

Han, X., & Becker, S. (2014). One spatial map or many? Spatial coding of connected environments. *Journal of Experimental Psychology: Learning, Memory, & Cognition, 40,* 511–531.

Researchers sought to clarify which of two competing theories best explained how people develop mental maps in complex environments. Using a virtual driving simulator, participants explored two virtual neighbourhoods under different conditions (e.g., sequentially or being free to navigate back and forth). Based on participants' memories of the neighbourhoods (which were tested later), researchers concluded support for hierarchical theory: People tended to form separate mental maps of regions, and later developed overarching connections across regions as a second step. The alternative theory, which proposed that maps of regions develop along with their interconnections, was not supported.

Test yourself! Which goal(s) does this research address?

Applied Research

Applied research is conducted to address practical problems and potential solutions. There is a range of how immediately "applied research" is expected to be applied; some offers insight into problems or solutions, and some offers specific tools to address those problems in specific settings (Klatzky, 2009). Consider how both of the following studies are examining applications of virtual reality to inform the practical issue of treating anxiety disorders: the first explores many different effects of this potential new treatment, and the second pits it head-to-head against the standard.

Côté, S., & Bouchard, S. (2005). Documenting the efficacy of virtual reality exposure with psychophysiological and information processing measures. *Applied Psychophysiology and Biofeedback, 30,* 217–232.

One well-established way for clinical psychologists to treat spider phobia is *exposure therapy*, which includes gradually exposing people to live spiders over weeks of treatment until they can hold one and not feel afraid. Researchers tested whether five weeks of exposure therapy using virtual spiders could decrease cognitive, physiological, and emotional symptoms of spider phobia. Participants had all been officially diagnosed with spider phobia. After virtual exposure therapy, people no longer fixated on images of spiders, their heart rate did not jump when presented with a live spider, and they reported having less spider-related anxiety.

Michaliszyn, D., Marchand, A., Bouchard, S., Martel, M.-O., & Poirier-Bisson, J. (2010). A randomized, controlled clinical trial of *in virtuo* and *in vivo* exposure for spider phobia. *Cyberpsychology, Behavior, and Social Networking, 13,* 689–695.

Researchers recruited clients who were seeking treatment for spider phobia, and after gaining their consent, randomly assigned them to receive
either the standard treatment using live spiders or matched exposure
using virtual spiders. Results showed that virtual reality treatment produced the same anxiety reduction as did live exposure, both by the end
of treatment and extending three months beyond, supporting its use in
clinical practice.

Both of these studies are grounded in the same applied issue, but they
differ in how quickly and easily the results of the study can actually be used.
The first study is aimed toward understanding the potential of virtual reality
in treatment, yet it is the second study that specifically offers a test of its use
in contrast to the pre-existing standard. Both of these studies are useful for
clinicians trying to provide treatment, but the specificity of the second means
it has the most applied relevance. Because the first study was used as a foundation for the second, these two examples also illustrate the idea of a program
of research that builds on prior work. We will explore the idea of using prior
research in Chapter 2.

Careers in Applied Research   Some applied research is conducted at universities, and some occurs in settings such as large business firms, market
research companies, government agencies, and public polling organizations.
Some industry-based applied research is not published but rather is used
within the company or by the company's clients. Whether or not such results
are published, however, they are used to help people make better decisions
about problems that require immediate action. Your training in research methods could help you pursue a career in many of these fields.

A major area of applied research–and a growing career opportunity–is
called **program evaluation.** Program evaluation research tests the efficacy
of social reforms and innovations that occur in government, education, the
criminal justice system, industry, health care, and mental health institutions.
(See also Chapter 11.) Social programs are designed to achieve certain outcomes, and social scientists should evaluate each program to determine
whether it is having its intended effect (Campbell, 1969). If it is not, alternative programs should be tried. Here is a sample published journal article
involving program evaluation research for which program administrators col-
laborated with university researchers:

Hayashi, K., Wood, E., Wiebe, L., Qi, J., & Kerr, T. (2010). An external evaluation of a peer-run outreach-based syringe exchange in Vancouver, Canada.
International Journal of Drug Policy, 21, 418–421.

Researchers analyzed data from an ongoing interviewer-administered
survey of Vancouver's injection drug users, and showed that a syringe
exchange program was effectively reducing the frequency of needle reuse
among people who were most at-risk for shared needle use and its consequences (i.e., HIV infection).

Integrating Basic and Applied Research

Progress in science is dependent on a synergy between basic and applied research. Much applied research is guided by the theories and findings of basic research investigations. For example, the creation of virtual reality crucially depended on earlier psychology research into basic processes of sensation and perception (e.g., depth); likewise, applied research on expert testimony in jury trials is guided by basic research in perception and cognition. In turn, the findings obtained in applied settings often suggest modification of existing theories and thereby spur more basic research. Such applied research is fed back into richer and more accurate knowledge of basic perceptual and cognitive processes.

Some people, including legislators who control the budgets of governmental research-granting agencies, have demanded that research be directly relevant to specific social issues. The problem with this attitude is that we can never predict the ultimate applications of basic research. Psychologist B. F. Skinner, for example, conducted basic research in the 1930s on operant conditioning, which carefully described the effects of reinforcement on such behaviours as bar-pressing by pigeons. Years later, this research led to many practical applications in therapy, education, and the workplace. Research with no apparent practical value ultimately can be very useful. No one can predict the eventual impact of basic research; therefore, support of basic research is necessary both to advance science and to benefit society.

Behavioural research is important in many fields and has significant applications to public policy. All researchers use scientific methods, whether they are interested in basic or applied questions. The themes and concepts we explored in this chapter will be expanded in the remainder of the book. In Chapter 2, we will consider how scientists find inspiration for research ideas and contribute to the body of knowledge by writing research reports. As you learn more about the scientific approach throughout this book, we invite you to engage in scientific skepticism and insist that claims be tested empirically.

STUDY TERMS

Test yourself! Define and generate an example of each of these key terms.

Alternative explanation (p. 11)

Applied research (p. 13)

Authority (p. 4)

Basic research (p. 12)

Covariation of cause and effect (p. 11)

Empiricism (p. 5)

Falsifiable (p. 7)

Goals of scientific research (p. 9)

Intuition (p. 4)

Peer review (p. 7)

Program evaluation (p. 14)

Pseudoscience (p. 8)

Replicate (p. 6)

Scientific skepticism (p. 5)

Temporal precedence (p. 11)

REVIEW QUESTIONS

Test yourself on this chapter's learning objectives. Can you answer each of these questions?

1. What are some of the benefits of learning about research methods?
2. Why is scientific skepticism useful in furthering our knowledge of behaviour? How does the scientific approach differ from other ways of gaining knowledge about behaviour?
3. Define and generate examples of the four goals of scientific research in psychology: description of behaviour, prediction of behaviour, determination of the causes of behaviour, and explanation of behaviour.
4. How does basic research differ from applied research?

DEEPEN YOUR UNDERSTANDING

Develop your mastery of these concepts by considering these application questions. Compare your responses with those from other people in your study group.

1. Read several blog posts or editorials in a local newspaper and identify the sources used to support the assertions and conclusions. Did the writer use intuition, appeals to authority, scientific evidence, or a combination of these? Give specific examples.
2. Suppose you were assigned to participate in a debate about the following claim: Behavioural scientists should conduct only research that has immediate practical applications. Develop arguments that support and oppose the claim.
3. Suppose you were assigned to participate in a debate about the following claim: Knowledge of research methods is unnecessary for students who intend to pursue careers in clinical and counselling psychology. Develop a few arguments that support and oppose the claim. Next, use skills from Chapter 2 and Appendix D to find the following article, and use it to evaluate your arguments:

   Lilienfeld, S. O., Ritschel, L. A., Lynn, S. J., Cautin, R. L., & Latzman, R. D. (2013). Why many clinical psychologists are resistant to evidence-based practice: Root causes and constructive remedies. *Clinical Psychology Review, 33,* 883–900.

4. A newspaper headline says that "Obesity Is More Common Outside Major Cities." You read the article to discover that a researcher found that the rates of obesity are lower in cities such as Vancouver, Toronto, and Montreal than in less urban centres across the country. Based on this information, is it appropriate to infer cause and effect and explanations of behaviour? Why or why not? Come back to this question after you have read the next few chapters. For more information, see:

   Vanasse, A., Demers, M., Hemiari, A., & Courteau, J. (2006). Obesity in Canada: Where and how many? *International Journal of Obesity, 30,* 677–683.

2

Where to Start

LEARNING OBJECTIVES

Keep these learning objectives in mind as you read to help you identify the most critical information in this chapter.

By the end of this chapter, you should be able to:

1	Describe different sources of ideas for research, including questioning common assumptions, observation, practical problems, theories, and past research.
2	Identify the two functions of a theory.
3	Summarize the information included in the abstract, introduction, method, results, discussion, and references sections of research articles.
4	Compare and contrast different ways to find past research.
5	Discuss how a research hypothesis differs from a prediction and a theory.

The motivation to conduct scientific research comes from a natural curiosity about the world. People may have their first experience with research when their curiosity leads them to ask, "I wonder what would happen if . . . " or "I wonder why . . . ," followed by an attempt to answer the question. What are the sources of inspiration for such questions? How do you find out about other people's ideas and past research? How do you structure your question so you can design a study to test it? In this chapter, we will explore the first three steps in the process of conducting research depicted in Figure 1.1: identifying some sources of scientific ideas, how to find and read past research on the topic, and how to convert your question into a testable hypothesis.

LO1

WHAT DO YOU WANT TO KNOW? SOURCES OF RESEARCH IDEAS

Good research ideas can come from anywhere. Many people are capable of coming up with worthwhile ideas but find it difficult to verbalize the process by which they are generated. Cartoonists know this–they show a brilliant idea as a light bulb flashing over the person's head. But where does the electricity come from? When student researchers are just starting out, their research ideas might come from what they are studying in their courses, or from the professors they work with in their research labs. Let's consider five broad sources of ideas: common assumptions, observation of the world around us, practical problems, theories, and past research.

Questioning Common Assumptions

One source of ideas that can be tested is common assumptions that people make to explain the world. For example, researchers can question *common-sense* or *folk-wisdom* beliefs within a culture (Stanovich, 2013). Do "opposites attract" or do "birds of a feather flock together"? Do friends or parenting practices affect children the most? Is a "picture worth a thousand words"? Asking questions such as these can lead to research programs studying attraction, social development, and the role of visual images in learning and memory, respectively.

Testing widely held assumptions can be valuable. Such notions don't always turn out to be correct, or research may show that the real world is much more complicated than our assumptions would have it. For example, despite the common belief that opposites attract, decades of research has shown that people tend to be attracted to others who are similar to themselves (Montoya, Horton, & Kirchner, 2008; Newcomb, 1961). Nonetheless, Heine, Foster, and Spina (2009) questioned whether this common finding would translate to non-Western cultures. Indeed, Japanese participants did not show this biased preference toward people who were similar to rather than different from them. Conducting research to test common assumptions often forces us to go beyond a common-sense theory of behaviour.

Observation of the World Around Us

Observations of personal and social events can lead us to develop intuitions about the world. As people taking on a *scientifically skeptical* mindset (see Chapter 1), we push those intuitions to fuel research ideas. For example, have you ever had the experience of setting aside a certain amount of time to complete a project, only to find that it takes much longer than you had anticipated it would? Such an experience could inspire research exploring how and why people underestimate task completion times. In fact, Roger Buehler at Wilfred Laurier University and his colleagues have conducted a series of experiments on this very topic (see Buehler, Griffin, & Ross, 2002, for a review). Carefully designed studies showed that people are particularly likely to underestimate how long a project will take when it involves many steps (and therefore can be interrupted easily), rather than when the task can be completed in one seating (Buehler, Peetz, & Griffin, 2010). Studying for exams and writing papers are exactly the kind of projects that take many steps. Be especially careful to give yourself enough time to complete them well!

Part-time jobs or volunteer positions can provide another rich source of material for scientific investigation. When he was a university student, psychologist Michael Lynn worked as a server in a restaurant, dependent upon tips from customers. The experience sparked an interest that fuelled an academic career (Crawford, 2000). For many years, Lynn has studied tipping behaviour in restaurants and hotels in the United States and in other countries (Lynn & Sturman, 2010). He has looked at factors that increase tips, such as posture, touching, and phrases written on a cheque, and his research has had an impact on the hotel and restaurant industry (Lynn & McCall, 2009). If you have ever worked in restaurants, you have undoubtedly formed many of your own hypotheses about tipping behaviour. Lynn went one step further and took a scientific approach to testing his ideas. His research illustrates that taking a scientific approach to an everyday problem can lead to new discoveries and useful applications.

Claims people make in books or other media can also trigger research ideas. For example, in her popular book on "tiger mothers," Chua (2011) proposed that extremely strict parenting practices produce the most productive children. A researcher might ask whether there is evidence for such a claim in all cultures or contexts, just some, or none at all.

Keenly observing the world can help people take advantage of *serendipity*. Sometimes the most interesting discoveries are the result of accident or sheer luck. Ivan Pavlov is best known for discovering what is called *classical conditioning*—a neutral stimulus (such as a tone), if paired repeatedly with an unconditioned stimulus (food) that produces a reflex response (salivation), will eventually produce the response when presented alone. Pavlov did not set out to discover classical conditioning. Instead, he was studying the digestive system in dogs by measuring their salivation when given food. His student happened to notice that the dogs were salivating prior to the actual feeding, and Pavlov then studied the ways that the stimuli preceding the feeding could produce a salivation response (Windholz, 1997). Of course, such accidental discoveries are made only when viewing the world with an inquisitive eye.

Practical Problems

Recall from Chapter 1 that the purpose of applied research is to address practical problems directly; the very existence of those real problems can trigger a research project idea. Groups of city planners and citizens might survey bicycle riders to determine the most desirable route for a city bike path, for example. On a larger scale, researchers have guided public policy by conducting research on graphic warning labels on cigarette packages (Hammond et al., 2007) and other social and health issues. Researchers who tend to conduct more basic research (see Chapter 1) may also draw inspiration from societal problems. Much of what is known about the psychology of prejudice and conformity, for example, can be traced to researchers attempting to understand the horrors of World War II (Aronson, 2012).

LO2

Theories

Much research in the behavioural sciences tests theories of behaviour. A **theory is a system of logical ideas that are proposed to explain a particular phenomenon and its relationship to other phenomena** (Fiske, 2004; Popper, 1968). In everyday conversation, people sometimes use the term *theory* to simply denote an idea that may or may not be true. In scientific usage, the term *hypothesis* comes closer to that idea. We will explore the concept of hypothesis in more detail later in this chapter. For now, what is most important to remember is that a scientific theory is grounded in–and helps to explain– actual data from prior research, and it specifies numerous hypotheses that are consistent with the broader theory. These specific hypotheses can then be tested through further research, to help evaluate the broader theory.

Theories serve two important functions in science. First, theories *organize and explain* a variety of specific facts or descriptions of behaviour. Such facts and descriptions are not very meaningful by themselves, and so theories are needed to meaningfully relate them to each other. Theories can make the world more comprehensible by providing a few abstract concepts around which we can organize and explain a variety of behaviours. Consider how Charles Darwin's theory of evolution by natural selection organized and explained a variety of facts concerning the characteristics of animal species. In psychology, one theory of memory asserts that there are separate systems of working memory and long-term memory. This theory organizes many specific observations about learning and memory, including the different types of memory deficits that result from damage to different areas of the brain (e.g., the hippocampus versus the amygdala), and the rate at which a person forgets material he or she has just read.

Second, theories *generate new knowledge* by focusing our thinking so that we notice new aspects of behaviour. Theories help us generate many hypotheses about behaviour, which are then evaluated in studies. If the studies support the hypotheses, then by extension, the theory is also supported. As a theory accumulates more and more supporting evidence, we become more confident that the theory is correct as it enables us to explain many observations. Research may reveal a weakness in a theory when part of it is not supported by evidence. When this happens, the theory can be modified to account for the new data. Sometimes a researcher will develop a new theory to account for both new data and an existing body of knowledge. When theories are informed by new data, the process of science expands our knowledge of the world around us.

Theories often are modified as new research defines their boundaries. The necessity of modifying theories is illustrated by the theory of working versus long-term memory mentioned previously. Originally, the long-term memory system was described as a storehouse of permanent, fixed memories. However, research by cognitive psychologists has shown that memories are easily reconstructed and reinterpreted. In a classic study, participants watched a film of an automobile accident and later were asked to tell what they saw in the film (Loftus, 1979). Participants' memories were influenced by the way they were questioned. For example, participants who were asked whether they saw "the" broken headlight were more likely to answer yes than were participants who were asked whether they saw "a" broken headlight. Results such as these required a more complex theory of how long-term memory operates.

If multiple theories are equally successful at explaining the same phenomenon, the scientific principle of **parsimony** dictates that the *least* complex theory is most desirable, because it is easiest to entirely *falsify* (Popper, 1968; see Chapter 1). Consider the case of two theories that differ in how many variables are used to explain the same phenomenon. Theory A is a complex theory with multiple variables, and Theory B is a simpler theory that focuses on just the variables that are necessary (and therefore is more parsimonious than Theory A). Now let's suppose that both theories really are wrong. It will be easier to show that the entire Theory B is wrong because it has fewer variables involved than Theory A, which will require more studies to completely disprove it. The theory with the fewest links among variables is better because it is easier to entirely falsify than is the theory with many links.

Consider the following theory as another way to think about *parsimony*. The meaning maintenance model (MMM; Heine, Proulx, & Vohs, 2006; Proulx & Inzlicht, 2012) is a broad theory that offers a single way to explain a vast array of research findings spanning developmental, social, clinical, personality, and cognitive psychology. *Meaning* is defined as a collection of mental representations that allows a person to understand their experiences. According to the MMM, events that violate meaning (e.g., witnessing explicit prejudice, absurdist art, sudden loss of a loved one) trigger a biologically aversive state of general physiological arousal. People are then motivated to reduce this state, and to recruit any of various meaning-maintenance strategies to do so (e.g., affirm other personal values, reinterpret the event in a way that makes it make sense). The MMM offers parsimony to the psychology literature: Rather than *un*-parsimoniously pursuing dozens of theories, MMM posits that the basic process underlying various phenomena *is the same*, regardless of whether one is considering schema development, cognitive dissonance reduction, coping with trauma, or the need for cognitive closure. One broad theory–if it holds up to further testing–might successfully explain findings from many other theories. Why is that a good thing? It more *parsimoniously* accounts for behaviour than the collection of narrower theories.

Notice also that the MMM meets the two major criteria for a theory: It organizes a vast array of past research findings as examples of a common meaning-maintenance phenomenon, and it triggers new questions (e.g., What types of maintenance strategies do people use after minor meaning violations like absurdist art versus after major meaning violations like a near-death experience?). Keep in mind that we do not know if the MMM is "right." Future research designed to test even more of its implications will reveal its limits.

Past Research

Another rich source of ideas is past research, which may or may not already include theories. Becoming familiar with a body of research already published on a topic is perhaps the best way to generate ideas for new research. Virtually every study raises questions that can be addressed in subsequent research. The research may lead to an attempt to apply the findings in a different setting, to study the topic with a different age group, or to use a different methodology to replicate the results. Recall from earlier that Steven Heine and colleagues (2009) found a result that replicated well in North America did not hold in Japan. Results like these have led to important qualifications of past research about many psychological phenomena.

As you become familiar with the research literature on a topic, you may notice inconsistencies in research results that need to be investigated, and you may want to study alternative explanations for the results. You may want to propose a new theory to account for existing results and spur new ideas, like Travis Proulx and colleagues did when developing the MMM (see above), or you may want to use what you know about one research area (e.g., alcohol consumption) to inform what is known about another area (e.g., self-control; see Rawn & Vohs, 2011).

Let's look at an example of a study that was designed to address methodological flaws in previous research. The study examined a method of helping children who are diagnosed with autism. Childhood autism is characterized by multiple symptoms, including severe impairments in language and communication ability, and is now subsumed under the diagnosis of autism spectrum disorder as of the *Diagnostic and Statistical Manual of Mental Disorders, Fifth Edition*. Parents and caregivers had been encouraged by a technique called *facilitated communication* that apparently allows an autistic child to communicate with others by pressing keys on a keyboard showing letters and other symbols. A facilitator holds the child's hand to enable the child to determine which key to press. With this technique, many autistic children seem to communicate their thoughts and feelings and answer questions posed to them. Many people who see facilitated communication in action consider it to be a miraculous breakthrough.

The original conclusion that facilitated communication was effective was based on comparing autistic children's ability to communicate with and without the facilitator. The difference is impressive to many observers. Recall, however, that science invites skepticism, including examining all evidence carefully and asking whether claims are justified (see Chapter 1). In the case of facilitated communication, Montee, Miltenberger, and Wittrock (1995) noted that the original study design failed to rule out a crucial *alternative explanation*: the facilitator may be unintentionally guiding the child's fingers to type meaningful sentences. In other words, the facilitator, and not the person with autism, is controlling the communication. Montee and colleagues conducted a study to test this idea. In one condition, both the facilitator and the autistic child were shown pictures, and the child was asked to indicate what was shown in each picture by typing a response with the facilitator. In another condition, only the child saw the pictures. In a third condition, the child and facilitator were shown different pictures (but the facilitator was unaware of this fact). Consistent with the hypothesis that the facilitator was controlling the child's responses, the pictures were correctly identified only in the condition in which both saw the same pictures. Moreover, when the child and facilitator viewed different pictures, the child never made the correct response, and usually the picture the facilitator had seen was the one identified. Despite *replications* of this effect (e.g., Wegner, Fuller, & Sparrow, 2003), some practitioners have chosen to ignore this evidence and continue to believe that facilitated communication is an effective treatment option (Mostert, 2010). This example, while illustrating the use of past research to generate new research questions, also reminds us that scientific skepticism is an important skill that helps us evaluate claims in everyday life.

Researchers use any or a combination of these methods—questioning assumptions, observation, practical problems, theories, and past research—to develop an idea for a single study or a program of research. In all cases, researchers need to find out what other scientists have already learned about the topic. Next, we consider how to find that past research literature.

HOW DO WE FIND OUT WHAT IS ALREADY KNOWN?

Imagine you have used your acute observations of the world around you to come up with a research idea. What comes next? It is time to find out what past research has already revealed. You might find a large body of research literature, including well-developed theories that lead you to revise your original question so that you are asking something new. Or you might find that very little is known about the phenomenon or variables driving your curiosity. Investigating past research helps the researcher clarify the idea and design the study, and ensures that the study is making a new contribution to understanding behaviour. Past research can also help you in your everyday life when evaluating research reported in the media, and when solving personal problems. In this section, we will explore the types of papers you can expect to find and the ways to find them.

What to Expect in a Research Article

When a scientist has research results or a new theory to share with the scientific community, it is time to write up a report to submit for publication in a professional journal (see Figure 1.1 in Chapter 1). These reports usually share some common features. Becoming familiar with these features will help you get the most out of the research articles you find. As a new scientist, you might be asked to write up a research report that follows these features too. For now, we will focus on what to look for while *reading* articles. See Appendix A for more information about how to *write* articles.

Across all sciences, research articles that report the results of one study usually have six major sections: (1) an *abstract* summarizes the entire report; (2) an *introduction* explains the problem under investigation and the specific hypotheses being tested, if any; (3) a *method* section describes in detail the exact procedures used in the study; (4) a *results* section presents the specific findings; (5) a *discussion* section concludes the article, in which the researcher may speculate on the broader implications of the results, address potential alternative explanations for the results, discuss reasons that a particular hypothesis may not have been supported by the data, and/or make suggestions for further research on the problem; and finally, (6) the *references* section lists all the sources that were cited throughout the article. In psychology, all citations throughout the article, and all references in the references section follow the specific formatting rules found in the *Publication Manual of the American Psychological Association* (APA, 2010b). References in this textbook are formatted using those rules. These common formatting rules help scientists to communicate with each other efficiently. All scientists know where to find information about the specific methods the researcher used (the methods section), and where to find the researcher's thoughts about the potential implications of the work (the discussion section). Each section is elaborated below. Note that some research reports include methods and results sections from multiple studies, which are synthesized later in a *general discussion* section.

LO3

Abstract   The **abstract** is a summary of the research report. It typically runs no more than 120 words in length, although the word limit can vary by journal. It includes information about the hypothesis, the procedure, and the broad pattern of results. Generally, little information is abstracted from the discussion section of the paper.

Read the abstract to decide whether the article could help you learn about your research topic.

Introduction   In the **introduction,** the researcher outlines the problem that has been investigated. Past research and theories relevant to the problem are described, a gap in the existing knowledge is identified, and the current study is introduced as an attempt to fill this knowledge gap. The researcher will often end this section by stating the hypothesis, or by declaring the study to be exploratory yet guided by particular questions. In other words, the investigator introduces the research project by building a logical case that justifies why this study and the expected results will make an important contribution to understanding behaviour.

Read the introduction to find out the purpose of the study, the past research and theories relevant to the study, and the hypothesis.

Method   The **method** section provides information about exactly how the study was conducted, including any details necessary for the reader to *replicate* (repeat) the study. It is often divided into subsections, with the number of subsections determined by the author and dependent on the complexity of the research design. One subsection describes the characteristics of the participants. How many participants identified themselves as male or female or transgendered? What was the average age? How many participants were included? If the study used human participants, how were they recruited for the study? If the study used non-human animals, what species and genetic strain was used? The next subsection details the procedure used in the study. It is important that no potentially crucial detail be omitted while describing stimulus materials presented to the participants, the way participants' behaviour was recorded, and so on. Other subsections may be necessary to describe in detail any equipment or testing materials that were used.

We have been using the term *participants* to refer to the people who participate in research projects. An equivalent term in psychological research is *subjects*. The *Publication Manual of the American Psychological Association* (APA, 2010b) recommends using *participants* when describing humans who take part in psychological research. You will see both terms and others when you read about research, and both terms will be used in this book. You may also see the term *respondents,* to refer to people who take part in survey research (see Chapter 7), and *informants,* to refer to people who help researchers understand the dynamics of particular cultural and organizational settings, or who report on the personality characteristics of other people (e.g., Vazire, 2006).

Read the method section to find out characteristics of the participants, what they were asked to do, what materials were used, and the overall study design.

Results   In the **results** section, the researcher presents the findings, which have been based on statistical analyses. The results are often presented in three ways. First, there is a description in narrative form—for example, "The location of items was least likely to be forgotten when the location was both highly memorable and an unusual place for the item to be stored." Researchers try to avoid interpreting these results so that the readers can evaluate them for themselves. Comments about what the results mean are typically reserved for the discussion section. Second, the results are described in statistical language that reflects the analyses that were conducted to test the hypothesis, usually at the end of the narrative sentence. Third, results are often summarized in tables and/or graphs.

The statistical terminology of the results section may appear intimidating. Think of statistics as a tool the researcher uses to evaluate the outcomes of the study. You can build your ability to understand the logic behind the statistics, even before understanding the specific calculations. Chapters 12 and 13 and Appendix B provide a brief introduction to this powerful tool.

Read the results section for tables, graphs, and sentences that summarize the pattern of findings. This section will become easier to read as you increase your knowledge of statistics.

Discussion   In the **discussion** section, the researcher reviews the current study from various perspectives. Do the results support the hypothesis? If they do, the author should give all possible explanations for the results and discuss why one explanation is superior to another. If the hypothesis has not been supported, or has received only partial support, the author should suggest potential reasons. What might have been wrong with the methodology, the hypothesis, or both? The researcher also discusses how the results compare with past research results on the topic. This section may also include suggestions for possible practical applications of the research and for future research on the topic.

Read the discussion section for conclusions about the hypothesis, the study's strengths and limitations, and contributions it makes to understanding the topic.

References   Throughout any scientific article and many textbooks (including this one), you will notice **citations:** names and dates at the end of some of the sentences. These citations serve as a short form for the full reference, which is listed alphabetically (by the article's first author) in the **references** section at the end of the report. Consider why there are hyperlinks on websites or Facebook posts: to give readers a link to the source material being referred to in the post. Similarly, the purpose of citations in academic writing is to signal to readers that the idea or result described in that sentence was stated or found by the people cited, not the current author. In some disciplines it is common to include direct quotations along with citations in research articles, but writers in psychology and other sciences tend to paraphrase others' work instead (Madigan, Johnson, & Linton, 1995). *See what we just did there?* We signalled to you that Madigan and colleagues found that psychologists tend to paraphrase more than other disciplines. It's not our finding. We are using their finding to make a point. You can go to the references list in this book and find the full reference to this article, which you can use to find the full text. Then you can decide for yourself if we paraphrased their findings correctly.

Read the references section to look up specific citations you noticed in earlier sections. Use this information to find specific research articles that will help you learn more about what is known about your topic.

Other Types of Articles: Literature Reviews and Meta-Analyses

Articles that review and summarize research in a particular area may not typically follow the full six-section format described above. Depending on the way the research is summarized, this type of article might be called a **literature review** (if it uses narrative techniques) or a *meta-analysis* (if it uses statistical techniques; see Chapter 14). These articles might also propose new theories to better explain the existing research. Review articles will have abstract, introduction, discussion, and references sections, but the sections between the introduction and discussion will vary. The following article is an example of a literature review:

> Spence, I., & Feng, J. (2010). Video games and spatial cognition. *Review of General Psychology, 14,* 92–104. doi: 10.1037/a0019491
>
> The authors of this article reviewed past research investigating whether playing video games changes people's visual perception processes. They organize and describe a very large number of studies showing that playing action games influences basic capacities (e.g., object tracking) and complex spatial tasks (e.g., mental rotation). They also discuss new directions for the further understanding and application of these findings.

Reading Articles

Reading articles is a great way to become familiar with the way information is presented in reports. (Consider starting with the entire article that is published in Appendix A. It is in manuscript form, formatted the way a psychologist would submit it for potential publication, with notations to help you create your own manuscript in APA style.) As you read articles, you will develop ways of efficiently processing the information in them. You do not need to read every section in order. It is usually best to read the abstract first, and then skim the article to decide whether you can use the information provided. Sometimes it is appropriate to skip to the section you need most. For example, when searching for ways that other researchers have studied creativity, you might head straight to the methods section. Then go back and read the article carefully. Note the hypotheses and theories presented in the introduction, write down anything that seems crucial or problematic in the method, and read the results in view of the material in the introduction. Be critical when you read the article. As you read more research on a topic, you will become more familiar with the variables being studied, the methods commonly used to study those variables, the important theoretical issues being considered, and the problems that need to be addressed by future research. You just might find yourself generating your own research ideas and planning your own studies.

LO4

Where Are These Articles Published? An Orientation to Journals and Finding Articles

Once a researcher has written a paper using the norms of our discipline briefly summarized above, it is time to submit the article for publication to a professional journal. The journal's editor will then solicit reviews from other scientists in the same field and will use these reviews to decide whether the report is to be accepted for publication. This is the process of *peer review* introduced in Chapter 1. Each journal receives many more papers than it is willing to publish. To help ensure high standards in the quality of research conducted, most papers are rejected. Those that are accepted are published in print about a year later; however, many journals now provide online access shortly after a paper is accepted. Some journals are published entirely online and never in print (e.g., PLOS ONE). Once accepted for publication by a journal, these research reports are considered *primary sources* in our discipline.

There is an enormous number of professional journals. Some are published monthly, others quarterly or annually. Some publish original scientific research across the discipline (e.g., the journal called *Psychological Science*) or in a subfield (e.g., *Journal of Experimental Social Psychology*). Others publish only literature reviews and meta-analyses (e.g., *Psychological Bulletin*). Table 2.1 lists just a few of the journals in several areas of psychology.

There are so many journals it would be impossible to list them all—let alone read them all! This is why we need search engines and databases to help us find the articles we need most. Next we offer some tips for finding articles published in scholarly journals. For further information, we encourage you to consult your institution's library resources (e.g., your library's website, librarians, and workshops the library may offer), as well as more-detailed guides to library research in psychology and to preparing to write papers (e.g., Reed & Baxter, 2003; Rosnow & Rosnow, 2012). Some institutions have subject librarians, whose job involves helping students and faculty find the articles they

TABLE 2.1 Some major and specialized journals in psychology

General	
American Psychologist	*Journal of Experimental Psychology: General*
British Journal of Psychology	*Psychological Methods*
Canadian Journal of Behavioural Science	*Psychological Science*
Literature reviews and meta-analyses	
Current Directions in Psychological Science	*Psychological Science in the Public Interest*
Psychological Bulletin	*Revue Quebecoise de Psychologie*
Psychological Review	
Cognitive and behavioural neuroscience areas of psychology	
Behavioral Neuroscience	*Journal of Experimental Psychology: Animal Learning and Cognition*
Canadian Journal of Experimental Psychology	
Cognition	*Journal of Experimental Psychology: Learning, Memory, and Cognition*
Neuropsychology	
Clinical and counselling psychology	
Behavior Research and Therapy	*Journal of Abnormal Psychology*
Journal of Abnormal Child Psychology	*Journal of Consulting and Clinical Psychology*
Developmental psychology	
Child Development	*Developmental Review*
Developmental Psychology	*Journal of Experimental Child Psychology*
Personality and social psychology	
Journal of Experimental Social Psychology	*Journal of Research in Personality*
Journal of Personality and Social Psychology	*Personality and Social Psychology Bulletin*
Applied and interdisciplinary areas of psychology	
Journal of Applied Psychology	*Health Psychology*
Journal of Educational Psychology	*Evaluation and Program Planning*
Psychology, Public Policy, and Law	*Journal of Consumer Psychology*
Cyberpsychology, Behavior, and Social Networking	*Journal of Experimental Psychology: Applied*
Sexuality, gender, culture, and family studies	
Journal of Family Psychology	*Journal of Sex Research*
Journal of Marital and Family Therapy	*Journal of Cross-Cultural Psychology*
Psychology of Women Quarterly	*Psychology of Men and Masculinity*

need for their research projects. Check out what resources are available at your institution to help you.

While you can access some physical copies of printed and bound journals by visiting your institution's library, many articles are available online as PDF or HTML documents. Finding them—and finding the right articles—can be more challenging than it seems at first, especially if you are new to a topic and are just learning its precise terminology. It might take a few hours to find just the right keywords that will reveal articles relevant to your research project. We will consider a few different ways of searching for articles online, and how best to use each of them. Table 2.2 highlights some pros and cons of each type of search.

PsycINFO   There are many databases that cover a wide range of academic disciplines. The American Psychological Association's searchable computer database system is called **PsycINFO,** which includes coverage of journal publications in psychology and related fields from the 1800s to the present. Access to *PsycINFO* is purchased by and tailored to your institution, so the exact procedures you will use to search *PsycINFO* (or any other database, such as PubMed for biological psychology and biomedical literature) will depend on how your library has arranged to obtain access to the database. In all cases, you enter search terms into the dialogue boxes to obtain a list of abstracts that are related to your search terms. *PsycINFO* is useful because it allows us to limit our search results to improve the likelihood of finding exactly the articles we need. For example, we have the option to limit results to peer-reviewed articles published in a particular date range by a specific author.

Try it out! Examine Appendix D for specific steps to conducting a *PsycINFO* search. Try following along in the *PsycINFO* database you can access through your institution's library. Off-campus users may need to log in to access it (e.g., through a virtual private network, or VPN). Your library's website should include instructions for how to access these resources from off campus.

Web of Science   Another search resource is the *Web of Science*, which can be accessed directly or through the *Web of Knowledge* database. Like *PsycINFO*, **Web of Science** allows you to search through citation information such as the name of the author or the article title. It draws articles from disciplines such as biology, chemistry, biomedicine, and pharmacology, as well as social and behavioural sciences such as psychology, sociology, and criminal justice. One strength of *Web of Science* is the ability to use the "cited reference search" for articles spanning disciplines. Here you need to first identify a key article on your topic, usually one published a while ago that is particularly relevant to your interests. You can then search for more recent articles that cited the key article. This search will give you a list of articles that may be relevant to your topic and that are more recent than your key article. *PsycINFO* may offer a cited reference search service too, depending on your library's agreements. To provide an example of this cited reference search process, consider the following article:

Ross, M., Xun, W. Q. E., & Wilson, A. E. (2002). Language and the bicultural self. *Personality and Social Psychology Bulletin, 28,* 1040–1050. doi: 10.1177/01461672022811003

An article search using the *Web of Science* resulted in 102 articles that have cited this paper since it was published in 2002. Here is one of them:

Cheung, B. Y., Chudek, M., & Heine, S. J. (2011). Evidence for a sensitive period for acculturation: Younger immigrants report acculturating at a faster rate. *Psychological Science, 22,* 147–152. doi: 10.1177/0956797610394661

After becoming familiar with this article or others on the list, you might use it as a new key article for further searches. It is also possible to specify a key researcher in order to find all articles written by or citing a particular researcher after a given date.

Other Library Databases　　Your library may or may not have access to the *PsycINFO* or the *Web of Science* databases. The number of information databases that a library may purchase today is enormous; budget and other considerations determine which ones are available to you. You will need to take advantage of instructional materials that your library provides to help you learn how to best search for information available through your library. Other major databases include Academic Search Complete, Sociological Abstracts, MEDLINE, PubMed, and ERIC (Educational Resources Information Center). In addition, services such as PsycEXTRA, Canadian Newsstand Complete, and Access World News allow you to search general media resources such as newspapers.

Some of the information resources available provide the full text of articles in the database, whereas others provide only abstract or citation information. *PsycINFO* typically links to full-text access for most journals, depending on your library's subscriptions. If the full text of the article is not available via computer, you may be able to obtain it from another library. A reference librarian can help you use these and other resources available to you.

The Internet　　The most widely available information resource is the wealth of material that is freely available on the Internet. Search engines such as Google allow you to search through a variety of materials to help you find websites devoted to your topic, articles people have posted, book reviews, and online discussions. Although it is incredibly easy to search (just type something in a dialogue box and press the Enter key), you can improve the quality of your searches by learning (1) the differences in the way each search engine finds and stores information; (2) advanced search rules, including how to make searches more narrow and how to find exact phrases; and (3) ways to critically evaluate the quality of the information that you find. We also encourage you to make sure that you carefully record the search engine and search terms you used, the dates of your search, and the exact location of any websites that you will be using in your research. This information will be useful as you provide references in the papers that you prepare, and may help you avoid unintentional plagiarism (see Chapter 3).

TABLE 2.2   Comparing library databases with Internet searches

Source	Useful for...	Cautions and Caveats
Library databases (e.g., *PsycINFO*, *Web of Science*)	Finding specific articles Setting advanced search limits (e.g., keywords, peer-reviewed articles only, author, title, journal title) Reliable cited reference searches Complete, searchable bibliographic details Trusting that the database is monitored for accuracy Accessing many full-text articles when connected to campus library Learning disciplinary jargon by using thesaurus-suggested terms as well as keywords lists from articles that are useful to you	For full access, log in on campus or consult your library resources for how to log in while off campus Knowing the important terminology in your topic is helpful for choosing specific search terms
Internet search	Exploring a topic very broadly, including blog posts, magazine articles, videos, etc. Finding researchers' websites for original articles and their full publication records	Cannot set advanced search limits (e.g., to limit to peer-reviewed articles) Can be difficult to find peer-reviewed journal articles amid broad, general search results Not monitored for accuracy
Scholar.google.ca	Exploring topic fairly broadly within books, dissertations, peer-reviewed journal articles, patents, etc. Setting basic search limits (e.g., publication date) Accessing some full-text articles when connected to campus library Finding some references to journal articles for *PsycINFO* search Learning some important terminology for a new area of study Finding sources for multidisciplinary topics	For more full-text links, log in on campus or consult your library resources for how to log in while off campus Results include all disciplines (e.g., search for "power" yields entries from sociology, political science, psychology, statistics, physics, and all articles with an author whose last name is Power) Cannot set advanced search limits (e.g., for peer-reviewed articles) Can be difficult to find peer-reviewed journal articles amid dissertations and books Citation counts are unverified and can be falsely inflated Not monitored for accuracy
Wikipedia	Learning some important terminology for a new area of study Finding some references to journal articles for *PsycINFO* search	Not monitored for accuracy Entries often have greatly limited or absent references Not considered an acceptable source for most research papers and assignments

When using the Internet for research and in everyday life, it is essential to critically evaluate the quality of what you find. Your own library and a variety of websites have information on evaluating the quality of information found on the Internet. Some of the most important things to look for are listed here:

- Are credible references (e.g., peer-reviewed articles) provided for factual information?

- Is the site associated with a major educational institution or research organization? A site sponsored by a single individual or an organization with a clear bias should be viewed with extra skepticism.

- Is information provided about the people who are responsible for the site? Can you check the credentials of these people? Is contact information provided for the authors, to enable you to verify the credibility of the site?

- Is the information current?

- Do links from the site lead to legitimate organizations?

Google Scholar   Google has developed a specialized scholarly search engine that can be accessed at http://scholar.google.ca. When you conduct a Google Scholar search, you find papers and books from scholarly journals, universities, and academic book publishers. This can be a useful addition to searching *PsycINFO* to find sources, particularly for topics that span across disciplines (e.g., artificial intelligence spans psychology and computer science). However, one of the primary disadvantages is that Google Scholar does not allow you to narrow your search as precisely as *PsycINFO*. For example, you cannot limit your search to peer-reviewed research, but instead you have to search through books or dissertations or book reviews that are typically (although not always) less helpful for research projects than are peer-reviewed articles. Another disadvantage of searching using Google Scholar is that the full text of primary source articles is sometimes unavailable or available only for pay. Be careful not to pay for articles your library provides for free!

Wikipedia   The Internet is overflowing with content generated by anyone, with or without expertise. Wikis such as Wikipedia invite any user to adapt its content. Although the ultimate goal of Wikipedia is to be a trustworthy source of information (Wikipedia, 2011a), it is *not intended nor considered a credible source for academic research* (Harris & Cameron, 2010; Wikipedia, 2011b; Young, 2006). Sites like Wikipedia, as well as encyclopedias, can be useful starting points to learn about terminology or a key idea in your topic area (e.g., see http://en.wikipedia.org/wiki/Portal:Psychology). However, Wikipedia should never be the final stop of your research. For example, you might be interested in how people perceive depth. If you choose to search Wikipedia for *depth perception*, you can see that there are both monocular and binocular cues to distance. Scrolling down to the bottom of the page, there is a list of references that you can use as a starting point in your *PsycINFO* or *Web of Science* searches to investigate these types of cues using credible sources. If there are no academic journal articles listed (and especially if there are no references at all), this is a clue to be even more skeptical than usual about the quality of the posting.

Comparing and Evaluating Search Results   You may find the most effective strategy to find the past research you need is to combine results from the broader Internet (e.g., Google Scholar) and library databases (e.g., *PsycINFO*). The psychology subject librarian at the University of British Columbia recommends using *PsycINFO* for precision and Google Scholar for completeness. Refer back to Table 2.2 for a list of pros and cons for using library databases and broader Internet searches.

As you use different types of searches, you will learn more about the topic, which will make it easier to use search tools efficiently. As you search, note the keywords and researchers' names you see most often associated with the journal articles that are closest to your topic, and use those words and names in your subsequent searches.

DEVELOPING HYPOTHESES AND PREDICTIONS

LO5

So far, you have come up with an idea and have refined it using the past research you found with the above search strategies. Now it might be time to create a hypothesis. After conducting a literature review, researchers will know whether enough is already known about the topic to create a hypothesis. A **research hypothesis** (often just called a *hypothesis*) is a statement about something that may or may not be true, is informed by past research or derived from a broader theory, and is waiting for evidence to support or refute it. If very little or no research has been conducted previously on a topic, a researcher might choose to conduct purely exploratory research that is not aimed to test a particular hypothesis. Yet as we have alluded to earlier, many studies are attempts to test a hypothesis about how two or more variables may relate to each other. Once the hypothesis is proposed, data must be gathered and evaluated in terms of whether the evidence is consistent or inconsistent with the hypothesis.

Consider the topic of food consumption among university students dining in groups in cafeterias. The research team of Young, Mizzau, Mai, Sirisegaram, and Wilson (2009) had several questions about this topic, such as "Do female undergraduates eat different amounts of food when sitting in mixed-sex groups versus female-only groups?" or "Do people eat a similar number of calories as the people with whom they are eating?" Such research questions form the basis of formal research hypotheses that propose how the variables (in this case, sex, group composition, and calorie consumption) may be related. Researchers converted the first question above into the following research hypothesis: "Females' calorie consumption differs depending on the sex composition of their eating companions."

Think about it! Imagine what it would be like to write an exam in a crowded lecture hall, squeezed in elbow-to-elbow. Now imagine what it would be like to write an exam in a room separated from other people by at least a metre in all directions. Do you think the crowding would have an effect on your performance? Based on this potential experience, now imagine that you wanted to conduct an experiment. You might make the following research hypothesis:

> *Hypothetical research hypothesis:* "A crowded environment results in worse performance on mental tasks compared to an uncrowded environment."

Once a research hypothesis is stated, it is time to design the specific study to test it. For example, you might invite research participants to complete a series of spatial rotation or memory tasks in either a crowded or an uncrowded room. Then, performance on these tasks is measured to assess whether crowding affected performance. After designing the study, the researcher would translate the more general hypothesis into a specific **prediction** concerning the outcome of this particular experiment (see Chapter 4). Importantly, predictions are stated in terms of the specific method chosen for the study. Note the differences between the general hypothesis above and the specific prediction stated below. One subtle shift you might notice is that predictions are often stated in the future tense (e.g., "will perform"), because they are referring to the specific study that is about to be conducted.

> *Potential prediction to test that hypothesis, phrased in the context of a specific research design:* "Participants in the uncrowded condition will perform better on a spatial rotation task than will participants in the crowded condition."

If the results of the study are consistent with this prediction, the more general research hypothesis is supported. If the results are not consistent with the prediction, the researcher will either reject the hypothesis (and conclude that crowding does not lead to poor performance) or conduct further research, testing the hypothesis using different methods. When the results of a study are consistent with a prediction, the hypothesis is only *supported*, not *proven*. Researchers often study the same hypothesis using a variety of methods, and each time this hypothesis is supported by a research study, we become more confident that the hypothesis reflects the truth rather than a fluke.

At this point, it is important to remember a key characteristic of all scientific hypotheses, which we discussed earlier in this chapter and in Chapter 1: **falsifiability** (Popper, 1968). This means that data could show that a hypothesis is false, *if* in fact it is false. Consider the hypothesis above that states that there is a difference in the amount of calories females consume at a given meal when eating with same-sex versus mixed-sex groups. It is certainly possible to measure and compare the amount of calories on the plates of females sitting in same-sex and mixed-sex groups. If the average amount of calories across these two groups was equal, this hypothesis would be *falsified*. If the average amount of calories for females eating with same-sex versus mixed-sex groups differs (as Young et al., 2009, found), the hypothesis is still capable of being falsified–but instead the data have supported it. In contrast, consider a hypothesis that is unfalsifiable: People have an invisible aura that changes colours depending on the person's health or illness. If the aura is invisible, how can it be measured at all, let alone relate to health and illness? What kind of data could ever support or disprove this hypothesis? Because scientists ascribe to *empiricism* (see Chapter 1), hypotheses are scientifically meaningful only if they can be falsified. This aura hypothesis cannot be falsified using objective data; therefore, it is a scientifically meaningless hypothesis.

In this chapter, we have elaborated the first three steps in the research process as depicted in Figure 1.1. We considered sources of research ideas, how to search for past research and what that looks like, and how to transform the idea into a research hypothesis. The next steps involve designing a study to test that hypothesis, collecting data, and evaluating whether the data support that hypothesis. We will explore many options for study designs throughout the rest of this book. But first, in Chapter 3, we consider the importance of ethics at all stages of the research design and reporting process.

STUDY TERMS

Test yourself! Define and generate an example of each of these key terms.

Abstract (p. 24)	Prediction (p. 35)
Citations (p. 26)	*PsycINFO* (p. 30)
Discussion (p. 26)	References (p. 26)
Falsifiability (p. 35)	Research hypothesis (p. 34)
Introduction (p. 25)	Results (p. 26)
Literature review (p. 27)	Theory (p. 20)
Method (p. 25)	*Web of Science* (p. 30)
Parsimony (p. 21)	

REVIEW QUESTIONS

Test yourself on this chapter's learning objectives. Can you answer each of these questions?

1. What are five different methods for generating ideas for research? Provide an example of each.

2. What are the two major functions of a theory?

3. What information does the researcher communicate in each of the sections of a research article?

4. Describe differences in the way past research is found when using *PsycINFO*, *Web of Science*, or Google Scholar, including pros and cons of each.

5. What is a research hypothesis? How does it differ from a prediction? What is the relationship between a theory and a hypothesis?

DEEPEN YOUR UNDERSTANDING

Develop your mastery of these concepts by considering these application questions. Compare your responses with those from other people in your study group.

1. Think of a few common-sense sayings about behaviour (e.g., "Spare the rod, spoil the child"; "Like father, like son"; "Absence makes the heart grow fonder"). For each saying, develop a hypothesis that is suggested by the saying and a specific prediction that could follow from the hypothesis (Gardner, 1988).

2. Choose one of the hypotheses you formulated in Question 1 and find existing research studies that relate to that topic using the online database from your library.

3. Recall that theories serve two purposes: (1) to organize and explain observable events, and (2) to generate new knowledge by guiding our way of looking at these events. Identify a consistent behaviour pattern in yourself or somebody close to you (e.g., you consistently get into an argument with your sister on Friday nights). Generate two possible theories that could explain these patterns (e.g., because you work long hours on Friday, you're usually stressed and exhausted when you get home; because your sister has a chemistry quiz every Friday afternoon and she's not doing well in the course, she is very irritable on Fridays). How would you gather evidence to determine which theory might be correct? Do the two theories make different hypotheses about behaviour change? If they do, they are considered competing theories. Is one more parsimonious than the other? Now consider each of your two theories, one at a time. Supposing your theory had been supported by empirical evidence, how would you change these behaviour patterns (e.g., to increase or decrease their occurrence)?

4. Use *PsycINFO* to find one journal article (use Appendix D for tips). Identify all six elements of the research article, and compare what you can find in each section. Note where the research was conducted and who the researchers were. Use the Internet to find out if the researchers have websites. Where do they work? What other articles have the researchers published?

Ethical Research

LEARNING OBJECTIVES

Keep these learning objectives in mind as you read to help you identify the most critical information in this chapter.

By the end of this chapter, you should be able to:

| 1 | Discuss the three core ethical principles for research with human participants, as outlined in the *Tri-Council Policy Statement*. |

| 2 | List and describe some of the potential risks and benefits of research. |

| 3 | Describe why informed consent is used despite the potential challenges to obtaining it. |

| 4 | Describe the purpose and process of debriefing research participants. |

| 5 | Describe the function of a Research Ethics Board (REB). |

| 6 | Contrast the categories of risk to participants: exempt, minimal risk, and greater than minimal risk. |

| 7 | Describe how the "Three Rs" are used to minimize harm to animals in research. |

| 8 | Discuss professional ethics issues, including scientific misconduct and transparency reform. |

Ethical decision making is crucial in all aspects of research and other academic activities, including when planning, conducting, analyzing, publishing, and evaluating research. As members of the academic community, students and faculty alike must act in accord with professional ethics. In this chapter, we will emphasize the ways that researchers strive to treat research participants with respect, including institutionalized guidelines and checks. We will also explore some broader ethical issues, including fraud and plagiarism. A note of warning: Although some guidelines will seem straightforward, applying them in new research contexts can be very challenging.

WERE MILGRAM'S OBEDIENCE EXPERIMENTS ETHICAL?

Let us begin by considering a familiar example. As you might recall, Stanley Milgram conducted a series of experiments (1963, 1964, 1965) to study the phenomenon of obedience to an authority figure. He placed an ad in a local newspaper in Connecticut, offering to pay $4.50 (approximately $37 in 2014 Canadian currency) to men to participate in a "scientific study of memory and learning" being conducted at Yale University. The participants reported to Milgram's laboratory at Yale, where they met a scientist dressed in a lab coat and another participant in the study, a middle-aged man named "Mr. Wallace." Mr. Wallace was actually a **confederate** (i.e., an accomplice) of the experimenter, but the participants didn't know this. The scientist explained that the study would examine the effects of punishment on learning. One person would be a "teacher" who would administer the punishment, and the other would be the "learner." Mr. Wallace and the volunteer participant then drew slips of paper to determine who would be the teacher and who would be the learner. The drawing was rigged, however: Mr. Wallace was always the learner, and the volunteer was always the teacher.

The scientist attached electrodes to Mr. Wallace and placed the teacher in front of an impressive-looking shock machine. The shock machine had a series of levers that, the individual was told, when pressed would deliver shocks to Mr. Wallace. The first lever was labelled 15 volts, the second 30 volts, the third 45 volts, and so on up to 450 volts. The levers were also labelled "Slight Shock," "Moderate Shock," and so on up to "Danger: Severe Shock," followed by red Xs above 400 volts.

Mr. Wallace was instructed to learn a series of word pairs. Then he was given a test to see if he could identify which words went together. Every time Mr. Wallace made a mistake, the teacher was to deliver a larger shock as punishment. The first mistake was supposed to be answered by a 15-volt shock, the second by a 30-volt shock, and so on. The learner, Mr. Wallace, never actually received any shocks, but the participants in the study didn't know that. Mr. Wallace made mistake after mistake. When the teacher "shocked" him with about 120 volts, Mr. Wallace began screaming in pain and eventually yelled that he wanted out. What if the teacher wanted to quit? This happened–the participants became visibly upset by the pain that Mr. Wallace seemed to be experiencing. The experimenter told the teacher that he could quit but urged him to continue, using a series of verbal prods that stressed the importance of continuing the experiment.

The study purportedly was to be an experiment on memory and learning, but Milgram really was interested in learning whether participants would continue to obey the experimenter by administering ever higher levels of shock to the learner. What happened? Approximately 65 percent of the participants continued to deliver shocks all the way to 450 volts. This study (and Milgram's many extended replications) received a great deal of publicity, and the results challenged many of our beliefs about our ability to resist authority. The results have implications for understanding obedience in real-life situations, such as the Holocaust in Nazi Germany and the Jonestown mass suicide (see Miller, 1986). Moreover, a recent partial replication of his studies suggests that many people in contemporary North American society continue to obey authorities viewed as legitimate (Burger, 2009).

But what about the ethics of the Milgram studies? Researchers immediately debated the ethics of his studies (Baumrind, 1964; Kaufmann, 1967), and Milgram's work has shaped the common practices we use in psychology to protect our participants (Korn, 1997). As we consider the major guidelines that researchers use to determine whether a study procedure treats participants ethically, we will explore some of those common practices.

ETHICAL RESEARCH IN CANADA

The Tri-Council and Its Policy Statement

In Canada, researchers and institutions adhere to the *Tri-Council Policy Statement: Ethical Conduct for Research Involving Humans* (Canadian Institutes, 2010). "Tri-Council" is a common way to refer to the three federally funded research-granting agencies: the Canadian Institutes of Health Research (CIHR), the Social Sciences and Humanities Research Council of Canada (SSHRC), and the Natural Sciences and Engineering Research Council of Canada (NSERC). In 1998 the Tri-Council published the first **Tri-Council Policy Statement (TCPS),** which became the first standard Canadian ethics code to guide all research involving humans, and replaced all guidelines developed as early as the 1970s. In 2010, the Tri-Council published the first major revision of the TCPS; these guidelines will continue to develop. All institutions whose researchers receive funding from the Tri-Council must have a *Research Ethics Board (REB)* that reviews each study to ensure it adheres to the TCPS ethical guidelines. Many colleges and universities require students and faculty to ensure they are up to date on current policies by completing the *TCPS 2 Course on Research Ethics,* an online tutorial freely available at http://tcps2core.ca. *Try it out!* We will further discuss REBs and their relationship to the Tri-Council later in this chapter.

Historical, Legal, and International Context

The 1949 Nuremberg Code, which was developed in response to horrific human experimentation during World War II, was a catalyst for modern international debate and policies for respecting human dignity in medical and behavioural research (Interagency Advisory Panel on Research Ethics, 2009). It emphasized heavily the importance of *informed consent* (see below), and paved the way for updated international codes of ethics, including the World Medical Association's Helsinki Declaration in 1964, which had a massive impact on the way medical research is conducted (McNeill, 1993). Countries and professional scientific societies also began codifying ethical practices for all research involving humans. For example, the core principles of Canada's TCPS are consistent with those outlined in the earlier American document *The Belmont Report: Ethical Principles and Guidelines for the Protection of Human Subjects of Research* (National Commission for the Protection of Human Subjects of Biomedical and Behavioural Research, 1979). This report defined the principles and applications that have guided more detailed regulations, and informed the American Psychological Association Ethics Code (American Psychological Association, 2010a), to be discussed later in this chapter.

The TCPS also reminds researchers to consult and follow the laws of the jurisdictions in which the research is conducted. In addition to adhering to the TCPS, researchers must comply with the *Canadian Charter of Rights and Freedoms*, Canadian privacy of information laws, and relevant provincial laws. Varying legal contexts is one of the reasons why the TCPS is considered a set of *guidelines* rather than rules. Moreover, having guidelines rather than rules reflects the reality of innovation in science. We cannot prepare hard rules governing the ethics of research that has not yet been conducted, but we can develop guidelines to help us evaluate those future innovations as they arise.

Core Principles Guiding Research with Human Participants   LO1

The aim of research ethics codes generally, including the TCPS, is to ensure that research is conducted in a way that respects the dignity and inherent worth of all human beings. Three basic ethical principles express the value of ensuring human dignity and are specified in the TCPS and other documents (e.g., the *Belmont Report*): respect for persons, concern for welfare, and justice. The TCPS specifies the following:

- To show *respect for persons*, researchers must respect the autonomy of research participants, and protect those who have "developing, impaired or diminished autonomy." Respecting autonomy means enabling people to choose participation freely and without interference.

■ To show *concern for welfare*, researchers must attempt to minimize risks associated with participating in research, while maximizing the benefits of that research to individual participants and to society. When coupled with respect for persons, participants must be free to choose whether the balance of risk and benefits is acceptable to them.

■ To show *justice*, researchers must treat people fairly and equitably by distributing the benefits and burdens of participating in research. Demonstrating justice includes recruitment methods that offer participation to people from a diverse range of social groups, and excluding groups only when scientifically justifiable.

These three principles provide ethical direction for all researchers who rely on human participants to help them make scientific discoveries. It is essential to continually consider the participant's perspective when applying these principles in specific research contexts.

DESIGNING RESEARCH TO UPHOLD THE CORE PRINCIPLES

Much of the TCPS is devoted to offering advice on how researchers and institutional Research Ethics Boards can implement the core principles effectively. Nonetheless, translating the core principles into practice can be challenging; interpretation is the source of ongoing discussion and debate. This section discusses some of the common research practices that promote each core principle, as well as related debates.

LO2

Promote Concern for Welfare by Minimizing Risks and Maximizing Benefits

The principle of **concern for welfare** refers to the need to maximize benefits and minimize any possible harmful effects of research participation. Think about the last time you made a big decision: Did you consider the relative risks (or costs) and benefits to yourself and others? In decisions about the ethics of research, we are required to calculate potential risks and benefits that are likely to result; this is called a **risk-benefit analysis.** Ethical research procedures minimize risk to participants.

Benefits to Participants and Society Participants may experience several benefits from participating in research, including education about the scientific process, acquisition of a new skill, or treatment for a psychological or medical problem. They may also receive material benefits such as a monetary payment, a gift, the possibility of winning a prize in a raffle, or points toward a course grade. Other less tangible benefits may include satisfaction from contributing to a scientific investigation that may yield results that benefit society. The knowledge gained through the research might improve future educational practices, psychotherapy, or social policy.

It may be important to consider the potential benefits to society and, relatedly, the cost of *not* conducting the study if the proposed procedure is the only way to collect potentially valuable data (cf., Christensen, 1988). For example, studying people's experiences of traumatic events may upset some participants, yet failure to study this topic can lead to misguided treatments and care (Newman, Risch, & Kassam-Adams, 2006). Although benefits and costs to society have a place in the risk-benefit analysis, they are typically considered secondary to ethical treatment of participants.

Risk of Physical Harm   Some procedures could cause some physical harm to participants. For example, researchers have administered alcohol to investigate the effects of intoxication on decision making (Assaad et al., 2006), and have deprived people of sleep during different sleep phases to investigate the effects on attention (Zerouali, Jemel, & Godbout, 2010). The risks in such procedures require that great care be taken to make them ethically acceptable. Moreover, there would need to be clear benefits of the research that would outweigh the potential risks.

Risk of Psychological Stress   Participants may experience psychological stress during research. Let's return to considering Milgram's research. It is not difficult to imagine feeling stress if one believes one is delivering intense shocks to an obviously unwilling learner. A film that Milgram made shows participants protesting, sweating, and even nervously laughing while delivering the shocks. When pursuing *concern for welfare*, we ask whether subjecting people to such a stressful experiment is justified, and whether the experience might have any long-range consequences for the participants. For example, would participants who obeyed the experimenter feel continuing remorse or begin to see themselves as cruel, inhumane people? A defence of Milgram's study follows, but first let's consider some potentially stressful research procedures that have been used more recently.

Participants have been told that they will deliver a speech in front of an evaluative audience, receive a few minutes to prepare the speech, and go on to deliver the speech (Kirschbaum, Pirke, & Hellhammer, 1993). This method has been used to increase our understanding of physiological responses to stress among people with chronic major depressive disorder (Harkness, Stewart, & Wynne-Edwards, 2011), and whether that response differs for males versus females with depression (Chopra et al., 2009). In a different procedure, researchers interested in self-esteem sometimes give participants bogus tests of personality or ability. Using *deception* (see below), the researchers provide false feedback indicating that the participant has an unfavourable personality trait or a low ability score. Participants' self-esteem drops, allowing researchers to examine consequences on, for example, relationship well-being (Cameron, Holmes, & Vorauer, 2009).

Procedures that ask people to think about the deaths of a parent, spouse, or friend or their memories of living through a disaster could trigger a stressful reaction. That said, asking people about traumatic or unpleasant events in their lives causes stress for only some participants, but not most (Newman & Kaloupek, 2004). Furthermore, well-conducted studies of people's traumatic life events tend to show little evidence of emotional distress, and may in fact offer participants benefits from talking about their experiences (Newman et al., 2006).

When stress is possible, even if just for a minority of participants, safeguards must be taken to help participants deal with the stress (Newman et al., 2006). Usually there is a *debriefing* session following the study that is designed in part to address potential stresses that may arise during the research. Debriefing is discussed later in this chapter.

Risk of Losing Privacy and Confidentiality   Another risk is the loss of expected privacy and confidentiality. Researchers must take care to protect the privacy of individuals, which includes "the right to control information about oneself" (Canadian Institutes, 2010). At a minimum, researchers should protect privacy by keeping all paper data locked in a secure place and encrypting all electronic data. Yet definitions of *privacy* and *confidentiality* are changing in the digital age (Richards & King, 2014), and those changing definitions will impact the way behavioural research is conducted. Ethical and legal policies are being redeveloped to accommodate this environment. For our purposes, it is important to be aware that using data for purposes other than what was agreed to in the *informed consent* process (see below) may breach participants' privacy and confidentiality, adding risk to the participants in the form of lost trust.

Confidentiality becomes particularly important when studying topics such as sexual behaviour, divorce, family violence, or drug abuse; in these cases, researchers may need to ask people very sensitive questions about their private lives. It is extremely important that individual responses to such questions be **confidential** (i.e., kept secret and used only for the purposes promised by the researcher). In many cases, the responses are completely **anonymous**—there is no way to connect any person's identity with the data. This happens, for example, when questionnaires are administered to groups of people, and no information is asked that could be used to identify an individual (such as name, student identification number, or phone number). In other cases, the identity of participants can be known, and therefore data are not completely anonymous. For example, it is usually impossible to guarantee complete anonymity in personal interviews or in online studies for which participants enter an e-mail address. The researcher must carefully plan ways of coding data, storing data, and explaining the procedures to participants to ensure complete confidentiality of responses.

In some research, there is a real need to be able to identify individual participants. This occurs when people are studied on multiple occasions over time, or when specific personal feedback, such as an accurate test score, must be given to individual participants. In such cases, the researcher should create a code to identify the individuals but should separate the information about their identity from the actual data. Thus, if questionnaires or the computerized data files were seen by anyone, the data could not be linked to specific people. In these cases where codes are used or participants can otherwise be identified, anonymity cannot be guaranteed and researchers must take extra precautions to safeguard the confidentiality of all data.

Privacy laws in the United States can affect research conducted using the Internet in Canada. In particular, the *Patriot Act* in the United States allows the government to access records of Internet service providers. Therefore, online studies that are hosted by servers located in the United States risk the privacy and confidentiality of Canadian participants. For this reason, REBs may require that online studies are conducted using companies whose servers are located in Canada. A similar issue occurs for research conducted over text messages or e-mail with servers hosted in the United States (e.g., Gmail). Researchers who conduct studies online must develop or seek services that provide safeguards such as encryption to protect participants' data from interception by unauthorized parties.

Another privacy issue concerns concealed observation of behaviour (see Chapter 6). In some studies, researchers make observations of behaviour in public places. Observing people in shopping malls (e.g., Ozdemir, 2008) or on sidewalks (e.g., Costa, 2010) does not seem to present any major ethical problems. However, what if a researcher wishes to observe behaviour online, in more private settings, or in ways that may violate individuals' privacy (see Wilson & Donnerstein, 1976)? For example, would it be ethical to rummage through people's trash or watch people in public washrooms?

In one famous study, Middlemist, Knowles, and Matter (1976) measured the time to onset of urination and the duration of urination of males in washrooms at a college. The purpose of the research was to study the effect of personal space on a measure of physiological anxiety (urination times). The students were observed while alone or with a confederate of the experimenter, who stood at the next stall or a more distant stall in the washroom. The presence and closeness of the confederate did have the effect of delaying urination and shortening the duration of urination. In many ways, this is an interesting study; also, the situation is one that males experience on a regular basis. However, one can question whether the invasion of privacy was justified (Koocher, 1977). The researchers used pilot studies, roleplaying, and discussions with potential participants to conclude that ethical problems with the study were minimal (Middlemist, Knowles, & Matter, 1977). *Do you agree?*

FIGURE 3.1
Analysis of
risks and
benefits

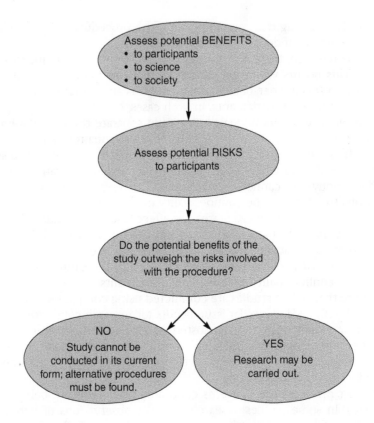

To uphold the TCPS principle of *concern for welfare* means that researchers seek to minimize risks and maximize benefits to participants. Figure 3.1 depicts a decision tree to help think through these complex issues, considering also the impact on society. Once a study has sufficiently demonstrated concern for welfare, the next principle comes into action: potential participants must be given the opportunity to assess their comfort with the risks and benefits involved.

Promote Respect for Persons through Informed Consent

The TCPS principle of **respect for persons** states that participants are treated as autonomous; they are capable of making deliberate decisions about whether to participate in research. The key way to apply this principle is **informed consent:** Potential participants in a research project should be provided with all information that might influence their decision about whether to participate. Thus, research participants should be informed about the purposes of the study, the risks and benefits of participation, and their rights to refuse or terminate participation in the study. They can then freely consent or refuse to participate in the research, and can withdraw at any time without penalty.

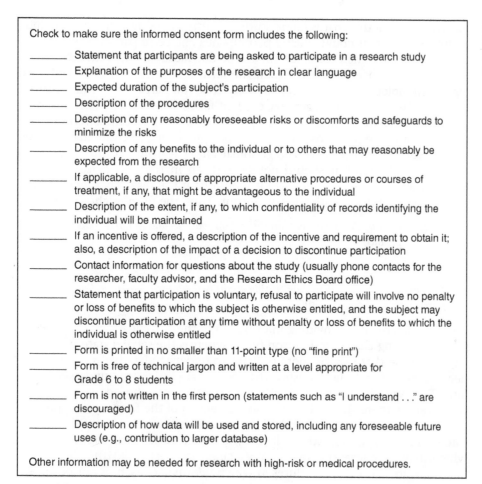

FIGURE 3.2
Checklist
for informed
consent form

Check to make sure the informed consent form includes the following:

_____ Statement that participants are being asked to participate in a research study

_____ Explanation of the purposes of the research in clear language

_____ Expected duration of the subject's participation

_____ Description of the procedures

_____ Description of any reasonably foreseeable risks or discomforts and safeguards to minimize the risks

_____ Description of any benefits to the individual or to others that may reasonably be expected from the research

_____ If applicable, a disclosure of appropriate alternative procedures or courses of treatment, if any, that might be advantageous to the individual

_____ Description of the extent, if any, to which confidentiality of records identifying the individual will be maintained

_____ If an incentive is offered, a description of the incentive and requirement to obtain it; also, a description of the impact of a decision to discontinue participation

_____ Contact information for questions about the study (usually phone contacts for the researcher, faculty advisor, and the Research Ethics Board office)

_____ Statement that participation is voluntary, refusal to participate will involve no penalty or loss of benefits to which the subject is otherwise entitled, and the subject may discontinue participation at any time without penalty or loss of benefits to which the individual is otherwise entitled

_____ Form is printed in no smaller than 11-point type (no "fine print")

_____ Form is free of technical jargon and written at a level appropriate for Grade 6 to 8 students

_____ Form is not written in the first person (statements such as "I understand . . ." are discouraged)

_____ Description of how data will be used and stored, including any foreseeable future uses (e.g., contribution to larger database)

Other information may be needed for research with high-risk or medical procedures.

Informed Consent Form   Potential participants are usually provided with some type of informed consent form that contains the information they need to make their decision. Commonly, the form is printed for the participant to read and sign. There are numerous examples of informed consent forms available on the Internet. Your university may have developed examples through its research office. A checklist for creating an informed consent form is provided in Figure 3.2. Note that the checklist addresses both content and format. The content typically will cover (1) the purpose of the research; (2) the procedures that will be used, including time involved; (3) the risks and benefits to the participant and in general; (4) any compensation; (5) how confidentiality will be protected; (6) the assurance of voluntary participation and permission to withdraw; and (7) contact information for questions about the research and about the ethics of the research. Researchers do not need to tell participants exactly what is being studied, but the consent form must include all information that could affect a participant's choice to participate.

A sample informed consent form can be downloaded from ▣ connect.

There have been cases in which the form is so technical or loaded with legal terminology that it is very unlikely that the participants fully realized what they were signing. In general, consent forms should be written in simple and straightforward language that avoids jargon and technical terminology (generally a Grade 6 to 8 reading level; word processing software may provide grade-level information with the grammar check feature). To make the form easier to understand, it should not be written in the first person. Instead, information should be provided as it would be if the researcher were simply having a conversation with the participant. Thus, the form might say

> *Participation in this study is voluntary. You may decline to participate without penalty.*

instead of

> *I understand that participation in this study is voluntary. I may decline to participate without penalty.*

The first statement is providing information to the participant in a straightforward way using the second person (you), whereas the second statement has a legalistic tone that may be more difficult to understand. Other measures may need to be taken to help ensure that potential participants understand the form. For example, if participants do not fluently speak the language the form is written in, there should be a translated version of the form. Special populations must be especially considered. For example, researchers have developed careful methods to help street drug users better understand the research to which they are consenting (e.g., HIV vaccine trials; Fisher, 2010).

There are research procedures in which informed consent is not necessary or even possible. If you choose to observe the number of same-gender and mixed-gender study groups in your library, you probably don't need to announce your presence or obtain anyone's permission. If you study the content of the self-descriptions that people write for an online dating service, do you need to contact each person to include their information in your study? When planning research without informed consent, it is important to make sure that you have good reasons for that decision. If informed consent is considered impossible to achieve the goal of science, the researcher's responsibilities to participants are increased.

Autonomy Issues   Informed consent seems simple enough; however, there are important issues to consider. The first concerns lack of autonomy. What happens when the participants may lack the ability to make a free and informed decision to voluntarily participate? Special populations such as minors, patients in psychiatric hospitals, or adults with cognitive impairments require special precautions. When minors are asked to participate, for example, a written consent form signed by a parent or guardian is generally required in addition to agreement by the minor; this agreement by a minor is formally called *assent*. The Division of Developmental Psychology of the American Psychological Association and the Society for Research in Child Development have established guidelines for ethical research with children.

Coercion is another threat to autonomy. Any procedure that limits an individual's freedom to consent is potentially coercive. For example, a supervisor who asks employees to fill out a survey during a staff meeting, or a professor who requires students to participate in a specific study in order to pass a course is applying considerable pressure on potential participants. The employees may believe that the supervisor will somehow punish them if they do not participate; they also risk embarrassment if they refuse in front of co-workers. Sometimes benefits are so great that they become coercive. For example, a prisoner may believe that increased privileges or even a favourable parole decision may result from participation; a person with extremely low income offered $100 to participate in a study may feel pressure to participate out of financial need, even if she is uncomfortable with the risks involved. Researchers must consider these issues and make sure that autonomy is preserved.

Massive data sets are proliferating as we move about our digitally enhanced lives, and government, businesses, and researchers are interested in analyzing them. Such secondary use of data can threaten people's ability to decide whether to participate in research. When you click "I accept the terms and conditions" when you sign up for an online service, is that equivalent to informed consent for any use of your data? Consider just the tip of the iceberg of your contribution to "big data": text and search histories, downloads and uploads, music and e-book purchases, Netflix watching habits, e-mail, Facebook friends and followers, constant location information, and application usage patterns. Human behaviour is being captured constantly, raising deep questions about the ethical use of these data.

Think about it! Consider a controversial experiment that involved collaboration between researchers working at a profit-based company (Facebook) and a university (Cornell). In 2012, unbeknownst to users, the Facebook researcher (a social psychologist) manipulated the emotional content of 689,003 users' news feeds. Anonymous data were provided to researchers at Cornell, and the whole team analyzed the data and published a peer-reviewed research paper in a reputable journal (Kramer, Guillory, & Hancock, 2014). The results showed evidence of spreading emotions across social networks: When people's news feeds contained fewer positive posts, their own posts were less positive and more negative; when their feeds contained fewer negative posts, their own posts were more positive and less negative. Controversy erupted (Albergotti & Dwoskin, 2014; Felten, 2014), and the journal editor issued an "Editorial Expression of Concern" (Verma, 2014). Why was this study controversial? Do you consider this study a violation of core principles? Why or why not?

Withholding Information   All ethics codes since the Nuremberg Code have stressed the importance of informed consent as a fundamental part of ethical research. However, it may have occurred to you that providing all information about the study might be problematic. Providing too much information could potentially invalidate the results of the study. Researchers usually will withhold information about the hypothesis of the study or the particular condition in which the person is participating (see Sieber, 1992). It is generally acceptable to withhold information when the information would not affect the decision to participate and when the information will later be provided, usually during a *debriefing* (see below) when the study is completed.

Deception   **Deception** occurs when researchers actively misrepresent information to participants. Milgram's experiments illustrate two types of deception: (1) misleading participants about the study's purpose and (2) staging a situation. First, there was deception about the purpose of the study. Participants in Milgram's experiments agreed to take part in a study of memory and learning, but they actually took part in a study on obedience. Who could imagine that a memory and learning experiment (that title does sound tame, after all) would involve delivering high-intensity, painful electric shocks to another person? Participants didn't know what they were agreeing to do. Milgram's experiments also illustrate a second type of deception: Participants became part of a series of events staged for the purposes of the study. A *confederate* of the experimenter played the part of another participant; Milgram created a reality for the participant in which obedience to authority could be observed.

Researchers typically use the first type of deception by creating a false purpose or a cover story to make the experiment seem plausible and involving (Gross & Fleming, 1982; Hertwig & Ortmann, 2008). For example, a researcher might tell participants that they are reading newspaper stories for a study on readability when the true purpose is to examine mind-wandering. Note that deception is not limited to laboratory research. Procedures in which observers conceal their purposes, presence, or identity are also deceptive (see Chapter 6).

Why do researchers use deception? Sometimes researchers are concerned that the informed consent procedure would affect the outcome of the study. Research indicates that providing informed consent may actually bias participants' responses, at least in some research areas (Dill, Gilden, Hill, & Hanslka, 1982; Gardner, 1978). In Milgram's case, knowledge that the research is designed to study obedience would likely alter the behaviour of the participants; some participants may seek to demonstrate how *dis*obedient they are. Milgram's study was conducted before informed consent was routine, yet Burger's (2009) partial replication suggests that fully informed consent would have changed the results: Participants' data had to be excluded from analyses if they had previously learned about Milgram's work.

It is also possible that the informed consent procedure may bias sample characteristics. In Milgram's experiment, if participants had prior knowledge that they would be asked to give severe shocks to another person, some might have declined to be in the experiment. Therefore, we might limit our ability to *generalize* the results only to people who would agree to participate in such a study. If this were true, anyone could say that the obedient behaviour seen in the Milgram experiment occurred simply because the people who agreed to participate were sadists in the first place! Researchers use deception when they are concerned that fully informed consent may affect who agrees to participate or how they behave once the study begins.

Practical Difficulties of Deception　Researchers still use elaborate deception setups like Milgram's, but they have become less common since the 1980s (Hertwig & Ortmann, 2008; Sieber, Iannuzzo, & Rodriguez, 1995). We speculate four potential reasons for a decrease in elaborate deception. First, researchers became interested in cognitive variables and so used methods that were similar to those used by researchers in memory and cognitive psychology. Second, the general level of awareness of ethical issues as described in this chapter has led researchers to conduct studies in other ways (some alternatives to deception are described below). Third, ethics committees (i.e., REBs) at universities and colleges now review proposed research more carefully, so elaborate deception is likely to be approved only when the research is important and there are no alternative procedures available. Fourth, such elaborate setups are very difficult to achieve successfully, sometimes because participants' suspicions can undermine the value of deception in the first place (Hertwig & Ortmann, 2008). However, this effect depends on the variables: Some physiological measures have shown no difference between people who were suspicious about deception and people who were not (Linden, Talbot Ellis, & Millman, 2010). Nonetheless, elaborate deception is sometimes ruled out as impractical.

The Importance of Debriefing　**Debriefing** occurs after the completion of the study. It is an opportunity for the researcher to deal with issues of withholding information, deception, and potential harmful effects of participation, as well as to further educate participants about the nature and purposes of the research. Researchers are required to debrief participants when using partial disclosure or deception (Canadian Institutes, 2010).

　If participants were deceived in any way, the researcher needs to explain why the deception was necessary. If the research altered a participant's physical or psychological state in some way–as in a study that produces stress–the researcher must make sure that the participant has calmed down and is comfortable about having participated. If the participant wants to receive additional information or to speak with someone else about the study, the researcher should be prepared to provide access to these resources. The participants should leave the experiment without any ill feelings toward the

LO4

field of psychology, as research suggests they may become distrustful of researchers after experiencing deception (Blatchley & O'Brien, 2007). After a thorough debriefing, participants may even leave with some new insight into their own behaviour or personality.

Debriefing also provides an opportunity for the researcher to explain the purpose of the study, tell participants what kinds of results are expected, and discuss any foreseeable practical implications. In some cases, researchers may contact participants later to inform them of the actual results of the study. Thus, debriefing serves both educational and ethical functions.

Is debriefing sufficient to remove any negative effects when stress and elaborate deception are involved? Little research has investigated the impact of debriefing in general (Sharpe & Faye, 2009), but what has occurred has concluded that it effectively deals with deception and other ethical issues that arise in research (Oczak, 2007; Smith, 1983; Smith & Richardson, 1983). In the case of Milgram's research, a thorough debriefing session was provided. Participants who were obedient were told that their behaviour was normal under strong situational pressures; they had acted no differently from most other participants. Participants were assured that no shock was actually delivered, and there was a friendly reconciliation with the confederate. Milgram later mailed participants a report of his research findings along with a survey about their reactions to the experiment. Most participants (84 percent) reported they were glad that they had participated, and 74 percent said they had benefited from the experience. Only 1 percent said they were sorry they had participated. When a psychiatrist interviewed participants a year later, no ill effects of participation could be detected. Analysts of Milgram's methods have concluded that debriefing helped his participants (Ring, Wallston, & Corey, 1970).

Alternatives to Deception The Windsor Deception Checklist was developed to help researchers and REB members decide whether the specific way in which they are considering using deception raises ethical concerns enough to reconsider its use (Pascual-Leone, Singh, & Scoboria, 2010). If that use of deception is considered sufficiently problematic, a researcher may consider alternatives such as role-playing, simulation studies (a variation on role-playing), and "honest" experiments.

Role-Playing In one role-playing procedure, the experimenter describes a situation to participants and then asks them how they would respond to the situation (Kelman, 1967). Sometimes participants are asked to predict how real participants in such a situation would behave. Role-playing is not generally considered to be a satisfactory alternative to deception (Freedman, 1969; Miller, 1972). One problem is that simply reading a description of a situation does not involve the participants very deeply–they are not part of a real situation. Also, because the experimenter gives the participants a complete description of the situation, the experimenter's hypothesis may become transparent to the participants. When people can figure out the hypothesis, they may try to behave in a way that is consistent with the hypothesis (see *demand characteristics*, Chapter 9).

The most serious defect of role-playing is that no matter what results are obtained, critics can always claim that the results would have been different if the participants had been in a real situation. This criticism is based on data showing that people aren't always able to accurately predict their own behaviour or the behaviour of others (Aknin, Norton, & Dunn, 2009; Nisbett & Wilson, 1977). In fact, Milgram asked a group of psychiatrists to predict the results of his study and found that even these experts could not accurately anticipate what would happen. Nonetheless, role-playing can yield some interesting results when there are no reasonable alternatives. For example, Canadians who vividly imagined what it would be like to live with many social restrictions showed increased empathy for members of minority status groups (Hodson, Choma, & Costello, 2009).

Simulation Studies   A different type of role-playing involves simulating a real-world situation. Simulations can be used to examine conflict between competing individuals, driving behaviour using driving simulators, or jury deliberations, for example. Such simulations can highly involve participants and can effectively mimic many elements of a real-life experience. (See Mayhew et al., 2011, for a comparison of driving simulators with real driving.)

You may recall one unusually dramatic example of a simulation study so involving that it had to be terminated early: the Stanford Prison Study (Zimbardo, 1973; Haney & Zimbardo, 1998). Student participants were paid $15 per day (approximately $89 in 2014 Canadian currency) and were randomly assigned to act as guards or prisoners in a simulated prison in the basement of the psychology building at Stanford University. Participants became so deeply involved in their roles, the simulation was stopped after six days (instead of two weeks) because of the cruel behaviour of the "guards" and the stressful reactions of the "prisoners." This was only a simulation—participants knew that they were not really prisoners or guards. Yet they became so involved in their roles that the study produced extremely high levels of stress. The Stanford Prison Study is an unusual case—most simulation studies do not raise the ethical issues seen in this particular study.

Honest Studies   Honest studies include any research design that does not try to misinform or hide information from participants (Rubin, 1973). For example, studies of actual speed-dating events have been a very useful way to study romantic attraction (Finkel, Eastwick, & Matthews, 2007; Provost, Kormos, Kosakoski, & Quinsey, 2006). Participants can be recruited to engage in a speed-dating setting held on campus or at a local restaurant; they complete numerous questionnaires and make choices that can lead to possible dates. The situation enables the systematic examination of many factors that might be related to date selection without deceiving anyone about the purpose of the study.

Another way to conduct research without deception is to recruit people who are seeking out information or services that they need. Students who volunteer for a study skills improvement program at their university may be assigned to either an in-class or an online version of the course. The researcher can administer measures to both groups to examine whether one version is superior to the other.

Another strategy that can avoid deception entirely is to notice naturally occurring events that present research opportunities. For example, Baum, Gachtel, and Schaeffer (1983) studied the stressful effects associated with nuclear power plant disasters by asking people about their experiences living near a nuclear plant that had or had not accidentally released radioactive gases. Science depends on *replicability* of results (see Chapter 14), so it is notable that the same pattern of results was obtained following the September 11, 2001, terrorist attacks (Schlenger et al., 2002). More than 2,000 adult residents of New York City and other metropolitan areas throughout the United States completed a post-traumatic stress disorder (PTSD) checklist to determine incidence of the disorder. PTSD was indicated in 11.2 percent of the New York residents in contrast with 2.7 to 3.6 percent of the residents living in other metropolitan areas. Such naturally occurring events can be valuable sources of data.

Promote Justice by Involving People Equitably in Research

As defined in the TCPS, the principle of **justice** addresses issues of fairness in receiving the benefits of research as well as bearing the burdens of risk. Any decisions to include or exclude certain people from a research study must be justified on scientific grounds. Thus, if age, ethnicity, gender, or other criteria are used to select participants, there must be a scientific rationale. The history of medical research includes too many examples of high-risk research that was conducted with individuals selected because they were powerless and marginalized within the society. One of the most horrific is the Tuskegee Syphilis Study in which 399 poor African-American people in Alabama were not treated for syphilis in order to track the long-term effects of this disease (Reverby, 2000). This study took place from 1932 to 1972, when the details of the study were made public. The outrage over this study's targeted exploitation of a disadvantaged social group spurred scientists to overhaul ethical regulations in both medical and behavioural research. Yet examples continue to emerge. In Canada between 1942 and 1952, nutritionists and the federal government experimented with nutrients and food provided to malnourished members of Aboriginal communities and residential schools–without consent (Mosby, 2013). Requiring a specific group of people to bear all the risks of research is unacceptable.

The benefits of research must also be equitably shared across groups. It is unethical for a researcher to study a particular group of people to advance science if that particular group will not have access to the benefits associated with that research. Researchers from relatively wealthy nations have often investigated the health and psychology of people in developing nations; the research participants in developing nations should (but have not always) directly benefit from what is learned (Glantz, Annas, Grodin, & Mariner, 2001). In Canada, the Tri-Council has made a clear statement that research with First Nations, Inuit, and Métis peoples must engage and benefit the involved communities. In addition to extending knowledge, whenever possible, research should be relevant to and "benefit the participating community (e.g., training, local hiring, recognition of contributors, return of results)" (Canadian Institutes, 2010, Article 9.13). These examples are tangible, immediate ways that research can benefit participants individually as well as the entire community. A full chapter in the TCPS expands on how researchers can uphold all three core principles specifically when working with Aboriginal peoples.

Evaluating the Ethics of Research with Human Participants

When you make decisions about how to treat research participants ethically, you can use the core principles of the TCPS as a compass. To put all three principles into practice, researchers need to consider many factors. Who are the participants? How will results be shared with the participant community? Are there risks of physical or psychological harm, or loss of confidentiality? What types of deception, if any, are used in the procedure? How will informed consent be obtained? What debriefing procedures are appropriate? Researchers also need to weigh the direct benefits of the research to the participants, the scientific importance of the research, and the educational benefits to the students who may be participating in the research for a class requirement (see Figure 3.1).

Think about it! These are not easy decisions. Consider a study in which a male confederate insults a male participant who grew up in either the northern or southern United States (Cohen, Nisbett, Bowdle, & Schwarz, 1996). The purpose was to investigate whether males in the South had developed a "culture of honour" that expects them to respond aggressively when insulted. Indeed, the students from the North had little response to a verbal insult while the Southerners responded with heightened physiological and cognitive indicators of anger. The fact that so much violence in the world is committed by males who are often avenging some perceived insult to their honour makes this topic relevant to society. An ethics committee reviewing this study concluded that the researchers had sufficiently minimized risks to the participants such that the benefits outweighed the costs. Do you think that the potential benefits of the study to society and science outweigh the risks involved in the procedure?

If you ultimately decide that the costs outweigh the benefits, you must conclude that the study cannot be conducted in its current form. There may be alternative procedures that could be used to make it acceptable. If the benefits outweigh the costs, you will likely decide that the research should be carried out. However, your calculation might differ from another person's calculation, which is precisely why having Research Ethics Boards, which are discussed next, is such a good idea.

MONITORING ETHICAL STANDARDS AT EACH INSTITUTION

LO5

Individual researchers working at Canadian universities often compete for research funding from one of the Tri-Council agencies; which of the three agencies depends on the topic of research they conduct. Once a researcher is awarded a research grant, the agency transfers the funds to the university, which administers it to the researcher for use on that project. Individual researchers are ultimately responsible for complying with the ethical standards in the TCPS. However, just as the Tri-Council relies on individual universities to administer funds, it also involves universities in the process of ensuring that the TCPS is upheld in funded research. Each institution that receives any funding from any of the Tri-Council agencies must have a **Research Ethics Board (REB),** whose mandate is to review all research projects for compliance with ethical standards. Before starting any research project involving humans, researchers must apply for and receive ethical approval from their institution's REB. All research involving participants that is conducted by faculty, students, and staff associated with the institution is reviewed in some way by the REB. This includes research that may be conducted at another location—such as a school, a community agency, a hospital, or online. Systematic review of research proposals reduces the chance that research that treats participants unethically will be conducted.

Consistent with regulations in other countries (e.g., U.S. Department of Health and Human Services) and professional societies (e.g., Canadian Psychological Association), the TCPS categorizes research according to the amount of risk involved. Researchers need to understand which level of risk their research entails to participants. A brief description of each risk level and examples are provided below. However, because individual institutions' REBs will differ in specifically how these categories are determined, it is difficult to provide concrete rules for determining what kinds of research would fall in each category. Consult your institution's REB to learn precisely how it defines these categories.

Exempt Research

LO6

Research in which there is absolutely no risk is typically exempt from REB review. Researchers often are not permitted to decide by themselves that research is exempt; instead, the institutional REB may create a procedure to allow a researcher to apply for exempt status. According to the TCPS, **exempt research** does not require REB review when it (1) only uses publicly available information that is legally accessible; (2) only involves observing people in public places without any intervention or interaction by the researcher, and no individuals can be identified when presenting the results; or (3) uses data that have already been collected and are completely anonymous. For example, archival research that uses anonymous data from Statistics Canada public use files (e.g., Stermac, Elgie, Dunlap, & Kelly, 2010) or published parliamentary archives (e.g., Suedfeld & Jhangiani, 2009) would be considered exempt. Also, *naturalistic observation* in public places when there is no threat to anonymity and no expectation of privacy would also be exempt. This type of research does not require informed consent. Keep watch for continued debate of exempt status in the context of big data issues discussed earlier.

Minimal Risk Research

According to the TCPS, **minimal risk research** means that the risks of harm to participants are no greater than risks encountered in daily life. The TCPS calls researchers to err towards a conservative interpretation of what constitutes "daily life," in the interest of protecting participants. Minimal risk research still adheres to the core principles, but elaborate safeguards are not of high concern, and approval by the REB can be delegated to a single member rather than considered by the whole committee. Individual REBs may vary in the specific criteria they use to determine minimal risk, but will likely consider the type of risk, the probability it will occur, the amount of risk, and the vulnerability of the intended participants. For example, the minimal risk designation may apply to research using questionnaires or interviews with competent adults on non-sensitive topics (e.g., the Big Five personality traits).

Greater Than Minimal Risk Research

Any research procedure that places participants at *greater than minimal risk* is subject to thorough review by the full REB committee. In addition to informed consent, other safeguards may be required before approval is granted. Using questionnaires or interviews would become classified as greater than minimal risk if the topic of those questionnaires or interviews was of a sensitive nature (e.g., sexual practices), or if the intended participants were members of vulnerable populations, even if the topic was not sensitive. In cases where it is ambiguous about whether the research is minimal risk or greater than minimal risk, REBs will likely tend to categorize research as greater than minimal risk. This conservative approach reflects their mandate to uphold the core principles of respect for persons, concern for welfare, and justice.

Researchers planning to conduct an investigation that involves minimal risk or greater than minimal risk are always required to submit an application to the institution's REB. The specific application will vary by institution, but typically requires a description of risks and benefits, procedures for minimizing risk, procedures for recruiting participants, the exact wording of the informed consent form, how participants will be debriefed, and procedures for maintaining confidentiality and anonymity whenever possible. Even after a project is approved, there is continuing review. If it is a long-term project, it will be reviewed at least once each year. If there are any changes in procedures or materials, researchers are required to obtain approval from the REB before implementing them.

REB Impact on Research

Some researchers have voiced frustration about the procedures necessary to obtain REB approval for research. The review process can take a long time (sometimes months), and the REB may ask for revisions and clarifications. Moreover, the policies and procedures that govern REB operations apply to all areas of research, so the extreme caution necessary for medical research is often applied to psychology research (Collins, 2002). Researchers must plan carefully, allow time for the approval process, and submit all materials requested in the application.

With the TCPS guidelines and review of research by the REB, the rights and safety of human participants seem well-protected. Researchers and review board members tend to be very cautious in terms of what is considered ethical, causing some researchers to argue that a high degree of caution among REBs is decreasing the value of science, particularly on controversial topics (Bernhard & Young, 2009; Fiske, 2009). Consider the following challenging and controversial example. Bernhard and Young (2009) attempted to study the experiences over time of illegal immigrants to Canada–a highly vulnerable group who could be deported if discovered–using a longitudinal, in-depth interview approach. It was legally possible that their records could be subpoenaed by immigration authorities, which prevented them from guaranteeing complete confidentiality to their participants. As they report it in their article, they were denied REB approval for their original research design because they could not fully guarantee complete confidentiality for this high-risk group under Canadian laws. However, other researchers argue that Canada's legal system would have allowed the researchers to maintain participants' confidentiality, and has in fact ruled in support of maintaining researcher's confidentiality commitments to participants in a similar case (Palys & Lowman, 2010). Legal support of researcher-participant confidentiality would mean supporting the integrity of science in the interest of society (in this case, to understand the experiences of a vulnerable group). Possibly in response to this controversy, the revised TCPS permits researchers to "maintain their promise of confidentiality to participants within the extent permitted by ethical principles and/or law. This may involve resisting requests for access, such as opposing court applications seeking disclosure" (Canadian Institutes, 2010, Article 5.1 Application). Clearly, the interaction among research ethics, REBs, and the law is a complex one that must be considered on a case-by-case basis.

REBs have a primary responsibility to protect participants, and in some cases, this protection may influence the progression of scientific discovery.

Is such high caution by REBs warranted, particularly when participants are considered low in vulnerability (e.g., a typical university student)? Several studies have shown that students who have participated in research studies are more lenient in their judgments of the ethics of experiments than are researchers or REB members (Epstein, Suedfeld, & Silverstein, 1973; Smith, 1983; Sullivan & Deiker, 1973), suggesting that REBs may perhaps be too cautious. However, there remains mixed evidence regarding participants' attitudes toward deception (Hertwig & Ortmann, 2008). People who have taken part in research that used deception report that they did not mind the deception and evaluated the experience positively (Christensen, 1988). Another study showed that participants who had experienced deception were less likely to volunteer for more research than those who had not participated in a study that used deception (Blatchley & O'Brien, 2007), suggesting they were dissatisfied. More research is needed to evaluate how participants feel about being deceived. Until that time, it is the most ethically defensible position for REBs to overprotect rather than underprotect participants, even if that means affecting the way science is conducted. The debate continues.

ETHICS AND ANIMAL RESEARCH

LO7

Although this chapter has been concerned with the ethics of research with humans, you are no doubt well aware that psychologists sometimes conduct research with animals (Akins, Panicker, & Cunningham, 2004). Animals are used for various reasons. The researcher can carefully control the environmental conditions of the animals, study the same animals over a long period, and monitor their behaviour 24 hours a day if necessary. Animals are also used to test the effects of drugs and to study physiological and genetic mechanisms underlying behaviour. About 7 percent of the articles in the database *Psychological Abstracts* in 1979 described studies involving animals (Gallup & Suarez, 1985), and data indicate that the amount of research done with animals has been steadily declining (Gauthier, 2004; Thomas & Blackman, 1992). According to one survey of animal research in psychology, over 95 percent of the animals used were rats, mice, and birds (see Gallup & Suarez, 1985).

Animal research, although controversial (Henry & Pulcino, 2009; Knight, Vrij, Bard, & Brandon, 2009; Plous, 1996a, 1996b), benefits humans and continues to lead to discoveries that would not have been possible otherwise (Carroll & Overmier, 2001; Miller, 1985; see also www.apa.org/science/leadership/care/guidelines.aspx). Strict laws and ethical guidelines govern both research with animals and teaching procedures in which animals are used. Such regulations deal with the need for proper housing, feeding, cleanliness, and health care. The research must avoid any cruelty in the form of unnecessary pain to the animal. Across all Tri-Council-funded research with animals—not just in psychology—the most common category of invasiveness is research that involves little or no discomfort or stress to animals (accounting for 34 percent of research on animals in 2011; Canadian Council on Animal Care, 2013).

The **Canadian Council on Animal Care (CCAC)** is an organization sponsored primarily by CIHR and NSERC and whose purpose is to "oversee the ethical use of animals in science in Canada" (Canadian Council on Animal Care, 2014). It is responsible for certifying institutions and specifying guidelines for ethical animal care for all research and teaching purposes across all disciplines (e.g., psychology, biology, medicine). In addition, institutions in which animal research is carried out must have an *Animal Care Committee (ACC)* composed of at least one scientist and/or teacher with experience in animal use, one institutional member who does not use animals, one experienced veterinarian, a community member, and others. The ACC is charged with reviewing animal research procedures and ensuring that all regulations are followed, including animal care training by all researchers and technicians involved in animal research (see Canadian Council on Animal Care, 2006). This mandate includes promotion of the widely accepted **Three Rs** of "Good Animal Practice in Science" (Russell & Burch, 1959), which aim to minimize harm to animals:

- *Replacement* involves replacing the use of animals or avoiding the use of animals altogether (e.g., by instead using mathematical modelling, humans, or meta-analyses on past research).
- *Reduction* involves minimizing the number of animals being used.
- *Refinement* involves modifying procedures to minimize pain and distress.

For more information, see the CCAC's Three Rs microsite (http://3rs.ccac .ca/en/), which aims to provide researchers with ideas and resources for following the Three Rs.

The Canadian Psychological Association (CPA) was an early leader among academic disciplines in creating ethical guidelines for the use of animals; their work has been superseded by the CCAC guide. The American Psychological Association (APA) has also developed a detailed set of *Guidelines for Ethical Conduct in the Care and Use of Nonhuman Animals in Research* (American Psychological Association, 2012), which offer some specific ways psychologists seek to apply the Three Rs and otherwise treat animals humanely. In addition to *replacing, reducing,* and *refining,* APA guidelines state that psychologists using animals are expected to supervise all procedures and ensure that animals' comfort and health are considered appropriately. Moreover, they must ensure that all personnel involved in the study (e.g., students, technicians, assistants) have received training in research methods as well as how to properly care for the species involved. The purpose of this book is to explore research with humans; please consult the resources on the CCAC website (www.ccac.ca) and your institution's Animal Care Committee for more information about the ethics of animal research.

PROFESSIONAL ETHICS IN ACADEMIC LIFE

Treating participants and nonhuman animals ethically is just part of what it means to conduct research ethically. It is expected that psychologists' commitment to ethical conduct extends across all areas of professional activity, including writing, teaching, clinical work, administration, and communicating with the general public. As members of the academic community, students are also expected to engage in ethically sound practices. In this section we will explore some further issues in professional ethics.

Professional Associations: Ethics Codes of the APA and CPA

Both the APA and the CPA have provided leadership in formulating **ethics codes**—ethical principles and standards for all aspects of a professional academic career. The preamble to the APA Ethics Code provides an overview of how far professional ethics extends for all psychologists, beyond what we have considered in this chapter:

> Psychologists are committed to increasing scientific and professional knowledge of behavior and people's understanding of themselves and others and to the use of such knowledge to improve the condition of individuals, organizations, and society. Psychologists respect and protect civil and human rights and the central importance of freedom of inquiry and expression in research, teaching, and publication. They strive to help the public in developing informed judgments and choices concerning human behavior. In doing so, they perform many roles, such as researcher, educator, diagnostician, therapist, supervisor, consultant, administrator, social interventionist, and expert witness. This Ethics Code provides a common set of principles and standards upon which psychologists build their professional and scientific work.

Both the APA and CPA Ethics Codes offer standards for ethical conduct by professional psychologists across all of the roles listed above (see American Psychological Association, 2010a, and Canadian Psychological Association, 2000, for web addresses to these codes). Koocher (2009) suggests that when prioritizing these various roles, psychologists' primary responsibility is toward the most vulnerable members of society (rather than, for example, toward the government or a corporation). The APA Ethics Code is longer and more detailed than the CPA Ethics Code, yet the two complement each other. Canadian psychologists can benefit from relying on both codes for ethical guidance; the benefit to consulting the CPA Ethics Code is that it will ensure consistency with the TCPS and highlight the Canadian context of research, teaching, clinical work, and other activities.

Scientific Misconduct and Publication Ethics

LO8

Ethical decision making in data collection, data analysis, and publication has recently taken centre stage in psychology and science more broadly, partly in response to some high-profile cases of scientific misconduct coming to light (Pashler & Wagenmakers, 2012). The bottom line is that *we must be able to believe the reported results of research*, otherwise the entire foundation of the scientific method as a means of knowledge is threatened. Yet there are many points in the publication process where scientists have been freely trusted to collect, analyze, and report data. Although we continue to assume that the vast majority of scientists act ethically in their search for real truths, we can no longer assume that scientific misconduct is extremely rare and of little concern (Stroebe, Postmes, & Spears, 2012).

Fabricating Data and Altering Collected Data Is Fraud   Two of the ways to commit **fraud** in science include (1) fabricating (i.e., making up) data sets and (2) collecting data from real participants but altering the numbers to fit the hypothesis. The Ethics Codes of both the APA and CPA have clearly stated standards prohibiting these actions. Yet some researchers in biomedicine, chemistry, psychology, and other sciences have been caught doing both of these things (Stroebe et al., 2012). Three major cases in social psychology have received much media attention. In 2001, Karen Ruggiero (a former McGill University undergraduate) was caught after having fabricated data in many studies that had been published in high-profile journals. Ruggiero subsequently resigned from her academic position and retracted her publications (Murray, 2002). More recently, Dirk Smeesters resigned after seven papers showed evidence of fabrication of data or analyses (Report of the Smeesters Follow-Up Investigation Committee, 2014).

Details of a massive case of fraud were released in November 2012. Evidence showed that Diederik Stapel committed fraud from 1996 to 2011 across 55 publications, including his own PhD dissertation and the dissertations of ten graduate students (Levelt Committee, 2012). After having received many early career awards and great prestige for his work, his graduate students developed suspicions (e.g., how perfectly his data always fit his predictions; Stroebe et al., 2012). Three of his graduate students eventually reported Stapel to their department head. Affected papers were retracted, he was fired, he relinquished his PhD, and he underwent a criminal investigation that ended in a community service settlement (Bhattacharjee, 2013). Stapel, Ruggiero, Smeesters, and all others who have been caught have destroyed their own reputations and careers, and in some cases have hurt the reputations of their collaborators and students.

How is fraud in science detected? It is possible that fraudulent results might be detected when other scientists fail to replicate the results of a study, or through the peer review process. However, data show that fraud is often detected by colleagues or students working with the researcher (as was the case with Ruggiero and Stapel; Stroebe et al., 2012). Alternatively, Simonsohn (2013) has developed methods to detect fraud using statistical analysis of published results. His analysis was a trigger for the investigation into Smeesters' work.

Why do some researchers commit fraud? One possible reason is that scientists occasionally find themselves seeking or holding academic positions with extreme pressure to produce impressive results. This is not a sufficient explanation, of course, because many researchers maintain high ethical standards under such pressure. Another reason may be that researchers who feel a need to produce fraudulent data have an exaggerated fear of failure, plus a great need for success and admiration. If you wish to explore further the dynamics of fraud, you might wish to begin with Goodstein's (2010) *On Fact and Fraud: Cautionary Tales from the Front Lines of Science.*

We should make one final point: Allegations of fraud should not be made lightly. If you disagree with someone's results on philosophical, political, religious, or other grounds, it does not mean that they are fraudulent. Even if you cannot *replicate* the results, the reason may lie in aspects of the study's methods rather than deliberate fraud. However, the fact that fraud could be a possible explanation of results stresses the importance of keeping careful records and documentation of all procedures and results.

Ethical Data Analysis   As you may notice in Chapters 12 and 13, statistical analysis of data can be complex and include a level of judgment that may surprise you. Mistakes like rounding errors occur sometimes in published reports of analyses. Although it is difficult to know whether mistakes are accidental or intentional, data show that they tend to occur in favour of the researcher's hypothesis (Bakker & Wicherts, 2011). Knowingly changing the numbers in your analysis is unethical and constitutes fraud. To avoid unintentional errors, it is good practice to double-check your analyses as well as your final report to ensure accuracy. Ask someone else whom you trust, and who is knowledgeable enough, to check them as well.

Improving Science through Publication Reform   Psychologists and other scientists are making progress as they seek to improve the trustworthiness of published research, but much progress lies ahead (Miguel et al., 2014). Recent reform has emphasized improving transparency (e.g., see the Open Science Framework at https://osf.io/). Three practices that individual researchers can take might help build a more honest and accurate science if they become the norm: disclosure, pre-registration of studies, and open data and materials (Miguel et al., 2014). Disclosing full information about the study (e.g., all measures used, reasons for excluding any participants) will promote accurate records of how research was conducted. Pre-registering methods and data analysis plans online will help honest researchers avoid misremembering hypotheses made before seeing the data. Posting data files and study materials online will help other researchers replicate a paper's analyses and entire study, which may help catch fraud or unintentional errors (Simonsohn, 2013). Importantly, these practices are being promoted and sometimes mandated by editors of major journals (e.g., *Psychological Science;* Eich, 2014). These and other reforms will develop further as more researchers dedicate effort to the honest pursuit of truth via science.

Plagiarism Is Unethical and Threatens the Integrity of Academic Communication

Plagiarism refers to presenting another person's work or ideas as your own, and is another form of scientific misconduct. All members of the academic community–students and professors alike–must give proper citation to all sources to signal where others' ideas end and our own ideas begin. Plagiarism can take the form of submitting an entire paper written by someone else. It can also mean including a paragraph or even a sentence that is copied without using quotation marks and a reference to the source of the quotation. Also, paraphrasing the actual words used by a source can become plagiarism if the source is not cited. Learning how to fairly represent the ideas of others is a skill that is essential to the academic conversation–a conversation in which you engage every time you submit coursework.

Although plagiarism is certainly not a new problem, access to Internet resources and the ease of copying material from the Internet may be increasing its prevalence. Szabo and Underwood (2004) report that more than 50 percent of a sample of British university students believe that using Internet resources for academically dishonest activities is acceptable. (To be clear, it is not.) Because of plagiarism concerns, many schools are turning to computer-based mechanisms of detecting plagiarism (e.g., www.turnitin.com). Plagiarism is ethically wrong and can lead to many strong sanctions. These include academic sanctions such as a failing grade or expulsion from the school. Because plagiarism is often a violation of copyright law, it can be prosecuted as a criminal offence as well.

One reason why students engage in cheating may be poor writing ability (Williams, Nathanson, & Paulhus, 2010). Poor writing skill is *not* an acceptable excuse for plagiarism. Instead, seek assistance to improve your writing from your instructor, your institution's writing centre, and numerous websites, such as Purdue University's extensive Online Writing Lab, available at http://owl.english.purdue.edu. Another reason why students may plagiarize is the belief that citing sources weakens their papers–that they are not being sufficiently original. In contrast, Harris (2002) notes that student papers are actually strengthened when sources are used and properly cited. Not knowing

TABLE 3.1 Plagiarism

Test yourself! Read the following examples and identify which counts as plagiarism and which does not. For each example you identify as plagiarism, specifically outline what changes you could make to avoid plagiarism in that case. If you are unsure of any example, discuss it with your instructor, writing centre staff, or librarian.

	Plagiarism	Not Plagiarism
1. Copying an entire essay and presenting it as original work.		
2. Compiling phrases, sentences, or paragraphs from a variety of sources to create a piece of work.		
3. Taking words from another author without acknowledging that they are not your own.		
4. Taking words from another author and noting that they are not your own (e.g., using quotation marks).		
5. Paraphrasing ideas from another author without acknowledging that they are not your own.		
6. Submitting work with incomplete source information (e.g., an incomplete References section).		
7. Using material from other sources as if it were the results of your own research.		

how plagiarism is defined in Canada is not an excuse to plagiarize. Practise identifying what constitutes plagiarism using Table 3.1.

Ethical guidelines and regulations are constantly developing. The TCPS and the APA and CPA Ethics Codes, as well as federal, provincial, and local regulations, are revised periodically. Researchers always need to be aware of the most current policies and procedures. In the following chapters, we will be discussing many specific procedures for studying behaviour. As you read about these procedures and apply them to research that interests you, remember that ethical considerations are always paramount.

STUDY TERMS

Test yourself! Define and generate an example of each of these key terms.

Anonymous (p. 44)

Canadian Council on Animal Care (CCAC) (p. 60)

Concern for welfare (p. 42)

Confederate (p. 39)

Confidential (p. 44)

Debriefing (p. 51)

Deception (p. 50)

Ethics codes (p. 61)

Exempt research (p. 57)

Fraud (p. 62)

Informed consent (p. 46)

Justice (p. 54)

Minimal risk research (p. 57)

Plagiarism (p. 64)

Research Ethics Board (REB) (p. 56)

Respect for persons (p. 46)

Risk-benefit analysis (p. 42)

Three Rs (p. 60)

Tri-Council Policy Statement (TCPS) (p. 40)

REVIEW QUESTIONS

Test yourself on this chapter's learning objectives. Can you answer each of these questions?

1. Discuss the three major ethical principles in behavioural research, and how they are related to risks, benefits, deception, debriefing, informed consent, and participant recruitment. How can researchers weigh the need to conduct research against the need for ethical procedures?

2. How does informed consent address respect for persons? What are the potential challenges involved in obtaining fully informed consent?

3. What are the purposes of debriefing participants after deception? What are some alternatives to deception?

4. What is a Research Ethics Board, and what does it do?

5. What are the differences among "no risk," "minimal risk," and "greater than minimal risk" research?

6. Summarize the ethical principles and procedures for research with animals.

7. What constitutes fraud? Why does it occur? What practices are being promoted to help avoid and detect it?

8. What activities do psychologists do that require upholding professional ethical standards?

DEEPEN YOUR UNDERSTANDING

Develop your mastery of these concepts by considering these application questions. Compare your responses with those from other people in your study group.

1. Consider the following experiment, similar to one that was conducted by Smith, Lingle, and Brock (1978). Each participant interacted for an hour with another person who was actually a confederate. After this interaction, both people agreed to return one week later for another session with each other. When the real participants returned, they were informed that the person they had met the week before had died. The researchers then measured reactions to the death of the person.

   a. Discuss the ethical issues raised by the experiment.

   b. Would the experiment violate any of the three core ethical principles for research with human participants? In what ways?

   c. What alternative methods for studying this problem (reactions to death) might you suggest?

Now consider these same three questions regarding a study conducted with final-year medical students (Fraser et al., 2014). In a live but simulated situation, a 70-year-old woman had ingested a poison and was suffering from lack of consciousness. For half the participants, the patient unexpectedly died. The researchers measured participants' emotional responses and cognitive load after the event, and their competence in a similar simulated situation three months later. *How have your responses changed? Why?*

2. In a procedure described earlier, participants are given false feedback that they have an unfavourable personality trait or a low ability level. What are the ethical issues raised by this procedure? Consider risks versus benefits. What if people are given false feedback that they possess a very favourable personality trait or a very high ability level, instead of negative false feedback? Does that change your reaction to this method?

3. A social psychologist conducts a field experiment (i.e., an experiment that occurs outside of the laboratory) at a local bar that is popular with university students. Interested in observing flirting techniques, the investigator instructs male and female confederates to smile and make eye contact with customers at the bar for varying amounts of time (e.g., two seconds, five seconds, etc.) and varying numbers of times (e.g., once, twice, etc.). The investigator observes the responses of those receiving the gaze. What ethical considerations, if any, do you perceive in this field experiment? Is there any deception involved? Should these field experiment participants be debriefed? Write a list of arguments supporting the pro position and another list supporting the con position.

4. Assess the level of risk for the following research activities. Why did you choose that level of risk? Could you argue for a different level of risk?

	No Risk	Minimal Risk	Greater Than Minimal Risk
a. Researchers conducted a study on a university campus examining the physical attractiveness level among peer groups by taking pictures of students on campus and then asking students at another university to rate the attractiveness levels of each student in the photos.			
b. A group of researchers plan to measure differences in depth-perception accuracy with and without binocular cues. In one condition, participants could use both eyes, and in another condition, one eye was covered with an eye patch.			
c. Researchers conducted an anonymous survey on attitudes toward gun control among shoppers at a local mall.			
d. University students watched a ten-minute video recording of either a male or female newscaster presenting the same news content. While the video played, an eye movement recording device tracked the amount of time the students were viewing the video.			

Research Design Fundamentals

LEARNING OBJECTIVES

Keep these learning objectives in mind as you read to help you identify the most critical information in this chapter.

By the end of this chapter, you should be able to:

1	Compare and contrast non-experimental and experimental research methods.
2	Define *operational definition* of a variable.
3	Give examples of confounding variables and describe how to avoid them.
4	Describe different possible relationships between variables: positive, negative, curvilinear, no relationship, and mediating.
5	Distinguish between an independent variable and a dependent variable.
6	Discuss how the three criteria for inferring causation are achieved (or not) in experimental and non-experimental methods.
7	Describe why multiple methods are used for research, including advantages and disadvantages of the basic designs.

This chapter offers an overview of the two major types of studies you will encounter in psychology: non-experiments and experiments. Discussing them together can help highlight important differences. We aim to offer enough detail here so you can start working on your own research project or proposal ideas, and we leave some of the more complex issues and variations for later chapters. We start with an overview of how researchers turn variables into studies. Then we unpack key concepts in non-experimental and experimental designs, respectively, and consider the value of using multiple types of studies.

INTRODUCTION TO BASIC RESEARCH DESIGN

In Chapter 2 we explored some ways researchers come up with ideas and begin to turn them into falsifiable hypotheses and predictions. In this section, we will break down those steps further by considering ideas as variables that researchers arrange in particular ways to ask research questions. How researchers arrange those variables influences the entire design. With a design in mind, researchers can state a hypothesis and use *operational definitions* to convert it into a prediction.

Variables

A research idea can be broken down into a set of variables. A **variable** is any event, situation, behaviour, or individual characteristic that can take more than one value (i.e., it varies). A researcher interested in the effects of sleep on memory is interested in two variables: sleep and memory. Other examples of variables a psychologist might study include prejudice, heart rate, intelligence, gender, reaction time, rate of forgetting, aggression, attractiveness, happiness, stress, age, and self-esteem. Each of these variables will have at least two specific *levels* or *values*. For some variables, the values will have true numeric, or quantitative, properties. Suppose that memory is measured using a 50-question test on which the values can range from a low of 0 correct to a high of 50 correct; these values have numeric properties. The values of other variables are not numeric, but instead simply identify different categories. An example is sex; common values for sex are male and female. These are different, but they do not differ in amount or quantity. We will consider variable properties further in Chapter 5.

Two Basic Research Designs

LOI

With variables of interest in mind, along with an idea about how they might be related, researchers must select a study design that will help them answer their questions about those variables. There are two general approaches to the study of relationships among variables: the non-experimental method and the experimental method. With the **non-experimental method,** relationships are studied by observing or otherwise measuring the variables of interest. Using this approach may include asking people to describe their behaviour, directly observing behaviour, recording physiological responses, or examining various public records such as census data. Once data on both variables are collected, the researcher uses statistics to determine whether there is a relationship between them. As values of one variable change, do values on the other change as well? For example, Gaudreau, Miranda, and Gareau (2014) measured how often undergraduate students used their laptops in class for unrelated tasks (e.g., visiting social network sites), and related this variable to academic average. The two variables did vary together: The more students admitted to more frequent non-school-related computer use in class, the lower their grades.

The **experimental method** involves direct manipulation and control of variables. The researcher manipulates the first variable of interest and then observes the response. For example, as mentioned in Chapter 2, Loftus (1979) used the experimental method. Participants viewed a film of an auto accident and were later asked whether they saw either "a" broken headlight or "the" broken headlight. The wording of the question (i.e., the *independent variable*) was manipulated, and participants' answers (i.e., the *dependent variable*) were then measured. With this method, the two variables do not merely vary together; one variable is introduced first to see whether it affects the second variable. The differences between non-experimental and experimental methods have important implications for the conclusions we can draw.

[LO2] Operationally Defining Variables: Turning Hypotheses into Predictions

Once the researcher decides on a method to study the variables of interest, these abstract variables must be translated into concrete forms of observation or manipulation. Thus, a variable such as "aggression," "cognitive task performance," "amount of reward," "self-esteem," or even "word length" must be defined in terms of the specific method used to measure or manipulate it. Scientists refer to the **operational definition** of a variable–a definition of the variable in terms of the operations or techniques used to measure or manipulate it in a specific study.

When considering options for operational definitions, sometimes it is helpful to think about variables in three general categories. A **situational variable** describes characteristics of a situation or environment: the length of words that you read in a book, the number of people who are squeezed into a classroom, the credibility of a person who is trying to persuade you, and the number of bystanders to an emergency. Situational variables can be *measured* in any design, or *manipulated* in experimental designs. **Response variable** refers to the responses or behaviours of individuals, such as reaction time, performance on a cognitive task, and degree of helping a victim in an emergency. Response variables are *measured* in either experimental or non-experimental designs. **Participant variable** describes a characteristic that individuals bring with them to a study, including cultural background, intelligence, and personality traits such as extraversion. Sometimes participant variables are related to other variables in non-experiments, and sometimes they are used to group participants for comparison on a response variable (see Chapter 10).

Variables must be operationally defined so that they can be studied empirically. Recall from Chapter 2 that hypotheses are more abstract than predictions. A prediction is a statement of the hypothesis that has been translated into the specific operational definitions of that particular study. Consider the *hypothesis:*

Hunger predicts aggression.

To test this hypothesis, researchers need to decide exactly what they mean by the terms *hunger* and *aggression* because there are many ways of operationally defining them. For example, aggression could be defined as (1) the volume and duration of noise blasts delivered to another person, (2) the number of times a child punches an inflated toy clown, (3) the number of times a child fights with other children during recess, (4) a city's homicide statistics gathered from police records, (5) a score on a personality measure of aggressiveness, (6) the number of times a batter is hit with a pitch during baseball games, and so on. Bushman, DeWall, Pond, and Hanus (2014) chose (1), which, along with their specific operational definition of hunger (i.e., lower blood glucose), led to the following *prediction:*

> Frustrated participants with lower blood glucose levels will give louder and longer noise blasts to their spouses than those with higher blood glucose levels.

You may debate whether their operational definitions (see Chapter 5) really measure hunger and aggression accurately. Indeed, different researchers may operationally define similar variables in different ways, depending on the research questions, the resources they have available, and their own creativity. In their research reports, researchers must describe precisely how they operationally define all variables, and provide other details of their study design, so other researchers can evaluate and attempt to *replicate* their study.

There may be several levels of abstraction when studying a variable, which adds complexity when researchers try to operationally define it. A variable such as "word length" is concrete and easily operationalized in terms of numbers of letters or syllables, but the exact words for the study must still be selected. The concept of "stress" is very general and more abstract. When researchers study stress, they might focus on any number of stressors—noise, crowding, major health problems, job burnout, and so on. A researcher interested in stress would probably choose one stressor to study and then develop operational definitions of that specific stressor. He or she would then carry out research investigations pertaining both to the specific stressor and to the more general concept of stress. The key point is that researchers must always translate variables into specific operations to manipulate or measure them.

Avoiding Confounds in Operational Definitions   Precise operational definitions are crucial for making claims about particular variables. Poor operational definitions capture more than just the variable of interest. Consider operationally defining the variable "intelligence" as "academic average." You might argue that academic average captures more than just intelligence; for example, it might also capture the personality trait conscientiousness, as well as motivation. In this case, if intelligence, conscientiousness, and motivation are all related to the outcome variable we are interested in (e.g., career success), conscientiousness and motivation can be called **confounding variables,** or simply *confounds*. Confounds are variables that are intertwined with another variable

LO3

so that you cannot determine which of the variables is operating in a given situation. Therefore, they impede our ability to make claims. One way (but not the only way) confounds occur in research is when they are introduced by imprecise operational definitions (Greenland & Morgenstern, 2001; Weisberg, 2010). Confounds can occur in operational definitions of variables that are measured, as in the intelligence example above. They can also occur in experimental designs that manipulate the independent variable imprecisely. When measuring naturally occurring variables, such as schizophrenia symptom severity, researchers must try to anticipate potential confounding variables, such as past psychiatric assistance, and measure them alongside the main variable of interest (e.g., Sarlon, Millier, Aballéa, & Tourni, 2014).

Consider an example. Researchers hypothesized that thinking about fast food causes people to be impatient (Zhong & DeVoe, 2010). The independent variable was operationally defined in terms of what was flashing on a computer screen while participants were doing an unrelated task: either fast-food logos (e.g., McDonald's, KFC) or same-sized squares. *Before reading further: Can you spot a potential confound?* Researchers concluded that exposure to fast-food logos causes impatience, yet alternative explanations remain viable. Not only did "logo versus square" change across levels of the independent variable, but so did the complexity of the image. Shape complexity is a confounding variable; it is possible that shape complexity influences impatience, not exposure to fast-food logos. In a follow-up study, the same researchers replaced the squares with logos of non-fast-food restaurants. The basis for their conclusion is now stronger because they replicated the result after changing the operational definition to avoid the shape complexity confound (see Chapter 14 for more about *conceptual replications* like this one).

Debating and Adapting Operational Definitions   There is rarely a single, infallible method for operationally defining a variable. A variety of methods may be available, each of which has advantages and disadvantages. Researchers must decide which one to use given the particular problem under study, the goals of the research, and other considerations such as ethics and costs. Concepts that were once untestable are now able to be operationally defined because of advances in technology. For example, the concept of "brain activation" has not always existed. The methods that researchers use to measure brain activity have changed dramatically since the early days of the first computed tomography (CT) scans. Rather than providing only a static image, as earlier imaging techniques had done, functional magnetic resonance imaging (fMRI) enables researchers to monitor brain activity as participants are doing something (e.g., viewing violent images on a screen or thinking about a loved one). Technology can change the operational definitions that are available to researchers.

Researchers sometimes disagree about whether an operational definition is an acceptable approximation of the variable under investigation. To illustrate how complex it can be to develop an operational definition of a variable, consider the choices faced by a researcher interested in studying crowding. The researcher could study the effects of crowding on university students in a carefully controlled laboratory experiment. However, the focus of the researcher's interest may be the long-term effects of crowding; if so, it might be a good idea to observe the effects of crowding on laboratory animals such as rats. The researcher could examine the long-term effects of crowding on aggression, eating, sexual behaviour, and maternal behaviour. But what if the researcher wants to investigate the effects of crowding on cognitive or social variables such as intellectual performance or family interaction? Here, the researcher might decide to compare the test results of people who are assigned to take a test in a crowded classroom versus alone. Alternatively, the researcher might conduct a quasi-experiment (see Chapter 11) and study people who live in crowded housing and compare them to people who live in less crowded circumstances. Because no one method is perfect, complete understanding of any variable often involves studying it using a variety of operational definitions. Next, let us explore further the foundational features of non-experimental and experimental methods.

NON-EXPERIMENTAL METHOD

Suppose a researcher is interested in the relationship between exercise and happiness. How could this topic be studied? Using the non-experimental method, the researcher would devise operational definitions to measure both the amount of exercise that people engage in and their level of happiness. There is a variety of ways to operationally define both of these variables; for example, the researcher might simply ask people to provide self-reports of their exercise patterns and current happiness level. *The important point to remember here is that both variables are <u>measured</u> when using the non-experimental method.* Now suppose that the researcher collects data on exercise and happiness from many people and finds that exercise is positively related to happiness; that is, the people who exercise more also have higher levels of happiness. The two variables *covary* or *correlate* with each other: Observed differences in exercise are associated with amount of happiness. Because the typical non-experimental design allows us to observe covariation between variables, another term that is frequently used to denote some non-experiments is the *correlational method*. With this method, we examine whether the variables correlate or vary together, but we cannot make statements of causation.

Relationships between Variables

LO4

Much research investigates the relationship between two variables to reveal whether different values of one variable are associated with different values of the other variable. That is, do the levels of the two variables vary systematically together? As children's age increases, does the amount they cooperate with playmates increase as well? Does viewing more television violence result in greater aggressiveness? Is depression related to obesity?

Non-experiments enable consideration of different kinds of relationships between variables. Recall that some variables have true numeric values (e.g., distance between people standing next to each other), whereas the levels of other variables are simply different categories (e.g., ethnicity). For current purposes, let's consider cases when both variables have values along a numeric scale. (We discuss different kinds of variable scales further in Chapter 5.) Many different "shapes" can describe their relationship. We begin by focusing on the four most common relationships found in research: the positive linear relationship, the negative linear relationship, the curvilinear relationship, and the situation in which there is *no relationship* between the variables. These relationships are best illustrated by line graphs that show the way changes in one variable are accompanied by changes in a second variable. The four graphs in Figure 4.1 show these four types of relationships. We will also briefly consider *mediated relationships*, which are used to

FIGURE 4.1
Four types of relationships between variables

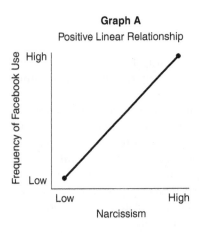

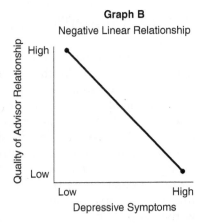

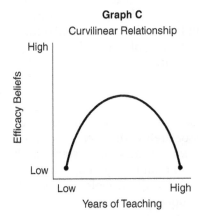

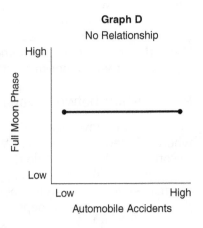

TABLE 4.I   Types of Relationship between Variables

Test yourself! Read the following examples and identify the type of relationship: positive, negative, or curvilinear.

	Positive	Negative	Curvilinear
a. Increased caloric intake is associated with increased body weight.			
b. As people gain experience speaking in public, their anxiety level decreases.			
c. Performance of basketball players increases as arousal increases from low to moderate levels, then decreases as arousal becomes extremely high.			
d. Increased partying behaviour is associated with decreased grades.			
e. Reducing the number of hours slept is associated with a decrease in the ability to pay close attention during class the next day.			
f. Amount of education is associated with higher income.			
g. Liking for a song increases the more you hear it, but then after a while you like it less and less.			
h. The more you exercise your puppy, the less your puppy chews on things in your house.			

help understand psychological processes. Table 4.1 provides an opportunity to review types of relationships.

In addition to knowing the general type of relationship between two variables, it is also necessary to know the strength of the relationship. In non-experimental designs, this means we need to know the size of the correlation between the variables. Sometimes two variables are strongly related to each other and there is little deviation from the general pattern. Other times the two variables are not highly correlated because many individuals' scores deviate from the general pattern. A numerical index of the strength of relationship between variables is called a **correlation coefficient** (see Chapter 12).

Positive Linear Relationship   In a **positive linear relationship,** increases in the values of one variable are accompanied by increases in the values of the second variable. In a study conducted by Mehdizadeh (2010), students at York University reported on their Facebook use and completed self-report measures of personality traits such as narcissism. High levels of narcissism indicate a person holds grandiose, exaggerated positive self-views and tends to seek out admiration. Graph A in Figure 4.1 shows a positive linear relationship between narcissism scores and Facebook use similar to what was found in this study. In a graph like this, we see a horizontal and a vertical axis, termed the *x* axis and *y* axis, respectively. Values of one variable are placed on the horizontal axis, labelled from low to high. Values of the other variable are placed on the vertical axis. Graph A shows that higher narcissism scores are associated with greater amounts of time spent on Facebook per session. Narcissism was also positively related to the number of times people checked their Facebook accounts per day.

Negative Linear Relationship   Variables can also be negatively related. In a **negative linear relationship,** *increases* in the values of one variable are accompanied by *decreases* in the values of the other variable. For an example, consider a study by Peluso, Carleton, and Asmundson (2011). They investigated depression among graduate students working in Canadian psychology departments. The researchers sent a survey to students that included a measure of depressive symptoms, as well as questions about their journal publication record, funding, and relationship with their academic advisor. Graph B in Figure 4.1 illustrates a negative relationship similar to what was found in the study. As satisfaction with their advisor *increased*, the number of depressive symptoms that graduate students reported *decreased*. The two variables are systematically related, just as in a positive relationship; only the direction of the relationship is reversed.

Curvilinear Relationship   In a **curvilinear relationship,** *increases* in the values of one variable are accompanied by *both increases and decreases* in the values of the other variable. In other words, the direction of the relationship changes at least once. Graph C in Figure 4.1 shows a curvilinear relationship between elementary and high school teachers' years of teaching experience and their beliefs that they are effective at engaging students (Klassen & Chiu, 2010). This particular relationship is called an inverted-U relationship. Greater years of experience are accompanied by *increases* in believing they are effective at engaging students, but only up to a point. The relationship then becomes negative, as further increases in experience are accompanied by *decreases* in believing they are effective at engaging students.

No Relationship   When there is no relationship between the two variables, the graph is simply a flat line. Graph D in Figure 4.1 illustrates the relationship between automobile accidents and the full moon phase (e.g., Laverty & Kelly, 1998). Unrelated variables vary independently of one another. Despite popular beliefs that the full moon influences human behaviour, lunar phase is *not* associated with automobile accidents or many other behaviours (see Foster & Roenneberg, 2008, for a review). A flat line describes the lack of relationship between the two variables: As one variable changes, the other does not change in any systematic way.

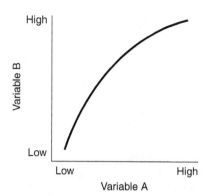

FIGURE 4.2
Positive non-
linear function

Keep in mind that these graphs depict the basic, clearest examples for illustration only. Almost any shape can describe the relationship between two variables. Other relationships are described by more complicated shapes than those in Figure 4.1. For example, some variables are positively related to each other, but not in a linear way as depicted in Graph A in Figure 4.1. Figure 4.2 depicts a positive relationship that is not strictly linear.

Mediated Relationship   A **mediating variable** is a psychological process that occurs between two variables that helps to explain the relationship between them (Baron & Kenny, 1986). For an example, Andrade and Tannock (2013) found the more that children were unable to keep focused attention, the more problems they had relating to their peers. Two mediating variables were used to help explain this relationship (see Figure 4.3). The more inattentive the children were, the less they showed prosocial concern for their peers and the more behaviour problems they had, which then both related to more peer problems. In other words, prosocial concern and behaviour problems *mediated* the relationship between inattention and peer problems. Models of *mediated relationships* like this one help provide insight into how variables (like inattention and peer problems) relate to each other, and can suggest possible interventions that can be tested using experiments to help inattentive children make friends (e.g., through training in prosocial concern). Note that all four variables in this study could be described as *participant variables*, and all were measured using questionnaires completed by the children's teachers. If you have concerns about whether those questionnaires were the best choice here, you are questioning the researcher's *operational definitions*. As you may be noticing, none is ever perfect.

Relationships and Reduction of Uncertainty   Relationships between variables are rarely perfect. Remember that the graphs in Figure 4.1 depict general patterns of relationships between two variables. Even if, in general, a

FIGURE 4.3
Prosocial concern and behaviour problems are *mediating* variables that help explain the relationship between inattention and peer problems.

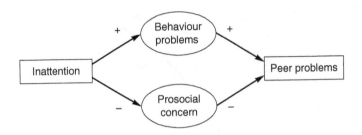

Adapted from Andrade, B.F., & Tannock, R. (2013). The direct effects of inattention and hyperactivity/impulsivity on peer problems and mediating roles of prosocial and conduct problem behaviors in a community sample of children. *Journal of Attention Disorders, 17,* Figure 1, p. 674.

positive linear relationship exists, it does not necessarily mean that everyone who scores high on one variable will also score high on the second variable. The purpose of the correlation is to capture the overall trend across many people's data; individual deviations from the general pattern are likely. For example, although narcissism is *generally* related positively to frequency of Facebook activity (Mehdizadeh, 2010), not everyone who shows a high degree of Facebook activity will be highly narcissistic. There are high and low narcissists who do not fit the general pattern.

Another way to think about this general point is to consider that when we detect a relationship between variables, we reduce uncertainty about the world by increasing our understanding of the variables we are examining. The term *uncertainty* implies that there is randomness in events; scientists refer to this as *random variability* or *error variability* in events that occur in the world. Research is aimed at reducing error variability by identifying systematic relationships between variables. To continue with our example, people's scores on a narcissism questionnaire and self-reported ratings of Facebook use will not be absolutely perfect indicators of their narcissism and Facebook use. Instead, each person's scores will be affected somewhat by various influences (e.g., memory biases when they try to recall how often they are on Facebook, misreading a question on the narcissism questionnaire, etc.) that are summarized by the term "error."

Correlations allow us to consider the trend across many people's data, reducing the uncertainty involved in interpreting each individual score. The error variability still exists, but now we can see the overall trend. The relationship between the variables is stronger when there is less error variability—for example, if 90 percent of high narcissists and only 10 percent of low narcissists used Facebook constantly, the relationship would be much stronger (with less uncertainty or randomness) than if 60 percent of high narcissists but 40 percent of low narcissists used Facebook constantly.

One way researchers seek to reduce this *random* or *error variability* is to conduct additional research. With further studies, you may be able to identify other variables that are also related to Facebook use. For example, Mehdizadeh (2010) also found that having lower self-esteem *in addition* to higher narcissism predicted greater Facebook use. Adding the variable self-esteem to the analysis gave her an additional way to reduce uncertainty, although realistically some uncertainty will always remain. We will revisit this idea of reducing error variability again in Chapter 5 when we discuss reliability, and in Chapter 12 when we discuss the correlation coefficient.

Interpreting Non-experimental Results

The non-experimental method is a reasonable approach to studying relationships between variables. A relationship is established by finding that the variables change together–the variables are said to covary or correlate with each other. Recall that this *covariation* is one of the three criteria for causal claims (see Chapter 1). Yet the non-experimental method does *not* help us answer questions about cause and effect. We know the two variables are related (i.e., they covary), but we cannot say anything about the causal impact of one variable on the other. There are two problems preventing researchers from making causal statements when the non-experimental method is used:

1. It can be difficult to determine the direction of cause and effect.
2. The third-variable problem–that is, extraneous variables may be causing an observed relationship.

Both problems are illustrated in Figure 4.4; arrows are used to depict possible causal links among variables.

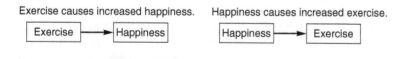

Exercise causes increased happiness.   Happiness causes increased exercise.

A third variable such as income is associated with both variables, creating an apparent relationship between exercise and happiness.

Higher levels of income result in more exercise; higher income also leads to increased happiness.

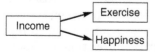

FIGURE 4.4
Possible causal directions in a hypothetical non-experimental study

Direction of Cause and Effect   With the non-experimental method, it is difficult to determine which variable causes the other—if there is any causal link at all. Consider this example: After finding a positive relationship between exercise and happiness, it cannot be said that exercise causes an increase in happiness. Although there are plausible reasons why this particular direction of cause and effect might be true, we must also consider that there are reasons why the opposite pattern might be true. Perhaps increasing happiness causes people to be more open to exercise. The issue here is one of *temporal precedence*, another of the three criteria necessary to make causal inferences (see Chapter 1). Knowledge of the correct direction of cause and effect in turn has implications for applications of research findings: If exercise increases happiness, then starting an exercise program would be a reasonable way to increase happiness. However, if increased happiness causes people to exercise more, simply forcing someone to exercise may not increase happiness levels.

Another possibility is that both causal directions might be true. Consider the case of similarity and liking. Research has shown that similarity causes people to like each other, and mutual liking causes people to become more similar. We need to gather data using an experimental design before we know if a causal arrow should be drawn in one, both, or neither direction.

The Third-Variable Problem   It is possible that the two variables measured are not directly related to each other. Exercise may not cause changes in happiness, and happiness may have no causal effect on exercise. Instead, a relationship between the two variables may appear in the study because some other variable that was not measured causes both exercise *and* happiness. This is known as the **third-variable problem.** Any number of other *third variables* may be responsible for an observed correlation between two variables. In the exercise and happiness example, one such third variable could be income level. Perhaps high income allows people more free time to exercise (and the ability to afford a health club membership) and also increases happiness. If data show that income is indeed the critical third variable, there might or might not be a direct cause-and-effect relationship between exercise and happiness; the relationship found in the study was really caused (or partially caused) by the third variable, income level. Because third variables offer an *alternative explanation* for the observed relationship, correlations can never be considered evidence of cause. Recall from Chapter 1 that the ability to *eliminate alternative explanations* for the observed relationship between two variables is another important factor when we try to infer that one variable causes another.

The third-variable problem can be considered a different issue from *confounding variables* discussed earlier. Sometimes these terms have been used interchangeably (Greenland & Morgenstern, 2001), but we distinguish them in a manner consistent with common use in psychology. Consider an example. Imagine you wanted to explore the relationship between weekly alcohol consumption and academic grades. After asking many people to report both values, you analyze the data and find a negative correlation: the more alcohol people consume per week, the lower their grades. What is the causal direction here? We do not know. It is possible that alcohol consumption causes low grades, and it is possible that people with low grades try to drown their sorrows by drinking more alcohol. Moreover, at least one *third variable* might be at work. For example, poor decision-making skills might be causing people to drink more alcohol while simultaneously causing them to have low grades. Compare this third variable to a potential confound. What if people who drink more alcohol are also more socially active than people who drink less alcohol? Based on your operational definitions, you can't disentangle alcohol consumption from social activity. If you were to find a negative relationship between alcohol consumption and grades, you cannot tell whether you are just measuring alcohol consumption or time spent socializing. In other words, time spent socializing is *confounded* with alcohol consumption. Third variables cause the apparent relationship between two other variables, whereas confounding variables are intertwined with another variable in your study so that you cannot tell which is at work.

As you can see, direction of cause and effect and potential third variables represent serious limitations of the non-experimental method. However, these limitations are often not considered in media reports of research results. For instance, a news website reported the results of a non-experimental study with the headline, "Father's attitude towards women shapes daughter's career ambitions" (Anderson, 2013), implying causation by using the word "shapes." The study actually found a positive relationship between fathers' traditional gender-role beliefs and their daughters' aspirations toward gender-stereotypical occupations (Croft, Schmader, Block, & Baron, 2014). You now know that there is not necessarily a cause-and-effect relationship between the two variables just because they are related to each other. Numerous third variables (e.g., socio-economic status, mother's occupation) could cause both fathers' beliefs and the types of occupations toward which girls aspire. The research team discussed these third variables as alternative explanations of the correlational finding. However, as is common in media reports of correlations, the headline oversimplified the case and implied causation without considering the impact of potential third variables. The results of such reports are ambiguous and should be viewed with skepticism. In order to claim cause-and-effect, we must rely on the experimental method.

EXPERIMENTAL METHOD

L05

When researchers use the experimental method to investigate the relationship between variables, the **independent variable** is considered to be the "cause" and the **dependent variable** the "effect." For example, speaker credibility is hypothesized to *cause* attitude change; exercise is hypothesized to *cause* changes in happiness. The independent variable is expected to *cause* changes in the dependent variable. One way to remember these terms is to consider that the dependent variable *depends* on the level of the independent variable. It is often helpful to actually draw a relationship between the independent and dependent variables using an arrow, as we did in Figure 4.4. The arrow always indicates your hypothesized causal direction:

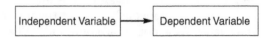

In an experiment, the manipulated variable is the independent variable, and the variable that is measured is the dependent variable. Another way to remember this crucial distinction is to relate the terms to what happens to participants in an experiment. The researcher devises a situation to which participants are exposed, such as watching a violent versus a non-violent program, or exercising versus not exercising. This situation is the manipulated variable; it is called the independent variable because the participant has nothing to do with its occurrence. In the next step of the experiment, the researcher measures the participant's response to the manipulated variable. The participant is responding to what happened to him or her; the researcher assumes that what the individual does or says is caused by, or dependent on, the effect of the independent variable.

Does sitting behind someone multitasking on a laptop in class affect learning? Sana, Weston, and Cepeda (2013) conducted an experiment to test this research question. We will rely on this study to illustrate the features of an experiment here, as well as corresponding statistical analyses in Chapter 13. The researchers hypothesized that exposure to the flickering laptop screen of a multitasking classmate (i.e., the independent variable) would decrease learning (i.e., the dependent variable). All participants took handwritten notes while attending a lecture in a classroom set up for the study. The independent variable was operationally defined as having two *levels* or *conditions;* participants were *randomly assigned* (see below) to experience one or the other. In the experimental condition, participants sat behind two *confederates* of the experimenter who were using their laptops to multitask during the lecture. In the control condition, participants sat behind two confederates without laptops. The dependent variable, learning, was operationally defined as the percent of questions answered correctly on a lecture comprehension test given right after the lecture. Participants who sat behind classmates multitasking on laptops scored 17 percent lower on the comprehension test than those who sat behind classmates without laptops. The researchers concluded that sitting behind flickering laptops impairs student learning. *Can you think of any confounds in this research design? If so, do they influence the conclusion or your willingness to sit behind someone using a laptop?*

When the relationship between an independent and a dependent variable is plotted in a graph, the independent variable is always placed on the horizontal (*x*) axis and the dependent variable is always placed on the

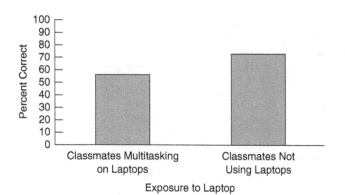

Based on Sana, F., Weston, T., & Cepeda, N.J. (2013). Laptop multitasking hinders classroom learning for both users and nearby peers. *Computers & Education, 62,* Figure 3.

FIGURE 4.5
Results of an
experiment

vertical (*y*) axis. Figure 4.5 illustrates this method. The independent variable, "exposure to laptop," is placed on the horizontal axis; the dependent variable, "percent correct," is placed on the vertical axis. A bar graph is used because the experimental conditions are separate categories. (The graphs in Figure 4.1 were line graphs because the variable on the horizontal axis is continuous; see Chapter 12.)

Note that some research focuses primarily on the independent variable, with the researcher studying the effect of a single independent variable on numerous behaviours. Other researchers may focus on a specific dependent variable and study how various independent variables affect that one behaviour. Consider experiments examining the relationship between jury size and juror decision making. One researcher studying this issue might vary group size to test its effect on a variety of behaviours, including jury decisions as well as risk taking among business managers. Another researcher interested solely in jury decisions might study the effects that different jury sizes, judge's instructions, and other aspects of trials have on juror decision making. Both emphases lead to important knowledge. Figure 4.6 presents an opportunity to test your knowledge of the types of variables we have described.

Designing Experiments That Enable Cause-and-Effect Inferences   L06

In the experimental method, the independent variable is manipulated and the dependent variable is then measured. To study whether exercise increases happiness using an experiment, exercise would be manipulated–perhaps by having one group of people exercise each day for a week and another group refrain from exercise. Happiness would then be measured in both groups. Suppose that people in the exercise group report greater happiness than the people in the no-exercise group. The researcher could now say something about the direction of cause and effect because *temporal*

FIGURE 4.6
Test yourself!
Types of
variables

Researchers conducted a study to examine the effect of music on exam scores. They hypothesized that scores would be higher when students listened to soft music compared to no music during the exam because the soft music would reduce students' test anxiety. One hundred (50 male, 50 female) students were randomly assigned to either the soft-music or no-music conditions. Students in the soft-music condition listened to music using headphones during the exam. Fifteen minutes after the exam began, researchers asked students to complete a questionnaire that measured test anxiety. Later, when the exams were completed and graded, the scores were recorded. As hypothesized, test anxiety was significantly lower and exam scores were significantly higher in the soft-music condition compared to the no-music condition.	Review the lists of variables below and link each study variable to the type of variable it represents.

Study variable	Type of variable
Sex of participant	Independent variable
Exam score	Participant variable
Headphones	Dependent variable
Music condition	Mediating variable
Test anxiety	Confounding variable

precedence is there: In the experiment, exercise came first in the sequence of events. Thus, happiness level could not influence the amount of exercise that the people engaged in.

Another characteristic of the experimental method is that it attempts to eliminate the influence of all variables *except* the one that is being manipulated. Such control is usually achieved by making sure that every feature of the environment except the independent variable is held constant. Any variable that cannot be held constant is controlled by ensuring its effects are random. Through random assignment of people to condition, the influence of extraneous variables is approximately equal across the experimental conditions, as long as there are enough participants in the study. Both procedures (i.e., control and random assignment) are used to try to *eliminate alternative explanations* by ensuring that any differences between the groups are due to the manipulated variable. Let us unpack these critical features of experiments in more detail.

Causality and Internal Validity   The experimental method enables researchers to make causal claims about how variables are related to each other. Recall from Chapter 1 that inferences of cause and effect have three requirements. First, there must be *temporal precedence:* The causal variable must come first in the temporal order of events and then be followed by the effect. The experimental method addresses temporal order by first manipulating the independent variable and then observing whether it has an effect on the dependent variable. In other situations, you may observe the temporal order or you may logically conclude that one order is more plausible than another. In the laptop study by Sana et al. (2013), laptop exposure came before the comprehension test.

Second, there must be *covariation* between the two variables. Covariation is demonstrated with the experimental method when participants in an experimental condition (e.g., classmates multitasking on laptops) show a different effect (e.g., lower test scores) relative to participants in a control condition (e.g., classmates not using laptops). In some studies, this requirement is met when the dependent variable is "present or not present" depending on the level of the independent variable; it may also be met by comparing amounts of the variable, such as levels of accuracy.

Third, there is a need to *eliminate plausible alternative explanations* for the observed relationship. One alternative explanation is based on the possibility that some confounding variable is responsible for the observed relationship. In the laptop study, you may have noticed that two things were present in the experimental condition but not in the control condition: a laptop and a multitasking screen. Is it the multitasking laptop or just the laptop that affected participants' performance? The researchers argued that this confound does not present an alternative explanation for their results, but instead offers a realistic comparison that mimics actual classroom experiences. You might disagree. When designing research, a great deal of attention is paid to identifying and eliminating plausible alternative explanations. The experimental method begins by attempting to keep such variables constant through random assignment and experimental control (see below). Other issues of control will be discussed in later chapters. Inferences about causal relationships are stronger when there are fewer alternative explanations for the observed relationships.

When a researcher designs a study that effectively meets all three criteria for cause and effect, the study is said to have high internal validity. *Validity* in research refers to "truth" and the degree to which a claim is accurate; we will consider many types of validity throughout this book. **Internal validity** refers to the ability to draw accurate conclusions about causal relationships from our data. A study has high internal validity when data support the inference that one variable caused changes in the other variable; alternative explanations are implausible. We have seen that strong causal inferences can be made when the experimental method is used rather than the non-experimental method. Internal validity is achieved in experiments by using random assignment to condition and ensuring that only the independent variable of interest changes across conditions.

Achieving Internal Validity: Experimental Control and Random Assignment to Condition   One way to eliminate alternative explanations is through **experimental control:** treat participants in all groups in the experiment identically so that the only difference between groups is the independent variable. In the Loftus experiment on memory (discussed in Chapter 2), both groups witness the same accident, the same experimenter provides the same instructions to both groups, the questions are identically worded except for the single word manipulation, and so on. When there is a difference between the groups in reporting memory, one can be sure that the difference is the result of the question wording rather than some other variable that was not held constant across conditions.

If a variable is "held constant" across conditions, it cannot explain the changes in the dependent variable. In the example experiment on the effect of exercise, the researcher would want to make sure that the only difference between the exercise and no-exercise groups is the exercise. If people in the exercise group are removed from their daily routine to engage in exercise, the people in the no-exercise group should be removed from their daily routine as well. Perhaps people in the no-exercise group could be asked to read a book for an hour instead of exercise. Because both groups now have a break in their daily routine, having a break cannot be an alternative explanation for any group differences in happiness levels.

To see the contrast, consider what would happen if the no-exercise group is not given a break like those in the exercise group. Suppose researchers find that people in the exercise condition later have higher happiness levels than people in the no-exercise group. Instead of being sure that exercise caused increased happiness, an alternative explanation is that the exercise group simply had a break from their daily routine, which caused increased happiness. The no-exercise group did not benefit from such a break, and therefore maintained their existing happiness levels. The break is a *confounding variable* that changes along with our variable of interest, exercise, which makes it impossible to know whether exercise or the break caused changes in happiness. In other words, the break is a variable that is *confounded* with exercise. Consider another variation: Everyone in the exercise condition spent the hour with a group talking to other people while they exercised, and everyone in the no-exercise condition spent a break hour alone. This manipulation would introduce a different confound: Socializing varies across conditions. It would be impossible to know whether exercise or socializing is affecting happiness. Achieving high experimental control means avoiding such confounds and making sure only the independent variable of interest changes across conditions.

Sometimes it is difficult to keep a variable constant across all conditions of the independent variable. The most obvious such variable is any characteristic of the participants. Consider an experiment in which half the research participants choose the exercise condition and the other half choose the no-exercise condition; the participants in the two conditions might be different on some extraneous participant variable, such as income. It is possible that all the participants with higher income choose the exercise condition, and all the participants with lower income choose the no-exercise condition. This difference could cause an apparent relationship between exercise and happiness that could be explained by income. How can the researcher eliminate the influence of such extraneous variables in an experiment?

The experimental method attempts to eliminate the influence of such variables by **random assignment** to condition. Random assignment ensures that extraneous variables are just as likely to affect one experimental group as they are to affect the other group, as long as there are enough participants in the study. To eliminate the influence of individual characteristics, the researcher assigns participants to the two groups randomly. In actual practice, this means that assignment to groups is determined by a list randomizer, like the one that is available at www.random.org.

Try it out! Imagine you are running a study and you expect to have 60 participants who are randomly assigned to either the experimental condition of the independent variable or to the control condition. Create a list in a word processor that includes "experimental" 30 times and "control" 30 times. Then, cut and paste that entire list of 60 words into the list randomizer at www.random.org/lists, and click Randomize. The program will re-sort that list in random order. As each participant arrives to your study, follow the randomly ordered list to place each participant in a condition.

By using a random assignment procedure with a large enough sample, you can be confident that many characteristics of the participants in the two groups will be virtually identical. For example, people with lower, medium, and higher incomes will be distributed equally in the two groups. As long as there are many people in the study, random assignment ensures that the individual characteristic composition of the two groups will be approximately identical in every way.

Besides participant variables, any other variable that cannot be held constant is also controlled by random assignment. For instance, many experiments are conducted over a period of several days or weeks, with participants arriving for the experiment at various times during each day. In such cases, the researcher uses a random order for scheduling the sequence of the various experimental conditions. This procedure prevents a situation in which one condition is scheduled only during the mornings while the other is studied only during the afternoons. If that happened, time of day would be *confounded* with condition, potentially interfering with the ability to make a causal claim.

Experimental control and random assignment to condition eliminate the influence of confounding and extraneous variables. Thus, the experimental method allows a relatively unambiguous interpretation of the results. A researcher can make a strong argument that any difference between groups on the dependent (measured) variable can be attributed only to the influence of the independent (manipulated) variable. The experiment has high internal validity.

Further Criteria for Claiming Cause   Recall the three criteria for cause we have emphasized here: temporal precedence, covariation, and elimination of alternative explanations. Sometimes we impose even more stringent requirements before concluding that there is a causal relationship. Some philosophers, scientists, and students argue that a cause-and-effect relationship is established only if the cause is both necessary *and* sufficient for the effect to occur. Suppose you have determined that reading the material for an exam is related to exam score; students who read the material score higher than students who do not read the material. To be *necessary*, the cause *must* be present for the effect to occur. To prove that reading the material is the cause of the high exam score, it must be shown that reading the material must occur to do well on the exam. To be *sufficient*, the cause will *always* produce the effect. To prove that reading the material is the cause, it must always result in a high exam score.

Let's analyze this situation further. If we are talking about a course in which the exam is based only on material in the book, reading the book is probably *necessary* for a good exam score. Is reading the material *sufficient* to do well on the exam? That is, does just reading the material always result in a high exam score? You may be thinking right now that there are many times when you read the material but did *not* excel on an exam. Simply reading the material is not a sufficient cause; instead, research has shown that you are most likely to retain the material when you actively study it by paying attention, relating the information to other things you know, and practise recalling the material (for a review, see Dunlosky, Rawson, Marsh, Nathan, & Willingham, 2013).

The "necessary *and* sufficient" requirement for establishing cause is rare in psychology. Whenever psychologists assert that there is a necessary and sufficient cause of a behaviour, research soon reveals that this simply isn't so. For example, psychologists once asserted that "frustration causes aggression": Whenever frustration occurs, aggression will result, and whenever aggression occurs, frustration must be the preceding cause. This assertion was shown to be inaccurate. Frustration may lead to aggression, but other responses, such as passive withdrawal or increased effort to overcome the frustration, are possible as well. Also, aggression may result from frustration, but other events may produce aggression as well, including pain, insult, or direct attack.

Behavioural scientists are not unduly concerned with the issues of ultimate cause and effect. Rather, they are more interested in carefully describing behaviour, studying how variables affect one another, and developing theories that explain behaviour. Moreover, relationships among variables are rarely completely explained; there is almost always room for more than one cause to produce a particular effect. The general consensus is that there are few interesting "necessary and sufficient" causes of behaviour. Instead, research on numerous variables eventually leads to an understanding of a whole "causal network" in which a number of variables are involved in complex patterns of cause and effect. This book will not focus on these difficult questions, but instead examines the fundamental methods used to study behaviour.

CHOOSING A METHOD: ADVANTAGES OF MULTIPLE METHODS

LO7

There are advantages and disadvantages to both experimental and non-experimental designs. Researchers sometimes use both methods to test relationships among variables in different ways and with different operational definitions. Let's examine some of the issues that arise when choosing a method.

Artificiality of Experiments

In a laboratory experiment, the independent variable is manipulated within the carefully controlled confines of a laboratory. This procedure can permit relatively unambiguous inferences concerning cause and effect, and reduces the possibility that extraneous variables could influence the results. Laboratory experimentation is an extremely valuable way to study many problems. However, the high degree of control and the laboratory setting can sometimes create an artificial atmosphere that may limit either the questions that can be addressed or the generality of the results. Adding non-experimental studies may help address these concerns.

Another alternative is to try to conduct an experiment in a field setting. In a **field experiment,** the independent variable is manipulated in a natural setting. As in any experiment, the researcher attempts to control extraneous variables via random assignment, experimental control, or both when possible. Many field experiments take place in public spaces such as street corners, shopping malls, parking lots, or online. For example, consider a field experiment that tested for discrimination in Vancouver's rental housing market (Lauster & Easterbrook, 2011). Researchers replied via e-mail to 1,669 rental housing listings. The independent variable was manipulated by varying the status of the sender, while keeping the rest of the e-mail content the same. Rental agents were randomly assigned to receive an e-mail from one of five senders: heterosexual couple, same-sex male couple, same-sex female couple, single mother, or single father. The dependent variable (discrimination) was operationally defined as whether the rental agent replied to the e-mail. This field experiment revealed evidence of discrimination: Same-sex male couples were least likely to receive a response to their rental inquiry than members of any other group.

The advantage of the field experiment is that the independent variable is investigated in a natural context. The disadvantage is that the researcher loses the ability to directly control many aspects of the situation. The laboratory experiment permits researchers to more easily keep extraneous variables constant, thereby eliminating their influence on the outcome of the experiment. Of course, it is precisely this control that leads to the artificiality of the laboratory investigation. Fortunately, when researchers have conducted experiments in both lab and field settings, the results of the experiments have been very similar (Anderson, Lindsay, & Bushman, 1999).

Ethical and Practical Considerations

Sometimes the experimental method is not a feasible alternative because experimentation would be either unethical or impractical. Consider child-rearing practices. Even if it were practically possible to randomly assign parents to one of two child-rearing conditions, such as using withdrawal of love versus physical types of punishment, the manipulation would be unethical. Non-experimental methods in natural settings are crucial for understanding variables like this. Many important research areas present similar problems—for example, studies of the effects of alcoholism and divorce, or the impact of a cancer diagnosis on risk-taking. Such problems need to be studied, and non-experimental designs can offer insights into relationships among these variables.

When such variables are studied, people are often categorized into groups based on their experiences. When studying the effects of maternal employment on child development, for example, one group would consist of children whose mothers work outside the home and another group would consist of children whose mothers do not work outside the home. Groups are formed on the basis of some actual difference rather than through random assignment as in an experiment. It is extremely important to study these differences. However, this is not experimental research because there is no random assignment to the groups, and therefore causation cannot not be established. See Chapter 11 for quasi-experimental designs useful to compare groups when true experiments are impossible.

Describing Behaviour

When the research goal is to describe events accurately, causal claims are irrelevant, and therefore, experiments are unnecessary. For example, to describe the nature and extent of gambling in Prince Edward Island, Doiron and Nicki (2001) used non-experimental survey techniques (see Chapter 7 on creating surveys). Another example of descriptive research in psychology comes from Jean Piaget, who carefully observed the behaviour of his own children as they matured, and described in detail the changes in their ways of thinking about and responding to their environment (Piaget, 1952). Piaget's descriptions and his interpretations of his observations resulted in an important theory of cognitive development that triggered much experimental research and greatly increased our understanding of this topic (Flavell, 1996).

Predicting Future Behaviour

In many everyday situations, it can be helpful to successfully predict a person's future behaviour–for example, success in school, ability to learn a new job, or criminal activity. In such circumstances, issues of cause and effect may be of little concern. It is possible to design measures that increase the accuracy of predicting future behaviour. School counsellors can give tests to decide whether students should be in "enriched" classroom programs, employers can test applicants to help determine whether they should be hired, and forensic psychologists can evaluate convicted criminals to estimate their likelihood of committing another crime. These types of tests can lead to better decisions for many people. When researchers develop tests and questionnaires designed to predict future behaviour, they must conduct research to demonstrate that the measure does, in fact, relate to the behaviour in question (see Chapter 5).

Advantages of Multiple Methods

A complete understanding of any phenomenon requires study using multiple methods, both experimental and non-experimental. No method is perfect, and no single study is definitive. To illustrate, consider this research question: Do music lessons enhance intelligence? Much anecdotal evidence suggested yes, but empirical research findings had been mixed. Glenn Schellenberg, a researcher at the University of Toronto, set out to solve this conundrum. His first approach was to establish a causal relationship linking music lessons to improved intelligence (Schellenberg, 2004). Children entering Grade 1 were recruited to participate in free arts lessons for a year. Participants were randomly assigned to one of four conditions of the independent variable: keyboard lessons, voice lessons, drama lessons, or no lessons. Thus, there were two music conditions (voice and keyboard) and two control conditions for comparison (drama and no lessons–note that these children received keyboard lessons the following year). Change in intelligence was operationally defined as the difference between intelligence scores before lessons (in September) versus after lessons (the next summer). The intelligence test he chose was a common, standardized measure designed for children (i.e., the Weschler Intelligence Scale for Children-III). The hypothesis was supported: Although intelligence scores for all groups of children increased from September to the summer, those children who had received music lessons showed a greater boost in intelligence scores than either of the two control groups. Music lessons cause increases in intelligence.

Does the effect of music lessons on intelligence increase with more training? Does it last over time? These questions remained unanswered after the experiment, so Schellenberg (2006) switched to non-experimental methods to examine the impact of music lessons on intelligence over time. In one study, he asked first-year university undergraduates to complete an intelligence test and to report on their history of music lessons and family background. Indeed, how long people had taken music lessons in childhood was positively related to their high school average and their current intelligence test scores in first year. You may be wondering if family income might be a confounding variable here. If people come from a high-income family, they may be able to take music lessons for longer than people who come from a low-income family. Perhaps then it is income, rather than music lessons, that predicts intelligence test scores. Schellenberg was concerned about this too. Therefore, he asked participants to report their family income, and he was able to remove the effect of this potential confound in the statistical analysis. In Chapter 12 we will discuss a statistical technique researchers can use to do that. For now, consider the effect of income removed from the equation. Using a non-experimental method, Schellenberg showed that music lessons in childhood are related to intelligence in early adulthood. We can't make a causal claim here, but when coupled with the experiment reported in Schellenberg (2004), his studies build a case that music lessons impact intelligence.

No study is a perfect test of a hypothesis. However, when multiple studies using multiple methods all point to the same conclusion, our confidence in the findings and our understanding of the phenomenon are greatly increased.

A variety of methods, each with advantages and disadvantages, are available for researchers to use. Researchers select the method that best enables them to address the questions they wish to answer, while considering the problem under investigation, ethics, cost and time constraints, and issues associated with internal validity. In the remainder of this book, many specific

methods will be discussed, all of which are useful under different circumstances. In fact, all are necessary to understand the wide variety of behaviours
that are of interest to behavioural scientists. Complete understanding of any
issue requires research using a variety of methodological approaches.

STUDY TERMS

Test yourself! Define and generate an example of each of these key terms.

Confounding variables (p. 71)   Negative linear relationship (p. 76)
Correlation coefficient (p. 75)   Non-experimental method (p. 69)
Curvilinear relationship (p. 76)   Operational definition (p. 70)
Dependent variable (p. 81)   Participant variable (p. 70)
Experimental control (p. 85)   Positive linear relationship (p. 75)
Experimental method (p. 70)   Random assignment (p. 86)
Field experiment (p. 89)   Response variable (p. 70)
Independent variable (p. 81)   Situational variable (p. 70)
Internal validity (p. 85)   Third-variable problem (p. 80)
Mediating variable (p. 77)   Variable (p. 69)

REVIEW QUESTIONS

Test yourself on this chapter's learning objectives. Can you answer each of these questions?

1. What are the major differences between non-experimental and experimental research methods?
2. What is an "operational definition" of a variable? List three variables and
   give at least two operational definitions for each.
3. How do confounds relate to operational definitions? Are any of your
   operational definitions in Review Question 2 confounded with another
   variable? Can you change your operational definition to eliminate the
   confound?
4. Distinguish among positive linear, negative linear, and curvilinear
   relationships.
5. How do direction and third variables qualify our interpretation
   of correlations?
6. What is the difference between an independent variable and a dependent variable?
7. How do experimental control and random assignment influence
   causal claims?

8. Describe the three elements for inferring causation. Which one(s) are achieved by experimental methods? By non-experimental methods? How are they achieved?

9. What are some advantages and disadvantages of the two basic research designs?

DEEPEN YOUR UNDERSTANDING

Develop your mastery of these concepts by considering these application questions. Compare your responses with those from other people in your study group.

1. Researchers have found that elementary school students who sit at the front of the classroom tend to get higher grades than students who sit at the back of the classroom (Tagliacollo, Volpato, & Pereira, 2010). What are three possible cause-and-effect relationships for this non-experimental result?

2. Consider the hypothesis that work stress causes family conflict.

   a. How might you investigate the hypothesis using the experimental method? How would you operationally define each variable?

   b. Identify the independent variable and the dependent variable in the statement of the hypothesis.

   c. How could you translate this experimental hypothesis into a non-experimental hypothesis? What type of relationship between stress at work and family conflict at home is proposed (e.g., positive linear, negative linear)?

   d. Graph the proposed relationship.

   e. How might you investigate your non-experimental hypothesis? How would you operationally define each variable?

   f. Would you prefer to use the experimental or non-experimental method to study the relationship between work stress and family conflict? What are the strengths and weaknesses of each approach?

3. Identify the independent and dependent variables in the following descriptions of experiments. Once you have identified the independent variable, also identify its levels. Can you spot any confounds?

   a. Students watched a cartoon either alone or with others and then rated how funny they found the cartoon.

   b. A comprehension test was given to students after they had studied textbook material either in silence or with the television turned on.

   c. Some elementary school teachers were told that a child's parents were university graduates, and other teachers were told that the child's parents had not finished high school; they then rated the child's academic potential.

    d. Workers at a company were assigned to one of two conditions: One group of workers completed a stress-management training program; another group of workers did not participate in any training. For the next two months, the number of sick days that workers took was recorded.

4. The limitations of non-experimental research were dramatically brought to the attention of the public by the results of an experiment on the effects of postmenopausal hormone replacement therapy (part of a larger study known as the Women's Health Initiative). In the experiment, participants were randomly assigned to receive either hormone replacement therapy or a placebo (no hormones). The hormone replacement therapy consisted of estrogen plus progestin. In 2002, the investigators concluded that women taking the hormone replacement therapy had a higher incidence of heart disease than did women in the placebo (no hormone) condition. At that point, they stopped the experiment and informed both the participants and the public that they should talk with their physicians about the advisability of this therapy. The finding dramatically contrasted with the results of non-experimental research in which women taking hormones had a lower incidence of heart disease; in these non-experimental studies, researchers compared women who were already taking the hormones with women not taking hormones. Why do you think the results were different with the experimental research and the non-experimental research?

5

Measurement Concepts

LEARNING OBJECTIVES

Keep these learning objectives in mind as you read to help you identify the most critical information in this chapter.

By the end of this chapter, you should be able to:

1 Define *reliability* of a measure of behaviour and describe the differences among test-retest, internal consistency, and interrater reliability.

2 Compare and contrast reliability and validity.

3 Describe how a researcher can build a case for construct validity, including predictive validity, concurrent validity, convergent validity, and discriminant validity.

4 Describe the problem of reactivity of a measure of behaviour and discuss ways to minimize reactivity.

5 Describe the properties of the four scales of measurement: nominal, ordinal, interval, and ratio.

Every variable that is studied must be *operationally defined*. Recall from Chapter 4 that operational definitions are the specific methods used to manipulate or measure the variable. How could you predict how long relationships will last, using people's satisfaction with their romantic relationships? Operationally defining length of relationship requires that you specify a time frame: Are you interested in whether relationships last a few days, months, or years? One way to operationally define satisfaction would be to ask people how satisfied they feel in that relationship using a scale ranging from 1 (*not at all satisfied*) to 9 (*very satisfied*). In fact, LeBel and Campbell (2009) at Western University used that kind of self-report measure of satisfaction and found that it was able to predict whether people were still in that same romantic relationship after four months. The key to this chapter is recognizing that some operational definitions are higher quality than others. We will focus on the primary criteria researchers use to evaluate the quality of their own and each others' operational definitions: *reliability* and *validity*. We will also consider some other characteristics that are important when operationally defining variables, including reactivity of measures and scales of measurement.

SELF-REPORT TESTS AND MEASURES

In this chapter, much of the discussion of reliability and validity will refer to self-report measures (also commonly called *scales*). Although reliability and validity are important characteristics of all operational definitions, systematic and detailed research on reliability and validity is often carried out on self-report measures of personality and individual differences. Psychologists often use self-report measures to study psychological attributes such as intelligence, self-esteem, extraversion, and depression; they also measure abilities, attributes, and potential. They study compatibility of couples and cognitive abilities of children. Some research is aimed at informing us about basic personality processes. For example, Costa and McCrae (1985) developed the self-report *NEO Personality Inventory* (*NEO-PI*) to measure five major dimensions of personality: neuroticism, extraversion, openness to experience, agreeableness, and conscientiousness. Other measures are important in applied settings. Clinical, counselling, and personnel psychologists use scales to help make better clinical diagnoses (e.g., *MMPI-II*), career-choice decisions (e.g., *Vocational Interest Inventory*), and hiring decisions.

When doing research in these areas, it is usually wise to use existing measures of psychological characteristics rather than develop your own. Existing measures should have reliability and validity data to help you decide which measure to use. You will also be able to compare your findings with prior research that uses the measure. Many existing measures are owned and distributed by commercial test publishers and are primarily used by professional psychologists in applied settings such as schools and clinical practices. Many other measures are freely available for researchers to use in their basic research investigations. Sources of information about psychological tests that have been developed include the *Mental Measurements Yearbook* available as a database from your library (similar to *PsycINFO*), and descriptions that you can find with an Internet search. Understanding the concepts of reliability and validity will help you evaluate the quality of existing measures as well as those operational definitions you create.

RELIABILITY OF MEASURES

The first step to a quality operational definition is **reliability,** which refers to the consistency or stability of a measure of behaviour. Your everyday definition of reliability is quite close to the scientific definition. For example, you might say that Professor Fuentes is "reliable" because she begins class exactly at 10 a.m. each day; in contrast, Professor Finkel might be called "unreliable" because she sometimes begins class exactly on the hour, but on any given day she may appear any time between 10 and 10:20 a.m.

Similarly, a reliable measure of a psychological variable such as intelligence will yield the same result each time you administer the intelligence test to the same person. The test would be unreliable if it measured the same person as average one week, low the next, and bright the next. Put simply, a reliable measure does not fluctuate from one measurement instance to the next. If the measure *does* fluctuate, there is error in the measurement device.

A more formal way to understand reliability is to use the concepts of true score and measurement error. Any measurement that you take can be thought of as comprising two components: (1) a **true score,** which is the person's real score on the variable, and (2) **measurement error.** To the extent that a measure of intelligence is unreliable, it contains measurement error and so cannot provide an accurate indication of an individual's true intelligence. In contrast, a reliable measure of intelligence contains little measurement error—it will yield an identical (or nearly identical) intelligence score each time the same individual is measured. Increasing the reliability of a measure *reduces uncertainty* or error associated with that measure (see Chapter 4).

Imagine that you know someone whose "true" intelligence score is 100. Now suppose that you administer two intelligence tests to this person each week for a year. You want to find out which test is more reliable than the other. After the year, you calculate the person's average score on *each* test based on the 52 scores you obtained. What might your data look like? Hypothetical data are shown in Figure 5.1. For each test, the average score is 100. However, scores on one test range from 85 to 115 (a 30-point spread), whereas scores on the other test range from 97 to 103 (a 6-point spread). *Think about it!* Which test is *more* reliable? The test with the least variability (6-point spread) is more reliable. In other words, it contains less *measurement error* than the test that had more variability in scores (30-point spread).

When conducting research, often you can measure each person only once; you can't give the measure 50 or 100 times to discover a true score. Thus, it is very important that you use a reliable measure. To the extent that your measure is reliable, your single administration of the measure will reflect the person's true score.

Reliability is crucial for any operational definition. An unreliable measure of length would be useless in building a table; an unreliable measure of a variable such as intelligence is equally useless in studying that variable.

FIGURE 5.1
Comparing
data of a
reliable and
unreliable
measure

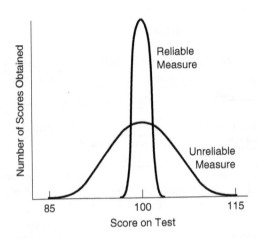

Researchers cannot use unreliable measures to systematically study variables or the relationships among variables. Trying to study behaviour using unreliable measures is a waste of time; conclusions will be meaningless, and results will not be able to be repeated.

Reliability is most likely to be achieved when researchers use careful measurement procedures. In some research areas, this might involve carefully training observers to record behaviour; in other areas, it might mean paying close attention to the way questions are phrased or the way recording electrodes are placed on the body to measure physiological reactions. In many areas, reliability can be increased by making multiple observations of the same variable. This approach is most commonly seen when assessing personality traits and cognitive abilities. A personality scale, for example, will typically have ten or more questions (called *items*) designed to assess the trait. Reliability is increased when the number of items increases.

How can we know how reliable a measure is? We cannot directly observe the true score and error components of an actual score on the measure. However, we can assess the stability of measures using correlation coefficients. Recall from Chapter 4 that a correlation coefficient is a number that tells us how strongly two variables are related to each other. There are several ways of calculating correlation coefficients; the most common correlation coefficient when discussing reliability is the **Pearson product-moment correlation coefficient.** The Pearson correlation coefficient (symbolized as *r*) can range from 0.00 to +1.00 and 0.00 to −1.00. A correlation of 0.00 tells us that the two variables are not related at all. The closer a correlation is to either +1.00 or −1.00, the stronger is the relationship. The positive and negative signs provide information about the direction of the relationship. When the correlation coefficient is positive (a "plus" sign), there is a positive linear relationship–high scores on one variable are associated with high scores on the second variable. A negative linear relationship is indicated by a "minus"

Reliability
A reliable measure is consistent.
Reliability coefficient: correlation coefficient ranging from 0.00 to 1.00.

Test-Retest Reliability	**Internal Consistency Reliability**	**Interrater Reliability**
How consistent is the measure across time?	*How consistent is the measure across items intended to measure the same concept?*	*How consistent is the measure when different people are rating?*
Take measure two times.	Cronbach's alpha: based on correlation of each item on test with every other item.	Extent to which raters agree in their observations (e.g., using Cohen's kappa).
Correlation of score at time one with score at time two; scores should be similar.		

FIGURE 5.2
Indicators of reliability of a measure

sign—high scores on one variable are associated with low scores on the second variable. The Pearson correlation coefficient will be discussed further in Chapter 12. When you read about reliability, the correlation will usually be called a *reliability coefficient*. Let's examine specific methods of assessing reliability (organized in Figure 5.2).

Test-Retest Reliability

Test-retest reliability is assessed by giving many people the same measure twice. For example, the reliability of a test of intelligence could be assessed by giving the measure to a group of people on one day and again a week later. We would then have two scores for each person, and a correlation coefficient could be calculated to determine the relationship between the first test score and the retest score. High reliability is indicated by a highly positive correlation coefficient showing that the two sets of scores are very similar. If many people have very similar scores, we conclude that the measure reflects more true score rather than measurement error. It is difficult to say how high the correlation should be before we accept the measure as reliable, but for most measures, the reliability coefficient should probably be at least .80.

Given that test-retest reliability involves administering the same test twice, the correlation might be artificially high because the people remember how they responded the first time. *Alternate forms reliability* is sometimes used to avoid this problem. Alternate forms reliability involves administering two different forms of the same test to the same people at two points in time.

Intelligence is a variable that can be expected to stay relatively constant over time; thus, we expect the test-retest reliability for intelligence to be very high. However, some variables may be expected to change from one test period to the next. For example, a mood scale designed to measure a person's current mood state is a measure that might easily change from one test period to another, and so test-retest reliability might not be appropriate. On a more practical level, obtaining two measures from the same people at two points in time may be difficult sometimes. To address these issues, researchers have devised methods to assess reliability without two separate assessments.

Internal Consistency Reliability

It is possible to assess reliability by measuring people at only one point in time. We can do this because most psychological measures are made up of a number of different questions, often called *items*. Think of each item as a repeated attempt to measure that same concept; when people respond similarly across these repeated items, it suggests the measure is reliable. An intelligence test might have 100 items, a measure of extraversion might have 15 items, or a multiple-choice examination in a class might have 50 items. A person's test score would be based on the total of his or her responses on all items. In the class, an exam consists of a number of questions about the material, and the total score is the number of correct answers. An extraversion measure might ask people to agree or disagree with items such as "I enjoy a lively party." An person's extraversion score is obtained by finding the total number of such items that are endorsed.

Internal consistency reliability assesses how well a certain set of items relate to each other. Because all items measure the same variable, they should yield similar or consistent results. Importantly, responses are gathered at only one point in time. We will briefly consider one common indicator of internal consistency below, but there are others (e.g., split-half reliability). Calculating internal consistency reliability is complex; a full treatment of the calculations and underlying theory is beyond the scope of this book. Consult a text on psychological measurement for technical procedures and theoretical considerations if you need to perform the calculations.

One common indicator of internal consistency is a value called **Cronbach's alpha.** In this analysis, the researcher calculates how well each item correlates with every other item, which produces a large number of *interitem correlations*. The value of Cronbach's alpha is based on the average of all interitem correlations and the number of items in the measure. It is also possible to examine the correlation of each item score with the total score based on all items. Such *item-total correlations* are very informative because they provide information about each individual item. Items that do not correlate with the other items can be eliminated from the measure to increase the measure's reliability. This information is also useful when it is necessary to remove some items to construct a brief version of a measure. Even though reliability can increase with longer measures, a shorter version can be more convenient to administer and also have acceptable reliability.

Interrater Reliability

In some research, raters observe behaviours and make ratings or judgments. To do this, a rater uses instructions for making judgments about the behaviours–for example, by rating whether the behaviour of a child on a playground is compassionate. You could have one rater make judgments about compassion, but the single observations of one rater might be unreliable, so it is common to use at least two raters of each behaviour. **Interrater reliability is the extent to which raters agree in their observations.** Thus, if two raters are judging whether behaviours are compassionate, high interrater reliability is obtained when most of the observations result in the same judgment. A commonly used indicator of interrater reliability is called *Cohen's kappa*.

Reliability and Accuracy of Measures

LO2

It is necessary for a high-quality operational definition to be reliable, but reliability is not the only characteristic of a measure that researchers worry about. Reliability tells us about the amount of error in the measurement, but it does not tell us about whether our measure accurately reflects the variable of interest. To use a silly but illustrative example, suppose we want to measure intelligence. The measure we develop looks remarkably like the device that is used to measure shoe size at the shoe store. We ask you to place your foot in the device and we use the gauge to measure your intelligence. There are numbers that provide a scale of intelligence, so we can immediately assess a person's intelligence level. Will these numbers result in a *reliable* measure of intelligence? Yes! Consider what a test-retest reliability coefficient would be. If we administer the "foot intelligence scale" on Monday, it will be almost the same the following Monday; the test-retest reliability is high. But is this an *accurate* measure of intelligence? No! Obviously, the scores have nothing to do with intelligence; just because we labelled that device as an intelligence test does not mean that it is a good measure of intelligence. The foot-based measure is not a *valid* indicator of intelligence. Yes, it is a consistent measure of intelligence–but it is consistently wrong.

Let's consider a less silly example. Do young infants have expectations about the physical properties of objects? For example, can a doll that hides behind a block suddenly reappear from behind a different block? These types of questions are often investigated using a *reliable* measure: looking time. Infants as young as 2.5 months will consistently stare longer at events that should not be physically possible, like the doll emerging from behind a different block, compared to events that are physically possible, like the doll emerging from behind the same block (Baillargeon, 2004). Yet does "looking longer" at the physically impossible event accurately indicate that babies can understand lay physics? That inference is an issue of the operational definition's *validity* (Jackson & Sirois, 2009). The difference between the reliability and accuracy of measures leads us to a consideration of the validity of measures.

VALIDITY OF MEASURES

Once shown to be reliable, the second requirement of a quality operational definition is validity. Typically, if we consider something to be valid, it is "true" in the sense that it is supported by available evidence. In Chapter 4, we have already encountered one type of validity, *internal validity*, which reflects the degree to which a claim of causation can be drawn from an experiment. **Construct validity** refers to the adequacy of a variable's operational definition. *Construct* is a term that is commonly used to denote an abstract variable that needs an operational definition, such as social anxiety, speaker credibility, or psychopathy. *Construct validity*, then, is the degree to which the operational definition of a variable actually reflects the true theoretical meaning of the variable. A measure of a personality characteristic such as shyness should be an accurate indicator of that trait, and a measure of lay physics understanding should accurately indicate that understanding. In terms of measurement, construct validity is a question of whether the measure that is employed actually measures the construct it is intended to measure.

Applicants for graduate school are required to take the Graduate Record Exam (GRE); this measure is supposed to predict an individual's ability to succeed in graduate school, rather than some other construct such as test-taking ability or extraversion. The validity of such a test is determined by whether it actually does measure this ability to succeed. A self-report measure rating the severity of past shy behaviour is an operational definition of the shyness variable; the validity of this measure is determined by whether it does measure this construct. Because variables can be measured and manipulated in a variety of ways, there is never a perfect operational definition of a variable. Thus, a variety of indicators of construct validity are used to build an argument that a construct has been accurately operationalized.

Indicators of Construct Validity

How do we know that a measure is a valid indicator of a particular construct? We gather construct validity information using a variety of methods. Ways that we can build a case toward construct validity are summarized in Figure 5.3. To illustrate each method, we will consider relevant research from some common measures of the construct of psychopathy. Some characteristics of psychopathy include charm, low empathy, impulsivity, and willingness to break rules and manipulate others without remorse. Some psychopaths are violent serial killers (think Ted Bundy or Paul Bernardo), but many others are not violent and can be found in everyday contexts such as in classrooms and in the business world.

Face Validity   The simplest way to argue that a measure is valid is to suggest that the measure *appears* to accurately assess the intended variable. This is

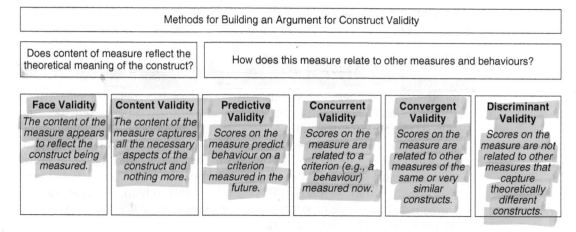

FIGURE 5.3
Indicators of construct validity of a measure

called **face validity**—the evidence for validity is that the measure appears "on the face of it" to measure what it is supposed to measure. Face validity is not very sophisticated; it involves only a judgment of whether, given the theoretical definition of the variable, the content of the measure appears to actually measure the variable. That is, do the procedures used to measure the variable appear to be an accurate operational definition of the abstract variable? A measure of a variable such as psychopathy will usually appear to measure that variable. The *Psychopathy Checklist-Revised (PCL-R*; Hare, 1991) includes assessments of low empathy, pathological lying, impulsive behaviours, and charm. All of these items appear closely related to the concept of psychopathy, suggesting this measure has high face validity. For the sake of example only, let's pretend that research had shown psychopaths reliably prefer the colour red to other colours; thus, an item assessing colour preference might appear on this measure. Including this colour preference item would reduce the face validity of this measure, because on the surface it doesn't make intuitive sense that colour preference has anything to do with psychopathy. Note that the assessment of face validity is a very subjective process. A way to improve the process somewhat is to systematically seek out experts in the field to judge face validity.

Face validity is *not* sufficient to conclude that a measure has construct validity. Appearance is not a very good indicator of accuracy. Some very poor measures may have face validity; for example, most personality measures that appear in popular magazines typically have several questions that look reasonable but often don't tell you anything meaningful. Interpreting the scores may make fun reading, but there is no empirical evidence to support the conclusions that are drawn from them. In addition, many good measures of variables do not have obvious face validity. For example, although research has shown that rapid eye movement (REM) sleep is an accurate (i.e., valid) indicator of dreaming, it is not obviously apparent that it should be so; therefore, eye movement is an indicator of dreaming that has low face validity.

Content Validity   **Content validity** is based on comparing the content of the measure with the theoretical definition of the construct. Consider psychopathy. Hare argues that psychopathy involves interpersonal callousness and unemotionality, as well as impulsivity and antisocial behaviour (i.e., rule breaking) (Guay, Ruscio, Knight, & Hare, 2007); therefore, to contribute to the case for content validity, his widely used *PCL-R* (Hare, 1991) includes questions intended to measure all four of those aspects—and nothing more. Researchers have disagreed about what should be included and excluded (e.g., Cooke, Michie, Hart, & Clark, 2004). Further research in response to this disagreement has made a strong case for Hare's original components (e.g., Neumann, Hare, & Newman, 2007).

Both face validity and content validity focus on assessing whether the content of a measure reflects the meaning of the construct being measured. Other indicators of validity rely on research that examines how scores on a measure relate to other measures (as is typical when gathering evidence of convergent and divergent validity) and behaviours (as is typical when gathering evidence of predictive and concurrent validity).

Predictive Validity   Using the measure to predict some future behaviour takes a **predictive validity** approach to construct validity. The criterion used to support construct validity is some future behaviour. Predictive validity is clearly important when studying measures that are designed to improve our ability to make predictions. The construct validity of such measures is supported when scores on the measure predict future behaviours that are relevant to the construct. For example, adult male Canadians who had been convicted of at least one criminal offence were tracked for ten years (Wormith, Olver, Stevenson, & Girard, 2007). Participants' original *PCL-R* scores successfully predicted whether they were later convicted of another offence, and how long their sentence length was. One can argue that future convictions are exactly what one would expect from criminals who are truly psychopathic; therefore, a scale that intends to measure psychopathy among criminals should be able to predict future convictions.

Concurrent Validity   **Concurrent validity** is assessed by research that examines the relationship between the measure and a criterion behaviour at the same time (i.e., concurrently). Research using the concurrent validity approach can take many forms. A common method is to study whether two or more groups of people (e.g., people who plagiarized and people who did not plagiarize) differ on the measure in expected ways. A self-report psychopathy scale intended for use in non-criminal populations identified more psychopathic tendencies among university students who plagiarized on essays than among those who did not plagiarize on essays (Williams, Nathanson, & Paulhus, 2010). Scores on the scale that intended to measure non-criminal psychopathy effectively distinguished people who acted unethically from people who did not, thereby demonstrating concurrent validity.

Another approach to concurrent validity is to study how people who score either low or high on the measure behave in different situations. For example, you could ask people who score high versus low on a measure of psychopathy to divide 20 dollars worth of loonies between themselves and another participant (i.e., the ultimatum game). You may expect people who score low on your psychopathy measure to divide the money evenly, responding to a sense of fairness and empathy for the other; psychopaths would likely take all the money and not feel badly about doing so (see Osumi & Ohira, 2010, for a similar design). Finding this kind of *concurrent* behavioural result would lend support for the construct validity of the psychopathy measure.

Convergent Validity   Any given measure is but one particular operational definition of the variable being measured. Often there will be other operational definitions–other measures–of the same or similar constructs. **Convergent validity** is the extent to which scores on the target measure in question are related to scores on other measures of the same construct or similar constructs. Measures of similar constructs should "converge"–for example, one measure of psychopathy should correlate highly with another psychopathy measure or a measure of a similar construct. Convergent validity was demonstrated when the original *PCL* correlated positively with antisocial personality disorder (ASPD), as diagnosed using the criteria in the *Diagnostic and Statistical Manual of Mental Disorders-III* (Hart & Hare, 1989). What is critical to note here is that ASPD and psychopathy are often considered distinct but related constructs. They share some aspects (i.e., antisocial behaviours and impulsivity), but not others (i.e., lack of remorse and empathy). Researchers found a strong positive correlation between ASPD scores and specifically that part of the *PCL* that measures antisocial, rule-breaking behaviours. This specific *convergence* increased researchers' confidence in the construct validity of the *PCL*.

Discriminant Validity   When the measure is *not* related to variables with which it should not be related, **discriminant validity** is demonstrated. The measure should *discriminate* between the construct being measured and other unrelated constructs. Therefore, it was important that Hart and Hare (1989) found that participants' ASPD scores were only weakly related to the part of the *PCL* measuring the unique, emotional aspects of psychopathy (e.g., lack of remorse and empathy). Further support for construct validity was gained by the zero correlations with other mental illnesses (e.g., schizophrenia). Such discriminant data was important because it, along with other evidence (e.g., convergence), helped to show that the *PCL* was not measuring "presence of mental illness" generally, but instead was measuring psychopathy specifically.

Collecting Evidence for Construct Validity   To build a strong argument that a measure is a valid operational definition of a particular construct, a researcher uses as many of the above methods as possible to gather as much evidence as possible. Even then, a measure may be considered well-validated for use in one population or context, but that does not mean it will be a valid indicator of that construct in a different population or context. For example, a self-report scale developed to identify psychopathy in criminal populations (Hare, Harpur, & Hemphill, 1989) is not necessarily appropriate to measure psychopathic tendencies among undergraduate students. It was possible that the construct of psychopathy could have manifested quite differently in criminal versus undergraduate populations. Researchers at the University of British Columbia investigated this question and provided evidence toward validating the measure among undergraduates (Williams, Paulhus, & Hare, 2007). They built an argument for convergent validity by showing that the measure correlated highly with other measures of psychopathy, and for concurrent validity by showing this measure correlated positively with self-reported behaviours one would expect of people scoring high on a psychopathy measure (e.g., bullying, drug abuse). Further evidence could be gained by investigating predictive and discriminant validities. Construct validity is built from various sources of evidence, and must be reconsidered whenever a measure is used for a new purpose.

REACTIVITY OF MEASURES

LO4

A potential problem when measuring behaviour is **reactivity.** For some operational definitions of variables, awareness of being measured changes an individual's behaviour. A reactive measure tells what the person is like when he or she is aware of being observed, but it doesn't tell how the person would behave under natural circumstances. Simply having various devices such as electrodes and blood pressure cuffs attached to your body may change the physiological responses being recorded. Knowing that a researcher is observing you or recording your behaviour might change the way you behave (see also Chapter 6). A person might lie on a questionnaire to avoid feeling embarrassed. Measures of behaviour vary in terms of their potential reactivity. There are ways to minimize reactivity, such as allowing time for people to become used to the presence of the observer or the recording equipment.

A book by Webb, Campbell, Schwartz, Sechrest, and Grove (1981) drew attention to a number of operational definitions that are called *nonreactive* or *unobtrusive.* Many such measures involve clever ways of indirectly recording a variable. For example, one way to measure preferences for paintings at an art gallery would be to ask patrons, but they might not report accurately, or they might not fully realize what captured their interest. An unobtrusive measure of preferences for paintings in an art museum is the frequency with which tiles around each painting must be replaced–the most popular paintings are the ones with the most tile wear. Levine (1990) studied the pace of life in cities, using indirect measures such as the accuracy of bank clocks and the speed of processing standard requests at post offices. Unobtrusive measures must be valid indicators of the constructs they purport to measure. Despite its age, the book by Webb and his colleagues is a rich and unparalleled source of creative nonreactive ways to operationally define variables. Importantly, it draws attention to the problem of reactivity and sensitizes researchers to the need to reduce reactivity whenever possible. We will return to this issue at several points in this book (e.g., Chapters 6 and 9).

VARIABLES AND MEASUREMENT SCALES   LO5

Recall from Chapter 4 that there must be at least two values or levels of any variable. The values may be quantitatively different or they may reflect categorical differences. In actuality, the world is a bit more complex. A variable's *levels* can be conceptualized in terms of four kinds of measurement scales: nominal, ordinal, interval, and ratio (summarized in Table 5.1). A variable's scale will depend on the way it is measured or manipulated (i.e., its operational definition). As we will discuss, the type(s) of scales you use will affect the rest of

TABLE 5.1   Scales of measurement

Scale	Defining Features	Example	Distinction
Nominal	Categories with no numeric scales	Males/females Experimental condition/control condition	Impossible to define any quantitative values and/or differences between/across categories
Ordinal	Rank ordering Numeric values have limited meaning	2-, 3-, and 4-star restaurants Birth order	Intervals between items not known or inconsistent
Interval	Numeric properties are literal Assume equal interval between values	Intelligence Temperature (Fahrenheit or Celsius)	No true zero
Ratio	Zero indicates absence of variable measured Assume equal interval between values	Reaction time Age Frequencies of behaviours	Can form ratios (e.g., someone responds twice as fast as another person)

your research, including the conclusions you can draw, the options available for establishing construct validity, and the kinds of statistical analyses that are possible and appropriate to use when analyzing your data (see Chapter 13).

Nominal Scales

A **nominal scale** has no numerical or quantitative properties. Instead, categories or groups simply differ from one another (sometimes nominal variables are called *categorical* variables). An example is the variable of sex. Animals are typically classified as either male or female. Being male does not imply a greater amount of "sexness" than being female; the levels are merely different. This is called a nominal scale because we assign names to different categories within a variable. Another example is the classification of undergraduates according to major. A psychology major would not be entitled to a higher number than a history major, for instance. In developmental psychology research, young children's behaviour patterns can be categorized into different attachment styles (secure, ambivalent, avoidant). Even if you were to assign numbers to the different categories, the numbers would be meaningless, except for identification.

In an experiment, the independent variable is often a nominal or categorical variable. For example, Cianci, Klein, and Seijts (2010) studied a variable that can be called "type of goal." Students about to take an analogy test were motivated with either a performance goal to earn the highest score possible, or a learning goal to use the test as an opportunity to learn how to answer analogy-style questions effectively. The "type of goal" variable is nominal because the two levels are merely different categories; the goals have no numerical properties. Results of this study showed that after everyone was told they failed on the first attempt, those who had the learning goal in mind performed better after failure than did those with the performance goal.

Ordinal Scales

An **ordinal scale** allows us to rank order the levels of the variable being studied. Instead of having categories that are simply different, as in a nominal scale, the categories can be ordered from first to last. One example of an ordinal scale is Olympic medals (gold, silver, and bronze); another is birth order (first, second, third, and so on). Developmental stage models also form ordinal scales. Piaget proposed that children's intellectual development progresses sequentially through sensorimotor, preoperational, concrete operational, then formal operational stages (Piaget, 1952). Consider a different, applied example: A restaurant that just made a major staffing change might ask diners to rate its service quality on an ordinal scale:

_____ Was the service *better than* the last time you were here?

_____ Was the service *about the same as* the last time you were here?

_____ Was the service *worse than* the last time you were here?

This information allows us to rank order a diner's visits by perceived quality of service. This rating system is not a nominal scale because the ratings are meaningful in terms of a continuum of quality. However, we cannot say anything about *how much* service differed between the last time patrons visited the restaurant and this time. Similarly, although we may have quantitative information about a person's birth order, we cannot say that the difference in age between a first-born and a second-born is always the same or that it is the same as the difference between a second-born and a third-born. In health psychology, researchers might distinguish among high, medium, and low socioeconomic status. The categories are ranked but they are not necessarily equally distributed in a population. No particular value is attached to the intervals between the numbers used in ordinal scales.

Interval Scales

In an **interval scale,** the difference between the numbers on the scale is equal in size. The difference between 1 and 2 on the scale, for example, is the same as the difference between 2 and 3. Interval scales generally have five or more quantitative levels. For example, a household thermometer (Fahrenheit or Celsius) measures temperature on an interval scale. The difference in temperature between 15° and 17° is equal to the difference between 26° and 28°. However, there is no absolute zero on the scale that would indicate the absence of temperature. The zero on any interval scale is only an arbitrary reference point. Without an absolute zero point on interval scales, we cannot form ratios of the numbers. That is, we cannot say that one number on the scale represents twice as much (or three times as much, and so forth) temperature as another number. You cannot say that 20° Celsius is twice as warm as 10° Celsius. This point becomes clear when these very values are converted to Fahrenheit: 68° is clearly not twice as warm as 50°. In fact, 0° Celsius equals 32° Fahrenheit!

Weschler's intelligence tests can be considered interval scales. The difference between an IQ score of 85 and 90 is the same as a difference between 105 and 110–but there is no absolute zero point that indicates an absence of all intelligence. Moreover, ratings scales (e.g., 7 points ranging from 1 to 7; see Chapter 7) are often assumed to be interval scales. These kinds of scales are often used to measure personality traits such as agreeableness, or attitudes toward different groups of people. If the measurement is an interval scale, we cannot make a statement such as "the person who scored 6 is twice as extraverted as the person who scored 3" because there is no absolute zero point that indicates an absence of the trait being measured.

Ratio Scales

A **ratio scale** does have an absolute zero point that indicates the absence of the variable being measured. The "absence of temperature" is defined on the

Kelvin scale as the point at which all molecular movement stops: 0° Kelvin (which equals −273° Celsius). Many physical measures, such as length, weight, or time, also use ratio scales. Ratio scales enable statements such as "a person who weighs 220 pounds weighs twice as much as a person who weighs 110 pounds" or "on average, participants in the experimental group responded twice as fast as participants in the control group" that are not possible when using other scales.

Ratio scales are often used in the behavioural sciences when variables that involve physical measures are being studied—particularly, time measures such as reaction time, rate of responding, and duration of response. However, many variables in the behavioural sciences are less precise and so use nominal, ordinal, or interval scale measures.

The Importance of the Measurement Scales

When you read about the operational definitions of variables, you can learn to recognize the levels of the variable in terms of these types of scales. As we will consider in Chapters 12 and 13, the scale determines the types of statistics that are appropriate to use when analyzing the results of a study. The statistical tests for interval and ratio scales are the same. Moreover, the conclusions one draws about the meaning of a particular score on a variable depend on which type of scale was used. With interval and ratio scales, you can make quantitative distinctions that allow you to talk about amounts of the variable. With nominal scales, there is no quantitative information. To illustrate, suppose you are studying perceptions of physical attractiveness. In an experiment, you might show participants pictures of people with different characteristics such as their waist-to-hip ratio (waist size divided by hip size). How should you measure the participants' physical attractiveness judgments? You could use a nominal scale:

_____ Not Attractive _____ Attractive

These scale values allow participants to state whether they find the person attractive or not, but do not allow you to know about the amount of attractiveness. As an alternative, you could use an interval scale that asks participants to rate amount of attractiveness:

Very Unattractive _____ _____ _____ _____ _____ _____ _____ Very Attractive

This rating scale provides you with quantitative information about amount of attractiveness because you can assign relatively meaningful numeric values to each of the response options on the scale; in this case, the values would range from 1 to 7. You may be interested to note that human males tend to prefer females with a 0.70 waist-to-hip ratio as more attractive than females with higher ratios (Singh, 1993; Suschinsky, Elias, & Krupp, 2007). This finding has been interpreted in terms of evolutionary theory. This ratio presumably is a signal of reproductive capacity.

We are now ready to consider approaches to operationally defining behaviour. A variety of observational methods are described in Chapter 6; questionnaires and interviews are the focus of Chapter 7.

STUDY TERMS

Test yourself! Define and generate an example of each of these key terms.

Concurrent validity (p. 104)

Construct validity (p. 102)

Content validity (p. 104)

Convergent validity (p. 105)

Cronbach's alpha (p. 100)

Discriminant validity (p. 105)

Face validity (p. 103)

Internal consistency
    reliability (p. 100)

Interrater reliability (p. 101)

Interval scale (p. 109)

Measurement error (p. 97)

Nominal scale (p. 108)

Ordinal scale (p. 108)

Pearson product-moment correlation
    coefficient (p. 98)

Predictive validity (p. 104)

Ratio scale (p. 109)

Reactivity (p. 106)

Reliability (p. 97)

Test-retest reliability (p. 99)

True score (p. 97)

REVIEW QUESTIONS

Test yourself on this chapter's learning objectives. Can you answer each of these questions?

1. How is the quality of an operational definition affected by low reliability and low validity?

2. What is meant by the reliability of a measure? Distinguish between true score and measurement error.

3. Compare and contrast the three ways to determine the reliability of a measure. When would a researcher use each kind of reliability?

4. Discuss the concept of construct validity, including how a researcher builds an argument for it.

5. Compare and contrast convergent and discriminant validity, predictive and concurrent validity.

6. Why isn't face validity sufficient to establish the validity of a measure?

7. What is a reactive measure?

8. Distinguish among nominal, ordinal, interval, and ratio scales.

DEEPEN YOUR UNDERSTANDING

Develop your mastery of these concepts by considering these application questions. Compare your responses with those from other people in your study group.

1. Find a reference book on psychological measurement such as the one by Robinson, Shaver, and Wrightsman (1999), or do a *PsycINFO* search (see Appendix D) using a keyword search for "scale" AND "validity." Identify a measure that interests you and describe the ways the researchers built a case for its reliability and validity.

2. Here are a number of references to variables. For each, identify whether a nominal, ordinal, interval, or ratio scale is being used:

   a. Today's temperatures in the eight biggest cities across Canada.

   b. The birth weights of babies who were born at Whitehorse General Hospital last week.

   c. The number of hours you spent studying each day during the past week.

   d. The amount of tip left after each meal served at a restaurant during a three-hour period.

   e. The number of votes received by each candidate for provincial parliament in your riding in the last election.

   f. The brand listed third in a consumer magazine's ranking of tablet computers.

   g. In a sportswriter opinion poll, the Montreal Canadiens were listed as the number one Canadian hockey team, with the Calgary Flames listed number two.

   h. Your friend's score on an intelligence test.

   i. Yellow walls in your office and white walls in your boss's office.

   j. The type of programming on each radio station in your city (e.g., in Winnipeg, CITI plays rock, CBW is talk radio).

   k. Ethnic group categories of people in a neighbourhood.

3. Take a personality test on the Internet. Based on the information provided, what can you conclude about reliability, construct validity, and reactivity?

4. Think of an important characteristic that you would look for in a potential romantic partner, such as humorous, intelligent, attractive, hard-working, religious, and so on. How might you measure that characteristic? Describe two methods that you might use to assess construct validity of that measure.

6

Observational Methods

LEARNING OBJECTIVES

Keep these learning objectives in mind as you read to help you identify the most critical information in this chapter.

By the end of this chapter, you should be able to:

1. Compare quantitative and qualitative approaches to investigating behaviour.
2. Describe naturalistic observation and discuss methodological issues such as participation and concealment.
3. Describe systematic observation and discuss methodological issues such as the use of coding systems, reactivity, equipment, reliability, and sampling.
4. Describe the features of and appropriate uses for a case study.
5. Describe archival research and sources of archival data: statistical records, survey archives, and written records.

Have you ever "people-watched"? Think about the wide variety of behaviours you have observed in university dormitories, on public transit, at the grocery store, on the street, on social media, at concerts or sporting events, and so on. In this chapter, we will explore various techniques that behavioural scientists have developed to turn everyday observations into knowledge. Sometimes these observation techniques are used to generate hypotheses for further research; sometimes they are used with the goal of in-depth description (see Chapter 1); sometimes they are used for non-experimental research (in which behaviour is always measured or observed rather than manipulated); and sometimes they are used in experimental designs (e.g., when measuring the dependent variable; see Chapter 4).

Many of the methods described in this chapter are used in different ways by a variety of researchers within and outside psychology. For example, you may have encountered some of these methods in your anthropology or sociology courses. Therefore, it will be helpful to start by situating these methods in terms of quantitative and qualitative perspectives.

QUANTITATIVE AND QUALITATIVE APPROACHES

LO1

How does a researcher learn to explore and understand behaviour? How does a researcher learn what methods are appropriate to use to collect and interpret data? How does a researcher know what "data" look like? Consider the training this text is offering you. Exploring and understanding behaviour involves the scientific method: developing theories; generating hypotheses to test those theories; designing experiments or non-experiments to test those hypotheses, including operationally defining variables; collecting numerical data from many participants; and analyzing those data using statistics. This approach is one way of learning about the world, often summarized as an *empirical* or **quantitative approach.** It is the perspective most often used in psychology, but it is not the only approach.

Consider another way to learn about the world, often called an *interpretive* (Poulin, 2007) or **qualitative approach.** Used widely in counselling psychology, anthropology, education, and sociology, a qualitative approach offers deep description of people's behaviour in natural settings, people explaining their experiences in their own words, collecting in-depth information on relatively few individuals or within a very limited setting, and conclusions that are based on careful interpretations drawn by the investigator. Instead of using one single, common set of rules like the scientific method, there is great variety in the research paradigms and sets of rules captured by the term *qualitative* (e.g., ethnography, phenomenology, grounded theory, narrative; see Creswell, 2007).

Imagine that you are interested in describing how the lives of teenagers are affected by working outside of school. You might take a quantitative approach by developing a questionnaire and asking a sample of teenagers to complete it (see Chapter 7). You could ask about the number of hours they work, the type of work they do, their stress levels, and their school grades. After assigning numerical values to the responses, you would analyze the data using statistics. A quantitative report of the results may include average levels of stress, and the relationship between hours worked and academic average.

Suppose, instead, that you take a qualitative approach to describing behaviour. You might conduct a series of focus groups in which you engage groups of eight teenagers in a discussion about their perceptions and experiences with the world of work. You would ask the teenagers to tell you about the topic using their own words. You might record the focus group discussions and have a transcript prepared later, or you might have observers take detailed notes during the discussions. A qualitative report of the results may describe themes that emerge from the discussions and the manner in which the teenagers considered the issues. Such description is qualitative because it is expressed in non-numerical terms using language and images. Other methods, both qualitative and quantitative, could also be used to study teenage employment. For example, a quantitative study could examine archival data collected from Statistics Canada; a qualitative study might use concealed naturalistic observation while working as a trainee in a fast-food restaurant.

As we explore various methods in this chapter and in Chapter 7, consider how each may be used from quantitative and qualitative perspectives. Some of the methods are used more commonly by investigators using a qualitative approach (e.g., naturalistic observation, focus groups), whereas some are used more commonly by investigators using a quantitative approach (e.g., systematic observation, closed-ended surveys). Many of these methods are used for both qualitative and quantitative purposes but in different ways (e.g., case studies, archives). Keep in mind that what counts as "data" is one of the keys to distinguishing the two approaches: The quantitative approach requires statistical analysis (and hence numerical data), whereas the qualitative approach often involves interpreting people's experiences within a specific context. Whether a researcher uses quantitative or qualitative approaches to learning about the world—or uses the rare mix of both—can depend on the kind of training he or she received as a student. Because it often takes years of training to become an expert in using either approach to research, qualitative and quantitative researchers sometimes fail to appreciate the strengths of the other. In the big picture, a thorough understanding of behaviour will likely require both qualitative and quantitative ways of knowing.

NATURALISTIC OBSERVATION

LO2

Naturalistic observation demands that researchers immerse themselves in a particular natural setting (sometimes called *the field*). Observations are typically made over an extended period of time using a variety of information-collection techniques. The field researcher, if taking a qualitative approach, observes everything—the setting, the patterns of personal relationships, people's reactions to events, and so on—without a hypothesis in mind. The goal is to provide a complete and accurate picture. To achieve this goal, the researcher must keep detailed field notes—that is, write or dictate everything that has happened at least once each day. Qualitative field researchers use a variety of techniques to gather information: observing people and events, interviewing key "informants" to provide inside information, talking to people about their lives, and examining documents produced in the setting, such as newsletters, e-mails, text messages, or manuals. Audio and video recordings, as well as photographs, are also used. Naturalistic observation has roots in anthropology and the study of animal behaviour and is used in the social sciences to study many phenomena in all types of social and organizational settings.

The researcher's first goal is to describe the setting, events, and persons observed. The second, equally important goal is to interpret what was observed. Depending on the specific qualitative approach used, this interpretation may involve identifying common themes (as in phenomenology) or developing a theory with hypotheses for future work (as in grounded theory; see Creswell, Hanson, Clark, & Morales, 2007). The final report might reflect the chronological order of events (as in the narrative approach), or it can be organized around the theory developed by the researcher (as in grounded theory). Specific examples of events that occurred during observation are used to support the researcher's interpretations. A good naturalistic observation report will support the validity (i.e., accuracy) of the interpretation by using multiple confirmations (Creswell, 2007). For example, similar events may occur several times, similar information may be reported by two or more people, and several different events may occur that all support the same conclusion. The published qualitative report includes specific observations and the researcher's interpretations.

Researchers can use naturalistic observation to describe and understand how people in a social or cultural setting live, work, and experience the setting. To learn about the hotel community, qualitative researchers have spent months visiting hotels, talking to people, observing interactions, and becoming accepted as "regulars" (Prus & Irini, 1980). To learn about practical mathematical thinking in everyday contexts, Scribner (1997) and her research team embedded themselves in the routines of machine operators, cashiers, and milk truck drivers, gathering all notes and photographing all devices people actually used to help them make complex calculations quickly. Thorough data analysis revealed some strategies that could often not be predicted from formal problem-solving models, thereby contributing new knowledge to the practical-thinking literature. In another particularly illuminating naturalistic observation study, eight psychologically healthy people were admitted to psychiatric hospitals after claiming to "hear voices" but no other symptoms, in order to learn about the conditions and treatment (Rosenhan, 1973). This study revealed deep and long-lasting stigmatization that comes with a diagnosis of mental illness.

Naturalistic observation tends to be used by researchers using a qualitative approach, as noted above. Therefore, the data from naturalistic observation studies are primarily qualitative descriptions of the observations themselves rather than quantitative statistical summaries. Such qualitative descriptions can be richer and closer to the phenomenon being studied than are statistical representations. Sometimes researchers use a mixed approach, gathering some quantitative data while engaging in naturalistic observation. If circumstances allow it, data can be gathered on income, family size, education levels, and other easily quantifiable variables. A researcher using a mixed approach might report and interpret such quantitative data along with qualitative data gathered from interviews and direct observations.

Researchers using a fully quantitative approach may employ naturalistic observation sometimes too. Some quantitative researchers have used naturalistic observation to generate hypotheses for later experiments. For example, to learn about how people persuade or influence others, psychologist Robert Cialdini was hired and trained in many sales positions (e.g., selling cars) before developing his theories he later tested using experiments (see Cialdini, 2008). Other quantitative researchers use naturalistic observation to collect data that they later translate into numerical data using a *coding system* (described below).

Issues in Naturalistic Observation

Participation and Concealment   Two related issues facing the researcher are whether to be a participant or non-participant in the social setting, and whether to conceal his or her purposes from the other people in the setting. Do you become an active participant in the group, or do you observe from the outside? Do you conceal your purposes or even your presence, or do you openly let people know what you are doing?

A non-participant observer is an outsider who does not become an active part of the setting. In contrast, a participant observer assumes an active, insider role. Because **participant observation** allows the researcher to observe the setting from the inside, he or she may be able to experience events in the same way as natural participants. Participant observation may facilitate friendships and other insider experiences that offer valuable data for the qualitative researcher aiming to completely describe the context. For example, Nathan (2005), who studied the first-year university experience using participant observation, describes critical insights she gained from friendships she made while living in a dormitory. A potential problem with participant observation, however, is that the observer may lose the objectivity necessary to conduct scientific observation. Remaining objective may be especially difficult when the researcher already belongs to the group being studied (e.g., a researcher who belongs to a city's Pride Society who undertakes a study of that group). If a researcher has some prior reason to either find fault with people in the setting or to report only positive behaviours of a particular group, there is great risk that the observations will be biased and the conclusions will lack objectivity (see Creswell & Miller, 2000).

Should the researcher remain concealed or be open about the research purposes? **Concealed observation** may be preferable because the presence of the observer may influence the behaviour of those being observed. Imagine how a non-concealed observer might change how a classroom of high school students behave. Concealed observation is less *reactive* (see Chapter 5) than non-concealed observation because people are not aware that their behaviours are being observed and recorded. Still, non-concealed observation may be preferable from an ethical viewpoint: Consider the ethical principles that were stretched when researchers perched in a bathroom stall to record hand-washing practices among university women (Drankiewicz & Dundes, 2003).

Reactivity can sometimes subside quickly; people can become used to the observer and behave naturally in the observer's presence–particularly when the observer is not present in person. By asking participants to wear a subtle device called an Electronically Activated Recorder (EAR), researchers have recorded thousands of 30-second audio clips of people's daily lives, providing rich naturalistic observation-style data sets (Mehl, Pennebaker, Crow, Dabbs, & Price, 2001). People seem to quickly forget about the recording device and spontaneously reveal many private aspects of their lives while wearing it.

The decision of whether to conceal one's purpose or presence depends both on ethical concerns and on the nature of the particular group and setting being studied. Sometimes a participant observer is non-concealed to certain members of the group, who give the researcher permission to be part of the group as a concealed observer. Often a concealed observer decides to say nothing directly about his or her purposes but will completely disclose the goals of the research if asked by anyone. Non-participant observers are also not concealed when they gain permission to "hang out" in a setting or use interview techniques to gather information. In actuality, then, there are degrees of participation and concealment: A non-participant observer may not become a member of the group, for example, but may over time become accepted as a friend or simply part of the ongoing activities of the group. Researchers who use naturalistic observation to study behaviour must carefully determine what their role in the setting will be.

You may be wondering about informed consent in naturalistic observation. Recall from Chapter 3 that observation in public places when anonymity is not threatened is typically considered *exempt research*. In these cases, informed consent is usually unnecessary. Nevertheless, researchers must be sensitive to ethical issues when conducting naturalistic observation. Of particular interest is whether the observations are made in a public place with no clear expectations that behaviours are private. For example, should a bar be considered public or private? What about a person's Facebook page? Kraut et al. (2004) discuss the ethically problematic issue that information written on Internet discussion boards is public, but people who post on these boards may perceive that they are part of a private community. Issues of informed consent also resurface when collecting data with the EAR device mentioned earlier, precisely because participants become so used to it. To ensure ongoing informed consent, sometimes participants are given all audio files before data analysis, so they can delete any they are uncomfortable sharing with researchers (Holleran, Whitehead, Schmader, & Mehl, 2011).

Defining the Scope of the Observation   A researcher employing naturalistic observation may want to study *everything* about a setting. However, this may not be possible simply because settings are so complex. Thus, researchers often must limit the scope of their observations to behaviours that are relevant to the central issues of the study. For example, a naturalistic observation of skateboarders might focus on their intrinsic motivation (as did Seifert & Hedderson, 2009), while ignoring other aspects of behaviour such as their use of public spaces, their social interactions, or the experience of gender. For another example, when Graham and colleagues (2006) used naturalistic observation to study behaviour in bars, they specifically focused on expressions of aggression, rather than attempting to record alcohol consumption, expressions of sexuality, and friendship.

Limits of Naturalistic Observation Naturalistic observation obviously cannot be used to study all issues or phenomena. From a qualitative perspective, the approach is most useful when investigating complex social settings to understand the settings and to develop theories based on the observations. From a quantitative perspective, it is useful for gathering data in real-life settings and generating hypotheses for later experiments. The inability to control the setting makes it challenging to test well-defined hypotheses under precisely specified conditions.

Naturalistic observation in the field is also very difficult to do (cf., Green & Wallaf, 1981). Unlike a typical laboratory experiment, data collection in the field cannot always be scheduled at a convenient time and place. Consider Graham and colleagues' (2013) extremely well-trained research assistants who stayed in and around bars until 3:30 a.m. over a thousand times! In fact, field research in general (whether it is naturalistic observation or a *field experiment*, see Chapter 4) can be extremely time-consuming, often placing the researcher in an unfamiliar setting for extended periods. Also, in laboratory research, the procedures are well-defined and the same for each participant, and the data analysis is planned in advance. In naturalistic observation research, however, there is an ever-changing pattern of events, some important and some unimportant; the researcher must record them all and remain flexible in order to adjust to them as research progresses. Finally, the process of data interpretation is not simple. The researcher must repeatedly sort through the vast amounts of data to identify common themes, to develop hypotheses to explain the data, or to code the data into meaningful categories for statistical analysis, depending on the approach being used (e.g., phenomenology, grounded theory, versus quantitative). Although naturalistic observation research is a difficult and challenging technique, it can yield valuable knowledge when done well (e.g., Rosenhan, 1973; Cialdini, 2008).

SYSTEMATIC OBSERVATION

LO3

Systematic observation refers to the careful observation of one or more specific behaviours in a particular setting, usually contrived by the researcher. This research method is much less global than naturalistic observation research, and is used more often from a quantitative rather than qualitative perspective. The researcher is interested in only a few very specific behaviours, the observations are quantifiable, and the researcher typically has hypotheses about the behaviours.

For example, a team of researchers at Dalhousie University in Halifax were interested in how young children develop empathy for others who are expressing pain or sadness (Bandstra, Chambers, McGrath, & Moore, 2011). Children aged 18 to 36 months were videotaped in a room while they played with an experimenter who either pretended to hurt herself and expressed pain, or broke a toy and expressed sadness. In this experimental design, the experimenter's emotion (pain versus sadness) was the independent variable. After the study was over, observers viewed the videotapes and coded each child's behaviour during the 30 seconds the experimenter expressed the emotion. Observers used the *coding system* depicted in Table 6.1.

The coded behaviours were the researchers' way of operationally defining the dependent variable: children's empathic responses. What Bandstra et al. found was opposite to what had been found among adults in a previous study: Children seemed more affected by witnessing another's sadness rather than pain. Specifically, children showed more self-distress, prosocial acts, and global concern after the experimenter expressed sadness than when she expressed pain. These findings suggest that children may develop empathy for different emotions at different rates.

Coding Systems

In systematic observation, the researchers must decide which behaviours are of interest, choose or create a specific setting in which the behaviours can

TABLE 6.1   Coding system for children's empathic responses (Bandstra et al., 2011)

Code	Definition	Frequency
Prosocial acts	Child attempts to comfort the experimenter through distraction, by sharing a new toy, or with verbal sympathy.	
Attempts to understand the distress	Child imitates the experimenter's emotional expression.	
Self-distress	Child engages in self-soothing behaviour (e.g., sucks thumb, seeks parental comforting).	
Unresponsive/ inappropriate affect	Child shows little concern (e.g., ignores experimenter, plays, laughs).	
Global concern	Overall level of concern (0 = *no concern evident* to 4 = *variety of responses clearly indicating concern*).	

be observed, and develop a **coding system,** such as the one in Table 6.1, to measure the behaviours. In general, the purpose of a coding system is to summarize qualitative observations–be it live actions, written responses, or images produced by participants. Sometimes the researcher develops the coding system to fit the needs of the particular study (see Boyatzis, 1998). Coding systems should be as simple as possible, allowing observers to easily categorize behaviours (e.g., presence or absence of thumb-sucking). The need for simplicity is especially important when observers are coding live behaviours rather than viewing videotapes that can be reviewed or even coded on a frame-by-frame basis; Bandstra et al. videotaped the children so that observers could carefully review their coding using the system in Table 6.1. For another example, Holleran et al. (2011) used a straightforward coding system for their EAR recordings to examine sources of job dissatisfaction among women who are faculty in the STEM disciplines (i.e., science, technology, engineering, and mathematics). Faculty members' conversations were coded on two dimensions: topic (social or research related) and gender of the person to whom they were speaking. One result from this study was that faculty were less likely to discuss research with female colleagues than with male colleagues.

Developing a coding system can be a very complex process. Researchers might first choose to conduct a naturalistic observation study to help them come up with meaningful categories for their coding system, which they could then use to code behaviours observed in a controlled, systematic way. This strategy was pursued by Graham et al. (2006). After observing people in 118 Toronto bars for 1,334 nights, the researchers created a coding system identifying many forms of physical aggression (e.g., pushing, restraining) and non-physical aggression (e.g., swearing, glaring). This coding system was later used in quantitative research investigating people's motives for different types of aggressive barroom acts (e.g., Graham et al., 2013).

Sometimes researchers use coding systems that have been developed by others. For example, the Facial Action Coding System (FACS; see Ekman & Friesen, 1978) is a way to categorize subtle, fleeting facial muscle movements based on specific "action units" of the upper face, lower face, and other areas (e.g., head movements). One way that the FACS has been used in psychology is to code emotion expressions, including surprise and shame (Tracy, Robins, & Schriber, 2009). Another coding system is the MICS, the Mealtime Interaction Coding System (Dickstein et al., 1994). The MICS provides a way of coding interactions of family members during mealtimes, including communication and behaviour standards. It has been used to explore how family interactions during mealtime relate to childhood attachment (Dubois-Comtois & Moss, 2008) and to children's (over)eating behaviour (Czaja, Hartmann, Rief, & Hilbert, 2011). A major advantage of using a previously developed coding system is that research already exists that *validates* the system's use for particular purposes, and training materials are usually available.

Issues in Systematic Observation

Reliability   Recall from Chapter 5 that *reliability* refers to the degree to which a measurement reflects a true score rather than a measurement error. Reliable measures are stable, consistent, and precise. When conducting systematic observation, two or more raters are usually used to code behaviour. Reliability is indicated by high agreement among the raters. Very high levels of agreement are reported in virtually all published research using systematic observation (generally 80 percent agreement or higher; e.g., Bandstra et al., 2011). For some research (e.g., using the FACS), observers must be trained extensively, including practising on prior data and discussing coding decisions, before coding new data (see Bakeman & Gottman, 1986).

It can be difficult to achieve high interrater reliability with live coding, unless the coding system is very simple (e.g., counting the number of times a participant touches her face during an interview). Video recording behaviour has the advantage of providing a permanent record that can be coded later by many observers. Depending on the study, computer programs can also be used to count and time observed behaviours.

Reactivity   Just as in naturalistic observation, the presence of the observer (be it a video camera or a live person) can affect people's behaviours (see also Chapter 5). As noted previously, reactivity can be reduced by concealed observation. The use of one-way mirrors and hidden cameras can conceal the presence of an observer in the laboratory. As mentioned in Chapter 3, gaining participants' informed consent to use their data is crucial after such deception. Especially if observation tools such as concealed cameras are used, participants should be fully debriefed and offered the opportunity to forbid researchers to use their data. (See Chapter 9 for more details on debriefing.) Alternatively, reactivity can be reduced by allowing enough time for people to become used to the presence of the observer and any recording equipment.

Sampling   Researchers must make decisions about how to sample behaviours. For many research questions, samples of behaviour taken over a long period provide more accurate and useful data than single, short observations. Consider a study on parents' behaviour at youth hockey games that used systematic observation in a field setting (Bowker et al., 2009). The researchers wanted to know whether parents promoted violence at hockey games, as is sometimes reported in the media. They could have studied a single hockey game or two; however, such data can be distorted by short-term trends—time of day, a particular team combination, or whether a particularly vocal parent happened to show up that day. A better method of addressing the question is to observe spectator behaviour over time, which is exactly what the researchers did. Observers attended 69 youth hockey games (which was approximately 10 percent of all games played by 11- to 14-year-olds in Ottawa between November 2006 and February 2007), and recorded all comments made by spectators for each team. Then, researchers systematically coded all comments into one of five categories (e.g., positive and directed specifically at one player, instructions for plays). Among other findings, results revealed that comments tended to be positive, especially at recreational (rather than competitive) games. The general positivity of comments collected in this systematic way offers evidence against a common assumption that parents fuel violence in youth hockey.

CASE STUDIES

LO4

A **case study** provides a description of an individual. This individual is usually a person, but it may also be a setting such as a business, school, or neighbourhood. A naturalistic observation study can sometimes be treated like a case study, but case studies do not necessarily involve naturalistic observation. Instead, the case study may be a description of a patient by a clinical psychologist or a historical account of an event such as a model school or program that failed. A *psychobiography* is a type of case study in which a researcher applies psychological theory to explain the life of an individual, usually an important historical figure (cf., Elms, 1994; see Runyan, 2006, for brief psychobiographies of famous psychologists). Case studies can involve library research and interviews with people familiar with the case, and may or may not include direct observation of the case (cf., Yin, 1994).

Depending on the purpose of the investigation, the case study may present the individual's history, symptoms, characteristic behaviours, reactions to situations, or responses to treatment. The case study method is useful when an individual possesses a particularly rare, unusual, or noteworthy condition. One famous case study involved a man with an amazing ability to recall information (Luria, 1968). The man, called "S.," could remember long lists and passages with ease, apparently using elaborate mental imagery. Luria also described some of the drawbacks of S.'s ability. For example, he frequently had difficulty concentrating because mental images would spontaneously appear and interfere with his thinking. A more recent case study investigated language development, which is typically slower among deaf children than among hearing children. York University researchers Ruggirello and Mayer (2010) compared the language development of fraternal twin girls, only one of whom was born with profound deafness, but who received two cochlear implants and therapy starting at age 1. Researchers spent two years thoroughly investigating this case using naturalistic observations in the home, formal language assessments, systematic observation in the lab, and structured interviews with the twins' mother. Researchers found that the implants and therapy were able to successfully reverse the early language delay experienced by the deaf twin; within about two years, her language development had caught up to her sister. This study contributed to the literature showing the importance of early implants among profoundly deaf infants.

Sometimes, case studies of people with particular types of brain damage can allow researchers to test hypotheses. For one example, consider research by Kwan, Craver, Green, Myerson, & Rosenbaum (2013). Previous research had shown that imagining future events activates the hippocampus, suggesting the hippocampus is required. However, past case studies had showed mixed findings: Of those with hippocampus damage, only some people showed difficulty imagining some future experiences such as consequences of different choices. Using four case studies considered simultaneously, Kwan and colleagues sought to test the hypothesis that a fully functioning hippo-campus is *not required* to imagine future outcomes of decisions. Just like participants without brain damage, the four people with hippocampal damage made decisions that benefited them in the future: They chose larger rewards to come later rather than smaller immediate rewards. This research provided evidence that hippocampus damage doesn't necessarily prevent all types of future-oriented thought. Because the same pattern was found (i.e., was *replicated*) in people with four different presentations of brain damage, the hypothesis received more support than if just one person was studied.

Case studies are valuable for learning about conditions that are rare or unusual and thus providing unique data about some psychological phenomena, such as memory, language, or decision making. Insights gained through a case study may also lead to the development of hypotheses that can be tested using other methods. Nonetheless, extreme caution must be taken when interpreting the results of a case study; it is inappropriate to generalize the results from one case to the population. This issue of *external validity* (i.e., the extent to which results generalize beyond the study) will be discussed in Chapter 14.

ARCHIVAL RESEARCH
[LO5]

Archival research involves using previously compiled information to answer research questions. The researcher does not actually collect the original data. Instead, he or she analyzes existing data such as public records (e.g., number of divorce petitions filed), reports of anthropologists, newspaper articles, personal diaries, social media posts, data published online for public access (e.g., NHL player statistics), or even other researchers' published reports (e.g., for a *meta-analysis;* see Chapter 14). The type of data extracted from the archival sources differs depending on whether the researcher is using a qualitative approach (e.g., common themes) or a quantitative approach (numerical data ready for statistical analysis). Three sources of archival research data are statistical records, survey archives, and written records.

Statistical Records

Statistical records are collected by many public and private organizations. Statistics Canada maintains the most extensive set of Canadian statistical records available to researchers for analysis; the U.S. Census Bureau maintains comparable records. Some of the many other sources include provincial-level vital statistics (e.g., birth and marriage records) and test score records kept by testing organizations such as the Educational Testing Service, which administers standardized tests such as the Graduate Record Exam.

Public records can also be used as sources of archival data. For example, Anderson and Anderson (1984) demonstrated a relationship between average monthly temperature and violent crime statistics in two U.S. cities. Data on both variables are readily available from agencies that keep these statistics. Moulden, Firestone, Kingston, and Wexler (2010) obtained access to a Royal Canadian Mounted Police database to describe the characteristics of teachers who have committed sexual offences against youth.

Sports, including baseball and hockey, keep and publish extensive records on many aspects of every game. These statistics are available to anyone who wants to examine them (e.g., mlb.com, nhl.com). Gee and Leith (2007) used archives from the National Hockey League (NHL) to test their hypothesis that players born in North America are more aggressive than players born in Europe. Despite earning, on average, the same number of points per season, North American–born players received significantly more aggressive penalties than European-born players. As European-born players gained NHL experience, they tended to receive more aggressive penalties than European-born rookies. Researchers suggested aggressive acts are learned through experience playing hockey in North America, but this is only one way to interpret the data. It is also possible that European players who do not like the aggressive style opt to leave the NHL. Like any non-experimental finding, we must be careful to avoid inferring causality.

Survey Archives

Survey archives consist of data from surveys that are made available online to researchers who wish to analyze them. Major polling organizations make many of their surveys available. Over 700 universities worldwide, including many Canadian schools, are part of the Inter-university Consortium for Political and Social Research (ICPSR), which also makes survey archive data available. Other very useful data sets intended as resources for social scientists include the World Values Survey (WVS)–which we examine in Chapters 12 and 13–and the General Social Survey (GSS). The GSS is a series of surveys funded in Canada by Statistics Canada and in the United States by the National Science Foundation. Each survey includes over 200 questions covering a range of topics such as attitudes, life satisfaction, health, religion, education, age, gender, and race. Using data from the Canadian GSS, Eagle (2011) investigated religious service attendance from 1986 to 2008. Results showed a 20 percent overall decrease in weekly and monthly attendance, which was linked to a 13 percent increase in the number of people reporting no religion, coupled with a drop in the number of self-reported Catholics attending religious services, particularly in Quebec. Eagle highlighted the need to consider many variables, including geographic region, when studying religious attendance in Canada. Survey archives are extremely important because most researchers do not have the financial resources to conduct surveys of randomly selected national samples, which, as we will see in Chapter 7, are crucial for making descriptive claims about specific populations. Archives allow researchers to access such samples to test their ideas.

Written and Mass Communication Records

Written records are documents including diaries and letters that have been preserved by historical societies; public documents, such as speeches by politicians; and ethnographies, which are detailed descriptions of other cultures written by anthropologists (for examples of the latter, see the Human Relations Area Files, available at www.yale.edu/hraf). Mass communication records include books, magazine articles, movies, television programs, newspapers, and websites. Recent technology-driven records are countless, including every status updated on social media, every photo uploaded, and every e-mail sent. Behind-the-scenes meta-data are being collected constantly by companies, including online search terms used, GPS coordinates of posts, date and time stamps for every click, as well as time spent on each application, web page, and phone call. In Chapter 3 we discussed some ethical considerations related to large-scale data sets in our emerging "big data" society. Here we focus on their use as archival records of human behaviour, which may be fuelling the emergence of a subfield in psychology called *psychoinformatics* (Markowetz, Blaszkiewicz, Montag, Switala, & Schlaepfer, 2014; Yarkoni, 2012).

Relying on existing written and mass communication archives can be a rich source of data for non-experimental research (see Chapter 4). Records can be used to predict political action; analysis of the cognitive structure embedded in politicians' speeches has helped understand and predict decisions of war and peace (see Suedfeld, 2010, for a review). Records can be used to understand mental illness; smartphone data including social interactions, physical movement (via GPS), and usage of apps track symptoms of major depressive disorder and Internet addiction (Markowetz et al., 2014). Records can be used to describe representations of gender; Gonzalez and Koestner (2005) studied the different emotions conveyed in infants' newspaper birth announcements. Records can be used to explore culturally-relevant events; *content analysis* (see the following section) of Twitter posts regarding CBC's *Hockey Day in Canada* revealed themes of Canadian culture, corporatization, and Don Cherry (a controversial commentator; Norman, 2012). Records can be used to understand personality; Yarkoni (2010) linked personality traits to word use in a sample of 694 blogs, both replicating past relationships and offering new findings suggesting ways that personality is embedded in language. In all these cases, previously existing data-based records were analyzed to learn something new about human behaviour.

Because they are used for non-experiments, archives can illuminate relationships, but causation cannot be claimed. Consider an analysis of existing Facebook groups related to breast cancer (Bender, Jimenez-Marroquin, & Jedad, 2011). Coding 620 groups revealed that most existed to promote fundraising or awareness. Of the relatively few support-oriented groups, half of them were created by young adults. These and other results can describe how social networks are being used for health information and support. However, experimental research is needed to explain or claim any effect of these groups on well-being or awareness. It is possible that fundraising groups might provide social support to people affected by breast cancer, making support-oriented groups redundant. Alternatively, face-to-face support groups may be more effective than online groups for older adults, but affected young people may have separate special needs that could be better met online. These and other questions require further research, including experiments, into social media as a venue for health information and support.

Working with Archival Data: Content Analysis and Interpretation

Content analysis is the systematic analysis of existing documents such as the ones described in this section (see Weber, 1990). It is the term used when *coding systems*, like those described in the systematic observation section earlier in this chapter, are used to quantify information in archival documents such as speeches, magazine articles, television shows, blogs, social media posts, and letters. Sometimes the coding is quite simple and straightforward; for example, it is easy to code how many people subscribe to a group on Facebook. Sometimes, the researcher must work to define categories in order to code the information. Just like when using *coding systems*, raters typically need to be trained in content analysis, especially when categories are subtle. Interrater reliability coefficients are always computed to ensure that there is high agreement among the raters.

Recently, computer programs have been developed to help with complex content analysis. For example, the computer program Linguistic Inquiry and Word Count (LIWC; Pennebaker, Booth, & Francis, 2007) helps researchers learn about psychological processes based on the words people choose to use and how they arrange them (see Tausczik & Pennebaker, 2010, for discussion, and Yarkoni, 2010, for an example). Although computer programs can help with some aspects of content analysis—particularly with big data–style massive data sets—nuanced coding and interpretation likely will continue to require human thought (Lewis, Zamith, & Hermida, 2013).

Archival data allows researchers to study interesting questions, some of which could not be studied in any other way. Some hypotheses can be generated or tested on data derived naturally. Archival data are a valuable supplement to more traditional data-collection methods, offering an enhanced ability to generalize results (i.e., *external validity*, see Chapter 14). There are at least three major problems with the use of archival data, however. First, the desired records may be difficult to obtain: They may be placed in long-forgotten storage places; they may have been destroyed; or they may exist behind password or paywall protection online. For example, Bender et al. (2011) could not analyze demographic characteristics of different types of Facebook groups because of privacy settings (see Chapter 3 for a discussion of online privacy ethics). Second, we have no control over what data were collected and the way they were recorded; we can never be completely sure of the accuracy of information collected by someone else. Third, many alternative explanations for observed relationships exist, so they cannot be used to make causal claims.

This chapter explored important observational techniques that can be used to study a variety of questions about behaviour from a quantitative or qualitative perspective. In the next chapter, we will examine a very common way of finding out about human behaviour—simply asking people to tell us about themselves.

STUDY TERMS

Test yourself! Define and generate an example of each of these key terms.

Archival research (p. 124)

Case study (p. 123)

Coding system (p. 121)

Concealed observation (p. 117)

Content analysis (p. 127)

Naturalistic observation (p. 115)

Participant observation (p. 117)

Qualitative approach (p. 114)

Quantitative approach (p. 114)

Systematic observation (p. 119)

REVIEW QUESTIONS

Test yourself on this chapter's learning objectives. Can you answer each of these questions?

1. Contrast the major differences between qualitative and quantitative approaches to research. Describe how a researcher taking either perspective might use naturalistic observation.

2. What is naturalistic observation? How does a researcher collect data when conducting naturalistic observation research?

3. Distinguish between participant and non-participant observation, and then between concealed and non-concealed observation. Compare the pros and cons for using each kind of observation.

4. What is systematic observation? What makes the data from systematic observation primarily quantitative?

5. What is a coding system? What are some important considerations when developing a coding system? How does it differ from a content analysis?

6. What is a case study? Why are case studies used?

7. What is archival research? What are the major sources of archival data?

8. Consider all observational techniques described in this chapter. What limitations do they have in common? What unique limitations or challenges does each have?

DEEPEN YOUR UNDERSTANDING

Develop your mastery of these concepts by considering these application questions. Compare your responses with those from other people in your study group.

1. Suppose you are interested in how a parent's alcoholism affects the life of an adolescent, and that you are open to considering both qualitative and quantitative approaches.

   a. Develop a research question best answered using quantitative techniques, and then another research question better suited to qualitative techniques. For example, a quantitative question could be, "Are adolescents with alcoholic parents more likely to have criminal records than adolescents with non-alcoholic parents?" whereas a qualitative question could be, "What issues do alcoholic parents introduce in their adolescent's peer relationships?"

   b. What techniques discussed in this chapter could you use to collect data that would help you answer those questions? What kind of data would you seek?

2. Devise a simple coding system to do a content analysis of a set of photographs. You could use your own uploads (e.g., Instagram or Facebook) or a publicly available collection (e.g., image search for "powerful"). Begin by examining the photographs to identify the content dimensions you wish to use. For example, if all the photographs in your set of images have people in them, you can use or adapt the list below as your coding system. Apply the system to many photographs (e.g., 20) and describe your results. What hypotheses can you develop based on your results?

Criterion	Photo 1	Photo 2	Photo . . .
Number of people depicted (e.g., 1, 2)			
Facial expression (e.g., smiling, crying, showing a furrowed brow); *repeat per person*			
Activity (e.g., reading, hiking); *repeat per person*			
Indoors or outdoors			
Occasion (if known; e.g., birthday)			
Type of props (e.g., drink, book)			
Geographic location (if known)			
Posed or candid			

3. Read each scenario below and determine whether a case study, naturalistic observation, systematic observation, or archival research was most likely used.

	Case Study	Naturalistic Observation	Systematic Observation	Archival Research
a. Researchers conducted an in-depth study of two 9/11 survivors to understand the psychological impact of the attack on the World Trade Center in 2001.				
b. Researchers recorded the time it took drivers in parking lots to back out of a parking stall. They also measured the apparent age and sex of the drivers, and whether another car was waiting for the space.				
c. Contents of mate-wanted personal ads in three major cities were coded to determine whether men and women differ in their self-descriptions.				
d. The researcher spent over a year interviewing Aileen Wuornos, the infamous serial killer who was the subject of the 2003 film *Monster*, to construct a psychobiography.				
e. Researchers examined unemployment rates and the incidence of domestic violence police calls in six cities.				
f. A group of researchers spent six months studying recycling behaviour at three local parks. They concealed their presence and kept detailed field notes.				

7

Asking People about Themselves: Survey Research

LEARNING OBJECTIVES

Keep these learning objectives in mind as you read to help you identify the most critical information in this chapter.

By the end of this chapter, you should be able to:

| 1 | Discuss reasons for conducting survey research.

| 2 | Identify features to consider when writing questions for interviews and questionnaires, including defining research objectives, question wording, and response options.

| 3 | Describe different ways to construct questionnaires, including open-ended questions and closed-ended questions that use various rating scales.

| 4 | Compare two ways to administer surveys: written questionnaires and verbal interviews.

| 5 | Explain the relationship between sample size and precision.

| 6 | Describe the ways that samples are evaluated for potential bias, including sampling frame and response rate.

| 7 | Compare and contrast three kinds of probability and three kinds of non-probability sampling techniques.

Survey research uses questionnaires and interviews to ask people to provide information about themselves–their attitudes and beliefs, demographics (age, sex, income, marital status, and so on) and other facts, as well as past or intended future behaviours. Researchers from both qualitative and quantitative approaches use surveys to collect data. Based on our discussion from Chapter 6, you may already suspect that the kinds of questions asked and what researchers do with the data will differ depending on the approach. In the first half of this chapter, we will emphasize methods of designing and conducting surveys. In the second half, we will discuss major considerations for interpreting survey results appropriately, including sampling techniques.

[LOI]

WHY CONDUCT SURVEYS?

A multitude of surveys are being conducted all the time. Just look at your daily news sources. Statistics Canada is reporting results of a survey of mental health symptoms in the Canadian Forces. A university student newspaper is reporting results of an online survey of sexual practices and preferences. Angus Reid Public Opinion is reporting results of eligible voter polls. Surveys are clearly a common and important method of studying behaviour.

Surveys provide us with a methodology for asking people to tell us about themselves. They have become extremely important as society demands data about issues rather than only intuition and anecdotes. University departments need data from graduates to help determine changes that should be made to the curriculum. Software companies want feedback from buyers to assess and improve product quality and customer satisfaction. Depending on how the data are collected, surveys may be much more useful sources of information than stories we might hear or letters that a graduate or customer might write. Other surveys can be important for lawmakers and public agencies when making policy decisions. For example, the McCreary Centre Society in British Columbia (www.mcs.bc.ca) surveys young people across the province about health issues. Data are used by the government and schools to create effective policies and programs. In basic research, many important variables, including attitudes, current emotional states, and self-reports of behaviours, are easily studied using questionnaires or interviews.

Surveys can be used in many ways. Often they are used to provide a "snapshot" of how a particular group of people think and behave at a given point in time. Surveys can also be used to gather data for studying relationships among variables, as well as ways that attitudes and behaviours change over time or among different groups of people. For example, Dumont, Leclerc, and McKinnon (2009) examined the relationship between academic average and the number of hours that high school students work outside of school. The sample consisted of 187 students in Grade 9 and another 144 students in Grade 11 at a high school in Quebec. Consistent with previous American

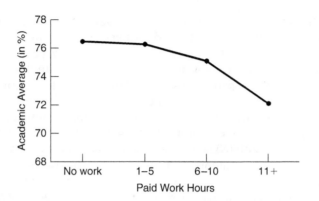

FIGURE 7.I
Relationship
between
hours of work
and academic
average

Source: Adapted from Dumont, M., Leclerc, D., & McKinnon, S. (2009). Consequences of part-time work on the academic and psychosocial adaptation of adolescents. *Canadian Journal of School Psychology, 24*(1), Figure 1, p. 67. © 2009 Sage Publications.

research (Steinberg & Dornbusch, 1991), the more students worked outside of school, the lower their academic average was (see Figure 7.1). However, unlike earlier research, Dumont et al. found this pattern only among Grade 9 students; among Grade 11 students, average grades were unrelated to the amount they worked. In addition, students who decreased the amount they worked from Grade 9 to Grade 11 experienced an increase in their academic average over the same period. These survey results are non-experimental. We cannot claim that grades suffer because of non-school work (see Chapter 4), yet we learn that variables can relate differently for different groups of people. This study highlights a major benefit to survey methods: Asking students about their work provides an efficient way to gather data. It would be impossible to visit each student's place of work and measure their work hours directly.

The National Survey of Student Engagement (NSSE; http://nsse.iub.edu) offers an example of a very large survey. Every year since 2000, thousands of students from hundreds of universities across Canada and the U.S. have rated their schools. Because the questions are the same each year, it is possible to track a university's changes over time on such variables as level of academic challenge, active and collaborative learning, student-faculty interaction, supportive campus environment, and enriching educational experiences. Universities whose students participate in the NSSE are given quantitative and qualitative data that can help guide administrative decisions about how to improve undergraduate education. *Closed-ended* data analysis (see below) includes tracking their own institution's scores over time, as well as comparisons with similar institutions. *Open-ended* responses to the "additional comments" respondents provide can be content analyzed (see Chapter 6) for additional insight into what undergraduates feel can enrich their education (Chambers, 2006).

When the same people are tracked and surveyed at two or more points in time, the design is sometimes called a **panel study** or is simply called a *longitudinal design* (see Chapter 11). In a "two-wave" panel study, people are surveyed at two points in time; in a "three-wave" panel study, there are three surveys; and so on. Panel studies are particularly important when the research question addresses the relationship between one variable at "time one" and another variable at some later "time two." For example, Arim, Dahinten, Marshall, and Shapka (2011) used survey data from the Canadian National Longitudinal Survey of Children and Youth (NLSCY) to examine children's aggressive behaviours. The NLSCY surveys new parents–and the children themselves when they are old enough–every two years on a variety of variables relating to family life, health, and development. Arim et al. showed that children who reported feeling more nurtured and loved by their parents right before puberty (10 years old for girls, 12 years old for boys) engaged in less direct aggression (e.g., fist fights) and less indirect aggression (e.g., spreading rumours) two years later.

Survey research is also important as a complement to experimental research findings. In a set of studies, Wood, Perunovic, and Lee (2009) investigated the phenomenon of repeating positive affirmations to oneself (e.g., "I'm a lovable person," "I will win!"), like those that are often recommended in self-help pop psychology. These researchers first used a survey of undergraduates to confirm that people actually do repeat these kinds of affirmations and believe that they are effective. Only 3 percent of participants reported they had never used affirmations; over half said they used them daily. Once it was established that affirmations were common, they conducted experiments to understand their effects. Whether these affirmations actually made people feel good depended on their self-esteem. People who had low self-esteem and were randomly assigned to repeat positive affirmations actually felt *worse* about themselves than those who were randomly assigned to the control (i.e., no self-statement) condition. People with high self-esteem felt a little bit better about themselves after repeating the affirmation than those in the control condition. This set of studies illustrates a point emphasized throughout this book: Multiple methods are needed to understand any behaviour. Surveys were a useful starting point to explore this phenomenon.

Response Bias in Survey Research

An assumption that underlies the use of questionnaires and interviews is that people are willing and able to provide truthful and accurate answers; this assumption is the source of much debate over the value of survey research. Researchers have addressed this issue by studying possible biases in the way people respond. A **response set** is a tendency to respond to all questions from a particular perspective rather than to provide answers that are directly related to the questions. Thus, response sets can reduce the usefulness of data obtained from self-reports. For example, people from different cultural backgrounds can differ in how they use response scales (e.g., tend to use the middle versus the extremes; see Hamamura, Heine, & Paulhus, 2008).

One of the most common response sets is called social desirability, or "faking good." The *social desirability response set* leads the individual to answer in the most socially acceptable way–the way that the person thinks "most people" would respond, or the way that would present themselves most favourably. Social desirability can be a problem in many research areas, but it is probably most acute when the question concerns a sensitive topic such as violent behaviour, substance abuse, or sexual practices. To deal with this problem, one option is to try to detect instances of dishonesty. Some scales are available to measure the extent to which people are trying to present themselves in a favourable way. As a clever alternative, Paulhus, Harms, Bruce, and Lysy (2003) operationally defined social desirable response bias as the extent to which people claim familiarity with fake "facts" (e.g., that "plates of parallax" is a real term) that are hidden in longer lists of true facts (e.g., that "nuclear fusion" is a real term) across a variety of domains (these examples are from physics; history is one of the other domains). Researchers can use their method to detect which participants may be showing a social desirability response set.

To increase accuracy in survey reports of sensitive topics, researchers can ensure privacy while completing the survey, assure confidentiality and anonymity, and employ other methods to increase motivation to respond accurately (see Tourangeau & Yan, 2007). Advanced statistical methods can be used to create tangible incentives for responding accurately (Prelec, 2004). John, Loewenstein, and Prelec (2012) effectively used an incentive method to encourage researchers to admit to ethically questionable research practices (e.g., conducting many studies but reporting only those with significant results). Higher accuracy meant greater donations to charity.

We turn now to the major considerations in survey research: constructing the questions that are asked, choosing how to present the questions, and deciding how to sample people to survey. While it is preferable to try to find surveys that have been used and *validated* by other researchers (see Chapter 5), sometimes it is necessary to construct them for a particular purpose. Knowing these major considerations will help you to critique the surveys you encounter as well as to design your own, should you need to do so.

CONSTRUCTING QUESTIONS TO ASK

LO2

A great deal of thought must be given to writing questions for questionnaires and interviews. This section describes some of the most important features to consider when constructing questions.

Defining the Research Objectives

When constructing questions for a survey, the first thing the researcher must do is explicitly determine the research objectives: What is it that he or she wishes to know? The survey questions must be tied to the research questions that are being addressed. Surveys get out of hand when researchers begin to ask any question that comes to mind about a topic without considering exactly what useful information will be gained by doing so. It is potentially unethical to ask questions if you have no real reason to use the information. Thus, researchers must carefully decide on the questions to ask. There are three general types of survey questions (Judd, Smith, & Kidder, 1991).

Attitudes and Beliefs   Questions about attitudes and beliefs focus on the ways people evaluate and feel and think about issues. Should more money be spent on mental health services? Are you satisfied with the way that police responded to your call? How do you evaluate this instructor?

Facts and Demographics   Factual questions ask people to indicate things they know about themselves and their situation. In most studies, asking some demographic information (e.g., age, gender identification) is necessary to adequately describe your sample. Depending on the topic of the study, questions about ethnicity, income, marital status, employment status, and number of siblings might be included. Obviously, if you are interested in making comparisons across groups, such as males and females, you must ask the relevant information about group membership.

Other factual information you might ask will depend on the topic of your survey. Each year, *Consumer Reports* magazine asks readers to report any repairs that have been necessary on many products, such as their cars and electronic devices. Factual questions about illnesses and other medical information would be asked in a survey of health and quality of life.

Behaviours   Other survey questions can focus on past behaviours or intended future behaviours. How many times last week did you exercise for 20 minutes or longer? Have you ever been so depressed that you called in sick to work? How many courses do you plan to take next year?

Question Wording

Care is necessary to write the very best questions for a survey. Cognitive psychologists have identified many potential problems with question wording (see Graesser, Kennedy, Wiemer-Hastings, & Ottati, 1999). Many problems stem from difficulties understanding the question, including (a) unfamiliar technical terms, (b) vague or imprecise terms, (c) ungrammatical sentence structure, (d) phrasing that overloads working memory, and (e) embedding the question with misleading information. Here is a question that illustrates some of the problems identified by Graesser et al.:

> Did your mother, father, full-blooded sisters, full-blooded brothers, daughters, or sons ever have a heart attack or myocardial infarction?

There is memory overload because of the length of the question and the need to keep track of all those relatives while reading the question, and the respondent must consider two different diagnoses with regard to each relative.

Further, the term *myocardial infarction* may be unfamiliar to many people. How do you write questions to avoid such problems? The following considerations are important to keep in mind. Later, test your understanding by reviewing the examples in Table 7.1.

Unnecessary Complexity   The questions asked in a survey should be relatively simple. People should be able to understand and respond to the questions easily. Avoid jargon and technical terms that people won't understand. Sometimes, however, you have to make the question a bit more complex to make it easier to understand. Usually this occurs when you need to define a term or describe an issue prior to asking the question. Thus, before asking whether someone approves of Bill S-4, you will probably want to provide a brief description of the legislation's contents.

Double-Barrelled Questions   Avoid "double-barrelled" questions that ask two things at once. A question such as "Should senior citizens be given more money for recreation and food assistance programs?" is difficult to answer because it taps two potentially very different attitudes. If you are interested in both issues, ask two questions.

TABLE 7.1   Question wording: What is the problem?

Test yourself! Read each of the following questions and identify which question wording problem(s) applies to each.

	Negative Wording	Unnecessary Complexity	Double-Barrelled	Loaded
a. To what extent do you agree that professors should not be required to take daily attendance?				
b. I enjoy studying and spending time with friends on weekends.				
c. Do you support the legislation that would unfairly tax hard-working farmers?				
d. I would describe myself as attractive and intelligent.				
e. Do you believe the relationship between cellphone behaviour and consumption of fast food is orthogonal?				
f. Restaurants should not have to be inspected each month.				
g. Are you in favour of the boss's whim to cut lunchtime to 30 minutes?				

Loaded Questions   A loaded question is written to lead people to respond in one way. For example, the questions "Do you favour eliminating the wasteful excesses in the public school budget?" and "Do you favour reducing the public school budget?" will likely elicit different answers. Questions that include emotionally charged words such as *rape, waste, immoral,* or *dangerous* may influence the way that people respond and thus lead to biased conclusions. Men are less likely to say they have "raped" someone than that they have "forced sex"; similarly, women are less likely to say they have been raped than forced to have unwanted sex (Koss, 1992).

Negative Wording   Avoid phrasing questions with negatives. This question is phrased negatively: "Do you believe that the city should not approve the proposed women's shelter?" Agreement with this question means disagreement with the proposal. Researchers caution against the use of such negatively worded items, as the confusion and errors they create have been shown to reduce scale *reliability* and *validity* (e.g., Woods, 2006; see Chapter 5). A better format would be: "Do you believe that the city should approve the proposed women's shelter?"

"Yea-Saying" and "Nay-Saying"   When you ask several questions about a topic, a respondent may either agree (yea) or disagree (nay) with all the questions. This tendency is called a **"yea-saying" or "nay-saying" response set.** The respondent may in fact be expressing true agreement, but an alternative explanation is that the person may simply be (dis)agreeing with anything you ask. One possible way to detect this response set is to word the questions so that consistent agreement is unlikely. For example, a measure of loneliness (e.g., Russell, Peplau, & Cutrona, 1980) phrases some questions so that agreement means the respondent is lonely (e.g., "I feel isolated from others") and others with the meaning reversed so that disagreement indicates loneliness (e.g., "I feel part of a group of friends"). It is possible that someone could legitimately (dis)agree with all related questions regardless of whether they are phrased in a standard way or reversed. However, such consistent (dis)agreement may indicate "yea-saying" or "nay-saying." Although the logic is sound, recent research on questionnaire design has demonstrated that including a few reversed items actually decreases scale *reliability* (Roszkowski & Soven, 2010).

| LO3 |

RESPONSES TO QUESTIONS: WHAT KIND OF DATA ARE YOU SEEKING?

Closed- versus Open-Ended Questions

Response options may be either closed- or open-ended. With **closed-ended questions,** a limited number of response alternatives are given; with **open-ended questions,** respondents are free to answer in any way they like. Thus you could ask, "What is the most important thing children should learn to prepare them for life?" followed by a list of answers from which to choose (a closed-ended question), or you could leave this question open-ended for respondents to provide any answer.

Closed-ended questions are easier to code and the response alternatives are the same for everyone. Open-ended questions require time to code the responses using content analysis or other qualitative methods (see Chapter 6) and are therefore more costly. Sometimes a respondent's response cannot be categorized at all because the response doesn't make sense or the person couldn't think of an answer. Still, an open-ended question can yield valuable insights into what people are thinking. Open-ended questions are most useful when the researcher needs to know what people are thinking and how they naturally view their world; closed-ended questions are more likely to be used when the dimensions of the variables are well-defined. As you may have suspected, closed-ended questions tend to be favoured from a quantitative approach, whereas open-ended questions tend to be used by both, yet favoured from a qualitative approach.

Closed- versus open-ended questions can sometimes lead to different conclusions. Schwarz (1999) cites the results of a survey question about preparing children for life. When "To think for themselves" was one alternative in a closed-ended list, 62 percent chose this option; however, only 5 percent gave this answer when the open-ended format was used. Using the closed-ended format may give the researcher the impression that most people thoughtfully consider preparing children to think for themselves, when open-ended responses suggest this is not the case. This finding highlights the need to have a good understanding of people's natural responses to the topic when asking closed-ended questions.

Rating Scales for Closed-Ended Questions

With closed-ended questions, there are a fixed number of response alternatives. **Rating scales** ask people to provide "how much" judgments on any number of dimensions—amount of agreement, liking, or confidence, for example. Rating scales can have many different formats and use various measurement scales (e.g., ordinal; see Chapter 5). The format that is used depends on factors such as the topic being investigated. Perhaps the best way to gain an understanding of the variety of formats is simply to look at a few examples. The simplest and most direct scale presents people with five or seven response alternatives with labels defining just the endpoints or all points. Consider the following examples:

Students at the university should be required to pass a comprehensive examination to graduate.

1	2	3	4	5	6	7
Strongly Disagree	Disagree	Slightly Disagree	Neither Agree nor Disagree	Slightly Agree	Agree	Strongly Agree

How confident are you that the defendant is guilty of attempted murder?

0	1	2	3	4
Not at All Confident				Very Confident

Labelling Response Alternatives   The second example above labelled only the endpoints on the rating scale. Respondents decide the meaning of the other response alternatives. Although people are usually able to use such scales without difficulty, research shows that fully labelled scales, as in the first option above, are more *reliable* than are partially labelled scales (Krosnick, 1999). Labels help to more clearly define the meaning of each alternative and reduce *measurement error* from relying on each person's idiosyncratic interpretations (see Chapter 5). The first example above represents a fairly standard way of labelling response alternatives for an agreement measure (Likert, 1932).

Number of Response Alternatives   In public opinion surveys, a simple "yes or no" or "agree or disagree" dichotomy can be sufficient. In more basic research, it is often preferable to have more alternatives to allow people greater opportunity to express themselves. Researchers often choose 5- or 7-point scales, allowing a middle "neutral" option, as in the first example above. This type of scale assumes that the middle alternative is a "neutral" point halfway between the endpoints, but sometimes respondents use it when they don't know how to respond, which can cause problems for reliability and validity. Therefore, it is sometimes recommended to offer an "I don't know" or "Not applicable" option to participants. Another issue is whether to have an odd or even number of alternatives. It is possible to force participants to choose one side or the other by dropping the "Neither agree nor disagree" option and keeping a 6-point rather than a 7-point scale, although this decision can substantially impact the way participants respond to a questionnaire (Nowlis, Kahn, & Dhar, 2002).

Sometimes a perfectly balanced scale may not be possible or desirable. Consider a commonly used scale asking a professor to rate a student for a job or graduate program. This particular scale asks for comparative ratings of students:

In comparison with other graduates, how would you rate this student's potential for success?

Lower 50%	Upper 50%	Upper 25%	Upper 10%	Upper 5%

Notice that most of the alternatives are asking people to make a rating in terms of the top 25 percent of students. This is done because students who apply for such programs tend to be very bright and motivated, and so professors rate them favourably. The wording of the alternatives attempts to force the respondents to make finer distinctions among generally very good students.

Labelling alternatives is particularly interesting when asking about behaviour frequencies. For example, you might ask, "How often do you exercise for at least 20 minutes?" What kind of scale should you use to collect responses? You could list (1) never, (2) rarely, (3) sometimes, and (4) frequently. These terms convey your meaning but they are vague. Here is a more precise set of alternatives, similar to ones described by Schwarz (1999):

_____ Less than twice a week

_____ About twice a week

_____ About four times a week

_____ About six times a week

_____ At least once each day

A different scale might be as follows:

_____ Less than once per month

_____ About once a month

_____ About once every two weeks

_____ About once a week

_____ More than once per week

Schwarz (1999) calls the first scale a *high-frequency scale* because most alternatives indicate a high frequency of exercise. The other scale is referred to as *low frequency*. Schwarz points out that the labels should be chosen carefully because people may interpret the meaning of the scale differently, depending on the labels used. If you were actually asking the exercise question, you might decide on alternatives different from the ones described here. Moreover, your choice should be influenced by factors such as the population you are studying. If you are studying people who generally exercise a lot, you will be more likely to use a high-frequency scale than you would if you were studying people who generally don't exercise much.

Graphic Rating Scale   A **graphic rating scale** requires a mark along a continuous 100 mm line that is anchored with descriptions at each end.

How would you rate the movie you just saw?

Not very enjoyable _____ Very enjoyable

The researcher uses a ruler to measure the score on a scale that ranges from 0 to 100.

Semantic Differential Scale   The **semantic differential scale** is a way to measure the meaning that people ascribe to concepts (Osgood, Suci, & Tannenbaum, 1957). Respondents rate any concept–people, objects, behaviours, ideas–on a series of bipolar adjectives using 7-point scales. In the example below, a respondent who felt that smoking cigarettes was totally bad and not at all good would place a check mark on the line closest to "bad." If she felt that smoking cigarettes had some redeeming qualities, she would place a check mark on a line closer to "good." Using multiple adjective pairs can help measure different aspects of attitudes toward smoking. Respondents struggling to quit smoking might rate smoking as bad, strong, and passive, whereas those content to smoke might rate smoking differently.

Smoking cigarettes

Good	___	___	___	___	___	___	___	Bad
Strong	___	___	___	___	___	___	___	Weak
Active	___	___	___	___	___	___	___	Passive

Research on the semantic differential shows that virtually anything can be measured using this technique. Ratings of specific things (marijuana), places (the student centre), people (the prime minister), ideas (abortion), and behaviours (using public transit) can be obtained. Research shows that concepts rated using semantic differential scales are rated along three basic dimensions: The first and most important is *evaluation* (e.g., adjectives such as good-bad, wise-foolish, kind-cruel); the second is *activity* (active-passive, slow-fast, excitable-calm); and the third is *potency* (weak-strong, hard-soft, large-small).

Non-verbal Scale   In some circumstances, a researcher might want to offer images instead of words or numbers. For example, young children may not understand the types of scales we've just described, but they are able to give ratings. For example, you could ask children to "Point to the face that shows how you feel about the toy."

FINALIZING THE QUESTIONNAIRE

Formatting the Questionnaire

The final questionnaire, whether distributed on paper or online, should appear attractive and professional. It should be typed in a clear font and free of spelling errors. Respondents should find it easy to identify questions and corresponding response alternatives. Leave enough space between questions so that people don't become confused when reading the questionnaire. If you have a particular scale format, such as a 5-point rating scale, use it consistently. Don't change from 5- to 4- to 7-point scales, for example, because statistical analyses will become much more difficult and potentially meaningless.

Carefully consider the order of your questions. In general, it is best to ask the most interesting and important questions first to capture the attention of your respondents and motivate them to complete the survey. Roberson and Sundstrom (1990) obtained the highest return rates in an employee attitude survey when important questions were presented first and demographic questions were asked last.

In a literature review, Vicente and Reis (2010) identified many specific formatting recommendations to improve response rates in online surveys. For example, split up questions so that a few appear on many pages, rather than have one long page to scroll down. A progress indicator bar at the top of the screen can help ensure completion, as long as participants perceive they are moving through the survey at a fast-enough rate. Use radio buttons rather than drop-down menus for response options to closed-ended scales. Lastly, because shorter questionnaires produce higher response rates than longer ones, carefully consider the necessity of every question. If you are conducting an online survey, you may want to use survey data collectors such as SurveyMonkey (surveymonkey.com) or its Canadian subsidiary FluidSurveys (fluidsurveys.com), which has domestic servers (important for legal aspects of data privacy).

Refining Questions

Before actually administering the survey, it is a good idea to give the questions to a few people and have them "think aloud" while answering them. These participants might be chosen from the population being studied, or they could be friends or colleagues who can give reasonable responses to the questions. Ask them to tell you how they interpret each question and how they respond to the response alternatives. This procedure can provide valuable information you can use to improve the questions. (The importance of pilot studies such as this is discussed further in Chapter 9.)

ADMINISTERING SURVEYS   LO4

There are two ways to administer surveys. In questionnaire format, respondents read the questions and indicate their responses on a paper or online form. In interview format, an interviewer asks the questions and records responses in a verbal interaction. In this section, we will explore unique issues raised by each method.

Keep in mind that there are additional administrative challenges when either survey format is used to repeatedly measure the same participants. In Chapter 3, we discussed options for maintaining confidential records in such designs. Additionally, societal or institutional changes might interfere with responses over time (e.g., a university might make a major policy change or experience drastic funding cuts one year, affecting interpretation of NSSE scores). Another major concern is that participants drop out of the study over time. A sample that starts out *random* (see below) can become biased over time because of non-random differences in the people who remain versus those who leave the study. These issues are common to all studies that use a repeated measures or *longitudinal* component; therefore, you will see related discussions in Chapters 8 and 11.

Questionnaires

Questionnaires present respondents with questions in written format, and respondents write or type their answers. Questionnaires can be administered in person to groups or individuals, through the mail, on the Internet, and with other technologies. A major benefit to using questionnaires is cost: They are generally inexpensive. They also allow the respondent to be completely anonymous as long as no identifying information (e.g., name, Social Insurance number, driver's licence number) is asked, and Internet protocol (IP) addresses are not recorded in online surveys. However, questionnaires require that respondents are motivated and attentive enough to complete them. Some respondents may have difficulty reading and understanding the questions. In these cases, it may be important to administer the survey in person so that the researcher is there for assistance.

Personal Administration to Groups or Individuals   Often researchers are able to distribute questionnaires to groups of individuals. This might be a university class, parents attending a school meeting, people attending a new employee orientation, or people waiting in line. An advantage of this approach is that you have a captive audience that is likely to complete the questionnaire once they start it. Also, the researcher is present, so people can ask questions if necessary.

Mail Surveys   Surveys can be mailed to individuals at a home or business address. One major drawback to the mail format is low response rates. The questionnaire can easily be placed aside and forgotten among all the other tasks that people must attend to at home and work. Even if people start to fill out the questionnaire, something may happen to distract them, they may have difficulty with a question, or they may become bored and simply throw the form in the recycling bin. Some methods for increasing response rates are described later in this chapter.

Internet Surveys   Administering questionnaires online is very easy and inexpensive. Responses are immediately downloadable for analysis (rather than requiring manual data entry). Researchers and major polling organizations sometimes build databases of people interested in participating in surveys who they can e-mail with an invitation to participate and, if appropriate, to forward the link to other potential participants. Also, online surveys can be advertised using social networking sites. One advantage to using the Internet is that it is possible to target advertisements and posts to obtain very large samples of people with particular characteristics, such as an illness, marital status, or occupational group. For example, one study was able to reach a sample of over 650 people, all of whom have a family member or friend who suffers from hoarding behaviour, to find out how that illness burdens them (Tolin, Frost, Steketee, & Fitch, 2008).

Internet surveys can be combined with other technologies to gather data. Hanson and Chen (2010) asked a sample of University of British Columbia students to complete an online survey about their day's stressors at the end of each day for a week. Participants then wore an *Actiwatch* to bed, which measured their sleep quality each night. Researchers learned that experiencing many hassles during the day predicted interrupted sleep quality among university students who had difficult childhoods, but the sleep of those who had experienced easier childhoods was not predicted by daily hassles. Although asking participants to complete a daily paper-and-pencil measure was an option, using a website enabled researchers to confirm exactly when their participants completed the survey. Technology played a vital role in this research.

One concern about Internet data collection is whether the results will be similar to what might be found using traditional methods. Researchers are increasingly finding that Internet results are comparable to paper-and-pencil measures (e.g., Howell, Rodzon, Kurai, & Sanchez, 2010, on measures of happiness; see also Gosling, Vazire, Srivastava, & John, 2004). A problem that remains with Internet data is that the true characteristics of the people providing information for the study are ambiguous. To meet ethical guidelines, the researcher will usually state that only people 18 years of age or older are eligible, but that cannot be controlled. People may also misrepresent their sex or ethnicity. We simply do not know if this is a major problem. For most research topics, it seems unlikely that people will go to the trouble of misrepresenting themselves on the Internet to a greater extent than they would with any other method of collecting data. For further consideration of ethical issues with Internet research, see Kraut et al. (2004).

Other Technologies Researchers are continually exploring new technologies to assist with the collection of survey data. For example, consider studies seeking to sample people's behaviours or emotions over an extended period of time. Instead of asking people to remember how they felt or acted over the past week, researchers using computerized experience sampling contact participants at various times through the day on their cellphone or other mobile device and ask them to provide an immediate report of their current activities and emotional experiences (e.g., Feldman-Barrett & Barrett, 2001). Researchers have found that people report feeling more risk (e.g., of physical harm) in their daily lives when they are asked to report it via text message throughout their day than when they rely on their memories to report feelings of risk on a paper-and-pencil measure (Hogarth, Portell, & Cuxart, 2007).

Interviews

The fact that an interview involves an interaction between people has important implications. First, people are often more likely to agree to answer questions for a real person than to answer a mailed questionnaire. Thus, response rates tend to be higher when interviews rather than questionnaires are used. The interviewer and respondent can establish a rapport that helps motivate the person to answer all questions, rather than leave questions unanswered. An important advantage of an interview is that the interviewer can address any problems the person might have in understanding questions. Further, an interviewer can ask follow-up questions if needed to help clarify answers.

One potential problem in interviews is called **interviewer bias.** This term summarizes all of the biases that can arise from the fact that the interviewer is a person interacting with another person. Thus, one potential problem is that the interviewer could subtly influence the respondent's answers by inadvertently showing approval or disapproval of certain answers. Personal characteristics of the interviewers (e.g., level of physical attractiveness, age, or race) might influence respondent's answers. Another problem is that interviewers may have expectations that could lead them to "see what they are looking for" in the respondent's answers. Such expectations could bias their interpretations of responses or lead them to probe further for an answer from some respondents but not from others—for example, when questioning people of Asian heritage but not people from other groups, or when testing girls but not boys (see also *experimenter expectancy effects* in Chapter 9). Careful screening and training of interviewers help to limit such biases.

There are three methods of conducting interviews: face-to-face and telephone interviews, which are used for both qualitative and quantitative research, and focus groups, which are mainly used for qualitative research.

Face-to-Face Interviews   Face-to-face interviews require that the interviewer and respondent meet to conduct the interview. The interviewer may travel to the respondent's home or office, or the respondent may go to the interviewer's office. Such interviews tend to be quite expensive and time-consuming. Therefore, they are most likely to be used when the sample size is fairly small and there are clear benefits to a face-to-face interaction.

Telephone Interviews   Interviews for large-scale surveys are commonly completed using telephone or equivalent online programs (e.g., Skype). Telephone interviews are less expensive than face-to-face interviews, and they allow data to be collected relatively quickly because many interviewers can work on the same survey at once. With a computer-assisted telephone interview system, the interviewer's questions are prompted on the computer screen, and the interviewer enters the data directly into the computer database, ready for analysis.

Focus Group Interviews   A **focus group** is an interview with a group of about six to ten people brought together for a period of usually two to three hours. Often the group members are selected because they have particular knowledge or interest in the topic. Because the focus group requires people to spend time and money travelling to the focus group location, there is usually some sort of monetary or gift incentive to participate.

The questions tend to be open-ended and they are asked of the whole group. Group interaction is considered an advantage in this method: People can respond to one another, and one comment can trigger a variety of responses. The interviewer must be skilled in working with groups to facilitate communication and to deal with problems that may arise, such as one or two people trying to dominate the discussion or hostility between group members. The group discussion is usually recorded and may be transcribed. The recordings and transcripts are then analyzed to find themes and areas of group consensus and disagreement (i.e., a more qualitative approach; see Chapter 6). Sometimes the transcripts are content analyzed to search for certain words and phrases (i.e., a more quantitative approach). Researchers usually prefer to conduct at least two or three focus groups on a given topic to make sure that the information gathered is not unique to one group of people. However, because each focus group is time-consuming and costly, and provides a great deal of information, researchers typically don't conduct many groups on any one topic.

INTERPRETING SURVEY RESULTS: CONSIDER THE SAMPLE

Of the methods discussed in this book, surveys are used most frequently to gather responses from very large groups of people and to make claims about the characteristics of specific groups of people. These two features highlight some particular issues in interpretation centred around sample size and sampling techniques. Although some of those issues will be explored more generally elsewhere (e.g., Chapter 13), let's briefly examine them in the special context of surveys.

Population and Samples

A **population** is a set of people of interest to the researcher. One population of interest for a large public opinion poll, for instance, might be all eligible voters in Canada. This implies that the population of interest does not include people under the age of 18, convicted prisoners, visitors from other countries, and anyone else not eligible to vote. You might conduct a survey in which your population consists of all students at your university, or all people who have immigrated to Canada from India. With enough time and money, a survey researcher could conceivably contact everyone in the national population. Canada attempts to do this every five years with an official census of the entire population.

With a relatively small population of interest, you might find it easy to study everyone. In most cases, however, studying the entire population of interest would be a massive undertaking. Because of financial and time constraints, researchers typically collect data on a sample to learn something about a larger population. With proper **sampling,** we can use information obtained from the respondents who were sampled to estimate characteristics of the population as a whole. Statistical theory allows us to infer what the population is like, based on data obtained from a sample (we will explore this idea further in Chapter 13).

Confidence Intervals   When researchers make inferences about populations using samples, they do so with a certain degree of confidence. Suppose you read about a survey that asked students to indicate whether they preferred to study at home or at school, and 61 percent of respondents preferred to study at home. You might see the following accompanying statement: "Results from the survey are accurate within 3 percentage points, 19 times out of 20." *What does this tell you?* The actual percentage of people in the student population who prefer to study at home probably falls between 58 and 64 percent. This is called a **confidence interval,** which is a range of plausible values for the population value; values outside the confidence interval are implausible (Cumming & Finch, 2005).

The best estimate of the population value is the sample value (which is 61 percent in the example above). The confidence interval helps us account for the error that exists in the estimate because only a sample and not the entire population was measured. The formal term for this error is **sampling error,** although you may have seen the term *margin of error* instead. Recall that the concept of measurement error was discussed in Chapter 5: When you measure a single individual on a variable, the obtained score deviates from the true score whenever there is a measurement error. Similarly, when you study one sample, the obtained result deviates from the true population value whenever there is a sampling error. The confidence interval gives you information about the likely amount of the error: For every 20 confidence intervals calculated in this way, 19 will include the true population value, but one will not (Cumming & Finch, 2005). The topic of confidence intervals is revisited more broadly in Chapter 13. For now, remember that narrower confidence intervals indicate more precise estimates with less sampling error.

LO5

For More Precise Estimates, Use a Larger Sample

Larger sample sizes reduce measurement error, and therefore reduce the size of the confidence interval. Although the size of the interval is determined by several factors, sample size is key. In general, larger samples are more likely to yield data that accurately reflect the true population value. This statement should make intuitive sense to you; a sample of 200 people from your school should yield more accurate data about your school than a sample of 25 people (although such accuracy also crucially depends on how you selected those 200 people; more on that later).

How large should the sample be? The sample size can be determined using a mathematical formula that takes into account the size of the confidence interval and the size of the population you are studying (Cumming & Finch, 2005). Table 7.2 helps us predict how large a sample we need to draw from particular population sizes, for different degrees of accuracy: within plus or minus 3 percent, 5 percent, and 10 percent, given a 95 percent level of confidence. Look across the rows to notice that greater accuracy (±3 percent) requires larger sample sizes than worse accuracy (±5 percent and ±10 percent). With a population size of 10,000, you need a sample of 370 for accuracy within ±5 percent, but to increase accuracy to ±3 percent, the required sample size increases to 964. Look down the columns in Table 7.2 to notice that sample size is *not* a constant percentage of the population size. Many people believe that proper sampling requires a certain percentage of the population; these people often complain about survey results when they discover that a survey of an entire province was done with "only" 700 or 1,000 people. However, you can see in the table that the needed sample size does not change much even as the population size increases from 5,000 to 100,000 or more. As Fowler (1984) notes, "A sample of 150 people will describe a population of 1,500 or 15 million with virtually the same degree of accuracy . . ." (p. 41), as long as the technique used to sample participants is appropriate (see below).

TABLE 7.2 Sample size needed for population estimates at three levels of precision (95% confidence level)

Size of Population	Precision of Estimate		
	±3%	±5%	±10%
2,000	696	322	92
5,000	879	357	94
10,000	964	370	95
50,000	1,045	381	96
100,000	1,056	383	96
Over 100,000	1,067	384	96

Note: The sample sizes were calculated using conservative assumptions about the nature of the true population values.

To Describe a Specific Population, Sample Thoroughly

Some research questions aim to describe the characteristics of a specific population. When such description is the primary research goal (see Chapter 1), it is crucial that findings based on a sample can be generalized to the broader population; in other words, the research must have high **external validity.** In the survey context, achieving external validity means ensuring that the sample is highly representative of the population from which it is drawn. To create such a completely *unbiased* sample, first you would randomly sample from a population that contains *all* people in the population of interest. Second, you would contact and obtain completed responses from *all* people selected to be in the sample. Such standards are rarely achieved. Various non-random sampling methods (described later in this chapter) introduce different biases into the sample, but are used out of necessity when random sampling is impossible.

Regardless of the sampling method used, the sampling frame used and poor response rates introduce bias. Let us consider these major sources of bias before considering a variety of sampling techniques in more detail.

Sampling Frame   The **sampling frame** is the *actual* population of people (or clusters) from which a random sample will be drawn. Rarely will this perfectly coincide with the population of interest—some biases will be introduced. How severe these biases are will impact how *externally valid* the survey results are. If you define your population as "residents of Saskatoon," the sampling frame may be a list of home telephone numbers that you will use to contact residents between 5 p.m. and 9 p.m. This sampling frame excludes people whose schedule prevents them from being at home when you are making calls. Also, if you are using the telephone directory to obtain numbers, you will exclude people who have unlisted numbers, who exclusively use a cellphone and do not have a home phone number, or who do not have a telephone at all. Consider another example: Suppose you want to know what lawyers think about the portrayal of the legal profession on television. A reasonable sampling frame would be all lawyers listed on Canada411.ca. You might limit your sample to lawyers in a particular geographical area or to lawyers who work in established firms—lawyers who work in other locations or as consultants have been excluded. When evaluating survey results, consider how well the sampling frame matches the population of interest. Often the biases introduced are quite minor; however, they could be consequential.

In a rare case, all major election polling companies were shocked when they wrongly predicted the results of the 2013 British Columbia provincial election. Instead of celebrating the predicted sizable majority government, NDP leader Adrian Dix lost to Liberal leader (and incumbent Premier) Christy Clark. Months of post-election analysis revealed that *sampling frame* was one of the key flaws. The sampling frame was defined as "eligible voters in British Columbia," rather than "people who will vote in this election" (Reid, 2013). Voters aged 18 to 35 tend to support the NDP but do not tend to vote. Because this age group represents a larger proportion of eligible voters compared to actual voters, they were overrepresented in the sample used to make predictions. Consequently, those predictions were useless.

Response Rate   The **response rate** in a survey is the percentage of people in the sample who actually completed the survey. Thus, if you mail 1,000 questionnaires to a random sample of adults in your community and 500 are completed and returned to you, the response rate is 50 percent. Response rate is one indicator of how much bias there might be in the final sample of respondents. Non-respondents may differ from respondents in any number of ways, including age, income, marital status, and education. The lower the response rate, the greater the likelihood that such biases may distort the findings and in turn limit the ability to generalize the findings to the population of interest. In other words, the study will have low *external validity*.

The response rate bias was introduced in 2010 when the Canadian government cancelled the mandatory long-form version of the census that was sent to a random sample of citizens. Instead, the new National Household Survey (NHS) is optional. Data from 2011 showed lower response rates with the NHS than with the former long-form census. Importantly, the decreases were uneven across different groups (e.g., across regions; Statistics Canada, 2013). Certain groups may be unrepresented entirely; others may be heavily overrepresented. Some people have argued that the sample no longer reflects the demographics of Canadians, thereby reducing the ability of innumerable agencies and businesses to provide the most appropriate services in particular regions across the country (Cain & Mehler Paperny, 2013). The controversy continues to unfold (Cain, 2013).

In general, mail surveys have lower response rates than Internet and telephone surveys. With all methods, however, steps can be taken to maximize response rates. Researchers might motivate some people to respond by highlighting the importance of the survey and that their participation will make a valuable contribution. With mail surveys, an explanatory letter can be sent a week or so prior to mailing the survey. Follow-up reminders, second mailings of the questionnaire, and including a personally stamped return envelope are often effective in increasing response rates. Even the look of the cover page of the questionnaire can be important (Dillman, 2000). With Internet surveys, follow-up e-mails are critical. With telephone surveys, people who aren't home can be called again, and people who can't be interviewed today can be scheduled for a call at a more convenient time. Sometimes an incentive may be necessary to increase response rates. Such incentives can include cash, a gift, a gift certificate, or a chance to win a prize in exchange for participation.

SAMPLING TECHNIQUES

LO7

There are two basic techniques for sampling individuals from a population: probability sampling and non-probability sampling. The sampling technique you use has implications for what conclusions you can draw, as discussed above. In **probability sampling,** each member of the population has a specifiable probability of being chosen. Probability sampling is very important when you want to make precise statements about a specific population based on your survey results. In **non-probability sampling,** we don't know the probability of any particular member of the population being chosen. Although this approach is not as sophisticated as probability sampling, we shall see that non-probability sampling is quite common and useful in many circumstances.

Probability Sampling

Simple Random Sampling   With **simple random sampling,** every member of the population has an equal probability of being selected for the sample. If the population has 1,000 members, each has one chance out of a thousand of being selected. Suppose you want to sample students who attend your school. A list of all students would be needed; from that list, students would be chosen at random to form the sample. Whenever people are randomly selected from a specific population to participate in a study, the resulting sample is called a **random sample.**

Stratified Random Sampling   A somewhat more complicated procedure is **stratified random sampling.** The population is divided into subgroups (or strata), and then simple random sampling is used to select sample members from each stratum. Any number of dimensions could be used to divide the population, but the dimension (or dimensions) chosen should be relevant to the problem under study. For instance, a survey of sexual attitudes might stratify on the basis of age, sex, sexual orientation, and amount of education because these factors are related to sexual attitudes. Stratification on the basis of height or hair colour would be meaningless.

Stratified random sampling has the advantage of a built-in assurance that the sample will accurately reflect the numerical composition of the various subgroups. This kind of accuracy is particularly important when some sub-groups represent very small percentages of the population. For instance, the Canadian NLSCY mentioned earlier stratifies its sample on the basis of province, age, and sex to reflect the population characteristics. If Aboriginal people make up 5 percent of a city of 100,000, a simple random sample of 100 people might not include any Aboriginal people; a stratified random sample divided by race would include five Aboriginal people chosen randomly from the Aboriginal population. In practice, when it is important to represent a small group within a population, researchers will typically "oversample" that group to ensure that a representative sample of the group is surveyed; a large-enough sample must be obtained to be able to make inferences about the sub-population. Thus, if your campus has a distribution of students similar to the city described here, and you need to compare attitudes of Aboriginal people and Whites, you will need to sample a large percentage of the Aboriginal students and only a small percentage of the White students to obtain a reasonable number of respondents from each group.

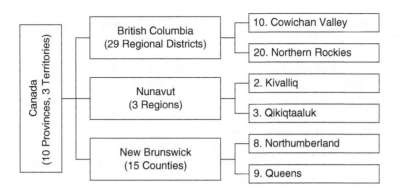

FIGURE 7.2
Multistage
cluster
sampling of
six Canadian
regions

Cluster Sampling   It might have occurred to you that obtaining a list of all members of a population might be difficult. What if officials at your school decide that you cannot have access to a list of all students? What if you want to study a population that has no list of members, such as people who work in regional health care agencies? In such situations, a technique called **cluster sampling** can be used. Rather than randomly sampling from a list of people, the researcher can identify "clusters" of people and then sample from these clusters. After the clusters are chosen, all people in each cluster are included in the sample. For example, you might conduct the survey of students using cluster sampling by identifying all classes being taught–the classes are the clusters of students. You could then randomly sample from this list of classes and ask all members of the chosen classes to complete your survey (making sure that no one completes the survey twice).

Most often, use of cluster sampling requires a series of samples from larger to smaller clusters–a "multistage" approach. For example, a researcher interested in studying regional health care agencies might first randomly determine which provinces to sample and then randomly select regions from each province chosen. Figure 7.2 shows six regions selected using this method. All random selections were made using the "list randomizer" feature of www.random.org described in Chapter 4. First, three provinces/territories were randomly selected, then two census regions were randomly selected from each. The researcher would then survey people working in the health care agencies in each of these regions. Note that the main advantage of cluster sampling is that the researcher does not have to sample from lists of people to obtain a truly random sample. However, as you may notice, this method can produce uneven representation of certain members of a population.

Non-probability Sampling

In contrast, non-probability or *non-random* sampling techniques are quite arbitrary. A population may be defined, but little effort is expended to ensure that the sample accurately represents the population; therefore, results may not generalize beyond the sample. However, non-probability samples are cheap and convenient. Three types of non-probability sampling are convenience sampling, purposive sampling, and quota sampling.

Convenience Sampling   One form of non-probability sampling is **convenience sampling** (sometimes called *haphazard sampling*). Participants are recruited wherever you can find them. To select a sample of students from your school, you might stand in front of the student union building at 9 a.m., ask people who sit around you in your classes to participate, or visit a couple of on-campus residences. Unfortunately, such procedures are likely to introduce biases into the sample so that the sample may not accurately represent the population of all students. For example, if you selected your sample from students walking by the student centre at 11 a.m., your sample excludes students who don't frequent this location, and it may also eliminate afternoon and evening students. On some campuses, this sample would differ from the population of all students by being younger and working fewer hours at paid employment. Sample biases such as these limit your ability to use your sample data to estimate the actual population values. Your results may not generalize to your intended population but instead may describe only the biased sample that you obtained. As we discuss later, this bias is typically more problematic for research with the goal of description than for research aiming toward other goals (e.g., explanation; see Chapter 1).

Purposive Sampling   A second form of non-probability sampling is **purposive sampling.** The *purpose* is to obtain a sample of people who meet some predetermined criterion. Sometimes researchers will use purposive sampling while asking certain customers at the cinema to fill out a questionnaire about one or more movies. Instead of sampling anyone walking toward the theatre, they look at each person to make sure that they fit some criterion—under the age of 30 or an adult with one or more children, for example. This is one way to limit your sample to a certain group of people. However, it is not a probability sample, so it limits conclusions.

Quota Sampling   A third form of non-probability sampling is **quota sampling.** A researcher who uses this technique chooses a sample that reflects the numerical composition of various subgroups in the population. Thus, quota sampling is similar to the stratified sampling procedure previously described, but without the randomness. To illustrate, suppose you want to ensure that your sample of students includes 19 percent first years, 23 percent second years, 26 percent third years, 22 percent fourth years, and 10 percent graduate students because these percentages reflect the distribution in your school's total population. A quota-sampling technique would make sure you have these percentages, but you would still collect your data using convenience techniques. If you didn't get enough graduate students in front of the student union, perhaps you could go to a graduate class to complete the sample. Although quota sampling is a bit more sophisticated than convenience sampling, the problem remains that no restrictions are placed on how people in the various subgroups are chosen. The sample does reflect the numerical composition of the whole population of interest, but respondents within each subgroup are selected in a haphazard manner. All techniques are summarized in Table 7.3.

TABLE 7.3 Advantages and disadvantages of sampling techniques

Sampling Technique	Example	Advantages	Disadvantages
Probability sampling			
Simple random sampling	A computer program randomly chooses 100 students from a list of all 10,000 students at University X.	Representative of population.	May cost more. May be difficult to get full list of all members of any population of interest.
Stratified random sampling	The names of all 10,000 University X students are sorted by major, and a computer program randomly chooses 50 students from each major.	Representative of population.	May cost more. May be difficult to get full list of all members of any population of interest.
Cluster sampling	Psychology majors are identified at 100 schools all over Canada. Out of these 100 clusters, 10 clusters are chosen randomly, and every psychology major in each cluster is sampled.	Researcher does not have to sample from multiple lists of people in order to get a random sample.	May cost more. May be difficult to get full list of all members of any randomly chosen cluster.
Non-probability sampling			
Convenience sampling	Ask students around you at lunch or in class to participate.	Inexpensive, efficient, convenient.	Likely to introduce bias into the sample. Results may not generalize to intended population.
Purposive sampling	In an otherwise convenience sample, select people who meet a criterion (e.g., an age group).	Relatively convenient. Sample includes only types of people you are interested in.	Likely to introduce bias into the sample. Results may not generalize to intended population.
Quota sampling	Identify the proportion of each important subgroup within a population, and then use convenience sampling within each subgroup.	Inexpensive, efficient, convenient. Slightly more sophisticated than convenience sampling.	Likely to introduce bias into the sample. Results may not generalize to intended population. No method for choosing individuals in subgroups.

Reasons for Using Convenience Samples

Much research in psychology uses non-probability sampling techniques to obtain participants for surveys, experiments, and other studies. The advantage of these techniques is that the investigator can obtain research participants without spending a great deal of money or time to select the sample. For example, it is common practice to invite students in introductory psychology classes to participate in studies being conducted by faculty at their institution. Often, these students are offered bonus points in exchange for participating in studies of their choosing. To promote the TCPS principle *respect for persons*, students may be offered an alternative way to earn the bonus points besides research participation (see Chapter 3).

Even in studies that do not use university students, the sample is often based on convenience rather than concern for obtaining a random sample. It is common for researchers who study children to draw from one or two particular elementary schools. Once they have established a good relationship with the teachers and administrators, obtaining permission to conduct the research is relatively easy. This method introduces some bias because only children from particular neighbourhoods with certain social and economic characteristics are included, but (depending on research goals) this isn't usually considered a major concern.

Why aren't researchers more worried about obtaining random samples from the "general population" for their research? Most basic psychological research is focused on studying the relationships between variables. The sample may be biased (e.g., will include more university students, be younger, etc. than the general Canadian population), but consider that even a random sample of the general population of Canadian residents may tell us little about citizens of other countries. Our research findings can provide important information even though the data cannot be strictly generalized beyond the population defined by the sample that was used. For example, the relationship between working and grades among high school students that is shown in Figure 7.1 is a useful finding even though the sample was drawn from a certain type of neighbourhood located in a particular province. Importantly, results from the study were generally consistent with those found in the U.S. (Steinberg & Dornbusch, 1991). *Replicating* results with multiple samples and multiple methods is one way to increase *external validity* while using non-probability sampling (see Chapter 14). The results of many studies can then be synthesized to gain greater insight into the phenomenon being investigated (cf., Albright & Malloy, 2000).

Keep in mind that some non-probability samples are more representative than others. Introductory psychology students seem fairly representative of university students in general, and most university student samples seem fairly representative of young adults. Other samples might be much less representative of an intended population. Every week of singing competitions like *American Idol* or *The Voice*, viewers could telephone or text a vote for whom they wanted to win. The sampling problems here are obvious: People from a particular contestant's hometown can rally together and vote for that person, regardless of his or her actual singing ability, and there are no limits on how many times someone can respond. It is likely that this sample's preferences do not represent the views of the North American population or even represent all viewers of the program, many of whom are not compelled to vote. We will revisit this discussion about the *external validity* of our samples in Chapter 14 in greater detail.

We have considered many issues that are important when asking people about themselves. If you engage in this type of research, you may need to design your own questions by following the guidelines described in this chapter and consulting sources such as Judd et al. (1991); Gosling and Johnson (2010); and Bradburn, Sudman, and Wansink (2004). You can also adapt questions and entire questionnaires that have been used in previous research. For example, Greenfield (1999) studied Internet addiction by adapting questions from a large body of existing research on addiction to gambling. Consider using previously developed questions, particularly if they have been useful in other studies (make sure you don't violate copyrights, however). For examples, see compilations of various measures of social and political attitudes developed by others (e.g., Robinson, Rusk, & Head, 1968; Robinson, Shaver, & Wrightsman, 1991; Registry of Scales and Measures, www.scalesandmeasures.net; Positive Psychology Questionnaires, http://www.ppc.sas.upenn.edu/ppquestionnaires.htm).

We noted in Chapter 4 that both non-experimental and experimental research methods are necessary to fully understand behaviour. Chapters 6 and 7 have focused on techniques that commonly form the backbone of many non-experimental designs, yet are also useful in operationally defining dependent variables in experiments. In the next chapter, we begin to explore experimental research design in detail.

STUDY TERMS

Test yourself! Define and generate an example of each of these key terms.

Closed-ended questions (p. 138)	Panel study (p. 134)
Cluster sampling (p. 153)	Population (p. 147)
Confidence interval (p. 148)	Probability sampling (p. 151)
Convenience sampling (p. 154)	Purposive sampling (p. 154)
External validity (p. 150)	Quota sampling (p. 154)
Focus group (p. 147)	Random sample (p. 152)
Graphic rating scale (p. 141)	Rating scales (p. 139)
Interviewer bias (p. 146)	Response rate (p. 151)
Non-probability sampling (p. 152)	Response set (p. 134)
Open-ended questions (p. 138)	Sampling (p. 148)

Sampling error (p. 148)   Stratified random sampling (p. 152)
Sampling frame (p. 150)   Survey research (p. 132)
Semantic differential scale (p. 142)   "Yea-saying" or "nay-saying" response
Simple random sampling (p. 152)   set (p. 138)

REVIEW QUESTIONS

Test yourself on this chapter's learning objectives. Can you answer each of these questions?

1. What is a survey? List some research questions you might address with a survey.

2. What are some features to consider when constructing questions for surveys (including both questions and response alternatives)?

3. What is a social desirability response set? What can a researcher do to identify and/or minimize it?

4. Compare the different ways to administer a survey using questionnaires and interviews. What are the advantages and disadvantages of each method?

5. How do sample size, sampling frame, response rate, and sampling technique affect the interpretation of survey results?

6. Distinguish between probability and non-probability sampling techniques. When would a researcher use each of these techniques? What are the costs and benefits involved in each technique?

7. Compare and contrast convenience sampling, purposive sampling, and quota sampling.

8. Compare and contrast simple random sampling, stratified random sampling, and cluster sampling.

9. Under what research circumstances is it most important to achieve random sampling?

DEEPEN YOUR UNDERSTANDING

Develop your mastery of these concepts by considering these application questions. Compare your responses with those from other people in your study group.

1. In the Dumont et al. (2009) study on teenage employment (see Figure 7.1), longer work hours were associated with lower grade point averages. Can you conclude that working longer hours *causes* lower grades? Why or why not? How might you expand the scope of this investigation using a panel study? An experiment?

2. Select a topic for a survey. Write at least five closed-ended questions that you might include. For each question, write one "good" version and one "poor" version. For each poor question, state what elements make it poor and why the good version is an improvement.

3. Suppose you want to know how many books in a bookstore have only male authors, only female authors, or both male and female authors. (You might operationally define the "bookstore" as a large retail store, the textbook section of your university bookstore, or all books in the stacks of your library.) Because there are thousands of books in the store, you decide to study a sample rather than examine every book there. Describe how you might sample books using a non-probability sampling technique. Then describe a possible probability sampling technique. How might your results differ using the two techniques?

8

Experimental Design

LEARNING OBJECTIVES

Keep these learning objectives in mind as you read to help you identify the most critical information in this chapter.

By the end of this chapter, you should be able to:

1	Describe how confounding variables affect the internal validity of an experiment.
2	List and explain three major steps toward planning a basic experiment.
3	Describe the pretest-posttest design, including the advantages and disadvantages of using a pretest.
4	Contrast an independent groups design with a repeated measures design, including advantages and disadvantages of each.
5	Describe the matched pairs design, including reasons to use this design.

The experimental method is a vital and versatile tool in the researcher's toolbox. The next four chapters showcase its versatility by building on the basic concepts you first learned in Chapter 4 (e.g., *independent variable, dependent variable, random assignment*). Suppose you want to test the hypothesis that crowding impairs cognitive performance. To do this, you might put one group of people in a crowded room and another group in an uncrowded room; crowded versus uncrowded are the two *levels* or *conditions* of the *independent variable.* The participants in each of the groups would then complete the same cognitive tests (i.e., the *dependent variables*). Now suppose that the people in the crowded condition do not perform as well on the cognitive tests as those in the uncrowded condition. Can the difference in test scores be attributed to the difference in crowding? Yes, *if* there is no other difference between the conditions. What if participants in the crowded condition were tested in a room with nine other participants, but those in the uncrowded condition were tested in a room with one other participant? Both the crowding and the number of people in the room changed. Therefore, it would be impossible to know whether the poor scores of the participants in the crowded condition were due to the experience of feeling crowded or to being distracted by nine other people. *How might you avoid this problem?*

CONFOUNDING AND INTERNAL VALIDITY

LOI

Recall from Chapter 4 that a critical advantage of experiments over non-experiments is that researchers can, relatively unambiguously, interpret results in terms of causality: altering one variable *causes* another to change. The researcher manipulates the independent variable to create groups that differ in the levels of that variable and then compares the groups in terms of their scores on the dependent variable. All other variables are kept constant, through direct *experimental control* and *random assignment* (or an equivalent procedure). If the scores of the groups are different, the researcher concludes that the independent variable caused the results because the only difference between the groups is the manipulated, independent variable.

Although the task of designing an experiment is logically simple, there are many possible pitfalls. Reconsider the hypothetical crowding experiment described above. Both group size and crowding change between conditions, and both might influence cognitive performance. Because we are interested in crowding, group size becomes a potential *confounding variable.* Recall from Chapter 4 that a confounding variable varies along with the independent variable; confounding occurs when the effects of the independent variable and an uncontrolled variable are intertwined so that you cannot determine which of the variables is responsible for the observed effect. One way to avoid the group size confound might be to test all participants in groups of ten, and vary crowding by the seating arrangement (spread apart or tightly packed).

Anticipating confounding variables is not always easy. Consider the following example from the self-control literature. First, a brief introduction to the standard *two-task* paradigm (Baumeister, Bratslavsky, Muraven, & Tice, 1998). The *independent variable* is manipulated by randomly assigning people to one of two levels: Complete a task that either requires self-control (e.g., eating bitter radishes while staring at delicious chocolates) or, in the neutral condition, does not (e.g., eating delicious chocolates while staring at bitter radishes). The *dependent variable* is then measured in a second task where performance requires self-control (e.g., persistence on difficult puzzles). Consistently, people in the self-control condition perform more poorly on the next act of self-control compared to people in the neutral condition (see Hagger, Wood, Stiff, & Chatzisarantis, 2010, for a meta-analysis of 198 studies).

But why does this result occur? For years, the most common explanation was that self-control is a limited resource. In an attempt to explain this "resource" idea further, Gailliot et al. (2007) proposed a hypothesis that exerting self-control depletes the body's energy reserves (in the form of blood glucose), leaving fewer "resources" left for the next self-control attempt. In the crucial studies, participants were given lemonade to drink between the two tasks in the standard paradigm. This lemonade had been sweetened either with sugar (i.e., glucose) or a sugar substitute (i.e., a *placebo*). The self-control resources of people who had consumed the sugary lemonade seemed to rebound: They performed just as well as people in the neutral condition! Glucose seemed to be the "resource" of self-control.

Other researchers were skeptical. Five years later, Molden et al. (2012) demonstrated that merely rinsing out one's mouth with a glucose-based solution can boost self-control. In Gailliot et al.'s (2007) studies, participants *drank* the sugary lemonade, which necessarily included passing it through their mouths. Molden et al. (2012) identified a *confounding variable* (i.e., rinsing) and isolated it. Surprisingly, people who simply rinsed their mouths with sugary water (but not sugar substitute) seemed to rebound: They performed just as well as people in the control condition. Because rinsing cannot boost blood glucose, Molden and colleagues' research helped *falsify* the glucose-based theory (see Chapter 1 for more about falsifiable ideas). Since then, researchers have focused on developing motivation-based theories to explain the two-task results (e.g., Inzlicht, Schmeichel, & Macrae, 2014).

Good experimental design allows researchers to make causal claims because competing, alternative explanations (e.g., confounding variables) are eliminated. When the results of an experiment can confidently be attributed to the effect of the independent variable, the experiment is said to have high *internal validity* (see Chapter 4). To achieve high internal validity, the researcher must design and conduct the experiment so that only the independent variable can be the cause of the results. As the self-control studies demonstrate, eliminating confounds and other *threats to internal validity* is not always easy. We will revisit this idea of threats to internal validity in Chapter 11 in the context of *quasi-experimental designs*, which are used when random assignment (or an equivalent procedure, see below) is impossible. For now, let us continue considering essential features of experiments.

| LO2 |

PLANNING A BASIC EXPERIMENT

The simplest possible experimental design has two variables: the independent variable, which has two levels (e.g., an experimental group and a control group), and the dependent variable. (In Chapter 10, we will explore more complex experimental designs that have more than two levels of an independent variable and more than one independent variable.) Researchers must make every effort to ensure that the only difference between the two groups is the manipulated variable. Using any experimental design involves three broad steps: (1) obtaining two equivalent groups of participants, (2) introducing the independent variable, and (3) measuring the effect of the independent variable on the dependent variable. When there are only two levels of the independent variable, the design can be diagrammed like this:

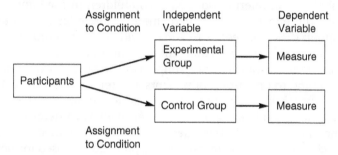

The first step in planning a basic experiment is to decide how to assign participants to the levels of the independent variable. The procedures used must achieve equivalent groups to eliminate any potential **selection differences:** The people selected to be in the conditions should not differ in any systematic way. For example, you cannot assign only high-income participants to the self-control condition and only low-income participants to the neutral condition because income would become confounded with the independent variable. There are three basic ways to assign participants to experimental conditions so that groups are equivalent (see Figure 8.1). In one procedure, called the *independent groups design*, groups are made equivalent by randomly assigning participants to experience only one of the conditions of the independent variable. In another procedure, called the *repeated measures design*, participants are assigned to participate in all levels of the independent variable. A third method, *matched pairs design*, makes groups equivalent by first selecting pairs of participants who score the same (i.e., are matched) on some variable of interest, and then uses

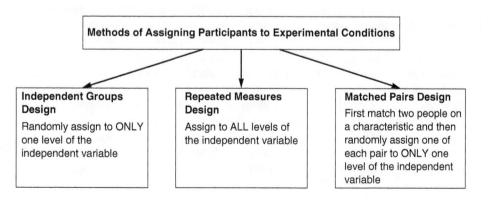

FIGURE 8.1
Three experimental designs

random assignment within each pair to determine which participant will experience which level of the independent variable. We will examine each of these designs in detail throughout this chapter.

The second step in planning a basic experiment is to *operationally define* the independent variable (see Chapter 4), creating at least two levels. Sometimes, these levels include an experimental group that receives a treatment and a control group that does not. For example, a researcher might study the effect of reward on motivation by offering a reward to one group of children before they play a game and offering no reward to children in the control group. A study testing the effect of a treatment method for reducing smoking could compare a group that receives the treatment with a control group that does not. Other times, researchers use two different amounts of the independent variable. They may use more reward in one group than the other, or offer one hour of relaxation training to one group of patients and ten hours to the other group. Any of these approaches would provide a basis for comparing the two groups.

The third step in planning a basic experiment is to determine a way to measure the effect of the independent variable by *operationally defining* the dependent variable. The same measurement procedure is used for both groups so that they can be compared. When the groups were equivalent to begin with and there were no confounding variables, we can conclude that any difference between the groups on the dependent variable was caused by the independent variable. This elegant, basic experimental design has a high degree of internal validity. In actuality, a statistical significance test would be used to assess the difference between the groups (see Chapter 13). Yet an experiment must be well-designed, and confounding variables must be eliminated before we can draw conclusions from statistical analyses.

INDEPENDENT GROUPS DESIGN

In an **independent groups design** (also called *between-subjects design*), different participants are assigned to each level of the independent variable using *random assignment*. This means that the decision to assign people to a particular level is completely due to chance. In practice, researchers often use a list randomizer like the one available on www.random.org to assign participants to condition (see Chapter 4 for instructions). Especially as the number of participants in the study increases, random assignment ensures the groups will be equivalent in terms of a whole host of participant characteristics, such as income, intelligence, age, or political attitudes. In this way, participant characteristics cannot be an alternative explanation for the experiment's results. To borrow an example from Chapter 4, in an experiment on the effects of exercise on happiness, higher levels of happiness in the exercise group than in the no-exercise group cannot be explained by saying that people in the groups are somehow different on characteristics such as income, education, or personality. With a sufficiently large sample of participants, random assignment will produce groups that are equivalent in all respects.

You may be wondering how many participants are needed in each group to make sure that random assignment has made the groups equivalent. The larger the sample, the less likely it is that the groups will differ in any systematic way prior to the manipulation of the independent variable. In Chapter 13, we will mention formal procedures for determining the sample size needed to detect a statistically significant effect if one exists, but as a rule of thumb, you will probably need a minimum of 30 to 50 participants per condition (Simmons, Nelson, & Simonsohn, 2013). In some areas of research, many more participants may be necessary.

Pretest-Posttest Design

LO3

Sometimes a researcher needs to be extra cautious that random assignment to condition created groups that were equivalent on some particular variable (e.g., intelligence, amount of exposure to a particular language). Therefore, the researcher may choose to add a *pretest* to measure that variable. Pretest scores for the two groups are then compared to ensure that the two groups were equivalent on that critical variable before the manipulation was introduced. This design is sometimes called the **pretest-posttest design;** when no pretest is given, an independent groups design is sometimes called a **posttest-only design.** The pretest-posttest design makes it possible for researchers to be absolutely sure that the groups were equivalent at the beginning of the experiment on a crucial variable. In this terminology, the *posttest* refers to the dependent variable that is measured after the experimental manipulation.

Advantages and Disadvantages of a Pretest The pretest is a precaution that is usually not necessary if participants have been randomly assigned to the two groups. However, there are three main reasons why a researcher may add a pretest: small sample size, to select appropriate participants, and when participants might drop out of the study. First, although random assignment is likely to produce equivalent groups, as sample size decreases, the less likely it is that the groups actually will be equal on all variables. Thus, a pretest enables the researcher to assess whether the groups were already equivalent on some critical variable before the manipulation began.

Second, a pretest may be used to select the participants to include in the experiment. A researcher might need to give a pretest to find the lowest or highest scorers on measures of smoking, math anxiety, or prejudice, for example. Once the target participants are identified, they would be randomly assigned to the experimental or control group. However, this selection method may introduce another problem: the threat to internal validity called *regression toward the mean* (see Chapter 11).

Third, a pretest also may be necessary whenever there is a possibility that participants will drop out of the experiment; this is most likely to occur in a study that lasts over a long time period. The dropout factor in experiments is called **mortality** (another threat to internal validity; see

Chapter 11 for others). People may drop out for reasons unrelated to the experimental manipulation, such as illness; sometimes, however, mortality is related to the experimental manipulation. Even if the groups are equivalent at the beginning, different mortality rates can make them non-equivalent by the time the dependent variable is measured at the end of the study. How might mortality affect a treatment program designed to reduce smoking? One possibility is that the heaviest smokers in the experimental group might leave the program. Therefore, when the posttest is given, only the light smokers would remain, so a comparison of the experimental and control groups would show less smoking in the experimental group even if the program had no effect. In this way, mortality becomes an alternative explanation for the results. A pretest enables researchers to examine whether mortality is a plausible alternative explanation for differences between groups on the dependent variable.

Thus, pretests may offer some advantages in the independent groups experimental design. One disadvantage of a pretest, however, is that it may be time-consuming and awkward to administer in the context of the particular experimental procedures being used. Perhaps most important, a pretest can sensitize participants to what you are studying, enabling them to figure out your hypothesis (i.e., it may create a *demand characteristic*; see Chapter 9). They may then react differently to the manipulation than they would have without the pretest. When a pretest influences the way participants react to the manipulation, it is very difficult to generalize results to people who have not received a pretest. That is, the independent variable may not have an effect in the real world, where pretests are rarely given (see Chapter 14).

For researchers who decide a pretest is useful, there are a few ways to avoid or measure its impact on results of the study. If awareness of the pretest is a problem, the pretest can be disguised using deception (see Chapter 3). One way to do this is to administer it in a completely different situation with a different experimenter. Another approach is to embed the pretest in a set of irrelevant measures so that it is not obvious that the researcher is interested in a particular topic (see Chapter 5 for additional tips for dealing with *reactivity*).

Alternatively, the *Solomon four-group design* is a type of complex experimental design that allows a researcher to assess the impact of the pretest directly. Essentially, the pretest is treated as a second independent variable. As shown in Figure 8.2, the first step in this design is to randomly assign half the participants to either the pretest condition or the no pretest condition. Next, participants are randomly assigned to one of the levels of the independent variable. Ultimately, then, participants are randomly assigned to one of four possible combinations. If there is no impact of the pretest, the average posttest scores will be the same in the two control groups (one with and one without the pretest) and in the two experimental groups (one with and one without the pretest).

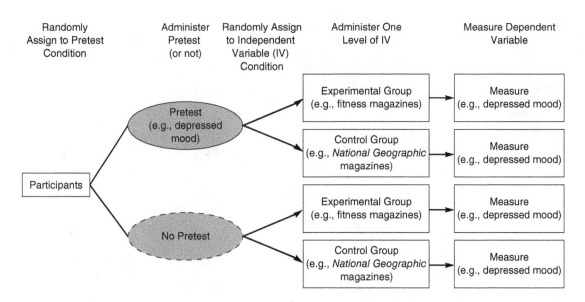

FIGURE 8.2
Solomon four-group design (examples from Wertz Garvin & Damson, 2008)

Wertz Garvin and Damson (2008) chose a Solomon four-group design to test the effect of exposure to idealized bodies in fitness magazines on depressed mood. Participants spent 30 minutes viewing either fitness magazines or control magazines such as *National Geographic;* these two kinds of magazines comprised the two levels of the main independent variable. They wanted to measure levels of depressed mood in a pretest before administering the independent variable, but were concerned that just asking these questions might introduce a confound: Responding to questions about depressed mood might make the idealized bodies in the fitness magazines condition seem more depressing than they would have been without first answering those questions. Therefore, only half the participants completed a measure of depressed mood before viewing the magazine materials (see Figure 8.2).

Figure 8.3 shows two different hypothetical results of the Solomon four-group design. The top graph illustrates an outcome in which the pretest has no impact, which is what was found in Wertz Garvin and Damson's (2008) study: People who viewed fitness magazines reported a more depressed mood than people who viewed control magazines, regardless of whether they received a pretest. The lower graph shows a different hypothetical outcome in which the pretest seems to enhance people's experience of the treatment condition. Without the pretest, the treatment condition results in the same outcome as the control condition. Although complex, the Solomon four-group design helps detect whether a pretest has an effect.

FIGURE 8.3
Examples of
outcomes of a
Solomon four-
group design;
Outcome 1
(top panel) is
similar to
results from
Wertz Garvin
and Damson
(2008).

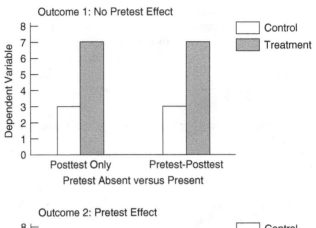

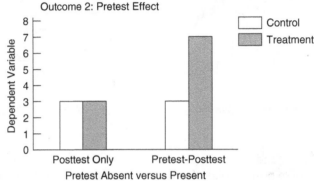

REPEATED MEASURES DESIGN

Instead of random assignment to condition, an alternative procedure for ensuring that groups are equivalent is to have the *same* individuals participate in all conditions. This is called a **repeated measures design** (also called *within-subjects design*); participants are measured on the dependent variable after being in each condition of the experiment. Pretests can also be used for repeated measures designs, for reasons mentioned earlier.

Let's consider an example. Have you ever thought about listening to audio books rather than reading? How often do you read out loud? University of Waterloo researchers used a repeated measures design to test whether these different exposures to material influence people's mind-wandering and memory (Varao Sousa, Carriere, & Smilek, 2013). Three passages were taken from the same book. The different ways in which the participants encountered the passages formed the independent variable: listening to it read by someone else, reading it silently, and reading it aloud. While experiencing the *listen* condition, participants were interrupted regularly and asked to report whether they were mind-wandering. Afterward, they completed a short memory test.

This procedure was repeated for the *read silently* condition and the *read aloud* condition, until each participant experienced all three exposures. Results showed the least mind-wandering and greatest memory for material that people read aloud, followed by material that is read silently, followed by material encountered by listening (regardless of the order they were administered, see below). Consider using audio books only for material you don't need to remember!

Advantages and Disadvantages of the Repeated Measures Design [LO4]

The repeated measures design has several advantages and disadvantages when compared to the independent groups design. A major advantage is that fewer research participants are needed because everyone participates in all conditions. When participants are scarce or when it is costly to run each participant through the study procedure, a repeated measures design can maximize the amount of data collected. Consider the importance of these issues for research relying on specialized machinery (e.g., fMRI) costing hundreds of dollars per participant, or specific populations (e.g., people with rare conditions) that take years of searching to find just a few people who meet the criteria and choose to participate.

An additional advantage of repeated measures designs is that they are extremely sensitive to detecting differences between levels of the independent variable. When the same people are in both conditions, less of the variance in the data is attributed to error. To illustrate what this means, consider hypothetical data from the reading experiment described above. Using an independent groups design, the first three participants in the read silently condition had memory scores of 58, 71, and 82. The first three participants in the listen condition had scores of 54, 68, and 75. The average memory score was higher when people read silently (average of 70.33) rather than listened (average of 65.66). However, there is a lot of variability in the scores in both groups. Not everyone in the read silently condition had good memory and not everyone in the listen condition had poor memory. A major reason for this variability is that people differ; there are individual differences in memory, so there is a range of scores in both conditions. This is part of the *error* in the scores; we cannot explain it, and it affects our statistical analyses (see Chapter 13). Just like when we considered reliability of measures (Chapter 5), we want as little error as possible.

However, if the same scores were obtained from the first three participants in a repeated measures design, the conclusions would be much different. Let's line up the hypothetical memory scores for the two conditions:

	Listen	Read Silently	Difference
Participant 1	54	58	+4
Participant 2	68	71	+3
Participant 3	75	82	+7

Regardless of condition, Participant 1 seems to have worse memory overall than does Participant 3; these overall patterns are what we mean by individual differences in memory. In a repeated measures design, we have measured these systematic individual differences and separated them from random error and from the effect of the independent variable. The *difference* column shows us that scores are higher for every participant in the read silently condition compared to the listening condition. Not every difference score is the same, so there is still some unexplained random error. Nonetheless, by accounting for individual differences in a repeated measures design, we are better able to detect an effect of the independent variable on the dependent variable, if one exists.

The major challenge with a repeated measures design stems from the fact that the different conditions must be presented in a particular sequence—a problem that is non-existent in the independent groups design. Sequence can become a confound if left unaddressed. Imagine, hypothetically, that the read aloud task always came third in the order in which conditions were presented, and participants remembered it best of all other conditions. Although this result could be caused by the manipulation of the independent variable, the result could also simply be an **order effect**—the order of presenting the treatments affects the dependent variable. Memory on the third task might be strongest merely because of the practice gained on earlier tasks.

There are several types of order effects. Order effects that are associated simply with the passage of time during the study include practice effects and fatigue effects. Time-related order effects are possible whenever there is a sequence of tasks to perform. A **practice effect** occurs when performance improves because of repeated practice with a task. A **fatigue effect** occurs when performance worsens as participants become tired, bored, or distracted. If the listening condition was always presented third, an alternative explanation for worse memory scores could be fatigue or boredom. If the repeated measures involved video game playing, for example, participants might improve performance by the third condition because of practice—instead of (or in addition to) any effect of the independent variable.

Other types of order effects occur when the effect of the first treatment carries over to influence the way people respond to the second treatment. A **contrast effect** occurs when the response to the second condition in the experiment is altered because the two conditions are contrasted to one another. To help explain, consider that visual contrast effects occur when the background influences our perception of the foreground, as in Figure 8.4. The dot on the left looks lighter than the dot on the right, but they are both the same shade of grey. The context (in this case, the background) affects our perception of the dot. Like the background in the optical illusion, the first condition in a repeated measures experiment can affect how participants experience the second condition. Suppose the independent variable is crime severity, and the dependent variable is assigned punishment. After reading about murder in the first condition, reading about theft in the second condition might seem much milder to participants than it would have seemed if presented first.

FIGURE 8.4
Visual contrast
effect

People might punish the thief less harshly when it follows murder than if it comes first. Order is confounded with crime severity.

There are two ways to deal with order effects in repeated measures designs: (1) using counterbalancing techniques and (2) ensuring the time between conditions is long enough to minimize the influence of the first condition on the second. These strategies can also be combined. We consider each in turn.

Counterbalancing

Complete Counterbalancing   In a repeated measures design using complete **counterbalancing,** all possible orders of presentation are included in the experiment. Let us consider counterbalancing for just two of the conditions in the mind-wandering and memory study discussed earlier (Varao Sousa et al., 2013). Half of the participants would be randomly assigned to the "listen then read silently" order, and the other half would be assigned to the "read silently then listen" order. This design is illustrated as follows:

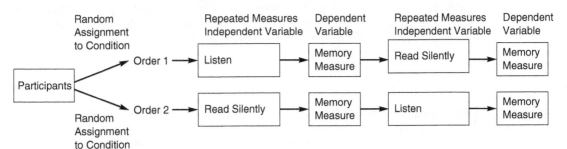

By counterbalancing the order of conditions, it is possible to determine the extent to which order is influencing the results. Compare average memory scores for the listen condition when it comes first and second; if they are the same, results suggest no order effects. A fatigue effect might be operating if memory is always worse for the second condition, regardless of whether it is listen or read silently.

Counterbalancing principles can be extended to experiments with three or more levels of the independent variable. With three levels, there are six possible orders (3! = *three factorial* = 3 × 2 × 1 = 6). With four levels, the number of possible orders increases to 24 (4! = 4 × 3 × 2 × 1 = 24); you would need a minimum of 24 participants to include each order, and you would need 48 participants to have only 2 participants per order. The number of possible orders increases quickly as more conditions are added. In an experiment with 10 conditions, there are 3,628,800 possible orders! Fortunately, there are alternatives to complete counterbalancing that still allow researchers to draw valid conclusions about the effect of the independent variable.

Partial Counterbalancing   One technique to control for most order effects without having all possible orders is to construct a **Latin square:** a limited set of orders constructed to ensure that (1) each condition appears at each ordinal position (i.e., first, second, third, and so on), and (2) each condition precedes and follows each condition once. Varao Sousa and colleagues (2013) chose a Latin square to counterbalance conditions and passages in the mind-wandering and memory study. For another example, consider an experiment in which participants' memory and reaction time were measured after eight, six, four, and zero hours of sleep the previous night (Roehrs, Burduvali, Bonahoom, Drake, & Roth, 2003). Results showed that both memory and reaction time were impaired after sleep loss. Instead of having 24 different orders in this repeated measures design, researchers used a Latin square. The number of orders in a Latin square is equal to the number of conditions; there were four repeated measures conditions, so there were four orders, as depicted in Table 8.1.

We should note that in an experiment in which people are tested over a series of trials, as in many learning studies, *trials* is a repeated measures variable. In this situation, counterbalancing is not an issue; the researcher is actually interested in the order effect of changes in performance over trials.

TABLE 8.1   A Latin square with four order conditions, based on Roehrs et al. (2003)

Ordinal Position of Repeated Measures Conditions			
	First	**Second**	**Third**	**Fourth**
Order 1	*Zero hours of sleep*	*Four hours of sleep*	*Eight hours of sleep*	*Six hours of sleep*
Order 2	*Four hours of sleep*	*Six hours of sleep*	*Zero hours of sleep*	*Eight hours of sleep*
Order 3	*Six hours of sleep*	*Eight hours of sleep*	*Four hours of sleep*	*Zero hours of sleep*
Order 4	*Eight hours of sleep*	*Zero hours of sleep*	*Six hours of sleep*	*Four hours of sleep*

Time Interval between Treatments

To ensure experimental control, researchers must carefully determine the time interval between the presentation of treatments and possible activities between them. A rest period may counteract a fatigue effect; attending to an unrelated task between treatments may reduce the possibility of a contrast effect. If the treatment is the administration of a drug or other physiological event that takes time to wear off, the interval between treatments may have to be a day or more. For example, because it takes time for the effects of sleep loss to wear off, Roehrs et al. (2003) gave participants three to seven days to recover between conditions. A similarly long time interval may be needed with procedures that produce emotional changes such as heightened anxiety or anger. Introducing an extended time interval may create a separate problem: Participants will have to commit to the experiment for a longer period of time. This can make it more difficult to recruit volunteers, and *mortality* may become a problem as some participants drop out of the experiment.

Choosing between Independent Groups and Repeated Measures Designs

Repeated measures designs have two major advantages over independent groups designs: First, fewer participants are required to complete the experiment, and second, removing some error variance means that any effect of the independent variable that exists will be easier to detect using statistics. As noted previously, in certain areas of research, these advantages are very important. However, researchers need to deal with the challenges of repeated measures designs, including *order effects*. In addition, repeated measures may give participants more clues to the specific hypothesis, which might affect their behaviour (see our discussion of *demand characteristics* in Chapter 9). Independent groups designs are preferable when experimental procedures are expected to produce relatively permanent changes, such as surgical procedures like the removal of brain tissue, or some psychotherapies.

Similarity to people's experiences in the "real world" may be another consideration when choosing a design (Greenwald, 1976). In actual everyday situations, we sometimes encounter variables in an independent groups fashion: We encounter only one condition without a contrasting comparison. For example, if you are interested in how characteristics of a defendant affect jurors, an independent groups design may be most appropriate because actual jurors focus on a single defendant in a trial. However, we encounter some variables in everyday life in a repeated measures fashion, like when employers consider several job applicants at once. Thus, to study topics like characteristics of job applicants, a repeated measures design might be more appropriate. Whether to use an independent groups or repeated measures design may be partially determined by these *external validity* issues (see Chapter 14).

LO5

MATCHED PAIRS DESIGN

A somewhat more complicated way to assign participants to conditions in an experiment is called a **matched pairs design.** Instead of simply randomly assigning participants to groups, the goal is to first match people on a crucial participant characteristic. The matching variable will be either the dependent variable itself or another variable that is strongly related to it. For example, a researcher interested in studying the effect of aging on cognitive functioning might start by recruiting identical twins matched on genotype; one twin from each pair is randomly assigned to each condition of an experiment (see McGue, Osler, & Christensen, 2010).

Matched pairs designs are complex and are used less frequently than the other experiments we have considered. In one rare example, Hockey and Earle (2006) chose a matched pairs design. Results revealed that when people control their own work schedules, they are less tired after working than people who are told exactly what to do. In the first step of matching, all participants were measured on some variables the researchers expected would crucially affect how tiring the work would be (e.g., general need for control, gender, typing speed). Participants were matched to create pairs of people who were similar to each other on all of these variables. All participants were then given numerous office tasks to complete (e.g., scheduling). One member of each pair was randomly assigned to have control over their own schedule; the matched participant was told to complete the tasks in the same order and duration as their match. Matching was used to achieve equivalency of groups as in a repeated measures design, without the necessity of having the same participants in both conditions.

Matching is most likely to be used when only a few participants are available or when it is very costly to run large numbers of people in the experiment. Like repeated measures designs, matched pairs designs help remove some random error to reveal a potential effect of the independent variable. Therefore, matched pairs and repeated measures designs may be particularly useful when individual differences on the dependent variable are expected to be very large, especially when the expected sample size is very small. (Remember, random assignment to condition only produces equivalent groups with large samples.)

However, matching procedures can be costly and time-consuming because they require measuring participants on the matching variable(s) prior to the experiment, or recruiting both members of identical twin pairs. Such efforts are worthwhile only when you are certain, prior to conducting the study, that the matching variable is strongly related to the dependent measure. For these reasons, matched pairs is not a commonly used design.

This chapter explored basic experimental design. Revisit Figure 8.1 to review the three designs we discussed—independent groups, repeated measures, and matched pairs. In the next chapter, we will consider various issues that arise when you decide how to actually conduct a study.

STUDY TERMS

Test yourself! Define and generate an example of each of these key terms.

Contrast effect (p. 170)

Counterbalancing (p. 171)

Fatigue effect (p. 170)

Independent groups design (p. 164)

Latin square (p. 172)

Matched pairs design (p. 174)

Mortality (p. 165)

Order effect (p. 170)

Posttest-only design (p. 165)

Practice effect (p. 170)

Pretest-posttest design (p. 165)

Repeated measures design (p. 168)

Selection differences (p. 163)

REVIEW QUESTIONS

Test yourself on this chapter's learning objectives. Can you answer each of these questions?

1. What is a confounding variable?

2. What is meant by the internal validity of an experiment? When designing a study, how does a researcher achieve internal validity?

3. How are independent groups, repeated measures, and matched pairs experiments designed to ensure that groups differ only in terms of the independent variable and nothing more?

4. Describe the differences between a basic independent groups design and the pretest-posttest design. What are the advantages and disadvantages of each?

5. What is a repeated measures design? What are the advantages and disadvantages of using a repeated measures design versus an independent groups design?

6. How do researchers overcome the unique challenges of repeated measures designs?

7. When and why might a researcher decide to use the matched pairs design?

8. What is the difference between random sampling (see Chapter 7) and random assignment?

DEEPEN YOUR UNDERSTANDING

Develop your mastery of these concepts by considering these application questions. Compare your responses with those from other people in your study group.

1. Design a repeated measures experiment that investigates the effect of report presentation style on the grade received for the report. Use two

levels of the independent variable: a *professional-style* presentation (high-quality paper, consistent use of margins and fonts, carefully constructed tables and charts) and a *non-professional style* (average-quality paper, frequent changes in the margins and fonts, tables and charts lacking proper labels). Is counterbalancing necessary? Why or why not? Create a diagram illustrating the experimental design.

2. Professor Foley conducted a cola taste test. Each participant in the experiment first tasted two ounces of Coca-Cola, then two ounces of Pepsi, and finally two ounces of President's Choice brand cola. Participants rated the cola's flavour after each taste. What are the potential problems with this experimental design and the procedures used? Revise the design and procedures to address these problems. Consider several alternatives and think about the advantages and disadvantages of each.

3. Design an experiment to test the hypothesis that single-sex math classes are beneficial to adolescent girls. Operationally define both the independent and dependent variables. Your experiment should have two groups and use the matched pairs design. What variable will you use to match participants? Why? In addition, defend your choice of either a posttest-only design or a pretest-posttest design.

9

Conducting Studies

LEARNING OBJECTIVES

Keep these learning objectives in mind as you read to help you identify the most critical information in this chapter.

By the end of this chapter, you should be able to:

1	Describe issues to consider when manipulating independent variables.
2	Describe and give examples of ways to measure dependent variables.
3	Contrast floor effects and ceiling effects while discussing sensitivity of a dependent variable.
4	Discuss what it means to "set the stage" for participants.
5	Describe ways to control participant expectations and experimenter expectations.
6	Summarize steps for preparing for ethical approval and running a study.

Previous chapters have laid the foundation for planning basic studies. Before we consider advanced topics, here we focus on some practical aspects of conducting research. How does a researcher turn a design into an actual study for gathering data? We will follow the process first depicted in Chapter 1, with emphasis on the middle three steps: finalizing the study design, applying for ethical approval, and collecting data (see Figure 9.1). Although most of these steps apply to experiments as well as non-experiments, some issues are specific to experiments (e.g., manipulating the independent variable). This chapter will be particularly useful if you are conducting a study for a course project, volunteering as a research assistant, or completing an honours project, or if you will conduct research in your future career. For everyone, this chapter is intended as a guide to help tie together the practical aspects of the research process presented throughout this book.

FIGURE 9.1
Overview of research, with emphasis on this chapter's topics

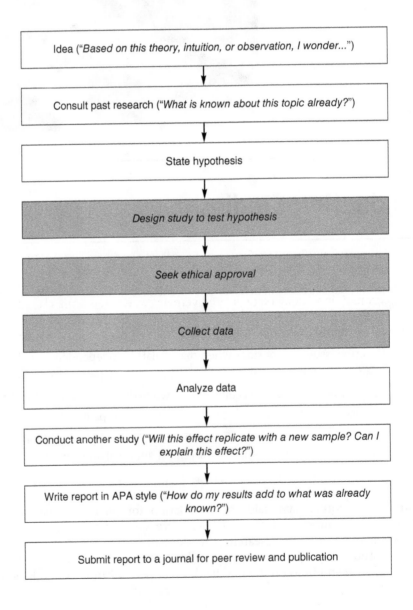

Idea ("*Based on this theory, intuition, or observation, I wonder...*")

Consult past research ("*What is known about this topic already?*")

State hypothesis

Design study to test hypothesis

Seek ethical approval

Collect data

Analyze data

Conduct another study ("*Will this effect replicate with a new sample? Can I explain this effect?*")

Write report in APA style ("*How do my results add to what was already known?*")

Submit report to a journal for peer review and publication

FINALIZING A STUDY DESIGN FOR DATA COLLECTION

Once you have a research idea, stated your hypothesis, and decided on a research design to test it (see Figure 9.1), the next steps involve detailing the operational definitions for each variable and creating an experience for your participants. Throughout this process, all efforts must be made to control as many elements of the situation as possible to ensure internal validity (see Chapter 8). All these details should be determined before applying for ethical approval.

To manipulate independent variables in experiments, and to measure variables in any study, you have to construct an *operational definition* of each variable; that is, you must turn a conceptual variable into a set of operations–specific instructions, events, and stimuli to be presented to participants. In Chapter 4, we considered some examples of operational definitions. Here, we emphasize various options a researcher has when creating them. There are no clear-cut rules for translating conceptual variables into specific operations. Exactly how the variable is operationally defined depends on the variable, cost, practicality, ethical concerns, and the researcher's creativity.

Options for Manipulating the Independent Variable

LOI

In experimental designs, researchers must decide on a way to manipulate the independent variable. One way to think about these operational definitions is to distinguish straightforward from staged manipulations.

Straightforward Manipulations   Researchers can manipulate a variable simply by presenting material to the participants. Such **straightforward manipulations** operationally define independent variables using instructions and stimulus presentations. Stimuli may be presented verbally, in written form, via videotape, or with a computer. Let's look at two examples.

Gaucher, Friesen, and Kay (2011) studied the impact of gendered language in job advertisements on job appeal. Both male and female participants were asked to read and rate job advertisements. In one condition, the advertisements were worded using masculine words (e.g., *dominant, independent, determined*); in the other condition, those words were replaced with feminine ones (e.g., *sensitive, collaborate, commitment*). To ensure experimental control, all details about the job were the same except those words. Female participants rated the femininely worded advertisements as more appealing than masculinely worded advertisements, whereas male participants preferred masculinely worded advertisements. The fact that researchers simply presented participants with stimulus material (i.e., the advertisements) makes this a straightforward manipulation. Researchers were able to conclude that job advertisements should be worded very carefully to avoid turning off potentially excellent candidates from particular demographic groups.

Much memory research relies on straightforward manipulations. For example, researchers at Dalhousie University showed participants words or pictures (e.g., of a kite) on a computer screen, one at a time (Quinlan, Taylor, & Fawcett, 2010). After each word or picture, participants were asked to remember or forget it. These materials (pictures versus words) and specific instructions (remember or forget) constitute two independent variables operationally defined using straightforward manipulations. Later, participants completed the dependent variable in the form of a recognition memory task. Overall, pictures were more memorable than words, even when participants had been asked to forget the pictures. These results suggested that intentionally trying to forget an image is more difficult than trying to forget a text-based description of that image. Think of that the next time you are considering whether to read a horror novel or see the movie!

Straightforward manipulations are used to operationally define many independent variables in all areas of behavioural research. Researchers vary the difficulty of material to be learned, the way questions are asked, the characteristics of people to be judged, and various other factors by presenting specific materials to participants and asking them to respond. Whenever the tasks involved in a study mimic experiences and conditions present in everyday life, the study is said to have high *mundane realism*. Reading job advertisements and judging how appealing they are (as participants did in Gaucher et al., 2011) is a task that job seekers do in everyday life. Deliberately trying to forget information and then trying to remember it (as participants did in Quinlan et al., 2010) is arguably less realistic. Therefore, we could argue that the job advertisement study has greater *mundane realism* than the memory study.

Staged Manipulations   Sometimes it is necessary to create a series of events that occur during the experiment to manipulate the independent variable successfully. These **staged manipulations** can be elaborate situations involving actors; at other times, they simply take the form of a cover story. Deception—with all its ethical concerns we explored in Chapter 3—is often involved in staged manipulations.

Staged manipulations are most frequently used for two reasons. First, the researcher may be trying to create some psychological state in the participants, such as frustration, anger, or a temporary lowering of self-esteem. For example, researchers have created situations where people believed they were interacting with another person, although the other person's contribution was actually a pre-recorded video (e.g., Cameron, Stinson, Gaetz, & Balchen, 2010). Nonetheless, that recording effectively influenced people's feelings.

Second, staged manipulations can be used to simulate some situation that occurs in the real world. White and Caird (2010) used the University of Calgary Driving Simulator to study the effects of conversing with a passenger on driving errors. Participants were randomly assigned to drive either alone or with a passenger. The passenger, a *confederate* (see below), engaged the participant in conversation throughout the driving simulation. Relative to the "alone" condition, the presence of this conversation did not affect how much time people spent looking at the road. However, it did reduce participants' ability to actually notice and respond to road hazards (e.g., pedestrian, motorcycle), especially for people who were attracted to the confederate. The conditions simulated common real-world environments that people experience while driving.

Staged manipulations sometimes employ a *confederate* (sometimes termed an *accomplice*). In the driving study by White and Caird (2010), the confederate was present and acting live; in the acceptance study by Cameron et al. (2010), the confederate's contribution was pre-recorded. Usually, the confederate is introduced as another participant in the experiment. A confederate may be useful to create a particular social situation and, sometimes, administer the independent variable. For example, in one study, sedentary women were randomly assigned to exercise on a treadmill alongside a confederate trained to give either positive or negative comments, depending on which condition the participant was in (Scarapicchia, Sabiston, Andersen, & Bengoechea, 2013). When the confederate expressed that she enjoyed running, participants chose to work out harder than when the confederate expressed hating running.

The staging involved in the running study was relatively minimal. For a more complex example of staging, consider a study conducted in a bar in the Netherlands (Larsen, Overbeek, Granic, & Engels, 2012). Participants were run in pairs in the campus bar; however, the second participant was actually a confederate. The experimenter offered the pair the chance to get acquainted before starting the study, during which time they could order two drinks paid for by the researchers. The confederate always chose first, and chose drinks that were either non-alcoholic (in one condition) or alcoholic (in the other condition). Participants drank more alcohol when the confederate ordered alcoholic beverages than when the confederate did not, demonstrating social influence in alcohol consumption in a field setting.

Staged manipulations demand a great deal of ingenuity and some acting ability. For example, look up Cameron et al.'s (2010) acceptance study to appreciate the importance of acting by the confederate and research assistants. The methods sections include multiple scripts! Staged manipulations are used to involve the participants in an ongoing social situation, which the individuals perceive not as an experiment but as a real experience. When a study engages and involves participants in this deep way, the study is said to have *experimental realism;* it is often easier to have high experimental realism in staged rather than straightforward manipulations. Researchers assume that the result will be natural behaviour that truly reflects the feelings and intentions of the participants. However, such procedures allow for a great deal of subtle interpersonal communication that is hard to put into words; this may make it difficult for other researchers to *replicate* the experiment. Also, a complex manipulation is difficult to interpret. If many things happened during the experiment, what *one* thing was responsible for the results? In general, it is easier to interpret results when the manipulation is relatively straightforward. However, the nature of the variable you are studying sometimes demands complicated procedures.

Additional Considerations When Manipulating the Independent Variable

Strength of the Manipulation   When deciding on precise operational definitions for each level of the independent variable, researchers consider **manipulation strength.** In general, try to make the manipulation as strong as possible. Essentially, this means making the levels of the independent variable maximally different, while keeping everything else between the two groups the same. This strong manipulation will increase the chances that your results will reveal an effect of the independent variable on the dependent variable, if one really exists.

To illustrate, consider two different ways University of Manitoba researcher Jessica Cameron and her colleagues (2010) manipulated the riskiness of social interactions in a set of elaborately staged manipulations. The purpose of these experiments was to examine the effects of self-esteem and risk of negative evaluation on feeling socially accepted by strangers. Riskiness of the interaction was the independent variable, and self-reported feelings of acceptance was the dependent variable. The strength of the manipulation differed in the two studies. In one study, the two levels of risk were *high risk* and *no risk*, whereas in the other study, the two levels were *high risk* and *less risk*. How were these variables operationally defined? In the first study, participants were led to believe that another participant (actually a confederate) had recorded a video to introduce themselves, and the person in this video was very warm and inviting. The video was the same in both conditions. Risk was manipulated by changing how the video was presented to the participant. It was presented as either a response to the participant's own introduction video that they had recorded earlier that session (i.e., *high-risk* condition) or as a response to someone else's introduction video (i.e., *no-risk* condition). Participants with high self-esteem rated the person in the video as more accepting of them (*high risk*) than of someone else (*no risk*). In contrast, low self-esteem participants rated the person in the video as being more accepting of someone else (*no risk*) than of themselves (*high risk*). In other words, the strong manipulation of risk produced an effect on feelings of acceptance that *interacted* with self-esteem (see Chapter 10 for further practice interpreting *interactions*).

A weaker manipulation of risk did not show differences in perceptions of social acceptance. In a second study, all participants interacted with a live confederate (who they thought was another participant). Risk was manipulated by providing people with different information about the confederate before the interaction. In the *high-risk* condition, participants were given some demographic information about the person. In the *less-risk* condition, participants were given a statement written by the person that admitted to a serious personal flaw. Researchers expected low self-esteem people to feel more accepted by someone who had just admitted a flaw, but the risk manipulation did not seem to influence feelings of acceptance. Of course, there are many possible reasons why results supported the hypothesis in the first study but not in the second. Elaborately staged manipulations are inherently challenging to control, and this summary provides only a snapshot of the whole context. Yet these studies illustrate how operational definitions can differ in strength. Across the two studies, *high-risk* social situations focused on whether someone likes you, a *less-risk* social situation focused on whether a flawed person likes you, and a *no-risk* social situation focused on whether someone likes someone else. Comparing high to low can lead to different conclusions than comparing high to no.

A note of caution: The strongest manipulation possible can sometimes be ethically problematic. Consider the bar study by Larsen and colleagues (2012) described earlier. People might have consumed even more alcohol if the confederate had ten drinks rather than two in the alcohol condition. Yet promoting that much alcohol consumption during an hour may put participants at risk of physical and psychological harm, thereby violating the ethical principle of *concern for welfare* (see Chapter 3). *Do you think this study already does violate that principle?*

Cost of the Manipulation   Cost is another issue when deciding how to manipulate the independent variable. Some government and private agencies offer grants for research (e.g., SSHRC, NSERC; see Chapter 3); because much research is costly, continued public support of these agencies is very important. Researchers who have limited monetary resources may not be able to afford expensive equipment, salaries for confederates, or payments to participants in long-term experiments. Also, a manipulation in which participants must be run individually (as in Cameron and colleagues' studies, 2010) requires more of the researcher's time than a manipulation that allows running many individuals at once. Straightforward manipulations are often much less costly than complex, staged, experimental manipulations.

Manipulation Checks   Researchers sometimes use a **manipulation check** to attempt to directly measure whether the independent variable manipulation induced the intended psychological state among participants. Manipulation checks can provide evidence for the *construct validity* of the manipulation (see Chapter 5). If you are manipulating anxiety to study its effect on memory, for example, a manipulation check will tell you whether participants in the high-anxiety group really were feeling more anxious than those in the low-anxiety condition. The manipulation check might involve a self-report of anxiety, a behavioural measure (e.g., number of arm and hand movements), or a physiological measure (e.g., heart rate change). Because a manipulation check might distract participants or inform them about the purpose of the experiment, it is difficult to decide when to administer it. If the effects of the independent variable are expected to last long enough, manipulation checks can be placed after measuring the dependent variable.

A manipulation check has two advantages. First, if the manipulation check is used in a pilot study and reveals that your manipulation was not effective, you can change the procedures before running the actual experiment. For instance, if the manipulation check shows that neither the low- nor the high-anxiety group was very anxious, you could change your procedures to increase anxiety further in the high-anxiety condition. In other words, you could increase the *strength* of the independent variable.

Second, a manipulation check is advantageous if the results show no effect of the independent variable on the dependent variable. If your manipulation did not successfully manipulate the independent variable, it is only reasonable that you will not find an effect. If both groups are equally anxious after you manipulate anxiety, anxiety can't affect the dependent measure. What if the check shows that the manipulation was successful, but you still do not find an effect? Then you know at least that the results were not due to a problem with the manipulation; the reason for not finding a relationship lies elsewhere. Perhaps you had a poor dependent measure, or perhaps there really is no relationship between the variables.

LO2

Options for Measuring Variables

In previous chapters, we have discussed various aspects of measuring variables, including reliability, validity, and reactivity, and observational and survey methods. Here, we emphasize some additional practical concerns when operationally defining variables that are measured, starting by outlining three broad categories: self-report, behavioural, and physiological. See Table 9.1 for a summary.

TABLE 9.1   Some ways to operationally define measured variables

Types of Measures	Some Examples of Techniques or Tools	Some Examples of Variables Operationally Defined Using These Techniques/Tools
Self-report	Paper-and-pencil questionnaire, face-to-face interview, online questionnaire	Attitudes, intentions to do something, rating someone's attractiveness, values, self-esteem, mood, recall, anxiety, preferences, attachment, depression, family conflict, relationship satisfaction, anxiety, personality
Behavioural	Counter, timer, audio or video recorder, eye tracker, measuring tape, Electronic Activated Recorder, weigh scale, camera, writing sample	Self-control (amount of ice cream eaten, length of persistence on boring task), creativity (number of ideas generated per minute), reaction time (speed of detecting a flashing light), facial expression of emotion (coded photographs), attention (eye tracker, number of hazards avoided in driving simulator), language complexity (writing sample), liking (distance seated apart from someone), efficacy of a bulimia intervention (weight gained or lost), memory (number of items recalled), generosity (amount of money donated)
Physiological	GSR, EMG, ECG, EEG, blood analysis, saliva analysis, heart rate, breathing rate, blood pressure, MRI, fMRI	Stress (sweating from GSR, cortisol in saliva), genetic marker for mental illness (blood analysis), physical fitness (heart rate change during exercise), size of amygdala or damage to hippocampus (MRI), brain activation when looking at image of romantic partner (fMRI)

Self-Report Measures   A **self-report measure** can be used to measure explicit attitudes, liking for someone, judgments about someone's personality characteristics, intended behaviours, emotional states, attributions about why someone performed well or poorly on a task, confidence in one's judgments, and many other aspects of human thought and behaviour. Rating scales with descriptive anchors are commonly used. For example, in Cameron and colleagues' self-esteem and social acceptance study described earlier in this chapter, after the independent variable was applied during the interaction with the confederate, participants were asked five questions about perceived social acceptance. All questions used a 7-point scale, like this one:

The other participant probably likes me.

1	2	3	4	5	6	7
Strongly Disagree	Disagree	Slightly Disagree	Neither Agree nor Disagree	Slightly Agree	Agree	Strongly Agree

If you are opting for this kind of self-report operational definition, use an existing scale that has been validated and published (see Chapter 5), or see Chapter 7 for question wording tips if creating your own.

Behavioural Measures   A **behavioural measure** is a direct observation of behaviours. As with self-reports, measurements of an almost endless number of behaviours are possible. Sometimes the researcher may record whether a given behaviour occurs–for example, whether an individual responds to a request for help, makes an error on a test, chooses to engage in one activity rather than another, or orders an alcoholic beverage. Often the researcher must decide whether to record the number of times a behaviour occurs in a given time period, the *rate* of a behaviour; how quickly a response occurs after a stimulus, a *reaction time*; or how long a behaviour lasts, a measure of *duration*. Deciding which aspect of behaviour to measure depends on which is most theoretically relevant to address the problem, or which measure logically follows from the independent variable manipulation. See Chapter 6 to further explore ways to code behaviours to count them.

Sometimes the nature of the variable being studied requires a particular type of measure. A measure of helping is almost by definition a behavioural measure, whereas a measure of perception of the personality characteristics of someone will employ a self-report measure. For many variables, however, both self-reports and behavioural measures could be appropriate. Interpersonal attraction could be measured on a self-report rating scale, or with behavioural measures of the physical distance two people place between themselves or the amount of time they spend looking into each other's eyes. A series of studies may be conducted to explore the effects of an independent variable on different types of measures.

Physiological Measures   A **physiological measure** is a recording of a response of the body. Many such responses are available (see Cacioppo, Tassinary, & Berntson, 2007). Consider some examples. The *galvanic skin response (GSR)* is a measure of general emotional arousal and anxiety. It measures the electrical conductance of the skin, which changes when sweating occurs. The *electromyogram* (EMG) measures muscle tension, and the *electrocardiogram* (ECG) measures heartbeat regularity and rate; both are used as measures of tension or stress. The *electroencephalogram* (EEG) is a measure of electrical activity of brain cells. It can be used to record general brain arousal as a response to different situations, activity in different parts of the brain as learning occurs, or brain activity during different stages of sleep. Reactions to stressors can be measured by analyzing the hormone cortisol in saliva (e.g., Pruessner et al., 2013). Blood sample analysis can reveal genetic aberrations associated with mental illness (e.g., Uher & Weaver, 2014). *Magnetic resonance imaging (MRI)* captures images of brain structures. It allows scientists to compare brain structures of people with a particular condition (e.g., a cognitive impairment or schizophrenia) with brain structures of people without the condition. A *functional MRI* (fMRI) scans the brain while a participant performs a physical or cognitive task. The data provide evidence for what brain processes are involved in these tasks. For example, researchers can see which areas of the brain are most active when judging whether other people are lying to us (Wu, Loke, Xu, & Lee, 2011).

Additional Considerations When Measuring Variables

[LO3]

Sensitivity   Recall that it is typically important to create strong independent variables that maximize the differences between groups. Likewise, the dependent variable should be sensitive enough to detect resulting differences between groups. A self-report measure of liking that asks, "Do you like this person?" with a simple "yes" or "no" response alternative is less sensitive than one that asks, "How much do you like this person?" on a 5- or 7-point scale. With the first measure, people may say yes even if they have some negative feelings about the person. The second measure is more sensitive by enabling a gradation of liking; such a scale would make it easier to detect differences in the amount of liking. Consider another example: reaction time. Changes in reaction time typically occur at the level of milliseconds (i.e., thousandths of seconds). A timer that measures only to the nearest second would not be *sensitive* enough to detect small differences in reaction time across conditions.

   The issue of **sensitivity** is particularly important when using behavioural measures of performance. Memory can be measured using recall, recognition, or reaction time; cognitive task performance might be measured by examining speed or number of errors during a proofreading task. Such tasks vary in their difficulty. Sometimes a task is so easy that everyone does well regardless of the independent variable condition. This results in what is called a **ceiling effect**— the independent variable might *appear* to have no effect on the dependent measure only because participants quickly reach the maximum performance level (i.e., the task is too easy). The opposite problem occurs when a task is so difficult that hardly anyone can perform well; this is called a **floor effect.**

Consider the example of a study investigating people's helping behaviour towards robots (Beran, Ramirez-Serrano, Kuzyk, Nugent, & Fior, 2011). Aware of the future expansion of robotics in society, the researchers wanted to test whether previous findings on helping behaviour would *generalize* beyond humans to human-like robots. The dependent measure was operationally defined using a simple coding scheme of *help* or *not help.* What would happen if all participants always helped the robot (i.e., a ceiling effect) or never helped the robot (i.e., a floor effect)? The researchers would be stuck! Any impact of manipulating the independent variable would not be detectable, because every-one would have acted in the same extreme way. Instead, researchers found that the dependent variable was appropriately sensitive: There was sufficient varia-bility in helping behaviour so that they could detect changes in helping caused by various independent variables. Specifically, 53 percent of children who were personally introduced to the robot helped it stack blocks, compared to only 28 percent of children who were not personally introduced to the robot.

Multiple Measures   Because any variable can be measured using various oper-ational definitions, researchers sometimes include multiple different measures of the same variable in their studies. In an experiment investigating music performance stress among young children, for example, researchers included three operational definitions of their dependent variable, stress: the children's self-reported stress about an upcoming performance, levels of the hormone cortisol in the children's saliva immediately after the performance, and observer ratings of anxious behaviours during the videotaped performances (Boucher & Ryan, 2011). If the independent variable has the same effect on several opera-tional definitions of the same dependent variable, our confidence in the results is increased. It is also useful to know whether the same independent variable affects some operational definitions of dependent variables but not others. For example, an independent variable designed to affect liking of a target person might influence people's self-reports of willingness to date them, but might not affect their willingness to work with them on a project. Researchers also may be interested in studying the effects of an independent variable on several entirely different dependent variables. For example, an experiment on the effects of a new active-learning technique might examine academic performance, quality of interaction among classmates, and teacher satisfaction.

When you have more than one measure, the question of *order* arises. Is it possible that responses to a measure will be different if it comes before or after another measure? The issue is similar to order effects in repeated measures designs (see Chapter 8). Perhaps responding to the first measures will some-how affect responses on the later measures; or perhaps people attend to the first measures more closely than later measures. There are two ways to deal with this issue. One strategy is to present the most important measures first and the less important ones later. Order will not be a problem in interpreting the results on the most important variables. Even though order may be a potential problem for some of the measures, the overall impact on the study is minimized. Another strategy is to *counterbalance* the order of presenting the measures (see Chapter 8).

Making multiple measurements in a single study can be efficient. However, it may be necessary to conduct a series of studies to explore the relationships between one variable and many others. To ensure ethical, open disclosure whenever multiple measures are used, it is important to include all of them in the research report, even if results are mixed (see Chapter 3).

Cost of Measures   Some measures are more expensive than others. Paper-and-pencil self-report measures are generally inexpensive; measures that require trained observers or elaborate equipment can become quite costly. A researcher studying attention, for example, might use an eye-tracking device to record each participant's eye movements while watching a film clip. Advanced statistical software would need to be purchased (and learned) to analyze the resulting data. Thus, there would be expenses for both equipment and personnel. Physiological data also can be expensive to obtain and analyze. Researchers need resources from the university or outside agencies to carry out such research.

Setting the Stage

LO4

Once you have decided on specific operational definitions for all variables, consider asking another researcher for feedback before moving forward. The next step will then be to plan the experience from the participant's viewpoint, or "set the stage" (Aronson, Brewer, & Carlsmith, 1985). There are no clear-cut rules for setting the stage, except that the study's setting must seem plausible to the participants. What is the exact procedure? How will you present and explain the sequence of tasks to participants? Will the participants fully understand what you are asking them to do?

In most cases, you will need to prepare the *informed consent* form (see Chapter 3) and explain to participants why the experiment is being conducted. Sometimes the rationale given is completely truthful, although only rarely will you want to tell participants the actual hypothesis (see *demand characteristics*, below). For example, you might say in a general way that you are conducting an experiment on memory when you are actually studying a specific aspect of memory, such as working memory capacity. If you decide that any deception is necessary, you will need to plan a debriefing session at the end of the experiment (see below).

If collecting data online, prepare the website including a welcoming message and a closing message thanking participants for their time. If collecting data in person or over the telephone, we recommend preparing a step-by-step script that starts with welcoming the participant to the study and finishes with debriefing and thanking the participant. Ensure that anyone who will be acting as an experimenter has practised using the script and is fluent in using it. Practice is important to ensure experimental control, especially when using elaborately staged manipulations. Once you have prepared all materials and set the stage for participants, there are just a few more issues to consider before applying for ethical approval from your institution's Research Ethics Board.

ADVANCED CONSIDERATIONS FOR ENSURING CONTROL

LO5

Good research design means eliminating as many alternative explanations for the results as possible. For example, researchers want to avoid operational definitions that *confound variables* (see Chapter 4). Additional control procedures may be necessary to address other types of alternative explanations. Two general control issues concern expectations on the part of both the participants and the experimenters. They tend to appear in experimental designs rather than non-experiments, so that is the context in which they are discussed.

Controlling for Participant Expectations

Demand Characteristics   Sometimes experimenters do not wish to inform participants about the specific hypotheses being studied or the exact purpose of the research. The reason for this lies in the problem of **demand characteristics** (Orne, 1962). A demand characteristic is any feature of a study that might inform participants of its purpose and consequently affect their behaviour. When participants form particular expectations about the hypothesis of the study, they might deliberately act in ways to confirm or undermine the hypothesis. Participants tend to act cooperatively, although not everyone does: Orne (1962) asked participants to repeatedly tear up their work, and many (but not all) complied. More recently, Nichols and Maner (2008) found that participants who had been told the hypothesis tended to act in ways that confirmed it, especially among participants who reported liking the experimenter.

One way to control for demand characteristics is to use *deception*—while "setting the stage," lead participants to think that the experiment is studying one thing when actually it is studying something else. The experimenter may devise elaborate cover stories to explain the purpose of the study and to disguise what is really being studied (see Laney et al., 2008, for a clever example in the context of false memory research). The researcher may also attempt to disguise the dependent measure by using an unobtrusive measure or by placing the measure among a set of unrelated **filler items** on a questionnaire. Another approach is to assess whether demand characteristics are a problem by asking participants about their perceptions of the purpose of the research (see Laney et al., 2008, for an example). It may be that participants do not have an accurate view of the purpose of the study; or if some individuals do guess the hypotheses of the study, their data may be analyzed separately.

Demand characteristics may be eliminated when people are not aware that an experiment is taking place or that their behaviour is being observed. Thus, observational research in which the observer is concealed or is using unobtrusive measures can minimize the problem of demand characteristics.

Placebo Effects   A special kind of participant expectation arises in research on the effects of treatments, including drugs. Consider an experiment investigating whether a drug such as Prozac reduces depression. People who have been diagnosed with depression are randomly assigned to receive the drug or not. Now suppose that the drug group shows an improvement. We do not know whether the improvement was caused by the properties of the drug or by what participants expect to feel after taking the drug–what is called a *placebo effect*. In other words, just administering a pill or an injection or another treatment may be sufficient to cause an observed improvement in behaviour. To control for this possibility, a **placebo group** can be added. To continue the drug example, participants in the placebo group receive a pill or injection containing an inert, harmless substance; they do not receive the drug given to members of the experimental group. If the improvement results from the active properties of the drug, the participants in the experimental group should show greater improvement than those in the placebo group. If the placebo group improves as much as the experimental group, the improvement is a placebo effect.

Sometimes, participants' expectations are the primary focus of an investigation. For example, Darredeau and Barrett (2010) conducted an experiment to determine whether nicotine inhalers reduce cigarette cravings because they contain nicotine or because users expect them to reduce cravings. The experimental design had four groups: (1) given nicotine–told nicotine, (2) given no nicotine–told no nicotine, (3) given nicotine–told no nicotine, (4) given no nicotine–told nicotine. This design is called a *balanced placebo design*. People who believed they had inhaled nicotine (Groups 1 and 4) reported very similar intentions to reduce smoking, although people in Group 4 were not actually given any nicotine. Believing nicotine was inhaled was more important than actually inhaling nicotine for reducing future intentions to smoke.

In some areas of research, the use of placebo control groups has ethical implications. Suppose you are studying a treatment that really has a positive effect on people (for example, by reducing symptoms of depression). It is important to use careful experimental procedures to make sure that the treatment is administered correctly, that the dependent variables are appropriately sensitive, and that alternative explanations, including a placebo effect, are eliminated. It is also important to help those people who are in the control conditions. Participants in the control conditions may be given the treatment after the study is completed. This practice is sometimes called a *waitlist control condition*.

Placebo effects are real and must seriously be studied in many areas of research. There has been much research and debate on the extent to which beneficial effects of antidepressant medications such as Prozac are due to placebo effects. Two *meta-analyses* (i.e., studies that combine the results of many single experiments; see Chapter 14) indicate that antidepressant medications may not have much greater effect than a placebo among people experiencing mild or moderate levels of depression, but that medication works better than a placebo among people with severe depression (Fournier et al., 2010; Kirsch et al., 2008).

Controlling for Experimenter Expectations

Experimenters are usually aware of the purpose of the study and thus may develop expectations about how participants should respond. These expectations can bias the results. This general problem is called **experimenter bias** or *experimenter expectancy effects* (Rosenthal, 1967, 2003).

Expectancy effects may occur whenever the experimenter knows which condition the participants are in. There are two potential sources of experimenter bias. First, the experimenter might unintentionally treat participants differently in the various conditions of the study. For example, certain words might be emphasized when reading instructions to one group but not the other, or the experimenter might smile more when interacting with people in one of the conditions. The second source of bias can occur when experimenters record participants' behaviours; there may be subtle differences in the way the experimenter interprets and records the behaviours.

Research on Expectancy Effects   Hundreds of studies have been conducted, many during the 1960s and 1970s, investigating the behavioural impact of expectations by experimenters, teachers, interviewers, and so on (Rosenthal, 2003). Perhaps the earliest demonstration of the problem is the case of Clever Hans, a horse whose alleged brilliance was revealed by Pfungst (1911) to be an illusion. Rosenthal (1967) describes Clever Hans:

> Hans, it will be remembered, was the clever horse who could solve problems of mathematics and musical harmony with equal skill and grace, simply by tapping out the answers with his hoof. A committee of eminent experts testified that Hans, whose owner made no profit from his horse's talents, was receiving no cues from his questioners. Of course, Pfungst later showed that this was not so, that tiny head and eye movements were Hans' signals to begin and to end his tapping. When Hans was asked a question, the questioner looked at Hans' hoof, quite naturally so, for that was the way for him to determine whether Hans' answer was correct. Then, it was discovered that when Hans approached the correct number of taps, the questioner would inadvertently move his head or eyes upward—just enough that Hans could discriminate the cue, but not enough that even trained animal observers or psychologists could see it. (p. 363)

An example of more systematic research on expectancy effects is a classic study by Rosenthal (1966). In this experiment, graduate students trained rats that were described as coming from either "bright" or "dull" genetic strains. The animals actually came from the same strain and had been randomly assigned to the bright and dull categories; however, the "bright" rats *did* perform better than the "dull" rats. Subtle differences in the ways the students treated the rats or recorded their behaviour must have caused this result.

If horses and rats can respond to subtle cues, it is reasonable to suppose that humans can too. Research has shown that experimenter expectancies can be communicated to humans by both verbal and nonverbal means (Doyen, Klein, Pichon, & Cleeremans, 2012; Jones & Cooper, 1971). In a controversial study, experimenters were told during their training that a manipulation would either cause participants to walk more quickly or more slowly (Doyen et al., 2012). It seems that experimenters unintentionally influenced participants' responses: Participants walked more slowly when experimenters expected them to do so than when they did not.

Expectations can also influence evaluations of behaviour, as illustrated in an experiment by Bruchmüller, Margraf, and Schneider (2012) that used a straightforward manipulation. Therapists were mailed a realistic case vignette in which an adolescent had enough symptoms to suggest attention-deficit/hyperactivity disorder (ADHD), but did not fully meet diagnostic criteria. The adolescent was more likely to be misdiagnosed with ADHD when presented as a boy than as a girl, when all other information was the same. The therapists' gendered expectations affected their diagnoses.

Solutions to the Expectancy Problem   There are a number of ways to address expectancy effects. One solution is to run everyone in all conditions simultaneously so that the experimenter's behaviour is exactly the same for all participants. This solution is feasible only under certain circumstances, such as when the study relies on printed materials and the experimenter's instructions to participants are the same for everyone. Alternatively, researchers can design computer programs to administer the independent variables and record responses. Such automated procedures leave little room for experimenter's expectations to influence results.

Other solutions target the experimenters. All experimenters should be well-trained and should practise behaving consistently with all participants. When they are particularly concerned about expectancy effects, researchers will use experimenters who are unaware of the hypothesis. The person conducting the study or making observations is blind regarding what is being studied or which condition the participant is in. In a **single-blind procedure,** the participants are unaware of which condition they are in (e.g., whether a placebo or the actual drug is being administered); in a **double-blind procedure,** neither the participant nor the experimenter knows the participant's condition. Double-blind procedures usually require two different experimenters—one who administers the independent variable, and another who takes over and administers the dependent variable.

Because researchers are aware of the problem of expectancy effects, solutions such as the ones just described are often incorporated into the procedures of the study. In addition, there are ways to design studies to specifically measure potential expectancy effects (see Klein et al., 2012). Sometimes these effects can be difficult to anticipate. Ask experienced colleagues to read your study's procedures or experience them as a mock participant. Their feedback may help you avoid expectancy effects, demand characteristics, or other problems before collecting data. Once your study is fully designed and materials are prepared, the next step before collecting data is to seek ethics approval.

SEEKING ETHICS APPROVAL

LO6

Ethical concerns are important throughout the research process. Recall from Chapter 3 that before collecting data, researchers must seek approval from their institution's *Research Ethics Board (REB)*. The REB will examine the procedure, materials, and informed consent form. Deception and other anticipated risks must be explained and justified. Researchers must also explain how they will ensure confidentiality and anonymity (if possible). In this section, we will emphasize two additional decisions that usually must be made before applying for ethics approval: the participant selection process and debriefing procedures. Table 9.2 offers a checklist summarizing common decisions that need to be made before applying for ethics approval. Consult your institution's REB to ensure you meet their criteria.

TABLE 9.2   Checklist: What to do before applying for ethics approval

_____	*Specifically operationally defined your independent variable (if applicable)*
_____	*Specifically operationally defined all measures (including dependent variables)*
_____	*Sought feedback from colleagues on the method (e.g., to avoid confounds)*
_____	*Listed the exact procedure each participant will experience*
_____	*Created all materials participants will use (e.g., online or paper-and-pencil questionnaire)*
_____	*Created the informed consent form*
_____	*Planned a way to debrief participants (if necessary)*
_____	*Justified who will be included and excluded from participating (if targeting a particular population, explain why)*
_____	*Determined the number of participants to be run in the study*
_____	*Prepared participant recruitment materials (e.g., poster, e-mail)*
_____	*Determined how confidentiality and anonymity will be maintained during and after data collection*
_____	*Minimized any foreseeable risks; noted any foreseeable benefits*
_____	*Completed institutional Research Ethics Board's application form*

Selecting Research Participants

The focus of your study may be children, university students, elderly adults, rats, pigeons, primates, or even bees or flatworms; in all cases, the participants or subjects must somehow be selected. The method used to select participants must be justified to the REB (in the case of humans) or the Animal Care Committee (in the case of non-human animals), and has implications for *generalizing* research results. In the case of human participants, the procedures you plan to use to recruit participants will likely need to be approved by your REB (to ensure they are not coercive or misleading). Prepare these procedures thoughtfully before applying for approval.

Recall from Chapter 7 that most research projects involve *sampling* research participants from a *population* of interest. For example, a researcher might be interested in the population of people who suffer from schizophrenia, or the population of people who are bilingual, or the population of all Canadians living in Canada. Samples may be drawn from any population using probability (i.e., random) sampling or non-probability sampling techniques (see Chapter 7). A brief refresher: Whenever it is important to accurately *generalize* characteristics to a specific population, probability sampling is essential; research aimed at testing hypotheses tends to rely on non-probability convenience samples such as university undergraduates. The issue of generalizing results is discussed in more detail in Chapter 14.

Whenever a specific population is targeted, it must be justified. Recall from Chapter 3 that the principle of *justice* requires that the benefits and burdens of research participation are fairly distributed. Special procedures will be needed when studying experiences of members of sensitive populations, such as Aboriginal peoples, people with mental illnesses, children, or people living in institutions (e.g., prisons). Consult your institution's REB for advice on conducting such research ethically.

How many participants will you need in your study? In general, increasing your sample size increases the likelihood that you will find an effect, assuming there is one to be found, because larger samples provide more accurate estimates of population values (see Table 7.2). Most researchers select sample sizes typical for studies in the topic area they are studying, although recent recommendations suggest using many more than has been the norm (Simmons, Nelson, & Simonsohn, 2013). A more formal approach to selecting a sample size is discussed in Chapter 13.

Planning the Debriefing

After all data are collected, a *debriefing* session provides an opportunity for the researcher to explain the ethical and educational implications of the study, verbally and/or in writing (*debriefing letters* are common in research fully conducted online). Debriefing sessions should always occur whenever any form of deception has been used (see Chapter 3). These sessions include an explanation of why the deception was considered necessary, reassurance that believing the deception does not reflect poorly on the person, and an apology to attempt to repair negative feelings. Debriefing sessions are also especially important whenever participants are put at any sort of risk. If the study is expected to trigger psychological disturbance, researchers may offer contact information for campus counselling services.

When running participants in person, the debriefing session can also provide an opportunity to learn more about what participants were thinking during the study, including what they believed to be the purpose of the study. After experiments, participants can be asked how they interpreted the independent variable manipulation, and what they were thinking when they responded to the dependent measures. Chartrand and Bargh (2000) offer a specific set of questions to probe for suspicion after using deception, called a *funnelled debrief*. Resulting information can prove useful in interpreting the results and planning future studies.

Researchers may ask the participants to refrain from discussing the study with others. Such requests are typically made when more people will be participating and they may talk with one another in classes or residence halls. People who have already participated are aware of the general purposes and procedures; it is often important that these individuals avoid revealing this information to potential future participants.

COLLECTING DATA

LO6

Once you have received ethical approval, you are almost ready to collect data! Examine Table 9.3 for a final checklist to be sure you are ready for your first participants. There are two additional issues to keep in mind: (1) whether to complete a pilot study, and (2) commitments that researchers have to the participants.

Pilot Studies

When procedures are particularly elaborate or costly, or when there will be only a single opportunity to collect data, researchers sometimes choose to conduct a **pilot study** in which the researcher does a "trial run" with a small number of participants drawn from the same population as the sample he or she ultimately hopes to test. Because data are collected from participants, the pilot study must be included in the ethics application.

The pilot study will reveal whether participants understand the instructions, whether the total experimental setting seems plausible, whether any questions are confusing, and so on. The pilot study can be especially important when using a staged manipulation of the independent variable, to ensure that the scenario is meaningful and believable for participants. Sometimes, participants in the pilot study are questioned in detail about the experience following the experiment. Another method is to use the "think aloud"

TABLE 9.3   Checklist: What to do before collecting data

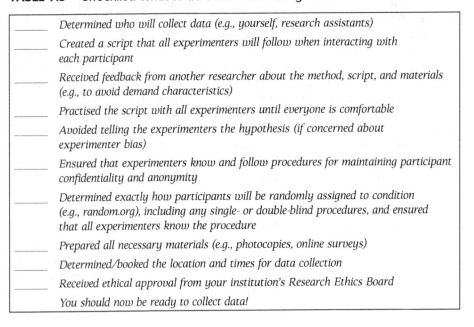

_____	*Determined who will collect data (e.g., yourself, research assistants)*
_____	*Created a script that all experimenters will follow when interacting with each participant*
_____	*Received feedback from another researcher about the method, script, and materials (e.g., to avoid demand characteristics)*
_____	*Practised the script with all experimenters until everyone is comfortable*
_____	*Avoided telling the experimenters the hypothesis (if concerned about experimenter bias)*
_____	*Ensured that experimenters know and follow procedures for maintaining participant confidentiality and anonymity*
_____	*Determined exactly how participants will be randomly assigned to condition (e.g., random.org), including any single- or double-blind procedures, and ensured that all experimenters know the procedure*
_____	*Prepared all necessary materials (e.g., photocopies, online surveys)*
_____	*Determined/booked the location and times for data collection*
_____	*Received ethical approval from your institution's Research Ethics Board*
	You should now be ready to collect data!

protocol (described in Chapter 7) in which participants in the pilot study are instructed to verbalize their thoughts about everything that is happening during the study. Such procedures provide the researcher with an opportunity to make any necessary changes in the method before conducting the entire study. Moreover, a pilot study allows experimenters who are collecting the data to become comfortable with their roles and to standardize their procedures. If you wish to make changes to the method or materials after the pilot study, submit an *amendment* to your original ethics application for updated approval.

Researcher Commitments

Researchers make several implicit "contracts" with participants during the course of a study. For example, if participants agree to be present for a study at a specific time, it is crucial that the researcher or research assistant collecting data is there. Participants notice punctuality and list it as important when asked about the obligations of the researcher (Epstein, Suedfeld, & Silverstein, 1973). If researchers promise to send a summary of results to participants, they should do so. If participants are to receive course credit for participation, the researcher must immediately follow through on this promise. These are little details, but they are very important in maintaining trust between participants and researchers, thereby supporting the advancement of science.

WHAT COMES NEXT?

Analyzing and Interpreting Results

After data have been collected, the next step is to analyze them. Statistical analyses allow the researcher to examine and interpret the pattern of data obtained in the study. Are the variables *significantly* related to each other? Does the independent variable have a large, small, or no effect on the dependent variable? We will explore basic statistical concepts in Chapters 12 and 13; some additional calculations are provided in Appendix B. Depending on the results of the study, the researcher might choose to conduct a follow-up study to see if the results can be *replicated* using a new sample of participants (see Chapter 14), to rule out alternative explanations or deal with problems in the first study, and to extend knowledge even further.

Communicating Research to Others

The final step is to write a report that details why you conducted the research, how you obtained the participants, what procedures you used, and what you found (see Chapter 2 for the common APA style format and Appendix A for further tips). Researchers report their results at scientific conferences, and by submitting them for publication in journals.

Professional Conferences   National and regional professional associations such as the Canadian Psychological Association (CPA), the American Psychological Association (APA), and the Association for Psychological Science (APS) hold annual meetings at which psychologists and psychology students present their own research and learn about the latest research being done by their colleagues. Journalists also attend so that they can write articles communicating the latest research to the public. Frequently, researchers deliver verbal presentations to an audience. Poster sessions are also common; here, researchers display posters summarizing the research and are available for discussion. See Appendix A for an example poster layout.

Journal Articles   There are many journals in which research papers are published (see Chapter 2 for examples). When a researcher submits a paper to a journal, the editor sends it for *peer review:* two or more other scientists read the paper and recommend acceptance (often with the stipulation that revisions be made) or rejection (which is much more common than acceptance). As many as 90 percent of papers submitted to the more prestigious journals are rejected. Many rejected papers are submitted to other journals and eventually accepted for publication, but much research is never published. Although such rejection can be a negative experience for individual researchers, it is good for science to ensure the separation of high-quality research from that of lesser quality.

This chapter emphasized the process that researchers take to convert their research designs into studies ready for participants to experience. As you can see, there are many decisions that must be made while specifying operational definitions and procedures, applying for ethical approval, and preparing experimenters to interact with participants. No study will ever be designed or executed perfectly, but careful planning along with advice from experienced colleagues will help you draw meaningful conclusions from your results.

STUDY TERMS

Test yourself! Define and generate an example of each of these key terms.

Behavioural measure (p. 185)

Ceiling effect (p. 186)

Demand characteristics (p. 189)

Double-blind procedure (p. 192)

Experimenter bias (p. 191)

Filler items (p. 189)

Floor effect (p. 187)

Manipulation check (p. 183)

Manipulation strength (p. 182)

Physiological measure (p. 186)

Pilot study (p. 195)

Placebo group (p. 190)

Self-report measure (p. 185)

Sensitivity (p. 186)

Single-blind procedure (p. 192)

Staged manipulations (p. 180)

Straightforward manipulations (p. 179)

REVIEW QUESTIONS

Test yourself on this chapter's learning objectives. Can you answer each of these questions?

1. Compare and contrast staged versus straightforward options for manipulating an independent variable.

2. Why is it important to consider the strength of the independent variable manipulation? How might a researcher determine whether it is strong enough?

3. Contrast three different ways to measure dependent variables.

4. When a dependent variable is *sensitive*, what does that mean? What are ceiling and floor effects?

5. What are demand characteristics? Describe ways to minimize demand characteristics.

6. What does "setting the stage" involve? How might it determine the content of the debriefing?

7. What are experimenter expectancy effects? What are some solutions to the experimenter bias problem?

8. What are all the decisions that need to be made before applying for ethical approval? Are pilot studies included in the ethics application?

9. How would you train someone to be the experimenter for your study?

DEEPEN YOUR UNDERSTANDING

Develop your mastery of these concepts by considering these application questions. Compare your responses with those from other people in your study group.

1. Dr. Turk studied the relationship between age and reading comprehension, specifically predicting that older people will show lower comprehension than younger people. Groups of participants who were 20, 30, 40, and 50 years old read a chapter from a popular book written by physicist Stephen W. Hawking (1988) for general audiences entitled *A Brief History of Time: From the Big Bang to Black Holes.* After reading the chapter, participants were given a comprehension measure. Results showed no relationship between age and comprehension scores; all age groups had equally low comprehension scores. Why do you think no relationship was found? Identify at least two possible reasons.

2. Revisit the experiment on facilitated communication by children with autism (Montee, Miltenberger, & Wittrock, 1995) that was described in Chapter 2 as an example of using past research to generate ideas. Interpret the findings of that study in terms of experimenter expectancy effects.

3. Your lab group has been assigned the task of designing an experiment to investigate the effect of time spent studying on a recall task. Thus far, your group has come up with the following plan: "Participants will be randomly assigned to two groups. People in one group will study a list of five words for five minutes, and those in the other group will study the same list for seven minutes. Immediately after studying, participants will read a list of ten words and circle those that appeared on the original study list." Make at least two improvements to this experiment, and explain why those changes are useful.

4. Design an experiment using a staged manipulation to test the hypothesis that when people are in a good mood, they are more likely to contribute to charity. Include a manipulation check in your design.

Complex Experimental Designs

LEARNING OBJECTIVES

Keep these learning objectives in mind as you read to help you identify the most critical information in this chapter.

By the end of this chapter, you should be able to:

1	Define a *factorial design* and discuss reasons why a researcher would use this design.
2	Describe what information is provided by main effects and interaction effects in a factorial design.
3	Interpret a graph depicting results from a 2 × 2 experimental design. Use this graph to estimate whether there is one main effect, two main effects, and/or an interaction effect on the dependent variable.
4	Discuss the role of simple main effects in interpreting interactions.
5	Describe an IV × PV design.
6	Compare the assignment of participants in an independent groups design, a repeated measures design, and a mixed factorial design.

So far we have focused primarily on the simplest experimental design, in which one independent variable is manipulated with two levels, and one dependent variable is measured. Researchers often investigate problems that demand more complicated designs, including the complex experimental designs we explore in this chapter. The fundamental aspects of all experimental research, such as internal validity and procedures for assigning participants to conditions, still hold true.

AN INDEPENDENT VARIABLE CAN HAVE MORE THAN TWO LEVELS

In the simplest experimental design, the independent variable has only two **levels** (also called *groups* or *conditions*). However, a researcher might want to design an experiment with three or more levels for several reasons. Researchers are frequently interested in comparing more than two groups. For example, in a study examining the use of virtual reality in stress reduction, participants who were experiencing stress were randomly assigned to explore one of three virtual reality environments: nature, a city, or a geometric shape control condition (Valtchanov & Ellard, 2010). People who explored a virtual natural environment showed the greatest decrease in stress and increase in attention span, compared to people in both the city and shape conditions. Adding the shape condition helped researchers gain some insight into why people react differently to natural versus city environments.

A design with only two levels of the independent variable may not provide enough information about the exact form of the relationship between the independent and dependent variables. Consider a study where two groups of people are compared on their performance on a motor task. One group is promised $40.00 for high performance, whereas the control group is not promised a reward. Figure 10.1 depicts the results of this hypothetical study. The solid line connects the points representing the average score on the motor task for

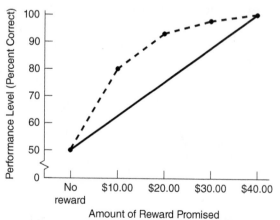

FIGURE 10.1
Results of a hypothetical experiment: positive linear versus positive non-linear functions

participants in the "no reward" group and the "$40.00" group. Because there are only two levels of the independent variable, the relationship can be described only with a straight line. We do not know what the relationship would be if other amounts were included as levels of the independent variable. The broken line in Figure 10.1 shows possible results when $10.00, $20.00, and $30.00 are also included as levels of the independent variable. This result is a more nuanced description of the relationship between the amount of reward promised (i.e., the independent variable) and performance (i.e., the dependent variable).

In this hypothetical experiment, the amount of reward is very effective in increasing performance up to a point (i.e., $20), after which only modest increases in performance accompany increases in reward. Thus, the relationship is a non-linear positive relationship rather than a strictly linear relationship (see Chapter 4). Such a result would be useful for deciding how much money you needed to pay employees or participants, for example. An experiment with only two levels of the independent variable could not yield such nuanced information. To foreshadow upcoming concepts (see Chapter 13), you may note that when an experiment with a single independent variable has two levels, it can be analyzed using a statistical technique called a *t test;* when there are three or more levels (or more than one independent variable), an *analysis of variance (ANOVA)* is the required test.

Recall from Chapter 4 that variables are sometimes related in a curvilinear fashion; that is, the direction of relationship changes. Figure 10.2 shows an example of a type of curvilinear relationship called an *inverted-U,* so named because the relationship has an upside-down U shape. An experimental design with only two levels of the independent variable cannot detect curvilinear relationships between variables. If a curvilinear relationship is predicted, at least three levels must be used. As Figure 10.2 shows, if only levels 1 and 3 of the independent variable had been used, no relationship between the variables would have been detected. Many such curvilinear relationships exist in psychology. The relationship between fear arousal and attitude change is one example. Increasing the amount of fear aroused by a persuasive message increases attitude change up to a moderate level of fear; further increases in fear arousal actually reduce attitude change.

FIGURE 10.2
Curvilinear
relationship

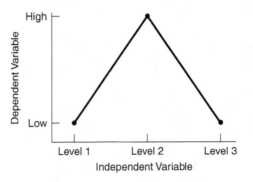

Note: At least three levels of the independent variable are required to show curvilinear relationships.

AN EXPERIMENT CAN HAVE MORE THAN ONE INDEPENDENT VARIABLE: FACTORIAL DESIGNS

LOI

Researchers often manipulate two or three independent variables in a single experiment. This type of experimental design is a closer approximation of real-world conditions, in which independent variables interact with other variables to produce behaviour. Recall the hypothetical crowding experiment that was described in Chapter 8. For experimental control, the number of people need to be kept constant; all participants should be run with the same number of other people in the room. Another option is to study whether the number of people influences test performance when people are crowded together. You could design an experiment with two independent variables–in this case, you could study the effects of crowding and number of people at the same time. Complex experimental designs–called *factorial designs*–allow you to do that.

A **factorial design** has more than one independent variable (or *factor*), and all levels of each independent variable (IV) are combined with all levels of the other independent variables. The simplest factorial design has two independent variables, each with two levels. The general format for describing factorial designs is

Number of levels of first IV × Number of levels of second IV.

When there are two independent variables, each with two levels, it is often expressed as a "2 × 2," which reads "two by two" factorial design.

An experiment by McFerran, Dahl, Fitzsimons, and Morales (2010) nicely illustrates a 2 × 2 factorial design. These researchers studied the effects of body type on others' food consumption. Participants (all students at the University of British Columbia) were told that the study was about experiences viewing movies, and they were offered a snack while they were viewing these movies. All participants were run in pairs, but the other "participant" was actually a *confederate*. One independent variable was the amount of snack food the confederate selected (30 candies or 2 candies). The other independent variable was the confederate's body size, which also had two levels: thin versus obese. Researchers had a suit created by an award-winning costume designer, which increased the confederate's natural size from a 00 to a 16, adding approximately 80 pounds (34 kg) to her frame. (If you'd like to see pictures of this amazing transformation, use the reference to find this article.) The dependent variable is the number of candies the participant ate.

This 2 × 2 design results in four experimental conditions (literally multiply two by two), each with a different combination of the two independent variables (see Table 10.1). Participants were randomly assigned to experience one of these four combinations: (1) thin confederate–30 candies, (2) thin confederate–2 candies, (3) obese confederate–30 candies, and (4) obese confederate–2 candies. We will use this study throughout this chapter to illustrate key concepts in factorial designs.

TABLE 10.1   2 × 2 factorial design: Results of the body type and food choices study

Confederate food selection (independent variable A)	Confederate body type (independent variable B)		Marginal means (shows main effect of A)
	Thin	Obese	
30 candies	9.82	6.25	8.12
2 candies	3.20	4.26	3.72
Marginal means (shows main effect of B)	6.51	5.26	

Based on McFerran, B., Dahl, D.W., Fitzsimons, G.J., & Morales, A.C. (2010). I'll have what she's having: Effects of social influence and body type on the food choices of others. *Journal of Consumer Research, 36,* 915-929.

LO2

Interpreting Factorial Designs

Factorial designs yield two distinct kinds of information. The first is information about the effect of each independent variable taken by itself: the **main effect** of each independent variable. In a design with two independent variables, there are two main effects, one for each independent variable. The second type of information is called an **interaction.** If there is an interaction between two independent variables, the way that one independent variable affects the dependent variable depends on the particular level of the other variable. Interactions are a completely different and very valuable source of information that cannot be obtained in a simple experimental design in which only one independent variable is manipulated.

To illustrate main effects and interactions, we can look at the results of McFerran and colleagues' (2010) study on the influence of others on food choices. Table 10.1 illustrates a common method of presenting outcomes for the various groups in a factorial design. The number in each **cell** of the table represents the mean number of candies people ate. (The *mean* is the formal term for "arithmetic average"; see Chapter 12.) The mean score on the dependent variable for participants who received the *thin confederate–30 candies* combination of independent variables can be found in that corresponding cell: It is 9.82. As we explore main effects and interactions, it may be helpful to refer back to Table 10.1 each time a variable or value is discussed.

Main Effects   A main effect is the effect that each independent variable *by itself* has on the dependent variable. The main effect of independent variable A (i.e., confederate food selection in the example above) captures its overall effect on the dependent variable (i.e., participants' candy consumption). Similarly, the main effect of independent variable B captures the effect of this independent variable (i.e., confederate body type) on the dependent variable.

Essentially, the main effect pretends that the other independent variable didn't exist in the experiment. Consider independent variable B: Is there a relationship between confederate body type and candy consumption? We can find out by looking at the **marginal mean** in the thin and obese conditions. These means are shown in the bottom row (which, along with the rightmost column, are called the *margins* of the table) of Table 10.1. The overall amount of candy eaten by all participants in the thin confederate condition (regardless of how much she ate) is 6.51, and the amount of candy eaten in the obese confederate condition (regardless of how much she ate) is 5.26. Note that the marginal mean of 6.51 in the thin confederate condition is the average of 9.82 in the *thin confederate–30 candies* group and 3.20 in the *thin confederate–2 candies* group. (This calculation assumes equal numbers of participants in each group.) You can see that overall, people ate more candy when in the company of someone who is thin rather than obese. Statistical tests would enable us to determine whether this is a significant main effect, but those calculations are beyond the scope of this chapter.

The main effect for independent variable A (confederate food selection) is the overall relationship between that independent variable, by itself, and the dependent variable. Examine Table 10.1 to see that the marginal mean in the 30 candies condition (regardless of confederate body type) is 8.12, and the marginal mean in the 2 candies condition (regardless of confederate body type) is 3.72. Thus, in general, people eat more candy when in the company of someone who takes 30 rather than 2 candies for herself.

Interactions   The two main effects tell us that, overall, people eat more candy (A) when their companion takes lots of candy rather than a little candy and (B) when their companion is thin rather than obese. There is also the possibility that an interaction exists; if so, interpreting the interaction is most important, as it indicates that the main effects must be qualified. An interaction between independent variables indicates that the effect of one independent variable is different at different levels of the other independent variable.

Examine Table 10.1 to try to find an interaction. Look at the vertical columns to see that the effect of confederate food selection is different depending on whether she is thin or obese. When a person's eating companion is thin, people eat more candy when she takes many rather than few candies (9.82 in the 30 candies condition and 3.20 in the 2 candies condition). However, when the eating companion is obese, the amount of food she takes has a much smaller effect (6.25 for 30 candies versus 4.26 for 2 candies). Thus, the relationship between eating companion's body type and food consumption can be understood only by considering both independent variables simultaneously. To know how eating is affected, we must consider the companion's body type *and* whether she takes a lot of food or only a little.

Sometimes it helps to see interactions when the means for all conditions are presented in a graph. So you can compare graph styles, Figure 10.3 shows

FIGURE 10.3
Interaction
between com-
panion's body
type and food
selection on
amount eaten,
graphed in
two ways

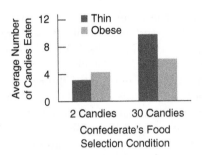
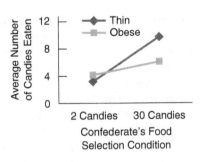

Adapted from McFerran, B., Dahl, D.W., Fitzsimons, G.J., & Morales, A.C. (2010). I'll have what she's having: Effects of social influence and body type on the food choices of others. *Journal of Consumer Research, 36,* 915–929.

both a bar graph and a line graph of the same results of the body type and food choices experiment that are displayed in Table 10.1. Note that all four cell means have been graphed. Two bars (on the left) compare the body types in the 2 candies condition; the same comparison is shown for the 30 candies condition. You can see that an eating companion's body type does not influence candy consumption much when she eats only 2 candies; however, when she eats 30 candies, her body type has a greater influence on how much people eat.

You probably use the concept of interaction all the time without realizing it. When we say "it depends," we are usually indicating that some sort of interaction is operating—it depends on some other variable. Suppose, for example, that a friend asks you if you want to go to a movie. The likelihood that you will go may reflect an interaction between two variables, such as (1) Is an exam coming up? and (2) Who stars in the movie? If there is an exam coming up, you won't go under any circumstance. If you do not have an exam to worry about, you may be more likely to go if your favourite actor is in the movie, but less likely to go if your least favourite actor is in the movie. The variables *exam* and *actor* interact to affect the likelihood you will go to the movie.

Try it out! For practice, you could try graphing the movie example in the same way we graphed the food study example in Figure 10.3. The dependent variable (going to the movie) is always placed on the vertical (Y) axis. It could have values ranging from 0 (absolutely will not go) to 100 (absolutely will go); 50 would indicate a 50/50 chance of going. The levels of one independent variable (e.g., upcoming exam) are placed on the horizontal (X) axis. Bars are then drawn to represent each of the levels of the other independent variable. Graphing the results in this manner is a useful method of visualizing interactions in a factorial design.

Interactions Illuminate Moderator Variables

In many studies, interactions are discussed in terms of a **moderator variable.** A moderator variable influences the relationship between two other variables (Baron & Kenny, 1986). In the study by McFerran et al. (2010), the main effect of a companion's food selection enables us to state the relationship between this variable and consumption generally: *People eat more food when an eating companion takes more rather than less food to eat.* However, because we have an interaction, we must then make a qualifying statement that the companion's body type influences (or *moderates*) this relationship: *People eat more food when an eating companion overindulges only when the companion is thin; when the companion takes little food, the amount people eat is not influenced by the companion's body type.* The body type variable is a moderator variable because it *moderates* (changes) the relationship between the other variables. Moderator variables may be aspects of the situation, as in this food study, or they may be participant variables (discussed later).

Depicting Possible Outcomes of a 2 × 2 Factorial Design Using Tables and Graphs

LO3

Recall that a 2 × 2 factorial design has two independent variables, each with two levels. When analyzing the results, there are several possibilities: (1) There may or may not be a main effect for independent variable A; (2) there may or may not be a main effect for independent variable B; and (3) there may or may not be an interaction between the independent variables. (Note that for each of these three possible effects, a researcher would run a statistical test to see if any difference noted is *statistically significant.* We will discuss statistical significance in Chapter 13. For now, we consider these three effects conceptually.)

Figure 10.4 illustrates eight possible outcomes in a 2 × 2 factorial design. This figure might look a bit alarming at first—we will walk you through interpretation and we encourage you to practise. For each outcome, the means are given in a table and then graphed using a line graph. The means that are given in the figure are idealized examples; such perfect outcomes rarely occur in actual research. Nevertheless, you should explore the graphs to determine for yourself why, in each case, there is or is not a main effect for A, a main effect for B, and an A × B interaction. Before you begin studying the graphs, it will help to think of concrete variables to represent the two independent variables and the dependent variable. You might want to think about the example of crowding and group size. Suppose that independent variable A is crowding (A_1 is *low crowding,* operationally defined as chairs placed 1 metre apart; A_2 is *high crowding,* operationally defined as chairs placed 1 centimetre apart), and independent variable B is group size (B_1 is *ten people* per room; B_2 is *two people* per room). The dependent variable is performance on a cognitive task, with higher numbers indicating better performance.

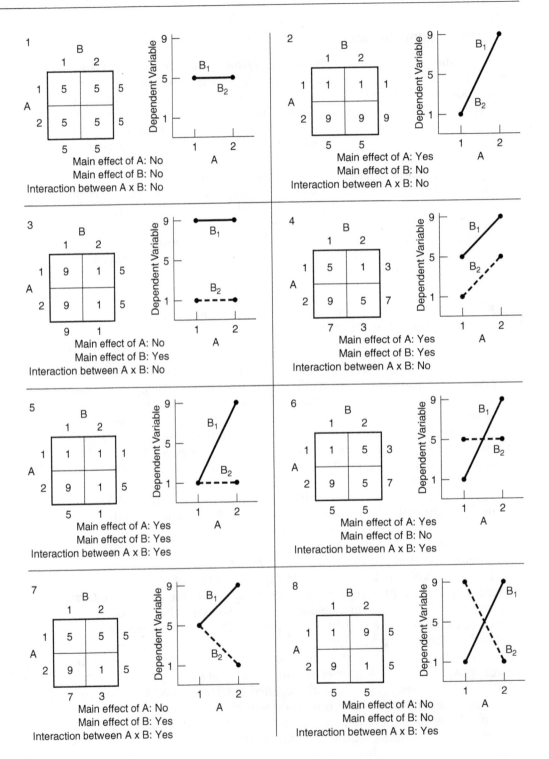

FIGURE 10.4
Outcomes of a factorial design with two independent variables

How can you tell what effects are present, given a graph? An interaction effect is easiest to spot: Are the two lines in the graph parallel to each other? If the lines are *not parallel*, there *is* an interaction–the effect of one variable is different at different levels of the other variable. To detect main effects, it is easiest to examine the table rather than the graph because the *marginal means* stand out. Examine whether each graph in Figure 10.4 is depicting a main effect of factor A and/or a main effect of factor B.

The first four graphs in Figure 10.4 illustrate outcomes in which there is no A × B interaction (note the parallel lines), and the last four graphs depict outcomes in which there is an interaction between independent variables A and B (note the non-parallel lines). When there is an interaction, you need to carefully examine the means, which are given in the corresponding tables, to understand the specific pattern of the interaction. In some cases, there is a strong relationship between the first independent variable and the dependent variable at one level of the second independent variable; however, there is no relationship or a weak relationship at the other level of the second independent variable (e.g., panel 5). In other studies, the interaction may indicate that an independent variable has opposite effects on the dependent variable, depending on the level of the second independent variable. This pattern is shown in panel 8, the last graph in Figure 10.4.

Test yourself! The independent and dependent variables in Figure 10.4 do not have concrete variable labels. As an exercise, interpret each of the graphs using actual variables from two different hypothetical experiments (described below). This test works best if you draw the graphs on paper, including labels for the variables (but not the answers!), separately for each experiment. For each hypothetical experiment, after you have labelled each graph with the variable names, consider whether the graph depicts a main effect of A, a main effect of B, and/or an A × B interaction. Once you have identified what effects are represented, try explaining in words what each graph would tell us about the relationships of those independent variables with the dependent variable.

You can try depicting the data as either line graphs or bar graphs. The data points in both types of graphs are the same and both have been used in this chapter (see Figure 10.3 for a direct comparison). In general, line graphs are used when the levels of the independent variable on the horizontal axis (independent variable A) are quantitative–low and high amounts. Bar graphs are more likely to be used when the levels of the independent variable are nominal, representing different categories, such as one type of therapy compared with another type.

Hypothetical experiment 1: Effect of age of defendant and type of substance use during an offence on months of sentence. Participants read a scenario of a male, age 20 or 50, who was found guilty of causing a traffic accident while under the influence of either alcohol or marijuana, and then assigned him a jail sentence.

Independent variable A: Type of offence (alcohol versus marijuana)

Independent variable B: Age of defendant (20 versus 50 years of age)

Dependent variable: Months of sentence (range from 0 to 10 months)

Hypothetical experiment 2: Effect of previously seen violence and sexual content on recall of advertisements. Participants viewed on a computer screen a video that was either violent or not violent. Next, they were then asked to read print ads for eight different products over the next three minutes. Ads featured either scantily clad models or fully clothed models. The dependent variable was the number of ads correctly recalled.

Independent variable A: Exposure to violence (non-violent versus violent video)

Independent variable B: Ad content (scantily clad models versus fully clothed models)

Dependent variable: Number of ads recalled (range from 0 to 8)

LO4

Breaking Down Interactions into Simple Main Effects

If you take a look at Table 10.1 and Figure 10.3 once again, there appears to be an interaction between the two independent variables. To find out whether any apparent main effects and/or the interaction are statistically significant, we would use a procedure called *analysis of variance* (see Chapter 13). Whenever there is a significant interaction, we need to break it down further to understand it. The next step is to look at the simple main effects. A **simple main effect** analysis examines the mean differences at *each level* of one independent variable. Take a moment to contrast two similar-sounding ideas. The *main effect* of an independent variable takes the average *across* the levels of the other independent variable; with *simple main effects*, the results are analyzed as if we had separate experiments *within* each level of the other independent variable. Additional analyses would reveal whether these comparisons are statistically significant.

Simple Main Effect of Independent Variable A   In Figure 10.3 (or Table 10.1, whichever you prefer), we can look at the simple main effect of A (food selection) *within* each level of B. Here, we compare the average food selections when the companion is either obese or thin. In this case, statistical tests showed that the *simple main effect* of food selection is not statistically significant when the eating companion is obese (means of 6.25 versus 4.26), but the *simple main effect* of food selection is significant when the eating companion is thin (means of 9.82 versus 3.20) (McFerran et al., 2010). We ignore the marginal means of food selection, and instead interpret the cell means within each level of confederate body type.

Simple Main Effect of Independent Variable B   Alternatively, we could examine the simple main effect of B, body type, *within* each level of A. This will tell us whether the difference between the thin and obese eating companion is significant when she eats 2 candies or 30 candies. In this case, the *simple main effect* of body type is not significant when the eating companion eats 2 candies (means of 3.20 versus 4.26), nor is the *simple main effect* significant when the eating companion eats 30 candies (means of 9.82 and 6.25).

Because these analyses overlap, you must choose to analyze only one of the simple main effects above (A or B, but not both). Which analysis you will be most interested in will depend on the predictions you made when you designed the study. The key point to remember here is that a significant interaction in a factorial design must be decomposed by examining cell means using a simple main effect analysis.

VARIATIONS ON 2 × 2 FACTORIAL DESIGNS

Factorial Designs with Manipulated and Non-manipulated Variables

LO5

One common type of factorial design includes both experimental (manipulated) and non-experimental (measured or non-manipulated) variables. This kind of design–sometimes called an **IV × PV design** (i.e., independent variable by participant variable)–allows researchers to investigate how different types of people respond to the same manipulated variable. These *participant variables* are often personal attributes such as sex, age, ethnic group, personality characteristics, or clinical diagnostic category. Participant variables cannot be randomly assigned or controlled: Participants bring those characteristics with them to the study. Therefore, the IV × PV design is not fully a true experiment.

The simplest IV × PV design includes one manipulated independent variable that has two levels and one participant variable with two levels. The two levels of the participant variable might be different age groups, groups of low and high scorers on a personality measure, or groups of males and females. An example of this design is a study by Klaver, Lee, and Hart (2007) investigating non-verbal behaviour among British Columbia prison inmates. The diagnosis of each inmate (either psychopathic or non-psychopathic) was the participant variable, and the story they told (either truth or a lie) was the manipulated independent variable. One of the dependent variables was the number of head movements participants made while telling the story. The results are shown in Figure 10.5. There was a significant interaction between psychopathy diagnosis and story on head movements. Overall, participants moved their heads more when telling a lie rather than telling the truth (in other words, there was a main effect of story condition). However, there was an interaction between story and psychopathy diagnosis that reveals a more complex picture.

FIGURE 10.5
Interaction in
IV × PV
design

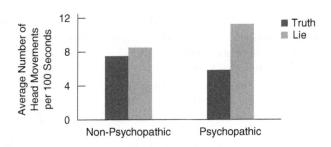

Adapted from Klaver, J.R., Lee, Z., & Hart, S.D. (2007). Psychopathy and nonverbal indicators of deception in offenders. *Law and Human Behavior, 31*, Figure 1, p. 345.

Among non-psychopathic participants, the number of head movements made was almost the same regardless of which story they were telling. However, psychopathic participants moved their heads much more often while telling a lie than when telling a truthful story. Head movements may not be very helpful when trying to tell whether a criminal is lying, unless that person is a psychopath!

Factorial designs that combine manipulated independent variables and participant variables are useful for investigating many interesting research questions. Fully understanding behaviour requires knowledge of both the situational variables that are able to be manipulated and the personal attributes of individuals. Nonetheless, because participant variables can never be manipulated and randomly assigned, we must be cautious not to make unwarranted causal claims when interpreting these results.

LO6

Assignment Procedures and Sample Size

Techniques for assigning participants to conditions can be generalized to factorial designs. Recall from Chapter 8: (1) In an independent groups design, different participants are randomly assigned to each of the conditions in the experiment; (2) in a repeated measures design, the *same* people participate in all conditions in the experiment. These two types of assignment procedures have implications for the number of participants necessary to complete the experiment. We can illustrate this fact by looking at a 2 × 2 factorial design. The design can be completely independent groups, completely repeated measures, or a **mixed factorial design**—that is, a combination of the two.

Independent Groups   In a 2 × 2 factorial design, there are four conditions. If we want a completely independent groups design, different participants will be assigned to each of the four conditions. Studies by McFerran and colleagues (2010) on food consumption (described above) and Darredeau and Barrett (2010) on intentions to smoke (described in Chapter 9) both illustrate factorial designs with different people randomly assigned to each of the conditions.

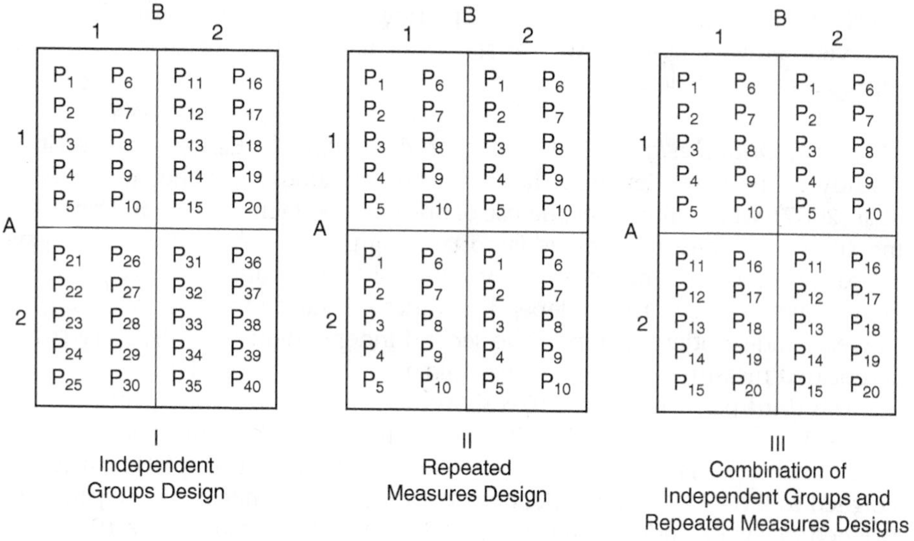

FIGURE 10.6
Number of participants (P) required for 10 observations in each condition in a 2 × 2 design

Suppose you have planned a 2 × 2 design and want to have 10 participants in each condition; you will need a total of 40 *different* participants, as shown in the first panel in Figure 10.6.

Repeated Measures   In a completely repeated measures procedure, the same people will participate in *all* conditions. Suppose you have planned a study on the semantic priming effect similar to the one by University of Waterloo researchers (Ferguson, Robidoux, & Besner, 2009). Semantic priming happens when exposure to one concept (e.g., bird) activates a meaningfully related concept (e.g., wings). Ferguson and colleagues used a complicated design to study this phenomenon; let's consider part of their method as an example. As quickly as possible, participants read out loud words that were displayed, one at a time, on a computer screen. One independent variable was meaning: Words that appeared in sequence were either meaningfully related to each other (e.g., wood, tree) or not (e.g., tree, bath). Another independent variable was visual clarity: Words were presented in either a clear font or a fuzzy font. Both *factors* showed main effects on reading speed. People read faster when the words were related to each other than when they were not. Also, people read faster when words were clearer than when they were not. There was also evidence of an interaction: People read especially quickly when the words were related *and* clear, and they read especially slowly when the words were unrelated *and* fuzzy.

In this completely repeated measures design, each person participated in all of the conditions by reading words in both clear and fuzzy fonts under both meaning conditions. If you wanted 10 participants in each condition, a total of 10 participants would be needed, as illustrated in the second panel in Figure 10.6. Compared to an independent groups design, this design offers considerable savings in the number of participants required. Revisit Chapter 8 to review other benefits as well as special challenges (e.g., order effects) with repeated measures designs.

Mixed Factorial Design Using Combined Assignment   Earlier, we described a study on lie detection from head movements among psychopaths (Klaver et al., 2007), which illustrates the use of both independent groups and repeated measures procedures in a mixed factorial design. The participant variable, psychopathy, is an independent groups variable (although note that mixed factorial designs typically use a true independent variable instead of a participant variable to create independent groups). The second independent variable, story truth, is repeated measures; all participants told a truthful story and a lie.

The third panel in Figure 10.6 shows the number of participants needed to have 10 per condition in a 2 × 2 mixed factorial design. In this table, independent variable A is an independent groups variable. Ten participants are assigned to level 1 of this independent variable, and another 10 participants are assigned to level 2. Independent variable B is repeated measures. The 10 participants assigned to A_1 receive both levels of independent variable B. Similarly, the other 10 participants assigned to A_2 receive both levels of the B variable. Thus, a total of 20 participants are required.

INCREASING THE COMPLEXITY OF FACTORIAL DESIGNS

The 2 × 2 is the simplest factorial design. Building on this basic design, the researcher can arrange experiments that are more and more complex. One way to increase complexity is to increase the number of levels of one or more of the independent variables; another way is to increase the number of independent variables. Let's expand the general format for describing factorial designs:

Number of levels of first IV × Number of levels of second IV × Number of levels of third IV

and so on. A 2 × 3 design, for example, contains two independent variables: Independent variable A has two levels, and independent variable B has three levels. Thus, the 2 × 3 design has 2 × 3 = 6 conditions. Following this logic, a 3 × 3 design has nine conditions. A 2 × 2 × 2 design contains three independent variables, each with two levels, for a total of 2 × 2 × 2 = 8 conditions.

Beyond Two Levels per Independent Variable

Table 10.2 shows a hypothetical 2 × 3 factorial design with the independent variables of task difficulty (easy, hard) and anxiety level (low, moderate, high). The dependent variable is performance on the task. The numbers in each of the six *cells* of the design indicate the mean performance score across participants assigned to that group. Just like when we considered the 2 × 2 design,

TABLE 10.2   2 × 3 factorial design

Task Difficulty	Anxiety Level			Marginal Means (shows main effect of task difficulty)
	Low	**Moderate**	**High**	
Easy	4	7	10	7.0
Hard	7	4	1	4.0
Marginal Means (shows main effect of anxiety level)	5.5	5.5	5.5	

the marginal means (rightmost column and bottom row) show the main effects of each of the independent variables. The results in Table 10.2 indicate a main effect of task difficulty because the *overall* performance mean in the easy-task group (7.0) is higher than the hard-task mean (4.0). However, there is no main effect of anxiety because the mean performance score is the same in each of the three anxiety groups (5.5). Is there an interaction between task difficulty and anxiety? Notice that increasing the amount of anxiety increases performance when the task is easy (means on the dependent variable jump from 4 to 7 to 10) but *decreases* performance when the task is hard (means on the dependent variable jump from 7 to 4 to 1). The effect of anxiety is different, depending on whether the task is easy or hard; thus, there is an interaction.

This interaction can be seen in a graph. Figure 10.7 is a line graph in which the solid line shows the effect of anxiety for the easy task and the dotted line represents the effect of anxiety for the hard task. As noted previously, line graphs are used when the independent variable represented on the horizontal axis is quantitative (i.e., the levels of the independent variable are increasing amounts of the variable).

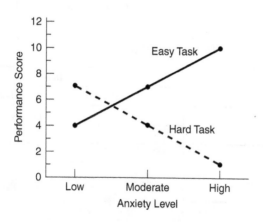

FIGURE 10.7
Line graph of data from 2 (task difficulty) × 3 (anxiety level) factorial design

Beyond Two Independent Variables

We can also increase the number of variables in the design. When we have more than two independent variables, these designs are typically called *higher-order factorials*. A 2 × 2 × 2 factorial design contains three variables, each with two levels. Thus, there are eight conditions in this design. In a 2 × 2 × 3 design, there are 12 conditions; in a 2 × 2 × 2 × 2 design, there are 16. The rule for constructing factorial designs remains the same throughout.

An example 2 × 2 × 2 factorial design is constructed in Table 10.3. The independent variables are (1) instruction method (online, face-to-face), (2) class size (small, moderate), and (3) student sex (male, female). Note that sex is a participant variable and the other two variables are manipulated variables. The dependent variable is performance on a standard test.

Notice that the 2 × 2 × 2 design can be seen as two 2 × 2 designs, one for the males and another for the females. The design yields three possible main effects: one for each independent variable. For example, let's consider the possible main effect of class size, which would be examined in the bottom row margin (not depicted). The overall mean for the small class size is obtained by considering all participants who experience the small class, regardless of instruction method or sex. Similarly, the moderate class size mean is derived from all participants in this condition. The two marginal means (small versus moderate class size) are then compared to see whether there is a significant main effect: Is one class size superior to the other, *overall?*

The design also allows us to examine interactions. In the 2 × 2 × 2 design, there could be interactions between (1) method and class size, (2) method and sex, and/or (3) class size and sex. There could also be a three-way ("higher-order") interaction that involves all three independent variables. Here, we want to determine whether the nature of the interaction between two of the variables differs depending on the particular level of the other variable. Three-way interactions are complicated and are less common in behavioural science than are two-way interactions.

Sometimes new researchers are tempted to include many independent variables in a single study. This practice is problematic because the design

TABLE 10.3   2 × 2 × 2 factorial design

	Class Size	
Instruction method	**Small (30)**	**Moderate (80)**
	Male	
Online		
Face-to-face		
	Female	
Online		
Face-to-face		

may become needlessly complex and require enormous numbers of partici- pants, especially with independent groups designs. The $2 \times 2 \times 2$ design had 8 groups; a $2 \times 2 \times 2 \times 2$ design has 16 groups; adding yet another indepen- dent variable with two levels means that 32 groups would be required. Also, when there are more than two independent variables, analyses become increas- ingly complex, and some of the particular conditions that are produced by the combination of so many variables may not make sense.

Experimental designs all use the same logic for determining whether the independent variable(s) cause a change on the dependent variable. In the next chapter, we will consider alternative designs that use somewhat different pro- cedures for examining relationships between variables under special circum- stances (e.g., when random assignment to condition is impossible).

STUDY TERMS

Test yourself! Define and generate an example of each of these key terms.

Cell (p. 204)	Main effect (p. 204)
Factorial design (p. 203)	Marginal mean (p. 205)
Interaction (p. 204)	Mixed factorial design (p. 212)
IV × PV design (p. 211)	Moderator variable (p. 207)
Levels (p. 201)	Simple main effect (p. 210)

REVIEW QUESTIONS

Test yourself on this chapter's learning objectives. Can you answer each of these questions?

1. Why would a researcher use more than two levels of the independent variable in an experiment?
2. What is a factorial design? Why would a researcher use a factorial design?
3. What are main effects? What is an interaction?
4. How do you use a graph to estimate whether there are any main effects, or if there is an interaction?
5. Cover the "yes" and "no" answers in Figure 10.4. For each graph, identify whether there is a main effect of factor A, a main effect of factor B, and/ or an interaction between factors A and B.
6. What information does a simple main effect analysis provide? How does it differ from a main effect?
7. Generate an example of an IV × PV factorial design. When might this design be useful?
8. What two pieces of information do you need to identify the number of conditions (or *cells*) in a factorial design?

DEEPEN YOUR UNDERSTANDING

Develop your mastery of these concepts by considering these application questions. Compare your responses with those from other people in your study group.

1. In a study by Chandler and Schwarz (2009), research participants read a description of a man named Donald. The description was ambiguous enough that his behaviour could be interpreted as being either assertive or hostile. Researchers were interested in whether a certain hand movement could cognitively prime the concept of hostility and influence personality ratings of Donald. Therefore, while reading about Donald, participants were asked to engage in a "motor task" that involved either extending their index finger or their middle finger upward (the latter is a signal of aggression in North American culture). Then participants rated Donald's personality on two kinds of trait dimensions: aggressive traits (e.g., hostile, unfriendly) and unrelated, control traits (e.g., intelligent, boring).

   a. Identify the independent variable(s) and dependent variable(s).

   b. Identify the design of this experiment.

   c. How many conditions are in the experiment?

   d. Is there a repeated measures variable in this experiment? If so, what are the levels?

   e. Is there a participant variable? If so, identify it. If not, can you suggest a participant variable that might be included?

2. Chandler and Schwarz (2009) reported the following mean personality ratings (higher numbers indicate greater amounts of that trait type): middle finger–aggressive traits (8.41), middle finger–unrelated traits (6.61), index finger–aggressive traits (6.74), and index finger–unrelated traits (6.38). Assume there are equal numbers of participants in each condition.

   a. Graph the means.

   b. Are there any main effects?

   c. Is there an interaction?

   d. Describe the results in a few sentences.

3. Assume that you want 15 participants in each condition of your experiment that uses a 3 × 3 factorial design. How many *different* participants do you need for (a) an independent groups design, (b) a repeated measures design, and (c) a mixed factorial design?

4. Read the following research scenarios and fill in the correct answer in each column of the table. It may be helpful to create a table or a graph like the ones depicted in this chapter.

	Number of Independent Variables	Number of Experimental Conditions	Number of Possible Main Effects	Number of Possible Interactions
a. Participants were randomly assigned to read a short story printed in either 12-point or 14-point font in one of three font style conditions: Calibri, Times New Roman, or Arial. Afterwards, they answered several questions designed to measure memory recall.				
b. Researchers conducted an experiment to examine sex and physical attractiveness biases in juror behaviour. Participants were randomly assigned to read a scenario describing a crime committed by either an attractive or unattractive woman or an attractive or unattractive man. The criminal was described as overweight or average weight.				

11

Research Designs for Special Circumstances

LEARNING OBJECTIVES
Keep these learning objectives in mind as you read to help you identify the most critical information in this chapter.

By the end of this chapter, you should be able to:

1	Describe single case experimental designs and discuss reasons to use these designs.
2	Describe the purpose of program evaluation research and five types of questions that program evaluations can seek to address.
3	Compare and contrast the one-group posttest-only design with the one-group pretest-posttest design.
4	Describe threats to internal validity that can be especially problematic in quasi-experimental designs.
5	Compare and contrast the non-equivalent control group design with the non-equivalent control group pretest-posttest design, and discuss the advantages of having a non-equivalent control group.
6	Distinguish between the interrupted time series design and control series design.
7	Compare cross-sectional, longitudinal, and sequential research designs, including the advantages and disadvantages of each design.

In the classic experimental design emphasized in Chapter 8, participants are randomly assigned to the levels of the independent variable, and a dependent variable is measured. The groups' responses on the dependent variable are then compared to determine whether the independent variable had an effect. Because all other variables are held constant, differences on the dependent variable must be due to the effect of the independent variable. This design has high *internal validity*, which means that we are very confident that the independent variable caused the observed responses on the dependent variable. You will frequently encounter this experimental design in the behavioural sciences.

Yet not all research can use a true experiment. This chapter focuses on ways that researchers have adapted the classic experimental design for special research circumstances. Single case experimental designs were developed for times when the effect of an independent variable must be evaluated with only one participant. Quasi-experimental designs can be used if a researcher has many participants, but true experimental designs are impossible (e.g., cannot use random assignment; see Chapter 8). Studying changes that occur with age requires yet another set of variations on the basic experimental design. Keep in mind that as we stray from true experiments, internal validity decreases, which reduces our ability to make a strong claim that the independent variable caused changes in the dependent variable. Throughout this chapter we will explore some specific threats to internal validity that are particularly worrisome in these special designs, but also can affect true experiments sometimes.

SINGLE CASE EXPERIMENTAL DESIGNS

LO1

Single case experiments were developed from a need to determine whether an experimental manipulation had an effect on a single research participant (Barlow, Nock, & Hersen, 2009; Shadish, Cook, & Campbell, 2002). In a **single case experimental design,** the participant's behaviour is first measured during a **baseline** control time period. The manipulation is then introduced during a treatment period, and the participant's behaviour continues to be observed. A change in the participant's behaviour from the baseline to treatment periods offers evidence for the effectiveness of the manipulation.

Much of the early interest in single case designs in psychology came from research on reinforcement schedules pioneered by B. F. Skinner (e.g., Skinner, 1953). Now these designs are often used in clinical, counselling, educational, and other applied settings (Kazdin, 2001; Morgan & Morgan, 2001). For example, Dolhanty and Greenberg (2009) documented the treatment of a woman battling anorexia nervosa. Her scores on measures of eating disorder and depression severity decreased drastically after she received 18 months of emotion-focused therapy. The problem, however, is that there could be many alternative explanations for the change other than the experimental treatment. For example, some other event may have coincided with the introduction of the treatment (i.e., a *history effect*, discussed later in this chapter). The single case designs described in the following sections attempt to address this problem.

Reversal Designs

The basic challenge in single case experiments is how to determine that the treatment–specifically–had an effect on the dependent variable. One method is to demonstrate that the effect can be undone, or reversed, by removing the treatment. A simple **reversal design** takes the following form:

A (baseline period) → B (treatment period) → A (baseline period)

This design, called an ABA design, requires that behaviour be observed and measured during the baseline control period (A), again during the treatment period (B), and also during a second baseline control period (A) after removing the experimental treatment. (Sometimes this is called a *withdrawal design*, in recognition of the fact that the treatment is removed, or withdrawn.) Some treatments produce an immediate change in behaviour; many other variables require a lengthy treatment period to show an impact (e.g., as in the case of the woman with anorexia nervosa mentioned above).

Consider how this type of design was used to measure the effect of a five-minute playtime intervention for preschool children in southern Ontario (Levine & Ducharme, 2013). The dependent variable was how often a child complied with their teacher's request. During the baseline period (A), a daily measure indicated the proportion of times a child complied. Then, a daily five-minute playtime intervention was introduced during the treatment period (B), during which the teacher joined the child one-on-one during the class's free play period, supporting and praising the child. The treatment was discontinued during the second baseline (A) period. Compliance was measured every day of each phase. Part of the data are shown in Figure 11.1. The fact that this child's behaviour was more consistently positive when the treatment was introduced and became more negative when the treatment was withdrawn can be considered evidence for the treatment's short-term effectiveness.

The ABA design can be greatly improved by extending it to an ABAB design, in which the experimental treatment is introduced a second time, or even to an ABABAB design that allows the treatment to be tested a third time. Adding more reversals can address two problems with the ABA reversal design. First, a single reversal could be caused easily by a random fluctuation in the person's behaviour; perhaps the treatment happened to coincide with some other event, such as a child's upcoming birthday, that caused the change (and the post-birthday reversal). Random or coincidental events are less likely to be responsible if the treatment has an effect two or more times. The second problem is ethical. As Barlow et al. (2009) warn, it doesn't seem right to end

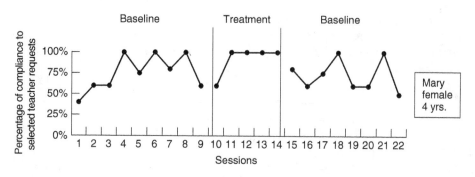

FIGURE II.I
Data from an
ABA reversal
design

Adapted from Levine, D.G., & Ducharme, J.M. (2013). The effects of a teacher-child play intervention on classroom compliance in young children in child care settings. *Journal of Behavioral Education, 22,* 50–65, Figure 1.

the design with the withdrawal of a treatment that may be very beneficial for the participant. An ABAB design provides the opportunity to observe a second reversal when the treatment is introduced again. The sequence ends with the treatment rather than its withdrawal.

Multiple Baseline Designs

In a **multiple baseline design,** the effectiveness of the treatment is demonstrated when a behaviour changes after the manipulation is introduced under *multiple* circumstances. There are several variations of the multiple baseline design (Barlow et al., 2009). In the multiple baseline *across participants,* the behaviour of several participants is measured over time; for each participant, though, the manipulation is introduced at a different point in time. Figure 11.2 shows data from four additional preschool participants in Levine and Ducharme's (2013) play intervention study. Note that reports of research using single case experimental designs typically present results like this, separately for each participant, rather than grouping data and presenting overall means across participants.

As you can see in Figure 11.2, introducing the play intervention did not have a perfectly uniform effect on children's compliance behaviour. However, on average, each child did improve compliance during the intervention phase. Because this change occurred across participants, and the intervention was introduced at a different time for each participant, some alternative explanations can be ruled out (e.g., that the result solely was based on random chance or historical events). By including additional children, researchers make a (slightly) stronger case for this intervention as a way to increase compliance in preschoolers.

In a multiple baseline *across behaviours,* several different behaviours of a single participant are measured over time. At different times, the same manipulation is applied to each of the behaviours. For example, a reward system

FIGURE 11.2
Data from a multiple baseline design across subjects

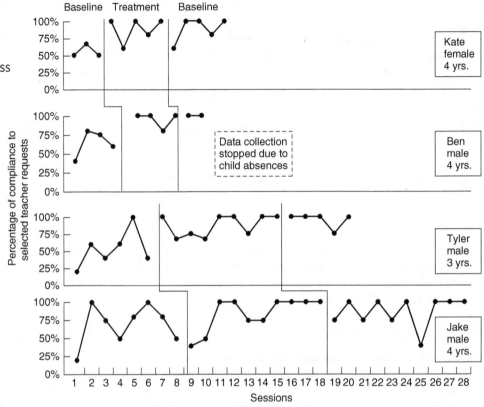

Adapted from Levine, D.G., & Ducharme, J.M. (2013). The effects of a teacher-child play intervention on classroom compliance in young children in child care settings. *Journal of Behavioral Education, 22,* 50-65, Figure 2.

could be instituted to increase the socializing, grooming, and reading behaviours of a person hospitalized for psychosis. The reward system would be applied to each of these behaviours at different times. Demonstrating improvement when the reward system was applied for each behaviour would be evidence for the effectiveness of the manipulation.

The third variation is the multiple baseline *across situations,* in which the same behaviour is measured in different settings, such as at home and at school. Again, a manipulation is introduced at a different time in each setting, with the expectation that a change in the behaviour in each situation will occur only after the manipulation. For example, researchers in Sherbrooke, Quebec, demonstrated that they were able to effectively teach a woman with early Alzheimer's disease to find her way around her seniors' residence; the researchers used an ABA design, where (B), the treatment, was applied to multiple locations (e.g., games room, laundry room; Provencher, Bier, Audet, & Gagnon, 2008).

Some multiple baseline designs include a reversal phase, and others do not. A reversal of some behaviours may be impossible or unethical. For example, it would be unethical to reverse treatment that reduces danger-ous or illegal behaviours, such as kleptomania (i.e., compulsive theft) or alcoholism, even if the possibility exists that a second introduction of the treatment might result in another change. Other treatments (e.g., surgery) might produce an irreversible change in behaviour. In such cases, multiple measures over time can be made before and after the manipulation. If the manipulation is effective, a change in behaviour may be observed immedi-ately, and the change should continue to be reflected in further measures of the behaviour.

Replications in Single Case Designs

Single case designs suffer from the same limitations as descriptive case studies, discussed in Chapter 6 (e.g., lack of generalizability). When the manipulation used with a single participant is *replicated* with other participants, the generaliz-ability of the results is enhanced. Consider the full dataset from Levine and Ducharme's (2013) play intervention study. The treatment was applied to eight children (three girls) from five different schools. For all children, average daily compliance increased during the intervention phase. For six of the eight chil-dren, compliance continued after the intervention ceased (e.g., see Figure 11.2); however, compliance dropped after the intervention for two children (e.g., see Figure 11.1). For these two children, compliance was maintained after repeat-ing the intervention (i.e., an ABABA design, not shown). Because the findings were replicated across different children at different schools, researchers con-cluded that this simple five-minute intervention can improve compliance among some children.

Single case designs can be especially valuable for someone who is apply-ing treatment to help someone in particular improve behaviour—for example, a parent who is trying a new way to reach a misbehaving child, or a clinician who is exploring therapeutic options for a new patient. They offer systematic ways to examine hypotheses when limited by one or a few participants. This sample size limitation has historically hindered statistical analyses, but statisti-cal techniques for single case designs are developing (see Shadish, 2014, for a review). Moreover, results from many single case designs can be combined using techniques of *meta-analysis* (see Chapter 14) to reveal overall patterns. For example, a University of Alberta team combined data from 115 single-case studies that each studied one to seven participants, for a total of 343 partici-pants (Wang, Parrila, & Cui, 2013). Combined data revealed that social skills interventions can effectively help people with autism spectrum disorder. Despite their limitations, single case designs can be a useful alternative to more traditional research designs when those are not possible.

LO2

PROGRAM EVALUATION

Researchers frequently investigate applied research questions and conduct evaluation research using true experimental designs, surveys, observational techniques, and other available methods, including quasi-experiments. Applied and evaluation research can present numerous practical problems that prevent researchers from using best practices and designs: True experiments are frequently impossible, the researchers are called in too late to decide on the best measurement technique, or the budget rules out many data collection possibilities (Bamberger, Rugh, Church, & Fort, 2004). Still, the research needs to be done. In the next section, we will focus on the use of quasi-experimental designs as a methodological tool that is particularly useful in applied research settings. Before doing so, we consider program evaluation research, which often uses these tools. Program evaluation is a viable career option for students like you who are majoring in social sciences. See www.evaluationcanada.ca for information about this professional designation and career opportunities.

Program evaluation is research on programs that are proposed and implemented to achieve some positive effect on a group of people (see also Chapter 1). Such programs may be implemented in schools, work settings, or entire communities. In schools, an example is the "At My Best" program designed to reduce obesity by teaching primary school children to make healthy diet and activity choices. This program is conducted by classroom teachers with supporting materials developed by Physical and Health Education Canada along with the AstraZeneca pharmaceutical company. Originally piloted in 2008 in 39 schools, it has since spread to over 1,000 schools across Canada. You may be wondering about the effectiveness of this program: so are we. Because research has yet to be published that examines the short-term and long-term impact of the "At My Best" program, it is worrisome that so many schools are readily adopting it. As you read about program evaluation and quasi-experimental designs in this chapter, consider how you would design a study to evaluate its effectiveness.

Influential social psychologist Donald Campbell (1969) urged a culture of evaluation in which all programs are thoroughly evaluated to determine whether they are effective. Accordingly, the initial focus of evaluation research was "outcome evaluation": Did the program result in the positive outcome for which it was designed (e.g., reductions in drug abuse, higher graduation rates, or lower absenteeism)? As the field of program evaluation has progressed, evaluation research has broadened its scope to many other questions. Five types of questions can guide program evaluations (Rossi, Freeman, & Lipsey, 2004). These questions are depicted in Figure 11.3 as elements of a sequential process, which is how Rossi and colleagues recommend they are considered (see Davidson, 2005, for an alternative approach to program evaluation research). Which questions are emphasized depends on the purpose of the evaluation.

The first type of question is the evaluation of need. Program evaluation that focuses on *needs assessment* asks whether there are, in fact, problems that need

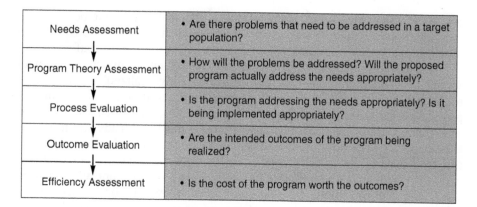

Needs Assessment	• Are there problems that need to be addressed in a target population?
Program Theory Assessment	• How will the problems be addressed? Will the proposed program actually address the needs appropriately?
Process Evaluation	• Is the program addressing the needs appropriately? Is it being implemented appropriately?
Outcome Evaluation	• Are the intended outcomes of the program being realized?
Efficiency Assessment	• Is the cost of the program worth the outcomes?

FIGURE II.3
Types of program evaluation research

to be addressed in a target population. For example, is there drug abuse by children and adolescents in the community? If so, what types of drugs are being used? What services do homeless people need most? Do repeat juvenile offenders have particular personal and family problems that could be addressed by an intervention program? Nunes (1998) conducted a needs assessment study among Portuguese-Canadians. Some of the most important overall needs identified were education (e.g., ensuring Portuguese-Canadians receive adequate education), economics (e.g., addressing high unemployment rates), and integration into Canadian society (e.g., including appropriate access to social services). Data for a needs assessment may come from surveys, interviews, and statistical data maintained by public health, criminal justice, and other agencies. Once a need has been established, programs can be planned to address the need.

The second type of program evaluation question addresses program theory. After identifying needs, a program can be designed to address them. The program must be based on valid assumptions about the causes of the problems and the rationale of the proposed program (Rossi et al., 2004). The *assessment of program theory* may involve the collaboration of researchers, service providers, and prospective program clients to ensure that the proposed program appropriately addresses the needs of the target population. Assessing program theory includes articulating the rationale for how members of the target population will benefit from the program, including, for example, how they will access and use the program's services. This rationale can then be evaluated: Will this program actually reach the target population as intended? Does it have appropriate goals?

The third type of program evaluation question is *process evaluation*, or program monitoring. When the program is under way, the evaluation researcher monitors it to determine whether it is reaching the target population, whether it is attracting enough clients, and whether the staff is providing the planned services. Sometimes, the staff has not received adequate training, or the services are being offered in a location that is undesirable or difficult to find. Overall, the researcher seeks evidence that the program is doing what it is supposed to do. This research is extremely important to avoid concluding that a program is ineffective when really it is not being implemented properly. Such research may involve questionnaires and interviews, observational studies, and analysis of records kept by program staff.

The fourth question concerns *outcome evaluation*, or impact assessment: Are the intended outcomes of the program being realized? Is the goal–to reduce drug use, increase literacy, decrease repeat offences by juveniles, or provide job skills–being achieved? To determine this, the evaluation researcher must devise a way of measuring the outcome and then study the impact of the program on the outcome measure. We need to know what participants of the program are like, and we need to know what they would be like if they had not completed the program. Ideally, a true experiment with random assignment to conditions (i.e., program, control) would be carried out to answer questions about outcomes. However, other research approaches, such as the quasi-experimental and single case designs described in this chapter, can be useful ways of assessing the impact of an intervention program when random assignment is not possible.

The final program evaluation question addresses *efficiency assessment*. Once it is shown that a program does have its intended effect, researchers must determine whether the benefits are worth the program's cost. Also, the researchers must determine whether the resources used to implement the program might be put to some better use.

As you may have noticed, a full program evaluation can be an extensive long-term undertaking, particularly if all of the above questions are to be addressed. Researchers such as Bamberger et al. (2004) are developing systematic approaches to respond to specific challenges that arise when doing evaluation research–they refer to doing "shoestring evaluation" when there are restraints of time, budget, and data collection options. Next we will consider quasi-experimental designs, which are sometimes incorporated into the program evaluation process.

QUASI-EXPERIMENTAL DESIGNS

Quasi-experimental designs address the need to study the effect of an independent variable in settings in which the control of true experimental designs cannot be achieved (*quasi* means "as if" in Latin). A quasi-experimental design allows us to examine the impact of a so-called "independent variable" on a dependent variable, but causal inference is much more difficult. Quasi-experiments lack important features of true experiments, such as control conditions and random assignment to conditions (hence the above qualifier of *so-called* independent variables). In other words, quasi-experimental designs have lower internal validity than do true experiments, so they are used only when true experiments are impossible to conduct.

There are many types of quasi-experimental designs, including both repeated measures and independent groups designs (Campbell, 1969; Campbell

& Stanley, 1966; Cook & Campbell, 1979; Shadish et al., 2002). Only six designs will be described here. As you read about each design, compare the design features and problems against the true experimental designs described in Chapter 8. See Table 11.1 to help organize and compare all of the designs described in this chapter. We start with the simplest and most problematic of the quasi-experimental designs. As you will see, data resulting from the first three designs are especially problematic to interpret. Nevertheless, all may be used in different circumstances when researchers have no other choice.

One-Group Posttest-Only Design

LO3

Suppose you want to investigate whether sitting close to a stranger will cause the stranger to move away. You might try sitting next to a number of strangers and measure the number of seconds that elapse before each leaves. Your design would look like this:

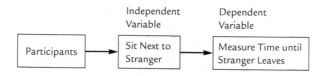

Now suppose that the average amount of time before people leave is 9.6 seconds. Without any sort of comparison, this finding is uninterpretable. You don't know if people would have stayed longer if you had not sat down, or if people would have stayed for 9.6 seconds anyway. Maybe they liked you and would have left sooner if you had not sat down!

This **one-group posttest-only design** lacks a crucial element of true experiments: a control group or other source of comparison. There must be some sort of comparison—and, ideally, random assignment to separate conditions—to enable you to interpret your results. With only one group and one measurement instance, this is not an experiment that will allow us to draw any causal inferences about the effect of an independent variable on a dependent variable because results are open to many potential alternative interpretations (e.g., many of the threats to internal validity discussed soon). In other words, it lacks *internal validity* entirely.

You may see this type of design used as (weak and insufficient) evidence for the effectiveness of programs or advertised products. For example, employees in a company might participate in a four-hour information session on emergency procedures, after which they score an average of 90 percent on a knowledge test. Without any sort of comparison, it would be inappropriate to conclude that the program is successfully educating employees. Remember, this design completely lacks internal validity. We do not know if the score on the dependent variable would have been equal, lower, or even higher without the program. Likewise, advertisers sometimes make claims about their products based on one-group posttest-only data. It is not enough to know only

TABLE II.I   Research designs for special circumstances, compared with a true independent groups experiment

Design Category	Design	Number of Groups/ Conditions	Random Assignment to Condition?	Number of Participants	Pretest?	Posttest?
True experiment	Independent groups	2+	Yes	Many (often 30+ per group)	Sometimes	Yes (dependent variable)
Single case	Reversal ABA(B)	1 (more if re-institute treatment, as in ABAB)	N/A	1	Yes (A, baseline)	Yes (reversal to baseline)
	Multiple baseline	1 (more if multiple settings or behaviours)	No	1 (more if multiple participants)	Yes (A, baseline)	Yes (B, treatment)
Quasi-experiment	One-group posttest-only	1	No	Many (often 30+)	No	Yes
	One-group pretest-posttest	1	No	Many (often 30+)	Yes	Yes
	Non-equivalent control group	2+	No	Many (often 30+ per group)	No	Yes
	Non-equivalent control group pretest-posttest	2+	No	Many (often 30+ per group)	Yes	Yes
	Interrupted time series	1	No	Many (often archival data)	Yes, multiple	Yes, often multiple
	Control series	2+	No	Many (often archival data)	Yes, multiple	Yes, often multiple
Developmental	Longitudinal	1	No	Many (often 30+)	Sometimes	Yes, multiple
	Cross-sectional	2+	No	Many (often 30+ per group)	Sometimes	Yes
	Sequential	2+	No	Many (often 30+ per group)	Sometimes	Yes, multiple

that children earned A grades after enrolling in an after-school enrichment class (maybe they already earned As), or that people reported high athletic performance after drinking a sport drink (maybe they would have performed even better if they drank water instead). People and companies sometimes report these kinds of results because they do not realize that these data are insufficient evidence, or because they are intentionally trying to mislead consumers. As scientists, we know that we need comparison data to be able to interpret any result.

One-Group Pretest-Posttest Design

One way to obtain a comparison (and therefore increase internal validity somewhat) is to measure participants before the manipulation (a pretest) and again afterward (a posttest). An index of change from the pretest to the posttest could then be computed. Although this **one-group pretest-posttest design** sounds fine relative to the one-group posttest-only design, there are still some major problems with it.

To illustrate, suppose you wanted to test the hypothesis that a relaxation training program will decrease cigarette smoking. If you were to use the one-group pretest-posttest design, you would select a group of people who smoke, measure their smoking rate, have them attend relaxation training, and then measure their smoking rate again. Your design would look like this:

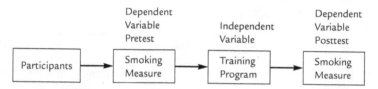

If you found a reduction in smoking, you could not assume that the result was due to the relaxation training program. This design has failed to take into account several potential alternative explanations, including history, maturation, testing, instrument decay, and possibly regression toward the mean. These alternative explanations are called "threats" to internal validity.

Threats to Internal Validity   [LO4]

Internal validity–our ability to claim that the independent variable is causing changes in the dependent variable–is threatened any time there is a reasonable alternative explanation for changes to the dependent variable. In Chapters 4 and 8 we explored many examples of confounding variables, which undermine internal validity. Yet many other threats to internal validity are possible, even for some true experiments. We will discuss some of the most common threats here in the context of quasi-experimental designs because these designs are particularly susceptible. These common threats are summarized in Table 11.2.

TABLE II.2   Some threats to internal validity

Threat	Summary	Ways It Can Undermine Internal Validity
History	Historical event that affects all or most participants (e.g., natural disaster, media event) and that is not of interest to the researcher.	Alternative explanation for change between pretest and posttest. If there are multiple groups and the event affects groups differently, this becomes a confound and therefore an alternative explanation for group differences.
Maturation	Natural changes to participants' short-term states (e.g., fatigue) or long-term development (e.g., education) not of interest to the researcher.	Alternative explanation for change between pretest and posttest. If there are multiple groups and the groups mature differently, this becomes a confound and therefore an alternative explanation for group differences.
Testing	Simply taking the pretest influences people's responses to the posttest.	Alternative explanation for change between pretest and posttest.
Instrument decay	Measurement instrument changes with repeated use.	Alternative explanation for change between pretest and posttest.
Regression toward the mean	May occur when participants are chosen or groups are divided based on extreme score on pretest, because extreme scores tend to become less extreme on repeated measures.	Alternative explanation for change between pretest and posttest.
Mortality	Participants leave the study.	Differences in mortality rate across groups may create (more) group differences by the end of the study, even if groups were initially randomly assigned, offering an alternative explanation for differences between groups.
Selection effects	Groups are divided based on any reason other than random assignment.	Pre-existing group differences offer alternative explanation for differences between groups.
Cohort effects	Groups are divided by different age. A special type of selection effect.	Instead of differences due to age in general, the unique characteristics of a particular cohort offer an alternative explanation for differences between groups.

History   **History effects** can be caused by virtually any event that occurs during or after the experimental manipulation, after the pretest (if there is one), but before the posttest. Any such event is confounded with the manipulation in the one-group design. Returning to our smoking example, suppose that a famous person dies of lung cancer during the time between the first and second measures. This event, and not the relaxation training, could be responsible for reduced smoking (in other words, the historical event becomes an alternative explanation). Consider a real study of an intervention program targeting the well-being of children whose families had recently immigrated to Montreal (Rousseau, Benoit, Lacroix, & Gauthier, 2009). Just after the pretest, the 2004 tsunami devastated many countries throughout the Indian Ocean region. Because many participants' families hailed from affected regions, researchers had to interpret the data in light of this historical event. The post-test showed a moderate improvement to well-being after the treatment, but it is impossible to know what the effect would have been (e.g., stronger, none) if the tsunami had not occurred at that time.

Maturation   People change over time. In a brief period, they become bored, fatigued, perhaps wiser, and certainly hungrier; over a longer period, people develop or recover from illnesses, adults change or start careers, and children become more coordinated and analytical. Changes that occur in participants systematically over time are called **maturation effects.** In the one-group pretest-posttest design, maturation is confounded with the manipulation. Maturation could be a problem in the smoking reduction example if people generally become more concerned about health as they get older and the posttest occurs after years of treatment. Any such time-related factor might result in a change from the pretest to the posttest, thereby offering an alternative explanation for the results. If this happens, you might mistakenly attribute the change to the treatment rather than to maturation.

Testing   **Testing effects** become a problem if simply taking the pretest changes the participant's behaviour, just as we discussed in Chapter 8. For example, the smoking measure might require people to keep a diary in which they note every cigarette smoked during the day. Simply keeping track of smoking might be sufficient to reduce the number of cigarettes a person smokes. Thus, rather than the program influencing posttest scores, the pretest may be an alternative explanation for the reduction. In other contexts, taking a pretest may sensitize people to the purpose of the experiment or make them more adept at a skill being tested. As a result, the experiment would have low internal validity.

Instrument Decay   Sometimes, the basic characteristics of the measuring instrument, or the way participants use it, change over time; this is called **instrument decay.** Instruments can literally deteriorate–timers fail as they lose battery power, or software programs develop bugs. Consider sources of instrument decay when human observers are used to measure behaviour: Over time, a person rating behaviour (who can be considered a "measuring instrument") may gain skill, become fatigued, or change the standards on which observations are based. In our smoking example, participants might be highly motivated to record all cigarettes smoked at first when the task is new and interesting, but by the end of the study, they may sometimes forget to record a cigarette. If so, instrument decay becomes an alternative explanation for an apparent reduction in cigarette smoking.

Regression toward the Mean   Sometimes called *statistical regression*, **regression toward the mean** can occur whenever participants are selected to participate because they score extremely high or low on some variable. When they are tested again, their scores tend to change in the direction of the mean. Extremely high scores are likely to become lower (closer to the mean), and extremely low scores are likely to become higher (again, closer to the mean).

Consider once again the smoking example. Regression toward the mean would be a problem if participants were selected because they were initially extremely heavy smokers. By choosing people for the program who scored highest on the pretest, the researcher may have selected many participants who were, for whatever reason, smoking much more than their usual at the particular time the measure was administered. Simply because of regression to the mean, the most extremely high smokers are, on average, likely to be smoking less when their smoking is measured again. If we then compare the overall amount of smoking before and after the program, it will appear that people are smoking less. The alternative explanation is that smoking reduction is due to regression toward the mean rather than the program.

Statistically speaking, extreme scores are likely to become less extreme over time, simply because they started out so extreme. The concept of regression toward the mean is sometimes challenging to grasp at first, so let's explore another example. Think about your worst grade in a course ever. Now think about your average grade across all your courses. Your average grade is higher than your worst grade. If we happened to select you for a study investigating an achievement intervention based on your worst course grade ever, that grade does not represent your typical performance. So regardless of whether our intervention works, your next course grade is probably going to be higher than your worst ever. Extreme scores tend to become less extreme with a repeated measurement. Consider what would happen if we had selected research participants only on the basis of their lowest grade, then gave them an intervention, and then measured their next course grade. Even if our intervention had no effect, our results would look like the achievement intervention helped; instead, regression toward the mean is an alternative explanation.

The problem of regression toward the mean is rooted in the reliability of the measure. Recall from Chapter 5 that any measure reflects a true score plus measurement error. If the measure is perfectly reliable, the two measures will be the same (if nothing happens to lower or raise the scores). If your course grades are a perfectly reliable reflection of your overall learning ability, every course grade will be the same. It would not matter on which course grade we based our study selection criteria—with such a perfectly reliable measure, they are all the same. Any change after the intervention could not be explained by regression toward the mean. However, if the two measures are not perfectly reliable and there is measurement error, most scores will be close to the true score but some will be higher and some will be lower. Most of your course grades are probably close to your average course grade, but there are probably some course grades that are much higher and some that are much lower. So if we select you to participate based on your most extreme grade, your grade will be different next time simply because that extreme grade is not doing a good job capturing your true abilities, and we won't be able to tell whether the intervention made an impact beyond that difference. Regression toward the mean is a problem when participants are selected because of extreme scores on an unreliable measure.

Regression toward the mean can help us explain everyday events as well. Sports commentators often refer to the hex that awaits an athlete who appears on the cover of *Sports Illustrated* magazine. The performances of a number of athletes have dropped considerably after they were the subjects of *Sports Illustrated* cover stories. Although these cover stories might cause the lower performance (perhaps the fame results in nervousness and reduced concentration), regression toward the mean is also a likely explanation. An athlete is selected for the cover of the magazine because of exceptionally high performance; regression toward the mean teaches us that very high performance is likely to deteriorate. If *Sports Illustrated* also did cover stories on athletes who were in a slump–i.e., creating a comparison group–and their performance then increased, we could more certainly conclude that regression toward the mean is driving the performance change.

Threats to Internal Validity in One Group Pretest-Posttest and Experimental Designs Given its severe susceptibility to the threats to internal validity explained above, is the one-group pretest-posttest design ever used? Sometimes in applied settings, a comparison group of any kind is impossible to obtain. Adding the pretest improved somewhat upon the one-group posttest-only design. Recall the example of the evaluation of a program to teach emergency procedures to employees. With a one-group pretest-posttest design, the knowledge test would be given before and after the training session. The ability to observe a change from the pretest to the posttest could rule out one alternative explanation about people's prior knowledge, even though other threats to internal validity remain. Forming a control group is always the best way to strengthen this design (see below). However, if no control group is possible, *replicating* the study at other times with other participants can help rule out some threats to internal validity (e.g., history).

It is important to note that many of these threats to internal validity can also affect other designs (e.g., longitudinal designs, single case designs, true experiments). Consider how these threats could affect a true experimental design that used random assignment to create equivalent groups initially. Even if the threat (e.g., history, maturation, instrument decay) affects both groups equally, it could still pose a problem for making causal claims. For example, if instrument decay means the dependent measure becomes less reliable for everyone between the pretest and the posttest, any genuine effect of the manipulation might be masked by all the error. In this way, the threat to internal validity is *not* in the form of an alternative explanation of differences between groups on the dependent variable. Instead, the threat is to the experiment's ability to detect a true effect that is there.

Overcoming Threats to Internal Validity   Many of the threats to internal validity can be addressed by the use of an appropriate control group. A group that does not receive the treatment provides some control for the effects of history, regression toward the mean, and so on. For example, if an outside historical event has the same effect on both the treatment and the control groups, any difference between the treatment and control groups on the dependent variable cannot be attributed to the historical event. The best way to create an equivalent group is using random assignment to condition, but that option is not always available.

When forming a control group, the participants in the experimental condition and the control condition should be equivalent. It is not always possible to use any of the three ways of assigning participants to groups to ensure they are equivalent (e.g., random assignment; see Chapter 8). If participants in the two groups differ *before* the manipulation, they will probably differ *after* the manipulation as well, but not necessarily because of your manipulation. The next design illustrates this problem.

LO5

Non-equivalent Control Group Design

The **non-equivalent control group design** has a separate control group, but the participants in the two conditions (e.g., an experimental group and a control group) are not equivalent. The participants were not randomly assigned, but are instead chosen from existing natural groups. **Selection differences** are pre-existing differences between these groups, which are *confounded* with the independent variable and provide an alternative explanation for the results. If the relaxation training program is studied with the non-equivalent control group design, the design can be diagrammed like this:

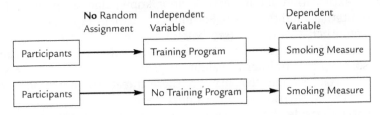

Participants in the first group are given the smoking frequency measure after completing relaxation training. Participants in the second group do not participate in any program. In this design, the researcher does not have any control over which participants are in each group. Suppose, for example, that a study is conducted in a division of a large company. All employees who smoke are recruited to participate in the training program. The people who volunteer for the program are in the experimental group, and the people in the control group are simply the smokers who did not sign up for the training. The problem of *selection differences* arises because smokers who choose to participate may differ in some important way from those who do not. For instance, non-volunteers may already be light smokers compared to the others, or they may be less confident that a program can help them. If so, any difference between the groups on the smoking measure may reflect pre-existing differences rather than the effect of the relaxation training.

Instead of comparing volunteers versus non-volunteers for a program, another option is to compare two similar groups. For example, a researcher might have all smokers in the engineering division of a company participate in the relaxation training program and smokers who work in the marketing division serve as a control group. Selection differences may still be a problem here: The smokers in the two divisions may have differed in smoking patterns *prior* to the relaxation program.

Non-equivalent Control Group Pretest-Posttest Design

Adding a pretest to the above design creates a **non-equivalent control group pretest-posttest design.** Although it can never be as internally valid as a true experiment, this is one of the most useful (i.e., internally valid) quasi-experimental designs. It can be diagrammed as follows:

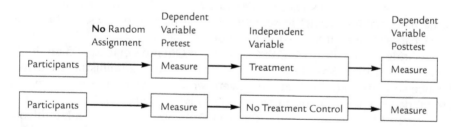

This is not a true experimental design because assignment to groups is not random; the two groups may not begin equivalent. We have the advantage of knowing pretest scores, so we can see whether the groups were the same on the pretest. Even if the groups are not equivalent, we can look at *changes* in scores from the pretest to the posttest. If the independent variable has an effect, the experimental group should show a greater change than the control group (see Kenny, 1979). Strategies for statistical analysis of such change scores are discussed by Trochim (2000).

Nelson, Ochocka, Janzen, and Trainor (2006) used a non-equivalent control group pretest-posttest design to study the effect of participation in mental health organizations on a variety of well-being measures. Participants were all people recovering from mental illness. Some participants were actively engaged in organizations where they could offer outreach to other people currently experiencing mental illness (called *Consumer/Survivor Initiatives*, or CSIs); other participants had signed up to participate in CSIs but were not actively engaged in them. Researchers asked participants to report on a variety of aspects of their life, and compared how the groups' reports changed over time. After 18 months, active CSI members maintained consistent engagement in employment and education activities, whereas non-active CSI members showed reduced engagement in these other important activities. Active CSI members also reported an increase in social support over time that was larger than the increase reported by non-active CSI members. Internal validity in this study is not as high as it would be if people had been randomly assigned to be active versus non-active CSI members. *Selection differences* still provide an alternative explanation for the results. To help partly address this concern, researchers used a pretest to demonstrate that these groups were similar in terms of demographics and symptom severity at the start of the study. Using the most internally valid design that was possible in this circumstance, results are consistent with the hypothesis that actively engaging in CSIs after experiencing a mental illness can promote various aspects of well-being.

Interrupted Time Series Design

The next two designs are similar to the one-group pretest-posttest design and the non-equivalent group pretest-posttest design, respectively. The key change is that there are multiple pretests and multiple posttests, instead of just one (see Table 11.1). These designs are commonly used to examine effects of natural "manipulations" in society, like the passing of laws. Archival data (see Chapter 6) are often used in these designs.

Asbridge and colleagues (2009) evaluated Ontario's crackdown on driving while intoxicated. Specifically, Ontario passed the administrative driver's licence suspension (ADLS) law in November 1996, which meant an immediate 90-day licence suspension to anyone caught driving while over the legal limit (i.e., a blood alcohol content of over 0.08 [80 mg per 100 mL of blood]), or for refusing to take a breathalyzer test to evaluate their blood alcohol content. Although seemingly an event in the distant past, the example offers a good illustration of an important methodological issue. The easiest way to evaluate the effect of this law is to compare the number of driver fatalities in 1996 (before the crackdown) with the number of fatalities in 1997 (after the crackdown). There was no immediate reduction in the number of driver deaths between 1996 and 1997. This single comparison is really a one-group pretest-posttest design with all of that design's problems of internal validity; there are many other reasons that traffic deaths might have declined or not.

One alternative is to use an **interrupted time series design** that would examine the traffic fatality rates over an extended period of time, both before

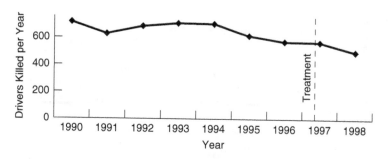

FIGURE 11.4
Ontario driver
fatalities,
1990–1998

Source: Adapted from Asbridge, M., Mann, R.E., Smart, R.G., Stoduto, G., Beirness, D., Lamble, R., & Vingilis, E. (2009). The effects of Ontario's administrative driver's licence suspension law on total driver fatalities: A multiple time series analysis. *Drugs: Education, Prevention, Policy, 16,* 140-151, Figure 1, p. 145.

and after the law was passed. Figure 11.4 shows this information for the years 1990 to 1998. There is a steady–and statistically significant–downward trend in fatalities after the crackdown, after many years of high fatality rates. Yet, you may notice a remaining problem in interpretation. The year just prior to the intervention, 1996, was already lower than all previous years. It is possible that citizens may have heard of the soon-to-pass law and had begun curbing their drinking and driving behaviour. It is also possible that 1996 was just a random fluctuation. Still, the data for the years extending before and after the crackdown allow for a less ambiguous interpretation than would be possible with data for only 1996 and 1997.

Control Series Design

One way to improve the interrupted time series design is to find some kind of control group and create a **control series design.** In the case of the Ontario ADLS law, this was possible because other provinces had not passed any similar law during that time period. Figure 11.5 shows the same data on driver fatalities in Ontario, plus the fatality rates for Manitoba and New Brunswick (combined) during the same years. The fact that fatality rates in the control provinces remained relatively constant while those in Ontario declined by 14.5 percent led Asbridge et al. (2009) to conclude that the law had some effect on reducing driver fatalities.

We have now explored some of the various single case and quasi-experimental designs for use in special data collection circumstances. Of course, these designs are never as high in internal validity as true experiments. While acknowledging their limitations, these designs can provide a valuable opportunity to gain some insight into how variables relate to each other. Next we consider some design options available for researchers interested in changes and growth over time.

FIGURE 11.5
Control series design comparing driver fatality rates for Ontario (dark line) and two comparable provinces (light line)

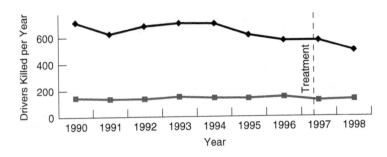

Source: Adapted from Asbridge, M., Mann, R.E., Smart, R. G., Stoduto, G., Beirness, D., Lamble, R., & Vingilis, E. (2009). The effects of Ontario's administrative driver's licence suspension law on total driver fatalities: A multiple time series analysis. *Drugs: Education, Prevention, Policy, 16,* 140–151, Figure 1, p. 145.

DEVELOPMENTAL RESEARCH DESIGNS

Developmental psychologists often study the ways people change as a function of age. A researcher might develop a hypothesis about changes in reasoning ability as children grow older, the age at which self-awareness develops in young children, or the values people report as they move from adolescence through old age. In all cases, the major variable is age. Developmental researchers use two general methods for studying people of different ages: the cross-sectional method and the longitudinal method. You will see that the cross-sectional method shares similarities with the independent groups design whereas the longitudinal method is similar to the repeated measures design. We will also examine a hybrid approach called the sequential method. The three approaches are illustrated in Figure 11.6.

Longitudinal Method

In the **longitudinal method,** the same group of people is observed at different points in time as they grow older. Most longitudinal studies study people over only a few years. For example, an eight-year study of Swedish children demonstrated positive effects of day care (Broberg, Wessels, Lamb, & Hwang, 1997). Other studies span much larger time frames. One famous longitudinal study is the Terman Life-Cycle Study that was begun by Stanford psychologist Lewis Terman in 1921. Terman studied 1,528 California schoolchildren who had intelligence test scores of at least 135. The participants, who called themselves "Termites," were initially measured on numerous aspects of their cognitive and social development in 1921 and 1922. Terman and his colleagues continued studying the Termites during their childhood and adolescence and

Cross-Sectional Method

	Year of birth (cohort)	Time 1: 2010
Group 1:	1955	55 years old
Group 2:	1950	60 years old
Group 3:	1945	65 years old

FIGURE II.6
Three designs
for develop-
mental
research

Longitudinal Method

	Year of birth (cohort)	Time 1: 2010	Time 2: 2015	Time 3: 2020
Group 1:	1955	55 years old ⟶	60 years old ⟶	65 years old

Sequential Method

	Year of birth (cohort)	Time 1: 2010	Time 2: 2015	Time 3: 2020
Group 1:	1955	55 years old ⟶	60 years old ⟶	65 years old
Group 2:	1945	65 years old ⟶	70 years old ⟶	75 years old

throughout their adult lives (cf., Terman, 1925; Terman & Oden, 1947, 1959). Terman's successors at Stanford continue to track the Termites until each one dies. The study has provided a rich description of the lives of highly intelligent people and offered evidence disputing many negative stereotypes of high intelligence—for example, the Termites were socially and emotionally well-adjusted. The data have been archived for use by other researchers. Friedman et al. (1995) used the Terman data to study social and health practice factors associated with age at death. One intriguing finding was that the personality dimension of "conscientiousness" is related to longevity. More recently, researchers found that sleeping more or less than the group's average during childhood predicted earlier deaths among male but not female Termites (Duggan, Reynolds, Kern, & Friedman, 2014).

A longitudinal study on aging and Alzheimer's disease called the Nun Study illustrates a different approach (Snowden, 1997). In 1991, all members of a particular religious order born prior to 1917 were asked to participate by providing access to their archived records as well as various annual medical and psychological measures taken over the course of the study. The sample consisted of 678 women with a mean age of 83. One fascinating finding from this study was based on autobiographies that all women wrote in 1930 (Donner, Snowden, & Friesen, 2001). The researchers devised a coding system (see Chapter 6) to measure positive emotional content in the autobiographies. Greater positive emotions were strongly positively correlated with actual survival rate during the course of the study.

Cross-Sectional Method

When using the **cross-sectional method,** people of different ages are studied at only one point in time. Suppose you are interested in examining how the ability to learn a computer application changes as people grow older. Using the cross-sectional method, you might study people who are currently 20, 30, 40, and 50 years of age. The participants in your study would be given the same computer learning task, and you would compare groups on their performance.

Comparing Longitudinal and Cross-Sectional Methods

The cross-sectional method is much more common than the longitudinal method, primarily because it is less expensive and immediately yields results. It would take 30 years to study the same group of people from age 20 to 50 with a longitudinal design, but with a cross-sectional design, comparisons of different age groups can be obtained relatively quickly.

There are, however, some disadvantages to cross-sectional designs. Most important, the researcher must infer that differences among age groups actually are due to age. Developmental change is not observed directly within the same group of people, but rather is based on comparisons among different cohorts. You can think of a *cohort* as a group of people born at about the same time, exposed to the same events in a society, and influenced by the same demographic trends such as divorce rates and family size. If you think about the hairstyles of people you know who are in their 30s, 40s, 50s, and 60s, you may recognize the importance of cohort effects. More crucially, differences among cohorts reflect different economic and political conditions in society, different music and technology, different educational systems, and different child-rearing practices. In a cross-sectional study, a difference among groups of different ages may reflect developmental age changes; however, an alternative explanation is that the differences may result from **cohort effects** (Schaie, 1986).

To illustrate this issue, let's consider the hypothetical study on learning to use computers. Suppose you found that age is associated with lower ability such that the 50-year-olds score lower on the learning measure than the 40-year-olds, and so on. Should you conclude that the ability to learn to use a computer application decreases with age? That may be an accurate conclusion. Alternatively, the differences could be due to a *cohort effect:* The older people had less experience with computers while growing up. We would not expect today's 20-year-olds to have as much difficulty learning to use a computer in 30 years, compared to today's 50-year-old person. The key point here is that the cross-sectional method confounds cohort effects with the variable of interest: age. Cohort effects are most likely to be a problem when the researcher is examining age effects across a wide range of ages (e.g., adolescents through older adults). The life experiences of adolescents versus retired adults are likely to be much more different than life experiences of people in their mid-teens versus early twenties, for example.

The only way to conclusively study changes that occur as people grow older is to use a longitudinal design. Longitudinal research is the best way to study how scores on a variable at one age are related to another variable at a later age. If a researcher wants to study how the home environment of children at age 5 is related to school achievement at age 13, a longitudinal study provides the best data. The alternative in this case would be to study 13-year-olds and ask them or their parents about their earlier home environment; this *retrospective* approach introduces other challenges, including the difficulty of accurately remembering events in the distant past.

Thus, the longitudinal approach, despite being expensive and difficult, has definite advantages. However, there is one major problem: Over the course of a longitudinal study, people may move, die, or lose interest in the study. In other words, there is a great risk of high participant *mortality* (see also Chapter 8). Researchers who conduct longitudinal studies become adept at convincing people to continue, often travel anywhere to collect more data, or scour social media sites (e.g., Facebook) to maintain connections over time (see Mychasiuk & Benzies, 2011). To appropriately analyze results, they must compare scores of people who drop out with those who stay. A researcher shouldn't embark on a longitudinal study without considerable resources and a great deal of patience and energy.

Sequential Method

The **sequential method** blends both longitudinal and cross-sectional methods. The first goal of the sequential study depicted in Figure 11.6 is to compare 55- and 65-year-olds. The first phase of the sequential method begins with the cross-sectional method; for example, you could study groups of 55- and 65-year-olds. All participants are then studied using the longitudinal method; each person is tested at least one more time. This method may take fewer years to complete than a longitudinal study, and cross-sectional data are ready to analyze and potentially publish while longitudinal data are being collected.

We have now described most of the major approaches to designing research. Earlier in this text we examined true experimental designs in increasing detail (Chapters 4, 8, and 10), as well as various methods typically used in non-experimental designs (correlations and surveys in Chapters 4 and 7, observational methods in Chapter 6). The current chapter addressed a variety of options available when a researcher wishes to conduct a true experiment but practical circumstances prevent it (e.g., no access to a control group, unable to randomly assign people to conditions). In the next two chapters, we introduce the foundations of data analysis using statistics.

STUDY TERMS

Test yourself! Define and generate an example of each of these key terms.

Baseline (p. 221)

Cohort effects (p. 242)

Control series design (p. 239)

Cross-sectional method (p. 242)

History effects (p. 232)

Instrument decay (p. 233)

Interrupted time series design (p. 238)

Longitudinal method (p. 240)

Maturation effects (p. 233)

Multiple baseline design (p. 223)

Non-equivalent control group design (p. 236)

Non-equivalent control group pretest-posttest design (p. 237)

One-group posttest-only design (p. 229)

One-group pretest-posttest design (p. 231)

Program evaluation (p. 226)

Quasi-experimental designs (p. 228)

Regression toward the mean (p. 234)

Reversal design (p. 222)

Selection differences (p. 236)

Sequential method (p. 243)

Single case experimental design (p. 221)

Testing effects (p. 233)

REVIEW QUESTIONS

Test yourself on this chapter's learning objectives. Can you answer each of these questions?

1. What is a reversal design? How is an ABAB design superior to an ABA design?

2. What is meant by *baseline* in a single case design?

3. What is a multiple baseline design? Why is it used? Distinguish among multiple baseline designs across participants, across behaviours, and across situations.

4. List five types of program evaluation research questions. What research goals does each address?

5. Why might a researcher use a quasi-experimental design rather than a true experimental design?

6. Why does adding a control group eliminate some problems associated with the one-group pretest-posttest design?

7. Describe the threats to internal validity discussed in this chapter. How do they threaten internal validity?

8. Describe the non-equivalent control group pretest-posttest design. What makes this design a quasi-experiment rather than a true experiment?

9. Contrast the interrupted time series from the control series designs. Which design has higher internal validity? Why?

10. Compare the features, advantages, and disadvantages of longitudinal, cross-sectional, and sequential methods. In which of these designs are cohort effects problematic? Explain your rationale.

DEEPEN YOUR UNDERSTANDING

Develop your mastery of these concepts by considering these application questions. Compare your responses with those from other people in your study group.

1. Your dog gets lonely while you are at work and consequently engages in destructive activities such as pulling down curtains or strewing garbage all over the floor. You decide that playing a radio while you are gone might help. How might you determine whether this "treatment" is effective?

2. The captain of each precinct of a metropolitan police service selected two officers to participate in a program designed to reduce prejudice by increasing sensitivity to racial and ethnic group differences. The training program took place every Friday morning for three months. At the first and last meetings, the officers completed a measure of prejudice. To assess the program's effectiveness, the average prejudice score at the first meeting was compared with the average score at the last meeting; the average score was in fact lower following the training program. What type of design is this? What specific problems arise if you try to conclude that the training program was responsible for the reduction in prejudice?

3. Many elementary schools have implemented a daily silent reading period during which students, faculty, and staff spend 20 minutes silently reading a book of their choice. Advocates of this policy claim that the activity encourages pleasure reading outside the required silent reading time. Design a non-equivalent control group pretest-posttest quasi-experiment to test this claim. Include a well-reasoned dependent measure. Is a true experiment possible in this case? Why or why not?

4. Dr. Cardenas studied political attitudes among different groups of 20-, 40-, and 60-year-olds. Political attitudes were found to be most conservative in the age-60 group and least conservative in the age-20 group.

   a. What type of method was used?

   b. Can you conclude that people become more politically conservative as they get older? Why or why not?

   c. Propose alternative ways of studying this topic.

12

Understanding Research Results: Describing Variables and Relationships among Them

LEARNING OBJECTIVES

Keep these learning objectives in mind as you read to help you identify the most critical information in this chapter.

By the end of this chapter, you should be able to:

1	Describe frequency distributions and ways to visually depict them.
2	Interpret measures of central tendency and variability.
3	Identify ways to describe and graph relationships involving nominal variable.
4	Identify and interpret an estimate of effect size between two groups.
5	Interpret correlation coefficients and scatterplots to describe relationships among continuous variables.
6	Describe how regression equations and multiple correlations are used to predict behaviour.
7	Discuss how a partial correlation addresses the third-variable problem.

Statistics help us understand the data collected in research investigations. In Chapter 12, we explore ways in which statistics and graphs are used to describe data. In Chapter 13, we discuss how statistics are used to help us make inferences, on the basis of sample data, about populations. We aim to introduce the underlying logic and general procedures for making statistical decisions. Specific calculations for various statistics are provided in Appendix B.

Concepts throughout this chapter are frequently illustrated using World Values Survey data (World Values Survey Wave 6, 2010-2014). These survey data were collected from 74,044 participants across 52 countries on various topics, including life satisfaction; perceived health, wealth, and safety; and religious and political views. You can download the dataset at www.worldvaluessurvey.org, and use it to practise some basic analyses and graphs.

REVISITING SCALES OF MEASUREMENT

Choosing the appropriate statistical analyses and graphs depends crucially on each variable's scale of measurement (see Chapter 5). A brief review of nominal, ordinal, interval, and ratio scales will help us throughout the next two chapters.

The levels of *nominal scale* variables are simply different categories or groups that have no numerical properties. For example, when behavioural and cognitive therapies are compared as treatments for depression, the two therapies are nominal categories. Variables using *ordinal scales* rank order the levels from lowest to highest, but the intervals between each rank order are not equal. Variables that use an *interval scale* have spaces between the levels that are equal in size. For example, intelligence quotient (IQ) tests often use an interval scale. The difference between 90 and 95 on the scale should be the same as the difference between 115 and 120. There is no absolute zero point that indicates an "absence" of intelligence. In contrast, *ratio scales* have equal intervals plus a true zero point. Response time and age are examples of ratio scales.

In the behavioural sciences, it is sometimes difficult to know precisely whether an ordinal or an interval scale is being used. For example, we assume that asking people to rate their state of health on a 4-point scale ranging from *very good* to *poor* uses an interval scale. Yet it is difficult to claim that, conceptually speaking, *very good* and *good* (represented by numbers 4 and 3) are equally distant as *fair* and *poor* (represented by numbers 2 and 1). But these anchors are not truly ordinal either. It is common practice to assume that variables measured like in this example use an interval scale because interval scales allow for more sophisticated statistical treatments than do ordinal scales.

The statistical procedures used to analyze data with interval and ratio variables are identical. Importantly, data measured on interval and ratio scales can be summarized using the *mean*, or arithmetic average. It is possible to provide a number that reflects the *mean* amount of a variable–for example, "on average, people rated their health as 2.1 on a 4-point scale" or the "mean age of the sample was 41.92 years." As we will see, the *mean* is used in many statistical analyses. Variables measured on interval and ratio scales are often referred to as *continuous variables* because the values represent an underlying continuum (at least in theory). They can be treated the same way statistically, so we will use that term as well.

DESCRIBING EACH VARIABLE

After collecting data, it is time to analyze the results. The first step a researcher may take is to explore each variable separately. Depending on measurement scale, different graphs and analyses will be appropriate. Let's consider some options.

LOI

Graphing Frequency Distributions

A **frequency distribution** indicates the number of participants who receive or select each possible score on a variable, and can be created for variables using any scale. Frequency distributions of exam scores are familiar to many students–they tell how many students received a given score on the exam, using either raw scores or percentages.

Frequency distributions are often depicted graphically to enable a quick visual inspection. You quickly can see what scores are most frequent and you can look at the shape of the distribution of scores. You can tell whether there are any **outliers**–scores that are unusual, unexpected, or very different from the scores of other participants. An outlier might reflect a data entry error (e.g., a person's age appears as 333) that can be corrected. Let's examine several types of graphs that are used to depict frequency distributions: pie chart, bar graph, histogram, and frequency polygon. Of these types, bar graphs and histograms are the most common.

Bar Graphs   A **bar graph** uses a separate and distinct bar for each piece of information. Bar graphs are commonly used for comparing group *means* (e.g., Figure 12.4) but can also be used for comparing *percentages*, as we have shown in Figure 12.1. World Values Survey respondents chose one of five responses to the question "Which of the following problems do you consider the most serious one for the world as a whole?" In this graph, the horizontal *x* axis shows the five possible responses. The vertical *y* axis shows the proportion of people who chose each response. Over half of the sample chose *poverty* over the other options.

Pie Charts   A **pie chart** divides a whole circle, or "pie," into "slices" that represent relative percentages. Pie charts are particularly useful when representing nominal scale information. Instead of using a bar graph for the data in Figure 12.1, we could have divided a circle into five sections corresponding to the five response options. The largest section would represent the *poverty* response option because it was selected most frequently. You will not see many pie charts in journal articles that you read. However, they are used frequently in applied research reports, infographics, newspapers, and magazines.

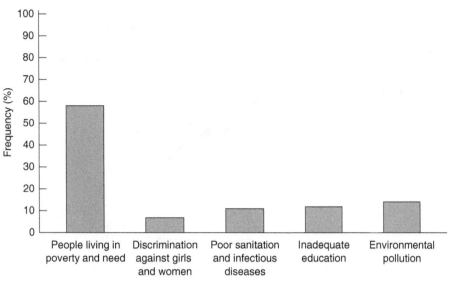

FIGURE 12.1
Most serious
problem for
the world as a
whole (World
Values Survey)

Data from World Values Survey Wave 6, 2010–2014. World Values Survey Association.
Retrieved from http://www.worldvaluessurvey.org.

Histograms A **histogram** uses bars to display a frequency distribution for a
continuous variable. In this case, the scale values along the *x* axis are continuous
and show increasing amounts of a variable such as blood pressure, stress, reaction
time, or number of correct responses. Figure 12.2 shows a histogram summarizing

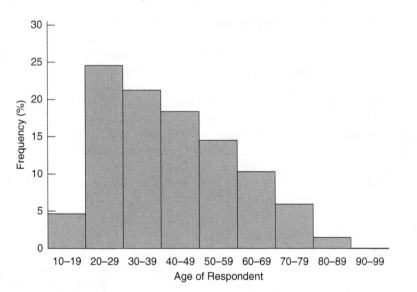

FIGURE 12.2
Histogram
showing fre-
quency of
respondents,
grouped by
age, to the
World Values
Survey

Data from World Values Survey Wave 6, 2010–2014. World Values Survey Association.
Retrieved from http://www.worldvaluessurvey.org.

FIGURE 12.3
Frequency polygons illustrating the distributions of respondents by age for the full World Values Survey sample, for the Australian sample, and for the Mexican sample

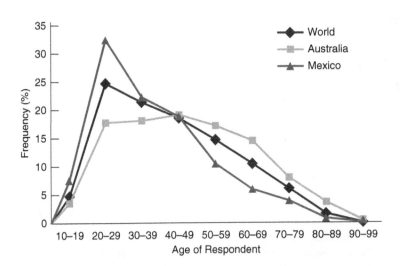

Note: Each frequency polygon is anchored at scores that were not obtained by anyone, just beyond the range of collected data.

Data from World Values Survey Wave 6, 2010–2014. World Values Survey Association. Retrieved from http://www.worldvaluessurvey.org.

the age of World Values Survey respondents. Notice that the histogram bars touch each other, reflecting the fact that the variable on the *x* axis is measured in *continuous* values. This display contrasts with the bar graph (see Figure 12.1), which is the correct graph to use when the values on the *x* axis are nominal categories.

Frequency Polygons **Frequency polygons,** an alternative to histograms, use a line to represent frequencies when the variable uses an interval or ratio scale. Frequency polygons are especially helpful when you want to examine frequencies for multiple groups simultaneously. Age data from the World Values Survey are depicted in Figure 12.3 using three frequency polygons—one for the total sample, one for the Australian sample, and one for the Mexican sample. This graph helps us to visualize the distribution of age in each group. When interpreting responses from different countries, it may be useful to note that the Australian sample represents an approximately even proportion of people in groups representing ages 20 through 59, but the Mexican sample includes more 20- to 29-year-olds than any other group. Layered frequency polygons make it easy to see this difference.

LO2

Descriptive Statistics

Visual frequency distributions are a good start, but are not yet useful for further statistical analyses. Researchers calculate **descriptive statistics** to make precise statements that summarize the data. *Central tendency* summarizes how participants scored overall, and *variability* summarizes how widely the distribution of scores is spread. These two values can be calculated to summarize each variable. If a study will be comparing across groups (e.g., an experiment with two conditions, participants' cultural background), descriptive statistics are calculated separately for each group.

Central Tendency   A **central tendency** statistic tells us what the sample is like as a whole, or on the average. There are three measures of central tendency–the mean, the median, and the mode. The **mean** of a set of scores is obtained by adding all the scores and dividing by the number of scores. For calculations, it is symbolized as $\bar{X}$ (pronounced "X bar"); in scientific reports, it is abbreviated as *M*. The mean is an appropriate indicator of central tendency only when scores are measured on an interval or ratio scale, because all of the actual values of the numbers are used in calculating the statistic. The mean age of all respondents to the World Values Survey was 41.92 years. The mean age of Australian respondents was 46.38 years, and it was 37.48 years for Mexican respondents. Figure 12.3 showed us visually that the Australian sample tended to be older than the Mexican sample. The mean provides us with a precise value that we can use to summarize each group.

The **median** is the score that divides the group in half (with 50 percent scoring below and 50 percent scoring above the median). In scientific reports, the median is abbreviated as *Mdn*. The median is appropriate when scores are on an ordinal scale because it takes into account only the rank order of the scores. It can be calculated with interval and ratio scale variables as well. The median age of all respondents to the World Values Survey was 40. The median for Australian respondents was 45, but it was only 35 for Mexican respondents. These values are consistent with what we learned from the mean but are less precise indicators of central tendency.

The **mode** is the most frequent score. The mode is the *only* measure of central tendency that is appropriate if a nominal scale is used. For example, in Figure 12.1, note that the mode choice for the most serious problem is *poverty*. The mode does not use most of the actual values on the scale, but simply indicates the most frequently occurring value (or values, if there is a tie for most frequent). The most frequently occurring age among World Values Survey respondents is 30 years (44 among Australians, 29 among Mexicans).

The median or mode can be a better indicator of central tendency than the mean if a few unusual scores bias the mean. For example, the median family income of a country is usually a better measure of central tendency than the mean family income. Because a relatively small number of people have extremely high incomes, using the mean would make it appear that the "average" person makes more money than is actually the case.

Variability   A measure of **variability** is a number that characterizes the amount of spread in a distribution of scores that are measured on interval or ratio scales. One such measure is the **standard deviation,** symbolized as *s,* which indicates how far away scores tend to be from the mean, on average. In scientific reports, the standard deviation is abbreviated as *SD*. The standard deviation is small when most people have scores close to the mean, and it becomes larger as more people have scores that lie further from the mean. For example, among Australian respondents to the World Values Survey, the standard deviation of age is 17.73, which tells us that most people in the sample are 17.73 units above and below the mean–that is, between 28.65 and 64.11 years of age. Among Mexicans, the standard deviation of age is 15.18, meaning that most people in the sample are between 22.30 and 52.66 years of age. Thus, the mean and standard deviation together provide much information about the way the scores are distributed in a group.

The standard deviation is derived by first calculating the **variance,** symbolized as s^2 (the standard deviation is the square root of the variance; see Appendix B for equations). Note that, as with the mean, the calculation of the standard deviation uses the actual values of all scores; thus, the standard deviation is appropriate only for interval and ratio scale variables. The variance is not interpreted in this way, but becomes an important value when calculating other statistics.

Another measure of variability is the *range*. In its simplest and most commonly used calculation, the range is the difference between the highest score and the lowest score. The age range for the Australian respondents in the World Values Survey is 77 (oldest = 95, youngest = 18), whereas it is 75 among Mexican respondents (oldest = 93, youngest = 18). The range is not as informative as the standard deviation because it tells us only about the difference between two scores, rather than indicating how the majority of scores compare with the mean.

LO3

DESCRIBING RELATIONSHIPS INVOLVING NOMINAL VARIABLES

Most research focuses on the study of relationships between variables. Depending on the way the variables are measured and the research questions being explored, there are different ways to describe the results. In this section we will consider comparing group percentages (when both variables have nominal scales) and comparing group means (when one variable has a nominal scale and the other is continuous). After describing data using percentages or means, the next step is typically a statistical analysis to determine whether there is a statistically significant difference between nominal groups (see Chapter 13 and Appendix B).

Comparing Groups of Participants

Comparing Group Percentages   Suppose you want to know whether Australians and Mexicans differ in what they consider to be the most serious problem facing the world. In the World Values Survey, people from each country were asked to choose one of five options (see Figure 12.1). How many people chose "discrimination against girls and women" as the most serious problem? Sixty-two of the 1,472 Australian respondents chose this option, whereas 283 of the 1,987 Mexican respondents did. To describe these results, calculate the percentage for each group: 4.2 percent of Australian respondents and 14.2 percent of Mexican respondents. There appears to be a relationship between nationality and perceived seriousness of discrimination against girls and women (at least when comparing these two nationalities specifically). Note that we are focusing on percentages because both variables (nationality and serious problem) are nominal.

Comparing Group Means   Much research is designed to compare mean responses to continuous variables made by participants in two or more nominal groups (including designs found in Chapters 8 and 10 as well as some in Chapter 11). For example, consider an experiment designed to study the effect of feeling powerful on feelings of well-being (Kifer, Heller, Perunovic, & Galinsky, 2013). Participants were randomly assigned to one of two conditions. All participants wrote about a situation from their past. Those in the high-power condition wrote about a time when they were able to control or evaluate another person; those in the low-power condition wrote about a time when someone else controlled or evaluated them. Each participant then rated their well-being. Researchers found that the mean well-being scores reported by people in the high-power condition were higher than the mean reported by people in the low-power condition. Looking to improve your well-being today? Consider remembering a time when you felt powerful!

Another way to form groups for comparison is using *participant variables* (see Chapter 10). Using data from the World Values Survey, we can compare different groups' mean life satisfaction. One question asks, "All things considered, how satisfied are you with your life as a whole these days?" Response options range from 1 (*completely dissatisfied*) to 10 (*completely satisfied*). As mentioned earlier, this type of scale is treated like an interval scale for analysis in behavioural sciences. The mean response for Australian respondents was 7.20; for Mexican respondents, it was 8.51.

Graphing Nominal Data

A common way to graph relationships between variables when one variable is nominal is to use a bar graph or a line graph (see Chapter 10 for more examples). Figure 12.4 is a bar graph depicting the mean life satisfaction scores for the Australian and Mexican groups. The levels of the nominal variable (in this case, Australian and Mexican) are represented on the horizontal x axis, and the dependent variable values are shown on the vertical y axis. For each group, a point is placed along the y axis that represents the mean for the groups, and a bar is drawn to visually represent the mean value. Bar graphs are often used when the values on the x axis are nominal categories (e.g., Australian and

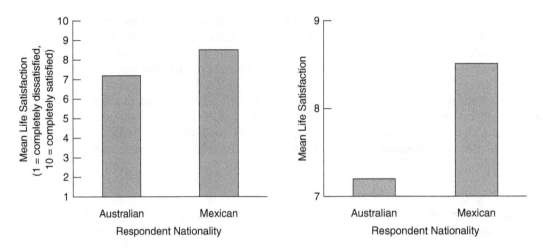

FIGURE 12.4
Honest and exaggerated graphs of mean life satisfaction scores comparing two nationalities

Data from World Values Survey Wave 6, 2010–2014. World Values Survey Association. Retrieved from http://www.worldvaluessurvey.org.

Mexican, or high-power condition and low-power condition). Line graphs are used when the values on the *x* axis are numeric (e.g., number of hours that teenagers work, as shown in Figure 7.1). In this case, a line is drawn connecting data points to represent the relationship between the variables.

Notice a common trick that is sometimes used to mislead readers. The trick is to exaggerate the distance between points on the *y* axis to make the results appear more dramatic than they really are. Suppose, for example, that a politician wanted to mislead people into thinking that Australians are dissatisfied with their lives compared with Mexicans (perhaps to argue in favour of some existing Mexican social program). They could use the same data in the left panel of Figure 12.4 to create the graph on the right. At first glance, it appears that Australians are dramatically dissatisfied with life. But look more closely: The scale on the *y* axis has been adjusted to exaggerate the difference between groups. It is always wise to look carefully at the numbers on the scales depicted in graphs.

LO4

Describing Effect Size between Two Groups

It is important to describe relationships among variables in terms of size, amount, or strength. **Effect size** is a general term for these indicators and is a vital descriptive tool to help us interpret the extent to which our study's results are meaningful. Effect size can be measured in many different ways, depending on the study design. When comparing two groups (e.g., two treatment conditions, two nationalities) on their responses to a variable measured on an interval or ratio scale, the appropriate way to calculate effect size is using **Cohen's *d*** (Cohen, 1988). In a true experiment, the Cohen's *d* value describes the magnitude of the effect of the independent variable on the dependent variable. In a study comparing naturally occurring groups, the Cohen's d value describes the magnitude of the effect of group membership on a continuous variable.

Cohen's d expresses effect size in terms of standard deviation units. A d value of 1.0 tells you that the means are 1 standard deviation apart; a d of .2 indicates that the means are separated by .2 standard deviations. The following rough guidelines are commonly used to interpret d values in the behavioural sciences: .2 indicates a small effect, .5 indicates a moderate effect, and .8 indicates a large effect. The smallest possible Cohen's d value is 0, indicating no effect, but there is no maximum value. Adding *confidence intervals* (see Chapter 7) around effect sizes offers even more valuable information about the range of effect sizes that are most likely to be true (Cumming, 2012, 2014; Kline, 2013).

Let's return to World Values Survey data comparing Australian versus Mexican nationality on life satisfaction. The mean life satisfaction among Australian respondents was 7.20 and the standard deviation was 2.05. The mean life satisfaction among Mexican respondents was 8.51 and the standard deviation was 1.93. Using these values and the formula in Appendix B, we can calculate that Cohen's $d = .66$. Life satisfaction among Mexican respondents was .66 standard deviations higher than life satisfaction among Australians, which indicates a moderately high effect size.

DESCRIBING RELATIONSHIPS AMONG CONTINUOUS VARIABLES: CORRELATING TWO VARIABLES

LO5

Different analyses are needed when you do not have distinct groups of subjects. In correlational designs, each participant is measured on at least two variables with a range of numerical values (see Chapter 4). The appropriate analysis involves a **correlation coefficient,** which is a statistic that describes whether, how, and how much two variables relate to each other. Is the relationship between variables relatively weak or strong, positive or negative, or is there no relationship at all? Whenever we use this type of analysis, it is critical to remember that a correlation tells us nothing about the potential causal relationship (see Chapter 4).

There are many different types of correlation coefficients. Each coefficient is calculated somewhat differently depending on the measurement scale that applies to the two variables (e.g., ordinal and interval). Because it is most common, we will focus on interpreting the **Pearson product-moment correlation coefficient** (usually just called the Pearson r). It is the correlation appropriate when both variables have interval or ratio scale properties.

Interpreting the Pearson r Correlation Coefficient

Recall from Chapter 5 that the value of a Pearson r can range from 0.00 to $\pm$ 1.00, which provides information about both the strength and the direction of the relationship. A correlation of 0.00 indicates that there is no relationship between the variables. The nearer a correlation is to 1.00 (positive or negative), the stronger is the relationship. Indeed, a ±1.00 correlation is sometimes called a *perfect relationship* because the two variables go together in a perfect fashion. The sign of the Pearson *r* tells us about the direction of the relationship; that is, it indicates whether there is a positive relationship or a negative relationship between the variables. A correlation coefficient of −.74 indicates a negative relationship that is stronger than the positive relationship indicated by a coefficient of +.21.

To calculate a correlation coefficient, we need to obtain pairs of observations: Each individual has two scores, one on each variable. Table 12.1 shows data for 10 fictitious World Values Survey respondents measured on the variables of life satisfaction and subjective feelings of physical health. Respondents rated their physical health on a scale that ranged from 1 (*poor*) to 4 (*very good*), and their life satisfaction on a scale that ranged from 1 (*completely dissatisfied*) to 10 (*completely satisfied*). Once we have collected our data, we can see whether the two variables are related. Do the variables go together systematically? To find out, we need to calculate a Pearson *r* correlation coefficient. See Appendix B for specific calculations; for now, we'll consider ways to interpret and graph these values.

The data in Table 12.1 correspond to a Pearson *r* value of .49, indicating a moderately positive relationship between life satisfaction and subjective physical health. (Note that actual data from all World Values Survey respondents indicate a smaller relationship: $r = .30$.)

Scatterplots

Data like those in Table 12.1 can be visualized in a **scatterplot** in which each pair of scores is plotted as a single point in a graph. Figure 12.5 shows two sample scatterplots. Values of the first variable are noted on the *x* axis; the values of the second variable are noted on the *y* axis. These scatterplots show

TABLE 12.1   Pairs of scores for 10 participants on subjective physical health and life satisfaction (fictitious data)

Participant Identification Number	Subjective Physical Health	Life Satisfaction
01	4	5
02	3	9
03	2	7
04	1	7
05	2	7
06	4	8
07	2	6
08	3	8
09	1	3
10	4	9

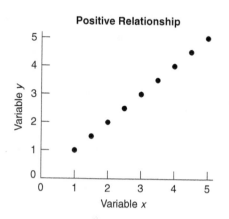

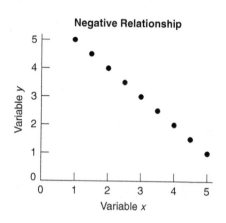

FIGURE 12.5
Scatterplots
of perfect
(±1.00)
relationships

a perfect positive relationship (+1.00) and a perfect negative relationship (−1.00). You can see the evidence of perfect relationships: The scores fall on a straight diagonal line. Each person's score on one variable goes perfectly with his or her score on the other variable. If we know a person's score on one of the variables, we can *predict* exactly what his or her score will be on the other variable. Such "perfect" relationships are rarely if ever observed in actuality.

The scatterplots in Figure 12.6 show patterns of correlation you are more likely to encounter. The relationships are not perfect. The first scatterplot shows pairs of scores that are positively correlated at +.65. You can make a general prediction that the higher the score on one variable, the higher the score on the second variable, but you cannot make an exact prediction. The second scatter-plot shows a negative relationship, −.77. There is a general but imperfect pattern that as scores on variable *y* increase, scores on variable *x* tend to decrease.

Whenever relationships are not perfect, if you know a person's score on the first variable, you cannot perfectly predict what that person's score will be on the second variable. To confirm this, take a look at value 1 on variable *x* (the horizontal axis) in the positive relationship scatterplot in Figure 12.6. You will see that two people had a score of 1. One of these people had a score of 1 on variable *y* (the vertical axis), and the other had a score of 3. The data points do not fall on the perfect diagonal. Instead, there is a variation (scatter) from the perfect diagonal line. Scatterplots allow a researcher to detect *outliers*, which are scores that are extremely distant from the rest of the data. Particularly when samples are small, outliers can skew correlation coefficients. As noted earlier, sometimes outliers indicate data entry errors; other times, a researcher may choose to analyze the data and report results both with and without the outlier.

The third graph (labelled No Relationship) shows a scatterplot in which there is absolutely no correlation (*r* = 0.00). The points fall in a completely random pattern. Scores on variable *x* are not related to scores on variable *y*. This type of random scatter would appear if we made a scatterplot of life satisfaction and age from World Values Survey data. These variables are almost completely uncorrelated: *r* = −.03. Based on these data, age has nothing to do with life satisfaction.

FIGURE 12.6
Scatterplots
depicting
patterns of
correlation:
Test yourself!

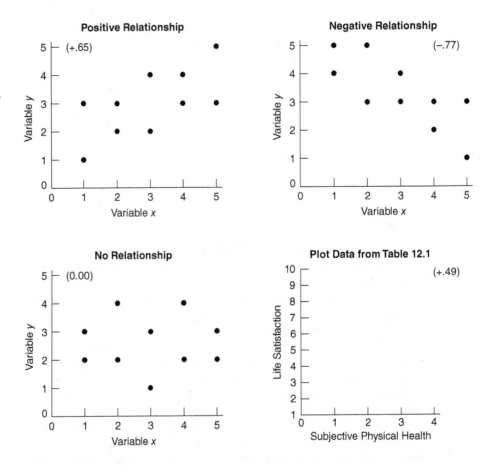

Test yourself! The fourth graph in Figure 12.6 has been left blank so that you can plot the data from Table 12.1. The horizontal *x* axis has been labelled for the subjective physical health variable, and the vertical *y* axis has been labelled for the life satisfaction variable. To complete the scatterplot, you will need to plot the 10 pairs of scores. For each individual in the sample, find the score on the subjective physical health variable, and then go up until you reach that person's life satisfaction score. A point placed there will describe the score on both variables. There will be 10 points on the finished scatterplot.

Important Considerations

Restriction of Range   It is important that the researcher sample from the full range of possible values of both variables. If the range of possible values is restricted, the correlation coefficient can be misleading. Examine the positive relationship depicted in Figure 12.6. Imagine the people in your sample had only scores of 1 or 2 on variable *x*; use your hand to cover the right side of that graph. Instead of showing a positive relationship, the variables now seem unrelated. With a "restricted range" of values, there is less variability in the scores and thus less variability that can be explained.

The problem of **restriction of range** occurs when the people in your sample are very similar on one or both of the variables you are studying. For example, in the World Values Survey data, age is negatively correlated with subjective feelings of health, $r = -.34$, as we might expect: As people get older, they tend to feel less healthy. However, when the range of age is restricted to respondents younger than 30, the relationship between age and subjective feelings of health shrinks to near zero, $r = -.07$. Restriction of range distorts relationships.

Curvilinear Relationship   The Pearson product-moment correlation coefficient (*r*) is designed to detect only linear relationships. If the relationship is curvilinear, as in the scatterplot shown in Figure 12.7, the correlation coefficient will not indicate the existence of a relationship. The Pearson *r* correlation coefficient calculated from these data is exactly 0.00, even though the two variables clearly are related.

Because the relationship between variables in your data might be curvilinear, it is important to inspect a scatterplot before looking at the magnitude of the Pearson *r*. The scatterplot is valuable because it gives a visual indication of the shape of the relationship. When the relationship is curvilinear, another type of correlation coefficient must be used to determine the strength of the relationship. Computer programs for statistical analysis can usually display scatterplots and can show you how well the data fit a linear or curvilinear relationship.

Correlation Coefficients as Effect Sizes

Recall that *effect size* is an important tool when describing research results. Each effect size indicator (e.g., Cohen's *d*) provides us with a scale of values that is consistent across studies, irrespective of the variables used, the particular research design selected, or the number of participants studied. The correlation

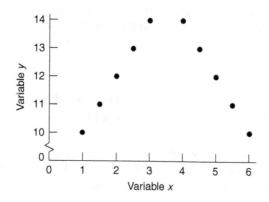

FIGURE 12.7 Scatterplot of a curvilinear relationship (Pearson correlation coefficient = 0.00)

coefficient can be considered an indicator of effect size; it indicates the strength of the linear association between two variables. When using the correlation coefficient as a measure of effect size, the values range from 0.00 to 1.00 (plus and minus values are not used). In the behavioural sciences, correlations near .15 (about .10 to .20) are considered small, those near .30 are medium, and correlations above .40 are large.

Results from studies examining eating-restraint scores among twins can illustrate the value of interpreting correlation coefficients as effect sizes. Eating restraint is the degree to which people monitor and restrict their food intake. The relationship between eating-restraint scores of identical twins is represented by a large correlation of .55, demonstrating that these pairs show a strong similarity in the degree to which they attempt to control their food. The correlation for fraternal twins is of medium size, $r = .31$. The fact that identical twins are more similar in their eating restraint than are fraternal twins led researchers to conclude that there is a genetic component to restrained eating (Schur, Noonan, Polivy, Goldberg, & Buchwald, 2009).

It is sometimes preferable to report the squared value of a correlation coefficient, noted as r^2. If the obtained $r = .50$, the $r^2 = .25$. Why square the value of r? This quick calculation changes the obtained r to a proportion, which can be converted to a percentage by multiplying by 100. Thus, the range of r^2 values can range from 0.00 (0 percent) to 1.00 (100 percent). The r^2, or **squared correlation coefficient,** value is sometimes referred to as the amount of *shared variance* between the two variables. In other words, it is the percent of variance in one variable accounted for by the second variable. Consider the relationship between life satisfaction and subjective feelings of health from the full World Values Survey. The correlation coefficient r is .30, which corresponds to a medium effect size. Convert that value to r^2 and multiply by 100, and we can state that 9 percent of the differences among people in life satisfaction are explainable using subjective feelings of health. Most (91 percent) of the variability in life satisfaction is *not* related to subjective feelings of health. This unexplained variability might be accounted for by other variables such as financial situation, opportunities for recreation, strong interpersonal relationships, and stress. You could account for 100 percent of the variability in life satisfaction if you had enough information on all other relevant variables: Each variable would make a contribution until all variability was accounted for.

DESCRIBING RELATIONSHIPS AMONG CONTINUOUS VARIABLES: INCREASING COMPLEXITY

The remainder of this chapter builds on your basic understanding of correlation by extending into the concept of prediction and accounting for additional variables. We will assume variables are measured on interval or ratio scales (i.e., they are continuous), although these analyses can be adapted for use with other types of variables.

Making Predictions Using the Regression Equation

Recall from Chapter 1 that one of the goals of psychological science is to predict behaviour. The statistical technique called *regression* allows us to pursue this goal. Like a correlation, regression analyzes relationships among variables. However, regression frames these as *predictive* relationships. Compare these two hypotheses:

> Subjective feelings of health are related to life satisfaction.
>
> Subjective feelings of health predict life satisfaction.

The first hypothesis indicates that a relationship between two variables is expected. The second hypothesis is framed in a different way: Scores on one variable are being used to make a prediction about people's scores on another variable. In both cases, the researcher would measure both life satisfaction and subjective feelings of health, but the frame of analysis would differ. A correlation would be used to test the first hypothesis, and regression would be used to test the second. The calculations for correlation and regression result in the same value when there are only two variables involved. However, the difference in the framing is important. As you will see, using the regression framework can be more powerful because it allows us to expand the analysis to include more variables, while describing relationships in terms of prediction.

Analyzing data using regression requires calculating a **regression equation,** which is the equation for a straight line. But not just any line–it's the line that best summarizes the data. Re-examine Figure 12.6. If we were to fit a regression line to the data in the top left graph, it would be angled upward, and it would have the smallest distance possible from all data points. Then we could use the corresponding regression equation to make specific predictions. If we already know the regression equation that summarizes the ability for subjective feelings of health to predict life satisfaction, we could plug in someone's score on subjective feelings of health and use it to predict that person's life satisfaction. Consider a different example. In a clinical setting, if we know the regression equation summarizing the relationship between symptom severity and treatment duration, we could measure a new client's symptom severity and use it to *predict* how long that client will need treatment before symptoms are reduced.

The general form of a regression equation is

$$Y = a + bX$$

where Y is the score we wish to predict, X is the known score, a is a constant, and b is a weighting adjustment factor that is multiplied by X (it is the slope of the line created with this equation). The equations for these values of a and b are beyond the scope of this book; consult a statistics textbook for formulae. For now, just get a sense of how the full regression equation can be used. Using World Values Survey data, we can use subjective feelings of health to predict life satisfaction, resulting in the following regression equation:

$$Y = 4.51 + (0.81)X$$

Thus, if we know a person's score on X (subjective feelings of health), we can insert that into the equation and predict what that person's score on Y (life satisfaction) will be. Let's say someone's X score is 4 (indicating very good feelings of health), we can predict that $Y = 4.51 + (0.81)(4)$, or that the person's life satisfaction score will be 7.65 out of 10. Her actual score may not be exactly 7.65, but this is our best estimate given the regression equation based on prior data.

In summary, when researchers are interested in predicting some behaviour (called the **criterion variable**) using a person's score on some other variable (called the **predictor variable**), it is first necessary to collect data on both variables from many people. Then the regression equation can be calculated. If a predictive relationship exists, the equation can be used to make predictions about the criterion using only the predictor variable score.

Multiple Correlation and Multiple Regression

Thus far we have focused on relating two variables at a time. Yet many different variables may be related to a given behaviour. A technique called **multiple correlation** (symbolized as R to distinguish it from Pearson r) provides the correlation between a combined set of predictor variables and a single criterion variable. Taking many predictor variables into account usually permits greater accuracy of prediction than if any single predictor is considered alone. In other words, the multiple correlation is usually stronger than the correlation between any one of the predictor variables and the criterion variable. Note that the **squared multiple correlation coefficient** (R^2) is interpreted in much the same way as the squared correlation coefficient (r^2). That is, R^2 tells you the proportion of variability in the criterion variable that is accounted for by the *combined set* of predictor variables.

Regression is more powerful than the correlation because it can be expanded to accommodate more than one *predictor* to predict scores on the *criterion*. This expanded model is often called **multiple regression.** This technique allows us to examine the unique relationship between each predictor and the criterion. For example, we may wish to use both subjective feelings of health *and* satisfaction with household income to predict life satisfaction. In its general form, the expanded multiple regression equation looks like this:

$$Y = a + b_1X_1 + b_2X_2 + \dots + b_nX_n$$

where Y is the criterion variable, X_1 to X_n are the predictor variables, a is a constant, and b_1 to b_n are weights that are multiplied by scores on the predictor variables. Using World Values Survey data, the equation predicting life satisfaction looks like this:

Predicted life satisfaction $= 2.95 + 0.54$(subjective feelings of health)
$+ 0.40$(satisfaction with household income)

Just like in regression with one predictor, we could plug someone's ratings for subjective health and income satisfaction to use both of them to predict life satisfaction. Consider an applied example. Clinical psychologists may use multiple correlation to identify how long clients need treatment. The predictor variables might be (1) symptom severity, (2) degree of social support, (3) sex, and (4) willingness to engage in treatment. No one of these variables is a perfect predictor of how long clients will likely need treatment, but this combination can yield a more accurate prediction than using just one.

When researchers use multiple regression to study basic research topics (see Chapter 1), predicting an individual's score is not a high priority. Instead, when exploring predictive relationships in basic research, a slightly different version of the multiple regression equation is often used. This "standardized" version of the equation allows us to consider the relative importance of each predictor when predicting scores on the criterion. Essentially, the adjusted mathematical calculations make it possible to assume that all variables are measured on the same scale. When this is done, each predictor's weight (symbolized by b) reflects the magnitude of the relationship between the criterion variable and that predictor variable in the context of that set of predictors.

Integrating Results from Different Analyses

Let us recap what we have learned so far by synthesizing our ongoing World Values Survey data example. In a first step, we note that life satisfaction is correlated with each of our two intended predictors. The *correlation coefficient* between life satisfaction and subjective feelings of health is .30; between life satisfaction and satisfaction with household income, the correlation is .48. Next we can calculate the *multiple correlation*. We learn that life satisfaction correlates highly with the combination of the other two variables at .52 (and therefore $R^2 = .27$). Thus, 27 percent of the variance in life satisfaction is explained using satisfaction with household income along with subjective feelings of health. Is one variable a better predictor of life satisfaction than the other? That question must be addressed using *multiple regression*. Using the two predictors of life satisfaction (i.e., subjective feelings of health and satisfaction with household income), the "standardized" version of the multiple regression equation is:

Predicted life satisfaction $= 0.20$(subjective feelings of health)
$+ 0.43$(satisfaction with household income)

We learn that in this large, worldwide sample, life satisfaction has more to do with being satisfied with household income than with feeling healthy, but both are important contributors. Notice that each analysis (correlations, multiple correlation, multiple regression) has provided different information about how our variables relate to each other.

You might encounter visual depictions of regression equations in journal articles. The life satisfaction multiple regression model could be diagrammed as follows:

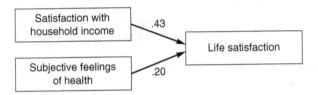

LO7

Partial Correlation and the Third-Variable Problem

As we have explored, the basic correlation coefficient can be adapted in many ways to address various research questions. Another technique–called *partial correlation*–is suited to address a specific issue: the third-variable problem. Recall that the *third-variable problem* occurs when two variables of interest are correlated with each other, but some uncontrolled third variable may be the reason why they are related to each other (see Chapter 4). This problem doesn't exist in experimental research because extraneous variables are controlled (e.g., by keeping the variables constant or by using random assignment).

Partial correlation provides a way of statistically controlling third variables in correlational studies. The result is a correlation between the two variables of interest, with the influence of the third variable removed from, or *partialed out of*, the original correlation. It estimates what the correlation between the primary variables would be if the third variable were *held constant*–in other words, if everyone responded in the same way to the third variable. This is not the same as actually keeping the variable constant, but it is a useful approximation. To calculate a partial correlation, you need to have scores on the two primary variables of interest as well as the third variable that you want to examine.

Suppose a researcher is interested in how much life satisfaction relates to people's perceptions of freedom of choice in their lives. After obtaining data–in this case from the World Values Survey–the researcher calculates that the correlation coefficient is .38, indicating a moderate positive effect. The researcher suspects that a third variable may be operating. Satisfaction with income could influence both life satisfaction and perceived freedom of choice. Because satisfaction with income was also measured, it can be included in a partial correlation calculation. The resulting value will indicate the relationship between life satisfaction and perceived freedom of choice while holding constant the effect of satisfaction with income.

When a partial correlation is calculated, you can compare the partial correlation with the original correlation to see if the third variable was influencing the original relationship. Is our original correlation of .38 substantially affected when satisfaction with income is held constant? The partial correlation is .29, indicating that a medium relationship between life satisfaction and perceived freedom of choice remains after removing the overlap from satisfaction with income.

Figure 12.8 shows two different visual depictions of correlations, for the sake of comparison. The correlation coefficient between each variable is indicated by the number near the line connecting those variables. Notice that both panels show the same .38 correlation between life satisfaction and perceived freedom of choice. The first panel shows that satisfaction with income correlated positively with both variables of interest. The partial correlation (removing the effect of satisfaction with income) drops from .38 to .29 because satisfaction with income is correlated with both of the primary variables. In the second panel, age is considered a potential third variable. However, this partial correlation remains almost the same at .37 because each variable is almost completely uncorrelated with age. Together, these examples show that the outcome of the partial correlation depends on the magnitude of the correlations between the third variable and both of the two variables of primary interest.

Advanced Modelling Techniques

Quantitative psychologists have developed many advanced statistical methods that are beyond our scope. Because it appears frequently in the research literature, let us just briefly explore one set of techniques called *structural equation modelling (SEM)*. SEM examines models that specify a set of relationships among many variables (see Kline, 2010; Ullman, 2007). A model is an expected pattern of relationships among many variables. The researcher starts by proposing a model based on a theory of how the variables may be causally related. After each variable has been measured, statistical methods are applied to examine how closely the proposed model actually "fits" the obtained data. Researchers typically present path diagrams to visually represent the models

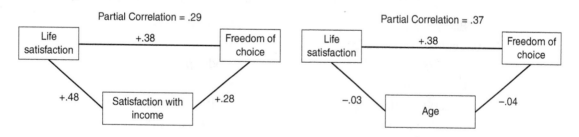

FIGURE 12.8

Two partial correlations between life satisfaction and freedom of choice

Data from World Values Survey Wave 6, 2010–2014. World Values Survey Association. Retrieved from http://www.worldvaluessurvey.org.

being tested. Such diagrams show the causal paths among the variables. The multiple regression diagram on life satisfaction shown earlier is an example of a path diagram of a very simple model.

There are many other applications of SEM. For example, SEM gives us the statistical tool to be able to evaluate mediating variables (see Chapter 4). SEM also enables researchers to compare two competing models in terms of how well each fits obtained data. Researchers can also use SEM to examine much more complex models that contain many more variables (for an example, see the analysis of job attitudes among women Canadian police officers by Tougas, Rinfret, Beaton, & de la Sablonnière, 2005). The major point here is that there are techniques to analyze data in complex ways, which can lead to a better understanding of the complex networks of relationships among variables.

COMBINING DESCRIPTIVE AND INFERENTIAL STATISTICS

The emphasis in this chapter has been on *describing* the data obtained in a study. We have included correlation, prediction, and effect size here because they emphasize describing the way the variables relate to each other. After describing the data, it is common practice to make decisions concerning the *statistical significance* of the results. Is the correlation coefficient statistically significant, given the sample size? Is the difference between the means of the high-power and low-power groups a statistically significant difference? In the next chapter, we turn to inferential statistics, which involves making decisions about statistical significance. Such decisions help us use data from a sample to estimate the way variables relate to each other in a population. Descriptive and inferential statistics are related, and you may find yourself returning to this chapter for some reminders about concepts that reappear (e.g., standard deviation, effect size).

STUDY TERMS

Test yourself! Define and generate an example of each of these key terms.

Bar graph (p. 248)

Central tendency (p. 251)

Cohen's *d* (p. 254)

Correlation coefficient (p. 255)

Criterion variable (p. 262)

Descriptive statistics (p. 250)

Effect size (p. 254)

Frequency distribution (p. 248)

Frequency polygons (p. 250)

Histogram (p. 249)

Mean (p. 251)

Median (p. 251)

Mode (p. 251)

Multiple correlation (p. 262)

Multiple regression (p. 262)

Outliers (p. 248)

Partial correlation (p. 264)

Pearson product-moment correlation coefficient (p. 255)

Pie chart (p. 248)

Predictor variable (p. 262)

Regression equation (p. 261)

Restriction of range (p. 259)

Scatterplot (p. 256)

Squared correlation coefficient (p. 260)

Squared multiple correlation
   coefficient (p. 262)

Standard deviation (p. 252)

Variability (p. 251)

Variance (p. 252)

REVIEW QUESTIONS

Test yourself on this chapter's learning objectives. Can you answer each of these questions?

1. What information does a frequency distribution provide?
2. Distinguish among a pie chart, bar graph, histogram, and frequency polygon. Construct one of each.
3. What information do measures of central tendency provide? Distinguish among the mean, median, and mode.
4. What information do measures of variability provide? Distinguish between the standard deviation and the range.
5. Under what circumstances would a researcher choose to compare percentages, compare means, or correlate scores?
6. What is a correlation coefficient? What do the size and sign of the correlation coefficient tell us about the relationship between variables?
7. What information does an effect size provide? Interpret Cohen's *d* and correlation coefficients as effect size indicators, and compare when each is used.
8. What is a scatterplot? What happens when a scatterplot shows a curvilinear relationship?
9. How does multiple correlation increase accuracy of prediction over a Pearson *r*?
10. What is a regression equation? How is regression similar to and different from a correlation?
11. What is the purpose of partial correlation?

DEEPEN YOUR UNDERSTANDING

Develop your mastery of these concepts by considering these application questions. Compare your responses with those from other people in your study group.

1. Hill (1990) studied correlations between final exam score in an introductory sociology course and several other variables (e.g., number of absences). The following Pearson *r* correlation coefficients with final exam score were obtained:

Overall college GPA	.72
Number of absences	−.51
Hours spent studying on weekdays	−.11
Hours spent studying on weekends	.31

Describe each correlation and draw graphs depicting the general shape of each relationship. Why do you think grades are differently correlated with hours spent studying on weekends versus weekdays?

2. Ask 20 students on campus to estimate how many hours per week they spend studying and how many hours per week they work in paid employment.

   a. Create a frequency distribution and find the mean for each of the two variables.

   b. Construct a scatterplot of these two variables. Does there appear to be a relationship between the variables? (*Note:* If there might be a restriction of range problem on your campus because few students work, ask different questions, such as number of Facebook friends or hours spent watching television each week.)

   c. Divide your sample into people who work in paid employment and people who do not. Calculate the mean number of hours spent studying separately for each group. Choose an appropriate graph to display your findings.

   d. What can you conclude about the relationship between these two variables? What can't you claim? Why?

3. Before the school year began, Ms. King reviewed the folders of students in her incoming Grade 4 class. She found that the standard deviation of students' scores on the Grade 3 reading comprehension test was exactly 0.00. What information does this provide her? How might that information prove useful for designing reading comprehension curriculum?

4. Select the correct answer(s) to questions a, b, and c.

   a. Which of the following numbers could *not* be a squared multiple correlation coefficient (R^2)?

   −.99   +.71   +1.02   −.01   −.38

   b. Which one of the following correlation coefficients indicates the strongest relationship?

   +.23   −.89   −.10   −.91   +.77

   c. Which of the following correlation coefficients indicates the weakest negative relationship?

   −.28   +.08   −.42   +.01   −.29

13

Understanding Research Results: Statistical Inference Basics

LEARNING OBJECTIVES

Keep these learning objectives in mind as you read to help you identify the most critical information in this chapter.

By the end of this chapter, you should be able to:

1	Explain the purpose of using inferential statistics to evaluate sample data.
2	Distinguish between the null hypothesis and the research hypothesis.
3	Discuss how a sampling distribution is used to determine statistical significance.
4	Describe when to use the t test, and explain the three basic steps to using it.
5	Describe the F test, including systematic variance and error variance.
6	Compare and contrast Type I and Type II errors, including elements that influence the probability of making them, and their impact on scientific progress.
7	Discuss multiple reasons non-significant results may occur.
8	Discuss how effect size and confidence intervals contribute to conclusion validity beyond hypothesis tests.

In the previous chapter, we examined ways of summarizing results of a study using descriptive statistics. Researchers are also interested in inferring whether the results that were obtained in a particular study are what we would find if we included the entire population instead of just a sample. In this chapter, we explore inferential statistics, which can be used to make this decision. We will also consider some of the many complex issues related to this decision. We have tried to simplify the discussion whenever possible. Nonetheless, if concepts in this chapter are challenging for you to grasp right away, you are not alone. Many of our students find this to be the most challenging chapter in this book. But fear not! Take your time, plan to read it more than once, complete the end-of-chapter questions, discuss the concepts with your classmates and instructor, and do your best.

INFERENTIAL STATISTICS: USING SAMPLES TO MAKE INFERENCES ABOUT POPULATIONS

LOI

The results of a given study are based on data obtained from a sample of research participants. Researchers rarely study entire populations, yet we want to make claims about populations. Would the results be similar if the study were conducted with the entire population? For example, would the difference in life satisfaction between Mexican and Australian respondents (see Figure 12.4 in Chapter 12) remain if we tested the whole population of each country? **Inferential statistics** are a way to help us infer whether a difference in sample means reflects a true difference in the population means.

Recall our discussion of making inferences using *confidence intervals* in Chapter 7. A sample of people in your province might tell you that 57 percent prefer the Conservative Party candidate for prime minister and 43 percent favour the Liberal Party candidate. The report then says that these results are accurate to within 3 percentage points, with a 95 percent confidence level. This means that out of 20 samples drawn from the population, 19 of the samples would show that 54 to 60 percent preferred the Conservative candidate, and 40 to 46 percent would prefer the Liberal candidate. In this case, the researcher could predict that the Conservative candidate will win because there is no overlap in the projected population values. Inferential statistics are a way to arrive at such conclusions on the basis of sample data. Is our result more likely to reflect a true effect in the population or just random chance?

It is important to note that inferential statistics have been heavily used—and criticized (see Cumming 2012, 2014; Kline, 2013). Concepts in this chapter will help you engage with the existing literature in psychology and the behavioural sciences. Some researchers are calling for increased reliance on other methods (including effect sizes and confidence intervals, and Bayesian techniques) to draw more thorough conclusions from our data. Therefore, we will revisit some of those topics at the end of this chapter.

Inferential Statistics: Ruling Out Chance

Much of our earlier discussion of experimental design centred on the importance of ensuring that groups are equivalent in every way except the independent variable manipulation (see Chapter 8). Equivalence of groups is achieved by experimentally controlling all other variables and by random assignment or repeated measures. If the groups are otherwise equivalent, any differences in the dependent variable are assumed to be caused by the independent variable.

In well-designed experiments, this assumption is often valid. However, it is also true that the difference between any two groups will almost never be zero, even when all of the principles of experimental design are used. This happens because we are dealing with samples rather than populations. Random error will be responsible for some difference in the means even if the independent variable had no effect on the dependent variable. Inferential statistics are a way to judge whether the difference between means reflects a real effect of the independent variable or simply random error. In other words, is the difference *statistically significant?*

Statistical Significance: An Overview

After collecting data and calculating descriptive statistics (e.g., means and standard deviations per group, or a correlation coefficient), a researcher must decide whether those values are **statistically significant.** In experimental designs, we ask: Are group differences most likely due to random error, or do they most likely reflect a real effect of the independent variable on the dependent variable in the population? To make this decision, a researcher subjects the data to a statistical test. There are many different kinds of statistical tests; which is most appropriate depends primarily on the study's design. The logic underlying the use of any statistical test rests on statistical theory, which is grounded in probability.

There are some general concepts that may help you understand what you are doing when you conduct a statistical test. (Don't worry if you don't understand right away; we will expand on these points throughout this chapter.) First, the goal of any statistical test is to allow you to make a decision about whether an effect that exists in a sample indicates the presence of a real effect in the population. Second, for each test, you need to decide how willing you are to be wrong if you say you really have captured an effect in the population. This is called the *significance level* (or *alpha level*). A .05 significance level says that you will conclude there is an effect in the population (when there really isn't) in 5 out of 100 times that the test is repeated on different samples from that population. Third, you are most likely to obtain significant results when you have a large sample size because larger sample sizes can provide better estimates of true population values. Finally, you are most likely to obtain significant results when the effect size is large (e.g., when differences between groups are large and variability of scores within groups is small). In the remainder of the chapter, we will expand on these concepts. We will start by considering the null hypothesis, which involves some basic concepts in probability.

LO2

NULL AND RESEARCH HYPOTHESES

Statistical inference begins with a statement of the null hypothesis and a research (or *alternative*) hypothesis. In Chapter 2 we discussed the *hypothesis* in general: the researcher's tentative idea about how variables are related (e.g., either causally or by correlation). In the framework of inferential statistics, this general hypothesis–that there is a relationship among variables in the population– is called the **research hypothesis.** In an experiment, the research hypothesis is that the means are *not* equal in the population. Notice that the hypothesis is framed in terms of the population because we are trying to *infer* whether our results would remain if everyone in the population participated in our study.

We also need to consider the possibility that any effect observed in our sample is due to error. This possibility is the focus of the **null hypothesis,** which assumes that there is no effect in the population. In correlation studies, the null hypothesis states that in the population the two variables are unrelated ($r = 0.00$); the research hypothesis states that in the population the two variables are related ($r \neq 0.00$). In experiments, the null hypothesis states that the independent variable has no effect on the dependent variable; the research hypothesis states that the independent variable does have an effect. These hypotheses capture the only two possibilities in the population: There either *is* or *is not* an effect, and we need to decide, using statistics on our sample data, which one is more likely to be true. Let us consider an example, using an experiment we discussed in Chapter 4 that was conducted at York University. This study compared people's lecture comprehension after listening to a lecture sitting either behind people who were multitasking on laptops or behind those who were not using laptops (Sana et al., 2013). The null and research hypotheses are as follows:

> H_0 (null hypothesis): The population mean comprehension for the "view of multitasking peers" group is equal to the population mean comprehension for the "no view of multitasking peers" group.
>
> H_1 (research hypothesis): The population mean comprehension for the "view of multitasking peers" group is *not* equal to the population mean comprehension for the "no view of multitasking peers" group.

The null hypothesis is rejected when there is a very low probability that the obtained results could be due to random error. This is what is meant by *statistical significance:* A "significant" result is one that has a very low probability of occurring if there is no effect in the population. It is unlikely that the difference between the sample means (or the non-zero correlation) was due to random error.

The logic of the null hypothesis is this: If we can determine, using statistics, that the null hypothesis is very unlikely to be true in the population, we reject it and conclude that our results are consistent with the research hypothesis. The null hypothesis is used in inferential statistics because it is a very precise statement–the population means are exactly equal or the correlation is exactly zero. This precision permits us to know the probability of the outcome of the study occurring if the null hypothesis is true in the population. Such precision isn't possible with the research hypothesis, so we infer that the research hypothesis is likely true in the population only by rejecting the null hypothesis as unlikely. Thus, *statistical significance* is a matter of probability.

PROBABILITY AND SAMPLING DISTRIBUTIONS

Probability is the likelihood that some event or outcome occurs. We all use probabilities frequently in everyday life. For example, if you say that you are likely to get an A in this course, you mean that this outcome has a high probability of occurring. Your probability statement is based on specific information, such as your grades on examinations. The weather forecaster says there is a 10 percent chance of rain today; this means that the likelihood of rain is very low. A gambler gauges the probability that a particular team will win the championship using past records of that team.

Probability in statistical inference is used in much the same way. We want to specify the probability that an event (in this case, a difference between means in the sample) will occur if there is no difference in the population. The question is: What is the probability of obtaining this result if only random error is operating? If this probability is very low, we reject the possibility that only random or chance error is responsible for the obtained difference in means–and we report our statistically significant results.

Probability: The Case of Mind Reading

The use of probability in statistical inference may be understood intuitively from an example. Suppose that a friend claims to have mind-reading ability (or ESP, extrasensory perception). You decide to test your friend by asking her to tell you which side of a coin lands up (heads or tails) when you toss it hidden from her view. In your single case experiment, you have 10 coin flip trials. Your task is to know whether your friend's answers reflect random error (guessing) or something more than random error. The null hypothesis in your study is that only random error is operating. The research hypothesis is that the number of correct answers shows more than random or chance guessing. (Note that rejecting the null hypothesis could mean that your friend has mind-reading ability, but it could also mean that the coin was weighted improperly, that you had somehow cued your friend when thinking about the head or tail, and so on.)

You can determine the number of correct answers to expect if the null hypothesis is correct. Just by guessing, one out of two answers (50 percent) should be correct. On 10 trials, five correct answers are expected under the null hypothesis. If, in the actual experiment, more (or fewer) than five correct answers are obtained, would you conclude that the obtained data reflect random error or something more than merely random guessing?

Suppose your friend gets six correct. You would probably conclude that only guessing is involved because you would recognize that there is a high probability of six correct answers *even though only five correct answers are expected under the null hypothesis.* You expect that exactly five answers in 10 trials would be correct in the long run, if you conducted this experiment with this participant over and over again. However, small deviations away from the expected five are highly likely in a sample of 10 trials.

Suppose, though, that your friend gets nine correct. You might conclude that the results indicate more than random error in this one sample of 10 observations. You might judge intuitively that an outcome of 90 percent correct when only 50 percent is expected is very unlikely. At this point, you may decide to reject the null hypothesis and state that the result is *significant*—it is very unlikely to occur if the null hypothesis is correct.

[LO3]

Sampling Distributions

You may have been able to judge intuitively that obtaining nine correct on the ten trials is very unlikely. Fortunately, we don't have to rely on intuition to determine the probabilities of different outcomes. Table 13.1 shows the probability of actually obtaining each of the possible outcomes in the mind-reading

TABLE 13.1   Exact probability of each possible outcome of the mind-reading experiment with 10 trials

Number of Correct Answers	Probability (Based on 50/50 Odds of Guessing Correctly)
10	.0010
9	.0098
8	.0439
7	.1172
6	.2051
5	.2461
4	.2051
3	.1172
2	.0439
1	.0098
0	.0010

experiment with 10 trials and a null hypothesis expectation of 50 percent correct. An outcome of five correct answers has the highest probability of occurrence (0.2461, or a 24.61 percent chance). Also, consistent with intuition, an outcome of six correct is highly probable, but an outcome of nine correct is highly unlikely (0.0098, or a 0.98 percent chance).

The probabilities shown in Table 13.1 were derived from a probability distribution called the *binomial distribution.* All statistical significance decisions are based on probability distributions such as this one. Such distributions are called *null hypothesis sampling distributions,* or simply sampling distributions (see Figure 13.1 for another example, displayed graphically). The **sampling distribution** is based on the assumption that the null hypothesis is true. In the mind-reading example, the null hypothesis is that the person is only guessing and should therefore get 50 percent correct. This sampling distribution assumes that if the null hypothesis is true, and you were to conduct the study with the same number of observations (ten) over and over again, the most frequent (but not every) finding would be 50 percent. Because of the random

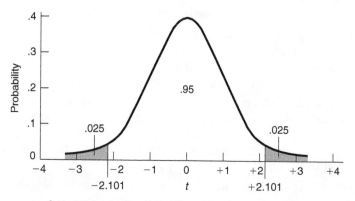

Critical Value for Two-Tailed Test with .05 Significance Level

FIGURE 13.1
Null hypothesis sampling distribution of *t* values with 18 degrees of freedom

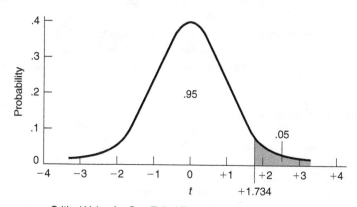

Critical Value for One-Tailed Test with .05 Significance Level

error possible in each sample, other outcomes are bound to happen. Outcomes that are close to the expected null hypothesis value of 50 percent are very likely. However, outcomes further from the expected result (e.g., a result of nine or one in your mind-reading experiment) are less and less likely if the null hypothesis is correct.

When your obtained results are highly unlikely in the null hypothesis sampling distribution, you decide to reject the null hypothesis. That is, you conclude that you have not sampled from the sampling distribution specified by the null hypothesis. Instead, you decide that your data are from a different sampling distribution, and you can argue that your research hypothesis captures the actual sampling distribution in the population. In the case of the mind-reading example, you could argue that you have found evidence that your friend can read minds.

Some basic features of a null hypothesis sampling distribution (see Figure 13.1 for a graphed example):

- Assumes the null hypothesis is actually true in the population.
- Is a frequency distribution of all possible results that would occur if you drew an infinite number of same-sized samples from the same population *in which the null hypothesis was true*, ran your study, and calculated the result (e.g., mean difference) for each one.
- Is a distribution, which means that even if the null hypothesis is true, results from the various samples will vary because of random error. It is more likely that samples will vary only a little from "no effect," but sometimes, even if there is no effect, random error will cause a big deviation from "no effect."
- "No effect" (e.g., a mean difference of zero) is the most frequently occurring result (because this sampling distribution is assuming that the null hypothesis is true).
- If a researcher finds a result that is far enough away from "no effect," a researcher can claim that the null hypothesis sampling distribution is unlikely to represent the truth in the population. Instead, there is a different distribution that captures the truth in the population (and the research hypothesis represents the researcher's best guess of what that truth is).

All statistical tests in the *null hypothesis significance testing (NHST)* framework rely on sampling distributions to determine the probability that the results are consistent with the null hypothesis. When the obtained data are very unlikely according to null hypothesis expectations (usually a .05 probability or less), the researcher decides to reject the null hypothesis and argue that the research hypothesis is true in the population.

Sample Size

The mind-reading example can help illustrate the impact of sample size—the total number of observations—on statistical significance. Suppose you had tested your friend on 100 trials instead of 10 and had observed 60 correct answers. Just as you had expected 5 correct answers in 10 trials, you would now expect 50 of 100 answers to be correct. However, 60 out of 100 has a much lower likelihood of occurrence than 6 out of 10. This is because, with more observations sampled, you are more likely to obtain an accurate estimate of the true population value. As the size of your sample increases, you are more confident that your outcome actually represents the true population, whether that is different from the null hypothesis or not.

How "Unlikely" Is Enough? Choosing a Significance (Alpha) Level

How unlikely does a result have to be before we decide to reject the null hypothesis? A decision rule is determined prior to collecting the data. The probability required for declaring significance is called the **alpha level,** and it is commonly set at .05. The outcome of the study is considered significant when there is less than a .05 probability of obtaining the results *if the null hypothesis is actually true* (Finch, Cumming, & Thomason, 2001). If it is very unlikely that random error is responsible for the obtained results, the null hypothesis is rejected.

Sometimes a researcher will choose a .01 alpha level. This means that the null hypothesis will be rejected if there is less than 1 percent chance of obtaining results like those from the sample *if the null hypothesis is actually true.* The decision has to do with the consequences of being wrong, and declaring a significant effect when it actually does not exist. We will consider the issue of such *Type I errors* later in the chapter. It is important to note here that there is nothing magical about a .05 or a .01 alpha level. In the null hypothesis significance testing framework, a null hypothesis rejected at .01 does not mean that a result is "more significant" than one rejected at .05. Many people have made this interpretation error (Kline, 2013). Remember that the significance test is pass/fail only. To discuss the strength of the effect, we need to calculate and interpret *effect size* (see Chapter 12).

EXAMPLE STATISTICAL TESTS

After specifying the null hypothesis and the research hypothesis, as well as the *alpha level* (usually .05, by convention), it is time to conduct a statistical test. Statistical tests use probability to help us decide whether to reject the null hypothesis. Different tests are used for different research designs. We will focus on the *t* test and the *F* test for independent groups designs. Each test can be adapted for use with repeated measures designs, including those we discussed in Chapter 8. The *t* test is most commonly used to examine whether two groups are significantly different from each other. In the experiment on the effect of viewing multitasking peers on comprehension, a *t* test was an appropriate option because Sana and colleagues (2013) asked whether the mean lecture comprehension score differed between two groups. The *F* test is a more general statistical test that can be used to ask whether there is a difference among three or more groups, including factorial designs, like those we discussed in Chapter 10. We will also revisit the Pearson *r* correlation coefficient, which is another statistic that can be evaluated for significance.

LO4

The *t* Test: Used When Comparing Two Means

The **t test** is a statistic that allows you to determine whether the mean difference found between two groups likely came from the null hypothesis sampling distribution for that sample size. The sampling distribution of all possible values of *t*, with a sample size of 20 (10 participants per group), is shown in Figure 13.1. (There is a different sampling distribution of *t* for each sample size.) The *x* axis contains all possible outcomes of *t* that we could find in our sample if we compare the means of two groups *and* the null hypothesis is true in the population. Regardless of sample size, the sampling distribution of *t* has a mean of 0 and a standard deviation of 1. Conceptually, the *t* value is a ratio of two aspects of the data: the difference between the group means and the variability within groups. The ratio may be described as follows:

$$t = \frac{\text{group difference}}{\text{within-group variability}}$$

The group difference is simply the difference between your obtained means; if the null hypothesis is true in the population, you expect this difference to be zero. Mathematically, the value of *t* increases as the difference between your obtained sample means increases. Note that the sampling distribution of *t* assumes that there is no difference in the population means; thus, the expected value of *t* under the null hypothesis is zero. (Notice in Figure 13.1 that zero has the highest probability of occurring.)

The denominator of the *t* formula is essentially an indicator of the amount of error in your dependent variable. Within-group variability captures the amount of variability of scores around each mean. Recall from Chapter 12 that *s*, the standard deviation, and s^2, the variance, are indicators of how much scores deviate from the group mean. The smaller the standard deviation in each group, the less error is influencing scores. Within the *t* statistic formula, smaller standard deviations mean a smaller denominator, which makes it easier to reject the null hypothesis than if the standard deviations (and therefore the denominator) were larger.

To use this sampling distribution to evaluate our data, we need to follow three steps. First, calculate a value of *t* from the obtained data using the formula below. Second, identify the *critical value* of *t* that reflects our chosen alpha level from the null hypothesis sampling distribution for our sample size.

Third, compare the obtained t to the critical value of t. If the obtained t exceeds the critical value, it has a low probability of occurring (less than .05) if the null hypothesis is true, and therefore the null hypothesis is rejected. If the obtained t is smaller than the critical value, we retain the null hypothesis. Such a t value is likely if chance is the only reason our means differ, rather than a true effect.

A concrete example of a t test calculation may help clarify these concepts. Let's use the results of the multitasking experiment (Sana et al., 2013) to illustrate the steps. Refer back to the null and research hypotheses stated earlier. The dependent variable, comprehension, was operationally defined as the proportion of questions answered correctly. For step one, the general formula for the t test for two independent groups is

$$t = \frac{\overline{X}_1 - \overline{X}_2}{\sqrt{\dfrac{s_1^2}{n_1} + \dfrac{s_2^2}{n_2}}}$$

We need three values for each group: the mean ($\overline{X}$), variance (s^2), and sample size (n). Because we are trying to re-create this analysis from a journal article, we need to decode this sentence from the results section:

"Participants in view of multitasking peers scored significantly lower on the test ($M = 0.56$, $SD = 0.12$, $n = 19$) than participants not in view of multitasking peers ($M = 0.73$, $SD = 0.12$, $n = 19$)" (Sana et al., 2013, p. 29).

The numerator is the difference between the means ($\overline{X}$) of the two groups, which is denoted as M in journal articles. For the denominator, we need to remember that to find the variance (s^2) of each group, we square the standard deviation, which is denoted as SD in journal articles. Here, the variance for people who viewed multitaskers is $0.12 \times 0.12 = 0.0144$. By coincidence, the variance in the other group happens to be exactly the same in this study. We divide each variance by the number of subjects (n) in that group, and then add these together. We then find the square root of the result; this converts the number from a squared score (the variance) to a combined version of the standard deviation. Finally, we calculate our obtained t value by dividing the mean difference by this denominator. When the formula is applied to the comprehension scores across the two conditions, we find

$$t = \frac{0.73 - 0.56}{\sqrt{\dfrac{0.0144}{19} + \dfrac{0.0144}{19}}}$$

$$t = \frac{0.17}{\sqrt{0.000758 + 0.000758}}$$

$$t = 4.37$$

Thus, the t value calculated from the data is 4.37. Is this a statistically significant result? A computer program analyzing the results would immediately tell you the probability of obtaining a t value of this size with a total sample size of 38 if only chance was operating. Without such a program, the next step is to use a table (such as Table C.2 in Appendix C) to find the appropriate *critical value* of t. Using an alpha level of .05, the critical value from the sampling distribution of t is 2.029. Any t value greater than 2.029 has less than a .05 probability of occurring if the null hypothesis is true. Note that the obtained result is *statistically significant*: 4.37 is greater than 2.029. Step three is decision time: Because our obtained value is larger than the critical value, we can reject the null hypothesis and conclude that the difference in means obtained in the sample is unlikely to reflect chance alone.

In the results sections of journal articles, you will see statements that summarize the results of statistical tests that look like this: $t(36) = 4.37, p < .05$. These statements appear at the end of sentences describing the effect (like the quote above) and provide the reader with four important pieces of information: the t test was used, with 36 degrees of freedom, resulting in an obtained t value of 4.37, which corresponds to a probability of less than .05 (our conventional alpha level) if the null hypothesis is true. The letter "p" indicates the probability of obtaining a result that extreme if the null hypothesis is true, and it is often reported precisely (e.g., $p = .02$). Specifically, p refers to the proportion of the null hypothesis sampling distribution that is more extreme than the obtained t value. Remember that these tests are pass/fail. We can ask only whether the p value is larger or smaller than *alpha*. A tiny p value cannot be interpreted as an indicator of effect size.

Finding the Critical Value of t

You may be wondering how we determined the critical value. See Appendix B for a more detailed description of how to use the tables in Appendix C. For now, consider three pieces of information we need to use the table: the degrees of freedom, whether we are using a one-tailed or two-tailed test, and our chosen alpha level (usually .05). We expand on the first two of these concepts here, as we have already discussed alpha level.

Degrees of Freedom   The **degrees of freedom (df)** are adjustments used in statistical analyses to account for the fact that we are estimating population values (e.g., group means, standard deviations) using data from small samples. The smaller our sample, the larger the impact degrees of freedom have on our critical value. When comparing two means, the degrees of freedom are equal to $(n_1 + n_2 - 2)$, or the total number of participants in the study minus the number of groups. In the multitasking experiment, the degrees of freedom were $(19 + 19 - 2) = 36$. To find the critical value above, we needed to interpolate between the values of 2.021 (for $df = 40$) and 2.042 (for $df = 30$), because our precise *degrees of freedom* (36) was not exactly represented in

Table C.2. Alternatively, we could have just used the higher (more conservative) value of 2.042.

Mathematically, degrees of freedom are the number of scores free to vary once the means are known. For example, if the mean of a group is 6.0 and there are five scores in the group, there are 4 degrees of freedom; once you have any four scores, the fifth score is known because the mean must remain 6.0.

One-Tailed versus Two-Tailed Tests   In Table C.2, you must choose a critical *t* that corresponds to your research hypothesis. Your research hypothesis either (1) specified a direction of difference between the groups (e.g., group 1 will be greater than group 2) or (2) did not specify a predicted direction of difference (e.g., group 1 will differ–in either direction–from group 2). Different critical values of *t* are used in the two situations: The first situation is called a one-tailed test, and the second situation is called a two-tailed test.

The issue can be visualized by looking at the sampling distribution of *t* values for 18 degrees of freedom, as shown in Figure 13.1. As you can see, a value of 0.00 is expected most frequently if the null hypothesis is true. Values greater than or less than zero are less likely to occur. The first distribution shows the logic of a *two-tailed test*. Try using Table C.2 to find that the critical value of *t* is 2.101, when the significance level is .05, degrees of freedom are 18, and a direction of difference is not predicted. This critical value is the point beyond which 2.5 percent of the positive values and 2.5 percent of the negative values of *t* lie (hence, a total probability of .05 combined from the two "tails" of the sampling distribution). The second distribution in Figure 13.1 illustrates a one-tailed test. If the researcher specifies a directional difference in the research hypothesis, the critical value is 1.734. This is the value beyond which 5 percent of the values lie in only one "tail" of the distribution. Whether to specify a one-tailed or two-tailed test will depend on whether you originally designed your study to test a directional hypothesis. Based on convention, most researchers default to using a two-tailed test, even if they specified a directional research hypothesis.

Test yourself! From Figure 13.1, adjust the critical *t* value to correspond to 36 degrees of freedom. The two-tailed critical *t* values are +2.029 and −2.029. The one-tailed critical *t* value is +1.689. Notice how increasing the sample size from 20 ($df = 18$) to 38 ($df = 36$) reduces the critical values, making it easier to reject the null hypothesis.

The *F* Test: Used When Comparing Three or More Group Means   LO5

The *t* test is limited to two-group designs. The **analysis of variance (ANOVA),** or ***F* test,** is an extension of the *t* test that can be used in many more research designs. When a study has only one independent variable with *two* groups, *F* and *t* are virtually identical–the value of *F* equals t^2 in this situation. However, ANOVA can be used when there are more than two levels of an independent variable or when a factorial design with two or more independent variables has been used (see Chapter 10). In Appendix B you can find the calculations necessary to conduct an F test.

The F statistic is a ratio of two types of variance (hence the term *analysis of variance*) that parallels the t ratio. **Systematic variance**–the numerator–is the deviation of the group means from the *grand mean* (which is the mean score of all participants across all conditions in the study). Systematic variance is small when the difference between group means is small, and increases as the group mean differences increase. **Error variance**–the denominator–captures how much individual scores in each group deviate from their respective group means. Because systematic variance is the variability of scores between groups, it is sometimes called *between-group variance*. Likewise, because error variance is the variability of scores within groups, it is sometimes called *within-group variance*. The larger the F ratio is, the greater the group differences are relative to the amount of error, and the more likely it is that the results are *statistically significant*. Then, follow-up tests are required to determine which group means differ from each other (e.g., using simple main effect analysis from Chapter 10).

Significance of a Pearson r Correlation Coefficient

Recall from Chapter 12 that the Pearson r correlation coefficient is used to describe the strength of the relationship between two variables when both variables have interval or ratio scale properties. Is the correlation statistically significant? The null hypothesis in this case is that the true population correlation is 0.00–the two variables are not related. What if you obtain a correlation of .27 (plus or minus)? A statistical significance test will allow you to decide whether to reject the null hypothesis and conclude that the true population correlation is greater or less than 0.00. The technical way to do this is to perform a different version of the t test that compares the obtained coefficient with the null hypothesis correlation of 0.00. The procedures for calculating a Pearson r and determining whether it is statistically significant are provided in Appendix B.

LO6

WE MADE A DECISION ABOUT THE NULL HYPOTHESIS, BUT WE MIGHT BE WRONG! INVESTIGATING TYPE I AND TYPE II ERRORS

The decision to reject the null hypothesis is based on probabilities rather than on certainties. We make a decision without actually ever knowing the truth in the population, because we almost never have access to the whole population. Thus, the decision might not be correct.

A decision matrix is shown in Figure 13.2. The two rows show the two possible decisions we make based on a statistical test: (1) Reject the null

	Population	
	Null Hypothesis Is True	Null Hypothesis Is False
Reject the Null Hypothesis	Type I Error (α)	Correct Decision $(1-\beta)$
Retain the Null Hypothesis	Correct Decision $(1-\alpha)$	Type II Error (β)

Decision

FIGURE 13.2 Decision matrix for Type I and Type II errors

hypothesis or (2) retain the null hypothesis. The two columns show the two possible truths about the population: (1) The null hypothesis is true or (2) the null hypothesis is false. There are two kinds of correct decisions and two kinds of errors.

Correct Decisions

One correct decision occurs when we reject the null hypothesis based on our sample statistics, and the null hypothesis is actually false in the population. We decide that the population means are not equal or there is a correlation between variables, and that is actually true in the population. This is the decision we hope to make when we begin our study.

The other correct decision is to retain the null hypothesis, and the null hypothesis is true in the population: The population means are in fact equal, or there is no relationship between the variables. There was no effect to find, and we did not accidentally find one in our sample.

Type I Errors

A **Type I error** is made when we reject the null hypothesis but the null hypothesis is actually true. We decide that the population means are not equal when they actually are equal. Type I errors occur when, simply by chance, we obtain a large value of t or F. For example, even though a t value of 4.37 is highly improbable if the population means are indeed equal (less than 5 chances out of 100), this *can* happen. When we do obtain such a large t value simply by chance, we *incorrectly* decide that the independent variable had an effect on the dependent variable.

The probability of making a Type I error is determined by the choice of significance or alpha level (which is symbolized as the Greek letter alpha α, as shown in Figure 13.2). When the significance level for deciding whether to reject the null hypothesis is .05, the probability of making a Type I error (alpha) is .05 if the null hypothesis is in fact true. If the null hypothesis is rejected (but it is really true), there are 5 chances out of 100 that the decision is wrong. The probability of making a Type I error can be changed by either decreasing or increasing the significance level. If we use a lower alpha level of .01, for example, there is less chance of making a Type I error if the null hypothesis is true. With a .01 significance level, the null hypothesis is rejected only when the probability of obtaining the results is .01 or less.

Remember the Type I error by thinking of a physician who reads a test result to a biologically male patient, announcing that he is pregnant. The physician is saying, "There is an effect!" when obviously that cannot be true.

Type II Errors

A **Type II error** occurs when the null hypothesis is retained based on our sample data, although in the population the null hypothesis is false. The population means are not equal, or the population correlation is not zero, but the study results do not lead to a decision to reject the null hypothesis.

Research should be designed so that the probability of a Type II error is relatively low, presuming an effect actually exists in the population. The probability of making a Type II error is called beta (symbolized β) and is related to three elements. The first is the significance (alpha) level. If we set a very low significance level to decrease the chances of a Type I error, we increase the chances of a Type II error. If we make it very difficult to reject the null hypothesis, the probability of incorrectly retaining the null hypothesis increases. The second factor is sample size. True differences that exist in the population are more likely to be detected as the sample size increases. The third factor is effect size. As the population effect size increases, the likelihood of making a Type II error decreases. A small effect size may go undetected, especially with a small sample. These three elements reappear in our discussion of power, which is directly related to the Type II error rate.

Remember the Type II error by thinking of a physician who reads a test result and tells a biologically female patient who is clearly pregnant that she is not. The physician is saying, "There is no effect!" when obviously that cannot be true.

The Everyday Context of Type I and Type II Errors

The decision matrix used in statistical analyses can be applied to the kinds of decisions people frequently make in everyday life. For example, consider the decision made by a juror in a criminal trial. As with inferential statistics, a decision must be made on the basis of evidence. Jurors must decide whether the defendant is innocent or guilty, but we never really know the truth.

The juror's decision matrix is illustrated in Figure 13.3. To align this example to statistical decisions, assume as the null hypothesis that the defendant is innocent (i.e., the dictum that a person is innocent until proven guilty). Thus, rejecting the null hypothesis means deciding to declare the defendant guilty, and retaining the null hypothesis means deciding to declare the defendant innocent. The null hypothesis may actually be true or false. There are

True State

	Null Is True (Innocent)	Null Is False (Guilty)
Reject Null (Find Guilty)	Type I Error	Correct Decision
Retain Null (Find Innocent)	Correct Decision	Type II Error

Decision

FIGURE 13.3
Decision matrix for a juror

two kinds of correct decisions and two kinds of errors, just like in statistical decisions. A Type I error is finding the defendant guilty when the person really is innocent; a Type II error is finding the defendant innocent when the person actually is guilty. In North America, Type I errors by jurors generally are considered to be more serious than Type II errors. Before finding someone guilty, the juror is asked to make sure that the person is guilty "beyond a reasonable doubt" or to consider that "it is better to have a hundred guilty persons go free than to find one innocent person guilty." Following this logic, to reduce Type I errors, a juror may interpret ambiguous evidence in favour of the defendant's innocence.

The decision that a doctor makes to operate or not operate on a patient provides another illustration of how a decision matrix works (see Figure 13.4). Here, the null hypothesis is that no operation is necessary. The decision is whether to reject the null hypothesis and perform the operation, or to retain the null hypothesis and not operate. In reality, the doctor is faced with two possibilities: Either the operation is unnecessary (the null hypothesis is true) or the patient will die without the operation (a dramatic case of the null hypothesis being false). Which error is more serious in this case? Doctors may believe that *not* operating on a patient who really needs the operation–making a Type II error–is more serious than making the Type I error of operating on

True State

	Null Is True (No Operation Needed)	Null Is False (Operation Is Needed)
Reject Null (Operate on Patient)	Type I Error	Correct Decision
Retain Null (Don't Operate)	Correct Decision	Type II Error

Decision

FIGURE 13.4
Decision matrix for a doctor

someone who does not really need it. Following this logic, to avoid a Type II error, a doctor may choose to interpret ambiguous symptoms as evidence that the patient does need the operation.

> *Try it out!* Now consider the important decision to marry someone. If the null hypothesis is that the person is "wrong" for you, and the true state is that the person is either "wrong" or "right," you must decide whether to marry the person. Try to construct a decision matrix for this particular problem. Which error do you think is more costly: a Type I error (marrying someone who is wrong for you) or a Type II error (failing to marry someone who is right for you)?

Type I and Type II Errors in the Published Research Literature

Researchers have generally believed that the consequences of making a Type I error are more serious than those associated with a Type II error. If the null hypothesis is rejected incorrectly, the researcher might publish the results in a journal, and the results might be reported in textbooks or in mass media. Researchers don't want to mislead people or risk damaging their own reputations by publishing results that are false and so cannot be *replicated*. One way to guard against the possibility of making a Type I error is to use a very low *alpha level* (.05 or .01). However, analyses of multiple scientific disciplines has shown that setting low alpha levels is not enough to ensure that false "effects" are not published (Ioannidis, 2005; Simmons, Nelson, & Simonsohn, 2011).

Publication Bias Inflates Overall Type I Error Rates   One of the problems made worse by Type I errors is **publication bias**–statistically significant results are much more likely than non-significant findings to be published in scientific journals (Kühberger, Fritz, & Scherndl, 2014). Thus, the probability of false "effects" making it into the literature may be higher than 5 percent, which is what the common alpha level would imply. Publication bias has created a problem for scientists, who have experienced pressure to seek *statistical significance* rather than *truth* in order to publish results, and consequently receive benefits such as jobs and awards. This pressure has made some problematic practices commonplace (e.g., relying on very small sample sizes, reporting results selectively; see Bakker, van Kijk, & Wicherts, 2012; Simonsohn, Nelson, & Simmons, 2014). Type I errors decrease the overall accuracy of our science.

Unreported Type II Errors Reduce Long-Term Accuracy   The consequences of a Type II error traditionally have not been considered as serious as Type I errors. It was thought that, at worst, a researcher gives up on finding an effect that actually is present in the population. Recent concern over *publication bias* has ignited discussion of the *file drawer*, which is a term used to describe the place where failed studies go to die, regardless of whether they have accurately found no effect or have made a Type II error. They can easily be excluded from *meta-analyses* that seek to combine results from many studies to describe an overall effect (see Chapter 14). When failed studies are not included, meta-analyses risk overestimating the overall effect size. It is tremendously difficult to interpret why a study failed to find statistical significance. One reason is that there truly is no effect to be found. But there are many reasons why Type II errors occur (see the upcoming section on interpreting non-significant results). Many Type II errors go unknown and unreported in file drawers because of publication bias, causing a problem for building a cumulative science.

Reform   As mentioned in Chapter 3, psychologists are developing ways to improve the accuracy of our science. Efforts to reduce Type I errors have emphasized the importance of replicating findings, increasing sample sizes whenever possible, and fully disclosing measures and analyses for others' verification (e.g., see Eich, 2014). Websites such as the Open Science Framework (https://osf.io/) and PsychDisclosure.org (LeBel et al., 2013) have been created for researchers to register research methods before data collection and post results that do not achieve *statistical significance* and therefore are not traditionally publishable. Rather than vanishing completely, failed studies are then available for other researchers to learn from. Importantly, these studies may be readily available for inclusion in meta-analyses, despite failing to find statistical significance. Although none is perfect, these and other reforms are striving to build a cumulative science that increases ethical practices (see Chapter 3) while minimizing both Type I and Type II errors.

INTERPRETING NON-SIGNIFICANT RESULTS

L07

Although "retaining the null hypothesis" is convenient terminology, it is important to recognize that researchers are not generally interested in retaining the null hypothesis. Research is designed to show that a relationship between variables does exist, not to demonstrate that variables are unrelated. As mentioned above, non-significant results are difficult to interpret. For this reason, researchers often say that they simply "fail to reject" the null hypothesis (Wilkinson et al., 1999).

When the results of a single study are non-significant, it is possible that there is no effect in the population. Yet, many alternative explanations remain. Sometimes, Type II errors can occur because of particular procedures used in the study. Assuming an effect really exists in the population, results of a study may be non-significant if unclear instructions are given to the participants, if the manipulation of the independent variable is very weak, or if the dependent measure is unreliable or insensitive (see Chapter 9). In these cases, a more carefully conducted study could find that the variables are related.

There are also statistical reasons for Type II errors. Recall that the probability of a Type II error is influenced by the significance (alpha) level, sample size, and effect size. If the researcher chooses to use a very cautious significance level of .001 rather than .05, it is more difficult to reject the null hypothesis (and make a Type I error if the null hypothesis is in fact true). However, that also means that there is a greater chance of retaining an incorrect null hypothesis (i.e., a Type II error is more likely if the null hypothesis is in fact false). In other words, a real effect is more likely to be overlooked when the significance level is very low.

Type II errors may also result from using a sample that is too small to detect the actual effect. Assuming a real effect exists, larger sample sizes are generally more likely to detect it. Very small effects are especially difficult to detect without very large sample sizes. Generally, larger effects in the population are easier to detect than smaller ones. Consider this metaphor: Imagine you are trying to find a tiny needle in a giant haystack. Now imagine trying to find a full-sized tractor in that same haystack. Both "effects" (i.e., the needle and the tractor) are in the haystack, but it is much easier to find the much larger tractor.

Given the many causes of Type II errors, researchers should not permanently retain a null hypothesis just because results from one study are non-significant. However, sometimes it is correct to retain the null hypothesis and conclude that two variables are *not* related. Several criteria can be used when deciding to retain the null hypothesis (Frick, 2005). Studies must be well-designed with sensitive dependent measures, and a manipulation check should indicate the independent variable was indeed manipulated effectively. A reasonably large sample should be used to rule out the possibility that the sample was too small to detect the effect. Further, evidence should come from multiple studies. Under such circumstances, a researcher may be justified in concluding that there is in fact no relationship. For an example, see Laverty and Kelly (1998), who argued to retain the null hypothesis that car accidents are unrelated to phases of the moon.

CHOOSING A SAMPLE SIZE: POWER ANALYSIS

We noted in Chapter 9 that researchers often select a sample size based on what is typical in a particular area of research. A more effective approach is to select—before your study begins—a sample size on the basis of a power analysis. The **power** of a statistical test is the probability of correctly rejecting the null hypothesis, presuming it is actually false (Wilkinson et al., 1999). It is directly related to the likelihood that you will retain a null hypothesis that is actually false:

$$\text{Power} = 1 - p(\text{Type II error})$$

where $p(\text{Type II error})$ means "the probability of making a Type II error." Assuming the effect really exists, power of .80 means that you will find an effect (i.e., correctly reject the null hypothesis) 80 percent of the time, but 20 percent of the time you will miss it (i.e., make a Type II error).

As noted earlier, the probability of a Type II error is related to the significance level (alpha), sample size, and effect size. A power analysis enables a researcher to choose a power probability, say at .80, and calculate the sample

TABLE 13.2   Total sample size needed to detect a significant difference for a t test

Population Effect Size d	Power = .80	Power = .90
.20 (a small effect)	788	1054
.50 (a moderate effect)	128	172
.80 (a large effect)	52	68
1.00	34	46
1.50	18	22

Note: Effect sizes are Cohen's d (see Chapter 12). Sample sizes are based on *a priori* power analysis for a two-group independent groups design using Cohen's d, two-tailed tests, and a significance level of .05.

size needed to detect an effect of the expected size (Cohen, 1988). Table 13.2 shows the total sample size needed for an experiment with two groups and a significance level of .05. In the table, expected effect sizes range from .20 to 1.50, and the desired power is shown at .80 and .90. Smaller effect sizes require larger samples to be significant at the .05 level. If a researcher is studying a relationship with an estimated effect size of .20, an extremely large sample size is needed for statistical significance at the .05 level. An inappropriately low sample size in this situation is likely to produce a non-significant finding, even though a small effect actually exists.

Higher desired power demands a greater sample size; you want to make it more likely that you will detect the effect that is there. Researchers usually use a power between .70 and .90 when using this method to determine sample size. Several computer programs have been developed for researchers to conduct power analysis easily and determine the sample size needed for their study. See Faul, Erdfelder, Lang, and Buchner (2007) for a free calculator.

COMPUTER ANALYSIS OF DATA

Although you can calculate statistics with a calculator using formulas from this chapter, Appendix B, and other sources, most data analysis uses computer programs. Sophisticated statistical software packages make it easy to calculate descriptive and inferential statistics quickly and accurately, including information on statistical significance. Computers also facilitate graphic displays of data.

Some of the major statistical software programs are SPSS, SAS, and R. Spreadsheet programs such as Microsoft Excel can also be used for some analyses. The general procedures for doing analyses are similar across statistics programs, but different steps are needed for inputting data, programming the test, and interpreting output.

Inputting data is the first step toward any computer-based analysis. Suppose you want to input the data for the multitasking experiment. Think of data for computer analysis as a matrix with horizontal rows and vertical columns. In Excel, it is usually easiest to set up a separate column for each group, as shown in Figure 13.5. Other programs may require somewhat different methods of data input.

The next step is to instruct the software to conduct the statistical analysis. Each program uses somewhat different steps to perform the analysis; most require you to choose from various menu options. Excel uses formulae that

FIGURE 13.5
Sample computer input and output.

	A	B	C	D
1	View of Multitasking Peers Condition		No View of Multitasking Peers Condition	
2	Participant #	Proportion Correct	Participant #	Proportion Correct
3	3	.4	1	.9
4	5	.65	2	.5
5	6	.575	4	.525
6	10	.625	7	.65
7	14	.325	8	.825
8	16	.45	9	.7
9	17	.625	11	.675
10	18	.625	12	.65
11	19	.45	13	.9
12	20	.55	15	.7
13	21	.725	23	.725
14	22	.6	25	.775
15	24	.675	28	.75
16	26	.8	29	.7
17	27	.55	31	.925
18	30	.55	32	.825
19	34	.425	33	.85
20	35	.475	37	.675
21	36	.5	38	.7

Excel method of data input

t Test: Two-Sample Assuming Equal Variances

	View	No View
Mean	0.556578947	0.734210526
Variance	0.014155702	0.01376462
Number of Observations	19	19
t Denominator	0.038333936	
Null hypothesis Mean Difference	0	
df	36	
t obtained	4.633794484	
t critical one-tail	1.6892	
p (t critical <=t obtained) one-tail	0.0000229	
t critical two-tail	2.0294	
p (t critical <=t obtained) two-tail	0.0000457	
Cohen's d effect size	1.503401453	

Output for a t test and Cohen's d using Excel

Data from study 2 of Sana, Weston, & Cepeda (2013).

are beyond the scope of this book (try Carlberg, 2011, for a primer). When the analysis is completed, the output shows the results of the statistical procedure you performed. You will need to learn how to interpret the output. Figure 13.5 shows the output for a t test using formulas in Excel. Note that the obtained t value is slightly different than the value we calculated earlier using means and standard deviations reported in the article—which had been rounded to two decimal places. Here, using the full data set and carrying many decimal places, we can calculate t more precisely.

Try it out! When you are first learning to use a statistical analysis program, try practising with some data from a textbook to make sure that you get the same results. This will ensure that you know how to properly input the data and request the statistical analysis.

SELECTING THE APPROPRIATE STATISTICAL TEST

How do you choose the appropriate statistical test for analyzing your data? There are many guides and tutorials you can access online, and SPSS has its own statistics coach to help with the decision. One important consideration is the scale properties of all variables in the study (nominal, ordinal, interval, or ratio). In tables below, we list some of the many statistical tests, some of which we have covered. We focus on variables that have (1) nominal scale properties, such as experimental and control conditions, or (2) interval/ratio scale properties with many values, such as reaction time or rating scales. Some examples of variables whose relationships could be analyzed using those methods are presented in *italics*.

Research Studying Two Variables

In these cases, the researcher is studying whether two variables are related, using non-experiments, quasi-experiments, or experimental designs. Chi-square is a statistical test appropriate only when both variables are on a nominal scale (see Appendix B for details). The table below lists tests appropriate for various combinations of independent and dependent variables.

IV (or Variable X)	DV (or Variable Y)	Statistical Test
Nominal *Buddhist-atheist*	Nominal *Vegetarian—yes/no*	Chi-square
Nominal (2 groups) *Experimental group-control group*	Interval/ratio *Academic average*	t test
Nominal (3 groups) *Study strategy (rereading, self-testing, and concept map conditions)*	Interval/ratio *Test score*	One-way analysis of variance
Interval/ratio *Optimism score*	Interval/ratio *Sick days last year*	Pearson correlation

Research with Multiple Independent or Predictor Variables

The following situations highlight some complex research designs. These designs have two or more independent or predictor variables that are studied with a single dependent or criterion variable. See Chapter 12 for a discussion of multiple regression.

IVs or Predictor Variables	DV or Criterion Variable	Statistical Test
Nominal (2 or more variables)	Interval/ratio	Analysis of variance (factorial design)
Interval/ratio (2 or more variables)	Interval/ratio	Multiple regression

There are many other types of designs and corresponding statistical analyses. Designs with multiple variables (that use multivariate statistics) are described in detail by Tabachnick and Fidell (2013). Consult Siegel and Castellan (1988) for procedures when using ordinal level measurement.

LO8

INTEGRATING DESCRIPTIVE AND INFERENTIAL STATISTICS

The null hypothesis test is pass/fail: The value of the statistic obtained from your data (e.g., t obtained) either exceeds the critical value (and the null hypothesis is rejected) or not (and the null hypothesis is retained). This hypothesis test tells us no information about whether an effect may be tiny or huge. For these judgments, effect sizes and confidence intervals are needed (Cumming, 2014; Wilkinson et al., 1999). Some radical researchers are proposing abandoning the hypothesis test altogether in favour of considering these more nuanced values. While the hypothesis test isn't likely to go out of style any time soon, effect sizes and confidence intervals are becoming increasingly valued for their rich information.

Effect Size

The concept of effect size was discussed in Chapter 12 because it is a way to *describe* the strength of the relationship between variables. In addition to reporting whether there was a statistically significant effect of the independent variable, it is becoming increasingly common in research articles to report and discuss the effect size, which offers much more information about the relationship among variables. For example, in two-group experiments, the effect size Cohen's *d* (see Chapter 12) is often reported alongside results of the pass/fail *t* test. There are other types of effect size calculations suitable for other research designs. See Appendix B for the formulae for Cohen's *d* as well as *omega squared*, which is used to calculate effect sizes in designs with three or more groups, including factorial designs.

It is possible for effects of any size to be *statistically significant* when using very large sample sizes. For example, data from the World Values Survey we examined in Chapter 12 show a statistically significant difference in life satisfaction between Australian and Mexican respondents. Australian respondents ($n = 1465$) rated their life satisfaction ($M = 7.20$, $SD = 2.05$) lower than Mexican respondents ($n = 2000$, $M = 8.51$, $SD = 1.93$), $t(3463) = 19.19$, $p < .0001$. Note the sample size (n) per group was far greater than the vast majority of research in the behavioural sciences. For the sake of example, let's assume we had only one-tenth the number of participants (15 Australians and 20 Mexicans), but the same standard deviations (SD). The result would no longer be statistically significant, $t(33) = 1.92$, $p > .05$. By traditional pass/fail standards, we learned nothing. This study would be lost to the *file drawer*. However, in both cases, our best estimate of the effect size, Cohen's d, is medium-large (.66). Our confidence that the true population effect size is actually near .66 would be much greater with the larger sample size, but in either case we can still learn something about the relationship between nationality and life satisfaction.

Some statistically significant differences might have very little *practical* significance. For example, if an expensive new psychiatric treatment technique significantly reduces the average hospital stay from 60 days to 59 days, it might not be practical to use the technique despite the evidence for its effectiveness. The additional day of hospitalization costs less than the treatment. There are other circumstances, however, in which a treatment with a very small effect size has considerable practical significance. Usually this occurs when a very large population is affected by a fairly inexpensive treatment. Suppose a simple flextime policy for employees reduces employee turnover by 1 percent per year. This doesn't sound like a large effect. However, if a company normally has a turnover of 2,000 employees each year and the cost of training a new employee is $10,000, the company saves $200,000 per year with the new procedure. This amount may have practical significance for the company. Thus, it is insufficient to consider only the result of the null hypothesis test without also considering effect size and, perhaps, the context for applying the result.

Confidence Intervals and Statistical Significance

After obtaining a sample value (e.g., a mean, a mean difference, or an effect size), we can calculate a confidence interval to define the most likely range of actual population values (see Cumming, 2012; Kline, 2013). As first discussed in Chapter 7, the interval has an associated confidence level: A 95 percent confidence interval indicates that 95 percent of the confidence intervals we calculate based on samples of that size will capture the population value; a 99 percent interval would provide greater certainty but the range of values would be larger.

For example, a confidence interval can be obtained for each of the means in the multitasking experiment by Sana and colleagues (2013). The calculations are beyond the scope of this book. For now, consider the .95 (95 percent) and .99 (99 percent) confidence intervals around the means of the two conditions:

	Viewing Multitasking Laptop Group	Not Viewing Multitasking Laptop Group
Obtained sample value (mean *proportion correct*)	.56	.73
.95 confidence interval around the mean (lower bound, upper bound)	(.50, .61)	(.68, .79)
.99 confidence interval around the mean (lower bound, upper bound)	(.48, .64)	(.66, .81)

The confidence intervals for the two means do not overlap, which is a clue that the difference is statistically significant. Examining confidence intervals is an alternative way of thinking about statistical significance. Interpreting confidence intervals around a statistic can be used as another way to conclude that the null hypothesis should be rejected.

Yet examining confidence intervals further enables greater understanding of the meaning of your obtained data. Although the obtained sample values (e.g., means, effect size) provide the best estimate of the population values for each group, you are able to see the range of possible values most likely to be true in the population. The size of the interval is related to both the size of the sample and the confidence level. As the sample size increases, the confidence interval narrows because the population value is being estimated more precisely.

Assuming the sample size stays the same, notice how the interval widens—becomes less precise—as the confidence level increases. If you want almost all of the confidence intervals calculated in this way to cover the true population mean (e.g., a 99 percent confidence interval), you will need to include more possibilities. Examining confidence intervals around values such as effect sizes and means can offer a richer alternative to the standard pass/fail null hypothesis approach (Cumming, 2012; Kline, 2013; Masson & Loftus, 2003).

Conclusion Validity

Conclusion validity is the extent to which the conclusions about the relationships among variables reached on the basis of the data are correct or reasonable (Trochim, 2006). Conclusion validity is a requirement for conclusions drawn from quantitative, statistical data as well as from qualitative data (see Chapter 6). When working with quantitative data, interpreting the effect size and confidence intervals along with significance test results and study design details, will help us to draw valid conclusions from our data.

THE IMPORTANCE OF REPLICATIONS

Throughout this discussion of statistical analysis, we have focused mainly on the results of a single study. What were the means and standard deviations? Was the mean difference between groups statistically significant? Confidence intervals around effect size estimates offer some idea about how results would turn out if we attempted to replicate the study (but p values do not; see the "Dance of the p Value" video available at http://www.latrobe.edu.au/psy/research/cognitive-and-developmental-psychology/esci). Scientists do not attach too much importance to the results of a single study. A rich understanding of any phenomenon comes from the results of numerous studies investigating the same variables. Instead of inferring population values on the basis of a single investigation, we can look at the results of several studies that replicate previous investigations (see Cohen, 1994). The importance of *replications* is a central concept in Chapter 14. In that final chapter, we will examine various issues of generalizing research findings beyond the specific circumstances in which the research was conducted.

STUDY TERMS

Test yourself! Define and generate an example of each of these key terms.

Alpha level (p. 277)

Analysis of variance (ANOVA) (p. 281)

Conclusion validity (p. 294)

Degrees of freedom (*df*) (p. 280)

Error variance (p. 282)

F test (p. 281)

Inferential statistics (p. 270)

Null hypothesis (p. 272)

Power (p. 288)

Probability (p. 273)

Publication bias (p. 286)

Research hypothesis (p. 272)

Sampling distribution (p. 275)

Statistically significant (p. 271)

Systematic variance (p. 282)

t test (p. 278)

Type I error (p. 283)

Type II error (p. 284)

REVIEW QUESTIONS

Test yourself on this chapter's learning objectives. Can you answer each of these questions?

1. Distinguish between the null hypothesis and the research hypothesis. When does the researcher decide to reject the null hypothesis? How are sampling distributions involved in this decision?

2. What is meant by statistical significance? What elements influence whether obtained results will be significant?

3. List and describe the three basic steps involved in using the *t* test.

4. Compare and contrast the *t* test and the *F* test. Consider their numerators and denominators, and reasons to choose either test.

5. Distinguish between Type I and Type II errors. How does significance level relate to the probability of making a Type I error if the null hypothesis is true?

6. How do Type I and Type II errors influence the accuracy of our published research overall?

7. What influences the probability of a Type II error?

8. What is the difference between statistical significance and practical significance?

9. Discuss reasons why a study might show non-significant results.

10. Compare information obtained using inferential statistics (e.g., a *t* test) with information from effect size and confidence intervals. What information does each analysis provide?

DEEPEN YOUR UNDERSTANDING

Develop your mastery of these concepts by considering these application questions. Compare your responses with those from other people in your study group.

1. In an experiment, one group of research participants is given ten pages of material to proofread for errors. Another group proofreads the same material on a computer screen. The dependent variable is the number of errors detected in a five-minute period. A .05 significance level is used to evaluate the results.

   a. What statistical test would you use? Why?

   b. What is the null hypothesis? The research hypothesis?

   c. What is the Type I error? The Type II error? Describe your answer in words.

   d. What is the probability of making a Type I error if the null hypothesis is false?

2. Professor Dre collected data using the design in Question 1. The average number of errors detected in the print and computer conditions was 38.4 and 13.2, respectively; this difference was not statistically significant. When Professor Seuss conducted the same experiment, the means of the two groups were 21.1 and 14.7, but the difference was statistically significant. Explain how two researchers using the same method could make these different conclusions about the null hypothesis.

3. Suppose that you work for the child social services agency in your province (e.g., Children's Aid Foundation). Your job is to investigate instances of possible child neglect or abuse. After collecting evidence from a variety of sources, you must decide whether to leave the child in the home or place the child in protective custody. Specify the null and research hypotheses in this situation. Describe in words what the Type I and Type II errors are. Is a Type I or Type II error more serious in this situation? Why?

4. A researcher investigated attitudes toward people in wheelchairs. Would people react differently to a person they perceived to be confined temporarily to the wheelchair compared to a person who had a permanent disability? Participants were randomly assigned to two groups. In one group, people worked on various tasks with a confederate in a wheelchair; in the other group, people worked with the same confederate in a wheelchair, but the confederate wore a leg cast. After the session was over, participants completed a questionnaire regarding their reactions to the study. One question asked, "Would you be willing to work with your test partner in the future on a class assignment?" with "yes" and "no" as the only response alternatives. What would be the appropriate significance test for this experiment? Why? Recalling our discussion from Chapter 9 regarding sensitivity, can you offer a critique of the dependent variable? If you changed the dependent variable, would it affect your choice of significance tests? If so, how?

Generalizing Results

LEARNING OBJECTIVES

Keep these learning objectives in mind as you read to help you identify the most critical information in this chapter.

By the end of this chapter, you should be able to:

1	Discuss four challenges when generalizing research results to other populations.
2	Identify three specific aspects of a study's procedure that may affect the ability to generalize beyond that study, and suggest possible solutions.
3	Discuss the importance of replications, distinguishing the procedures and uses of direct replications and conceptual replications.
4	Evaluate strengths and limits of using convenience samples, and identify ways to find more diverse samples.
5	Distinguish between narrative literature reviews and meta-analyses.
6	Identify ways to continue using your knowledge of research methods.

Our ability to generalize research findings has been a source of heated debate through the years. A single study is conducted with a particular sample and procedure. The **external validity** of that study is the extent to which the results can be generalized beyond that study to other populations and settings. The issue of external validity is complex, raising deep questions about the usefulness of the knowledge we create. Can results be generalized to other populations or to other study contexts? In this chapter, we will explore some ways to tackle these questions, and then will close by considering ways to generalize your knowledge beyond this book.

CHALLENGES TO GENERALIZING RESULTS

In this section, we consider two ways in which research results may or may not generalize beyond a study. Can results generalize beyond your sample of participants to other populations? Can results generalize beyond the particular situation of your study?

Can Results Generalize to Other Populations?

LO1

Except in rare cases, research is conducted on samples rather than entire populations. If we wish to generalize results to the entire population of humanity, the best–but completely impractical–method for doing so is to select participants randomly from the general population. As we noted in Chapters 7 and 9, the people who participate in psychological research are usually *convenience samples*, selected because they are available and willing. The most available population from which to sample is often university students. They may be volunteers, may be mostly males or mostly females, or may be from a particular culture. Are our research findings limited to these types of participants, or can we generalize our findings to a more general population?

Beyond University Students   Undergraduate students are studied in a substantial portion of research in psychology. Estimates based on numerous samples of top-tier psychology journals suggest about 68 percent of participants are university undergraduate students (Sears, 1986; Smart, 1966; Wintre, North, & Sugar, 2001); estimates based on lesser ranking journals suggest about 25 percent (Bodner, 2006). The potential problem is that university students represent a highly restricted population–typically, first- and second-year students taking an introductory psychology class (Sears, 1986; Wintre et al., 2001) in the United States (Bodner, 2006). They therefore tend to be young and to possess the characteristics of late adolescence: a developing sense of self-identity, social and political attitudes that are in a state of flux, a high need for peer approval, and unstable peer relationships. They also are intelligent, have high cognitive skills, and know how to win approval from authority (having done well enough in a school environment to get into university). What we know about "people in general" may actually be limited to a highly select and unusual group, both culturally and historically. Researchers at the University of British Columbia have dubbed this group WEIRD, which stands for *Western, Educated, Industrialized, Rich, and Democratic*, arguing that conclusions drawn from these participants are inappropriate to generalize to all humanity (Henrich, Heine, & Norenzayan, 2010a).

Beyond Volunteers   Researchers usually must ask people to volunteer to participate in their research. At many universities, introductory psychology students are required either to volunteer for experiments or to complete an alternative project. If you are studying populations other than university students, you are even more dependent on volunteers—for example, asking people at a hockey game to participate in a study of emotional experiences, or conducting research on the Internet for which people must go to your website. Research indicates that volunteers differ in various ways from non-volunteers (Rosenthal & Rosnow, 1975). For instance, volunteers tend to be more highly educated, more in need of approval, and more social (Rosenthal & Rosnow, 1975); they also tend to have higher levels of conscientiousness and lower levels of neuroticism than non-volunteers (Lönnqvist et al., 2007).

Further, different kinds of people volunteer for different kinds of studies. In universities, there may be a sign-up board or website with advertisements for many studies. Different types of people may be drawn to the study titled "problem solving" than to the one titled "interaction in small groups." Available evidence indicates that the title does influence who signs up (Hood & Back, 1971; Silverman & Margulis, 1973). Studies that recruit participants by emphasizing financial rewards tend to attract less-altruistic participants than studies emphasizing the potential learning opportunity (Krawczyk, 2011). Similarly, studies offering course credit for participating tend to attract less-motivated participants than studies that do not offer course credit (Sharp, Pelletier, & Lévesque, 2006), although offering either money or course credit boosts volunteer rates more than offering nothing. How the study is advertised attracts different volunteers.

Beyond Sex of Participants   Sometimes, researchers use either males or females (or a very disproportionate ratio of males to females) simply because this is convenient or the procedures seem better suited to either males or females. Given the possible differences between males and females, however, the results of such studies may not be generalizable (Denmark, Russo, Frieze, & Sechzer, 1988). For example, Barha, Paluwski, and Galea (2007) noted that in past research, male rats whose mothers exhibited high levels of maternal care (e.g., grooming) performed better on spatial memory tasks than those whose mothers exhibited low levels of maternal care. They wanted to know whether this finding would generalize to female rats. In fact, they found the opposite pattern: Female rats whose mothers groomed them *less* performed better than those whose mothers groomed them *more*.

In psychological research with humans, sex or gender could influence results or the conclusions drawn from them. Denmark et al. (1988) identify several ways that sex or gender bias may arise in many steps of the research process. If a sample is solely or predominantly male or female, it is best to avoid concluding that a generalizable truth has been found. It is possible that the variables relate differently, or that males and females interpret experimental materials differently. If you want to generalize, *replicate* the study (see below) including (more) people of the other sex, and include sex as a variable in your analyses to discover if results generalize across sexes.

Beyond Culture   Only a few years ago, participants in most studies were university students in the United States who were primarily White, reflecting the predominant population of university students. Today, however, many samples of university students are ethnically diverse because the population of university students across North America is increasingly diverse, and more research is being done around the world. The overall *external validity* of the research literature is enhanced, and it is now much easier to compare ethnic groups to examine group differences and similarities. In the late 1980s, fewer than 10 percent of studies in social psychology included comparisons of two or more cultures (Pepitone & Triandis, 1987). Since then, there has been an explosion of interest in studying different cultures. A special section in the journal *Perspectives on Psychological Science* was devoted to highlighting "the fundamental nature of culture research in psychological science," including how researchers are revising and developing new theories for a better, more global, and more relevant science (Gelfand & Diener, 2010, p. 390). Despite this progress in comparing psychological phenomena across cultures, psychology remains grounded in a Western perspective. A truly global psychology, arguably, will require greater influence of concepts and methods originating in non-Western cultures (Berry, 2013).

So far, much research has centred on identifying cross-cultural similarities and differences in responses to the same environments, as well as personality and other psychological characteristics (Matsumoto, 1994). For example, Buunk, Park, and Duncan (2010) conducted a series of studies to examine how much parents influence dating and marriage across cultures. They asked students in the Netherlands, Iraq, and Canada to rate the degree to which their parents controlled their mate choice. Because the Netherlands is highly individualistic and Iraq is highly collectivistic, researchers hypothesized that parents have much more say in selecting marriage partners in Iraq than in the Netherlands. Results supported their hypothesis and indicated a very large effect size (Cohen's $d = 2.23$; see Chapter 12). In their Canadian sample, Buunk and colleagues compared University of British Columbia students whose cultural background was East Asian (i.e., more collectivistic) versus European (i.e., more individualistic). Again, students with a collectivist cultural background reported more parental involvement in their mate choice than students with an individualist cultural background (Cohen's $d = 1.42$). This type of research informs us about the generality of effects across cultural groups.

Miller (1999) encourages psychologists to take a broad view of the importance of culture in which "culture is understood as shared meaning systems that are embodied in artifacts and practices and that form a medium for human development" (p. 86). Research on self-concept can help illustrate the benefits of incorporating cultural perspectives into psychological theory. Traditional theories of self-concept are grounded in the culture of North America and Western Europe; the "self" is an individualistic concept; people are independent from others and self-enhancement comes from individual achievements. From a cultural perspective, the Western meaning of self does not seem to generalize to other cultures, in which the "self" is a collective concept and self-esteem is derived from relationships with others (Kitayama, Markus, Matsumoto, & Norasakkunkit, 1997). Researchers have debated whether this difference in self-concept influences the degree to which people show a self-enhancing bias. Although some researchers have argued that self-enhancement is universal (Cai et al., 2011; Sedikides, Gaertner, & Toguchi, 2003), more data supports the view that people from East Asian countries tend to self-criticize rather than self-enhance (Falk, Heine, Yuki, & Takemura, 2009; Heine & Hamamura, 2007; see also Henrich, Heine, & Norenzayan, 2010b).

Operational definitions of the constructs we study are grounded in particular cultural meanings (Byrne & van de Vijver, 2010). A measure of self-esteem that is appropriate for an individualistic culture is probably not appropriate for use, and would yield misleading results, in a collectivistic culture (Hamamura, Heine, & Paulhus, 2008; Heine, Lehman, Peng, & Greenholtz, 2002). It is therefore crucial to reconsider *construct validity* (see Chapter 5) whenever using a familiar operational definition in a new population.

Can Results Generalize Beyond the Specific Study Situation?

LO2

Beyond the Experimenter   The person who actually conducts the experiment can trigger another generalization problem. In most research, only one experimenter is used to make sure that any influence the experimenter has on participants is constant throughout the experiment. Because little attention is typically paid to experimenters' personal characteristics (McGuigan, 1963; Strohmetz, 2008), it is possible that results are generalizable only to certain types of experimenters.

Some of the important characteristics of experimenters include personality, sex, and amount of practice in the role of experimenter (Kintz, Delprato, Mettee, Persons, & Schappe, 1965). A warm, friendly experimenter may produce different results than a cold, unfriendly experimenter. Participants are more productive (i.e., generate more words) with male and female experimenters who are dressed in line with stereotyped gender roles (i.e., males dressed professionally, females dressed casually) rather than opposite gender roles (Green, Sandall, & Phelps, 2005). It has even been shown that rabbits learn faster when trained by experienced experimenters (Brogden, 1962)! The influence of the experimenter also may depend on participants' characteristics. For example, participants seem to perform better when tested by an experimenter of the opposite sex (Stevenson & Allen, 1964).

One solution to the problem of generalizing to other experimenters is to use two or more experimenters, preferably both male and female (Rubin, 1975).

Another option is to deliver instructions using a computer, which minimizes experimenter–participant interaction–and therefore the potential for influence (Strohmetz, 2008; see also Chapter 9).

Beyond a Pretest   Recall from Chapter 8 that researchers must decide whether to give a pretest. Intuitively, pretesting seems to be a good idea. The researcher can examine whether groups are equivalent on the pretest, and sometimes it is important to examine changes in people's scores from pretest to posttest, rather than simply comparing group means on the posttest. In longitudinal studies that risk participants withdrawing from the study, a pretest allows assessment of *mortality* effects. You can determine whether the people who withdrew were different initially from those who completed the study.

Pretesting, however, may limit the ability to generalize to populations that did not receive a pretest. In the real world, people are rarely given a pretest. For example, people do not regularly take stock of their attitudes before listening to a political speech or viewing an advertisement (cf., Lana, 1969). Recall from Chapter 8 that a Solomon four-group design (Solomon, 1949) can be used when a pretest is desirable but there is concern that simply taking the pretest will affect later responses. In the Solomon four-group design, the same experiment is conducted with and without the pretest. The researcher can examine whether there is an *interaction* between the independent variable and the pretest variable (see Chapter 10). If the pretest has no effect, posttest scores on the dependent variable are the same regardless of whether or not the pretest was given.

Beyond the Laboratory   Research conducted in a laboratory setting has the advantage of allowing the experimenter to study variables under highly controlled conditions. In experiments, the goal of high *internal validity* (i.e., the ability to infer a causal relationship between variables) may sometimes conflict with the goal of external validity. Does the artificiality of the laboratory setting limit the ability to generalize results to real-life settings? *Field experiments* are one way that researchers try to counteract laboratory artificiality and therefore increase the external validity of their experiments (see Chapter 4). In a field experiment, the researcher manipulates the independent variable in some natural setting, like a factory, a school, or a cafeteria.

Conducting research in both laboratory and field settings provides the greatest opportunity for advancing our understanding of behaviour. Consider research on eyewitness testimony. Many important limits of the accuracy of eyewitness memory to a crime have been illuminated in the lab. For example, in one study, Carleton University students who viewed a videotaped crime were much less likely to correctly identify the perpetrator in a lineup if the perpetrator had changed his hair colour and style (Pozzulo & Marciniak, 2006). This finding is consistent with field research showing that perpetrator hair colour is among the most accurately remembered details for eyewitnesses, even in violent crimes (Wagstaff et al., 2003). Yet controversy remains over whether lab-based findings can be generalized to real events in which people witness live crimes (Yuille, Ternes, & Cooper, 2010), which are more stressful situations (Pozzulo, Crescini, & Panton, 2008). Both lab- and field-based studies are vital to understand eyewitness testimony.

Do laboratory and field experiments that examine the same variables generally produce the same results? To answer this question, Mitchell (2012) found 217 pairs of studies for which a laboratory investigation had a field-based counterpart. The studies were drawn from a variety of subfields in psychology, mostly from social and industrial/organizational, but also from developmental, marketing, education, and clinical. *Replicating* an earlier and much smaller study (Anderson, Lindsay, & Bushman, 1999), overall results showed the laboratory and field experiments were similar: The magnitude of the effect of the independent variable on the dependent variable was similar in the two types of studies. Lab-field correspondence was highest in industrial/organizational psychology, and when *effect sizes* (see Chapter 12) were large. Thus, even though lab and field experiments are conducted in different settings, the results are often complementary and only sometimes contradictory. As we discuss next, when findings are *replicated* in multiple settings, our confidence in the generalizability of the findings increases.

SOLUTIONS TO GENERALIZING RESULTS

LO3

Replicate the Study

Replication is an important way to overcome problems of generalization that occur in a single study. There are two types of replications to consider: direct replications and conceptual replications (Schmidt, 2009).

Replicate Directly   A **direct replication** is an attempt to replicate the procedures of a study as closely as possible to see whether the same results are obtained. In best practice, individual researchers attempt to directly replicate their own work when possible, especially when the results from the initial study are unexpected (Cesario, 2014). Direct replications are crucial for determining whether an original finding can generalize to other samples drawn from the same population (e.g., university undergraduates at the researcher's institution)—in other words, to offer evidence that the initial result was not a *Type I error* (see Chapter 13; Simons, 2014).

Researchers may also engage in direct replication when starting a new area of research. If you are starting your own work on a problem, you may try to replicate a crucial study to make sure that you understand the procedures and can obtain the same results. Often, direct replications occur when a researcher builds on the findings of a prior study—this can be called a *replication with extension* (Bonett, 2012). For example, suppose you are intrigued by research on waist-to-hip ratio mentioned in Chapter 5 (Singh, 1993; Suschinsky, Elias, & Krupp, 2007). These studies showed that males rate females with a ratio of 0.70 as most attractive. In your research, you might replicate the procedures used in the original study while expanding on the original research. For example, you might study this phenomenon with males similar to those in the original sample, as well as males from different cultures or age groups (see below). When you can replicate the original research findings using the same or very similar procedures, confidence in the generality of the original findings is increased.

Sometimes a researcher will be unable to replicate a previous finding. A single failure to replicate does not reveal much, though; it is unrealistic to assume, on the basis of a single failure to replicate, that the previous research was a *Type I error*. Failures to replicate share the same problems as non-significant results, discussed in Chapter 13. A failure to replicate could mean that the original results are invalid, but it could also mean that the replication attempt was flawed. For example, if the replication is based on the procedure as reported in a journal article, it is possible that the article omitted an important aspect of the procedure. For this reason, it is usually a good idea to contact the researcher to obtain detailed information on all materials and procedures used in the study.

The so-called "Mozart effect" offers another example of the importance of replications. In the original study, university students listened to ten minutes of a particular Mozart sonata (Rauscher, Shaw, & Ky, 1993). These students then showed increased performance on a spatial-reasoning measure drawn from the Stanford-Binet Intelligence Scale. Subsequently, the same research team replicated the effect using a different operational definition of spatial ability: the Stanford-Binet Paper Folding and Cutting task (Rauscher, Shaw, & Ky, 1995). Despite the fact that the effect was temporary, lasting about ten minutes, these findings received a great deal of attention in the press. People quickly generalized it to the possibility of increasing children's intelligence with Mozart sonatas. In fact, one U.S. governor began producing Mozart CDs to distribute in maternity wards, and entrepreneurs began selling Mozart kits to parents. Over the next few years, however, there were many failures to replicate the Mozart effect (see Steele, Bass, & Crook, 1999). Rauscher and Shaw (1998) responded to the many replication failures by precisely describing the conditions necessary to produce the Mozart effect. However, Steele et al. (1999) and McCutcheon (2000) were unable to obtain the effect even though they followed the detailed procedures. A *meta-analysis* (see below) compiled the results of 40 studies with 3,000 participants, concluding that there was a small effect of listening to Mozart on spatial task performance compared to not listening to music (Pietschnig, Voracek, & Formann, 2010). However, listening to *any* music resulted in an effect of equal size, likely due to music increasing arousal levels (e.g., Thompson, Schellenberg, & Husain, 2001). It seems there is nothing special about listening to Mozart after all.

A single failure to replicate is not adequate cause for discarding the original research finding. As in the case of the Mozart effect, attempts to replicate do not occur in isolation, as many researchers attempt replications. Repeated failures to replicate may lead to a conclusion that the original results were a fluke—a *Type I error* was made. Another possibility is that the research will demonstrate that the effect occurs only under certain limited circumstances. In a few cases, it may turn out that the original researcher misrepresented the results in some way (see Chapter 3 for a discussion of fraud).

Direct Replication and Disciplinary Reform   Several high-profile cases of failures to directly replicate research results in the last few years have shone a spotlight on the issue of replication. In one case, a paper published in a major journal purportedly offered evidence of psi phenomena (Bem, 2011). For example, participants were better than chance at guessing the on-screen location of hidden erotic pictures, but not at guessing the location of hidden nonerotic pictures: Their *future* emotions seemed to affect choices in the present. When skeptical researchers attempted to replicate it, many were unable to do so (see Baruss & Rabier, 2014, for a summary). In another case, several attempts failed to replicate some well-known studies of non-conscious priming. In one of the original studies, people who were primed with the concept of old age subsequently walked more slowly, suggesting that a subtle cognitive prime had a measurable behavioural effect (Bargh, Chen, & Burrows, 1996). Doyen, Klein, Pichon, and Cleeremans (2012) replicated this effect—but only when the experimenters believed that it would occur, suggesting that the original result may have resulted from an *experimenter expectancy effect* (see Chapter 9; for other failed replications of similar studies, see Harris, Coburn, Roher, & Pashler, 2013; Pashler, Coburn, & Harris, 2012; see Yong, 2012, for an overview of the controversy).

These failures to replicate precognition and behavioural priming effects were some of the major triggers of recent debate and reform efforts (see also Chapter 3 for cases of fraud). Many complex questions have been raised about the way research in psychology—and other disciplines—is conducted. Consider the following questions about replication in particular: Whose responsibility is it to replicate results? To what extent can we trust past literature that no one has attempted to replicate? What is the best way to replicate others' work? Which kinds of replications are most important? Answers to these questions will continue to emerge and change in the coming years; here we consider some recent attempts.

Historically, direct replications have been difficult to publish, particularly in the social sciences (Fanelli, 2012). Recent commitments made by journal editors in psychology are changing that norm by accepting particular types of replication studies after adequate *peer review*. Relatedly, researchers are developing best practices that are helping to ensure that direct replications are high quality and objective (see Brandt et al., 2013). Some recommendations for convincing replication attempts include ensuring high statistical *power* (including a very large sample size; see Chapter 13); following the original procedures as closely as possible, including original materials if obtainable; and making details public for other researchers (including the original study's authors) to verify. For an example, Earp, Everett, Madva, and Hamlin (2014) attempted to directly replicate a widely cited study examining morality and physical purity. They used the original materials and ensured that their samples were ethnically diverse and large enough to detect effects that exist. Yet they failed in three studies to find evidence of the effect. Instead of their work disappearing from record, they were able to successfully publish their methodologically rigorous– but failed–direct replication attempts.

It is becoming increasingly common for researchers from many labs to collaborate to conduct simultaneous direct replications. Earp et al. (2014) attempted replications in the United States, the United Kingdom, and India. Not only does a multi-labs approach add *external validity* to the results, it also promotes objectivity as researchers have less personal investment in the outcomes. The journal *Perspectives on Psychological Science* has created a special type of paper called a Registered Replication Report (RRR), which requires the cooperation of many labs to directly replicate important findings, as well as cooperation from the target study's original author whenever possible to approve the method and supply original materials (Simons, Holcombe, & Spellman, 2014). Importantly, the study design is pre-registered with the Open Science Framework (see https://osf.io/), undergoes *peer review* on the methodological protocol before data are collected, and is virtually guaranteed publication regardless of whether results support the original result. The first RRR was published in September 2014 (Alogna et al., 2014), involved over 30 labs from 10 countries, and ultimately replicated the original results with some qualifications (see Schooler, 2014, for a commentary from the original study's first author). The RRR and other published direct replications represent a major commitment to high-quality psychological science.

Replicate Conceptually   The use of different procedures to replicate a research finding is called a **conceptual replication.** In most research, the goal is to discover whether a relationship between conceptual variables exists. The music manipulation in the original Mozart effect study mentioned earlier used the first section of Mozart's *Sonata for Two Pianos in D Major (K. 448)*. This selection is a specific operational definition for the purposes of studying the effect of music on a spatial performance. Likewise, the specific task chosen as the dependent measure is an operational definition of the more general performance variable.

In a conceptual replication, the same independent variable is manipulated in a different way and/or the dependent variable is measured in a different way. A relationship that appears with one set of operational definitions should *generalize* to different ways of manipulating and measuring the variables. Sometimes a conceptual replication may involve an alternative stimulus (e.g., a different Mozart sonata, or music by a different composer) or an alternative dependent measure (e.g., a different spatial-reasoning task, as in Rauscher et al., 1995). When conceptual replications produce similar results as the original study, a case can be made that the relationship between the variables generalizes beyond the original operational definitions.

This discussion should also alert you to an important way of thinking about research findings. The findings represent relationships between conceptual variables but are grounded in specific operations. You may read about the specific methods employed in a study and speculate whether they are so unusual that they could never generalize to other situations or operational definitions. A conceptual replication, however, would demonstrate that the relationship between the conceptual theoretical variables is still present.

Conceptual replications can help develop theories of behaviour; however, they are not a substitute for direct replications (Schmidt, 2009). One problem with conceptual replications is the potential to promote Type I errors. If a conceptual replication fails to find an effect, it is possible to toss that study aside as methodologically problematic, and continue substituting operational definitions until the original effect is conceptually replicated (LeBel & Peters, 2011). This is one of the major criticisms of the psi phenomenon paper (Bem, 2011). Despite offering nine conceptual replications, apparently there were also many "pilot studies" that had failed to show effects and were dismissed as methodological problems–which increased the chance that the conceptual replications are simply Type I errors. Thus, for greater confidence in the generalizability of an effect, consider conducting a *direct replication* first to ensure that the original results generalize beyond the original sample. Then carefully substitute alternative operational definitions in a conceptual replication to develop your theory about how the variables relate.

Consider Different Populations

LO4

Recognize Limits of Convenience Samples and Seek Diverse Samples
Psychologists rely heavily on undergraduate students as research participants. As we noted earlier, this unique population has characteristics that make it unrepresentative of humanity generally (i.e., it is WEIRD; Henrich et al., 2010a, 2010b), which presents a challenge to the external validity of behavioural science. In Chapter 7 we emphasized the importance of randomly sampling from a population when you wish to generalize to a specific population (e.g., all Canadians). It would be ideal, then, to randomly sample participants for all studies that seek to generalize to all of humanity–yet this method is clearly logistically impossible!

Does that mean we must throw out all data using undergraduate samples as useless? No! But we can question whether our results would generalize beyond this specific population, and seek broader samples whenever possible. Before dismissing research that uses any particular type of participant, such as university students, consider the characteristics of the sample you do have. How well does it represent, demographically, the characteristics of your region or country? To the extent that a sample of undergraduates is diverse on various dimensions (e.g., socio-economic status, culture, age), making broader generalizations beyond them is less problematic.

Consider how results might differ or be similar in a sample drawing from a different population. University students, after all, *are* human–we simply need to be mindful about how far we extend our claims. How might older people, younger people, people from different cultural backgrounds or socio-economic statuses respond to these variables? Rather than assuming that processes operate universally, seek out disconfirming evidence. Then use factorial designs to test those hypotheses and adapt the theory accordingly. As noted in Henrich et al. (2010b), members of a small nomadic culture who live off of Burma have the ability to see clearly underwater because their pupils constrict (rather than dilate, as most peoples' pupils do underwater). A thorough theoretical understanding of vision—seemingly a basic process that could not differ across cultures—must be able to account for both underwater pupillary reactions (see Chapter 2 on theory development).

It is not always possible to collect data from diverse sources, but researchers should strive to do so whenever possible. Consider research conducted by Simon Fraser University's Lara Aknin and her colleagues. She has tested the relationship between giving to others and personal well-being in samples of university under-graduates, children, company employees; in vast international surveys; as well as in lab and field experiments run in Canada, the United States, Uganda, India, South Africa, and a tiny village in Vanuatu (see Aknin et al., 2013; Aknin, Broesch, Hamlin, & Van de Vondervoort, 2015; Aknin, Hamlin, & Dunn, 2012; Dunn, Aknin, & Norton, 2008). Results *replicate* across all of these groups, offering strong evidence that the positive effect of giving on well-being has high external validity.

The Internet is one relatively inexpensive way for researchers to reach samples beyond undergraduate students. Although such studies raise their own generalization issues, they frequently complement studies based on university student samples, while reaching a broader population (Gosling, Vazire, Srivastava, & John, 2004). Samples recruited using the Internet (e.g., using social media or Amazon's Mechanical Turk) show greater diversity on variables such as socio-economic status, ethnicity, age, and work experience (Behrend, Sharek, Meade, & Wiebe, 2011; Casler, Bickel, & Hackett, 2013). These latter two studies also revealed very similar responses on most measures when comparing university undergraduate and Internet samples, thereby adding external validity to their claims. As psychological science progresses further, seeking evidence of external validity in our samples will continue to be important.

Research with animals once suffered from the convenience sample criticism too: At one time, this work relied largely on the white rat, because rats were easy to obtain and study on a university campus (Beach, 1950). However, a more recent *replication* showed that research with animals now relies on a great diversity of species to explore rich questions in perception and cognitive processes (Shettleworth, 2009). As further evidence of external validity, many results from research using animal models have been successfully applied to humans. Research on reinforcement using rats and pigeons has been applied to treat mental illness through behaviour modification, to understand person-ality, and to study choice behaviour in humans. Various aspects of human psychology have been illuminated by animal research, including the biologi-cal bases of memory, food preferences, addiction, and sexual behaviour.

Examine the Influence of Group Membership Using Factorial Designs   One way to think about generalization to different populations is in the context of factorial designs (see Chapter 10). An interaction occurs when a relationship between variables exists under one condition but not another, or when the nature of the relationship is different in one condition than in another. Thus, if you question the generalizability of a study that used only males (or only adolescents or only Westerners), you are suggesting that there is an interaction between sex (or age or culture) and the independent variable. Suppose, for example, that a study examines the relationship between crowding and aggression among males and reports that crowding is associated with higher levels of aggression. You might then question whether the results are generalizable to females.

Figure 14.1 shows four potential outcomes of a hypothetical study on crowding and aggression that tested both males and females. In each graph, the relationship between crowding and aggression for males has been maintained. In Graph A, there is no interaction–the behaviour of males and females is virtually identical (the solid and dotted lines overlap). Thus, the results of the

FIGURE 14.1
Outcomes of a hypothetical experiment on crowding and aggression

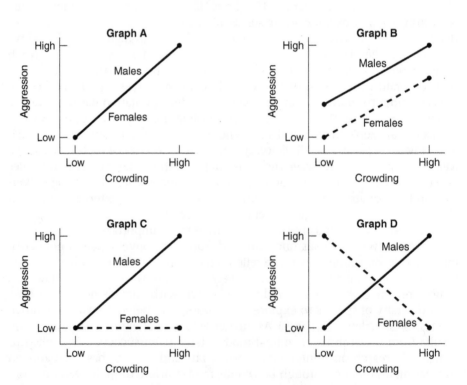

Note: The presence of an interaction (Graphs C and D) indicates that the results for males *cannot* be generalized to females.

original all-male study could be generalized to females. In Graph B, there is also no interaction; the effect of crowding is identical for males and females. However, in this graph, males are more aggressive than females (i.e., a main effect of sex). Although such a main effect of sex may be interesting, it does not prevent generalization because the overall positive relationship between crowding and aggression is present for both males and females.

Graphs C and D show interactions, which affect generalizations. In both, the results with males cannot be generalized to females. In Graph C, there is no relationship between crowding and aggression for females but there is for males. In Graph D, the interaction tells us that a positive relationship between crowding and aggression exists for males but that a negative relationship exists for females. As it turns out, Graph D describes the results of several studies (cf., Freedman, Levy, Buchanan, & Price, 1972).

Researchers can address generalization issues that stem from the use of different populations by including participant type as a variable. By including variables such as sex, age, or cultural background in the design of the study, results may be analyzed to determine whether there are interaction effects like the ones illustrated in Figure 14.1.

Rely on Multiple Studies to Draw Conclusions: Literature Reviews and Meta-Analyses

LO5

Researchers have traditionally drawn conclusions about the generalizability of research findings by conducting literature reviews. In a **literature review,** a researcher reads many studies that address a particular topic and then writes a paper that summarizes, organizes, and evaluates the literature, sometimes proposing advances to theory (see Chapter 2). The literature review offers a summary of existing results, indicating what findings are strongly versus weakly supported in the literature, identifying inconsistent findings and areas in which research is lacking, and discussing future directions for research. The conclusions in a narrative literature review are based on the subjective impressions of the reviewer.

A review paper that uses statistical techniques to combine results from many studies in an area is called a **meta-analysis** (Rosenthal, 1991). In a meta-analysis, the statistical procedures incorporate effect sizes, sample sizes, and other features to compare the strength of a given finding across many different studies that tested the same or similar variables; statistical conclusions are then drawn. As demonstrated earlier regarding the so-called Mozart Effect, a good meta-analysis (e.g., Pietschnig et al., 2010) can be extremely informative. General conclusions that can be reached using meta-analysis are very difficult to draw from traditional literature reviews. Anyone would find it difficult to integrate the results of so many studies with different experimental designs, participant types, and measures. If you read all the studies and someone asked you the simple question, "Does listening to Mozart improve spatial intelligence?"

you could spend a day telling the person about the specific studies and the complexities you noted while reading the literature. A meta-analysis is designed to integrate information from diverse sources.

Meta-analyses are used to examine relationships between variables, to test hypotheses, and to refine theories (Chan & Arvey, 2012). For example, University of Calgary researcher Piers Steel (2007) used a meta-analysis to investigate the predictors and outcomes of procrastination by gathering 691 correlation coefficients reported from 216 studies. Among many findings, Steel found that people's tendency to procrastinate was related to the personality trait conscientiousness (and similar concepts like organization and low distractibility), but not to neuroticism (or similar concepts like perfectionism). Moreover, people tend to procrastinate on tasks they find unpleasant and when the reward for completing the task is delayed. Given these results, it seems that studying for a test when completing your degree is years away presents a situation ripe for procrastinating!

Typical tables in meta-analyses will show information about the effect size obtained in a number of studies, often with a summary of the average effect size. Consider the information in Table 14.1. This table summarizes some results from a meta-analysis of 241 data sets examining correlates of academic performance in university (Richardson, Abraham, & Bond, 2012). Performance self-efficacy was the strongest correlate with GPA, with an average *r* of .59 across four samples that tested 1,348 participants. Notice the 95 percent *confidence interval:* The true population correlation most likely falls between .49 and .67. For contrast, consider the weak negative correlation between GPA and depression: average $r = -.10$. The confidence interval ranges from $-.17$ to $+.02$: Based on available data (drawing from 16 samples totalling 6,335 participants), the true population correlation is most likely in the zero to weakly negative range. By pooling results from dozens of studies from various researchers, meta-analysis can provide more-informative estimates of population values than when relying on a single study.

Both narrative literature reviews and meta-analyses provide valuable information and are often complementary. A meta-analysis allows statistical, quantitative conclusions, whereas the narrative review uses a more qualitative approach to help identify trends in the literature and directions for future study. However, the quality of conclusions drawn from either method reflects the accuracy and completion of the literature that is included (Chan & Arvey, 2012). *Publication bias*—the tendency to publish only *statistically significant* results—can lead to overestimating effect sizes (see Chapter 13). Therefore, researchers conducting these types of reviews often e-mail other researchers requesting any unpublished data that may be appropriate to include.

Even without conducting a meta-analysis ourselves, a background in meta-analysis is helpful when reviewing research findings. Simply knowing about meta-analysis can improve the way we interpret information for literature reviews, enabling us to discount flashy titles and focus on the effects for greater accuracy (Bushman & Wells, 2001).

TABLE I4.I   Some results from a meta-analysis of correlates of undergraduate grade point average (from Richardson, Abraham, & Bond, 2012)

Correlate of GPA	Effect Size *r*	95% Confidence Interval for *r*	Number of Samples	Total Sample Size
Socio-economic status	.11	[.08, .15]	21	75,000
High school GPA	.40	[.35, .45]	46	34,724
Conscientiousness personality trait	.19	[.17, .22]	69	27,875
Extraversion personality trait	−.04	[−.07, −.02]	58	23,730
Performance self-efficacy (belief in one's ability to use past experiences to succeed on familiar challenges)	.59	[.49, .67]	4	1,348
Academic self-efficacy (belief in one's ability to succeed on unfamiliar challenges)	.31	[.28, .34]	67	46,570
Academic intrinsic motivation	.17	[.12, .23]	22	7,414
Academic extrinsic motivation	.01	[−.06, .08]	10	2,339
Test anxiety	−.24	[−.29, −.20]	29	13,497
Goal commitment	.15	[.07, .22]	10	13,098
General stress	−.13	[−.19, −.06]	8	1,736
Depression	−.10	[−.17, .02]	17	6,335

Issues of generalizing our results are complex and important. Replication and meta-analyses are increasingly recognized as vital tools for generalizing results beyond individual laboratories and achieving more accurate estimates of effects. Whenever possible, seek large and diverse samples for participation in research, to enable more accurate and generalizable results. As psychology and other sciences engage in ongoing disciplinary reform, best research practices will continue to develop.

GENERALIZING YOUR KNOWLEDGE BEYOND THIS BOOK   `LO6`

This last chapter emphasizes the ability to generalize results from a study to a population. As you finish reading this book, you might also pause to consider ways you can "generalize" your knowledge of research methods. This section is intended to help you identify some of the ways you can do that.

Recognize and Use Your New Knowledge

In Chapter 1 we considered an overview of the research process. Examine Figure 14.2, which connects each chapter in this book to at least one broad aspect of this research process. Notice how we have emphasized study design

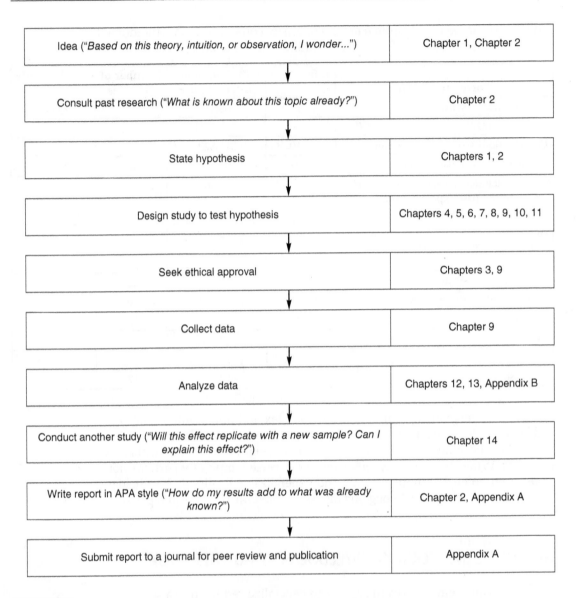

FIGURE 14.2
Overview of research process, with connections across chapters

across eight chapters. As you likely noticed, there are many features to consider and details to be decided when designing methodologically rigorous research! To the extent you have engaged with this book (and corresponding course), you have deepened your skills and understanding of good research design. You can use this knowledge to more effectively evaluate research reported in the media and to help you learn about research results in future courses. You can seek and use research literature to answer questions you might have about behaviour, such as "What are the best study strategies?" (Check out Dunlosky et al., 2013, for a thorough literature review.) You may also be interested in becoming more involved in doing research, seeking further research training, and perhaps pursuing a career path that relies on quantitative training (see Chapter 1).

Stay Connected to Building a Better Psychological Science

The primary goal for this updated Canadian edition was to address the current controversies, debates, and disciplinary reform initiatives related to research methods. These ongoing debates are particularly relevant to ethics (Chapter 3), statistics (Chapters 12 and 13), and generalization (this chapter). Best practices in research methods continue to be shaped right now. The *Association for Psychological Science*, and particularly its journal *Perspectives on Psychological Science*, is a good place to keep current on these ongoing issues (see www. psychologicalscience.org). It is an exciting time to be a psychological scientist!

You now have developed skills useful for accurately communicating psychological research results to the public. As president of the Association for Psychological Science, Mahzarin Banaji launched the *Wikipedia Initiative* "to improve the quality and quantity of the information about psychological science presented in Wikipedia" (Banaji, 2011; see also Banaji, 2010). By challenging all of us who are knowledgeable about psychological science–including students like you!–to update and clarify Wikipedia entries, more accurate information is reaching the broader public for the benefit of us all (Farzan & Kraut, 2013).

Use Research to Improve Lives

One reason why many students are drawn to psychology is the desire to help others. The topics we study and methods we use in our discipline make it well-positioned to "promote human welfare" (Miller, 1969) and to improve everyday life. Indeed, psychological research has long impacted many domains of life (Zimbardo, 2004). Impact can be seen in areas such as health (programs to promote health-related behaviours related to stress, heart disease, and sexually transmitted infections), law and criminal justice (providing data on the effects of 6- versus 12-person juries, and showing how law enforcement personnel can improve the accuracy of eyewitness identification), education (providing methods for encouraging academic performance or reducing conflict among different ethnic groups), and work environments (providing workers with more control, and improving the ways that people interact with computers in the workplace).

Psychologists have developed many websites to provide the public with information on parenting, education, mental health, and many other topics. Spread the word to your friends and families about ways to find research-based information to use in everyday life. For examples, share websites of the American Psychological Association (www.apa.org), the Association for Psychological

Science (www.psychologicalscience.org), the Canadian Psychological Association (www.cpa.ca), the Canadian Mental Health Association (www.cmha.ca), and the Greater Good Science Center (http://greatergood.berkeley.edu/).

Despite the potential challenges of generalizing research findings highlighted in this chapter, evidence suggests that we can use many findings profitably across various aspects of our lives. We hope that by engaging with this textbook, you have gained skills and knowledge that you can *generalize* beyond this course. Continue to use your skills to seek out, evaluate, and perhaps even create research evidence, so you can improve your life and the lives of others.

STUDY TERMS

Test yourself! Define and generate an example of each of these key terms.

Conceptual replication (p. 307)   Literature review (p. 311)

Direct replication (p. 304)   Meta-analysis (p. 311)

External validity (p. 298)   Replication (p. 304)

REVIEW QUESTIONS

Test yourself on this chapter's learning objectives. Can you answer each of these questions?

1. Why should a researcher be concerned about generalizing to other participant populations? What are some of the generalization problems that a researcher might confront?

2. What is the source of the problem of generalizing to other experimenters? How can this problem be solved?

3. Why might a pretest present a problem for generalization?

4. Distinguish between a direct replication and a conceptual replication. What is the value of each?

5. What is a meta-analysis? What is the purpose of a meta-analysis? How does it differ from a literature review?

6. List three ways you might continue to use your knowledge of research methods in the future.

DEEPEN YOUR UNDERSTANDING

Develop your mastery of these concepts by considering these application questions. Compare your responses with those from other people in your study group.

1. Participate in a psychological research study on the Internet (e.g., try https://implicit.harvard.edu/implicit/). What issues of generalization might arise when interpreting the results of such studies? Does the computer

aspect of the research make this research less generalizable than university lab-based research, or does the fact that people throughout the world can participate make it more generalizable? How could you design a study to answer this question empirically?

2. Use *PsycINFO* to find abstracts of articles that included race, ethnicity, sex, or nationality as a variable (consult Appendix D for strategies). What conclusions do the authors of these studies draw about generalization?

3. Find a meta-analysis published in a journal; two good sources are *Psychological Bulletin* and the *Review of Educational Research*. How were studies selected for the analysis? How was the concept of effect size discussed in the meta-analysis? What conclusions were drawn from the meta-analysis?

4. Find the most recent Registered Replication Report at *Perspectives on Psychological Science*, or another direct replication study. How many labs and participants were involved? How were issues of external validity and overall effect size addressed? What conclusions were drawn about the original study results?

Appendix A

Writing Research Reports in APA Style

This appendix offers an introduction to reporting research results using the conventions of APA style. Most recommendations–including a complete, annotated example–relate to preparing written reports; we also include a few tips for presenting posters and talks. Information in this appendix can be helpful for writing or otherwise presenting your research results in your courses, at conferences, or for possible publication in a professional journal. When preparing reports for a class, a thesis, or submission to a journal, always check whether you are required to follow APA style directly, or other variations.

The format presented here for writing research reports is drawn from the *Publication Manual of the American Psychological Association* (Sixth Edition, 2010). *APA style* is the term used to denote this set of specific rules for organizing and presenting research results, as well as for citing and referencing past research. APA style is considered the standard in many journals in psychology, child development, family relations, and education, regardless of where you conduct your research. Other disciplines use other styles (e.g., MLA, Chicago). (If you are unsure whether a particular journal uses APA style, examine a recent issue of that journal.) To deepen your knowledge of APA style beyond the brief treatment presented here, purchase the entire *Publication Manual* through your university bookstore or directly from the American Psychological Association. Tutorials at www.apastyle.org may also be helpful.

Overall, the APA manual is guided by principles of "specificity and sensitivity." First, papers should be written at a level of specificity and detail that will allow others to *replicate* the research. Second, papers should be free of inappropriate language that might be interpreted as biased and insensitive. The manual also includes manuscript preparation guidelines, including references. Throughout this appendix, examples that are intended to appear as you would type them in your papers appear in a unique font to make spacing and other rules clear; this convention is also used in the APA manual. When typing your own paper, you would not use this type of font (see below for details).

Why learn APA style? The purpose of APA style is to facilitate communication between writers and readers. Because APA style provides a uniform structure for written reports and other presentations, you will be better equipped to understand and evaluate them. By using APA style properly in your own work, you signal that you are a participant in this scholarly community while making it easier for other members of this community to understand your work. As you will notice throughout this appendix, attention to detail is crucial to mastering these rules. Mastering APA style provides an opportunity to develop your detail skills, which will prove helpful when you enter the job market.

Many additional resources might be helpful as you prepare to write your first research reports. In a brief book, former *Psychological Science* editor Robert Kail (2015) offers specific advice on how to effectively construct sentences, paragraphs, and APA style manuscripts. It serves as a tutorial by incorporating many examples, prompts to practise, and answers. For additional guidelines about writing compelling APA style research reports, see an article by Kazdin (1995) and a chapter by Bem (2003). Other brief books offer advice spanning many aspects of report writing, from conducting literature reviews through to preparing manuscripts for publication (see Rosnow & Rosnow, 2012; Sternberg & Sternberg, 2010).

The rest of this appendix is divided into sections: general writing style and word choice, writing each section of the APA style research report, formatting a manuscript, citing and referencing sources in APA style, and tips for conference presentations. Finally, an example paper is provided in manuscript format ready for submission to a journal.

WRITING STYLE AND WORD CHOICE

One way to think about writing style is as a way to signal membership in a community. Think about how you might communicate the same idea–say, about how prepared you are to write tomorrow's exam–differently depending on whether you are talking to your friend, a parent, or the course instructor. You might choose different words, emphasize different points, and omit different information. Similarly, writing about research effectively requires adapting your writing to fit in with the style of the academic community (e.g., psychology). Writing style that is appropriate for the psychology community would seem out of place in the history community, and vice versa. Learning to write effectively in the style of a discipline involves identifying and using subtle features that indicate membership in that community (Madigan, Johnson, & Linton, 1995).

Identifying and learning the subtle stylistic features of a discipline can be difficult, precisely because they are so subtle. Whenever you read published journal articles, try to notice how the authors choose to incorporate past research, summarize research results, and discuss the implications of their work. We provide some general suggestions for improving writing, and as much as possible tailor recommendations to the style of psychology. We recommend consulting Madigan et al. (1995) and Kail (2015) for further insight into the subtleties of this style.

Clarity and Intended Audience

Present ideas precisely and clearly, with your intended audience in mind. Words are a vehicle for communicating ideas. It is important to use straightforward sentences that avoid flowery language. Some students seem to believe that liberal use of a thesaurus and extremely long complex sentences makes their work sound smart. Instead, the sacrifice in clarity signals that the author is not a member of this scholarly community. As people become more effective writers in psychology, they are able to maintain clarity while injecting creativity into their reports. But clarity is crucial for writing effectively in this community.

The overall piece should be organized in such a way that the ideas flow coherently and logically. APA style provides an overall organizational structure for research reports that can also be used in other forms of professional communication (e.g., posters). Yet each section within the APA style written report needs to be organized by the author (particularly the introduction and discussion sections, see below). Creating an outline is one way to organize sections (as well as other works that do not use APA style). Many writers plan a paper by putting their thoughts and ideas into outline form. The outline then serves as a writing guide. This method forces writers to develop a logical structure before writing the paper.

Paragraphs should be well organized. It is a good idea for a paragraph to contain a topic sentence. Other sentences within a paragraph should develop the idea in the topic sentence by elaborating, expanding, explaining, or supporting the same idea. Kail (2015) recommends developing the outline for subsections of the report from topic sentences, then using those topic sentences to guide your writing of the rest of the paper. Avoid one-sentence paragraphs. If you find such paragraphs in your paper, expand the paragraph, include the idea in another paragraph, or delete the concept.

The amount of jargon and level of specificity you use will depend on your audience. When preparing any kind of writing in a class, ask your instructor whether the audience is other scholars knowledgeable about the topic and methods, other scholars unfamiliar with the topic and methods, the general public, or some other group. Use only the jargon that is appropriate for the audience you are intending to reach. For example, it would be appropriate to use the term *external validity* when writing a report for publication in a journal, but might be less appropriate when writing a blog post or a Wikipedia entry. In reports for publication, assume the reader is generally familiar with statistics and hypothesis testing. Statistical outcomes can usually be presented without defining terms such as the *mean, standard deviation,* or *significance.* Regardless of your audience, avoid creating unnecessary abbreviations your readers have to learn (e.g., *LM condition* to refer to the *laptop multitasking condition*).

Expect to write multiple drafts of your paper. After completing the first draft of your paper, it is a good idea to let it sit for a day or so before you reread it. Carefully proofread the paper, paying attention to grammar and spelling. Some grammatical considerations are described here; you can also use your word processor to check your spelling and grammar. We advise seeking feedback from others who will read your report carefully and suggest improvements. Ideally, these readers are knowledgeable with the type of writing you are preparing (e.g., APA style report) but not necessarily the topic. Thoughtfully consider what feedback will improve your final product.

Paraphrase and Cite Past Research

There are two important reasons to cite past research in your report. First, it connects your research to the rest of what is known about a topic. Acknowledging what other researchers have already found enables you to specify the contribution your research makes to knowledge (Giltrow, Gooding, Burgoyne, & Sawatsky, 2014). Second, acknowledging the work of others signals what ideas and results are theirs, and what ideas and results are yours. In other words, you avoid plagiarism (see Chapter 3).

In psychology and other sciences, it is common to include others' work by paraphrasing it and adding a citation at the end of the sentence. *Paraphrasing* means re-stating the original author's idea or result in different words. Learning to paraphrase can be challenging, particularly for students who are still building confidence in writing. Examples of effective paraphrasing are available online (e.g., see http://www.uc.utoronto.ca/paraphrase and https://owl.english.purdue.edu/owl/resource/619/1/ for practice exercises). Practise paraphrasing others' work as you use it to identify the contributions you are making. Indicating how your paper builds on previous research strengthens your paper by showing the reader that you are building on the existing body of scientific knowledge (Harris, 2002). Refer to the section on citing and referencing sources later in this appendix for details about how to cite using APA style.

Paraphrasing is a stylistic feature that psychology shares with other sciences, but is less common in the humanities (Madigan et al., 1995). If you have taken many courses in the humanities, you may be used to directly quoting your sources. The tendency to paraphrase rather than quote in the sciences reflects an assumption that an idea can be preserved regardless of the precise words used. To signal that you are participating in the scientific community, avoid using direct quotations and instead use paraphrasing with citations. Consult your instructor or the writing centre at your university for more advice on effective and honest use of sources to write in psychology.

Active versus Passive Voice

It is common for authors writing in psychology to use the passive voice (Madigan et al., 1995). Some argue that many writers rely too much on the passive voice in their reports, and risk lost clarity (Kail, 2015). Consider the following sentences:

It was found by Yee and Johnson (1996) that adolescents prefer . . .

Participants were administered the test after a 10-minute rest period.

Participants were read the instructions by the experimenter.

Now try writing those sentences in a more active voice. For example:

Adolescents prefer . . . (Yee & Johnson, 1996).

Participants took the test after a 10-minute rest period.

The experimenter read the instructions to participants.

Prose that seems stilted using the passive voice is much more direct when phrased in the active voice. Deliberately choose active or passive voice.

Sometimes authors refer to themselves in the third person. Thus, they might say "The experimenter distributed the questionnaires" instead of "I distributed the questionnaires." It is unclear whether "the experimenter" is in fact the author or someone else. When authors refer to themselves in the paper, APA style recommends using first person pronouns (e.g., "I" or "we").

Avoiding Biased Language

Recall that APA style is guided by the principles of specificity and sensitivity. The principle of specificity leads to the recommendation to use the term *participants* to refer to humans and *subjects* to refer to animals used in your study. Use other terms if they more accurately describe the people in the study (e.g., children, patients, clients, or *respondents* in survey research).

Be sensitive to the possibility that your writing might convey a bias, however unintentional, regarding gender, sexual orientation, and ethnic or racial group. As a general principle, be as specific as possible when referring to groups of people. For example, referring to the participants in your study as "Korean Canadians and Vietnamese Canadians" is more specific and accurate than describing them as "Asians." Also, be sensitive to the use of labels that might be offensive to members of certain groups. In practice, this means using the terms people prefer. Instead of writing "We tested groups of schizophrenics and normals," write "We tested people with and without schizophrenia."

The APA manual offers numerous examples of ways to be sensitive to gender, racial and ethnic identity, age, sexual orientation, and disabilities. The term *gender* refers to males and females as social groups. Thus, gender is the proper term to use in a phrase such as "gender difference in average salary." The term *sex* refers to biological aspects of men and women; for example, "sex fantasies" or "sex differences in the size of certain brain structures." The use of gender pronouns can be problematic. Do not use *he, his, man, man's,* and so on when both males and females are meant. Sentences can usually be rephrased or specific pronouns deleted to avoid linguistic biases. For example, "The worker is paid according to his productivity" can be changed to "The worker is paid according to productivity" or "Workers are paid according to their productivity." In the first case, *his* was simply deleted; in the second case, the subject of the sentence was changed to plural. Avoid substituting pronouns with *s/he*.

There are certain rules to follow when referring to racial and ethnic groups. The names of these groups are capitalized and never hyphenated; for example, Black, White, African American, Latino, South Asian, Chinese Canadian. The manual also reminds us that the terms that members of racial and ethnic groups use to describe themselves may change over time, and there may be a lack of consensus about a preferred term. You are urged to use the term most preferred by your participants. If you have any questions about appropriate language, consult the APA style manual and your instructor or colleagues whose opinions you respect.

WRITING EACH SECTION OF THE APA STYLE RESEARCH REPORT

A research report is organized into six major parts: Abstract, Introduction, Method, Results, Discussion, and References. The report may also include tables and figures used in presenting the results. We will consider the parts of the paper in the order prescribed by APA style, but you do not have to write them in this order. Consider starting with the Method section because it is relatively easy to describe what participants did. Refer to the sample paper at the end of this appendix as you read the material that follows. As you read the published literature, you will see variations on this basic structure to account for multiple studies in a single paper, meta-analyses, and literature reviews.

Title Page

The first page of the paper is the title page. It is a separate page and is numbered page 1. Note that in the sample paper the title page includes the title as well as other important information. The first line of the title page is the *running head* and a page number (1). The running head has a very specific meaning and purpose: It is an abbreviated title and should be no more than 50 characters (letters, numbers, spaces) long. The running head line from the example article appears as follows:. The running head has a very specific meaning and purpose: It is an abbreviated title and should be no more than 50 characters (letters, numbers, spaces) long. The running head line from the example article appears as follows:

Running head: GETTING A BIGGER SLICE

Note that all letters in the running head are capitalized, but only the R in Running head is capitalized (not the h). If the paper is published in a journal, the running head is printed as a heading at the top of pages (along with the page number) to help readers identify the article.

The running head and page number should be formatted so that the page number is flush to the right margin of the paper and the running head is flush to the left margin of the paper. Do not try to manually type the running head and number at the top of every page of your paper; check your word processing program for how to create a page header. Use the page header feature to create a header that prints approximately halfway between the text of the paper and the top of each page, usually 0.5 inch (1.25 cm) from the top. The same page header (including the running head and page number) appears on every page of your paper.

The remainder of the title page consists of the title, author, and institutional affiliation. All are centred on the page. The title should be fairly short (usually no more than 10 to 12 words) and should inform the reader of the nature of your research. A good way to do this is to include the names of your variables in the title. For example, the following titles are both short and informative:

Anxiety Impairs Mathematical Problem Solving

Laptop Multitasking Hinders Classroom Learning for Both Users and Nearby Peers

Sometimes a colon in the title will help to convey the nature of your research or even add a bit of "flair" to your title, as in the following:

Cognitive Responses in Persuasion: Affective and Evaluative Determinants

The Pen Is Mightier Than the Keyboard: Advantages of Longhand over Laptop Note Taking

Another method of titling a paper is to pose the question that the research addresses, as in these examples:

Do Rewards in the Classroom Undermine Intrinsic Motivation?

Does Occupational Stereotyping Still Exist?

Search engines (e.g., *PsycINFO*) are most likely to find your article if the title includes words and phrases that people are most likely to use when conducting a search on your topic. This consideration also applies to the abstract.

Abstract

The abstract is a brief summary of the research report and typically runs 100 to 120 words in length. The purpose of the abstract is to introduce the article, allowing readers to decide whether the article appears relevant to their own interests. The abstract should provide enough information so that the reader can decide whether to read the entire report, and it should make the report easier to comprehend when it is read.

Although the abstract appears at the beginning of your report, it is easiest to write the abstract last. Read a few abstracts to get some good ideas for how to condense a full-length research report down to eight or ten information-packed sentences. For practice, write an abstract for a published article, and then compare your abstract to the one written by the original authors.

Abstracts generally include a sentence or two about each of the four main sections in the body of the article. First, from the *Introduction* section, state the problem under study and the primary hypotheses. Second, from the *Method* section, include a brief summary of the procedure (e.g., self-report questionnaires, direct observation, repeated measurements), and possibly some information on participants' characteristics (e.g., number, age, sex, and any special characteristics). Third, from the *Results* section, describe the pattern of findings for major variables. This is typically done by reporting the direction of differences, omitting numerical values. Finally, the abstract will include implications of the study taken from the *Discussion* section. Informative comments about the findings are preferred to general statements such as "the implications of the study are addressed" (Kail, 2015; Kazdin, 1995).

The abstract is typed on a separate page numbered page 2. The word "Abstract" is centred at the top of the page. The abstract is always typed as a single paragraph with no paragraph indentation.

Introduction

The Introduction section begins on a new page (page 3), with the title of your report typed and centred at the top of the page. Note that the author's name does not appear on this page, which allows a reviewer to read the paper without knowing the name of the author. After reading the introduction, the reader should know why the research is important and how you decided to go about doing it. In general, the introduction progresses from broad theories and previous relevant research, to hypotheses and specifics of the current research.

The introduction has three components, although formal subsections are rarely used. The components are (1) the problem under study, (2) the literature review, and (3) the rationale and hypotheses of the study. The introduction should begin with an opening statement of the problem under study. In two or three sentences, give the reader an appreciation of the broad context and significance of the topic (Bem, 1981; Kazdin, 1995). Specifically stating what problem is being investigated helps readers, even those who are unfamiliar with the topic, to understand and appreciate why the topic was studied in the first place.

Following the opening statement, the introduction describes past research and theory most relevant to your hypothesis. This is called the *literature review.* An exhaustive review of past theory and research is not necessary. (If there are major literature reviews of the topic, you would refer the reader to the reviews.) Rather, you want to describe only the research and theoretical issues that are clearly related to your study. State explicitly what is already known about your topic, and identify what is not known yet. By specifying such a gap in the existing knowledge, you are preparing readers to understand the contribution your study will make by filling that gap. See Giltrow et al. (2014) for a thorough discussion of the purpose of an introduction.

The final part of the introduction tells the reader the *rationale* of the current study. Here you state what variables you are studying and what results you expect. Your hypothesis and the current research design should follow logically from your previous discussion of prior research and what knowledge is missing.

Method

The Method section begins immediately after you have completed the introduction (on the same page, if space permits). This section provides the reader with detailed information about how your study was conducted. Ideally, there should be enough information in the Method section to allow a reader to *directly replicate* your study.

The Method section is typically divided into subsections. Both the order and the number of subsections vary in published articles. Decisions about which subsections to include are guided by the complexity of the investigation. The sample paper in this appendix uses three subsections: *Participants*, *Materials*, and *Procedure*. Some of the most commonly used subsections are discussed next.

Overview   If the experimental design and procedures used in the research are complex, a brief overview of the method can help the reader understand the information that follows.

Participants   A subsection describing the participants is always necessary. Include the number of participants, as well as relevant characteristics such as age, sex, and ethnicity. Include any special characteristics that are relevant to your research question. For example, you may have limited your sample to first-born children, adolescent children of alcoholics, student teachers, or parents of children being treated for ADHD. State explicitly how participants were recruited and what incentives for participation were used, if any.

Apparatus   An Apparatus subsection may be necessary if special equipment is used in the experiment (e.g., an eye-tracking device). Specify the brand name and model number of special equipment. If the device is rare or has never been used for research before, consider describing it in detail. Include this information if it is needed to replicate the study.

Procedure   The Procedure subsection tells the reader exactly how the study was conducted. Include any detail that might be important in a direct replication of the study. One way to report this information is to describe, step by step, what occurred in the study from the perspective of the participant. Maintain the temporal sequence of events so that the reader is able to visualize the sequence of events the participants experienced.

The Procedure subsection tells the reader what instructions were given to the participants, how the independent variables were manipulated, and how the dependent variables were measured. The methods used to control extraneous variables also should be described. These include random assignment procedures, counter-balancing, and any special means that were used to keep a variable constant across all conditions. Describe how participants were debriefed, particularly if deception was used. If your study used a non-experimental method, provide details on exactly how you conducted the study and all measures you used. Ask a colleague to read your procedure to ensure it is appropriately detailed and clear.

Other Subsections   Include other subsections if they are needed to clearly present the method. For example, a subsection on testing materials (e.g., questionnaires) might be necessary instead of an Apparatus subsection. Other sections are customized by the authors to suit their study. If you glance through a recent issue of a journal, you will find that some studies have only two subsections and others have many more subsections. This reflects the varying complexity of the studies and the particular writing styles of the researchers.

Results

The Results section is a straightforward description of your results, supported by appropriate statistical analyses. Although it is tempting to explain your findings in the Results section, save that discussion for the next section of the paper. Focus on presenting the results as clearly and efficiently as possible.

The content of your Results section will vary according to the type and number analyses you conducted. If you stated more than one hypothesis in the Introduction section of the paper, consider presenting your results in the same order. If you conducted a manipulation check, consider presenting it before you describe the major results. Some authors include in the Results section a description of scoring or coding procedures performed on the data to prepare them for analysis. Other authors include such data transformations in a subsection of the Method section.

Summarize each finding in words, and use a statistical phrase at the end of the sentence to indicate the type of statistical test used to draw that conclusion. These statistical phrases indicate the type of test used, the degrees of freedom, the exact p value, and the effect size (see Chapter 13). Reserve the term "significant" to refer to findings that have a p value less than your alpha. Your readers will assume that you used an alpha (probability) level of .05 for decisions about statistical significance. If you did not, add a simple sentence such as "An alpha level of .01 was used for statistical analyses."

Report statistical values (e.g., mean, standard deviation, t) to two decimal places. Also, round probabilities to two decimals (e.g., $p = .03$); any value less than .01 should be reported as $p < .01$. This guideline has not been universally adopted, so you will read many articles in which statistics and/or probabilities are reported using three decimal places. Your instructor may require the use of three decimal places.

The results should be stated in simple sentences. For example, consider the difference in life satisfaction among Australian and Mexican respondents we considered in Chapter 12. We could express that difference as follows:

Contrary to predictions, Australian respondents reported lower life satisfaction ($M = 7.20, SD = 2.05$)

than Mexican respondents ($M = 8.51, SD = 1.93$), $t(3463) = 19.19, p < .01$, Cohen's $d = .66$.

These brief sentences inform the reader of the general patterns of the results, the obtained means, statistical significance, and effect size. Carefully note the precision of the statistical phrase. Each space (e.g., before and after $=$), comma, and the order that values are presented is specific to APA style.

If the results are relatively straightforward, they can be presented entirely in sentence form. If the study involved a complex design, use tables and figures to present your results clearly.

Tables and Figures   Tables are generally used to present large arrays of data. For example, a table might be useful in a design with several dependent measures; the means of the different groups for all dependent measures would be presented in the table. Tables are also convenient when a factorial design has been used. For example, in a $2 \times 2 \times 3$ factorial design, a table could be used to present all 12 cell means.

Figures are used when a visual display of the results would help the reader understand the outcome of the study, such as a significant interaction or a trend over time (see Chapter 12). Bar graphs are used when describing the responses of two or more groups (e.g., experimental and control conditions, or Australian versus Mexican respondents). Line graphs are useful when both variables have quantitative properties, e.g., the average response time of two groups on days 1, 2, 3, 4, and 5 of an experiment. Consult Nicol and Pexman (2010) for detailed information on creating figures and other visual displays of data.

When strictly adhering to APA style, each table and figure appears on a separate page at the end of the manuscript, rather than presented in the main body. Check with your instructor for variations in course assignments and theses. In the Results section text, refer to the table or figure number and briefly describe its main content. For example, make a statement such as "As shown in Figure 1, the laptop group . . ." or "Table 1 presents the demographic characteristics of the survey respondents." Describe the important features of the table or figure rather than using a generic comment such as "See Figure 3."

Avoid repeating the same data in more than one place. An informative table or figure supplements, not duplicates, the text. Using tables and figures does not diminish your responsibility to clearly state the nature of the results in the text of your report.

Discussion of the Results   It is usually *not* appropriate to discuss the implications of the results in the Results section. However, the Results and Discussion sections may be combined if the discussion is brief and greater clarity is achieved by the combination. This combination happens most often in papers with multiple studies. A General Discussion is then added at the end of all studies that aligns with the broader Discussion section described below.

Discussion

The Discussion section is the proper place to discuss implications of the results. Just like the introduction, it is important for the Discussion section to be logically organized (see Kail, 2015, for further tips). One way to organize the discussion is to begin by summarizing the original purpose and expectations of the study, and then to state whether the results were consistent with your expectations. If the results do support your original ideas, you should discuss how your findings contribute to knowledge of the problem you investigated. You will want to consider the relationship between your results and past research and theory. If you did not obtain the expected results, discuss possible explanations. The explanations would be quite different depending on whether you obtained results that were the opposite of what you expected or the results were not significant.

It is often a good idea to include your own criticisms of the study. No study is ever perfect; all have limitations. It is appropriate to address any major limitations in your study in the Discussion section. Try to anticipate what a reader might find wrong with your methodology. For example, if you used a non-experimental research design, you might acknowledge problems of cause and effect, and identify any specific possible extraneous variables you think might be operating. Sometimes there may be major or minor flaws that could be corrected in a subsequent study (if you had the time, money, and so on). You can describe such flaws and suggest corrections. You might argue whether the results would or would not generalize to other samples.

The results will probably have implications for future research. If so, discuss the direction that research might take. It is also possible that the results have practical implications—for example, for child-rearing or improving learning in the classroom. Discussion of these larger issues is usually placed at the end of the Discussion section. Finally, consider including a brief concluding paragraph that provides "closure" to the entire paper.

References

The list of references begins on a new page. The references must contain complete citations for all sources mentioned in your report. Do not omit any sources you cited from the list of references; also, do not include any sources that are not cited in your report. The exact procedures for citing sources within the body of your report and in your list of references follow the APA *Publication Manual* and are described later in this appendix. You can also follow examples in recent publications that use APA style.

Appendix

The APA *Publication Manual* notes that an appendix might be appropriate when necessary material would be distracting in the main body of the report. Examples of appendixes include the entire questionnaire or survey instrument, a complex mathematical proof, a long list of words used as stimulus items, or other materials employed in the study. If an appendix is provided in the manuscript itself, it begins on a new page with the word "Appendix" centred at the top. Sometimes journals provide appendixes as online supplements to articles; other times, individual authors upload these materials to their websites. Check with your instructor concerning the appropriateness of an appendix for your paper.

Author Note

The author note begins with a paragraph that gives the department affiliations of the authors. Another paragraph may give details about the background of the study (e.g., that it is based on the first author's master's thesis) and acknowledgments (e.g., grant support, colleagues who assisted with the study, and so on). A final paragraph begins with "Correspondence concerning this article should be addressed to . . ." followed by the mailing and e-mail addresses of the author people should contact if they wish to follow up directly. The author note usually begins on a new page. However, sometimes a journal editor will ask you to place the author note information at the bottom of the title page. This is done when the paper will have a *masked review:* The person reviewing the paper has no information about the author of the paper. In this case, the title page will be separated from the rest of the paper prior to review. An author note may be unnecessary for class research reports; consult your instructor.

Footnotes and Endnotes

Footnotes are rarely used in psychology. In unpublished manuscripts, all footnotes in the paper are treated as endnotes, and are typed on one page at the end of the paper. Avoid using footnotes unless they are absolutely necessary. They can be distracting to readers, and important information can and should be integrated into the body of the paper.

Tables

Each table should be on a separate page. As noted previously, APA style requires placement of the table at the end of the paper, but for a class you may be asked to place your tables within the body of the paper. When preparing your table, allow enough space so that the table does not appear cramped on a small portion of the page. Define areas of the table using horizontal lines (do not use vertical lines in APA style tables). Ensure that the title accurately and clearly describes the content of the table. You may wish to use an explanatory note at the bottom of the table to show significance levels or the range of possible values on a variable. There are common formats for many types of tables, including tables of means, correlation coefficients, multiple regression analyses, and so on (consult the *Publication Manual*; Nicol & Pexman, 2010; or a recent journal published by the APA). For example, below is a table of correlations. Note that the title of the table is typed in italics, and that the areas of the table are separated by horizontal lines.

Table I
Correlations between Dependent Measures

Measure	1	2	3	4
1. Attractiveness	–	.52	.35	.29
2. Extraversion		–	.11	.23
3. Conscientiousness			–	.49
4. Starting salary				–

Figures

According to APA style, figures are placed after the tables in papers. However, this rule may not be necessary for student reports or theses. You may be asked to place each figure on a separate page at the appropriate point in the body of the text. As on every page, the running head and page number appear at the top of each figure page.

Most spreadsheet, word processing, and statistical analysis programs have graphing features (e.g., Word, Excel, OpenOffice Calc, SPSS). Independent and predictor variables are placed on the horizontal axis; dependent and criterion variables are placed on the vertical axis. Both the horizontal and vertical axes must be labelled. When you print the graph on a separate piece of paper, a rule of thumb is that the horizontal axis should be about 5 inches (12.5 cm) wide, and the vertical axis should be about 3.5 inches (8.75 cm) long. If you are inserting a graph into the text of your report (not using APA style), your graphs may be smaller than this.

Remember that the purpose of a figure is to depict results clearly. If the graph is cluttered with information, it will confuse the reader and will not serve its purpose. Plan your graphs carefully to make sure that you are accurately and clearly informing the reader.

Summary: Order of Pages

To summarize, the organization of your paper is as follows:

1. Title page (page 1)
2. Abstract (page 2)
3. Pages of text (start on page 3)
   a. Title at top of first page begins the Introduction
   b. Method
   c. Results
   d. Discussion
4. References (start on new page)
5. Appendix (start on new page if included)
6. Author Note (start on new page)
7. Footnotes (start on new page if included)
8. Tables, with table captions (each table on a separate page)
9. Figures, with figure captions (each figure on a separate page)

You should now have a general idea of how to structure and write your report. The remainder of this appendix focuses on some of the technical rules that may be useful as you prepare your own research report.

FORMATTING A MANUSCRIPT

In APA style, the paper should be *entirely double-spaced*. The margins surrounding text should be 1 inch (2.5 cm) on all four sides of the page. Page headers, the information that appears at the top of each page including the page number, are set approximately 0.5 inch (1.25 cm) from the top of the page. All pages are numbered except for figure pages at the end of the paper. Paragraphs are indented 5 to 7 spaces or 0.5 inch (1.25 cm; use the tab keyboard function, not multiple spaces). Avoid using contractions (e.g., use *cannot* instead of *can't*). Rather than fully justifying text and breaking words with hyphens at the end of lines, justify your text to the left margin (creating a jagged edge of text along the right side of the page).

According to APA style, place only one space between sentences. Leaving two spaces is a convention left over from the days of manual typewriters; one space is more attractive and readable when using word processors with modern printer fonts. (If you automatically double space after a period without thinking, use your word processor's "replace" feature to replace instances of two spaces with one space.)

Take advantage of the features of your word processing application. Learn to use headers to place running heads and page numbers automatically at the top of each page. Use other features to insert tables, centre text, check spelling and grammar, insert tabs (rather than spaces), and so on.

The font should be 12-point size throughout the paper. Use a serif font for all text and tables. The serif font should usually be Times New Roman font style. Figures, however, should be prepared with a sans serif font, either Arial or Calibri font style. Serif fonts have short lines at the ends of the strokes that form the letters; sans serif literally means "without serif" and so does not have serif lines. Here are examples:

This is serif text.

This is sans serif text.

Use the italics feature of your word processor sparingly. Italics are used for (a) titles and volume numbers of periodicals in the References section; (b) titles of books in the References section; (c) most statistical terms; (d) anchors of a scale, such as 1 (*strongly disagree*) to 5 (*strongly agree*); and (e) when you need to emphasize a particular word or phrase when first mentioned in the paper. Pay attention to the use of italics in the examples used throughout this appendix. Use boldface type to denote some headings, as noted below.

Using Headings

Papers written in APA style use one to five levels of headings. Most commonly, you will use level 1 and level 2 headings, and you may need to use level 3 headings as well. These five levels are as follows:

(Level 1)   **Centred Heading**

(Level 2)   **Margin Heading**

                        The text begins indented on a new line.

(Level 3)   **First paragraph heading.** The heading is bold, and indented as a new paragraph.
                        The text begins on the same line.

(Level 4)   ***Second paragraph heading.*** The heading is bold and italicized. It is indented as
                        a new paragraph and the text begins on the same line.

(Level 5)   *Third paragraph heading.* The heading is italicized (only). It is indented as a new
                        paragraph and the text begins on the same line.

Level 1, or centred, headings are used to head major sections of the report: Abstract, Title (on page 3), Method, Results, Discussion, References. Level 1 headings are typed with uppercase and lowercase letters (i.e., the first letter of each major word is capitalized).

Level 2, or margin, headings are used to divide major sections into subsections. Level 2 headings are typed flush to the left margin, with uppercase and lowercase letters (i.e., the first letter of each major word is capitalized). For example, the Method section is divided into at least two subsections: Participants and Procedure. The correct format is as follows:

Method

Participants

The description of the participants begins on a new line.

Procedure

The procedure is described in detail.

Levels 3 to 5, or paragraph, headings are used to organize material within a subsection. For example, the Procedure subsection might be broken down into separate categories for describing instructions to participants, the independent variable manipulation, measurement of the dependent variable, and debriefing. Each of these could be introduced using level 3 paragraph headings. (For example, the Materials subsection in the sample paper at the end of this appendix uses three level 3 headings.) You may break these categories down further using heading levels 4 or 5, but these levels are rare.

Level 3 to 5 paragraph headings begin on a new line, indented 0.5 inch (1.25 cm). The first word begins with a capital letter; the remaining words are all typed in lowercase letters, except for proper nouns and the first word to follow a colon, which are capitalized. The heading ends with a period. All information that appears between a paragraph heading and the next heading (of any level) must be related to the paragraph heading. Both level 3 and level 4 headings are boldface; both level 4 and level 5 headings are italicized.

Abbreviations

Abbreviations are used sparingly in APA style papers. They can be distracting because the reader must constantly translate the abbreviation into its full meaning. However, APA style does allow for the use of abbreviations that are accepted as words in the dictionary (specifically, *Webster's Collegiate Dictionary*). These include IQ, REM, ESP, and AIDS. Scientific abbreviations for various measurement units are also acceptable (e.g., cm for centimetre, ms for millisecond).

Certain well-known terms may be abbreviated when it would make reading easier, but the full meaning should be given when first used in the paper. Examples of commonly used abbreviations are the following:

MMPI	Minnesota Multiphasic Personality Inventory
STM	short-term memory
CS	conditioned stimulus
RT	reaction time
CVC	consonant-vowel-consonant
ANOVA	analysis of variance

Statistical terms are sometimes used in their abbreviated or symbol form. These are always italicized in a manuscript, as in the following examples:

M	mean
SD	standard deviation
Mdn	median
df	degrees of freedom
n	number of individuals in a group or experimental condition
N	total number of participants or respondents
p	probability (significance) level
SS	sum of squares
MS	mean square
F	value of F in analysis of variance
r	Pearson correlation coefficient
R	multiple correlation coefficient

Finally, certain abbreviations of Latin and Middle English terms are regularly used in papers. Some of these abbreviations and their meanings are given below:

cf.	compare (from Latin *confer*)
e.g.	for example (from Latin *exempli gratia*)
et al.	and others (from Latin *et alia*)
etc.	and so forth (from Latin *et cetera*)
i.e.	that is (from Latin *id est*)
viz.	namely
vs.	versus

Reporting Numbers and Statistics

Virtually all research papers report numbers: number of participants, number of groups, the values of statistics such as t, F, or r. Should you use numbers (e.g., "*43*"), or should you use words (e.g., "*forty-three*")? The general rule is to use words when expressing the numbers zero through nine but to use numbers for 10 and above. There are some important qualifications, however.

If you start a sentence with a number, you should use words even if the number is 10 or larger (e.g., "*Eighty-five student teachers participated in the study.*"). Starting a sentence with a number is often awkward, especially with large numbers. Therefore, you should try to revise the sentence to avoid the problem (e.g., "*The participants were 85 students enrolled in teaching credential classes.*").

When numbers both above and below 10 are being compared in the same sentence, use numerals for both (e.g., "*Participants read either 8 or 16 paragraphs.*"). However, this sentence contains an appropriate mix of numbers and words: "*Participants read eight paragraphs and then answered 20 multiple-choice questions.*" The sentence is correct because the paragraphs and the questions are different entities and so are not being compared.

When reporting a percentage, always use numerals followed by a percent sign except when beginning a sentence. This is true regardless of whether the number is less than 10 (e.g., "*Only 6% of the computer games appealed to females.*") or greater than 10 (e.g., "*When using this technique, 85% of the participants improved their performance.*").

Always use numbers when describing ages (e.g., "*5-year-olds*"), points on a scale (e.g., "*a 3 on a 5-point scale*"), units of measurement (e.g., "*the children stood 2 m from the target*"), sample size (e.g., "*6 girls and 6 boys were assigned to each study condition*"), and statistics (e.g., "*the mean score in the control group was 3.10*"). An odd but sensible exception to the word–number rule occurs when two different types of numbers must appear together. An example is "*Teachers identified fifteen 7-year-olds as the most aggressive.*" This sentence avoids an awkward juxtaposition of two numbers.

For a multiplication sign, use either a lowercase x or the multiplication symbol used by your word processor. This is true whether you are describing a mathematical operation or a factorial design (e.g., a 2 × 2 design). For a minus sign, use a hyphen with a space both before and after the hyphen.

Statistical terms are abbreviated and typed with italics (e.g., *M, r, t, F, d*). When reporting the results of a statistical significance test, provide the name of the test, the degrees of freedom, the value of the test statistic, and the probability level. Here are two examples of sentences that describe statistical results:

As predicted, participants in the high-anxiety condition took longer to recognize the words ($M = 2.63$, $SD = .42$) than did the individuals in the low-anxiety condition ($M = 1.42$, $SD = .36$), $t(20) = 2.54$, $p = .02$, Cohen's $d = 3.09$.

Job satisfaction scores were significantly correlated with marital satisfaction, $r(50) = .48$, $p < .01$.

Recall that exact probabilities (p values) are reported as they appear in the computer output of your statistical analysis. Use the < (less than) symbol for probabilities less than .01, i.e., $p < .01$. Special symbols, including Greek letters (e.g., α) can be found using the *insert symbol* function in your word processor.

Pay attention to the way statistics are described in the articles you read. You will find that you can vary your descriptions of results to best fit your data and presentation, as well as vary your sentence constructions.

APA Style and Student Paper Formats

APA style is intended to provide a manuscript to a publisher who then prepares the paper for publication in a journal; several APA style requirements are for the convenience of the publisher. When you prepare a paper for a class report, an honours project, or a thesis, your paper may be the "final product" for your readers. When your intended audience is your instructor, you should pay close attention to what he or she has to say about expectations for the paper (Rosnow & Rosnow, 2012). In such cases, some aspects of APA style may be ignored so that your paper will closely resemble a printed report. For example, APA style calls for placement of tables and figures at the end of the paper; the publisher inserts the tables and figures in the body of the paper for the published article. However, if your report is the final version for your readers, you may need to insert tables and figures in the text or on separate pages within the body of your report. Some of the other ways that a student report may differ from APA style have been noted earlier. When you are getting ready to prepare your own report, be sure to check the particular requirements of your instructor or university.

CITING AND REFERENCING SOURCES

Citing Sources in the Body of the Report

Whenever you refer to information reported by other researchers, you must accurately identify the sources. APA journals use the author–date citation method: The author name(s) and year of publication are inserted at appropriate points. The citation style depends on whether the author names are part of the narrative or are in parentheses.

One Author   When the author's name is part of the narrative, include the publication date in parentheses immediately after the name:

> Gervais (2011) found that anti-atheist prejudice can be reduced by reminding believers how prevalent atheists are in society.

When the author's name is not part of the narrative, the name and date are cited in parentheses at the end of an introductory phrase or at the end of the sentence:

> Religious believers show lower anti-atheist prejudice after being reminded atheists are prevalent in society (Gervais, 2011).

> In one study (Gervais, 2011), religious believers were reminded that atheists are a prevalent group . . .

Two Authors   When the work has two authors, both names are included in each reference citation. The difference between narrative and parenthetical citations is in the use of the conjunction "and" and the ampersand "&" to connect authors' names. When the names are part of a sentence, use the word "and" to join the names of two authors. When the complete citation is in parentheses, use the "&" symbol:

> Adults' ability to remember to do something in the future (i.e., prospective memory) is predicted by personality traits, specifically conscientiousness (Cuttler & Graf, 2007).

> Cuttler and Graf (2007) found that adults' ability to remember to do something in the future (i.e., prospective memory) is predicted by personality traits, specifically conscientiousness.

Three to Five Authors   When a report has three to five authors, all author names are cited the first time the reference occurs. Thereafter, cite the first author's surname followed by "and colleagues" or the abbreviation et al. along with the publication date. The abbreviation may be used in narrative and parenthetical citations:

First citation

> Research suggests that repeating positive self-statements (e.g., "I'm a good person") may lead people with low self-esteem to feel negatively about themselves (Wood, Perunovic, & Lee, 2009).

> Wood, Perunovic, and Lee (2009) reported that people who have low self-esteem who repeated a positive self-statement (e.g., "I'm a good person") felt worse about themselves than if they did not repeat any statement.

Subsequent citations

> Among people with high self-esteem, repeating a positive self-statement has little impact on how they feel about themselves (Wood et al., 2009).

> Wood et al. (2009) also examined the impact of positive self-statements on those with high self-esteem.

Another question about subsequent citations is whether to include the publication date each time an article is referenced. Within a paragraph, you do *not* need to include the year in subsequent citations as long as the study cannot be confused with other studies cited in your report.

Citation within a paragraph

In a recent study, Sana, Weston, and Cepeda (2013) . . .

Sana and colleagues also reported that . . .

When subsequent citations are in another paragraph or in another section of the report, the publication date should be included.

Six or More Authors   Occasionally you will reference a report with six or more authors. In this case, use the abbreviation et al. after the first author's last name in *every* citation. Although you would not list all author names in the text, the citation in the references section of the report should include the names of the first six authors followed by et al. for additional authors.

References with No Author   When an article has no author (e.g., some newspaper or magazine articles), cite the first two or three words of the title in quotation marks, followed by the publication date:

Citation in text

In an article on smoking ("The decline of smoking," 2011), data obtained from Statistics Canada . . .

Which refers readers to this citation in the reference list

The decline of smoking in Canada. (2011, July 29). CBC News. Retrieved from http://www.cbc.ca

Multiple Works within the Same Parentheses   A convenient way to cite several studies on the same topic or several studies with similar findings is to reference them as a series within the same parentheses. When two or more works are by the same author(s), report them in order of year of publication, using commas to separate citations:

Mio and Willis (2003, 2005) found . . .

Past research (Mio & Willis, 2003, 2005) indicates . . .

When two or more works by different authors are cited within the same parentheses, arrange them in alphabetical order and separate citations by semicolons:

Investigations of why people procrastinate have revealed the importance of perceptions of the task. Risk factors for procrastination include optimistic predictions of how long a task will take to complete and expecting to dislike the task (Buehler, Griffin, & Ross, 2002; Buehler, Peetz, & Griffin, 2010; Steel, 2007).

Reference List Style

The APA *Publication Manual* provides examples of 97 different reference formats for journal articles, books, book chapters, technical reports, convention presentations, dissertations, Web pages, and videos, among many others. Only a few of these are presented here. When in doubt about how to construct a reference, consult the APA manual. The general format for a reference list is as follows:

1. The references are listed in alphabetical order by the first author's last name. Do not categorize references by type (i.e., books, journal articles, and so on). Note the spacing in the typing of authors' names in the examples.
2. Elements of a reference (authors' names, article title, publication date) are separated by periods.

The first line of each reference is typed flush to the left margin; subsequent lines are indented. This is called a "hanging indent." When you type the reference, it will appear as follows:

Stermac, L., Elgie, S., Dunlap, H., & Kelly, T. (2010). Educational experiences and achievements of war-zone immigrant students in Canada. *Vulnerable Children and Youth Studies, 5,* 97–107.

Each reference begins on a new line (think of each reference as a separate paragraph). Most word processors will allow you to easily format the paragraph with a hanging indent, so you do not have to manually insert spaces on the second and subsequent lines. Using Microsoft Word, for example, begin the paragraph with Ctrl-t (control key and t pressed simultaneously).

Format for Journal Articles   Most journals are organized by volume and year of publication (e.g., volume 66 of *American Psychologist* consists of all 12 journal issues published in 2011). A common confusion is whether to include the journal issue number in addition to the volume number. The rule is simple: If the issues in a volume are paginated consecutively throughout the volume, *do not* include the journal issue number. If each issue in a volume begins with page 1, the issue number should be included. Specific examples are shown next.

In the reference list, both the name of the journal and the volume number are italicized. Also, only the first letter of the first word in article titles is capitalized (except proper nouns and the first word after a colon or question mark). Here are some examples:

One author—no issue number

Gervais, W. M. (2011). Finding the faithless: Perceived atheist prevalence reduces anti-atheist prejudice. *Personality and Social Psychology Bulletin, 37,* 543–556.

Two authors—use of issue number

Nguyen, T., & Trimarchi, A. (2010). Active learning in Introductory Economics: Do MyEconLab and
Aplia make any difference? *International Journal for the Scholarship of Teaching and
Learning, 4*(1), 1–18.

Format for Books When a book is cited, the title of the book is italicized. Only the first word of the title is capitalized; however, proper nouns and the first word after a colon or question mark are also capitalized. The city of publication and the publishing company follow the title. If the city is not well known, include the U.S. Postal Service two-letter abbreviation for the state (e.g., AZ, NY, MN, TX); if the city is outside the United States, include the city and country (e.g., Toronto, Canada; Manchester, England).

One-author book

Carlberg, C. (2011). *Statistical analysis: Microsoft Excel 2010.* Indianapolis, IN: Que Publishing.

One-author book—second or later edition

Creswell, J. W. (2007). *Qualitative inquiry and research design: Choosing among five approaches*
(2nd ed.). Thousand Oaks, CA: Sage.

Edited book

Gosling, S. D., & Johnson, J. A. (Eds). (2010). *Advanced methods for behavioral research on the
Internet.* Washington, DC: American Psychological Association.

Format for Chapters in Edited Books For edited books, the reference begins with the names of the authors of the article, not the book. The title of the article follows. The name(s) of the book editor(s), the book title, the inclusive page numbers for the article, and the publication data for the book follow, in that order. Only the book title is italicized, and only the first letters of the article and book titles are capitalized. Here are some examples:

One editor

Brown, A. L., & Campione, J. C. (1994). Guided discovery in a community of learners. In K. McGilly
(Ed.), *Classroom lessons: Integrating cognitive theory and classroom practice* (pp. 229–270).
Cambridge, MA: MIT Press.

Two editors

Glantz, L. H., Annas, G. J., Grodin, M. A., & Mariner, W. K. (2001). Research in developing countries:
Taking "benefit" seriously. In Teays, W., & Purdy, L. (Eds.), *Bioethics, justice, and health care*
(pp. 261–267). Belmont, CA: Wadsworth.

Format for "Popular Articles"   The reference styles shown next should be used for articles from magazines and newspapers. As a general rule, popular press articles are used sparingly (e.g., when no scientific articles on a topic can be found or to provide an example of an event that is related to your topic).

Magazine–continuous pages

Carson, S. (2011, May/June). The unleashed mind. *Scientific American Mind, 22*(2), 22–29.

Newspaper–no author

Savannahs shaped human evolution, new study concludes. (2011, August 5). *The Vancouver Sun*, p. B3.

Newspaper–discontinuous pages

Bailey, I. (2011, August 5). Euthanasia issue won't be reopened, Nicholson says. *The Globe and Mail*, pp. S1, S2.

Format for Papers and Poster Sessions Presented at Conferences   Occasionally you may need to cite an unpublished paper or poster session that was presented at a professional meeting. Here are two examples:

Paper

Cheung, I., Conway, P. J., Maxwell-Smith, M., & Seligman, C. (2009, June). *Happiness and the outcome of the 2008 Canadian Federal Election.* Paper presented at the 70th annual meeting of the Canadian Psychological Association, Montreal, Canada.

Poster session

Kang, S. K., & Chasteen, A. L. (2011, January). *Beyond the double jeopardy hypothesis: The interaction between age- and race-based stereotypes across the lifespan.* Poster session presented at the meeting of the Society for Personality and Social Psychology, San Antonio, TX.

Secondary Sources   Sometimes you need to cite an article, book, or book chapter that you read about through a textbook, an abstract, or a book review. Although it is always preferable to read and cite primary sources, sometimes you may have to cite a secondary source instead if you have exhausted all possible options for finding the source.

Suppose you wish to cite an article that you read about in a book. When you refer to the article in your paper, you need to say that it was cited in the book. In the following example, a paper by Widmeyer and McGuire is the secondary source:

Widmeyer and McGuire (as cited in Gee & Leith, 2007) suggested that playing a defensive position in hockey is associated with increased frustration and aggression . . .

In the reference list at the end of the paper, simply provide the reference for the primary source you used (in this case, the Gee and Leith citation):

Gee, C. J., & Leith, L. M. (2007). Aggressive behavior in professional ice hockey: A cross-cultural

comparison of North American and European born NHL players. *Psychology of Sport and*

Exercise, 8, 567–583.

Reference Formats for Electronic Sources

The amount and types of information available via the Internet has exploded. The American Psychological Association provided guidelines in the *Publication Manual* and published updates for some formats in the *APA Style Guide to Electronic Resources* (APA, 2012). There are 70 different types of references described in this guide. Only a few are provided here. The primary goal of all references is to allow readers to easily find the original source material.

Citing a Website   Sometimes you simply want to cite a particular website in your paper without referring to a specific document. In this case, just provide the address of the website. No listing in the references is necessary. For example, the following citation might appear in the text of your paper.

Most professional associations in psychology maintain websites for their members and the public.

The site of the Canadian Psychological Association is http://www.cpa.ca and the Association for

Psychological Science site is http://www.psychologicalscience.org.

Citing Specific Web Documents/Pages   Many Web pages were written specifically for the Web and should not be considered as journal articles or books. For example, a document prepared by David Kenny provides information on mediating variables. In general, the rules for citing such documents are very similar to citations for journal articles. In our example, your text might read:

Kenny (2009) describes a procedure for using multiple regression to examine causal models that

include mediating variables.

Your actual reference to the document would be:

Kenny, D. A. (2009). *Mediation.* Retrieved from http://davidakenny.net/cm/mediate.htm

Note that the reference includes the author, a date that was provided in the document, and a title. Some Web documents do not include a date; in this case, simply substitute n.d. in parentheses to indicate that there is no date. Most important, information is provided on the file name (URL) of the document. Note also that there is no period at the end of the reference.

There is an important rule about typing the URL (location) of the document you are citing. It is acceptable to have the URL carry over two lines if it will not fit on a single line. However, never insert a hyphen because this is not part of the address. Instead, let the address carry over with no extra hyphen.

Citing Journal Articles   Final published versions of journal articles are increasingly available via searches in a variety of library and Internet full-text databases such as *PsycINFO*. When citing these articles, the primary new feature to look for is the DOI–the digital object identifier, which is intended to help others locate the article. The DOI is now used for research articles but not articles in the popular press. You can find the DOI as a field in databases such as *PsycINFO*; it may also appear in the text of the article, usually on the first or last page. It will appear as a long series of numbers and letters. Here is a citation that includes the DOI:

Mather, A. A., Stein, M. B., & Sareen, J. (2010). Social anxiety disorder and social fears in the

Canadian military: Prevalence, comorbidity, impairment, and treatment-seeking. *Journal of*

Psychiatric Research, 44, 887–893. doi:10.1016/j.jpsychires.2010.02.01

Do not provide information on the date retrieved or URL because this is the final, published version of the paper and will not change.

Some articles that you access online will not have a DOI. In such cases, provide the standard article information. Then include "Retrieved from URL" to provide the URL of the article. There is still no need to provide the date retrieved because it is the final version of the article.

Citation of an Abstract   Sometimes you may need to cite the abstract of an article that you found in a search of *PsycINFO* or another database. Although it is preferable to find the original article, you may find that the original article is not available online or at any nearby libraries or is published in a foreign language with only the abstract available in English. Here is an example:

Morisano, D., Hirsh, J. B., Peterson, J. B., Pihl, R. O., & Shore, B. M. (2010). Setting, elaborating, and

reflecting on personal goals improves academic performance. *Journal of Applied Psychology, 95,*

225–264. Abstract retrieved from PsycINFO database.

In this example, the complete reference is given. However, you also provide the crucial information that you have only examined the abstract of the article and you found the abstract through a search of the *PsycINFO* database.

There are many other examples in the *APA Style Guide to Electronic Resources*, including books, encyclopedias, newspaper articles, and presentation slides. The rules are consistent and rely on whether the source is a final, published version; whether the DOI is provided; and whether you need to have information on the database in order to make sure you can find the document.

CONFERENCE PRESENTATIONS

Students present their research findings in many different ways: in class, at regional and national meetings of professional psychology organizations, and at conferences specifically designed to highlight student research. If you are interested, ask faculty members at your institution to recommend conferences.

The presentation may take the form of a talk to an audience or a poster presentation in which other conference attendees may read the poster and engage in conversation with the presenter. Psi Chi, the International Honor Society in Psychology, has posted guidelines for paper and poster presentations on its website (www.psichi.org/?RES_ConvPresent#.Va1Rp_lVikp). We will explore the major points, but any student planning a presentation may wish to obtain more detailed advice. (As an aside: Psi Chi chapters are rare in Canada. If your university doesn't have a Psi Chi chapter, you may want to visit its website for information about how to become a member.)

Paper Presentations

Paper presentations are talks that are often only about 10 to 12 minutes long. Conference attendees typically see many of these talks during a conference. It is easy for attendees to become overloaded with information. The major thing to remember, then, is that you should attempt to convey only a few major ideas about why and how you conducted your research. Your audience wants the "big picture," so you can avoid describing the details of past research findings, discussing exactly how you did your data analysis, or listing every step in your procedure. Omit technical jargon inappropriate for a broad audience. Use clear language to convey why the topic is important, your hypothesis, the general methods you used, and the major results. Provide a quick summary at the end, and finish with a major conclusion or key implication of the results.

The Psi Chi guidelines also advise you to write the presentation in advance but not to read it to your actual audience. You can use the written version for practice and timing. Consider bringing copies of a written summary of your presentation that includes your name, the title of the presentation, when and where it was presented, and how you can be contacted. Interested audience members may wish to refer to it later.

Poster Sessions

A poster session can involve just a few or hundreds of presenters simultaneously. Each presenter is provided with space to display poster material. During the poster session, members of the audience may stop to read the poster, and some may have questions or comments. The chance to have conversations about your research with people who find your work interesting is the most valuable feature of a poster session.

Conference organizers will provide information in advance about the amount of space available for each poster. Typical dimensions are 3 to 4 feet high and 6 to 8 feet wide. The content of each poster will usually be divided up like an APA style manuscript, although it will contain much less information for each section. An example poster layout is provided in Figure A.1. The Psi Chi website has other suggested layouts. The actual construction of the poster may consist of a series of separate pages or a single professionally printed poster using large format printing technology.

Avoid providing too much detail–often a bulleted list of major points will be most effective. One or two easy-to-read figures can also be very helpful. There are probably no more than two major points that you would like someone to remember after viewing your poster. Make sure those points are obvious. The font that you use should be large enough to be read from a distance (usually the text will be 18-point font). Colour can be used to enhance the attractiveness of the poster. For interested readers, bring copies of a summary poster handout that includes your contact information as well as the date and location of the conference.

FIGURE A.I
A sample
poster

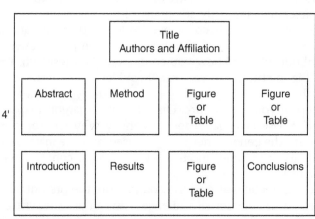

APPENDIX A SAMPLE PAPER

The remainder of this appendix consists of a typed manuscript of a paper that was published in a professional journal. This is intended to be a useful guide when you write your own reports in APA style. Read through the manuscript, paying particular attention to the general format, and make sure you notice the rules concerning page numbering, section headings, reference citation, and the format of figures. Writing your first research report is always a challenging task. It will become easier as you read the research of others and gain practice by writing reports of your own.

Janet Polivy, C. Peter Herman, and Rajbir Deo graciously gave their permission to reprint their paper to illustrate elements of APA style. The comments at the side alert you to features of APA style that you will need to know about when writing your own papers. Be aware, though, that every paper will include slightly different types of information depending on the particular topic, method, and results. Your paper will follow the general guidelines of APA style, but many of the details will be determined by the needs of your study.

You may note that the title of this paper is longer than the 10 to 12 words recommended by APA style. A briefer (but less intriguing) title might omit the part before the colon. Also note that the horizontal lines are meant to signal page breaks. Do not include these lines in your manuscript (except in a figure).

The running head is a shortened version of the title (up to 50 characters, including spaces). The title page shows the words "Running head:" followed by a shortened version of the title in CAPS.

1

Running head: GETTING A BIGGER SLICE

All pages are numbered consecutively, starting with the title page. Page numbers are flush right, on the same line as the running head. Running head is flush left and page number is flush right in header area of the page.

Getting a Bigger Slice of the Pie: Effects on Eating and Emotion

in Restrained and Unrestrained Eaters

Janet Polivy, C. Peter Herman, and Rajbir Deo

University of Toronto

The title is usually no more than 12 words.

Title, author(s), and affiliation are centred and appear in the upper half of the page.

The author note, if required, would begin below the authors' affiliations. Student papers usually do not require an author note. See pages 24 and 25 of the APA Publication Manual.

GETTING A BIGGER SLICE 2

Abstract

We investigated the influence of perceptions of the portion size of food on subsequent eating by restrained and unrestrained eaters. In the present study, all participants were served a same-sized slice of pizza. For one-third of participants, their slice appeared larger than the slice being served to another ostensible participant, another third perceived their slice as smaller, and the final third did not see a second slice. All participants then proceeded to "taste and rate" cookies in an ad lib eating opportunity. A significant interaction reflected the fact that when the pizza slice was perceived as large, restrained eaters tended to eat more cookies whereas unrestrained eaters tended to eat less cookies. Emotion data suggest that the differential responses of restrained and unrestrained eaters to the belief that they have overeaten relative to another eater influenced their subsequent dissimilar ad lib eating behavior.

The running head identified on the title page should be carried forward on every subsequent page. It should remain flush left in all uppercase letters. The words "Running head" are deleted on subsequent pages.

The section of a research report that summarizes the entire study.

There is no paragraph indentation in the abstract.

Getting a Bigger Slice of the Pie: Effects on Eating and Emotion in Restrained and Unrestrained Eaters

We often eat one food followed by another (e.g., main course and then dessert). How much we eat of the later food probably depends to a large extent on our intake of the earlier food. In the laboratory, we refer to the earlier food as a "preload." The effects of food preloads on subsequent eating are complex: Chronic dieters or restrained eaters generally respond quite differently than nondieters or unrestrained eaters do. Whereas unrestrained eaters typically compensate by eating less after a larger preload than after a smaller one, restrained eaters often "counter-regulate," eating more after a large preload than after a small preload or after no preload at all (Adams & Leary, 2007; Herman, Polivy, & Esses, 1987; Polivy, Heatherton, & Herman, 1988; Polivy, Herman, Hackett, & Kuleshnyk, 1986). Presumably, the larger preload is more likely to sabotage the restrained eater's diet for that day, undermining motivation for continued restraint and unleashing disinhibited eating (possibly potentiated by chronic perceived deprivation). If the preload is actually large and fattening, it is likely to produce disinhibited eating by restrained eaters (Herman et al., 1987; McCann, Perri, Nezu, & Lowe, 1992; Polivy et al., 1986, 1988), but disinhibition may be observed even when the restrained eater is merely led to believe that the preload is high in calories or otherwise forbidden (Polivy, 1976; Spencer & Fremouw, 1979) or when the restrained eater draws that implication from the nature of the food itself (Knight & Boland, 1989). Previous studies have manipulated the perceived size of the preload (holding actual size or caloric content constant) by either telling participants that the preloads are high in calories (Polivy, 1976; Spencer & Fremouw, 1979) or by implication. For example, Knight and Boland (1989), served iso-caloric preloads of milkshake or a cottage cheese and fruit mixture. Restrained eaters

---

Punctuation such as periods and commas appear inside the quotes. Punctuation such as question marks, exclamation marks, colons, and semicolons that are not part of the quote appear outside the quotes.

Standard form: Citation of two authors, parenthetically (Author & Author, Year).

Standard form: Citation of three to five authors, first citation, parenthetically (Author, Author, & Author, Year).

When several references are cited together, alphabetize, and separate with a semicolon.

Standard form: Citation of three or more authors, after first citation in text, parenthetically (Author et al., Year).

Standard form: Citation of a single author, parenthetically (Author, Year).

GETTING A BIGGER SLICE   4

displayed disinhibition only when served milkshake, because they
regard milkshake as inherently more caloric than the salad-like
cottage cheese and fruit mixture. More recently, Pliner and Zec
(2007) showed that thinking about a preload as a meal (rather than
as a snack) makes people perceive the preload as higher in calories
and affects eating accordingly.

Standard form for citation of two authors, in text: Name and Name (Year).

The present study was designed to further extend the exploration
of the effects of perceived preload/portion size on eating and,
moreover, to do this in a more externally valid meal setting. In
order to understand the source of these effects, we included
measures of affective responses, as it has been shown that affect
infl uences eating differently for restrained and unrestrained eaters
(Polivy & Herman, 1999), and eating, especially eating what is seen
as a large amount, affects emotions differently in restrained and
unrestrained eaters (Polivy & Herman, 2005).

We hypothesized that even with the preload/meal held constant,
restrained eaters who regard the portion as larger will subsequently
eat more than will those who regard it as normal sized or small,
because the "large" portion is more likely to break their diets and
lead to disinhibited eating. We also predicted that unrestrained
eaters will eat less after a perceived large portion than after what
they perceive to be a normal-sized meal, and less after a portion
perceived as normal sized than after one perceived as small. In the
present study, all participants received an identical, standard light
lunch meal, but some were led to perceive the portion they received
as large and some were led to perceive the portion as small simply
by means of social comparison (or more accurately, perceptual
contrast). If someone gets a larger portion than yours, your own
portion may appear to be "small," whereas, if someone gets a
portion that is smaller than yours, your own portion may appear to
be "large."

GETTING A BIGGER SLICE   5

Method

Participants

The participants were 106 female undergraduate students enrolled in an introductory psychology class at a large university. The participants were recruited via an experimental database, where they could sign up for a study entitled "Market Taste Test Study." Each experimental session lasted 1 hr; participants received credit toward a course requirement for their participation.

Materials

Food. Extra-large uncut cheese pizza was ordered from a local pizza chain for each day of experimentation. The slices were reheated in a microwave oven before they were served to the participants. Any leftover pizza was stored in a freezer for use on another day. Frozen cookie dough (from a manufacturer who supplies "fresh-baked" cookies to local restaurants) was stored in a freezer and used to bake bite-sized cookies regularly throughout the week. Three different types of cookies were baked as needed: oatmeal raisin, chocolate chip, and double chocolate chip.

Questionnaires. Pre- and post-pizza rating scales were completed by all participants immediately after the manipulation and again after the pizza but before the cookie taste test. The pizza rating scales included a section from the PANAS (Positive and Negative Affect Schedule; Watson, Clark, & Tellegen, 1988), which was designed to measure the participants' negative affect. Participants described their negative emotional states such as "guilty" and "angry" using rating scales ranging from 1 for *very slightly or not at all* to 5 for *extremely*. Other questions assessed hunger and various aspects of the pizza that they were about to eat or had just eaten using a 9-point Likert-type scale. These questions included a manipulation check that asked participants to rate the portion size (rating from 1 for *too small* to 5 for *just right* to 9 for *too big*). The

---

The Method section begins immediately after the Introduction (no new page). The word "Method" is centred and boldface.

*Subsection headings such as "Participants" are **boldface**, typed flush to the left margin, and set alone on the line.*

Use numerals to express numbers 10 and above.

Use numerals to express numbers that are immediately followed by a unit of measurement (in this case, hr for hour). Also abbreviate min (minute), s (second), ms (millisecond). Do not abbreviate day, week, month, year.

This section describes the measures and materials used to conduct the study. They make up a sort of "ingredients" list for the study.

*This additional level of subheadings begins the paragraph. They are **boldface**, indented, and separated from the text of the paragraph with a period.*

Define unfamiliar acronyms when they are first used.

The anchors of scales (e.g., very slightly or not at all) are italicized.

GETTING A BIGGER SLICE   6

questions were answered before and after eating the pizza (with wording changed appropriately). In addition, participants were asked at the end of the study to what extent they had noticed any difference in the size of the pizza slices ("How did your slice of pizza compare to the slice received by the other person in the study?" Response options were *smaller, the same,* and *larger*).

Restraint scale. The 10-item Herman and Polivy Revised Restraint Scale (Herman, Polivy, & Silver, 1979) was used to determine restraint status. Participants who scored 15 or less on the restraint scale were classified as unrestrained eaters, whereas participants who scored above 15 were classified as restrained eaters.

Procedure

Female participants were recruited for this study through a psychology experimental website advertisement that specified that the participants must have no food allergies, must not be lactose intolerant, and should refrain from eating for up to 3 hr prior to their experimental session.

This section describes exactly how the study was conducted.

Each participant was informed that she would be given a light vegetarian cheese pizza lunch in order to ensure that each participant had the same taste experience and same level of fullness before completing taste ratings for market research. She was told that she would be sampling various food products that were being proposed for the market by a large food company that targeted the university-student population. The participant was also informed that she would be completing some questionnaires to assess her mood and other variables to ensure that these factors were not influencing her food ratings. Furthermore, the participant was told that she would be discussing her food ratings with another female participant in a brief discussion at the end of their session. She then signed the consent form.

GETTING A BIGGER SLICE   7

Participants were randomly assigned to one of three pizza-slice conditions: smaller slice, larger slice, and no information. Regardless of which condition the participant was in, she always received a standard slice of pizza (1/6 of the pizza), but the size of the "other participant's" slice was varied. Each pizza was cut into six pieces consisting of four standard-sized slices (1/6 of the pizza), one larger slice (1/3 larger than a standard-sized slice), and one smaller slice (1/3 smaller than the standard slice). In order to ensure that each slice was consistently cut for all pizzas used in the study, the appropriate sized slices were drawn onto a piece of paper and cut out to be used as templates for all pizzas. Thus, in the "smaller" condition, the participant received a standard-sized slice of pizza, while the "other female participant" was supposedly receiving the slice 1/3 larger than the standard slice. Similarly, participants in the "larger" condition received the standard slice of pizza, while the "other female participant" appeared to be receiving the slice 1/3 smaller than the standard slice. In the "no information" control condition, participants were given a standard-sized slice of pizza, with no indication of the "other female participant's" slice.

When the experimenter presented the participant with the pizza slices, the pizza slices were placed on a tray with a glass of water next to each slice and brought into the experimental room. Each participant in the "smaller" condition was presented with her standard-sized slice of pizza next to the 1/3 larger slice belonging to the "other female participant," which was identified as such as it was situated further away from her. Each participant in the "larger condition" saw her standard-sized slice along with the "other" female participant's smaller slice. In the "no information" control condition, the participant was presented only with her standard-sized slice, along with a glass of water. The experimenter then left the room, leaving the slices in the room and explaining that she had to

Numbers less than 10 are expressed as words.

Numbers less than 10 are expressed as words.

GETTING A BIGGER SLICE 8

retrieve a questionnaire for the participants. The experimenter left the room for exactly 1 min, allowing a sufficient amount of time for the participant to observe the slices and perceive the differences in their sizes. When the experimenter returned, the participant's slice and water were placed on the table in front of her and the pre-pizza rating scale was handed to the participant. She was asked to complete the questionnaire before eating her pizza slice. The experimenter then left the room with the "other participant's" slice.

Numbers that are immediately followed by a unit of measurement are expressed as numerals, as are numbers that represent time.

The participant was given 7 min to complete the preeating questionnaire and to eat her entire pizza slice (supposedly to ensure equal fullness in all participants), after which time the experimenter returned to the experimental room and handed the participant another set of questionnaires (to maintain the cover story). These questionnaires included the post-pizza scales. The participant was instructed to ring a bell when she had completed the questionnaires. At that time, the experimenter returned with three heaping (preweighed) plates of each of three types of cookie and another glass of water, plus three cookie-rating sheets (one for each cookie type). Tasting these cookies was ostensibly the principal purpose of the experiment, but the cookies were actually provided as a measure of ad lib consumption. In order to measure how many cookies the participants ate, the cookies were weighed prior to the experimental session and again after the "taste-test task." A heaping amount of each cookie type (oatmeal raisin, chocolate chip, and double chocolate chip) was placed onto one of three separate plates and the weight of each plate was measured and recorded. The three plates of cookies were placed on the table in front of the participant, with oatmeal-raisin cookies always being first, chocolate-chip cookies second, and double chocolate-chip cookies third. The participant was instructed that she would now be participating in the taste-test portion of the study, wherein she would sample

GETTING A BIGGER SLICE   9

three different types of cookies that were about to be released on the market by a large food company that marketed its snack foods to the university-aged population. The participant was instructed to begin with the oatmeal-raisin cookies and take as many cookies as she required to be very sure of her taste ratings of the cookies. She was told to sample the oatmeal-raisin cookies first, followed by the chocolate chip cookies, and finally the double chocolate-chip cookies. It was emphasized that once she had completed the ratings for one cookie type, she was not to go back and resample the previous cookie type and she was not to change her ratings once she had moved on to a "new taste." The water was provided to permit the participant to "cleanse her palate" as she moved from cookie to cookie. Moreover, the participant was reminded to be sure of her ratings since she would be comparing her food ratings with the "other female participant" at the end of the session. Finally, the participant was informed that once she was finished making her ratings, there were plenty of cookies and she was free to have as many more of any type as she liked, as long as she did not change any ratings. After the instructions were clear to the participant, the experimenter left the room for 10 min.

The experimenter reentered the room with the final set of questionnaires to be completed (including the restraint scale). The cookie plates were removed from the room, where they were reweighed without the participants' knowledge, in order to measure how many grams of cookies the participant had consumed. When the participant had completed the last set of questionnaires, her height and weight were measured and recorded. The participant was debriefed as to the purpose of the study. She was also asked if she had noticed the size difference in the pizza slices that had been presented, when she last ate, and what she ate at that time. She was thanked and asked some questions about the experiment so that

GETTING A BIGGER SLICE 10

she could receive credit for her psychology course before being dismissed. The study was thus conducted in accordance with ethical principles and had full institutional ethical review and approval.

Results
Participant Characteristics

A series of 2 (restrained versus unrestrained) × 3 (control, "small slice," "large slice") ANOVAs indicated the usual restraint main effect on BMI, $F(1,98) = 9.77$, $p = .002$, with restrained eaters having higher BMIs ($M = 24.27$) than unrestrained eaters ($M = 21.63$). There was no effect of condition and no significant interaction; as well, there were no restraint or condition differences in preeating hunger.

Manipulation Checks

On the pre- and post-pizza questionnaires, participants were asked about the quantity of pizza that they had been served. A 2 (restrained versus unrestrained) × 3 (control, "small slice," "large slice") ANOVA on each of these questions yielded only main effects for condition, preeating $F(2,97) = 5.25$, $p = .008$, and posteating $F(2,100) = 8.16$, p < .001. In both analyses, the "small" slice was rated as close to 5 (which corresponded to "just right") ($Mpre = 5.22$; $Mpost = 5.43$), the control/no information slice was seen as bigger than the small one ($Mpre = 5.69$; $Mpost = 6.03$), and the "large" slice was seen as bigger than either of the others ($Mpre = 6.33$; $Mpost = 6.80$). All differences were significant at the .05 level.

Cookie Intake

A 2 (Restraint: restrained, unrestrained) × 3 (Condition: control, "small slice," "large slice") ANOVA on the amount of cookies eaten (in grams) yielded no main effects of restraint or condition; however, there was a significant interaction, $F(2,100) = 3.51$, $p = .034$, $\eta_2 = 0.066$. Post hoc t tests indicated that whereas neither restrained nor unrestrained participants in the "small slice" condition differed from those

The section of a research report in which the researcher presents the findings.

When the outcome of a statistical test is presented, the name of the test is italicized and followed by the degrees of freedom in parentheses. The p refers to the probability of obtaining the results if the null hypothesis is correct.

Generally, exact probabilities are shown except when p < .001. Sometimes it is appropriate to use "ns" to indicate that a result is nonsignificant.

Statistical symbols, such as M for the mean, are italicized.

Greek letter eta, an indicator of effect size (squared value).

GETTING A BIGGER SLICE   11

in the control condition or from each other, restrained and unrestrained eaters in the "large slice" condition differed significantly from
each other, $t(100) = 2.98, p = .005$. In addition, although not significant, restrained eaters in the "large slice" condition ate marginally
more than did restrained eaters in the control condition, $t(100) = 1.82$,
$p = .075$, and unrestrained eaters in the "large slice" condition ate
marginally less than did unrestrained eaters in the control condition, t
$(100) = 1.66, p = .10$ (see Table 1 for all means and standard deviations).

Any figures or tables must be mentioned in the text.

Negative Affect

A 2 × 3 ANOVA on total negative affect before eating the pizza
(but after the manipulation of perceived portion size) yielded no
significant main effects, but there was a significant interaction
between restraint and condition, $F(2,100) = 3.40, p = .037, \eta_2 = 0.066$
(see Figure 1). The only significant differences found in the post
hoc t tests were between the "small" versus "large" conditions for
the unrestrained eaters, with those receiving the large slice feeling
more negative emotion than those receiving the small slice, $t(100)$
$= 2.25, p = .026$, and between restrained and unrestrained eaters in
the "small" condition, $t(100) = 2.03, p = .045$, with restrained eaters
feeling more negative affect than did unrestrained eaters. The analysis comparing restrained and unrestrained participants in the
"large" slice condition indicated a trend in the opposite direction, t
$(100) = 1.49, p = .14$, as did the analysis comparing "small" versus
"large" for restrained eaters, $t(100) = 1.41, p = .17$. The negative
affect ratings made after eating the pizza were no longer significantly different. Also, there were no significant effects on hunger
ratings either before or after eating the pizza.

The section of a research report in which the researcher considers the research results from various perspectives.

Discussion

Participants clearly perceived the size of their portion of pizza
differently as a function of whether they saw a comparison slice

GETTING A BIGGER SLICE   12

and what they saw in the comparison. When they saw their slice
next to a larger one, they perceived their slice as smaller than did
those who did not see a comparison slice; and when they saw their
slice next to a smaller slice they perceived it as larger than did participants who saw only their own slice. The change in perception
occurred despite the fact that not only were all participants given
the same-sized slice, but this size is the standard slice sold on campus and at all other outlets of the major pizza chain that supplied
the pizza.

Based simply on these different perceptions of the identical
portion, participants went on to eat different amounts, as shown by
the significant interaction between restraint and condition. Those
who saw their pizza slice as smaller ate the same amount of cookies
as did those who did not have a comparison (regardless of restraint
status), but the cookie intake of those who thought that they had
eaten a larger slice of pizza was affected by this perception (in different ways depending on restraint status). That the effect was
more a matter of the "large slice" condition changing intake somewhat (relative to control) than of the "small slice" condition changing intake (relative to control) was probably due to the fact that in
the "small slice" condition, the slice was seen as close to—indeed,
slightly more than—"just right," but the "large slice" was seen as
significantly larger than "just right." In other words, it was the pizza
in the "large slice" condition that was seen as unusually large,
rather than the pizza in the "small slice" condition being seen as
unusually small.

Quotation marks are placed after the period.

The direction of the effect in the "large slice" condition
depended on restraint status, as was reflected in the significant
interaction. Restrained and unrestrained eaters ate the same
amount of cookies in the control and "small slice" conditions, but
unrestrained eaters tended to eat less in the "large slice" condition,

whereas restrained eaters tended to eat more in the "large slice" condition. (Restrained eaters ate significantly more than did unrestrained eaters in the "large slice" condition.) In other words, unrestrained eaters compensated by eating less cookies if they thought that they had eaten a lot of pizza, whereas restrained eaters counter-regulated and ate more cookies when they thought that they had already overeaten on pizza. This pattern corresponds to the effect obtained in previous research when preload size was actually manipulated or when perceived preload size was manipulated by telling participants that the preloads varied in caloric value (Polivy, 1976) or by implying that the preloads differed in caloric value because they were either "forbidden" or "allowed" foods (e.g., Knight & Boland, 1989). While subtle manipulations such as the smell of food have been shown to induce restrained eaters to eat more (Fedoroff, Polivy, & Herman, 1997, 2003; Jansen & Van den Hout, 1991), the present study involved arguably the subtlest manipulation yet. Nothing was said about size or caloric value of the preload, and the identical preload/meal was used in all conditions; only a visual comparison to someone else's smaller portion acted to render one's own portion relatively large, with predictable effects on subsequent intake. Moreover, the present "preload" was actually a meal ("light lunch") rather than extraneous eating. However, even simply perceiving one's meal as "larger than just right" seems to have been enough to push eating in opposite directions for restrained versus unrestrained eaters. Eating was thus more strongly influenced by social comparison and the perception this fostered (I'm eating more than she is) than by actual portion size.

The fact that restrained eaters ate somewhat more in the "large slice" condition is what we have come to expect from the literature in which restrained eaters typically overeat after a large preload (or a preload perceived as large). That they did not eat less in the

APA strongly encourages writers to use past tense when reporting procedures and results.

GETTING A BIGGER SLICE   14

"small slice" condition than in the control condition was consistent
with the finding that restrained eaters' eating is "dichotomous":
they ate either a small, reasonable amount, when they were not disinhibited (i.e., when the preload was not seen as large, or they were
not disinhibited by food cues, negative emotion, or other factors) or
they ate a large amount when they became disinhibited (i.e., when
the preload—or in the present case, meal—was large or perceived
as large). In the present study, the "large slice" condition was perceived as a large preload/meal whereas the other two conditions
were seen as appropriate sized.

The unrestrained eaters on the other hand did not compensate
for receiving the smaller piece of pizza by eating more cookies,
even though they perceived the smaller portion as smaller than the
other portions. They did, however, rate the small slice as "just right"
in size. They may possibly have simply responded to their internal
signals of satiety and thus ate the same amount of cookies as did
the unrestrained eaters who got no comparative information (and
also saw their slice as close to the "right" size). Of course, unrestrained eaters in the large slice condition presumably had the same
satiety signals, but unrestrained eaters may be more prepared to
eat less (after a preload/meal that they consider to be large) than to
eat more (after a preload/meal that they consider to be "just right").

Not surprisingly, because all participants were actually given
and ate the same amount of pizza, there were no group or condition
differences in hunger either before or after eating the pizza. There
were, however, some potentially interesting differences in the
extent of negative affect experienced upon realizing that one had
been given a larger or smaller portion of pizza. For unrestrained
eaters, getting a large slice made them more dysphoric, but for
restrained eaters, dysphoria was higher when they received a
smaller slice. Although small, these opposite emotional reactions

GETTING A BIGGER SLICE   15

may speak to the differential psychology of the restrained and unrestrained eaters. Unrestrained eaters may be responding to the prescriptive norm of not appearing to eat excessively (Herman, Roth, & Polivy, 2003), and feel worse if they think that they are violating the norm. Restrained eaters, on the other hand, may actually be more upset with being allowed to maintain their diets (by eating the smaller piece); apparently they feel somewhat better when "forced" by the experimenter to eat "more," break their diets, and indulge themselves with additional cookies. This interpretation comports with the assumption that fundamentally, people want to eat as much as possible, but are constrained by considerations of social propriety (not eating excessively so as not to look like a "pig") or their self-imposed dietary agendas (Herman et al., 2003). When forced by someone else to transgress against their diets, restrained eaters may well experience what we have called the "what the hell effect" (Herman & Polivy, 1984) and feel relieved to be pushed off their diets and allowed to unleash their eating.

The present study shows that the mere perception that one's meal was excessively large acts the same as a gratuitous preload to disinhibit eating in restrained eaters. The data also show that restrained and unrestrained eaters alike judge the amount that they are served in comparison to what those around them are eating. Such perceptions about the social context or meaning of one's portion apparently outweigh feelings of hunger in influencing the amount eaten, particularly if one sees oneself as having overeaten relative to others. Restrained eaters, when they perceive themselves as having eaten excessively compared to others, continue to eat liberally rather than curtail their intake. This indulgence undermines their stated dietary goals, but the fact that they feel worse when they do not (get to) overindulge provides a hint as to why dieters so often find themselves breaking their diets.

GETTING A BIGGER SLICE   16

References

Adams, C., & Leary, M. (2007). Promoting self-compassionate attitudes toward eating among restrictive and guilty eaters. *Journal of Social & Clinical Psychology, 26*, 1120–1144. doi :10.1521/jscp.2007.26.10.1120

Fedoroff, I., Polivy, J., & Herman, C. P. (1997). The effect of pre-exposure to food cues on the eating behavior of restrained and unrestrained eaters. *Appetite, 28*, 33–47. doi:10.1006/appe.1996.0057

Fedoroff, I., Polivy, J., & Herman, C. P. (2003). The specificity of restrained versus unrestrained eaters' responses to food cues: General desire to eat, or craving for the cued food? *Appetite, 41*, 7–13. doi:10.1016/S0195-6663(03)00026-6

Jansen, A., & Van den Hout, M. (1991). On being led into temptation: "Counterregulation" of dieters after smelling a preload. *Addictive Behaviors, 16*, 247–253. doi:10.1016/0306-4603(91)90017-C

Herman, C. P., & Polivy, J. (1984). A boundary model for the regulation of eating. *Psychiatric Annals, 13*, 918–927.

Herman, C. P., Polivy, J., & Silver, R. (1979). Effects of an observer on eating behavior: The induction of "sensible" eating. *Journal of Personality, 47*, 85–99. doi:10.1111/j.1467-6494.1979.tb00616.x

Herman, C. P., Polivy, J., & Esses, V. M. (1987). The illusion of counter-regulation. *Appetite, 9*, 161–169. doi:10.1016/S0195-6663(87)80010-7

Herman, C. P., Roth, D., & Polivy, J. (2003). Effects of the presence of others on food intake. A normative interpretation. *Psychological Bulletin, 129*, 873–886. doi:10.1037/0033-2909.129.6.873

A list of all sources cited in the body of a paper, sorted alphabetically by the last name of the first author of the cited material, formatted in APA style and including all information required to locate each source. Forms the last section of the APA format manuscript style.

A comma always follows the first author's initial, even if only two authors are listed.

A comma always follows the first author's initial, even if only two authors are listed.

APA recommends using the en-dash symbol between page numbers rather than a simple hyphen. The Microsoft Word shortcut to insert the en dash is Control-hyphen. This is probably not necessary for student papers.

Each reference begins on a new line and is considered a paragraph. The paragraph is a hanging indent, in which the first line is flush to the left margin and subsequent lines are indented.

GETTING A BIGGER SLICE   17

Knight, L., & Boland, F. (1989). Restrained eating. An experimental
    disentanglement of the disinhibiting variables of calories and
    food type. *Journal of Abnormal Psychology, 98,* 412–420.
    doi:10.1037/0021-843X.98.4.412

McCann, K. L., Perri, M. G., Nezu, A. M., & Lowe, M. R. (1992). An
    investigation of counterregulatory eating in obese clinic
    attenders. *International Journal of Eating Disorders, 12,*
    161–169. doi:10.1002/1098-108X(199209)12:2<161::AID-
    EAT2260120206>3.0.CO;2-A

Pliner, P., & Zec, D. (2007). Meal schemas during a preload decrease
    subsequent eating. *Appetite, 48,* 278–288. doi:10.1016/j.
    appet.2006.04.009

Polivy, J. (1976). Perception of calories and regulation of intake in
    restrained and unrestrained subjects. *Addictive Behaviors,
    1,* 237–243. doi:10.1016/0306-4603(76)90016-2

Polivy, J., Heatherton, T. F., & Herman, C. P. (1988). Self-esteem,
    restraint, and eating behavior. *Journal of Abnormal Psychol-
    ogy, 97,* 354–356. doi:10.1037/0021-843X.97.3.354

Polivy, J., & Herman, C. P. (1999). Distress and eating: Why do diet-
    ers overeat? *International Journal of Eating Disorders, 26,*
    153–164. doi:10.1002/(SICI)1098-108X(199909)26:2<153::AID-
    EAT4>3.0.CO;2-R

Polivy, J., & Herman, C. P. (2005). Mental health and eating behav-
    iours: A bi-directional relation. *Canadian Journal of Public
    Health, 96,* 43–48.

Polivy, J., Herman, C. P., Hackett, R., & Kuleshnyk, I. (1986). The
    effects of self-attention and public attention on eating in
    restrained and unrestrained subjects. *Journal of Personality
    and Social Psychology, 50,* 1203–1224. doi:10.1037/0022-
    3514.50.6.1253

Titles of books and journals are italicized, as are the volume numbers of journals.

Note that "&" (the ampersand symbol) is used for multiple authors throughout the References section.

Note capitalization: First word and first word following a colon, plus any proper nouns.

When the same set of authors is included multiple times, the entries are ordered by date, from oldest to newest.

Spencer, J. A., & Fremouw, W. J. (1979). Binge eating as a function of restraint and weight classification. *Journal of Abnormal Psychology, 88*, 262–267. doi:10.1037/0021-843X.88.3.262

Watson, D., Clark, L. A., & Tellegen, A. (1988). Development and validation of brief measures of positive and negative affect: The PANAS scale. *Journal of Personality and Social Psychology, 54*, 1063–1070. doi:10.1037/0022-3514.54.6.1063

The first line of the page should include the table number.

The next double-spaced line should include the table title, which should be italicized, with all major words capitalized. No period is required.

Only the first word of headings within the table are capitalized. Sections of the table are separated by horizontal lines. Do not use vertical lines.

A horizontal line should separate column headers from data presented in the table.

Include another horizontal line below the last row of information.

A note below the table is optional. The note may provide additional information such as an explanation of abbreviations or specific group differences.

GETTING A BIGGER SLICE   19

Table 1

Amount of Cookies Eaten (in Grams) in the Pizza Size Conditions

Restraint	Larger slice			Control/no info			Smaller slice		
	M	SD	n	M	SD	n	M	SD	n
Unrestrained eaters	50.39	6.83	25	67.89	8.04	18	61.20	7.12	23
Restrained eaters	84.36	9.13	14	59.94	9.86	12	62.12	9.13	14

Note. The number of participants (n) in the unrestrained eaters group is higher than the number in the restrained group when using the standard cutoff score on the Restraint Scale.

GETTING A BIGGER SLICE   20

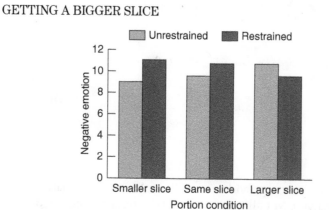

Figure 1. Total negative affect before eating pizza (but after seeing it). Post hoc *t* tests show a significant difference between the restrained and unrestrained eaters who were given the smaller slice. Unrestrained eaters getting the small slice felt better than those given the larger slice; restrained eaters given the small slice felt marginally worse than those given the large slice.

Figure caption. Note italics for figure number. Caption may include more than one sentence.

Appendix B

Statistical Tests

The purpose of this appendix is to provide some formulas and calculation procedures for some data analysis. Not all possible statistical tests are included, but a variety of tests are given that should be appropriate for many research designs you might use.

We will build on Chapters 12 and 13 to examine procedures for both descriptive and inferential statistics. You may recall from those chapters that the appropriate statistical analysis is determined by the type of design and by the measurement scale used in the study. Remember that there are four types of measurement scales: nominal, ordinal, interval, and ratio. Nominal scales have no numerical properties, ordinal scales provide rank-order information only, and interval and ratio scales have equal intervals between the points on the scale. In addition, ratio scales have a true zero point. As we consider each statistical test, we will note the relevant measurement scale restrictions that apply.

The examples here use small and simple data sets, so the calculations can be done easily by hand using a calculator. You will probably use a computer program such as SPSS, SAS, or Excel for your analyses. Practising the underlying calculations will help you understand the output from these computer programs.

DESCRIPTIVE STATISTICS

Measures of Central Tendency

A measure of central tendency gives a single number that describes how an entire group scores as a whole or on the average. Three different central tendency measures are available: the mode, the median, and the mean. Table B.1 shows a set of scores alongside the descriptive statistics.

The Mode The mode is the most frequently occurring score. The most frequently occurring score in Table B.1 data is 5. No calculations are necessary to find the mode. The mode can be used with any of the four types of

TABLE B.I   Descriptive statistics for a set of scores

Score	Descriptive Statistic
1	Mode = 5
2	
4	Median = 5
4	
5	$\bar{X} = \dfrac{\Sigma X}{N} = 4.5$
5	
5	
6	Range = 6
6	
7	$s^2 = \dfrac{\Sigma(X - \bar{X})^2}{N - 1} = \dfrac{\Sigma X^2 - N\bar{X}^2}{N - 1} = \dfrac{233 - 202.5}{9} = 3.388$
$\Sigma X = 45$	
$\Sigma X^2 = 233$	$s = \sqrt{s^2} = 1.84$
$N = 10$	

measurement scales. However, with nominal scale data, mode is the *only* measure of central tendency that can be used. If you are measuring sex of participants and find there are 100 females and 50 males, the mode is "female" because this is the most frequently occurring category on the nominal scale.

The Median   The median is the score that divides the group in half: 50 percent of the scores are below the median and 50 percent are above the median. When the scores have been ordered from lowest to highest (as in Table B.1), the median is easily found. If there are an odd number of scores, you simply find the middle score. (For example, if there are eleven scores, the sixth score is the median, because there are five lower and five higher scores.) If there is an even number of scores, the median is the average of the two middle scores. In the data in Table B.1, there are ten scores, so the fifth and sixth scores are the two middle scores. To find the median, we add the two middle scores and divide by 2. Thus, in Table B.1, the median is

$$\frac{5 + 5}{2} = 5$$

The median can be used with ordinal, interval, or ratio scale data. It is most likely to be used with ordinal data, however. This is because calculation of the median considers only the rank ordering of scores and not the actual size of the scores.

The Mean   The mean does take into account the actual size of the scores. Thus, the mean is based on more information about the scores than either the mode or the median. However, it is appropriate only for interval or ratio scale data. The mean is the sum of the scores in a group divided by the number of scores. The calculational formula for the mean can be expressed as

$$\overline{X} = \frac{\Sigma X}{N}$$

where $\overline{X}$ is the symbol for the mean. In this formula, X represents one person's score, and the Σ symbol indicates addition. The symbol ΣX can be read as "sum of the Xs," which indicates that everyone's scores are to be added. Thus, ΣX in the data from Table B.1 is

$$1 + 2 + 4 + 4 + 5 + 5 + 5 + 6 + 6 + 7 = 45$$

The N in the formula symbolizes the number of scores in the group. In our example, $N = 10$. Thus, we can calculate the mean:

$$\overline{X} = \frac{\Sigma X}{N} = \frac{45}{10} = 4.5$$

Measures of Variability

In addition to describing the central tendency of the set of scores, we want to describe how much the scores vary among themselves. How much spread is there in the set of scores?

The Range   The range is typically calculated as the highest score minus the lowest score, although some variations account for rounding. In our example, the range is 6. The range is not a very useful statistic, because it is based on only two scores in the distribution. It ignores all of the information about dispersion that is available across the entire set of scores.

The Variance and Standard Deviation   The variance and a related statistic called the standard deviation use all the scores to yield a measure of variability. The variance indicates the degree to which scores vary about the group mean. The formula for the variance (symbolized as s^2) is

$$s^2 = \frac{\Sigma(X - \overline{X})^2}{N - 1}$$

where $(X - \overline{X})^2$ is an individual score, X, minus the mean, $\overline{X}$, and then squared. Thus $(X - \overline{X})^2$ is the squared deviation of each score from the mean. The Σ sign indicates that these squared deviation scores are to be added together. Finally, dividing by $N - 1$ gives the mean of the squared deviations. The variance, then, is the mean of the squared deviations from the group mean. (Squared deviations are used because simple deviations would add up to zero. $N - 1$ is used in most cases for statistical purposes because the scores represent a sample and not an entire population. As the sample size becomes larger, it makes little difference whether N or $N - 1$ is used.)

The data in Table B.1 can be used to illustrate calculation of the variance. $\Sigma(X - \bar{X})^2$ equals

$$(1 - 4.5)^2 + (2 - 4.5)^2 + (4 - 4.5)^2 + (4 - 4.5)^2 + (5 - 4.5)^2 + (5 - 4.5)^2$$
$$+ (5 - 4.5)^2 + (6 - 4.5)^2 + (6 - 4.5)^2 + (7 - 4.5)^2 = 30.50$$

The next step is to divide $\Sigma(X - \bar{X})^2$ by $N - 1$. The calculation for the variance, then, is

$$s^2 = \frac{\Sigma(X - \bar{X})^2}{N - 1} = \frac{30.50}{9} = 3.388$$

You might encounter a different calculational formula for the variance:

$$s^2 = \frac{\Sigma X^2 - N\bar{X}^2}{N - 1}$$

where ΣX^2 is the sum of the squared individual scores, and $\bar{X}^2$ is the mean squared. You can confirm that the two formulas are identical by computing the variance using this simpler formula. (Remember that ΣX^2 tells you to square each score and then add the squared scores.)

The standard deviation is the square root of the variance. Because the variance uses squared scores, the variance does not describe the amount of variability in the same units of measurement as the original scale. The standard deviation (s) corrects this problem. Thus, the standard deviation is the average deviation of scores from the mean.

Pearson Product-Moment Correlation Coefficient

As explained in Chapters 4 and 12, the Pearson product-moment correlation coefficient (r) is used to describe the strength of the relationship between two variables that have been measured on interval or ratio scales.

Example   Suppose you want to know whether travel experiences are related to knowledge of geography. In your study, you give a 15-item quiz on North American geography, and you also ask how many American states and Canadian provinces participants have visited. After obtaining the pairs of observations from each participant, a Pearson r can be computed to measure the strength of the relationship between travel experience and knowledge of geography.

Table B.2 presents fictitious data from such a study along with the calculations for r. A formula to calculate r is

$$r = \frac{N\Sigma XY - \Sigma X/\Sigma Y}{\sqrt{N\Sigma X^2 - (\Sigma X)^2}\sqrt{N\Sigma Y^2 - (\Sigma Y)^2}}$$

where X refers to a participant's score on variable X, and Y is a participant's score on variable Y. In Table B.2, the travel experience score is variable X, and

TABLE B.2   Data for hypothetical study on travel and knowledge of geography: Pearson r

Subject Identification Number	Travel Score (X)	Knowledge Score (Y)	XY
01	4	10	40
02	6	15	90
03	7	8	56
04	8	9	72
05	8	7	56
06	12	10	120
07	14	15	210
08	15	13	195
09	15	15	225
10	17	14	238
	$\Sigma X =$ 106	$\Sigma Y =$ 116	$\Sigma XY =$ 1302
	$\Sigma X^2 =$ 1308	$\Sigma Y^2 =$ 1434	
	$(\Sigma X)^2 =$ 11236	$(\Sigma Y)^2 =$ 13456	

Computation:

$$r = \frac{N\Sigma XY - \Sigma X\Sigma Y}{\sqrt{N\Sigma X^2 - (\Sigma X)^2}\sqrt{N\Sigma Y^2 - (\Sigma Y)^2}}$$

$$= \frac{10(1302) - (106)(116)}{\sqrt{10(1308) - 11236}\sqrt{10(1434) - 13456}}$$

$$= \frac{13020 - 12296}{\sqrt{13080 - 11236}\sqrt{14340 - 13456}}$$

$$= \frac{724}{\sqrt{1844}\sqrt{884}}$$

$$= \frac{724}{1276.61}$$

$$= .567$$

the geography knowledge score is variable Y. In the formula, N is the number of paired observations (that is, the number of participants measured on both variables).

The calculation of r requires a number of arithmetic operations on the X and Y scores. ΣX is simply the sum of the scores on variable X. ΣX^2 is the sum of the squared scores on X (each score is first squared and then the sum of the squared scores is obtained). The quantity $(\Sigma X)^2$ is the square of the sum of the scores: The total of the X scores (ΣX) is first calculated and then this total is squared. It is important not to confuse the two quantities, ΣX^2 and $(\Sigma X)^2$. The same calculations are made, using the Y scores, to obtain ΣY, ΣY^2, and $(\Sigma Y)^2$. To find ΣXY, each participant's X score is multiplied by the score on Y; these values are then summed for all subjects. When these calculations have been made, r is computed using the formula for r given above.

At this point, you may wish to examine carefully the calculations shown in Table B.2 to familiarize yourself with the procedures for computing r. For practice, you might try calculating r from another set of data, such as the study shown in Table 12.1.

ADDITIONAL STATISTICAL SIGNIFICANCE TESTS

In Chapter 13, we examined the t test as one example of a statistical significance test. It is appropriate when comparing two groups' responses to a continuous dependent variable. This section describes several additional statistical significance tests. Like the t test, these tests are used to determine the probability that the results were due to random error. All these tests use the logic of the null hypothesis discussed in Chapter 13. We will first consider how to evaluate the statistical significance of Pearson's r, and then proceed to the chi-square test and the analysis of variance (F test).

Significance of Correlation Coefficient r

To test the null hypothesis that the population correlation coefficient is 0.00, we can consult a table of critical values of r. Table C.4 in Appendix C shows critical values of r for .10, .05, and .01 levels of significance. The critical value of r for any given study depends on the *degrees of freedom* (*df*; see Chapter 13). Degrees of freedom refers to the number of scores that are free to vary. The *df* for the significance test for r is $N - 2$. In our example study on travel and knowledge, the number of paired observations is 10, so the $df = 8$. For 8 degrees of freedom, the critical value of r at the .05 level of significance is .632 (plus or minus). The obtained r must be more extreme than the critical r to be significant.

Because our obtained r (from Table B.2) of .567 is closer to zero than the critical value, we do not reject the null hypothesis—even though the magnitude of r is fairly large. Recall the discussion of non-significant results from

Chapter 13. It is possible that the correlation would reach statistically significance if you used a larger sample size or more sensitive and reliable measures of the variables.

Chi-Square (χ^2)

The chi-square (Greek letter *chi*, squared) test is used when dealing with nominal scale data. It is used when the data consist of frequencies (i.e., the number of participants that fall into each of several categories). Chi-square can be used with either experimental or non-experimental data. The major requirement is that both variables are studied using nominal scales.

Example   Suppose you want to know whether there is a relationship between sex and hand dominance. To do this, you sample 50 males and 50 females and ask whether they are right-handed, left-handed, or ambidextrous (use both hands with equal skill). Your data collection involves classifying each person as male or female and as right-handed, left-handed, or ambidextrous.

Fictitious data for such a study are presented in Table B.3. The frequencies labelled as "O" (for "observed") in each of the six cells in the table refer to

TABLE B.3   Data for hypothetical study on hand dominance: Chi-square test

Sex of Subject	Hand Dominance			Row Totals
	Right	Left	Ambidextrous	
Male	$O_1 = 15$	$O_2 = 30$	$O_3 = 5$	50
	$E_1 = 25$	$E_2 = 20$	$E_3 = 5$	
Female	$O_4 = 35$	$O_5 = 10$	$O_6 = 5$	50
	$E_4 = 25$	$E_5 = 20$	$E_6 = 5$	
Column totals	50	40	10	$N = 100$

Computations:	Cell number	$\dfrac{(O-E)^2}{E}$	
	1	4.00	
	2	5.00	
	3	0.00	
			$\chi^2 = \Sigma\dfrac{(O-E)^2}{E}$
	4	4.00	
	5	5.00	$= 18.00$
	6	0.00	
		$\Sigma = 18.00$	

the number of male and female subjects who fall into each of the three hand-dominance categories. The frequencies labelled "E" (for "expected") refer to frequencies that are expected if the null hypothesis is correct. It is important that each subject falls into only one of the cells when using chi-square (that is, no subject can be counted as both male and female or both right- and left-handed).

The chi-square test examines the extent to which the frequencies that are actually observed in the study differ from the frequencies that are expected if the null hypothesis is correct. The null hypothesis states that there is no relationship between sex and hand dominance: Males and females do not differ on this characteristic.

The formula for computing chi-square is

$$\chi^2 = \Sigma \frac{(O - E)^2}{E}$$

where O is the *observed* frequency in each cell, E is the *expected* frequency in each cell, and the symbol Σ refers to summing over all cells. The steps in calculating the value of χ^2 are as follows:

Step 1: Arrange the observed frequencies in a table such as Table B.3. Note that in addition to the observed frequencies in each cell, the table presents row totals, column totals, and the total number of observations (N).

Step 2: Calculate the expected frequencies for each of the cells in the table. The expected frequency formula is

$$E = \frac{\text{row total} \times \text{column total}}{N}$$

where the row total refers to the row total for the cell, and the column total refers to the column total for the cell. Thus, the expected frequency for cell 1 (male right-handedness) is

$$E_1 = \frac{50 \times 50}{100} = 25$$

The expected frequencies for each of the cells are shown in Table B.3 below the observed frequencies.

Step 3: Calculate the quantity $(O - E)^2/E$ for each cell. For cell 1, this quantity is

$$\frac{(15 - 25)^2}{25} = \frac{100}{25} = 4.00$$

Step 4: Find the value of χ^2 by summing the $(O - E)^2/E$ values found in step 3. The calculations for obtaining χ^2 for the example data are shown in Table B.3.

Significance of Chi-Square   The significance of the obtained χ^2 value can be evaluated by consulting a table of critical values of χ^2, like Table C.1 in Appendix C. The critical χ^2 values indicate the value that the *obtained* χ^2 must exceed to be significant at the .10 level, the .05 level, and the .01 level.

As is the case for all statistical tests, the critical value of χ^2 for any given study depends on the degrees of freedom. For a chi-square test, the *degrees of freedom* are the number of cells in which the frequencies are free to vary once we know the row totals and column totals. The degrees of freedom for chi-square are calculated as

$$df = (R - 1)(C - 1)$$

where R is the number of rows in the table and C is the number of columns. In our example in Table B.3, there are two rows and three columns, so there are $(2 - 1)(3 - 1) = 2$ degrees of freedom. In a study with three rows and three columns, there are 4 degrees of freedom, and so on.

To use Table C.1, find the correct degrees of freedom and then determine the critical value of χ^2 necessary to reject the null hypothesis at the chosen significance level. With 2 degrees of freedom, the obtained χ^2 value must be greater than the critical value of 5.991 to be significant at the .05 level. There is only a .05 probability that a χ^2 beyond 5.991 would occur if only random error is operating. Because the obtained χ^2 from our example is 18.00, we can reject the null hypothesis that there is no relationship between sex and hand dominance. (Of course, the chi-square was based on fictitious data, but you could determine for yourself whether there is a relationship by gathering and analyzing your own data.)

Concluding Remarks   The chi-square test is used frequently across the behavioural sciences. The calculational formula described is generalizable to expanded studies in which there are more categories on either of the variables. One note of caution, however: When both variables have only two categories, so that there are only two rows and two columns, the formula for calculating chi-square changes slightly. In such cases, the formula is

$$\chi^2 = \Sigma \frac{(|O - E| - .5)^2}{E}$$

where $|O - E|$ is the absolute value of $O - E$, and .5 is a constant that is subtracted for each cell.

Analysis of Variance (*F* Test): Overview

As noted briefly in Chapter 13, the analysis of variance (ANOVA), or *F* test, is used to determine whether there is a significant difference among groups on a dependent measure that uses either an interval or ratio scale. ANOVA is a versatile test that can be adapted for various designs. Here we offer procedures for calculating F for the following designs: independent groups with one or two independent variables, and repeated measures with one independent variable.

Analysis of Variance: One Independent Variable, Independent Groups Design

To illustrate the use of the analysis of variance, let's consider a hypothetical experiment on physical distance and self-disclosure. You might predict that people will reveal more about themselves to an interviewer when they are sitting close to the interviewer than they will when sitting farther away. To test this idea, you conduct an experiment. Participants are told that interviewing techniques are being studied. Each participant is seated in a room; the interviewer comes into the room and sits at one of three distances from the participant: close (2 feet, or 0.61 metres), medium (4 feet, or 1.22 metres), or far (6 feet, or 1.83 metres). The interviewer's distance is the independent variable manipulation. Participants are randomly assigned to one of the three distance conditions, and the interviewer's behaviour is otherwise constant in all conditions. The interview consists of a number of questions, and the dependent variable is the number of personal, revealing statements made by the participant during the interview.

Fictitious data for this independent groups experiment are shown in Table B.4. Note there are five participants in each group. The first step in calculating the F ratio is to calculate different variance estimates called *sum of squares*.

Sum of Squares   Sum of squares stands for the *sum of squared deviations from the mean*. Computing an analysis of variance for the data in Table B.4 involves three sums of squares: (1) SS_{TOTAL}, the sum of squared deviations of each individual score from the grand mean; (2) SS_A, the sum of squared deviations of each of the group means from the grand mean; and (3) SS_{ERROR}, the sum of squared deviations of the individual scores from their respective group means. The "A" in SS_A is used to indicate that we are dealing with the systematic variance associated with independent variable A.

All three sums of squares are deviations from a particular mean. (Recall that we calculated deviations earlier when finding the variance in a set of scores.) We could calculate the deviations directly with the data in Table B.4, but such calculations are hard to work with, so we will use simplified formulas for computational purposes. The three computational formulas are explained below. The actual computations are shown in Table B.4. As you work through the example, note that $SS_{TOTAL} = SS_A + SS_{ERROR}$. The total *sum of squares* is being divided into two parts: variation attributable to the independent variable A, and variation attributable to error.

TABLE B.4   Data for hypothetical experiment on distance and
self-disclosure: Analysis of variance

	Distance (A)	
Close (A1)	Medium (A2)	Far (A3)
33	21	20
24	25	13
31	19	15
29	27	10
34	26	14
$T_{A1} = 151$	$T_{A2} = 118$	$T_{A3} = 72$
$n_{A1} = 5$	$n_{A2} = 5$	$n_{A3} = 5$
$X_{A1} = 30.20$	$X_{A2} = 23.60$	$X_{A3} = 14.40$
$\Sigma X_{A1}^2 = 4623$	$\Sigma X_{A2}^2 = 2832$	$\Sigma X_{A3}^2 = 1090$
$T_{A1}^2 = 22801$	$T_{A2}^2 = 13924$	$T_{A3}^2 = 5184$

$$SS_{TOTAL} = \Sigma X^2 - \frac{G^2}{N} = (4623 + 2832 + 1090) - \frac{(151 + 118 + 72)^2}{15}$$

$$= 8545 - 7752.07$$

$$= 792.93$$

$$SS_A = \Sigma \frac{T_a^2}{n_a} - \frac{G^2}{N} = \left[\frac{(151)^2}{5} + \frac{(118)^2}{5} + \frac{(72)^2}{5} \right] - 7752.07$$

$$= 8381.80 - 7752.07$$

$$= 629.73$$

$$SS_{ERROR} = \Sigma X^2 = \Sigma \frac{T_a^2}{n_a} = 8545 - 8381.80$$

$$= 163.20$$

SS_{TOTAL} The formula for SS_{TOTAL} is

$$\Sigma X^2 - \frac{G^2}{N}$$

where ΣX^2 is the sum of the squared scores of all subjects in the experiment.
Each of the scores is squared first and then added. Thus, for the data in Table
B.4, ΣX^2 is $33^2 + 24^2 + 31^2$ and so on until all of the scores have been squared
and added. If you are doing the calculations by hand or with a calculator, it may
be convenient to find the ΣX^2 for the scores in each group and then add these
up for your final computation. This is what we did for the data in the table. The
G in the formula stands for the grand total of all of the scores. This involves adding up the scores for all participants. The grand total is then squared and divided

by N, the total number of participants in the experiment. When computing the sum of squares, you should always keep the calculations clearly labelled, because you can simplify later calculations by referring to these earlier ones.

SS_A The formula for SS_A is

$$\Sigma \frac{T_a^2}{n_a} - \frac{G^2}{N}$$

The T_a in this formula refers to the total of the scores in Group a of independent variable A. (T_a is a shorthand notation for ΣX in each group. [Recall that we calculated ΣX for the mean.] The T_a symbol is used here to avoid having to deal with too many Σ signs in our calculation procedures.) The a is used to symbolize the particular group number; thus, T_a is a general symbol for T_1, T_2, and T_3. Looking at our data in Table B.4, $T_1 = 151$, $T_2 = 118$, and $T_3 = 72$. These are the sums of the scores in each of the groups. After T_a has been calculated, T_a^2 is found by squaring T_a. Now, T_a^2 is divided by n_a, the number of subjects in Group a. Once the quantity T_a^2/n_a has been computed for each group, the quantities are summed as indicated by the Σ symbol.

Note that the second part of the formula, G^2/N, was calculated as a step toward SS_{TOTAL}. Because we already have this quantity, it need not be calculated again when computing SS_A. After obtaining SS_A, we can now compute SS_{ERROR}.

SS_{ERROR} The formula for SS_{ERROR} is

$$\Sigma X^2 - \Sigma \frac{T_a^2}{n_a}$$

Both halves of this equation were calculated above in obtaining SS_{TOTAL} and SS_A. To obtain SS_{ERROR}, find these quantities and perform the proper subtraction.

To check your calculations, ensure that $SS_{TOTAL} = SS_A + SS_{ERROR}$.

Mean Squares   After obtaining the sum of squares, it is necessary to compute the *mean squares*. Mean square stands for the *mean of the sum of the squared deviations from the mean* or, more simply, the mean of the sum of squares. The mean square (MS) is the sum of squares divided by the degrees of freedom. The degrees of freedom are determined by the number of scores in the sum of squares that are free to vary. The mean squares are the variances that are used in computing the value of F. The necessary computations are shown in an analysis of variance summary table in Table B.5. Constructing a summary table is the easiest way to complete the computations.

From Table B.5, you can see that the mean squares that concern us are the mean square for A (systematic variance) and the mean square for error (error variance). The formulas are

$$MS_A = SS_A/df_A$$
$$MS_{ERROR} = SS_{ERROR}/df_{ERROR}$$

TABLE B.5   Analysis of variance summary table

Source of Variance	Sum of Squares	df	Mean Square	F
A	SS_A	$a - 1$	SS_A/df_A	MS_A/MS_{ERROR}
Error	SS_{ERROR}	$N - a$	SS_{ERROR}/df_{ERROR}	
Total	SS_{TOTAL}	$N - 1$		
A	629.73	2	314.87	23.15
Error	163.20	12	13.60	
Total	792.93	14		

where $df_A = a - 1$ (the number of groups minus one) and $df_{ERROR} = N - a$ (the total number of subjects minus the number of groups).

Obtaining the F Value   The obtained F is found by dividing MS_A by MS_{ERROR}. If only random error is operating, the expected value of F is 1.0. The greater the F value, the lower the probability that the results of the experiment were due to chance error.

Significance of F   To determine the significance of the obtained F value, it is necessary to compare the obtained F to a critical value of F. Table C.3 in Appendix C shows critical values of F for significance levels of .10, .05, and .01. To find the critical value of F, locate on the table the degrees of freedom for the numerator of the ratio (the systematic variance) and the degrees of freedom for the denominator of the F ratio (the error variance). The intersection of these two degrees of freedom on the table is the critical F value.

The appropriate degrees of freedom for our sample data are 2 and 12 (see Table B.5). The critical F value from Table C.3 is 3.89 for a .05 level of significance. For the results to be significant, the obtained F value must be equal to or greater than the critical value. Because the obtained value of F in Table B.5 (23.15) is greater than the critical value, we conclude that the results are significant and reject the null hypothesis that the means of the groups are equal in the population.

Concluding Remarks   The analysis of variance for one independent variable with an independent groups design can be used when there are two or more groups in the experiment. The calculations are the same whether participants are randomly assigned to condition or are grouped according to a participant variable (e.g., sex, low versus high self-esteem). The formulas are also applicable to cases in which the number of participants in each group is not equal (although you should try your best to have approximately equal numbers of participants in each group).

When the design of the experiment includes more than two levels of the independent variable (as in our example experiment, which had three groups), the obtained F value only tells us that there is a significant difference among means–but does not tell us whether any two specific groups are significantly different from one another. Follow-up tests are needed. One way to examine the difference between two groups in such a study is to adapt the formula for SS_A using only two of the groups (the df to use for the mean square would then be $2 - 1$). When calculating the F ratio in the final step, use MS_{ERROR} as the denominator. More complicated procedures for evaluating the difference between two groups in such designs are available, and easily calculated with statistical software.

Analysis of Variance: Two Independent Variables, Independent Groups Design

In this section, we will describe the computations for analysis of variance with a factorial design containing two independent variables (see Chapter 10). The formulas apply to an $A \times B$ factorial design with any number of levels of each independent variable. The formulas apply only to a completely independent groups design with different subjects in each group, and the number of subjects in each group must be equal. This analysis expands on the ANOVA for one independent variable we just explored, and can be adapted for use in more complicated designs (e.g., repeated measures or unequal numbers of participants across conditions). With these limitations in mind, let's consider example data from a hypothetical experiment.

The experiment uses a 2×2 IV $\times$ PV factorial design. Variable A is the type of instruction used in a course, and variable B is students' intelligence level. The students are classified as of either "low" or "high" intelligence on the basis of intelligence test scores and are randomly assigned to one of two types of classes. One class uses the traditional lecture method; the other class uses an individualized learning approach with frequent testing over small amounts of material, tutors to help individual students, and a requirement that students master each section of material before going on to the next section. The information presented to students in the two classes is identical. At the end of the course, all students take the same test, which covers all of the material presented in the course. The score on this examination is the dependent variable.

Table B.6 shows fictitious data for such an experiment, with five participants in each condition. This design allows us to evaluate three effects– the main effect of A, the main effect of B, and the $A \times B$ interaction (see Chapter 10). The main effect of A assesses whether one type of instruction is superior to the other; the main effect of B assesses whether high-intelligence students score differently on the test than do low-intelligence students; the $A \times B$ interaction examines whether the effect of one independent variable (e.g., instruction) is different depending on the particular level of the other variable (e.g., intelligence).

To compute the analysis of variance, begin by calculating the sum of squares for the following sources of variance in the data: SS_{TOTAL}, SS_A, SS_B, $SS_{A \times B}$, and SS_{ERROR}. The procedures for calculation are similar to the calculations performed for the analysis of variance with one independent variable. The numerical calculations for the example data are shown in Table B.7. Next, each formula is considered in turn.

SS_{TOTAL} The SS_{TOTAL} is computed in the same way as the previous analysis. The formula is

$$SS_{TOTAL} = \Sigma X^2 - \frac{G^2}{N}$$

where ΣX^2 is the sum of the squared scores of all subjects in the experiment, G is the grand total of all of the scores, and N is the total number of subjects. It is usually easiest to calculate ΣX^2 and G in smaller steps by calculating subtotals separately for each group in the design. The subtotals are then added. This is the procedure followed in Tables B.6 and B.7.

TABLE B.6   Data for hypothetical experiment on the effect of type of instruction and intelligence level on exam score: Analysis of variance

	Intelligence (B)		
	Low (B1)	High (B2)	
Traditional	75	90	
lecture (A1)	70	95	
	69	89	
	72	85	
	68	91	
	$T_{A1B1} = 354$	$T_{A1B2} = 450$	$T_{A1} = 804$
	$\Sigma \overline{X}^2_{A1B1} = 25094$	$\Sigma X^2_{A1B2} = 40552$	$n_{A1} = 10$
	$n_{A1B1} = 5$	$n_{A1B2} = 5$	$\overline{X}_{A1} = 80.40$
	$\overline{X}_{A1B1} = 70.80$	$\overline{X}_{A1B2} = 90.00$	
Individualized	85	87	
method (A2)	87	94	
	83	93	
	90	89	
	89	92	
	$T_{A2B1} = 434$	$T_{A2B2} = 455$	$T_{A2} = 889$
	$\Sigma X^2_{A2B1} = 37704$	$\Sigma X^2_{A2B2} = 41439$	$n_{A2} = 10$
	$n_{A2B1} = 5$	$n_{A2B2} = 5$	$\overline{X}_{A2} = 88.90$
	$\overline{X}_{A2B1} = 86.80$	$\overline{X}_{A2B2} = 91.00$	
	$T_{B1} = 788$	$T_{B2} = 905$	
	$n_{B1} = 10$	$n_{B2} = 10$	
	$\overline{X}_{B1} = 78.80$	$\overline{X}_{B2} = 90.50$	

TABLE B.7 Computations for analysis of variance with two independent variables

$$SS_{TOTAL} = \Sigma X^2 - \frac{G^2}{N}$$

$$= (25094 + 40552 + 37704 + 41439)$$
$$- \frac{(354 + 450 + 434 + 455)^2}{20}$$
$$= 144789 - 143312.45$$
$$= 1476.55$$

$$SS_A = \frac{\Sigma T_a^2}{n_a} - \frac{G^2}{N}$$

$$= \frac{(804)^2 + (889)^2}{10} - 143312.45$$
$$= 143673.70 - 143312.45$$
$$= 361.25$$

$$SS_B = \frac{\Sigma T_b^2}{n_b} - \frac{G^2}{N}$$

$$= \frac{(788)^2 + (905)^2}{10} - 143312.45$$
$$= 143996.90 - 143312.45$$
$$= 684.45$$

$$ss_{A \times B} = \frac{\Sigma T_{ab}^2}{n_{ab}} - \frac{G^2}{N} - SS_A - SS_B$$

$$= \frac{(354)^2 + (450)^2 + (434)^2 + (455)^2}{5}$$
$$- 143312.45 - 361.25 - 684.45$$
$$= 144639.40 - 143312.45 - 361.25 - 684.45$$
$$= 281.25$$

$$SS_{ERROR} = \Sigma X^2 - \frac{\Sigma T_{ab}^2}{n_{ab}}$$

$$= 144789 - 144639.40$$
$$= 149.60$$

SS_A The formula for SS_A is

$$ss_A = \frac{\Sigma T_a^2}{n_a} - \frac{G^2}{N}$$

where ΣT_a^2 is the sum of the squared totals of the scores in each of the groups of independent variable A, and n_a is the number of participants in each level of independent variable A. When calculating SS_A, the totals for each group of the A variable are obtained by considering all participants in that level of A, regardless of which condition of B the subject may be in. When we calculated SS_{TOTAL}, we already calculated G^2/N.

SS_B The formula for SS_B is

$$SS_B = \frac{\Sigma T_b^2}{n_b} - \frac{G_2}{N}$$

SS_B is calculated in the same way as SS_A. The only difference is that we are calculating group totals for independent variable B.

$SS_{A \times B}$ The formula for $SS_{A \times B}$ is

$$SS_{A \times B} = \frac{\Sigma T_{ab}^2}{n_{ab}} - \frac{G^2}{N} - SS_A - SS_B$$

The sum of squares for the $A \times B$ interaction is computed by first calculating the quantity ΣT_{ab}^2. This involves squaring the total of the scores in each of the ab conditions (*cells*) in the experiment. In our example experiment in Table B.6, there are four conditions; the interaction calculation considers all four of the groups. Each of the group totals is squared, and added together. This sum is divided by n_{ab}, the number of subjects in each group. The other quantities in the formula for $SS_{A \times B}$ have already been calculated, so the computation of $SS_{A \times B}$ is relatively straightforward.

SS_{ERROR} The quantities involved in the SS_{ERROR} formula have already been calculated. The formula is

$$SS_{ERROR} = \Sigma X^2 - \frac{\Sigma T_{ab}^2}{n_{ab}}$$

These quantities were calculated previously; perform the proper subtraction to complete the computation of SS_{ERROR}.

At this point, you may want to practise calculating the sums of squares using the data in Table B.6. To check the calculations, make sure that $SS_{TOTAL} = SS_A + SS_B + SS_{A \times B} + SS_{ERROR}$.

After obtaining the sums of squares, the next step is to find the mean square for each of the sources of variance. The easiest way to do this is to use an analysis of variance summary table like Table B.8.

TABLE B.8   Analysis of variance summary table: Two independent variables

Source of Variance	Sum of Squares	df	Mean Square	F
A	SS_A	$a - 1$	SS_A/df_A	MS_A/MS_{ERROR}
B	SS_B	$b - 1$	SS_B/df_B	MS_B/MS_{ERROR}
A × B	$SS_{A \times B}$	$(a - 1)(b - 1)$	$SS_{A \times B}/df_{A \times B}$	$MS_{A \times B}/MS_{ERROR}$
Error	SS_{ERROR}	$N - ab$	SS_{ERROR}/df_{ERROR}	
Total	SS_{TOTAL}			
A	361.25	1	361.25	38.64
B	684.45	1	684.45	73.20
A × B	281.25	1	281.25	30.08
Error	149.60	16	9.35	
Total	1476.55	19		

Mean Square The mean square for each of the sources of variance is the sum of squares divided by the degrees of freedom. The formulas for the degrees of freedom and the mean square are shown in the top portion of Table B.8, and the computed values are shown in the bottom portion of the table.

Obtaining the F Value The F value for each of the three sources of systematic variance (main effects for A and B, and the interaction) is obtained by dividing the appropriate mean square by the MS_{ERROR}. We now have three obtained F values and can evaluate the significance of each main effect and the interaction.

Significance of F To determine whether an obtained F is significant, we need to find the critical value of F from Table C.3 in Appendix C. For all of the Fs in the analysis of variance summary table, the degrees of freedom are 1 and 16. Let's assume that a .01 significance level for rejecting the null hypothesis was chosen. The critical F at .01 for 1 and 16 degrees of freedom is 8.53. If the obtained F is larger than 8.53, we can say that the results are significant at the .01 level. By referring to the obtained Fs in Table B.8, you can see that the main effects and the interaction are all significant. We will leave it to you to interpret the main effect means and to graph the interaction. Review Chapter 10 as needed.

Analysis of Variance: One Independent Variable, Repeated Measures Design

The analysis of variance computations considered thus far have been limited to independent groups designs. This section adapts these formulas for use in a repeated measures design with one independent variable.

Fictitious data for a hypothetical experiment using a repeated measures design are presented in Table B.9. The experiment examines the effect of a job candidate's physical attractiveness on judgments of the candidate's competence. The independent variable is the candidate's physical attractiveness; the dependent variable is judged competence on a 10-point scale. Participants in the experiment view two videotapes of different women performing a mechanical aptitude task that involved piecing together a number of parts. Both women do equally well, but one is physically attractive and the other is unattractive. The order of presentation of the two tapes is counterbalanced to assess order effects. For these analyses, assume order effects have already been ruled out.

The main difference between the repeated measures analysis of variance and the independent groups analysis described earlier is that the effect of participant (or *subject*) differences becomes a source of variance. There are four

TABLE B.9 Data for hypothetical experiment on attractiveness and judged competence: Repeated measures analysis of variance

Subjects (or subject pairs)	Condition (A)		T_s	T_s^2
	Unattractive candidate (A_1)	Attractive candidate (A_2)		
#1	6	8	14	196
#2	5	6	11	121
#3	5	9	14	196
#4	7	6	13	169
#5	4	6	10	100
#6	3	5	8	64
#7	5	5	10	100
#8	4	7	11	121
	$T_{A1} = 39$	$T_{A2} = 52$		$\Sigma T_s^2 = 1067$
	$\Sigma X_{A1}^2 = 201$	$\Sigma X_{A2}^2 = 352$		
	$\bar{X}_{A1} = 4.88$	$\bar{X}_{A2} = 6.50$		

$$SS_{TOTAL} = \Sigma X^2 - \frac{G^2}{N} = (201 + 352) - \frac{(39 + 52)^2}{16}$$
$$= 553 - 517.56$$
$$= 35.44$$

$$SS_A = \frac{\Sigma T_a^2}{n_a} - \frac{G^2}{N} = \frac{(39)^2 + (52)^2}{8} - 517.56$$
$$= 528.13 - 517.56$$
$$= 10.57$$

$$SS_{SUBJECTS} = \frac{\Sigma T_s^2}{n_s} - \frac{G^2}{N} = \frac{1067}{2} - 517.56$$
$$= 533.50 - 517.56$$
$$= 15.94$$

$$SS_{ERROR} = SS_{TOTAL} - SS_A - SS_{SUBJECTS} = 35.44 - 10.57 - 15.94$$
$$= 8.93$$

sources of variance in the repeated measures analysis of variance, and so four sums of squares are calculated:

$$SS_{TOTAL} = \Sigma X^2 - \frac{G^2}{N}$$

$$SS_A = \frac{\Sigma T_a^2}{n_a} - \frac{G^2}{N}$$

$$SS_{SUBJECTS} = \frac{\Sigma T_s^2}{n_s} - \frac{G^2}{N}$$

$$SS_{ERROR} = SS_{TOTAL} - SS_A - SS_{SUBJECTS}$$

The calculations for these sums of squares are shown in the lower portion of Table B.9. Refer to earlier calculations for reminders of how to calculate most quantities in these formulas. The only new quantity involves the calculation of $SS_{SUBJECTS}$. The term refers to the squared total score of each subject–that is, the squared total of the scores that each subject gives when measured in each of the different groups in the experiment. The quantity ΣT_s^2 refers to the sum of these squared totals for all subjects. The calculation of $SS_{SUBJECTS}$ is completed by dividing ΣT_s^2 by n_s and then subtracting by G^2/N. The term n_s refers to the number of scores that each subject gives. Because our hypothetical experiment has two conditions, $n_s = 2$, the total for each subject is based on two scores.

The repeated measures analysis of variance summary table is shown in Table B.10. The procedures for computing the mean squares and obtaining F are similar to our previous calculations. Note that the mean square and F for $SS_{SUBJECTS}$ are not computed. There is usually no reason to know or care whether subjects differ significantly from one another. The ability to calculate this source of variance does have the advantage of reducing the amount of error variance–in an independent groups design, subject differences are part of the error variance. Because there is only one score per subject in the independent groups design, it is impossible to estimate the influence of subject differences.

You can use the summary table and the table of critical F values to determine whether the difference between the two groups is significant. The procedures are identical to those discussed previously.

Analysis of Variance: Conclusion

The analysis of variance is a very useful test that can be extended to any type of factorial design, including those that use a combination of independent groups and repeated measures in the same design. The method of computing analysis of variance is much the same regardless of the complexity of the design. A section on analysis of variance as brief as this is not intended to

TABLE B.10 Analysis of variance summary table: Repeated measures design

Source of Variance	Sum of Squares	df	Mean Square	F
A	SS_A	$a - 1$	SS_A/df_A	MS_A/MS_{ERROR}
Subjects	$SS_{SUBJECTS}$	$s - 1$	—	
Error	SS_{ERROR}	$(a - 1)(s - 1)$	SS_{ERROR}/df_{ERROR}	
Total	SS_{TOTAL}	$N - 1$		
A	10.57	1	10.57	8.26
Subjects	15.94	7	—	
Error	8.93	7	1.28	
Total	35.44	15		

cover all of the many aspects of such a general statistical technique. However, you should now have the background to compute an analysis of variance and to understand the more detailed discussions of analysis of variance in advanced statistics texts.

EFFECT SIZE

In general, measures of effect size indicate the extent to which variables are associated. These are very important measures because they help assess the strength or amount of association across studies, and can be combined in *meta-analyses* (see Chapter 14) to determine overall patterns. Different effect size measures are appropriate for different data. See Grissom and Kim (2012) for a thorough discussion of various effect size measures.

Effect Size as Strength of Association

Correlation   Recall that correlation coefficients can be interpreted as effect sizes, because they indicate the magnitude of the relationship between two variables. These numbers range from 0.00, indicating no relationship, to 1.00; correlations above .50 are considered to be indicative of very strong relationships (Cohen, 1992). In much research, expect correlations between about .15 and .40. Correlations between about .10 and .20 are considered weak, but may be statistically significant with very large sample sizes. Typically, larger correlations are more useful. Nonetheless, weak correlations might be important for theoretical or practical reasons, depending on the context.

Cramer's V to Accompany Chi-Square Tests   In addition to determining whether there is a significant relationship using the chi-square (χ^2) test, an indicator of effect size tells you the strength of association between the variables. A common effect size indicator for nominal scale data is called Cramer's V (an adaptation of the *phi* coefficient; see Grissom & Kim, 2012). The V coefficient is computed after obtaining the value of chi-square. The formula is

$$V = \sqrt{\frac{\chi^2}{N(\kappa - 1)}}$$

In this formula, N is the total number of cases or subjects and κ is the smaller of the rows or columns in the table; thus, in our earlier example with three columns (hand dominance) and two rows (sex), the value of κ is 2, the lower value.

The value of V for the sex and hand dominance example in Table B.3 is

$$V = \sqrt{\frac{18}{100(2 - 1)}} = \sqrt{.18} = .42$$

Values of Cramer's V are interpreted as correlation coefficients. This result of .42 offers an estimate that in the population, hand dominance and sex would be moderately related (if these data weren't fictitious!).

Effect Size as Proportion of Variance Explained

Squared Correlation and Squared Multiple Correlation   Recall from Chapter 12 that we can square correlation coefficients (r) and multiple correlation coefficients (R). When squared, these values can be interpreted as a proportion of variance in one variable that is explained by the other (or by the combined set of predictors, as in the case of regression).

Omega Squared (ω^2) to Accompany ANOVA   After computing an analysis of variance and evaluating the significance of the F statistic, you need to examine effect size. One commonly used effect size measure is called *eta squared* (symbolized η^2). Although it can be easily interpreted like a correlation coefficient, this estimate is misleading unless the true population effect size is very large and the researcher has drawn a very large sample. A more robust alternative is called *omega squared* (symbolized ω^2). It can be adapted for use in independent groups designs with one independent variable, as well as to estimate the strength of main effects and interactions in factorial designs. The general formula is

$$\omega^2 = \frac{SS_{effect} - (df_{effect}MS_{error})}{SS_{Total} + MS_{error}}$$

In the 2×2 design described earlier, the effects of teaching method (Factor A) and student intelligence (Factor B) on test scores were investigated. We could use omega squared to estimate the effect size for the main effect of Factor A. We can extract the values we need from Table B.8: SS_A was 361.25, MS_{error} was 9.35, df_A was 1, and SS_{TOTAL} was 1479.55. The value of omega squared then would be

$$\omega^2 = \frac{361.25 - (1)(9.35)}{1476.55 + 9.35}$$

$$= .24$$

This result would indicate that 24 percent of the variance in final exam scores was explained by differences in the two teaching methods (again, if these data weren't fictitious!).

Effect Size as a Standardized Difference between Means

Recall from Chapter 12 that Cohen's d is the appropriate effect size measure when comparing two groups on a dependent variable. Cohen's d can be used to help interpret the nature of the effect, after a t test has evaluated whether two groups differ significantly on the dependent variable. This effect size measure results in a value interpreted in standard units. Calculate the value of Cohen's d using the means (M) and standard deviations (SD) of the two groups:

$$d = \frac{M_1 - M_2}{\sqrt{\dfrac{(SD_1^2 + SD_2^2)}{2}}}$$

Note that the formula uses M and SD instead of $\overline{X}$ and s. These abbreviations are used in APA style (see Appendix A). Try applying this formula to the (real!) data in Figure 13.5. You will see that the effect size estimating the relationship between viewing multitasking peers and lecture comprehension is very large ($d = 1.50$). In other words, sitting behind someone multitasking on a laptop during lectures decreases comprehension by an average of 1.5 standard deviations, compared to not sitting behind such a multitasker (see Sana et al., 2013).

Appendix C

Statistical Tables

TABLE C.I Critical values of chi-square

Degrees of Freedom	Probability Level		
	.10	.05	.01
1	2.706	3.841	6.635
2	4.605	5.991	9.210
3	6.251	7.815	11.345
4	7.779	9.488	13.277
5	9.236	11.070	15.086
6	10.645	12.592	16.812
7	12.017	14.067	18.475
8	13.362	15.507	20.090
9	14.684	16.919	21.666
10	15.987	18.307	23.209
11	17.275	19.675	24.725
12	18.549	21.026	26.217
13	19.812	22.362	27.688
14	21.064	23.685	29.141
15	22.307	24.996	30.578
16	23.542	26.296	32.000
17	24.769	27.587	33.409
18	25.989	28.869	34.805
19	27.204	30.144	36.191
20	28.412	31.410	37.566

Source: Table adapted from Fisher and Yates, *Statistical Tables for Biological, Agricultural, and Medical Research* (1963, 6th ed.), London: Longman. Reprinted by permission.

TABLE C.2   Critical values of *t*

df	.05 / .10	.025 / .05	.01 / .02	.005 / .01

	Significance Level[a]				one-tailed test
	.05	.025	.01	.005	one-tailed test
df	.10	.05	.02	.01	two-tailed test
1	6.314	12.706	31.821	63.657	
2	2.920	4.303	6.965	9.925	
3	2.353	3.182	4.541	5.841	
4	2.132	2.776	3.747	4.604	
5	2.015	2.571	3.365	4.032	
6	1.943	2.447	3.143	3.707	
7	1.895	2.365	2.998	3.499	
8	1.860	2.306	2.896	3.355	
9	1.833	2.262	2.821	3.250	
10	1.812	2.228	2.764	3.169	
11	1.796	2.201	2.718	3.106	
12	1.782	2.179	2.681	3.055	
13	1.771	2.160	2.650	3.012	
14	1.761	2.145	2.624	2.977	
15	1.753	2.131	2.602	2.947	
16	1.746	2.120	2.583	2.921	
17	1.740	2.110	2.567	2.898	
18	1.734	2.101	2.552	2.878	
19	1.729	2.093	2.539	2.861	
20	1.725	2.086	2.528	2.845	
21	1.721	2.080	2.518	2.831	
22	1.717	2.074	2.508	2.819	
23	1.714	2.069	2.500	2.807	
24	1.711	2.064	2.492	2.797	
25	1.708	2.060	2.485	2.787	
26	1.706	2.056	2.479	2.779	
27	1.703	2.052	2.473	2.771	
28	1.701	2.048	2.467	2.763	
29	1.699	2.045	2.462	2.756	
30	1.697	2.042	2.457	2.750	
40	1.684	2.021	2.423	2.704	
60	1.671	2.000	2.390	2.660	
120	1.658	1.980	2.358	2.617	
∞	1.645	1.960	2.326	2.576	

[a] Use the top significance level when you have predicted a specific directional difference (a one-tailed test; e.g., Group 1 will be greater than Group 2). Use the bottom significance level when you have predicted only that Group 1 will differ from Group 2 without specifying the direction of the difference (a two-tailed test).

TABLE C.3   Critical values of *F*

df for Denominator (Error)	α	*df* for Numerator (Systematic)											
		1	2	3	4	5	6	7	8	9	10	11	12
1	.10	39.9	49.5	53.6	55.8	57.2	58.2	58.9	59.4	59.9	60.2	60.5	60.7
	.05	161	200	216	225	230	234	237	239	241	242	243	244
	.01	4052	4999	5404	5624	5764	5859	5928	5981	6022	6056	6083	6107
2	.10	8.53	9.00	9.16	9.24	9.29	9.33	9.35	9.37	9.38	9.39	9.40	9.41
	.05	18.5	19.0	19.2	19.2	19.3	19.3	19.4	19.4	19.4	19.4	19.4	19.4
	.01	98.5	99.0	99.2	99.2	99.3	99.3	99.4	99.4	99.4	99.4	99.4	99.4
3	.10	5.54	5.46	5.39	5.34	5.31	5.28	5.27	5.25	5.24	5.23	5.22	5.22
	.05	10.1	9.55	9.28	9.12	9.01	8.94	8.89	8.85	8.81	8.79	8.76	8.74
	.01	34.1	30.8	29.5	28.7	28.2	27.9	27.7	27.5	27.3	27.2	27.1	27.1
4	.10	4.54	4.32	4.19	4.11	4.05	4.01	3.98	3.95	3.94	3.92	3.91	3.90
	.05	7.71	6.94	6.59	6.39	6.26	6.16	6.09	6.04	6.00	5.96	5.94	5.91
	.01	21.2	18.0	16.7	16.0	15.5	15.2	15.0	14.8	14.7	14.5	14.4	14.4
5	.10	4.06	3.78	3.62	3.52	3.45	3.40	3.37	3.34	3.32	3.30	3.28	3.27
	.05	6.61	5.79	5.41	5.19	5.05	4.95	4.88	4.82	4.77	4.74	4.71	4.68
	.01	16.3	13.3	12.1	11.4	11.0	10.7	10.5	10.3	10.2	10.1	9.96	9.89
6	.10	3.78	3.46	3.29	3.18	3.11	3.05	3.01	2.98	2.96	2.94	2.92	2.90
	.05	5.99	5.14	4.76	4.53	4.39	4.28	4.21	4.15	4.10	4.06	4.03	4.00
	.01	13.7	10.9	9.78	9.15	8.75	8.47	8.26	8.10	7.98	7.87	7.79	7.72
7	.10	3.59	3.26	3.07	2.96	2.88	2.83	2.78	2.75	2.72	2.70	2.68	2.67
	.05	5.59	4.74	4.35	4.12	3.97	3.87	3.79	3.73	3.68	3.64	3.60	3.57
	.01	12.2	9.55	8.45	7.85	7.46	7.19	6.99	6.84	6.72	6.62	6.54	6.47
8	.10	3.46	3.11	2.92	2.81	2.73	2.67	2.62	2.59	2.56	2.54	2.52	2.50
	.05	5.32	4.46	4.07	3.84	3.69	3.58	3.50	3.44	3.39	3.35	3.31	3.28
	.01	11.3	8.65	7.59	7.01	6.63	6.37	6.18	6.03	5.91	5.81	5.73	5.67
9	.10	3.36	3.01	2.81	2.69	2.61	2.55	2.51	2.47	2.44	2.42	2.40	2.38
	.05	5.12	4.26	3.86	3.63	3.48	3.37	3.29	3.23	3.18	3.14	3.10	3.07
	.01	10.6	8.02	6.99	6.42	6.06	5.80	5.61	5.47	5.35	5.26	5.18	5.11
10	.10	3.29	2.92	2.73	2.61	2.52	2.46	2.41	2.38	2.35	2.32	2.30	2.28
	.05	4.96	4.10	3.71	3.48	3.33	3.22	3.14	3.07	3.02	2.98	2.94	2.91
	.01	10.0	7.56	6.55	5.99	5.64	5.39	5.20	5.06	4.94	4.85	4.77	4.71

(continued)

TABLE C.3   (continued)

df for Denominator (Error)	α	\multicolumn{12}{c}{df for Numerator (Systematic)}											
		1	2	3	4	5	6	7	8	9	10	11	12
11	.10	3.23	2.86	2.66	2.54	2.45	2.39	2.34	2.30	2.27	2.25	2.23	2.21
	.05	4.84	3.98	3.59	3.36	3.20	3.09	3.01	2.95	2.90	2.85	2.82	2.79
	.01	9.65	7.21	6.22	5.67	5.32	5.07	4.89	4.74	4.63	4.54	4.46	4.40
12	.10	3.18	2.81	2.61	2.48	2.39	2.33	2.28	2.24	2.21	2.19	2.17	2.15
	.05	4.75	3.89	3.49	3.26	3.11	3.00	2.91	2.85	2.80	2.75	2.72	2.69
	.01	9.33	6.93	5.95	5.41	5.06	4.82	4.64	4.50	4.39	4.30	4.22	4.16
13	.10	3.14	2.76	2.56	2.43	2.35	2.28	2.23	2.20	2.16	2.14	2.12	2.10
	.05	4.67	3.81	3.41	3.18	3.03	2.92	2.83	2.77	2.71	2.67	2.63	2.60
	.01	9.07	6.70	5.74	5.21	4.86	4.62	4.44	4.30	4.19	4.10	4.02	3.96
14	.10	3.10	2.73	2.52	2.39	2.31	2.24	2.19	2.15	2.12	2.10	2.08	2.05
	.05	4.60	3.74	3.34	3.11	2.96	2.85	2.76	2.70	2.65	2.60	2.57	2.53
	.01	8.86	6.51	5.56	5.04	4.69	4.46	4.28	4.14	4.03	3.94	3.86	3.80
15	.10	3.07	2.70	2.49	2.36	2.27	2.21	2.16	2.12	2.09	2.06	2.04	2.02
	.05	4.54	3.68	3.29	3.06	2.90	2.79	2.71	2.64	2.59	2.54	2.51	2.48
	.01	8.68	6.36	5.42	4.89	4.56	4.32	4.14	4.00	3.89	3.80	3.73	3.67
16	.10	3.05	2.67	2.46	2.33	2.24	2.18	2.13	2.09	2.06	2.03	2.01	1.99
	.05	4.49	3.63	3.24	3.01	2.85	2.74	2.66	2.59	2.54	2.49	2.46	2.42
	.01	8.53	6.23	5.29	4.77	4.44	4.20	4.03	3.89	3.78	3.69	3.62	3.55
17	.10	3.03	2.64	2.44	2.31	2.22	2.15	2.10	2.06	2.03	2.00	1.98	1.96
	.05	4.45	3.59	3.20	2.96	2.81	2.70	2.61	2.55	2.49	2.45	2.41	2.38
	.01	8.40	6.11	5.18	4.67	4.34	4.10	3.93	3.79	3.68	3.59	3.52	3.46
18	.10	3.01	2.62	2.42	2.29	2.20	2.13	2.08	2.04	2.00	1.98	1.96	1.93
	.05	4.41	3.55	3.16	2.93	2.77	2.66	2.58	2.51	2.46	2.41	2.37	2.34
	.01	8.29	6.01	5.09	4.58	4.25	4.01	3.84	3.71	3.60	3.51	3.43	3.37
19	.10	2.99	2.61	2.40	2.27	2.18	2.11	2.06	2.02	1.98	1.96	1.94	1.91
	.05	4.38	3.52	3.13	2.90	2.74	2.63	2.54	2.48	2.42	2.38	2.34	2.31
	.01	8.18	5.93	5.01	4.50	4.17	3.94	3.77	3.63	3.52	3.43	3.36	3.30
20	.10	2.97	2.59	2.38	2.25	2.16	2.09	2.04	2.00	1.96	1.94	1.92	1.89
	.05	4.35	3.49	3.10	2.87	2.71	2.60	2.51	2.45	2.39	2.35	2.31	2.28
	.01	8.10	5.85	4.94	4.43	4.10	3.87	3.70	3.56	3.46	3.37	3.29	3.23

TABLE C.3 (continued)

df for Denominator (Error)	α	1	2	3	4	5	6	7	8	9	10	11	12
		\multicolumn{12}{c}{*df* for Numerator (Systematic)}											
22	.10	2.95	2.56	2.35	2.22	2.13	2.06	2.01	1.97	1.93	1.90	1.88	1.86
	.05	4.30	3.44	3.05	2.82	2.66	2.55	2.46	2.40	2.34	2.30	2.26	2.23
	.01	7.95	5.72	4.82	4.31	3.99	3.76	3.59	3.45	3.35	3.26	3.18	3.12
24	.10	2.93	2.54	2.33	2.19	2.10	2.04	1.98	1.94	1.91	1.88	1.85	1.83
	.05	4.26	3.40	3.01	2.78	2.62	2.51	2.42	2.36	2.30	2.25	2.21	2.18
	.01	7.82	5.61	4.72	4.22	3.90	3.67	3.50	3.36	3.26	3.17	3.09	3.03
26	.10	2.91	2.52	2.31	2.17	2.08	2.01	1.96	1.92	1.88	1.86	1.84	1.81
	.05	4.23	3.37	2.98	2.74	2.59	2.47	2.39	2.32	2.27	2.22	2.18	2.15
	.01	7.72	5.53	4.64	4.14	3.82	3.59	3.42	3.29	3.18	3.09	3.02	2.96
28	.10	2.89	2.50	2.29	2.16	2.06	2.00	1.94	1.90	1.87	1.84	1.81	1.79
	.05	4.20	3.34	2.95	2.71	2.56	2.45	2.36	2.29	2.24	2.19	2.15	2.12
	.01	7.64	5.45	4.57	4.07	3.75	3.53	3.36	3.23	3.12	3.03	2.96	2.90
30	.10	2.88	2.49	2.28	2.14	2.05	1.98	1.93	1.88	1.85	1.82	1.79	1.77
	.05	4.17	3.32	2.92	2.69	2.53	2.42	2.33	2.27	2.21	2.16	2.13	2.09
	.01	7.56	5.39	4.51	4.02	3.70	3.47	3.30	3.17	3.07	2.98	2.91	2.84
40	.10	2.84	2.44	2.23	2.09	2.00	1.93	1.87	1.83	1.79	1.76	1.73	1.71
	.05	4.08	3.23	2.84	2.61	2.45	2.34	2.25	2.18	2.12	2.08	2.04	2.00
	.01	7.31	5.18	4.31	3.83	3.51	3.29	3.12	2.99	2.89	2.80	2.73	2.66
60	.10	2.79	2.39	2.18	2.04	1.95	1.87	1.82	1.77	1.74	1.71	1.68	1.66
	.05	4.00	3.15	2.76	2.53	2.37	2.25	2.17	2.10	2.04	1.99	1.95	1.92
	.01	7.08	4.98	4.13	3.65	3.34	3.12	2.95	2.82	2.72	2.63	2.56	2.50
120	.10	2.75	2.35	2.13	1.99	1.90	1.82	1.77	1.72	1.68	1.65	1.62	1.60
	.05	3.92	3.07	2.68	2.45	2.29	2.17	2.09	2.02	1.96	1.91	1.87	1.83
	.01	6.85	4.79	3.95	3.48	3.17	2.96	2.79	2.66	2.56	2.47	2.40	2.34
200	.10	2.73	2.33	2.11	1.97	1.88	1.80	1.75	1.70	1.66	1.63	1.60	1.57
	.05	3.89	3.04	2.65	2.42	2.26	2.14	2.06	1.98	1.93	1.88	1.84	1.80
	.01	6.76	4.71	3.88	3.41	3.11	2.89	2.73	2.60	2.50	2.41	2.34	2.27
∞	.10	2.71	2.30	2.08	1.94	1.85	1.77	1.72	1.67	1.63	1.60	1.57	1.55
	.05	3.84	3.00	2.60	2.37	2.21	2.10	2.01	1.94	1.88	1.83	1.79	1.75
	.01	6.63	4.61	3.78	3.32	3.02	2.80	2.64	2.51	2.41	2.32	2.25	2.18

TABLE C.4   Critical values of r (Pearson product–moment correlation coefficient)

	Level of Significance for Two-Tailed Test[a]		
df	.10	.05	.01
1	.988	.997	.9999
2	.900	.950	.990
3	.805	.878	.959
4	.729	.811	.917
5	.669	.754	.874
6	.622	.707	.834
7	.582	.666	.798
8	.549	.632	.765
9	.521	.602	.735
10	.497	.576	.708
11	.476	.553	.684
12	.458	.532	.661
13	.441	.514	.641
14	.426	.497	.623
15	.412	.482	.606
16	.400	.468	.590
17	.389	.456	.575
18	.378	.444	.561
19	.369	.433	.549
20	.360	.423	.537
25	.323	.381	.487
30	.296	.349	.449
35	.275	.325	.418
40	.257	.304	.393
45	.243	.288	.372
50	.231	.273	.354
60	.211	.250	.325
70	.195	.232	.303
80	.183	.217	.283
90	.173	.205	.267
100	.164	.195	.254

[a]The significance level is halved for a one-tailed test.

Appendix D

How to Conduct a *PsycINFO* Search

As discussed in Chapter 2, *PsycINFO* is a database that allows you to find peer-reviewed journal articles in psychology and related disciplines. This appendix offers tips and strategies for using *PsycINFO* to find articles effectively.

THE USER SCREEN

The exact "look and feel" of the website you will use to search *PsycINFO* will depend on your institution's arrangements. Figure D.1 provides an example of a display; your *PsycINFO* screen will have its own appearance.

> *Try it out!* The best way to learn how to conduct a search is to actually conduct a search! Go to your institution's library website and find the *PsycINFO* database, keeping in mind that you might need to log in or use a virtual private network if you are off campus. Follow along with the search below to learn how to use *PsycINFO* to find psychological research.

FIGURE D.I
Example of a *PsycINFO* user screen

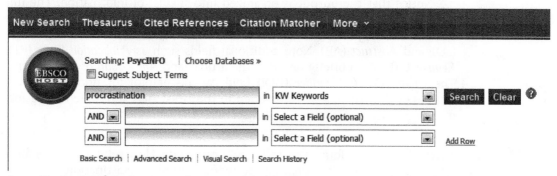

Source: The *PsycINFO*® database screen shots are reproduced with permission of the American Psychological Association, publisher of the *PsycINFO* database, all rights reserved. No further reproduction or distribution is permitted without written permission from the American Psychological Association.

SPECIFYING SEARCH TERMS AND FINDING RESULTS

Your most important task is to specify the search terms you want *PsycINFO* to use. These are typed into an input box. In most simple searches, such as the one shown in Figure D.1, you have some other options. For example, you can limit your search to articles that have a specific word or phrase in the title.

How do you know what terms to use? Most commonly, you will want to use standard psychological terms. Identifying the term that will yield results you are seeking may take many tries. To help you, consult the *Thesaurus of Psychological Index Terms*. This thesaurus lists all the standard terms that are used to index the abstracts, and it can be accessed directly within most *PsycINFO* systems. Also, your institution's subject librarian might be able to help you generate the best terms.

Suppose you are interested in the topic of procrastination. Entering *procrastination* into the *Thesaurus of Psychological Index Terms* reveals that *motivation* is a broader term that could be relevant to your search too. If you click on *motivation*, you will see many related terms, including *achievement motivation*, *temptation*, and *procrastination*. Let's assume that you are using a standard search window as in Figure D.1. Give the command to start the search for *procrastination*, and the results will be displayed.

Below, we have included some of the output of one of the articles found with a search on *procrastination*. The exact appearance of your output will depend on the computer system you are using as well as the information that you choose to display. The default output includes citation information along with the abstract itself. Some of the extra information shows how information is organized in the database (e.g., the numbers in the "population" section are codes). When you do the search, some fields will appear as hyperlinks to lead you to other information in your library database or to other websites. Systems are continually being upgraded to enable users to more easily obtain full-text access to the articles and find other articles on similar topics.

Notice that the output is organized into "fields" of information. The full name of each field is included here; many systems allow abbreviations. You will almost always want to see the *Title* (abbreviated as TI), *Author* (AU), *Source* (SO), and *Abstract* (AB). Note additional fields such as *Publication Type* (PT), *Keywords* (KW) to briefly describe the article, and *Age Group* of participants. The *Digital Object Identifier* (DOI) field can be helpful for finding full-text sources of the article, and is included in the latest APA style referencing format mentioned in Chapter 2 and Appendix A.

Title:	I forgive myself, now I can study: How self-forgiveness for procrastinating can reduce future procrastination.
Author(s):	Wohl, Michael J. A., Carleton University, Department of Psychology, Ottawa, ON, Canada

Pychyl, Timothy A., Carleton University, Department of Psychology, Ottawa, ON, Canada

Bennett, Shannon H., Carleton University, Department of Psychology, Ottawa, ON, Canada

Address: Wohl, Michael J. A., Carleton University, Department of Psychology, 1125 Colonel By Drive, B550 Loeb Building, Ottawa, ON, Canada, K1S 5B6

Source: Personality and Individual Differences, Vol 48(7), May, 2010. pp. 803–808.

Publisher: Netherlands: Elsevier Science.

Digital Object Identifier: 10.1016/j.paid.2010.01.029

Language: English

Keywords: self-forgiveness; procrastination; university students; psychology education

Abstract: In the present study, we examined the association between forgiving the self for a specific instance of procrastination and procrastination on that same task in the future. A sample of 119 first-year University students (49 male, 70 female) completed measures of procrastination and self-forgiveness immediately before each of two midterm examinations in their introductory psychology course. Results revealed that among students who reported high levels of self-forgiveness for procrastinating on studying for the first examination, procrastination on preparing for the subsequent examination was reduced. This relationship was mediated by negative affect, such that increased self-forgiveness reduced procrastination by decreasing negative affect. Results are discussed in relation to the impact of procrastination on self-directed negative affect. (PsycINFO Database Record (c) 2010 APA, all rights reserved)

Subjects: °Forgiveness; °Procrastination; College Students; Psychology Education

Classification: Personality Traits & Processes (3120)

Population: Human (10)
Male (30)
Female (40)

Location: Canada

Age Group: Adulthood (18 yrs & older) (300)

Methodology: Empirical Study; Quantitative Study

Publication
Type: Journal, Peer Reviewed Journal
Number of Citations
in Source: 32
Database: PsycINFO

COMBINING SEARCH TERMS AND NARROWING RESULTS

When you do a simple search with a single word or a phrase such as *procrastination*, the default search yields articles that have that word or phrase anywhere in any of the fields listed. This strategy can produce too many articles, including articles that are not directly relevant to your interests. One way to narrow the search is to limit it to certain fields. The simple search screen (see Figure D.1) may allow you to limit the search to one field, such as the title of the article. For example, you could specify *procrastination in TI* to limit your search to articles that have the term in the title of the article. Also note that there is often a "Set Limits" option within *PsycINFO*. This allows you to easily specify that the search should find only peer-reviewed journal articles (not books or doctoral dissertations) or include participants from certain age groups.

Most *PsycINFO* systems have advanced search functions that enable you to use the Boolean operators AND and OR and NOT. These can be typed as discussed below, but the advanced search screen uses prompts to help you design the search. Suppose you want to restrict the *procrastination in KEYWORD* search to students only. You can do this by asking for *(procrastination in KW) AND (students)*, all in the same search box, or in different search boxes if they appear. The AND forces both conditions to be true for an article to be included. The parentheses are used to separate different parts of your search specification and are useful when your searches become increasingly complicated. They could have been left out of this search but are included here for illustration.

The OR operation is used to expand a search that is too narrow. Suppose you want to find journal articles that discuss romantic relationships on the Internet. The last time we checked, a quick search for *Internet AND romance* resulted in 146 citations; when you select "limit to scholarly (peer reviewed) journals" that number dropped to 86 peer-reviewed articles. Changing the specification to *Internet AND (romance OR dating OR love)* yielded 346 peer-reviewed journal articles. Articles that have the term *Internet* as well as *any* of the other terms specified were included in the second search.

The NOT operation will exclude abstracts based on a criterion you specify, and is useful when you anticipate that the search criteria will be met by some irrelevant abstracts. In the Internet example, it is possible that the search will include articles on child predators. To exclude the term *child* from the search results, the following adjustment can be made: *Internet AND (romance*

TABLE D.I   Some *PsycINFO* search strategies

Strategy 1:	Use fields such as TI and AU.
	Example: [(divorce) in TI] requires that a term appear in the title.
Strategy 2:	Use AND to limit search.
	Example: [divorce AND child] requires both terms to be included.
Strategy 3:	Use OR to expand search.
	Example: [divorce OR breakup] includes both terms.
Strategy 4:	Use NOT to exclude search terms.
	Example: [shyness NOT therapy] excludes any shyness articles that have the term therapy.
Strategy 5:	Use the wildcard asterisk (°).
	Example: [child°] finds any word that begins with child (children, childhood, etc.).

OR dating OR love) NOT child. This search resulted in 318 abstracts instead of the 346 obtained previously.

Another helpful search tool is the wildcard asterisk (°). The asterisk stands for any set of letters in a word and so it can expand your search. Consider the word *romance* in the search above–by using *roman°*, the search will expand to include both *romance* and *romantic*. The wildcard can be very useful with the term *child°* to find *child, children, childhood,* and so on. You have to be careful when doing this, however; the *roman°* search would also find *Romania* and *romanticism*. In this case, it might be more efficient to simply add *OR romantic* to the search. These search strategies are summarized in Table D.1.

Give careful thought to your search terms. Consider the case of a student who decided to do a paper on the topic of "road rage." She wanted to know what might cause drivers to become so angry at other drivers that they will become physically aggressive. A search on the term *road rage* led to a number of interesting articles. However, when looking at the results from the search she noticed that the major keywords (KW) included *driving behaviour* and *anger* but not *road rage*. When she asked about this, we realized that she had found only articles that included the term *road rage* in the title or abstract. This term has become popular but it may not be used in all scientific studies of the topic. She then expanded the search to include *driving AND anger* and also *dangerous driving*. The new search yielded many articles not found in the original search.

SAVING RESULTS

When you complete your search, you can e-mail the results, save them to a flash drive, or upload them to a reference manager (e.g., Zotero, RefWorks, or

EndNote). When you save, you can often choose which of the fields to display. Some systems and reference managers allow you to print, copy, or save results in different formats, including APA style. Carefully note all the options available to you. When relying on automatically generated APA style references, be sure to double-check them.

Finding just the right articles can take time. Practise using the strategies in this appendix as well as other tips in Chapter 2, and over time your searches will become more efficient.

Appendix E

Constructing a Latin Square

Use a Latin square to determine order controls for most order effects without having to include all possible orders. A Latin square to determine the orders of any N number of conditions will have N arrangements of orders in a repeated measures design (see Chapter 8). Thus, if there are four conditions, there will be four orders in a 4×4 Latin square; eight conditions will produce an 8×8 Latin square. The method for constructing a Latin square shown below will produce orders in which (1) each condition or group appears once at each order and (2) each condition precedes and follows every other condition one time.

Imagine you have been hired by a new company to design its website. You design a repeated measures study to investigate the effect of different font types on ease of reading on a computer screen. Your four conditions are as follows: Times New Roman, Calibri, Arial, and Lucida Handwriting. A Latin square for these four conditions is shown in Figure E.1. Each row in the square is one of the orders of the conditions (the conditions are labelled A, B, C, and D).

FIGURE E.I   A Latin square with four conditions

	Order of Conditions			
	1	**2**	**3**	**4**
Row 1	A (Times New Roman)	B (Calibri)	D (Lucida Handwriting)	C (Arial)
Row 2	B (Calibri)	C (Arial)	A (Times New Roman)	D (Lucida Handwriting)
Row 3	C (Arial)	D (Lucida Handwriting)	B (Calibri)	A (Times New Roman)
Row 4	D (Lucida Handwriting)	A (Times New Roman)	C (Arial)	B (Calibri)

Note: The four conditions were randomly given the letter designations. A = Times New Roman, B = Calibri, C = Arial, and D = Lucida Handwriting. Each row represents a different order of running the conditions.

Use the following procedures for generating a Latin square when there is an even number of conditions:

1. Determine the number of conditions. Use letters of the alphabet to represent your N conditions: ABCD for four conditions, ABCDEF for six conditions, and so on.

2. Determine the order for the first row, using the following ordering:

$$A, B, L, C, L - 1, D, L - 2, E$$

and so on. L stands for the last or final treatment. Thus, if you have four conditions (ABCD), your order will be

$$A, B, D, C$$

With six conditions (ABCDEF), the order will be

$$A, B, F, C, E, D$$

because F is the final treatment (L), and E is the next to final treatment ($L - 1$).

3. Determine the order for the second row by increasing one letter at each position of the first row. The last letter cannot be increased, of course, so it reverts to the first letter. With six conditions, the order of the second row becomes

$$B, C, A, D, F, E$$

4. Continue this procedure for the third and subsequent rows. For the third row, increase one letter at each position of the second row:

$$C, D, B, E, A, F$$

The final 6 × 6 Latin square will be

$$
\begin{array}{cccccc}
A & B & F & C & E & D \\
B & C & A & D & F & E \\
C & D & B & E & A & F \\
D & E & C & F & B & A \\
E & F & D & A & C & B \\
F & A & E & B & D & C \\
\end{array}
$$

5. Randomly assign each of your conditions to one of the letters to determine which condition will be in the A position, the B position, and so on.

If you have an odd number of conditions, you must make two Latin squares. For the first square, simply follow the procedures we have shown. Now create a second square that reverses the first one; that is, in each row, the first condition becomes the last, the second condition is next to last, and so on. Join the two squares together to create the final Latin square (actually a rectangle!). Thus, if there are five conditions, you will have ten possible orders to run in your study.

When you conduct your study using the Latin square to determine order, you need at least one participant per row. Usually, you will have two or more participants per row; the number of participants run in each order must be equal.

Glossary

abstract   The section of a research report that summarizes the entire study.

alpha level   In a statistical analysis, the maximum probability that a result–having been declared significant by exceeding this value–has actually come from the null hypothesis sampling distribution. It is usually set at .05.

alternative explanation   Part of causal inference; a potential alternative cause of an observed relationship between variables.

analysis of variance (ANOVA)   *See F test.*

anonymous   In research, data are anonymous when, once collected, a researcher is completely unable to identify the participant who provided the data.

applied research   Research conducted to address practical problems and potential solutions.

archival research   The use of existing sources of information for research. Sources include statistical records, survey archives, and written records.

authority   As an alternative to the scientific method of acquiring knowledge, accepting anything learned from supposed authority figures (e.g., news media, books, government officials, or religious figures).

bar graph   Using bars to depict frequencies of responses, percentages, or means in two or more groups.

baseline   In a single case design, the participant's behaviour during a control period before introduction of the manipulation.

basic research   Research that attempts to answer fundamental questions about the nature of behaviour.

behavioural measure   An operational definition that involves directly observing and precisely recording a human's or animal's behaviour.

Canadian Council on Animal Care (CCAC)   A Canadian organization responsible for setting standards for the ethical treatment of animals in research and ensuring that they are upheld.

case study   A descriptive account of the behaviour, past history, and other relevant factors concerning a specific individual.

ceiling effect   The failure of a measure to detect a difference because it was too easy (*also see* floor effect).

cell   A term sometimes used to refer to one condition in an experiment, or to a combination of conditions in a complex factorial experimental design.

central tendency   A single number or value that describes the typical or central score among a set of scores.

citations   Names and dates that appear in the body of a text in order to accurately attribute ideas and results to the authors cited rather than the current paper's author. Refers reader to the corresponding entry in the *References* section for full source information.

closed-ended questions   Questions that offer respondents limited options. A multiple choice question is an example.

cluster sampling   A method of sampling in which clusters of individuals are identified. Clusters are sampled, and then all individuals in each cluster are included in the sample.

coding system   A set of rules used to categorize observations.

Cohen's *d*   A standardized calculation of effect size that is appropriate for two-group experimental designs.

cohort effects   A cohort is a group of people born at about the same time and exposed to the same societal events; cohort effects are confounded with age in a cross-sectional study.

concealed observation   A type of naturalistic observation in which the researcher assumes a participant role in the setting he or she is researching, but conceals the purpose of the research.

conceptual replication   Replication of research using different procedures for manipulating or measuring the variables.

concern for welfare   Principle that research should have beneficial effects while minimizing any harmful effects.

conclusion validity   The extent to which the conclusions about the relationships among variables reached on the basis of the data are correct.

concurrent validity   The construct validity of a measure is assessed by examining whether groups of people differ on the measure in expected ways.

confederate   A person posing as a participant in an experiment who is actually part of the experiment.

confidence interval   An interval of values that will capture the true population value a certain proportion of times (e.g., 95 percent) that the confidence interval is calculated in that way.

confidential   Principle that information is kept private; disclosure is limited only to the minimum number of people necessary.

confounding variables   An uncontrolled variable that is impossible to separate from a variable of interest. In an experiment, the experimental groups differ on both the independent variable and the confounding variable, making conclusions about the effect of the independent variable on the dependent variable impossible.

construct validity   The degree to which a measurement device accurately measures the theoretical construct it is designed to measure.

content analysis   Systematic analysis of the content of written records.

content validity   An indicator of the construct validity of a measure in which the content of the measure is compared to the universe of content that defines the construct.

contrast effect   In a repeated measures design, occurs when participants' responses in a later condition are affected by a particular experience they had in an earlier condition.

control series design   An extension of the interrupted time series quasi-experimental design in which there is a comparison or control group.

convenience sampling   Selecting participants in a haphazard manner, usually on the basis of availability, and not with regard to having a representative sample of the population; a type of non-probability sampling. Also called *haphazard sampling*.

convergent validity   The construct validity of a measure is assessed by examining the extent to which scores on the measure are related to scores on other measures of the same construct or similar constructs.

correlation coefficient   An index of how strongly two variables are related to each other.

counterbalancing   A method of controlling for order effects in a repeated measures design by either including all orders of treatment presentation or randomly determining the order for each participant.

covariation of cause and effect   Part of causal inference; observing that a change in one variable is accompanied by a change in a second variable.

criterion variable   The outcome variable that is being predicted in a multiple regression analysis.

Cronbach's alpha   An indicator of internal consistency reliability assessed by examining the average correlation of each item (question) in a measure with every other question.

cross-sectional method   A developmental research method in which persons of different ages are studied at only one point in time; conceptually similar to an independent groups design.

curvilinear relationship A relationship in which increases in the values of the first variable are accompanied by both increases and decreases in the values of the second variable.

debriefing Explanation of the purposes of the research that is given to participants following their participation in the research.

deception Any time a researcher misleads participants into believing something about the study that is not true.

degrees of freedom (*df*) A concept used in tests of statistical significance; the number of observations that are free to vary to produce a known outcome.

demand characteristics Cues that inform the participant how he or she is expected to behave.

dependent variable The variable that is the participant's response to, and dependent on, the level of the manipulated independent variable.

descriptive statistics Statistical measures that describe the results of a study; descriptive statistics include measures of central tendency (e.g., mean), variability (e.g., standard deviation), and correlation (e.g., Pearson *r*).

direct replication Replication of research using the same procedures for manipulating and measuring the variables that were used in the original research.

discriminant validity The construct validity of a measure is assessed by examining the extent to which scores on the measure are not related to scores on conceptually unrelated measures.

discussion The section of a research report in which the researcher considers the research results from various perspectives.

double-blind procedure An experiment in which neither the experimenter nor the participant knows to which condition the participant has been assigned.

effect size The extent to which two variables are associated; in experimental research, the magnitude of the impact of the independent variable on the dependent variable.

empiricism Use of objective observations to answer a question about the nature of behaviour.

error variance Random variability in a set of scores that is not the result of the independent variable; statistically, the variability of each score from its group mean.

ethics codes Documents created by research organizations and nations that offer guidance to researchers and professionals for ensuring the safety and welfare of research participants.

exempt research Research in which there is absolutely no risk, and thus may be exempt from REB review.

experimental control A feature of strong experimental designs. Occurs when only the precise independent variable varies across conditions; all other features of the experiment are the same across conditions.

experimental method A method of determining whether variables are related, in which the researcher manipulates the independent variable and controls all other variables either by randomization or by direct experimental control.

experimenter bias Any intentional or unintentional influence that the experimenter exerts on participants to confirm the hypothesis under investigation; also called *experimenter expectancy effects*.

external validity The degree to which the results of an experiment may be generalized.

***F* test** A statistical significance test for determining whether two or more means are significantly different; also known as *analysis of variance (ANOVA)*. *F* is the ratio of systematic variance to error variance.

face validity The degree to which a measurement device appears to accurately measure a variable.

factorial design A design in which all levels of each independent variable are combined with all levels of the other independent variables. A factorial design allows investigation of the separate main effects and interactions of two or more independent variables.

falsifiability The principle that a good scientific idea or theory should be capable of being shown to be false when tested using scientific methods.

falsifiable Capable of being shown to be false when tested using scientific methods; a good scientific idea or theory should be falsifiable.

fatigue effect When participants perform worse over the course of a study simply because of effort or the passage of time; particularly problematic in repeated measures designs.

field experiment An experiment that is conducted in a natural setting rather than in a laboratory setting.

filler items Items included in a questionnaire measure to help disguise the true purpose of the measure.

floor effect The failure of a measure to detect a difference because it was too difficult (*also see* ceiling effect).

focus group A qualitative method of data collection in which six to ten people are interviewed together about a particular topic.

fraud The intentional misrepresentation of any aspect of research (e.g., data, analyses, participants).

frequency distribution An arrangement of a set of scores from lowest to highest that indicates the number of times each score was obtained.

frequency polygons Graphic displays of a frequency distribution in which the frequency of each score is plotted on the vertical axis, with the plotted points connected by straight lines.

goals of scientific research Within psychology and the behavioural sciences are four general goals of scientific research: (1) to describe behaviour, (2) to predict behaviour, (3) to determine the causes of behaviour, and (4) to understand or explain behaviour.

graphic rating scale A type of closed-ended response where two words appear on either side of a solid line. Participants place a mark on the line indicating their relative preference for one or the other word.

histogram A type of graph used when the variable on the x-axis is continuous. A key feature is that the bars touch, unlike bar graphs.

history effects As a threat to the internal validity of an experiment, refers to outside events that are not part of the manipulation that could be responsible for the results.

hypothesis, null *see* null hypothesis

hypothesis, research *see* research hypothesis

independent groups design An experiment in which different participants are assigned to each group. Also called *between-subjects design.*

independent variable The variable that is manipulated to observe its effect on the dependent variable.

inferential statistics Statistics designed to determine whether results based on sample data are generalizable to a population.

informed consent In research ethics, the principle that participants in an experiment be informed in advance of all aspects of the research that might influence their decision to participate.

instrument decay As a threat to internal validity, the possibility that a change in the characteristics of the measurement instrument is responsible for the results.

interaction The differing effect of one independent variable on the dependent variable, depending on the particular level of another independent variable.

internal consistency reliability Reliability assessed with data collected at one point in time with multiple measures of a psychological construct. A measure is reliable when the multiple measures provide similar results.

internal validity The certainty with which results of an experiment can be attributed to the manipulation of the independent variable rather than to some other, confounding variable.

interrater reliability An indicator of reliability that examines the agreement of observations made by two or more raters (judges).

interrupted time series design A design in which the effectiveness of a treatment is determined by examining a series of measurements made over an extended time period both before and after the treatment is introduced. The treatment is not introduced at a random point in time.

interval scale A scale of measurement in which the intervals between numbers on the scale are all equal in size.

interviewer bias Intentional or unintentional influence exerted by an interviewer in such a way that the actual or interpreted behaviour of respondents is consistent with the interviewer's expectations.

introduction The section of a research report in which the researcher outlines the problem that has been investigated.

intuition Unquestioning acceptance of what your personal judgment or a single story about one person's experience tells you about the world.

IV × PV design A factorial design that includes both an experimental independent variable (IV) and a non-experimental participant variable (PV).

justice Principle that all individuals and groups should have fair and equal access to the benefits of research participation as well as the potential risks of research participation.

Latin square A technique to control for order effects without having all possible orders.

levels Term sometimes used to denote *conditions* in an experimental design.

literature review A narrative summary of the research that has been conducted on a particular topic.

longitudinal method A developmental research method in which the same persons are observed repeatedly as they grow older; conceptually similar to a repeated measures design.

main effect The direct effect of an independent variable on a dependent variable.

manipulation check A measure used to determine whether the manipulation of the independent variable has had its intended effect on a participant.

manipulation strength The degree to which levels of an independent variable differ from each other. In a weak manipulation, conditions are subtly different; conditions are maximally different in a strong manipulation.

marginal mean In a factorial design, the average score of all participants in one condition of one independent variable, collapsing across all other variables.

matched pairs design A method of assigning participants to groups in which pairs of participants are first matched on some characteristic and then individually assigned randomly to groups.

maturation effects As a threat to internal validity, the possibility that any naturally occurring change within the individual is responsible for the results.

mean A measure of central tendency, obtained by summing scores and then dividing the sum by the number of scores.

measurement error The degree to which a measurement deviates from the true score value.

median A measure of central tendency; the middle score in a distribution of scores that divides the distribution in half.

mediating variable A psychological process that occurs between an event and a behavioural response.

meta-analysis A set of statistical procedures for combining the results of a number of studies in order to provide a general assessment of the relationship between variables.

method The section of a research report in which the researcher provides information about exactly how the study was conducted, including any details necessary for the reader to *replicate* (repeat) the study.

minimal risk research Research that involves no greater risks to participants than they would encounter in their daily lives.

mixed factorial design A design that includes both independent groups (between-subjects) and repeated measures (within-subjects) variables.

mode A measure of central tendency; the most frequent score in a distribution of scores.

moderator variable A variable that influences the nature of the relationship between two other variables (an independent variable and a dependent variable). In a factorial design, the effect of the moderator variable is revealed as an interaction.

mortality The loss of participants who decide to leave an experiment. Mortality is a threat to internal validity when the mortality rate is related to the nature of the experimental manipulation.

multiple baseline design Observing behaviour before and after a manipulation under multiple circumstances (across different individuals, different behaviours, or different settings).

multiple correlation A correlation between one variable and a combined set of predictor variables.

multiple regression An extension of the correlation technique; analysis that models the extent to which one or more predictor variables is related to one criterion variable.

naturalistic observation Descriptive method in which observations are made in a natural social setting; sometimes called *field observation*.

negative linear relationship A relationship in which increases in the values of the first variable are accompanied by decreases in the values of the second variable.

nominal scale A scale of measurement with two or more categories that have no numerical (less than, greater than) properties.

non-equivalent control group design A quasi-experimental design in which non-equivalent groups of participants participate in the different experimental groups, and there is no pretest.

non-equivalent control group pretest-post-test design A quasi-experimental design in which non-equivalent groups are used, but a pretest allows assessment of equivalency and pretest-posttest changes.

non-experimental method Use of measurement of variables to determine whether variables are related to one another. Also called *correlational method*.

non-probability sampling Type of sampling procedure in which one cannot specify the probability that any member of the population will be included in the sample.

null hypothesis The hypothesis, used for statistical purposes, that the variables under investigation are not related in the population, that any observed effect based on sample results is due to random error.

one-group posttest-only design A quasi-experimental design that has no control group and no pretest comparison; a very poor design in terms of internal validity.

one-group pretest-posttest design A quasi-experimental design in which the effect of an independent variable is inferred from the pretest-posttest difference in a single group.

open-ended questions Questions that offer respondents no restrictions as to how to respond to the prompt (e.g., an essay question).

operational definition Definition of a concept that specifies the operation used to measure or manipulate the concept.

order effect In a repeated measures design, the effect that the order of introducing treatment has on the dependent variable.

ordinal scale A scale of measurement in which the measurement categories form a rank order along a continuum.

outliers Scores that are extremely distant from the rest of the scores in a data set.

panel study In survey research, questioning the same people at two or more points in time.

parsimony The scientific principle stating that if two theories are equally effective at explaining a phenomenon, the simpler of the two theories is preferable.

partial correlation The correlation between two variables with the influence of a third variable statistically controlled for.

participant observation A type of naturalistic observation in which the researcher assumes a role in the setting he or she is researching. The researcher's participation may or may not be concealed.

participant variable   A term sometimes used to denote a variable that groups participants on some pre-existing characteristics (e.g., sex, ethnicity). It is often treated as an independent variable in experimental designs, despite the lack of random assignment.

Pearson product-moment correlation coefficient   A type of correlation coefficient used with interval and ratio scale data. In addition to providing information on the strength of the relationship between two variables, the Pearson product-moment correlation coefficient indicates the direction (positive or negative) of the relationship.

peer review   The process of judging the scientific merit of research through review by peers of the researcher–other scientists with the expertise to evaluate the research.

physiological measure   An operational definition that involves observing and recording a response of the body.

pie chart   A graphic display of data in which frequencies or percentages are represented as "slices" of a pie.

pilot study   A small-scale study conducted prior to conducting an actual experiment; designed to test and refine procedures.

placebo group   In drug research, a group given an inert substance to assess the psychological effect of receiving a treatment.

plagiarism   The intentional or unintentional use of another person's work without adequately indicating the source.

population   The defined group of individuals from which a sample is drawn.

positive linear relationship   A relationship in which increases in the values of the first variable are accompanied by increases in the values of the second variable.

posttest-only design   A true experimental design in which the dependent variable (posttest) is measured only once, after manipulation of the independent variable.

power   The probability of correctly rejecting the null hypothesis.

practice effect   When participants perform better over the course of a study simply because they are more experienced with the task; particularly problematic in repeated measures designs.

prediction   A statement that makes an assertion concerning what will occur in a particular research investigation.

predictive validity   The construct validity of a measure is assessed by examining the ability of the measure to predict a future behaviour.

predictor variable   The variable used to predict changes in the criterion (or outcome) variable in a multiple regression analysis.

pretest-posttest design   A true experimental design in which the dependent variable is measured both before (pretest) and after (posttest) manipulation of the independent variable.

probability   The likelihood that a given event (among a specific set of events) will occur.

probability sampling   Type of sampling procedure in which one is able to specify the probability that any member of the population will be included in the sample.

program evaluation   Research designed to evaluate programs (e.g., social reforms, innovations) that are designed to produce certain changes or outcomes in a target population.

pseudoscience   Claims that are made on the basis of evidence that is designed to appear scientific; such evidence is not based on the principles of the scientific method, however.

PsycINFO   The American Psychological Association's searchable computer database system that includes coverage of journal publications from the 1800s to the present.

publication bias   The finding that statistically significant results are more likely to be published in journals than non-significant results.

purposive sampling   A type of convenience sampling procedure conducted to obtain predetermined types of individuals for the sample.

qualitative approach   A set of approaches to research that emphasizes people's lived experiences in their own words, and the researcher's interpretation of those experiences.

quantitative approach An approach to research that emphasizes scientific empiricism in design, data collection, and statistical analyses.

quasi-experimental designs Types of designs that approximate the control features of true experiments to infer that a given treatment did have its intended effect.

quota sampling A sampling procedure in which the sample is chosen to reflect the numerical composition of various subgroups in the population. A convenience sampling technique is used to obtain the sample.

random assignment Controlling for the effects of extraneous variables by ensuring that participants in an experiment are assigned to condition in a manner determined entirely by chance.

random sample When everyone in a given population is equally likely to have been selected to participate in the study, that sample is said to be random.

rating scales Closed-ended response options that enable participants to indicate the degree to which they endorse a particular statement.

ratio scale A scale of measurement in which there is an absolute zero point, indicating an absence of the variable being measured. An implication is that ratios of numbers on the scale can be formed (generally, these are physical measures such as weight or timed measures such as duration or reaction time).

reactivity A problem of measurement in which the measure changes the behaviour being observed.

references A list of all sources cited in the body of a paper, sorted alphabetically by the last name of the first author of the cited material, formatted in APA style and including all information required to locate each source. Forms the last section of the APA format manuscript style.

regression equation A mathematical equation that allows prediction of one behaviour when the score on another variable is known.

regression toward the mean Principle that extreme scores on a variable tend to be closer to the mean when a second measurement is made. Sometimes called *statistical regression*.

reliability The degree to which a measure is consistent.

repeated measures design An experiment in which the same participants are assigned to each group. Also called *within-subjects design*.

replicate To repeat a research study to determine whether the results can be duplicated.

replication Repeating a research study; a way of increasing confidence that the results of a single study represent the truth.

Research Ethics Board (REB) An ethics review committee established to review research proposals within a university. The REB is composed of scientists, non-scientists, and legal experts.

research hypothesis The hypothesis that the variables under investigation are related in the population–that the observed effect based on sample data is true in the population.

respect for persons Principle that all individuals should have the free and informed choice to participate in a study or not.

response rate The percentage of people selected for a sample who actually completed a survey.

response set A pattern of individual response to questions on a self-report measure that is not related to the content of the questions.

response variable Operational definitions that involve recording a participant's reaction to some event (e.g., reaction time, attitudes, choice, action).

restriction of range Occurs when the full set of a variable's possible values are not sampled, which can lead to incorrect inferences about that variable and its relationship to other variables.

results The section of a research report in which the researcher presents the findings.

reversal design A single case design in which the treatment is introduced after a baseline period and then withdrawn during a second baseline period. It may be extended by adding a second introduction of the treatment. Sometimes called a *withdrawal design*.

risk-benefit analysis   A researcher's or REB's evaluation of the potential hazards of conducting a study, weighed against the potential benefits to participants and to society.

sampling   The process of choosing members of a population to be included in a sample.

sampling distribution   A frequency distribution of the values of a statistic that would be obtained if a researcher took an infinite number of samples of a particular size, conducted the same study, and calculated the same statistic for each one. Used in inferential statistics to evaluate the likelihood of a given result if only chance is operating.

sampling error   The degree to which the statistic calculated from a sample deviates from the true population value.

sampling frame   The individuals or clusters of individuals in a population who might actually be selected for inclusion in the sample.

scatterplot   A graph in which individual scores are plotted based on their x-y coordinates; used to illustrate the relationship between two variables.

scientific skepticism   The concept that ideas must be evaluated on the basis of careful logic and results from scientific investigations.

selection differences   Differences in the type of participants who make up each group in an experimental design; this situation occurs when participants elect which group they are to be assigned to.

self-report measure   An operational definition of a variable that involves asking people to explicitly indicate something about themselves (e.g., personality, behaviour, attitudes).

semantic differential scale   A type of closed-ended response where two words appear on either side of a series of dashed lines. Participants place a mark on the dash indicating their relative preference for one or the other word.

sensitivity   The ability of a measure to detect differences between groups.

sequential method   A combination of the cross-sectional and longitudinal designs to study developmental research questions.

simple main effect   In a factorial design, the effect of one independent variable at a particular level of another independent variable.

simple random sampling   A sampling procedure in which each member of the population has an equal probability of being included in the sample.

single-blind procedure   An experiment in which participants do not know to which condition they have been assigned, but the experimenter does.

single case experimental design   A research design in which the effect of the independent variable is assessed using data from a single participant.

situational variable   A characteristic of some event or environment (e.g., lighting conditions, question wording, a confederate's actions).

squared correlation coefficient   A correlation coefficient (e.g., Pearson r) that has been multiplied by itself; can be interpreted as the proportion of variance shared between the two variables.

squared multiple correlation coefficient   In multiple regression, the proportion of variance in the criterion that can be explained by that set of predictors combined.

staged manipulations   Operational definitions that involve creating a situation in which the independent variable is manipulated; participants then experience the situation and their responses are recorded. Deception is often used to conceal the fact that the situation is a ruse.

standard deviation   The average deviation of scores from the mean (the square root of the variance).

statistically significant   Rejection of the null hypothesis when an outcome has a low probability of occurrence (usually .05 or less) if, in fact, the null hypothesis is correct.

straightforward manipulations   Operational definitions that involve manipulating the independent variable using instructions or other stimulus materials in a simple way.

stratified random sampling   A sampling procedure in which the population is divided into strata followed by random sampling from each stratum.

survey research Questionnaires and interviews carefully designed to ask people information about themselves.

systematic observation Observation of one or more specific variables, usually made in a precisely defined setting.

systematic variance Variability in a set of scores that is the result of the independent variable; statistically, the variability of each group mean from the grand mean of all participants.

t **test** A statistical significance test used to compare differences between means.

temporal precedence Part of causal inference; the cause precedes the effect in a time sequence.

testing effects A threat to internal validity in which taking a pretest changes behaviour without any effect on the independent variable.

test-retest reliability A reliability coefficient determined by the correlation between scores on a measure given at one time with scores on the same measure given at a later time.

theory A framework that attempts to organize and explain various findings relating to a particular phenomenon, and in doing so, generates new, testable hypotheses about that phenomenon.

third-variable problem When describing the relationship between two variables, a third variable is any other variable that is extraneous to the two variables of interest. True experiments control for the possible influence of third variables.

Three Rs In animal research, the principles of replacement (avoid using animals if possible), reduction (minimize the number of animals used), and refinement (modify procedures to minimize distress).

Tri-Council Policy Statement (TCPS) In Canada, the official statement of ethical conduct for research involving humans; researchers and institutions are expected to adhere to this document to receive federal research funds.

true score An individual's actual score on a variable being measured, as opposed to the score the individual obtained on the measure itself.

Type I error An incorrect decision to reject the null hypothesis when it is true.

Type II error An incorrect decision to accept the null hypothesis when it is false.

variability The amount of dispersion of scores about some central value.

variable Any event, situation, behaviour, or individual characteristic that varies–that is, has at least two values.

variance A measure of the variability of scores about a mean; the mean of the sum of squared deviations of scores from the group mean.

Web of Science A searchable database that allows searches for articles that cite a particular older article.

"yea-saying" and "nay-saying" response sets The tendency for some survey respondents to agree (yea) or disagree (nay) with the vast majority of questions being asked, regardless of the question; introduces error into the measure.

References

Akins, C. K., Panicker, S., & Cunningham, C. L. (2004). *Laboratory animals in research and teaching: Ethics, care, and methods.* Washington, DC: American Psychological Association.

Aknin, L. B., Barrington-Leigh, C. P., Dunn, E. W., Helliwell, J. F., Burns, J., Biswas-Diener, R., . . . Norton, M. I. (2013). Prosocial spending and well-being: Cross-cultural evidence for a psychological universal. *Journal of Personality and Social Psychology, 104,* 635-652.

Aknin, L. B., Broesch, T., Hamlin, J. K., & Van de Vondervoort, J. W. (2015). Prosocial behavior leads to happiness in a small-scale rural society. *Journal of Experimental Psychology: General.* Advance online publication. doi:10.1037/xge0000082

Aknin, L. B., Hamlin, J. K., & Dunn, E. W. (2012). Giving leads to happiness in young children. *PLoS ONE 7*(6): e39211. doi:10.1371/journal.pone.0039211

Aknin, L. B., Norton, M. I., & Dunn, E. W. (2009). From wealth to well-being? Money matters, but less than people think. *The Journal of Positive Psychology, 4,* 523-527.

Albergotti, R., & Dwoskin, E. (2014, 30 June). Facebook study sparks soul-searching and ethical questions. *Wall Street Journal* (online). Retrieved from http://search.proquest.com.ezproxy.library.ubc.ca/docview/1541549641?accountid=14656

Albright, L., & Malloy, T. E. (2000). Experimental validity: Brunswik, Campbell, Cronbach and enduring issues. *Review of General Psychology, 4,* 337-353.

Alhalal, E. A., Ford-Gilboe, M., Kerr, M., & Davies, L. (2012). Identifying factors that predict women's inability to maintain separation from an abusive partner. *Issues in Mental Health Nursing, 33,* 838-850.

Alogna, V. K., Attaya, M. K., Aucoin, P., Bahnik, S., Birch, S., Birt, A. R., . . . Zwaan, R. A. (2014). Registered replication report: Schooler & Engstler-Schooler (1990). *Perspectives on Psychological Science, 9,* 556-578.

American Psychological Association. (2010a). *Ethical principles of psychologists and code of conduct.* Retrieved May 9, 2011, from http://www.apa.org/ethics/code

American Psychological Association. (2010b). *Publication manual of the American Psychological Association* (6th ed.). Washington, DC: Author.

American Psychological Association. (2012). *Guidelines for ethical conduct in the care and use of animals.* Retrieved July 30, 2014, from http://www.apa.org/science/leadership/care/guidelines.aspx

American Psychological Association. (2012). *APA style guide to electronic resources* (6th ed.). Washington, DC: American Psychological Association.

Anderson, C. A., & Anderson, D. C. (1984). Ambient temperature and violent crime: Test of the linear and curvilinear hypotheses. *Journal of Personality and Social Psychology, 46,* 91-97.

Anderson, C. A., Lindsay, J. J., & Bushman, B. J. (1999). Research in the psychological laboratory: Truth or triviality? *Current Directions in Psychological Science, 8,* 3-9.

Anderson, C. A., Shibuya, A., Ihori, N., Swing, E. L., Bushman, B. J., Sakamoto, A., . . . Saleem, M. (2010). Violent video game effects on aggression, empathy, and prosocial behavior in Eastern and Western countries: A meta-analytic review. *Psychological Bulletin, 136,* 151-173.

Anderson, M. S., Ronning, E. A., DeVries, R., & Martinson, B. C. (2010). Extending the Mertonian norms: Scientists' subscription to norms of research. *Journal of Higher Education, 81,* 366-393.

Anderson, R. (2013, January 13). Father's attitude towards women shapes daughter's career ambitions. *Parent Herald*. Retrieved from http://www.parentherald.com/articles/730/20130121/fathers-attitude-towards-women-shapes-daughters-career.htm

Andrade, B. F., & Tannock, R. (2013). The direct effects of inattention and hyperactivity/impulsivity on peer problems and mediating roles of prosocial and conduct problem behaviors in a community sample of children. *Journal of Attention Disorders, 17,* 670–680.

Arim, R. G., Dahinten, V. S., Marshall, S. K., & Shapka, J. D. (2011). An examination of the reciprocal relationships between adolescents' aggressive behaviors and their perceptions of parental nurturance. *Journal of Youth and Adolescence, 40,* 207–220.

Aronson, E. (2012). *Not by chance alone: My life as a social psychologist.* New York: Basic Books.

Aronson, E., Brewer, M., & Carlsmith, J. M. (1985). Experimentation in social psychology. In G. Lindzey & E. Aronson (Eds.), *Handbook of social psychology* (3rd ed.). New York: Random House.

Asbridge, M., Mann, R. E., Smart, R. G., Stoduto, G., Beirness, D., Lamble, R., & Vingilis, E. (2009). The effects of Ontario's administrative driver's licence suspension law on total driver fatalities: A multiple time series analysis. *Drugs: Education, Prevention, Policy, 16,* 140–151.

Assaad, J.-M., Pihl, R. O., Séguin, J. R., Nagin, D. S., Vitaro, F., & Tremblay, R. E. (2006). Intoxicated behavioral disinhibition and the heart rate response to alcohol. *Experimental and Clinical Psychopharmacology, 14,* 377–388.

Baillargeon, R. (2004). Infants' physical world. *Current Directions in Psychological Science, 13,* 89–94.

Bakeman, R., & Gottman, J. M. (1986). *Observing interaction.* Cambridge, UK: Cambridge University Press.

Bakker, M., van Dijk, A., & Wicherts, J. M. (2012). The rules of the game called psychological science. *Perspectives on Psychological Science, 7,* 543–554.

Bakker, M., & Wicherts, J. M. (2011). The (mis)reporting of statistical results in psychology journals. *Behavior Research Methods, 43,* 666–678.

Bamberger, M., Rugh, J., Church, M., & Fort, L. (2004). Shoestring evaluation: Designing impact evaluations under budget, time and data constraints. *American Journal of Evaluation, 25,* 5–37.

Banaji, M. (2010, December). Wikipedia is the encyclopedia that anybody can edit. But have you? *Observer, 23*(10). Retrieved from www.psychologicalscience.org/index.php/publications/observer

Banaji, M. (2011, February). Harnessing the power of Wikipedia for scientific psychology: A call to action. *Observer, 24*(2). Retrieved from www.psychologicalscience.org/index.php/publications/observer

Bandstra, N. F., Chambers, C. T., McGrath, P. J., & Moore, C. (2011). The behavioural expression of empathy to others' pain versus others' sadness in young children. *Pain, 152,* 1074–1082.

Bargh, J. A., Chen, M. A., & Burrows, L. (1996). Automaticity of social behaviour: Direct effects of trait construct and stereotype activation on action. *Journal of Personality and Social Psychology, 71,* 230–244.

Barha, C. K., Pawluski, J. L., & Galea, L. A. M. (2007). Maternal care affects male and female offspring working memory and stress reactivity. *Physiology & Behavior, 92,* 939–950.

Barlow, D. H., Nock, M. K., & Hersen, M. (2009). *Single case experimental designs: Strategies for studying behavior change* (3rd ed). Boston: Allyn & Bacon.

Barnoy, S., Ofra, L., & Bar-Tal, Y. (2012). What makes patients perceive their health care worker as an epistemic authority? *Nursing Inquiry, 19,* 128–133.

Baron, R. M., & Kenny, D. A. (1986). The moderator-mediator variable distinction in social psychological research: Conceptual, strategic, and statistical considerations. *Journal of Personality and Social Psychology, 51,* 1173–1182.

Baruss, I., & Rabier, V. (2013). Failure to replicate retrocausal recall. *Psychology of Consciousness: Theory, Research, and Practice, 1,* 82–91.

Baum, A., Gachtel, R. J., & Schaeffer, M. A. (1983). Emotional, behavioral, and psychological effects of chronic stress at Three Mile Island. *Journal of Consulting and Clinical Psychology, 51,* 565–572.

Baumeister, R. F., Bratslavsky, E., Muraven, M., & Tice, D. M. (1998). Ego depletion: Is the active self a limited resource? *Journal of Personality and Social Psychology, 74,* 1252–1265.

Baumrind, D. (1964). Some thoughts on ethics of research: After reading Milgram's "behavioral study of obedience." *American Psychologist, 19,* 421-423.

Beach, F. A. (1950). The snark was a boojum. *American Psychologist, 5,* 115-124.

Behrend, T. S., Sharek, D. J., Meade, A. W., & Wiebe, E. N. (2011). The viability of crowdsourcing for survey research. *Behavioral Research, 43,* 800-813.

Bem, D. J. (1981). Writing the research report. In L. H. Kidder (Ed.), *Research methods in social relations.* New York: Holt, Rinehart & Winston.

Bem, D. J. (2003). *Writing the empirical journal article.* Retrieved July 16, 2008, from http://dbem.ws/WritingArticle2.pdf

Bem, D. J. (2011). Feeling the future: Experimental evidence for anomalous retroactive influences on cognition and affect. *Journal of Personality and Social Psychology, 100.* 407-425.

Bender, J. L., Jimenez-Marroquin, M.-C., & Jadad, A. R. (2011). Seeking support on Facebook: A content analysis of breast cancer groups. *Journal of Medical Internet Research, 13,* 221-232.

Beran, T. N., Ramirez-Serrano, A., Kuzyk, R., Nugent, S., & Fior, M. (2011). Would children help a robot in need? *International Journal of Social Robotics, 3,* 83-93.

Bernhard, J. K., & Young, J. E. E. (2009). Gaining institutional permission: Researching precarious legal status in Canada. *Journal of Academic Ethics, 7,* 175-191.

Berry, J. W. (2013). Achieving a global psychology. *Canadian Psychology, 54,* 55-61.

Bhattacharjee, Y. (2013, 28 June). Stapel gets community service for fabricating studies. *Science News.* Retrieved July 31, 2014, from http://news.sciencemag.org/europe/2013/06/stapel-gets-community-service-fabricating-studies

Blatchley, B., & O'Brien, K. R. (2007). Deceiving the participant: Are we creating the reputational spillover effect? *North American Journal of Psychology, 9,* 519-534.

Bodner, T. E. (2006). Designs, participants, and measurement methods in psychological research. *Canadian Psychology, 47,* 263-272.

Bonnet, D. G. (2012). Replication-extension studies. *Current Directions in Psychological Science, 21,* 409-412.

Boucher, H., & Ryan, C. A. (2011). Performance stress and the very young musician. *Journal of Research in Music Education, 58,* 329-345.

Bowker, A., Boekhoven, B., Nolan, A., Bauhaus, S., Glover, P., Powell, T., & Taylor, S. (2009). Naturalistic obervations of spectator behavior at youth hockey games. *Sport Psychologist, 23,* 301-316.

Boyatzis, R. E. (1998). *Transforming qualitative information: Thematic analysis and code development.* Thousand Oaks, CA: Sage.

Bradburn, N. M., Sudman, S., & Wansink, B. (2004). *Asking Questions: The Definitive Guide to Questionnaire Design–For Market Research, Political Polls, and Social and Health Questionnaires.* San Francisco, CA: Jossey-Bass.

Brandt, M. J., Ijzerman, H., Dijksterhuis, A., Farach, F. J., Geller, J., Giner-Sorolla, R., . . . van't Veer, A. (2014). The Replication Recipe: What makes for a convincing replication? *Journal of Experimental Social Psychology, 50,* 217-224.

Braver, S. L., Thoemmes, F. J, & Rosenthal, R. (2014). Continuously cumulating meta-analysis and replicability. *Perspectives on Psychological Science, 9,* 333-342.

Broberg, A. G., Wessels, H., Lamb, M. E., & Hwang, C. P. (1997). Effects of day care on the development of cognitive abilities in 8-year-olds: A longitudinal study. *Developmental Psychology, 33,* 62-69.

Brogden, W. J. (1962). The experimenter as a factor in animal conditioning. *Psychological Reports, 11,* 239-242.

Bruchmüller, K., Margraf, J., & Schneider, S. (2012). Is ADHD diagnosed in accord with diagnostic criteria? Overdiagnosis and influence of client gender on diagnosis. *Journal of Consulting and Clinical Psychology, 80,* 128-238.

Buehler, R., Griffin, D., & Ross, M. (2002). Inside the planning fallacy: The causes and consequences of optimistic time predictions. In T. Gilovich, D. Griffin, & D. Kahneman (Eds.), *Heuristics and biases: The psychology of intuitive judgment.* Cambridge: Cambridge University Press.

Buehler, R., Peetz, J., & Griffin, D. (2010). Finishing on time: When do predictions influence completion times? *Organizational Behavior and Human Decision Processes, 111,* 23-32.

Burger, J. (2009). Replicating Milgram: Would people still obey today? *American Psychologist, 64,* 1–11.

Bushman, B. J., DeWall, C. N., Pond, R. S., & Hanus, M. D. (2014). Low glucose relates to greater aggression in married couples. *PNAS Proceedings of the National Academy of Sciences of the United States of America, 111,* 6254–6257.

Bushman, B. J., & Wells, G. L. (2001). Narrative impressions of the literature: The availability bias and the corrective properties of meta-analytic approaches. *Personality and Social Psychology Bulletin, 27,* 1123–1130.

Buunk, A. P., Park, J. H., & Duncan, L. A. (2010). Cultural variation in parental influence on mate choice. *Cross-Cultural Research, 44,* 23–40.

Byrne, B. M., & van de Vijver, F. J. R. (2010). Testing for measurement and structural equivalent in large-scale cross-cultural studies: Addressing the issue of nonequivalence. *International Journal of Testing, 10,* 107–132.

Cacioppo, J. T., Tassinary, L. G., & Berntson, G. G. (Eds.). (2007). *Handbook of psychophysiology* (3rd ed.). New York: Cambridge University Press.

Cai, H., Sedikides, C., Gaertner, L., Wang, C., Carvallo, M., Xu, Y., . . . Jackson, L. E. (2011). Tactical self-enhancement in China: Is modesty at the service of self-enhancement in East Asian culture? *Social Personality and Personality Science, 2,* 59–64.

Cain, P. (2013, October 2). National Household Survey: More than 90% of Kelowna neighbourhoods would have been excluded from results if Statistics Canada hadn't dropped its standards. *Global News.* Retrieved August 11, 2014, from http://globalnews.ca/news/873012/who-filled-out-the-national-household-survey-and-why-did-statscan-cut-its-census-standards-in-half/#statscan

Cain, P., & Mehler Paperny, A. (2013, October 21). Fraser Health may cut programs to pay for data Statscan didn't get. *Global News.* Retrieved August 11, 2014, from http://globalnews.ca/news/911490/statscans-national-household-survey-missed-people-on-social-assistance-heres-why-thats-a-problem/

Cameron, J. J., Holmes, J. G., & Vorauer, J. D. (2009). When self-disclosure goes awry: Negative consequences of revealing personal failures for lower self-esteem individuals. *Journal of Experimental Social Psychology, 45,* 217–222.

Cameron, J. J., Stinson, D. A., Gaetz, R., & Balchen, S. (2010). Acceptance is in the eye of the beholder: Self-esteem and motivated perceptions of acceptance from the opposite sex. *Journal of Personality and Social Psychology, 99,* 513–529.

Campbell, D. T. (1969). Reforms as experiments. *American Psychologist, 24,* 409–429.

Campbell, D. T., & Stanley, J. C. (1966). *Experimental and quasi-experimental designs for research.* Chicago: Rand McNally.

Canadian Psychological Association (2000). *Canadian Code of Ethics for Psychologists* (3rd ed.). Canadian Psychological Association: Ottawa, Canada. Retrieved July 30, 2014, from http://www.cpa.ca/aboutcpa/committees/ethics/codeofethics/

Canadian Council on Animal Care. (2006). *Terms of Reference for Animal Care Committees.* Retrieved July 30, 2014, from http://www.ccac.ca/Documents/Standards/Policies/Terms_of_reference_for_ACC.pdf

Canadian Council on Animal Care. (2013). *Annual Report 2012-2013 Canadian Council on Animal Care.* Retrieved July 30, 2014, from http://www.ccac.ca/en_/publications/annual_reports

Canadian Council on Animal Care. (2014). *About the Canadian Council on Animal Care.* Retrieved July 30, 2014, from http://www.ccac.ca/en/about

Canadian Institutes of Health Research, Natural Sciences and Engineering Research Council of Canada, and Social Sciences and Humanities Research Council of Canada, (2010). *Tri-Council Policy Statement: Ethical Conduct for Research Involving Humans.* Retrieved July 30, 2014, from http://www.pre.ethics.gc.ca

Carlberg, C. (2011). *Statistical Analysis: Microsoft Excel 2010.* Indianapolis, IN: Que Publishing.

Carroll, M. E., & Overmier, J. B. (Eds.). (2001). *Animal research and human health: Advancing human welfare through behavioral science.* Washington, DC: American Psychological Association.

Casler, K., Bickel, L., & Hackett, E. (2013). Separate but equal? A comparison of participants and data gathered via Amazon's MTurk, social media, and face-to-face behavioural testing. *Computers in Human Behavior, 29,* 2156–2160.

Cesario, J. (2014). Priming, replication, and the hardest science. *Perspectives on Psychological Science, 9,* 40-48.

Chambers, T. (2006). What I hear you saying is . . . : Analysis of student comments from the NSSE. *College Student Journal, 44,* 3-24.

Chan, M. E., & Arvey, R. D. (2012). Meta-analysis and the development of knowledge. *Perspectives on Psychological Science, 7,* 79-92.

Chandler, J., & Schwarz, N. (2009). How extending your middle finger affects your perception of other: Learned movements influence concept accessibility. *Journal of Experimental Social Psychology, 45,* 123-128.

Chartrand, T. L., & Bargh, J. A. (2000). The mind in the middle: A practical guide to priming and automaticity research. In Reis, H. T., & Judd, C. M. (Eds.), *Handbook of research methods in social and personality psychology* (pp. 253-285). Cambridge, UK: Cambridge University Press.

Cheung, B., Y., Chudek, M., & Heine, S. J. (2011). Evidence for a sensitive period for acculturation: Younger immigrants report acculturating at a faster rate. *Psychological Science, 22,* 147-152.

Chopra, K. K., Ravindran, A., Kennedy, S. H., Mackenzie, B., Matthews, S., Anisman, H., et al. (2009). Sex differences in hormonal responses to a social stressor in chronic major depression. *Psychoneuroendocrinology, 34,* 1235-1241.

Christensen, L. (1988). Deception in psychological research: When is its use justified? *Personality and Social Psychology Bulletin, 14,* 664-675.

Chua, A. (2011). *Battle hymn of the Tiger Mother.* New York: Penguin.

Cialdini, R. B. (2008). *Influence: Science and practice* (5th ed.). Boston: Allyn & Bacon.

Cianci, A. M., Klein, H. J., & Seijts, G. H. (2010). The effect of negative feedback on tension and subsequent performance: The main and interactive effects of goal content and conscientiousness. *Journal of Applied Psychology, 95,* 618-630.

Cohen, D., Nisbett, R. E., Bowdle, B. F., & Schwarz, N. (1996). Insult, aggression, and the southern culture of honor: An "experimental ethnography." *Journal of Personality and Social Psychology, 70,* 945-960.

Cohen, J. (1988). *Statistical power analysis for the behavioral sciences* (2nd ed.). Hillsdale, NJ: Erlbaum.

Cohen, J. (1992). A power primer. *Psychological Bulletin, 112,* 155-159.

Cohen, J. (1994). The earth is round ($p < .05$). *American Psychologist, 49,* 997-1003.

Collaboration, Open Science, *The Reproducibility Project: A Model of Large-Scale Collaboration for Empirical Research on Reproducibility* (January 3, 2013). Available at SSRN: http://ssrn.com/abstract=2195999 or http://dx.doi.org/10.2139/ssrn.2195999

Collins, B. E. (2002). Coping with IRBs: A guide for the bureaucratically challenged. *APS Observer, 15*(10). Retrieved January 15, 2005, from http://www.psychologicalscience.org/observer/2002/1202/irb.cfm

Cook, T. D., & Campbell, D. T. (1979). *Quasi-experimentation: Design and analysis issues for field settings.* Boston: Houghton-Mifflin.

Cooke, D. J., Michie, C., Hart, S. D., & Clark, D. A. (2004). Reconstructing psychopathy: Clarifying the significance of antisocial and socially deviant behavior in the diagnosis of psychopathic personality disorder. *Journal of Personality Disorders, 18,* 337-357.

Cory, P. (2001). *The inquiry regarding Thomas Sophonow: The investigation, prosecution and consideration of entitlement to compensation.* Manitoba, Canada: Manitoba Justice.

Costa, M. (2010). Interpersonal distances in group walking. *Journal of Nonverbal Behavior, 34,* 15-26.

Costa, P. T., Jr., & McCrae, R. R. (1985). *The NEO Personality Inventory manual.* Odessa, FL: Psychological Assessment Resources.

Côté, S., & Bouchard, S. (2005). Documenting the efficacy of virtual reality exposure with psychophysiological and information processing measures. *Applied Psychophysiology and Biofeedback, 30,* 217-232.

Crawford, F. (2000). Researcher in consumer behavior looks at attitudes of gratitude that affect gratuities. *Cornell Chronicle.* Retrieved February 28, 2005, from http://www.news.cornell.edu/Chronicle/00/8.17.00/Lynn-tipping.html

Creswell, J. W. (2007). *Qualitative inquiry and research design: Choosing among five approaches* (2nd ed.). Thousand Oaks, CA: Sage.

Creswell, J. W., Hanson, W. E., Clark, V. L. P., & Morales, A. (2007). Qualitative research designs: Selection and implementation. *The Counseling Psychologist, 35*, 236-264.

Creswell, J. W., & Miller, D. L. (2000). Determining validity in qualitative inquiry. *Theory into Practice, 39*, 124-130.

Croft, A., Schmader, T., Block, K., & Baron, A. S. (2014). The second shift reflected in the second generation: Do parents' gender roles at home predict children's aspirations? *Psychological Science, 25*, 1418-1428.

Cumming, G. (2012). *Understanding the new statistics: Effect sizes, confidence intervals, and meta-analysis.* New York, NY: Routledge.

Cumming, G. (2014). The new statistics: Why and how. *Psychological Science, 25*, 7-29.

Cumming, G., & Finch, S. (2005). Inference by eye: Confidence intervals and how to read pictures of data. *American Psychologist, 60*, 170-180.

Cuttler, C., & Graf, P. (2007). Personality predicts prospective memory task performance: An adult lifespan study. *Scandinavian Journal of Psychology, 48*, 215-231.

Czaja, J., Hartmann, A. S., Rief, W., & Hilbert, A. (2011). Mealtime family interactions in home environments of children with loss of control eating. *Appetite, 56*, 587-593.

Darredeau, C., & Barrett, S. P. (2010). The role of nicotine content information in smokers' subjective responses to nicotine and placebo inhalers. *Human Psychopharmacology, 25*, 577-581.

Davidson, E. J. (2005). *Evaluation methodology basics: The nuts and bolts of sound evaluation.* Thousand Oaks, CA: Sage Publications.

Denmark, F., Russo, N. P., Frieze, I. H., & Sechzer, J. A. (1988). Guidelines for avoiding sexism in psychological research: A report of the Ad Hoc Committee on Nonsexist Research. *American Psychologist, 43*, 582-585.

Dickstein, S., Hayden, L.C., Schiller, M., Seifer, R., & San Antonio, W. (1994). *Providence family study mealtime family interaction coding system.* Unpublished classification manual, Bradley Research Center, East Providence, RI.

Dill, C. A., Gilden, E. R., Hill, P. C., & Hanslka, L. L. (1982). Federal human subjects regulations: A methodological artifact? *Personality and Social Psychology Bulletin, 8*, 417-425.

Dillman, D. A. (2000). *Mail and Internet surveys: The tailored design method* (2nd ed.). New York: Wiley.

Doiron, J. P., & Nicki, R. M. (2001). Epidemiology of problem gambling in Prince Edward Island: A Canadian microcosm? *Canadian Journal of Psychiatry, 46*, 413-417.

Dolhanty, J., & Greenberg, L. S. (2009). Emotion-focused therapy in a case of anorexia nervosa. *Clinical Psychology and Psychotherapy, 16*, 366-382.

Donner, D. D., Snowden, D. A., & Friesen, W. V. (2001). Positive emotions in early life and longevity: Findings from the Nun Study. *Journal of Personality and Social Psychology, 80*, 804-813.

Doyen, S., Klein, O., Pichon, C.-L., & Cleeremans, A. (2012). Behavioral priming: It's all in the mind, but whose mind? *PLoS ONE, 7*, e29081.

Drankiewicz, D., & Dundes, L. (2003). Handwashing among female college students. *American Journal of Infection Control, 31*, 67-71.

Dubois-Comtois, K., & Moss, E. (2008). Beyond the dyad: Do family interactions influence children's attachment representations in middle childhood? *Attachment & Human Development, 10*, 415-431.

Duggan, K. A., Reynolds, C. A., Kern, M. L., & Friedman, H. S. (2014). Childhood sleep and lifelong mortality risk. *Health Psychology, 33*, 1195-1203.

Dumont, M., Leclerc, D., & McKinnon, S. (2009). Consequences of part-time work on the academic and psychosocial adaptation of adolescents. *Canadian Journal of School Psychology, 24(1)*, 58-75.

Dunlosky, J., Rawson, K. A., Marsh, E. J., Nathan, M., & Willingham, D. T. (2013). Improving students' learning with effective learning techniques: Promising directions from cognitive and educational psychology. *Psychological Science in the Public Interest, 14*, 4-58.

Dunn, E. W., Aknin, L. B., & Norton, M. I. (2008). Spending money on others promotes happiness. *Science, 319*, 1687-1688.

Eagle, D. E. (2011). Changing patterns of attendance at religious services in Canada, 1986-2008. *Journal for the Scientific Study of Religion, 50*, 187-200.

Earp, B. D., Everett, J. A. C., Madva, E. N., & Hamlin, J. K. (2014). Out, damned spot: Can the "Macbeth Effect" be replicated? *Basic and Applied Social Psychology, 36*, 91-98.

Eich, E. (2014). Business not as usual. [Editorial]. *Psychological Science, 25,* 3-6.

Ekman, P., & Friesen, W. V. (1978). *Facial action coding system: A technique for the measurement of facial movement.* Palo Alto, CA: Consulting Psychologists Press.

Elms, A. C. (1994). *Uncovering lives: The uneasy alliance of biography and psychology.* New York: Oxford University Press.

Epstein, Y. M., Suedfeld, P., & Silverstein, S. J. (1973). The experimental contract: Subjects' expectations of and reactions to some behaviors of experimenters. *American Psychologist, 28,* 212-221.

Falk, C. F., Heine, S. J., Yuki, M., & Takemura, K. (2009). Why do Westerners self-enhance more than East Asians? *European Journal of Personality, 23,* 183-203.

Fanelli, D. (2012). Negative results are disappearing from most disciplines and countries. *Scientometrics, 90,* 891-904.

Farzan, R., & Kraut, R. E. (2013). Wikipedia classroom experiment: Bidirectional benefits of students' engagement in online production communities. *CHI'13, Proceedings of the SIGCHI Conference on Human Factors in Computing Systems,* 783-792.

Faul, F., Erdfelder, E., Lang, A.-G., & Buchner, A. (2007). G*Power 3: A flexible statistical power analysis program for the social, behavioral, and biomedical sciences. *Behavior Research Methods, 39,* 175-191.

Feldman-Barrett, L., & Barrett, D. J. (2001). Computerized experience-sampling: How technology facilitates the study of conscious experience. *Social Science Computer Review, 19,* 175-185.

Felten, E. W. (2014, June 6). Facebook's emotional manipulation study: When ethical worlds collide [Weblog]. *Huffington Post.* Retrieved from http://www.huffingtonpost.com/edward-w-felten/facebooks-emotional-manip_b_5545567.html

Ferguson, R., Robidoux, S., & Besner, D. (2009). Reading aloud: Evidence for contextual control over lexical activation. *Journal of Experimental Psychology: Human Perception and Performance, 35,* 499-507.

Finch, S., Cumming, G., & Thomason, N. (2001). Reporting of statistical inference in the *Journal of Applied Psychology:* Little evidence of reform. *Educational and Psychological Measurement, 61,* 181-210.

Finkel, E. J., Eastwick, P. W., & Matthews, J. (2007). Speed-dating as an invaluable tool for studying romantic attraction: A methodological primer. *Personal Relationships, 14,* 149-166.

Fisher, C. B. (2010). Enhancing HIV vaccine trial consent preparedness among street drug users. *Journal of Empirical Research on Human Research Ethics: An International Journal, 5,* 65-80.

Fiske, S. T. (2004). Mind the gap: In praise of informal sources of formal theory. *Personality and Social Psychology Review, 8,* 132-137.

Fiske, S. T. (2009). Institutional Review Boards: From bane to benefit. *Perspectives on Psychological Science, 4,* 30-31.

Flavell, J. H. (1996). Piaget's legacy. *Psychological Science, 7,* 200-203.

Foster, R. G., & Roenneberg, T. (2008). Human responses to the geophysical daily, annual and lunar cycles. *Current Biology, 18,* R784-R794.

Fournier, J. C., DeRubeis, R. J., Hollon, S. D., Dimidjian, S., Amsterdam, J. D., Shelton, R. C., & Fawcett, J. (2010). Antidepressant drug effects and depression severity: A patient-level meta-analysis. *Journal of the American Medical Association, 303,* 47-53.

Fowler, F. J., Jr. (1984). *Survey research methods.* Newbury Park, CA: Sage.

Fraser, K., Huffman, J., Ma, I., Sobczak, M., McIlwrick, J., Wright, B., & McLaughlin, K. (2014). The emotional and cognitive impact of unexpected simulated patient death: A randomized control trial. *CHEST, 145,* 958-963.

Freedman, J. L. (1969). Role-playing: Psychology by consensus. *Journal of Personality and Social Psychology, 13,* 107-114.

Freedman, J. L., Levy, A. S., Buchanan, R. W., & Price, J. (1972). Crowding and human aggressiveness. *Journal of Experimental Social Psychology, 8,* 528-548.

Frick, R. W. (1995). Accepting the null hypothesis. *Memory and Cognition, 25,* 132-138.

Friedman, H. S., Tucker, J. S., Schwartz, J. E., Tomlinson-Keasy, C., Martin, L. R., Wingard, D. L., & Criqui, M. H. (1995). Psychosocial and behavioral predictors of longevity: The aging and death of the "Termites." *American Psychologist, 50,* 69-78.

Gailliot, M. T., Baumeister, R. F., DeWall, C. N., Maner, J. K., Plant, E. A., Tice, D. M., . . . Schmeichel, B. J. (2007). Self-control relies on glucose as a limited energy source: Willpower is more than a metaphor. *Journal of Personality and Social Psychology, 92,* 325-336.

Gallup, G. G., & Suarez, S. D. (1985). Alternatives to the use of animals in psychological research. *American Psychologist, 40,* 1104-1111.

Gardner, G. T. (1978). Effects of federal human subjects regulations on data obtained in environmental stressor research. *Journal of Personality and Social Psychology, 34,* 774-781.

Gardner, L. E. (1988). A relatively painless method of introduction to the psychological literature search. In M. E. Ware & C. L. Brewer (Eds.), *Handbook for teaching statistics and research methods.* Hillsdale, NJ: Erlbaum.

Gaucher, D., Friesen, J., & Kay, A. C. (2011). Evidence that gendered wording in job advertisements exists and sustains gender inequality. *Journal of Personality and Social Psychology, 101,* 109-128.

Gaudreau, P., Miranda, D., & Gareau, A. (2014). Canadian university students in wireless classrooms: What do they do on their laptops and does it really matter? *Computers and Education, 70,* 245-255.

Gauthier, C. (2004). Overview and analysis of animal use in North America. *ALTA: Alternatives to Laboratory Animals, 32,* 275-285.

Gee, C. J., & Leith, L. M. (2007). Aggressive behavior in professional ice hockey: A cross-cultural comparison of North American and European born NHL players. *Psychology of Sport and Exercise, 8,* 567-583.

Gelfand, M. J., & Diener, E. (2010). Culture and psychological science: Introduction to the special section. *Perspectives on Psychological Science, 5,* 390.

Gervais, W. M. (2011). Finding the faithless: Perceived atheist prevalence reduces anti-atheist prejudice. *Personality and Social Psychology Bulletin, 37,* 543-556.

Gigerenzer, G., Gaissmaier, W., Kurz-Milcke, E., Schwartz, L. M., & Woloshin, S. (2007). Helping doctors and patients make sense of health statistics. *Psychological Science in the Public Interest, 8,* 53-96.

Gilovich, T. (1991). *How we know what isn't so: The fallibility of human reason in everyday life.* New York: Free Press.

Giltrow, J., Gooding, R., Burgoyne, D., & Sawatsky, M. (2014). *Academic writing: An introduction* (3rd ed.). Peterborough, ON: Broadview.

Glantz, L. H., Annas, G. J., Grodin, M. A., Mariner, W. K. (2001). Research in developing countries: Taking "benefit" seriously. In Teays, W., & Purdy, L. (Eds.), *Bioethics, justice, and health care* (pp. 261-267). Belmont, CA: Wadsworth.

Gonzalez, A. Q., & Koestner, R. (2005). Parental preference for sex of newborn as reflected in positive affect in birth announcements. *Sex Roles, 52,* 407-411.

Goodstein, D. (2010). *On fact and fraud: Cautionary tales from the front lines of science.* Princeton, NJ: Princeton University Press.

Goodstein, D. (2011). How science works. In Committee on Science, Technology, and Law Policy and Global Affairs, *Reference Manual on Scientific Evidence* (3rd ed.) (pp. 37-54). Washington, DC: The National Academies Press. Retrieved from http://www.fjc.gov/

Gosling, S. D., & Johnson, J. A. (Eds). (2010). *Advanced methods for behavioral research on the Internet.* Washington, DC: American Psychological Association.

Gosling, S. D., Vazire, S., Srivastava, S., & John, O. (2004). Should we trust web-based studies? A comparative analysis of six preconceptions about Internet questionnaires. *American Psychologist, 59,* 93-104.

Graesser, A. C., Kennedy, T., Wiemer-Hastings, P., & Ottati, V. (1999). The use of computational cognitive methods to improve questions on surveys and questionnaires. In M. G. Sirkin, D. J. Hermann, S. Schechter, N. Schwarz, J. M. Tanur, & R. Tourangeau (Eds.), *Cognition and survey methods research* (pp. 199-216). New York: Wiley.

Graham, K., Bernards, S., Osgood, D. W., Parks, M., Abbey, A., Felson, R. B., . . . Wells, S. (2013). Apparent motives for aggression in the social context of the bar. *Psychology of Violence, 3,* 218-232.

Graham, K., Tremblay, P. F., Wells, S., Pernanen, K., Purcell, J., & Jelley, J. (2006). Harm, intent, and the nature of aggressive behaviour:

Measuring naturally occurring aggression in barroom settings. *Assessment, 13,* 280-296.

Green, J., & Wallaf, C. (1981). *Ethnography and language in educational settings.* New York: Ablex.

Green, R. J., Sandall, J. C., & Phelps, C. (2005). Effect of experimenter attire and sex on participant productivity. *Social Behavior and Personality, 33,* 125-132.

Greenfield, D. N. (1999). *Nature of Internet addiction: Psychological factors in compulsive Internet use.* Paper presented at the meeting of the American Psychological Association, Boston, MA.

Greenland, S., & Morgenstern, H. (2001). Confounding in health research. *Annual Review of Public Health, 22,* 189-212.

Greenwald, A. G. (1976). Within-subjects designs: To use or not to use? *Psychological Bulletin, 83,* 314-320.

Grissom, R. J., & Kim, J. J. (2012). *Effect sizes for research: Univariate and multivariate applications* (2nd ed.). New York: Routledge.

Gross, A. E., & Fleming, I. (1982). Twenty years of deception in social psychology. *Personality and Social Psychology Bulletin, 8,* 402-408.

Guay, J.-P., Ruscio, J., Knight, R. A., & Hare, R. D. (2007). A taxometric analysis of the latent structure of psychopathy: Evidence for dimensionality. *Journal of Abnormal Psychology, 116,* 701-716.

Hagger, M. S., Wood, C., Stiff, C., & Chatzisanrantis, N. L. D. (2010). Ego depletion and the strength model of self-control: A meta-analysis. *Psychological Bulletin, 136,* 495-525.

Hamamura, T., Heine, S. J., Paulhus, D. L. (2008). Cultural differences in response styles: The role of dialectical thinking. *Personality and Individual Differences, 44,* 932-942.

Hammond, D., Fong, G. T., Borland, R., Cummings, K. M., McNeill, A., & Driezen, P. (2007). Text and graphic warnings on cigarette packages: Findings from the International Tobacco Control Four Country Study. *American Journal of Preventive Medicine, 32,* 202-209.

Han, X., & Becker, S. (2014). One spatial map or many? Spatial coding of connected environments. *Journal of Experimental Psychology: Learning, Memory, & Cognition, 40,* 511-531.

Haney, C., & Zimbardo, P. G. (1998). The past and future of U.S. prison policy: Twenty-five years after the Stanford Prison Experiment. *American Psychologist, 53,* 709-727.

Hanson, M. D., & Chen, E. (2010). Daily stress, cortisol, and sleep: The moderating role of childhood psychosocial environments. *Health Psychology, 29,* 394-402.

Hare, R. D. (1991). *The Hare Psychopathy Checklist-Revised (PCL-R).* Toronto: Multi-Health Systems.

Hare, R. D., Harpur, T. J., & Hemphill, J. D. (1989). Scoring Pamphlet for the Self-Report Psychopathy Scale: SRP-II. Unpublished manuscript, Simon Fraser University, Vancouver, British Columbia, Canada.

Harkness, K. L., Stewart, J. G., & Wynne-Edwards, K. E. (2011). Cortisol reactivity to social stress in adolescents: Role of depression severity and child maltreatment. *Psychoneuroendocrinology, 36,* 173-181.

Harris, C. M., & Cameron, S. L. (2010). Displacing *Wikipedia.* In D. S. Dunn, B. C. Beins, M. A. McCarthy, & G. W. Hill, IV (Eds.), *Best practices for teaching beginnings and endings in the psychology major.* New York: Oxford.

Harris, C. R., Coburn, N., Rohrer, D., & Pashler, H. (2013). Two failures to replicate high-performance-goal priming effects. *PLOSONE, 8,* e72467.

Harris, R. (2002). *Anti-plagiarism strategies for research papers.* Retrieved September 10, 2002, from http://www.virtualsalt.com/antiplag.htm

Hart, S. D., & Hare, R. D. (1989). Discriminant validity of the Psychopathy Checklist in a forensic psychiatric population. *Psychological Assessment: A Journal of Consulting and Clinical Psychology, 1,* 211-218.

Hawking, S. W. (1988). *A brief history of time: From the big bang to black holes.* New York: Bantam Books.

Hayashi, K., Wood, E., Wiebe, L., Qi, J., & Kerr, T. (2010). An external evaluation of a peer-run outreach-based syringe exchange in Vancouver, Canada. *International Journal of Drug Policy, 21,* 418-421.

Heine, S. J., Foster, J. A. B., & Spina, R. (2009). Do birds of a feature universally flock together? Cultural variation in the similarity-attraction effect. *Asian Journal of Social Psychology, 12,* 247-258.

Heine, S. J., & Hamamura, T. (2007). In search of East Asian self-enhancement. *Personality and Social Psychology Review, 11,* 4-27.

Heine, S. J., Lehman, D. R., Peng, K., & Greenholtz, J. (2002). What's wrong with cross-cultural comparisons of subjective Likert scales? The reference-group effect. *Journal of Personality and Social Psychology, 82,* 903-918.

Heine, S. J., Proulx, T., & Vohs, K. D. (2006). The Meaning Maintenance Model: On the coherence of social motivations. *Personality and Social Psychology Review, 10,* 88-110.

Henrich, J., Heine, S. J., & Norenzayan, A. (2010a). The weirdest people in the world? [Target Article]. *Behavioral and Brain Sciences, 33,* 1-23.

Henrich, J., Heine, S. J., & Norenzayan, A. (2010b). Beyond WEIRD: Towards a broad-based behavioural science. [Response]. *Behavioral and Brain Sciences, 33,* 111-135.

Henry, B., & Pulcino, R. (2009). Individual difference and study-specific characteristics influencing attitudes about the use of animals in medical research. *Society & Animals, 17,* 305-324.

Hertwig, R., & Ortmann, A. (2008). Deception in experiments: Revisiting the arguments in its defense. *Ethics & Behavior, 18,* 59-92.

Hill, L. (1990). Effort and reward in college: A replication of some puzzling findings. In J. W. Neuliep (Ed.), *Handbook of replication in the behavioral and social sciences* [Special issue]. *Journal of Social Behavior and Personality, 5*(4), 151-161.

Hockey, G. R., & Earle, F. (2006). Control over the scheduling of simulated office work reduces the impact of workload on mental fatigue and task performance. *Journal of Experimental Psychology: Applied, 12,* 50-65.

Hodson, G., Choma, B. L., & Costello, K. (2009). Experiencing alien-nation: Effects of a simulation intervention on attitudes toward homosexuals. *Journal of Experimental Social Psychology, 45,* 974-978.

Hogarth, R. M., Portell, M., & Cuxart, A. (2007). What risks do people perceive in everyday life? A perspective gained from the Experience Sampling Method (ESM). *Risk Analysis, 27,* 1427-1439.

Holleran, S. E., Whitehead, J., Schmader, T., & Mehl, M. R. (2011). Talking shop and shooting the breeze: A study of workplace conversation and job disengagement among STEM faculty. *Social Psychological and Personality Science, 2,* 65-71.

Hood, T. C., & Back, K. W. (1971). Self-disclosure and the volunteer: A source of bias in laboratory experiments. *Journal of Personality and Social Psychology, 17,* 130-136.

Howell, R. T., Rodzon, K. S., Kurai, M., & Sanchez, A. H. (2010). A validation of well-being and happiness surveys for administration via the Internet. *Behavior Research Methods, 42,* 775-784.

Interagency Advisory Panel on Research Ethics (PRE). (2009). *Introductory Tutorial for the Tri-Council Policy statement: Ethical Conduct for Research Involving Humans (TCPS).* Retrieved December 13, 2011, from http://www.pre. ethics.gc.ca/english/tutorial/welcome.cfm

Inzlicht, M., Schmeichel, B. J., & Macrae, C. N. (2014). Why self-control seems (but may not be) limited. *Trends in Cognitive Sciences, 18,* 127-133.

Ioannidis, J. P. (2005). Why most published research findings are false. *PLoS Medicine, 2,* 0696-0701.

Jackson, I., & Sirois, S. (2009). Infant cognition: Going full factorial with pupil dilation. *Developmental Science, 12,* 670-679.

John, L. K., Loewenstein, G., & Prelec, D. (2012). Measuring the prevalence of questionable research practices with incentives for truth telling. *Psychological Science, 23,* 524-532.

Jones, R., & Cooper, J. (1971). Mediation of experimenter effects. *Journal of Personality and Social Psychology, 20,* 70-74.

Judd, C. M., Smith, E. R., & Kidder, L. H. (1991). *Research methods in social relations* (6th ed.). Ft. Worth, TX: Holt, Rinehart & Winston.

Kail, R. V. (2015). *Scientific writing in psychology: Lessons in clarity and style.* Thousand Oaks, CA: SAGE.

Kaufmann, H. (1967). The price of obedience and the price of knowledge. *American Psychologist, 22,* 321-322.

Kazdin, A. E. (1995). Preparing and evaluating research reports. *Psychological Assessment, 7,* 228-237.

Kazdin, A. E. (2001). *Behavior modification in applied settings* (6th ed.). Belmont, CA: Wadsworth.

Kelman, H. C. (1967). Human use of human subjects: The problem of deception in social psychological experiments. *Psychological Bulletin, 67,* 1-11.

Kenny, D. A. (1979). *Correlation and causality.* New York: Wiley.

Kifer, Y., Heller, D., Perunovic, W. Q. E., & Galinsky, A. D. (2013). The good life of the powerful: The experience of power and authenticity enhances subjective well-being. *Psychological Science, 24,* 280-288.

Kintz, N. L., Delprato, D. J., Mettee, D. R., Persons, C. E., & Schappe, R. H. (1965). The experimenter effect. *Psychological Bulletin, 63*, 223-232.

Kirsch, I., Deacon, B. J., Huedo-Medina, T. B., Scoboria, A., Moore, T. J., & Johnson, B. T. (2008). Initial severity and antidepressant benefits: A meta-analysis of data submitted to the Food and Drug Administration. *PLoS Medicine, 5*, 260-268.

Kirschbaum, C., Pirke, K.-M., & Hellhammer, D. H. (1993). The 'Trier Social Stress Test': A tool for investigating psychobiological stress responses in a laboratory setting. *Neuropsychobiology, 28*, 76-81.

Kitayama, S., Markus, H. R., Matsumoto, H., & Norasakkunkit, V. (1997). Individual and collective processes in the construction of the self: Self-enhancement in the United States and self-criticism in Japan. *Journal of Personality and Social Psychology, 72*, 1245-1267.

Klassen, R. M., & Chiu, M. M. (2010). Effects of teachers' self-efficacy and job satisfaction: Teacher gender, years of experience, and job stress. *Journal of Educational Psychology, 102*, 741-759.

Klatzky, R. L. (2009). Giving psychological science away: The role of applications courses. *Perspectives on Psychological Science, 4*, 522-530.

Klaver, J. R., Lee, Z., & Hart, S. D. (2007). Psychopathy and nonverbal indicators of deception in offenders. *Law and Human Behavior, 31*, 337-351.

Klein, O., Doyen, S., Leys, C., Magalhães de Saldanha da Gama, P. A., Miller, S., Questienne, L., & Cleeremans, A. (2012). Low hopes, high expectations: Expectancy effects and the replicability of behavioural experiments. *Perspectives on Psychological Science, 7*, 572-584.

Kline, R. B. (2010). *Principles and practice of structural equation modeling* (3rd ed.). New York: Guilford Press.

Kline, R. B. (2013). *Beyond significance testing: Statistics reform in the behavioral sciences* (2nd ed.). Washington, DC: APA Books.

Knight, S., Vrij, A., Bard, K., & Brandon, D. (2009). Science versus human welfare? Understanding attitudes toward animal use. *Journal of Social Issues, 65*, 463-483.

Koocher, G. P. (1977). Bathroom behavior and human dignity. *Journal of Personality and Social Psychology, 35*, 120-121.

Koocher, G. P. (2009). Ethics and the invisible psychologist. *Psychological Services, 6*, 97-107.

Korn, J. H. (1997). *Illusions of reality: A history of deception in social psychology*. Albany: State University of New York Press.

Koss, M. P. (1992). The underdetection of rape: Methodological choices influence incident estimates. *Journal of Social Issues, 48*(1), 61-75.

Kramer, A. D. I., Guillory, J. E., & Hancock, J. T. (2014). Experimental evidence of massive-scale emotional contagion through social networks. *Proceedings of the National Academy of Sciences, 111*, 8788-8790.

Kraut, R., Olson, J., Banaji, M., Bruckman, A., Cohen, J., & Couper, M. (2004). Psychological research online: Report of Board of Scientific Affairs Advisory Group on the Conduct of Research on the Internet. *American Psychologist, 59*, 105-117.

Krawczyk, M. (2011). What brings your subjects to the lab? A field experiment. *Experimental Economics, 14*, 482-489.

Krosnick, J. A. (1999). Survey research. *Annual Review of Psychology, 50*, 537-567.

Kühberger, A., Fritz, A., & Scherndl, T. (2014). Publication bias in psychology: A diagnosis based on the correlation between effect size and sample size. *PLoS ONE, 9*, e105825.

Kwan, D., Craver, C. F., Green, L., Myerson, J., & Rosenbaum, R. S. (2013). Dissociations in future thinking following hippocampal damage: Evidence from discounting and time perspective in episodic amnesia. *Journal of Experimental Psychology: General, 142*, 1355-1369.

Lana, R. E. (1969). Pretest sensitization. In R. Rosenthal & R. L. Rosnow (Eds.), *Artifacts in behavioral research*. New York: Academic Press.

Laney, C., Kaasa, S. O., Morris, E. K., Berkowitz, S. R., Bernstein, D. M., & Loftus, E. F. (2008). The Red Herring technique: A methodological response to the problem of demand characteristics. *Psychological Research, 72*, 362-375.

Larsen, H., Overbeek, G., Granic, I., & Engels, R. C. M. E. (2012). The strong effect of other people's drinking: Two experimental observation studies in a real bar. *The American Journal on Addictions, 21*, 168-175.

Lauster, N., & Easterbrook, A. (2011). No room for new families? A field experiment measuring rental discrimination against same-sex couples and single parents. *Social Problems, 58*, 389-409.

Laverty, W. H., & Kelly, I. W. (1998). Cyclical calendar and lunar patterns in automobile property accidents and injury accidents. *Perceptual and Motor Skills, 86*, 299-302.

LeBel, E. P., Borsboom, D., Giner-Sorolla, R., Hasselman, F., Peters, K. R., Ratliff, K. A., & Smith, C. T. (2013). PsychDisclosure.org: Grassroots support for reforming reporting standards in psychology. *Perspectives on Psychological Science, 8*, 424-432.

LeBel, E. P., & Campbell, L. (2009). Implicit partner affect, relationship satisfaction, and the prediction of romantic breakup. *Journal of Experimental Social Psychology, 45*, 1291-1294.

LeBel, E. P., & Peters, K. R. (2011). Fearing the future of empirical psychology: Bem's (2011) evidence of psi as a case study of deficiencies in modal research practice. *Review of General Psychology, 15*, 371-379.

Levelt Committee, Noort Committee, Drenth Committee (2012, November 28). *Flawed science: The fraudulent research practices of social psychologist Diederik Stapel* [English translation]. Retrieved July 31, 2014, from https://www.commissielevelt.nl/wp-content/uploads_per_blog/commissielevelt/2013/01/finalreportLevelt1.pdf

Levine, D. G., & Ducharme, J. M. (2013). The effects of a teacher-child play intervention on classroom compliance in young children in child care settings. *Journal of Behavioral Education, 22*, 50-65.

Levine, R. V. (1990). The pace of life. *American Scientist, 78*, 450-459.

Lewis, S. C., Zamith, R., & Hermida, A. (2013). Content analysis in an era of Big Data: A hybrid approach to computational and manual methods. *Journal of Broadcasting & Electronic Media, 57*, 34-52.

Likert, R. (1932). A technique for the measurement of attitudes. *Archives of Psychology, 22*(140), 5-55.

Lilienfeld, S. O., Ritschel, L. A., Lynn, S. J., Cautin, R. L., & Latzman, R. D. (2013). Why many clinical psy-chologists are resistant to evidence-based practice: Root causes and constructive remedies. *Clinical Psychology Review, 33*, 883-900.

Linden, W., Talbot Ellis, A., & Millman, R. (2010). Deception in stress reactivity and recovery research. *International Journal of Psychophysiology, 75*, 33-38.

Lindsay, R. C., & Wells, G. L. (1985). Improving eyewitness identifications from lineups: Simultaneous versus sequential lineup presentation. *Journal of Applied Psychology, 70*, 556-564.

Loftus, E. (1979). *Eyewitness testimony.* Cambridge, MA: Harvard University Press.

Lönnqvist, J.-E., Paunonen, S., Verkasalo, M., Leikas, S., Tuulio-Henriksson, A., & Lönnqvist, J. (2007). Personality characteristics of research volunteers. *European Journal of Personality, 21*, 1017-1030.

Luria, A. R. (1968). *The mind of a mnemonist.* New York: Basic Books.

Lynn, M., & McCall, M. (2009). Techniques for increasing servers' tips. *Cornell Hospitality Quarterly, 50*, 198-208.

Lynn, M., & Sturman, M. J. (2010). Tipping and service quality: A within-subjects analysis. *Journal of Tourism and Hospitality Research, 34*, 269-275.

Madigan, R., Johnson, S., & Linton, P. (1995). The language of psychology: APA style as epistemology. *American Psychologist, 50*, 428-436.

Markowetz, A., Blaszkiewicz, K., Montag, C., Switala, C., & Schlaepfer, T. E. (2014). Psycho-informatics: Big data shaping modern psychometrics. *Medical Hypotheses, 82*, 405-411.

Masson, M. E. J., & Loftus, G. R. (2003). Using confidence intervals for graphically based data interpretation. *Canadian Journal of Experimental Psychology, 57*, 203-220.

Matsumoto, D. (1994). *Cultural influences on research methods and statistics.* Belmont, CA: Brooks/Cole.

Mayhew, D. R., Simpson, H. M., Wood, K. M., Lonero, L., Clinton, K. M., & Johnson, A. G. (2011). On-road and simulated driving: Concurrent and discriminant validation. *Journal of Safety Research, 42*, 267-275.

McCutcheon, L. E. (2000). Another failure to generalize the Mozart effect. *Psychological Reports, 87*, 325-330.

McFerran, B., Dahl, D. W., Fitzsimons, G. J., & Morales, A. C. (2010). I'll have what she's having: Effects of social influence and body type on the food choices of others. *Journal of Consumer Research, 36*, 915-929.

McGue, M., Osler, M., & Christensen, K. (2010). Causal inference and observational research: The utility of twins. *Perspectives on Psychological Science, 5*, 546-556.

McGuigan, F. J. (1963). The experimenter: A neglected stimulus. *Psychological Bulletin, 60,* 421-428.

McNeill, P. M. (1993). *The ethics and politics of human experimentation.* New York, NY: Cambridge University Press.

Mehdizadeh, S. (2010). Self-presentation 2.0: Narcissism and self-esteem on Facebook. *Cyberpsychology, Behavior, and Social Networking, 13,* 357-364.

Mehl, M. R., Pennebaker, J. W., Crow, D. M., Dabbs, J., & Price, J. H. (2001). The Electronically Activated Recorder (EAR): A device for sampling naturalistic daily activities and conversations. *Behavior Research Methods, Instruments, & Computers, 33,* 517-523.

Merton, R. K. (1973). *The sociology of science.* Chicago: University of Chicago Press.

Middlemist, R. D., Knowles, E. S., & Matter, C. F. (1976). Personal space invasion in the lavatory: Suggestive evidence for arousal. *Journal of Personality and Social Psychology, 33,* 541-546.

Middlemist, R. D., Knowles, E. S., & Matter, C. F. (1977). What to do and what to report: A reply to Koocher. *Journal of Personality and Social Psychology, 35,* 122-124.

Miguel, E., Camerer, C., Casey, K., Cohen, J., Esterling, K. M., Gerber, A., . . . Van der Laan, M. (2014). Promoting transparency in social science research. *Science, 343,* 30-31.

Milgram, S. (1963). Behavioral study of obedience. *Journal of Abnormal and Social Psychology, 67,* 371-378.

Milgram, S. (1964). Group pressure and action against a person. *Journal of Abnormal and Social Psychology, 69,* 137-143.

Milgram, S. (1965). Some conditions of obedience and disobedience to authority. *Human Relations, 18,* 57-76.

Miller, A. G. (1972). Role-playing: An alternative to deception? *American Psychologist, 27,* 623-636.

Miller, A. G. (1986). *The obedience experiments: A case study of controversy in social science.* New York: Praeger.

Miller, G. A. (1969). Psychology as a means of promoting human welfare. *American Psychologist, 24,* 1063-1075.

Miller, J. G. (1999). Cultural psychology: Implications for basic psychological theory. *Psychological Science, 10,* 85-91.

Miller, N. E. (1985). The value of behavioral research on animals. *American Psychologist, 40,* 423-440.

Mitchell, G. (2012). Revisiting truth or triviality: The external validity of research in the psychological laboratory. *Perspectives on Psychological Science, 7,* 109-117.

Molden, D. C., Hui, C. M., Scholer, A. A., Meier, B. P., Noreen, E. E., D'Agostino, P. R., & Martin, V. (2012). Motivational versus metabolic effects of carbohydrates on self-control. *Psychological Science, 23,* 1137-1144.

Montee, B. B., Miltenberger, R. G., & Wittrock, D. (1995). An experimental analysis of facilitated communication. *Journal of Applied Behavior Analysis, 28,* 189-200.

Montoya, R. M., Horton, R. S., & Kirchner, J. (2008). Is actual similarity necessary for attraction? A meta-analysis of actual and perceived similarity. *Journal of Social and Personal Relationships, 25,* 889-922.

Moretti, M. M., & Obsuth, I. (2009). Effectiveness of an attachment-focused manualized intervention for parents of teens at risk for aggressive behavior: The Connect Program. *Journal of Adolescence, 32,* 1347-1357.

Morgan, D. L., & Morgan, R. K. (2001). Single-participant research design: Bringing science to managed care. *American Psychologist, 56,* 119-127.

Mosby, I. (2013). Administering colonial science: Nutrition research and human biomedical experimentation in Aboriginal communities and residential schools, 1942-1952. *Histoire sociale/Social history, 46,* 145-172.

Mostert, M. (2010). Facilitated communication and its legitimacy–Twenty-first century developments. *Exceptionality, 18,* 31-41.

Moulden, H. M., Firestone, P., Kingston, D. A., & Wexler, A. F. (2010). A description of sexual offending committed by Canadian teachers. *Journal of Child Sexual Abuse, 19,* 403-418.

Murray, B. (2002). Research fraud needn't happen at all. *APA Monitor, 33*(2). Retrieved July 31, 2002, from http://www.apa.org/monitor/feb02/fraud.html

Mychasiuk, R., & Benzies, K. (2011). Facebook: An effective tool for participant retention in longitudinal researcher. *Child: Care, Health and Development, 38,* 753-756.

Nathan, R. (2005). *My freshman year: What a professor learned by becoming a student.* Ithaca, NY: Cornell University Press.

National Commission for the Protection of Human Subjects of Biomedical and Behavioral Research. (1979, April 18). *The Belmont Report: Ethical principles and guidelines for the protection of human subjects of research.* Retrieved May 9, 2011, from http://ohsr.od.nih.gov/guidelines/belmont.html

Nelson, G., Ochocka, J., Janzen, R., & Trainor, J. (2006). A longitudinal study of mental health consumer/survivor initiatives: Part 2—A quantitative study of impacts of participation on new members. *Journal of Community Psychology, 34,* 261-272.

Neumann, C. S., Hare, R. D., & Newman, J. P. (2007). The super-ordinate nature of the Psychopathy Checklist-Revised. *Journal of Personality Disorders, 21,* 102-117.

Newcomb, T. M. (1961). *The acquaintance process.* New York: Holt, Rinehart & Winston.

Newman, E., & Kaloupek, D. G. (2004). The risks and benefits of participating in trauma-focused research studies. *Journal of Traumatic Stress, 17,* 383-394.

Newman, E., Risch, E., & Kassam-Adams, N. (2006). Ethical issues in trauma-related research: A review. *Journal of Empirical Research on Human Research Ethics: An International Journal, 1,* 29-46.

Nichols, A. L., & Maner, J. K. (2008). The good-subject effect: Investigating participant demand characteristics. *The Journal of General Psychology, 135,* 151-165.

Nicol, A. A. M., & Pexman, P. M. (2010). *Displaying your findings: A practical guide for creating figures, posters, and presentations* (6th ed.). Washington, DC: American Psychological Association.

Nisbett, R. E., & Ross, L. (1980). *Human inference: Strategies and shortcomings of social judgment.* Englewood Cliffs, NJ: Prentice-Hall.

Nisbett, R. E., & Wilson, T. D. (1977). Telling more than we can know: Verbal reports on mental processes. *Psychological Review, 84,* 231-259.

Norman, M. (2012). Saturday night's alright for tweeting: Cultural citizenship, collective discussion, and the new media consumption/production of *Hockey Day in Canada. Sociology of Sport Journal, 29,* 306-324.

Nowlis, S. M., Kahn, B. E., & Dhar, R. (2002). Coping with ambivalence: The effect of removing a neutral option on consumer attitude and preference judgments. *Journal of Consumer Research, 29,* 319-334.

Nunes, F. (1998). *Portuguese-Canadians from sea to sea: A national needs assessment.* Toronto: Portuguese-Canadian National Congress.

Oczak, M. (2007). Debriefing in deceptive research: A proposed new procedure. *Journal of Empirical Research on Human Research Ethics, 2,* 49-59.

Orne, M. T. (1962). On the social psychology of the psychological experiment: With particular reference to demand characteristics and their implications. *American Psychologist, 17,* 776-783.

Osgood, C. E., Suci, G. J., & Tannenbaum, P. H. (1957). *The measurement of meaning.* Urbana, IL: University of Illinois Press.

Osumi, T., & Ohira, H. (2010). The positive side of psychopathy: Emotional detachment in psychopathy and rational decision-making in the ultimatum game. *Personality and Individual Differences, 49,* 451-456.

Ozdemir, A. (2008). Shopping malls: Measuring interpersonal distance under changing conditions and across cultures. *Field Methods, 20,* 226-248.

Palys, T., & Lowman, J. (2010). Going boldly where no one has gone before? How confidentiality risk aversion is killing research on sensitive topics. *Journal of Academic Ethics, 8,* 265-284.

Pascual-Leone, A., Singh, T., & Scoboria, A. (2010). Using deception ethically: Practical research guidelines for researchers and reviewers. *Canadian Psychology, 51,* 241-248.

Pashler, H., Coburn, N., & Harris, C. R. (2012). Priming of social distance? Failure to replicate effects on social and food judgments. *PLOS ONE, 7,* e29081.

Pashler, H., & Wagenmakers, E.-J. (2012). Editors' introduction to the special section on replicability in psychological science: A crisis of confidence? *Perspectives on Psychological Science, 7,* 528-530.

Paulhus, D. L., Harms, P. D., Bruce, M. N., & Lysy, D. C. (2003). The Over-Claiming Technique: Measuring self-enhancement independent of ability. *Journal of Personality and Social Psychology, 84,* 890-904.

Peluso, D. L., Carleton, R. N., & Asmundson, G. J. G. (2011). Depression symptoms in Canadian psychology graduate students: Do research productivity, funding, and the academic advisory relationship play a role? *Canadian Journal of Behavioural Science, 43,* 119-127.

Pennebaker, J. W., Booth, R. J., & Francis, M. E. (2007). Linguistic Inquiry and Word Count: LIWC [Computer software]. Austin, TX: LIWC.net.

Pepitone, A., & Triandis, H. (1987). On the universality of social psychological theories. *Journal of Cross-Cultural Psychology, 18,* 471-499.

Petty, R. E., & Cacioppo, J. T. (1986). *Communication and persuasion: Central and peripheral routes to attitude change.* New York: Springer-Verlag.

Pfungst, O. (1911). *Clever Hans (the horse of Mr. von Osten): A contribution to experimental, animal, and human psychology* (C. L. Rahn, Trans.). New York: Holt, Rinehart & Winston. (Republished 1965.)

Piaget, J. (1952). *The origins of intelligence in children.* New York: International Universities Press.

Pietschnig, J., Voracek, M., & Formann, A. K. (2010). Mozart effect-Shmozart effect: A meta-analysis. *Intelligence, 38,* 314-323.

Plous, S. (1996a). Attitudes toward the use of animals in psychological research and education: Results from a national survey of psychologists. *American Psychologist, 51,* 1167-1180.

Plous, S. (1996b). Attitudes toward the use of animals in psychological research and education: Results from a national survey of psychology majors. *Psychological Science, 7,* 352-363.

Popper, K. (1968). *The logic of scientific discovery.* New York: Harper & Row.

Poulin, K. L. (2007). Teaching qualitative research: Lessons from practice. *The Counseling Psychologist, 35,* 431-458.

Pozzulo, J. D., Crescini, C., & Panton, T. (2008). Does methodology matter in eyewitness identification research?: The effect of live versus video exposure on eyewitness identification accuracy. *International Journal of Law and Psychiatry, 31,* 430-437.

Pozzulo, J. D., & Marciniak, S. (2006). Comparing identification procedures when the perpetrator has changed appearance. *Psychology, Crime & Law, 12,* 429-438.

Prelec, D. (2004). A Bayesian Truth Serum for subjective data. *Science, 306,* 462-466.

Proulx, T., & Inzlicht, M. (2012). The five "A"s of Meaning Maintenance: Finding meaning in the theories of sense-making. *Psychological Inquiry, 23,* 317-335.

Provencher, V., Bier, N., Audet, T., & Gagnon, L. (2008). Errorless-based techniques can improve route finding in early Alzheimer's disease: A case study. *American Journal of Alzheimer's Disease & Other Dementias, 23,* 47-56.

Provost, M. P., Kormos, C., Kosakoski, G., & Quinsey, V. L. (2006). Sociosexuality in women and preference for facial masculinization and somatotype in men. *Archives of Sexual Behavior, 35,* 305-312.

Pruessner, M., Béchard-Evans, L., Boekstyn, L., Iyer, S. N., Pruessner, J. C., & Malla, A. K. (2013). Attenuated cortisol response to acute psychosocial stress in individuals at ultra-high risk for psychosis. *Schizophrenia Research, 146,* 79-86.

Prus, R., & Irini, S. (1980). *Hookers, rounders, and desk clerks: The social organization of the hotel community.* Toronto: Gage.

Public Prosecution Service of Canada (PPSC). (2011). Federal/Provincial/Territorial heads of Prosecutions Subcommittee on the Prevention of Wrongful Convictions. *The path to justice: Preventing wrongful convictions.* Retrieved from http://www.ppsc-sppc.gc.ca/eng/pub/ptj-spj/index.html

Quinlan, C. K., Taylor, T. L., & Fawcett, J. M. (2010). Directed forgetting: Comparing pictures and words. *Canadian Journal of Experimental Psychology, 64,* 41-46.

R. v. Berikoff, BCSC 1024 (CanLII). (2000). Retrieved from http://www.canlii.org/en/bc/bcsc/doc/2000/2000bcsc1024/2000bcsc1024.html

R. v. Lavallee, 1 SCR 852 (CanLII). (1990). Retrieved from http://www.canlii.org/en/ca/scc/doc/1990/1990canlii95/1990canlii95.html

R. v. Trochym, 1 SCR 239 (CanLII). (2007). Retrieved from http://www.canlii.org/en/ca/scc/doc/2007/2007scc6/2007scc6.html

Rasch, B., & Born, J. (2013). About sleep's role in memory. *Physiological Reviews, 93,* 681-766.

Rauscher, F. H., & Shaw, G. L. (1998). Key components of the Mozart effect. *Perceptual and Motor Skills, 86,* 835-841.

Rauscher, F. H., Shaw, G. L., & Ky, K. N. (1993). Music and spatial task performance. *Nature, 365*, 611.

Rauscher, F. H., Shaw, G. L., & Ky, K. N. (1995). Listening to Mozart enhances spatial-temporal reasoning: Towards a neurophysiological basis. *Neuroscience Letters, 185*, 44-47.

Rawn, C. D., & Vohs, K. D. (2011). People use self-control to risk personal harm: An intra-interpersonal dilemma. *Personality and Social Psychology Review, 15*, 267-289.

Reed, J. G., & Baxter, P. M. (2003). *Library use: A handbook for psychology* (3rd ed.). Washington, DC: American Psychological Association.

Reid, A. (2013, July 8). Angus Reid: What went wrong with the polls in British Columbia? *Maclean's.* Retrieved August 11, 2014, from http://www.macleans.ca/news/canada/angus-reid-what-went-wrong-with-the-polls-in-british-columbia/

Report of the Smeesters follow-up investigation committee. (2014). Retrieved July 31, 2014, from http://www.rsm.nl/fileadmin/Images_NEW/News_Images/2014/Report_Smeesters_follow-up_investigation_committee.final.pdf

Reverby, S. M. (Ed.). (2000). *Tuskegee's truths: Rethinking the Tuskegee syphilis study.* Chapel Hill, NC: University of North Carolina Press.

Richards, N. M., & King, J. H. (2014). Big data ethics. *Wake Forest Law Review, 49*, 393-432.

Richardson, M., Abraham, C., & Bond, R. (2012). Psychological correlates of university students' academic performance: A systematic review and meta-analysis. *Psychological Bulletin, 138*, 353-387.

Ring, K., Wallston, K., & Corey, M. (1970). Mode of debriefing as a factor affecting subjective reaction to a Milgram-type obedience experiment: An ethical inquiry. *Representative Research in Social Psychology, 1*, 67-68.

Roberson, M. T., & Sundstrom, E. (1990). Questionnaire design, return rates, and response favorableness in an employee attitude questionnaire. *Journal of Applied Psychology, 75*, 354-357.

Robinson, J. P., Rusk, J. G., & Head, K. B. (1968). *Measures of political attitudes.* Ann Arbor, MI: Institute for Social Research.

Robinson, J. P., Shaver, P. R., & Wrightsman, L. S. (1991). *Measures of personality and social psychological attitudes* (Vol. 1). San Diego, CA: Academic Press.

Roehrs, T., Burduvali, E., Bonahoom, A., Drake, C., & Roth, T. (2003). Ethanol and sleep loss: A "dose" comparison of impairing effects. *Sleep, 26*, 981-985.

Rosenhan, D. (1973). On being sane in insane places. *Science, 179*, 250-258.

Rosenthal, R. (1966). *Experimenter effects in behavior research.* New York: Appleton-Century-Crofts.

Rosenthal, R. (1967). Covert communication in the psychological experiment. *Psychological Bulletin, 67*, 356-367.

Rosenthal, R. (1991). *Meta-analytic procedures for social research* (rev. ed.). Newbury Park, CA: Sage.

Rosenthal, R. (2003). Covert communication in laboratories, classrooms, and the truly real word. *Current Directions in Psychological Science, 12*, 151-154.

Rosenthal, R., & Rosnow, R. L. (1975). *The volunteer subject.* New York: Wiley.

Rosnow, R. L., & Rosnow, M. (2012). *Writing papers in psychology* (9th ed.). Belmont, CA: Cengage Learning.

Ross, M., Xun, W. Q. E., & Wilson, A. E. (2002). Language and the bicultural self. *Personality and Social Psychology Bulletin, 28*, 1040-1050.

Rossi, P. H., Freeman, H. E., & Lipsey, M. W. (2004). *Evaluation: A systematic approach* (7th ed.). Thousand Oaks, CA: Sage.

Roszkowski, M. J., & Soven, M. (2010). Shifting gears: Consequences of including two negatively worded items in the middle of a positively worded questionnaire. *Assessment and Evaluation in Higher Educaiton, 35*, 117-134.

Rousseau, C., Benoit, M., Lacroix, L., & Gauthier, M.-F. (2009). Evaluation of a sandplay program for preschoolers in a multiethnic neighborhood. *Journal of Child Psychology and Psychiatry, 50*, 743-750.

Rubin, Z. (1973). Designing honest experiments. *American Psychologist, 28*, 445-448.

Rubin, Z. (1975). Disclosing oneself to a stranger: Reciprocity and its limits. *Journal of Experimental Social Psychology, 11*, 233-260.

Ruggirello, C., & Mayer, C. (2010). Language development in a hearing and deaf twin with simultaneous bilateral cochlear implants.

Journal of Deaf Studies and Deaf Education, 15, 274-286.

Runyan, W. M. (2006). Psychobiography and the psychology of science: Understanding relations between the life and work of individual psychologists. *Review of General Psychology, 10,* 147-162.

Russell, D., Peplau, L. A., & Cutrona, C. E. (1980). The revised UCLA Loneliness Scale: Concurrent and discriminant validity. *Journal of Personality and Social Psychology, 39,* 472-480.

Russell, W. M. S., & Burch, R. L. (1959). *The principles of humane experimental technique.* London: Methuen & Co.

Sana, F., Weston, T., & Cepeda (Wiseheart), N. J. (2013). Laptop multitasking hinders classroom learning for both users and nearby peers. *Computers & Education, 62,* 24-31.

Sarlon, E., Millier, A., Aballéa, S., & Tourni, M. (2014). Evaluation of different approaches for confounding in nonrandomized observational data: A case-study of antipsychotics treatment. *Community Mental Health Journal, 50,* 711-720.

Scarapicchia, T. M. F., Sabiston, C. M., Andersen, R. E., & Bengoechea, E. G. (2013). The motivational effects of social contagion on exercise participation in young female adults. *Journal of Sport and Exercise Psychology, 35,* 563-575.

Schaie, K. W. (1986). Beyond calendar definitions of age, time, and cohort: The general developmental model revisited. *Developmental Review, 6,* 252-277.

Schellenberg, E. G. (2004). Music lessons enhance IQ. *Psychological Science, 15,* 511-514.

Schellenberg, E. G. (2006). Long-term positive associations between music lessons and IQ. *Journal of Educational Psychology, 98,* 457-468.

Schlenger, W. E., Caddell, J. M., Ebert, L., Jordan, B. K., Rourke, K. M., Wilson, D., . . . Kulka, R. A. (2002). Psychological reactions to terrorist attacks: Findings from the National Study of Americans' Reactions to September 11. *Journal of the American Medical Association, 288,* 581-588.

Schmidt, S. (2009). Shall we really do it again? The powerful concept of replication is neglected in the social sciences. *Review of General Psychology, 13,* 90-100.

Schooler, J. W. (2014). Turning the lens of science on itself: Verbal overshadowing, replication,

and metascience. *Perspectives on Psychological Science, 9,* 579-584.

Schur, E., Noonan, C., Polivy, J., Goldberg, J., & Buchwald, D. (2009). Genetic and environmental influences on restrained eating behavior. *International Journal of Eating Disorders, 42,* 765-772.

Schwarz, N. (1999). Self-reports: How the questions shape the answers. *American Psychologist, 54,* 93-105.

Scribner, S. (1997). Studying literacy at work: Bringing the laboratory to the field. In E. Torbach, R. J. Falmagne, M. B. Parlee, L. M. W. Martin, & A. S. Kapelman (Eds.), *Mind and social practice: Selected writings of Sylvia Scribner.* Cambridge, UK: Cambridge University Press.

Sears, D. O. (1986). College sophomores in the laboratory: Influences of a narrow data base on social psychology's view of human nature. *Journal of Personality and Social Psychology, 51,* 515-530.

Sedikides, C., Gaertner, L., & Toguchi, Y. (2003). Pancultural self-enhancement. *Journal of Personality and Social Psychology, 84,* 60-70.

Seifert, T., & Hedderson, C. (2009). Intrinsic motivation and flow in skateboarding: An ethnographic study. *Journal of Happiness Studies, 11,* 277-292.

Shadish, W. R. (2014). Statistical analyses of single-case designs: The shape of things to come. *Current Directions in Psychological Science, 23,* 139-146.

Shadish, W. R., Cook, T. D., & Campbell, D. T. (2002). *Experimental and quasi-experimental designs for generalized causal inference.* Boston: Houghton Mifflin.

Sharp, E. C., Pelletier, L. G., & Lévesque, C. (2006). The double-edged sword of rewards for participation in psychology experiments. *Canadian Journal of Behavioural Science, 38,* 269-277.

Sharpe, D., & Faye, C. (2009). A second look at debriefing practices: Madness in our method? *Ethics & Behavior, 19,* 432-447.

Shettleworth, S. J. (2009). The evolution of comparative cognition: Is the snark still a boojum? *Behavioural Processes, 80,* 210-217.

Shoda, Y., Mischel, W., & Peake, P. K. (1990). Predicting adolescent cognitive and self-regulatory competencies from preschool delay of gratification: Identifying diagnostic conditions. *Developmental Psychology, 26,* 978-986.

Sieber, J. E. (1992). *Planning ethically responsible research: A guide for students and internal review boards.* Newbury Park, CA: Sage.

Sieber, J. E., Iannuzzo, R., & Rodriguez, B. (1995). Deception methods in psychology: Have they changed in 23 years? *Ethics and Behavior, 5,* 67-85.

Siegel, S., & Castellan, N. J. (1988). *Nonparametric statistics for the behavioral sciences.* New York: McGraw-Hill.

Silverman, I., & Margulis, S. (1973). Experiment title as a source of sampling bias in commonly used "subject-pool" procedures. *Canadian Psychologist, 14,* 197-201.

Simmons, J. P., Nelson, L. D., & Simonsohn, U. (2011). False-positive psychology: Undisclosed flexibility in data collection and analysis allows presenting anything as significant. *Psychological Science, 22,* 1359-1366.

Simmons, J. P., Nelson, L. D., & Simonsohn, U. (2013). Life after p-hacking. Meeting of the Society for Personality and Social Psychology, New Orleans, LA, 17-19 January 2013. Available at SSRN: http://ssrn.com/abstract=2205186 or http://dx.doi.org/10.2139/ssrn.2205186

Simons, D. J. (2014). The value of direct replication. *Perspectives on Psychological Science, 9,* 76-80.

Simons, D. J., Holcombe, A. O., & Spellman, B. A. (2014). An introduction to Registered Replication Reports at *Perspectives on Psychological Science, 9,* 552-555.

Simonsohn, U. (2013). Just post it: The lesson from two cases of fabricated data detected by statistics alone. *Psychological Science, 24,* 1875-1888.

Simonsohn, U., Nelson, L. D., & Simmons, J. P. (2014). *P*-curve: A key to the file drawer. *Journal of Experimental Psychology: General, 143,* 534-547.

Singh, D. (1993). Adaptive significance of female physical attractiveness: Role of waist-to-hip ratio. *Journal of Personality and Social Psychology, 65,* 293-307.

Skinner, B. F. (1953). *Science and human behavior.* New York: Macmillan.

Smart, R. (1966). Subject selection bias in psychological research. *Canadian Psychologist, 7,* 115-121.

Smith, C. P. (1983). Ethical issues: Research on deception, informed consent, and debriefing. In L. Wheeler & P. Shaver (Eds.), *Review of personality and social psychology* (Vol. 4). Newbury Park, CA: Sage.

Smith, R. J., Lingle, J. H., & Brock, T. C. (1978). Reactions to death as a function of perceived similarity to the deceased. *Omega, 9,* 125-138.

Smith, S. S., & Richardson, D. (1983). Amelioration of harm in psychological research: The important role of debriefing. *Journal of Personality and Social Psychology, 44,* 1075-1082.

Snowden, D. A. (1997). Aging and Alzheimer's disease: Lessons from the Nun Study. *Gerontologist, 37,* 150-156.

Solomon, R. L. (1949). An extension of control group design. *Psychological Bulletin, 46,* 137-150.

Spence, I., & Feng, J. (2010). Video games and spatial cognition. *Review of General Psychology, 14,* 92-104.

Stanovich, K. E. (2013). *How to think straight about psychology* (10th ed.). Toronto: Pearson.

Statistics Canada. (2013). *NHS user guide: National Household Survey 2011.* Retrieved August 11, 2014, from http://www12.statcan.gc.ca/nhs-enm/2011/ref/index-eng.cfm

Steblay, N., Dysart, J., Fulero, S., & Lindsay, R. C. L. (2001). Eyewitness accuracy rates in sequential and simultaneous lineup presentations: A meta-analytic comparison. *Law and Human Behavior, 25,* 459-473.

Steel, P. (2007). The nature of procrastination: A meta-analytic and theoretical review of quintessential self-regulatory failure. *Psychological Bulletin, 133,* 65-94.

Steele, K. M., Bass, K. E., & Crook, M. D. (1999). The mystery of the Mozart effect: Failure to replicate. *Psychological Science, 10,* 366-369.

Steinberg, L., & Dornbusch, S. M. (1991). Negative correlates of part-time employment during adolescence: Replication and elaboration. *Developmental Psychology, 27,* 304-313.

Stermac, L., Elgie, S., Dunlap, H., & Kelly, T. (2010). Educational experiences and achievements of war-zone immigrant students in Canada. *Vulnerable Children and Youth Studies, 5,* 97-107.

Sternberg, R. J., & Sternberg, K. (2010). *The psychologist's companion: A guide to scientific writing for students and researchers* (5th ed.). Cambridge, UK: Cambridge University Press.

Stevenson, H. W., & Allen, S. (1964). Adult performance as a function of sex of experimenter and sex of subject. *Journal of Abnormal and Social Psychology, 68,* 214–216.

Stroebe, W., Postmes, T., & Spears, R. (2012). Scientific misconduct and the myth of self-correction in science. *Perspectives on Psychological Science, 7,* 670–688.

Strohmetz, D. B. (2008). Research artifacts and the social psychology of psychological experiments. *Social and Personality Psychology Compass, 2,* 861–877.

Suedfeld, P. (2010). The cognitive processing of politics and politicians: Archival studies of conceptual and integrative complexity. *Journal of Personality, 78,* 1669–1702.

Suedfeld P., & Jhangiani, R. (2009). Cognitive management in an enduring international rivalry: The case of India and Pakistan. *Political Psychology, 30,* 937–951.

Sullivan, D. S., & Deiker, T. E. (1973). Subject-experimenter perceptions of ethical issues in human research. *American Psychologist, 28,* 587–591.

Suschinsky, K. D., Elias, L. J., & Krupp, D. B. (2007). Looking for Ms. Right: Allocating attention to facilitate mate choice decisions. *Evolutionary Psychology, 5,* 428–441.

Szabo, A., & Underwood, J. (2004). Cybercheats: Is information and communication technology fuelling academic dishonesty? *Active Learning in Higher Education, 5,* 180–199.

Tabachnick, B. G., & Fidell, L. S. (2013). *Using multivariate statistics* (6th ed.). New York: Pearson.

Tagliacollo, V. A., Volpato, G. L., & Pereira, A., Jr. (2010). Association of student position in classroom and school performance. *Educational Research, 1,* 198–201.

Tausczik, Y. R., & Pennebaker, J. W. (2010). The psychological meaning of words: LIWC and computerized text analysis methods. *Journal of Language and Social Psychology, 29,* 24–54.

Terman, L. M. (1925). *Genetic studies of genius: Vol. 1. Mental and physical traits of a thousand gifted children.* Stanford, CA: Stanford University Press.

Terman, L. M., & Oden, M. H. (1947). *Genetic studies of genius: Vol. 4. The gifted child grows up: Twenty-five years' follow-up of a superior group.* Stanford, CA: Stanford University Press.

Terman, L. M., & Oden, M. H. (1959). *Genetic studies of genius: Vol. 5. The gifted group in midlife: Thirty-five years' follow-up of the superior child.* Stanford, CA: Stanford University Press.

The decline of smoking in Canada (2011, July 29). *CBC News.* Retrieved from http://www.cbc.ca

Thomas, G. V., & Blackman, D. (1992). The future of animal studies in psychology. *American Psychologist, 47,* 1678.

Thompson, W. F., Schellenberg, E. G., & Husain, G. (2001). Arousal, mood, and the Mozart effect. *Psychological Science, 12,* 248–251.

Tolin, D. F., Frost, R. O., Steketee, G., & Fitch, K. E. (2008). Family burden of compulsive hoarding: Results of an Internet survey. *Behaviour Research and Therapy, 46,* 334–344.

Tougas, F., Rinfret, N., Beaton, A. M., & de la Sablonnière, R. (2005). Policewomen acting in self-defense: Can psychological disengagement protect self-esteem from the negative outcomes of relative deprivation? *Journal of Personality and Social Psychology, 88,* 790–800.

Tourangeau, R., & Yan, T. (2007). Sensitive questions in surveys. *Psychological Bulletin, 133,* 859–883.

Tracy, J. L., Robins, R. W., & Schriber, R. A. (2009). Development of a FACS-verified set of basic and self-conscious emotion expressions. *Emotion, 9,* 554–559.

Trochim, W. M. (2000). *The research methods knowledge base* (2nd ed.). Cincinnati, OH: Atomic Dog Publishing.

Trochim, W. M. (2006). *The research methods knowledge base* (2nd ed.). Retrieved May 1, 2008, from http://www.socialresearchmethods.net/kb/

Uher, R., & Weaver, I. C. G. (2014). Epigenetic traces of childhood maltreatment in peripheral blood: A new strategy to explore gene-environment interactions. *The British Journal of Psychiatry, 204,* 3–5.

Ullman, J. B. (2007) Structural equation modeling. In B. G. Tabachnick & L. S. Fidell (Eds.),

Using multivariate statistics (5th ed.). New York: Allyn & Bacon.

U.S. Department of Justice. (1999). *Eyewitness evidence: A guide for law enforcement.* Retrieved July 10, 2002, from http://www.ncjrs.org/pdffiles1/nij/178240.pdf

Valtchanov, D., & Ellard, C. (2010). Physiological and affective responses to immersion in virtual reality: Effects of nature and urban settings. *Journal of CyberTherapy & Rehabilitation, 3,* 359-373.

Vanasse, A., Demers, M., Hemiari, A., & Courteau, J. (2006). Obesity in Canada: Where and how many? *International Journal of Obesity, 30,* 677-683.

Varao Sousa, T. L., Carriere, J. S. A., & Smilek, D. (2013). The way we encounter reading material influences how frequently we mind wander. *Frontiers in Psychology, 4*(892), 1-8.

Varnhagen, C. K., McFall, G. P., Pugh, N., Routledge, L., Sumida-MacDonald, H., & Kwong, T. E. (2010). Lol: New language and spelling in instant messaging. *Reading and Writing, 23*(6), 719-733.

Vazire, S. (2006). Informant reports: A cheap, fast, and easy method for personality assessment. *Journal of Research in Personality, 40,* 472-481.

Verma, I. M. (2014). Editorial expression of concern and correction. *Proceedings of the National Academy of Sciences, 111,* 10779.

Vicente, P., & Reis, E. (2010). Using questionnaire design to fight nonresponse bias in web surveys. *Social Science Computer Review, 28,* 251-267.

Wagstaff, G. F., MacVeigh, J., Boston, R., Scott, L., Brunas-Wagstaff, J., & Cole, J. (2003). Can laboratory findings on eyewitness testimony be generalized to the real world? An archival analysis of the influence of violence, weapon presence, and age on eyewitness accuracy. *The Journal of Psychology, 137,* 17-28.

Wang, S.-Y., Parrila, R., & Cui, Y. (2013). Meta-analysis of social skills interventions of single-case research for individuals with autism spectrum disorders: Results from three-level HLM. *Journal of Autism and Developmental Disorders, 43,* 1701-1716.

Webb, E. J., Campbell, D. T., Schwartz, R. D., Sechrest, R., & Grove, J. B. (1981). *Nonreactive measures in the social sciences* (2nd ed.). Boston: Houghton Mifflin.

Weber, R. P. (1990). *Basic content analysis* (2nd ed.). Newbury Park, CA: Sage.

Wegner, D. M., Fuller, V. A., & Sparrow, B. (2003). Clever hands: Uncontrolled intelligence in facilitated communication. *Journal of Personality and Social Psychology, 85,* 5-19.

Weisberg, H. I. (2010). *Bias and causation: Models and judgment for valid comparisons.* Hoboken, NJ: John Wiley & Sons.

Wells, G. L. (2001). Police lineups: Data, theory, and policy. *Psychology, Public Policy, and Law, 7,* 791-801.

Wertz Garvin, A., & Damson, C. (2008). The effects of idealized fitness images on anxiety, depression and global mood states in college age males and females. *Journal of Health Psychology, 13,* 433-437.

White, C. B., & Caird, J. K. (2010). The blind date: The effects of change blindness, passenger conversation and gender on looked-but-failed-to-see (LBFTS) errors. *Accident Analysis and Prevention, 42,* 1822-1830.

Wikipedia, the free encyclopedia. (2011a). Retrieved May 4, 2011, from http://en.wikipedia.org/wiki/Wikipedia:About

Wikipedia, the free encyclopedia. (2011b). Retrieved May 4, 2011, from http://en.wikipedia.org/wiki/Wikipedia:What_Wikipedia_is_not

Wilkinson, L., & the Task Force on Statistical Inference. (1999). Statistical methods in psychology journals: Guidelines and explanations. *American Psychologist, 54,* 594-604.

Williams, K. M., Nathanson, C., & Paulhus, D. L. (2010). Identifying and profiling scholastic cheaters: Their personality, cognitive ability, and motivation. *Journal of Experimental Psychology: Applied, 16,* 293-307.

Williams, K. M., Paulhus, D. L., & Hare, R. D. (2007). Capturing the four-factor structure of psychopathy in college students via self-report. *Journal of Personality Assessment, 88,* 205-219.

Wilson, D. W., & Donnerstein, E. (1976). Legal and ethical aspects of nonreactive social psychological research. *American Psychologist, 31,* 765-773.

Windholz, G. (1997). Ivan P. Pavlov: An overview of his life and psychological work. *American Psychologist, 52,* 941-946.

Wintre, M. G., North, C., & Sugar, L. A. (2001). Psychologists' response to criticisms about research based on undergraduate participants: A developmental perspective. *Canadian Psychology, 42,* 216–225.

Wohl, M. J. A., Pychyl, T. A., Bennett, S. H. (2010). I forgive myself, now I can study: How self-forgiveness for procrastinating can reduce future procrastination. *Personality and Individual Differences, 48,* 803–808.

Wood, J. V., Perunovic, W. Q. E., & Lee, J. W. (2009). Positive self-statements: Power for some, peril for others. *Psychological Science, 20,* 860–866.

Woods, C. M. (2006). Careless responding to reverse-worded items: Implications for confirmatory factor analysis. *Journal of Psychopathology and Behavioral Assessment, 28,* 189–194.

WORLD VALUES SURVEY Wave 6 2010-2014 OFFICIAL AGGREGATE v.20140429. World Values Survey Association (www.worldvaluessurvey.org). Aggregate File Producer: Asep/JDS, Madrid SPAIN. Retrieved from http://www.worldvaluessurvey.org/

Wormith, J., Olver, M. E., Stevenson, H. E., & Girard, L. (2007). The long-term prediction of offender recidivism using diagnostic, personality, and risk/need approaches to offender assessment. *Psychological Services, 4,* 287–305.

Wu, D., Loke, I. C., Xu, F., & Lee, K. (2011). Neural correlates of evaluations of lying and truth-telling in different social contexts. *Brain Research, 1389,* 115–124.

Yarkoni, T. (2010). Personality in 100,000 words: A large-scale analysis of personality and word use among bloggers. *Journal of Research in Personality, 44,* 363–373.

Yarkoni, T. (2012). Psychoinformatics: New horizons at the interface of the psychological and computing sciences. *Current Directions in Psychological Science, 21,* 391–397.

Yarmey, A. D. (2003). Eyewitness identification: Guidelines and recommendations for identification procedures in the United States and in Canada. *Canadian Psychology, 44,* 181–189.

Yin, R. K. (1994). *Case study research: Design and methods.* Newbury Park, CA: Sage.

Yong, E. (2012, May 17). Replication studies: Bad copy. *Nature [News Feature], 485,* 298–300.

Young, J. (2006, June 12). Wikipedia founder discourages academic use of his creation. *The Chronicle of Higher Education.* Retrieved from http://chronicle.com/blogs/wiredcampus/ wikipedia-founder-discourages-academic-use-of-his-creation/2305

Young, M. E., Mizzau, M., Mai, N. T., Sirisegaram, A., & Wilson, M. (2009). Food for thought. What you eat depends on your sex and eating companions. *Appetite, 53,* 268–271.

Yuille, J. C., Ternes, M., & Cooper, B. S. (2010). Expert testimony on laboratory witnesses. *Journal of Forensic Psychology Practice, 10,* 238–251.

Zerouali, Y., Jemel, B., & Godbout, R. (2010). The effects of early and late night partial sleep deprivation on automatic and selective attention: An ERP study. *Brain Research, 1308,* 87–99.

Zhong, C.-B., & DeVoe, S. E. (2010). You are how you eat: Fast food and impatience. *Psychological Science, 21,* 619–622.

Zimbardo, P. G. (1973). The psychological power and pathology of imprisonment. In E. Aronson & R. Helmreich (Eds.), *Social psychology.* New York: Van Nostrand.

Zimbardo, P. G. (2004). Does psychology make a significant difference in our lives? *American Psychologist, 59,* 339–351.

Credits

Index